Information Sources in

Architecture and Construction

Guides to Information Sources

A series under the General Editorship of
Ia C. McIlwaine
M.W. Hill
and
Nancy J. Williamson

This series was known previously as 'Butterworths Guides to Information Sources'.

Other titles available include:

Information Sources in Chemistry (Fourth edition)
   edited by R.T. Bottle and J.F.B. Rowland
Information Sources in Physics (Third edition)
   edited by Dennis F. Shaw
Information Sources in Finance and Banking
   by Ray Lester
Information Sources in Environmental Protection
   edited by Selwyn Eagle and Judith Deschamps
Information Sources in Grey Literature (Third edition)
   by C.P. Auger
Information Sources in Music
   edited by Lewis Foreman
Information Sources in the Life Sciences (Fourth edition)
   edited by H.V. Wyatt
Information Sources in Engineering (Third edition)
   edited by Ken Mildren and Peter Hicks
Information Sources in Sport and Leisure
   edited by Michele Shoebridge
Information Sources in Patents
   edited by C.P. Auger
Information Sources for the Press and Broadcast Media
   edited by Selwyn Eagle
Information Sources in Information Technology
   edited by David Haynes
Information Sources in Pharmaceuticals
   edited by W.R. Pickering
Information Sources in Metallic Materials
   edited by M.N. Patten
Information Sources in the Earth Sciences (Second edition)
   edited by David N. Wood, Joan E. Hardy and
   Anthony P. Harvey
Information Sources in Cartography
   edited by C.R. Perkins and R.B. Barry
Information Sources in Polymers and Plastics
   edited by R.T. Adkins
Information Sources in Economics (Second edition)
   edited by John Fletcher

Information Sources in

Architecture and Construction

Second Edition

Editor
Valerie J. Nurcombe

BOWKER
SAUR ●

London · Melbourne · Munich · New Jersey

British Library Cataloguing in Publication Data
A catalogue record for this title is available from the British Library

Library of Congress Cataloging-in-Publication Data
A catalog record for this book is available from the Library of Congress

Published by Bowker-Saur, Maypole House, Maypole Road,
East Grinstead, West Sussex RH19 1HU, UK
Tel: +44(0)1342 330100 Fax: +44(0)1342 330191
E-mail: lis@bowker-saur.co.uk
Internet Website: http://www.bowker-saur.co.uk/service/

Bowker-Saur is part of REED REFERENCE PUBLISHING

ISBN 1-85739-094-6

Cover design by Calverts Press
Typesetting by The Castlefield Press
Printed on acid-free paper
Printed and bound in Great Britain by Bell & Bain Ltd, Glasgow

Series editors' foreword

The second half of the 20th century has been characterized by the recognition that our style of life depends on acquiring and using information effectively. It has always been so, but only in the information society has the extent of the dependence been recognized and the development of technologies for handling information become a priority. These modern technologies enable us to store more information, to select and process parts of the store more skilfully and transmit the product more rapidly than we would have dreamt possible only 40 years ago. Yet the irony still exists that, while we are able to do all this and are assailed from all sides by great masses of information, ensuring that one has what one needs just when one wants it is frequently just as difficult as ever. Knowledge may, as Johnson said in the well known quotation, be of two kinds, but information, in contrast, is of many kinds and most of it is, for each individual, knowable only after much patient searching.

The aim of each Guide in this series is simple. It is to reduce the time that needs to be spent on that patient searching, to recommend the best starting point and sources most likely to yield the desired information. Like all subject guides, the sources discussed have had to be selected, and the criteria for selection will be given by the individual editors and will differ from subject to subject. However, the overall objective is constant; that of providing a way into a subject to those new to the field or to identify major new or possibly unexplored sources to those already familiar with it.

The great increase in new sources of information and the overwhelming input of new information from the media, advertising, meetings and conferences, letters, internal reports, office memoranda, magazines, junk mail, electronic mail, fax, bulletin boards etc. inevitably tend to make one reluctant to add to the load on the mind and memory by consulting books and journals. Yet they, and the other traditional types of printed material, remain for many purposes the most reliable sources of information. Despite all the information that is instantly accessible via the new technologies one still has to look things up in databooks, monographs, journals, patent specifications, standards, reports both official and commercial, and on maps and in atlases. Permanent recording of facts, theories and opinions is still carried out primarily by publishing in printed form. Musicians still work from printed scores even though they are helped by sound recordings. Sailors still use printed charts and tide tables even though they have radar and sonar equipment.

However, thanks to computerized indexes, online and CD-ROM, searching the huge bulk of technical literature to draw up a list of references can be undertaken reasonably quickly. The result, all too often, can still be a formidably long list, of which a knowledge of the nature and structure of information sources in that field can be used to put in order of likely value.

It is rarely necessary to consult everything that has been published on the topic of a search. When attempting to prove that an invention is genuinely novel, a complete search may seem necessary, but even then it is common to search only obvious sources and leave it to anyone wishing to oppose the grant of a patent to bear the cost of hunting for a prior disclosure in some obscure journal. Usually, much proves to be irrelevant to the particular aspect of our interest and whatever is relevant may be unsound. Some publications are sadly lacking in important detail and present broad generalizations flimsily bridged with arches of waffle. In any academic field there is a 'pecking order' of journals so that articles in one journal may be assumed to be of a higher or lower calibre than those in another. Those experienced in the field know these things. The research scientist soon learns, as it is part of his training, the degree of reliance he can place on information from co-workers elsewhere, on reports of research by new and (to him) unknown researchers, on data compilations and on manufacturers of equipment. The information worker, particularly when working in a field other than his own, faces very serious problems as he tries to compile, probably from several sources, a report on which his client may base important actions. Even the librarian, faced only with recommending two or three books or journal articles, meets the same problem though less acutely.

In the Bowker-Saur Guides to Information Sources we aim to bring you the knowledge and experience of specialists in the field. Each chapter is written by someone who regularly uses the information sources and services described there. Any tricks of the trade that the author has learnt are passed on.

Nowadays, two major problems face those who are embarking upon research or who are in charge of collections of information of every kind. One is the increasingly specialized knowledge of the user and the concomitant ignorance of other potentially useful disciplines. The second problem is the trend towards cross-disciplinary studies. This has led to a great mixing of academic programmes – and a number of imprecisely defined fields of study. Courses are offered in Environmental Studies, Women's Studies, Communication Studies or Area Studies, and these are the forcing ground for research. The editors are only too aware of the difficulties raised by those requiring information from such hybrid subject fields, and this approach, too, is being handled in the series alongside the traditional 'hard disciplines'.

Guides to the literature have a long and honoured history. Marion Spicer of SRIS recently drew to our attention a guide written in 1891 for engineers. No doubt there are even earlier ones. Nowadays, with the information and even the publishing fields changing quite frequently, it is necessary to update guides every few years and this we do in this present series.

Michael Hill
Ia McIlwaine
Nancy Williamson

About the contributors

Peter Adderley qualified in architecture and town planning at University College London. Conventional architectural and planning practice, including six years with the GLC, was followed by 15 years providing a technical information service in a large private practice. Now a freelance information consultant, his work has included a wide range of writing and editing, notably for RIBA and RIBA Publications. He is the author of *Abbreviations guide: an ABC for the construction industry.*

John Barrick was Librarian and Information Officer of the Royal Town Planning Institute for 22 years, during which he made a valuable contribution to the bibliography of planning in the UK. Before that, he worked at the Architectural Association Library after qualifying as a Chartered Librarian. Sadly, John Barrick died in July 1995 before the publication of this book.

Sylvester Bone is an Architect and Information Consultant. He has been a senior architect in Local Government and a partner in private practice. He is author of several technical books on construction and writes a regular technical page for *Building design* magazine under the name of 'Henry Haverstock'. He is currently a principal in The Camden Consultancy, a grouping of independent consultants in the construction, planning and information fields.

Jeanne M. Brown received her MLS from the University of Illinois at Urbana-Champaign in 1973. Since then she has worked at several libraries including the University of Illinois, and the American University in Cairo, Egypt, where she was the Head of the Creswell Library of Islamic Art and Architecture. She is currently the Architecture Studies Librarian at the University of Nevada, Las Vegas. The focus of much of her research in the last several years has been Internet resources and use of the Internet in architecture and construction.

Katharine R. Chibnik is Associate Director of Avery Architectural and Fine Arts Library, Columbia University, New York, a post which she has held since 1994. She has been a librarian at Columbia since 1980, first as a book selector/reference librarian in urban planning and as cataloger in art and architecture (1980–1988), and then as Head of Access and Support Services in Avery (1988–1994). Previous to these positions, she was an editor at the R.R. Bowker Company for *Ulrich's International Periodicals Directory.*

Anthony J. Coulson is Liaison Librarian (Arts) at the Open University and has been involved in many aspects of picture research, production and writing of arts courses since 1970. Also involved in various capacities with ARLIS/Art Libraries Society/UK and Ireland and Design History Society, he currently serves on the Editorial Board of the *Journal of Design History.* Publications include *A Bibliography of Design in Britain 1851–1970* (1979), articles and reviews in *Art Libraries Journal, Audiovisual Librarian* and other journals as well as entries in *Contemporary Designers*, papers presented to IFLA Art Libraries Section, and picture research/editing for various books including the illustrated edition of Daniel Defoe's *A tour through the whole island of Great Britain* (1991).

Margaret Culbertson is head of the William R. Jenkins Architecture and Art Library at the University of Houston, USA. She is the author of *American House Designs, An Index to Popular and Trade Periodicals, 1850–1915*, as well as as articles on architectural history and design topics. She is an active member of the Art Libraries Society/North America, which awarded her its first research grant in 1991.

Gillian Edmonds, principal of Morgan Edmonds Associates, trained at Birmingham School of Architecture, and has been involved in technical writing and information management for the construction industry since 1978. Morgan Edmonds Associates provides a range of consultancy services to professionals and manufacturers in the construction industry, producing technical manuals, setting up information systems and carrying out research. She is a member of CIIG, the Construction Industry Information Group, and chairman of CIIG Freelance Group.

Malcolm Green is a chartered librarian, formerly Librarian with the Travers Morgan Consulting Group (1966–1993), and currently employed in the Information Centre at the London office of Building Design Partnership. Past Chairman of the Construction Industry Information Group, Malcolm Green has contributed to various committees, courses and publications on aspects of construction information.

Sheila Harvey is Librarian at the Landscape Institute and an editorial advisor to its journal, *Landscape Design.* In addition, she was editor of *Reflections on landscape* (1987) and co-editor of *Fifty years of 'Landscape Design' 1934–1984* (1985) and *Landscape design: an international survey* (1992).

Lorraine Jefferson has worked for Building Design Partnership in the position of Information Services Manager for five years. She is responsible for information provision in five UK offices and for supporting BDP's European offices. She has worked as an Academic Librarian in further and higher education, where she had a particular interest in user education. She obtained her professional qualifications at the now University of Northumbria and her degree from Manchester Metropolitan University.

Stephen Loyd qualified as a librarian at Brighton Polytechnic (now Brighton University) and after service in the public library field, joined BSRIA in 1974. He became Head of Information Services in 1985, responsible for BSRIA's online database and for developing new information products for the building services industry.

Mary Nixon has been Reader Services Librarian at the British Architectural Library of the Royal Institute of British Architects since 1990. After reading French and Italian at London University, she worked in the libraries of University College London and Lambeth Palace before joining the BAL as one of the contributors to the *Architectural Periodicals Index*.

Barry H. Nurcombe trained as a Mechanical Engineer with Parker Plant, builder's plant division, before moving on to design instrumentation for turbines. He is currently designing retrofit installation of instrumentation on rotating machinery. In particular, he is experienced in machinery and plant, construction and instrumentation, with special responsibility for conformity with standards and specification, hazardous area regulations and European directives. He has been involved with the development of *Sources of information in architecture and construction* since the first edition.

Valerie J. Nurcombe spent 14 years in polytechnic libraries teaching the use of, and running, information services for architects, builders, quantity surveyors, planners and estate managers. In 1984 she became freelance and since then has worked on a variety of projects ranging from retrieval of information in construction and commerce to the organization and re-development of professional practice and industrial libraries. This has included the design, development and maintenance of a variety of databases for information retrieval, document control and project management. She is currently serving on the Standing Committee on Official Publications (SCOOP), of the Library Associations Information Services Group (ISG) and is Advertising Manager for the ISGN journal, *Refer*. In the past she has also served on Aslib's Planning Environment and Transport Information Group (PETIG) and is a member of the Institute of Information Scientists (IIS).

Annette O'Brien has worked in construction information for over 20 years, of which for 12 she was a self-employed Information Consultant.

Clients included architects, structural and services engineers, quantity surveyors, manufacturers, research institutions and information providers, ranging in size from one-(wo)man- bands to practices of 60–70 technical staff. She is currently Chief Librarian to Ove Arup & Partners whose Library serves offices throughout the world.

Keith Parker graduated in languages at the University of Bristol and qualified as a librarian while working in Bristol Public Libraries. From there he moved to the University of York, where he has been responsible for the library of the Institute of Advanced Architural Studies since 1964.

Nancy J. Pistorius is Associate Director of the Fine Arts Library and the Humanities Co-ordinator for the General Library at The University of New Mexico. She is the collection development selector, information specialist, and bibliographic instruction librarian for the subject areas of architecture, art, photography and planning and holds the rank of Associate Professor. She is also the author of 'Drafting and implementing collection development policies in academic art libraries' in *Current issues in fine arts collection development of* the *Occasional Papers No. 3* (1984) of the Art Libraries Society of North America.

Vincent Powell-Smith is Professor of Law at the International Islamic University in Malaysia. He was formerly Professor of Law at the University of Malaya, and has been associated with the construction industry for over 25 years. He is qualified in both common law and Islamic law. A well-known author in the field of construction law, he has been legal correspondent of *Contract Journal* since 1974. He is Editor of *Asia-Pacific Construction Law Reports* and Joint Editor of *Construction Law Reports*, and sits frequently as an arbitrator in domestic and international building and civil engineering disputes.

Jacqueline Pugsley is Subject Librarian for building studies and architecture at De Montfort University, Leicester.

Robin Waters is the Data Products Manager of Longman Geo Information, and is responsible for publishing CD-ROM datasets of geographically distributed information in the UK and Europe. After several years surveying in Africa and the Caribbean, he worked on digital mapping development at Ordnance Survey and at Laser-Scan Ltd., as Marketing Director of Geonex (UK) and as GIS consultant. He has just completed his year as President of the Royal Institution of Chartered Surveyors.

Erik Winterkorn has a degree in Architecture from Cornell University, USA, and studied Building Science at the Technical University in Munich. Before joining CICA as a Computing Consultant for the construction industry he spent 12 years working in US and UK architectural and multi-disciplinary design firms. He regularly delivers papers at seminars and conferences all over the world and is the author of reports on CAD, GIS, Building Environment Analysis, Office Management and Software Quality Assurance.

Contents

Foreword

'Information' is nowadays frequently coupled with words such as 'jungle', 'mountain' or 'superhighway'. Such associations suggest that information is a terrain to be traversed or explored. Before setting off to explore new or unfamiliar territory it is essential to have a map or a guide. *Information sources in architecture and construction* is a textbook guide. For those who are already familiar with the territory it reveals new roads and byways. For those just starting out it indicates possible routes to follow.

The construction industry information terrain is constantly expanding and changing, reflecting the growing internationalism of the industry and the removal of barriers between different information provinces, encompassing legal, business, governmental, financial and legislative. *Information sources in architecture and construction* maps a very wide territory, taking in all forms of information (such as periodicals, databases, trade literature, standards, maps and drawings) and subject areas (among which are interior design, landscape, liability, and conservation) that the information traveller may wish to visit.

Since the first edition of this book in 1983 there have been major developments. Many new routes have opened; some old roads have closed. Electronic highways such as the internet and CD-ROM now provide new ways of travelling. All are thoroughly recorded in this guide.

All guidebooks have a built-in obsolescence. When this happens the explorer needs a survival manual, not merely a guide. The authors, all experts in their fields, provide this through instructions in methodology and hints on keeping up with advances in information. Anyone setting out on a journey to find information on architecture and construction would be advised to read this guide first.

Ruth H. Kamen
Director, British Architectural Library and Sir Banister Fletcher Librarian
Royal Institute of British Architects
August 1995

Preface to the second edition

The first edition of this book was published in 1983. During the intervening years there have been many changes in technology and in the construction industry. However, there has been a certain stability in some of the sources of information available. Titles may have changed and the means of supply diversified and developed but many of the suppliers remain the same. Had the *CIIG manual*, referred to throughout but particularly in the chapter on practice information provision, been published in 1981-2 this guide might never have seen the light of day – there was nothing else to refer to for this type of guidance on resources whether in architecture, building or most other branches of this industry. The Construction Industry Information Group in the UK worked long and hard to bring that manual to fruition and it has supplied the current useful information required for the practice librarian on a daily basis. An equivalent might perhaps be useful in all countries. However, it fortunately supplements and complements this guide as it takes a different angle looking at the establishment and maintenance of an information unit with national and local information sources, addresses and texts, which are not covered here. This book should form an essential reference guide for that unit to refer to regularly.

This guide had its origin when, as Academic Librarian at Leicester Polytechnic (now De Montfort University), I was asked to condense some of my teaching notes and leaflets into a format suitable for use with a group of experienced architects in a concentrated session on sources of information. The resultant large booklet was seen by others and the first edition developed from it. The aim remains the same – to assist all those involved in the construction process in understanding the nature and sources of information available. The guide is written with the professional in mind, and the language of the librarian is avoided as far as possible – but not entirely as many librarians in the construction industry, on both sides of the Atlantic, have intimated that they have found the first edition an invaluable starting point for various enquiries and research.

Depth coverage of both the information sources and the sources pertaining to particular sections of the industry, are essential to the information specialist in the construction industry, partly because the range of information usually required can be so broad. The guide attempts not only to indicate where to search over a broad range of topics but to give hints for those needing to go beyond its immediate sphere. It does not attempt at any time to list sources exhaustively.

Organization of the content is similar to the previous edition. Firstly, the various common types of resource and materials are considered before discussing the topics involved in the construction process. These are arranged broadly following their order of use during the design and construction process. However, a linear arrangement does not always give the most useful order. Landscape and interior design should be involved in the project from an early stage as are contracts and the office, its procedures, quality control and management, but they had to be placed either before or after the construction process. The latter was chosen. The three IT chapters, or sections, are placed first as they all come into play from the start of the process and continue throughout. Conservation and history are deemed important but placed last as they concern that which has already been built.

In editing the contributions to the guide the same principle has been followed. Data has been amplified, missing publishers and dates supplied in some cases – but only up to a point. Originally there were to be no bibliographies at the end of chapters, only references in the text. However, in certain situations this was not practicable: the text became confused with too many references obliterating the sense. The use of numbered references suited some authors' topic and style. In other cases the alphabetical bibliography was appropriate. Editorial has aimed to make each chapter a cohesive whole integrated with the others to provide a comprehensive guide.

Where information has fitted well in chapter it has been left provided it complemented, without undue duplication, that in another chapter; hence some standards information is left in the structures and materials chapter (15), and UnCover is mentioned in several sentences on several occasions. Thus, also, regulations are covered where most appropriate: the explanation of what regulations are and the building regulations appear in the official publications chapter (7), but the CPD regulations are mainly discussed under standards (6) and the CDM regulations are covered with structures and materials.

The length of the sections is variable – it did not seem appropriate, given their difference in outlook and scope, to limit the longer contributions and possibly make them less valuable. Thus the lengthy and excellent chapters on visual resources and on structures and materials remain substantially as contributed although the chapter on design data has been cut to a certain extent. Information has been left in, sometimes as appendices, where it is not generally widely accessible.

To make a text of this nature truly international is not easy. This has been attempted but is difficult where so much of the material is essentially local to a country. As far as possible Europe, USA and Canada, and other English speaking countries have been touched upon, but it was not possible to locate many authors with international experience and knowledge of their topics. The principles expressed remain true in most countries and the patterns of information supply, the types of publications and guide will be found in other countries, as will similar associations. Omissions and inclusions are bound to be controversial and this is acknowledged.

Editing an international text is never easy – the Bowker-Saur preferences have been adopted for spellings and citation format wherever possible. All chapters from both sides of the Atlantic have been edited to use standard spellings and layouts, with great care to ensure that phrases such as Internet addresses are not changed by the spell checker. In these days of word processed text, with spelling and grammar checks it is hoped that errors can be minimised but they still creep in. Bibliographic references follow a standard format set by the publishers but place of publication is usually only given for the lesser known publishers.

Many abbreviations, associations and organizations etc. are mentioned in all chapters and this sometimes becomes repetitive. To minimise the repetition almost all addresses and abbreviations have been compiled into two appendices at the end. These cover all chapters, although a few addresses have been left with specific chapters. Abbreviations common to the construction industry have not always been expanded but all those relating to associations have been. Addresses are usually given for only one side of the Atlantic, although there are branches occasionally on the other. Please see the introduction to that appendix for the limitations of the listing.

No guide will ever include everything – nor will every reference be up-to-date. It is not intended that all should be in print. Out-of-print references may remain vitally important. References will change during the time taken for editorial and printing processes. New publications of 1995 may become the standard reference texts of 1999 or they may fade into oblivion. It is difficult to judge at the present time. Most sections have been written to maintain currency for the life of the text and should not date too soon – new titles will be published from time to time which will supplement those cited. The references in the first edition will still assist those with a broad remit working backwards in time. Unfortunately, family and health difficulties as well as pressure of work have affected more than one of the contributors, causing delays. Others have taken advantage of this to update their contribution. Updates to items such as the CDM regulations have been added at page proof stage. The databases chapter was written after the majority of text was received – due to the illness of the original contributor – and hence does not go over ground known to be covered by others but has taken a broader outlook and provided background taken for granted by other authors.

With volume 23, January 1995, the renowned *Architectural periodicals index* changed its name to *Architectural publications index*. Most contributions referring heavily to this were already completed and the text remains as it was since all references cannot be fully amended to take into account any possible changes in coverage that the change of name implies. Reference is made here and in the index to the change, and also in one location in the text where it was practicable and appropriate.

Unfortunately the week after corrected page proofs were received from John Barrick he collapsed and died suddenly. This chapter must be his final work and an epitaph to the Librarian of the Royal Town Planning Institute for 22 years. He is already missed in the planning information world.

Thanks go to everyone who has been involved, in no matter how small a way, from the chapter authors to those who have helped with the typing, correction, reading and provision of further information. Special thanks go to my husband, who, as an engineer, understands some of the topics covered and has helped tremendously throughout and encouraged the project of revision in the first place.

Valerie J. Nurcombe
Winsford, October 1995

CHAPTER ONE

Introduction to information retrieval and presentation

VALERIE J. NURCOMBE

The production of data by the analysis and digestion of new information is usually the result either of research or of everyday work in the professional practice. Much of the work in architectural offices is not research in the academic sense but, in applying known facts to new situations and in analysing the results, new information is created. That information is used in creating a building, which may then be reviewed in professional literature. If it is not reviewed the information will be absorbed for internal use only – but if published information is created, then that information enters the 'information chain'. Once the chain of reporting, of literature creation, is understood then it is possible to select the most appropriate source for the information required. Figure 1.1 represents the stages of publication of information, showing the levels of 'digestion' and the names that are given to the retrieval tools appropriate to each level. The tertiary level of lists is not shown. These are the guides to using and finding literature as well as lists of bibliographies, databases, indexing services and so on which are useful to anyone requiring guidance in information retrieval.

This chapter aims to discuss the nature of the information usually required in construction processes, to examine suitable approaches to the information retrieval process, discussing the skills involved in information retrieval and giving hints on keeping records and presenting information.

The nature of searches

It is always easier to ask someone else to find information, but there are occasions when there is no-one to ask or when it is more profitable to do it yourself. Few can achieve the same understanding of the requirements as the originator, nor have others the same ability to recognize what may be useful, to assess and integrate the findings with the problem instantly, whilst assimilating additional information which might otherwise have been unnoticed.

Everyday information requirements are usually for established facts, design data, manufacturers' addresses, product names and features. Many are swiftly found by consulting desk collections, the office 'library' or colleagues. Sometimes these fail: the address is not there; the tables seem to give every figure except the one sought – then, one must look elsewhere. In performing these searches one goes through a process, or series of processes, without conscious thought, once the usual procedures have been learned. Finding more complex information entails thinking through those processes methodically. Information needs are also highly individual, depending upon the enquirer, the level of expertise in the profession (ranging from student architect, to recently qualified building surveyor, to experienced civil engineer), the usual field of interest, the depth of knowledge required and the subject characteristics of the information required. Thus, when seeking information, available sources may be used for their speed of access, although better, more detailed or more reliable data may lie unsuspected in a less accessible report or article. At some point a decision may be made that there is no necessity to search further, or time may prohibit the extension of a search. Awareness of more remote resources plays a significant part in their retrieval and use. Conscious efforts have been made to improve the understanding among construction professionals of the availability of information in order to improve the application of R&D to buildings. Many journals mention recent research reports in their columns, particularly under the heading 'current awareness'.

Basic data may be found quickly by turning to a reference handbook; the *Barbour technical microfile* or Neufert's *Architect's data*, perhaps. The need is clear and easily expressed. The answer is, or should be, obvious when it is found; for example, degree day data for this month, average rainfall at the new site. Such facts are usually located in handbooks, and discussions of their use can be located quickly in specialist journals or texts once the source is known or identified. Telephone enquiries for such information are easily answered, as they do not involve searching through a chain of information but just entering the right handbook at the appropriate point. The architect may choose to locate such facts through his computer terminal using an appropriate on-line or CD-ROM database. An instinct for the source of the answer develops. It cannot be easily taught. For a town plan most people will think of consulting a road atlas, the Ordnance Survey or the Geographia plan series. In a large library, the development plan or

Figure 1.1: Generation of information

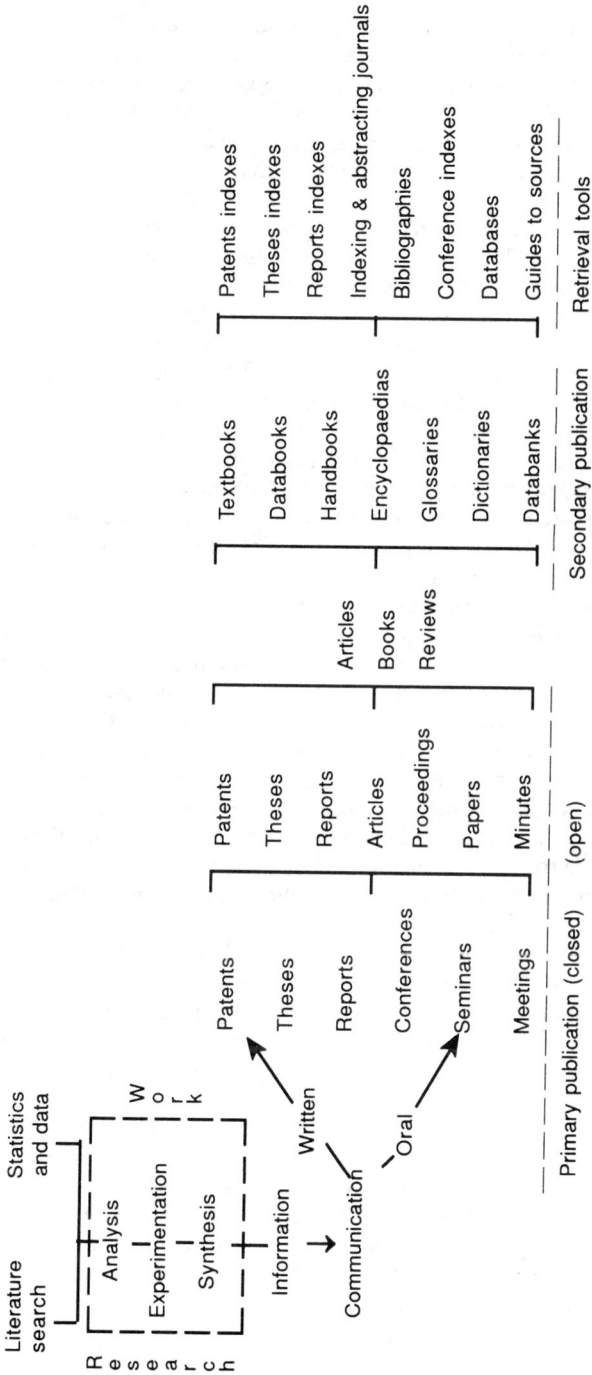

structure plan from the county council will be available, and may give the information required about the site environment in a form more suitable for the purpose. In the same way a dictionary will explain the meaning of a word, but an architecture or building dictionary will often be preferable to the *Oxford English dictionary* or *Webster's* and may include tables and other related information such as is found in Cowan's *Dictionary of architectural science* (Applied Science, 1973). Whatever the requirement, the data is sought, extracted from the source and the search ends. It is not necessarily a lengthy process.

More often the need is not just for facts but for descriptions of techniques, user requirements, materials, etc. A detailed answer is difficult to find. A new material has been advertized but in what situations has it been tested and used? To find manufacturer-independent information may require a long search through many different types of literature, involving not only time but lateral thinking. Success may be dependent upon the depth and quality of the indexing in the retrieval tools as much as upon the skill of the searcher. Mechanized databases can speed up such searches but, once references are found, the actual documents must be sought. Delays are sometimes inevitable. Precision in answering the enquiry may be vital.

An exhaustive search may be essential sometimes. An architect may make such a request figuratively, for example, when a client's brief calls for a new type of building with which he has little experience, or which he has not designed recently, and he requests 'all' information on that particular building type. This does not usually mean everything ever published but a selection of keynotes, relevant readings and examples of current thinking about that particular building type and the needs of its users. On occasion, especially when commencing research projects, an exhaustive search is needed. All possible sources must be investigated using the type of strategy outlined below in order to ascertain that the work has not been done before, is not currently in progress and has a firm background of established fact on which to build. Many references are sought, only some of which will be followed up. It is an exacting process requiring meticulous documentation. Such searches may continue for a considerable time.

Flexibility and an open mind are essential in order to exploit all approaches to a difficult problem when it may be useful to back-track, side-step or even start the search again. Records are therefore essential to save time, to remember what has been done and what has been found. A methodical and systematic approach to both searching and record keeping is essential. Even items which were rejected or useless should be recorded with a note of what was wrong with them, so that it is clear that they have been consulted and to save time back-tracking later. Answers may not always be found in the expected place. Resourcefulness will uncover alternative sources of information and persistence will be necessary where specific information is elusive, where dead-ends are met and when the whole process is dull. Browsing may bring rewards. Where index terms change not only is a thesaurus often necessary but so is a degree of lateral thinking – for instance, articles on nuclear fallout shelters have existed since World War II but, prior to the 1970s, they were usually indexed under 'civil defence shelters', 'air-raids', etc.

Definitions

Many architects have a small basic 'library' of information sources including books, pamphlets, catalogues and articles. Many items are selected individually and referred to again and again. Outline lists of such collections are given annually in the Building Bookshop catalogue and the *RIBA Reference annual*, formerly the *RIBA List of recommended books*. Lists are also given in the recent *CIIG Manual* mentioned in Chapter 22. The types of publication shown in Figure 1.2 are defined here and discussed in the following pages.

Guides to sources

This whole book is a guide. There are others like it on various topics, particularly in this series, in series from Mansell in the UK, and Gale and Meckler in the United States. While some guides tell you which publications to consult they are more than simple lists – they discuss methods and point the user down the right path to the source of the information required.

Bibliographies

A list of books and articles is usually called a bibliography. Each item is often called a 'reference'. Many bibliographies on technical topics also include institutional sources of information and research known to be in progress. Some are pure lists, while others are annotated, that is, they briefly describe the scope and sometimes comment on the merits of each item. The length of a bibliography may vary from six or seven references at the end of an article to a full-length hardback book such as John Smith's *Critical bibliography of building conservation*. The larger collections of these and of guides are usually found in professional and academic rather than public libraries.

References

As mentioned above, a reference is 'the item referred to', whether it is another book, a database, an institution or other source of information.

Figure 1.2: Information search chain

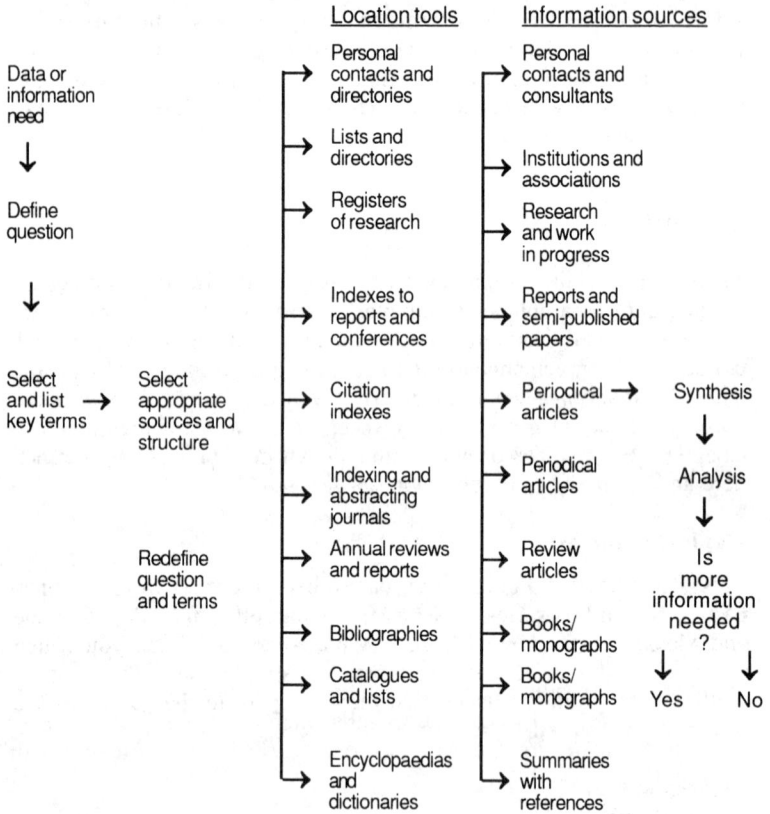

Process		Location tools	Information sources	
Data or information need		Personal contacts and directories	Personal contacts and consultants	
↓		Lists and directories	Institutions and associations	
Define question		Registers of research	Research and work in progress	
↓		Indexes to reports and conferences	Reports and semi-published papers	
Select and list key terms →	Select appropriate sources and structure	Citation indexes	Periodical articles →	Synthesis
		Indexing and abstracting journals	Periodical articles	↓ Analysis
	Redefine question and terms	Annual reviews and reports	Review articles	↓ Is more information needed ?
		Bibliographies	Books/ monographs	
		Catalogues and lists	Books/ monographs	↓ Yes ↓ No
		Encyclopaedias and dictionaries	Summaries with references	

There should always be adequate information given to locate any reference: for a book that is author, title, publisher and date; and for a journal, author, article, title, journal title, volume, issue, date and page numbers.

Reference works

These are specially designed handbooks, databooks, etc., to enable users to find specific information quickly. They are not meant to be read thoroughly.

Methodology

'Unfortunately the publishing world is not systematic' (Maltha, 1976), therefore any methodology has to take into account the need to skip stages and allow for exceptions. Bibliographies may now include books, periodical articles, the names of institutions and other sources of information. Some indexing journals include relevant reports and books. The following paragraphs give an outline of how to proceed; the essence is to start the snowball rolling, since once it is gathering momentum, and hopefully size, the order of procedure may vary. Figure 1.2 shows clear routes through the most rewarding channels, chosen initially according to the subject of the enquiry, then continuing into specific types of resource using the following hints on technique.

Some processes are automatic, that is, the brain proceeds with them when it recognizes the need for information. Skills must be developed. Initially, it is important to clarify exactly what information is required. This implies an awareness of any technical limitations, the terminology usually used and the level and amount of information needed at the particular time. Some books and articles may be too technical, too mathematical, or even too simple, or based on practices unique to a country. The exact time coverage and any relevant dates should be checked. For example, information on an event such as the Summerland (Isle of Man) fire has an exact date before which there will be no information. Although reports are usually published within a few years, reassessment may occur as, for example, the report in 1981 on the causes of the Ronan Point (London) failure which occurred in 1969. Nor will that information be found in many databases established more than a year or so after the date of the occurrence. At times, only very recent information will be required, such as standards, and the scope of a search should be narrowed accordingly. Foreign-language material may not be acceptable, or barriers between practices in different countries will prevent its use: for example, the application of solar energy systems depends on climate. However, some American publishing companies publish British texts, and vice versa, and many are multi-national, so that it is no longer possible to reject their output instantly as being based on local standards.

Searching, even using on-line, CD-ROM or Internet resources takes time; but intelligent guesses can save time. If a lot of information is required, use a bibliography as soon as possible. The index to the *Barbour technical microfile* is a type of classified bibliography, and many publications listed have references leading to other more specific information than that which appears on the microfiche file document. Stop when enough information has been found – most searches could go on forever but the rate of return diminishes.

Where current information is needed, be aware of the delays inherent in publishing processes. Books may be written four years before publication date and only partially updated after the submission of text. Publication usually takes six months to one year. Some journals which appear quarterly may also be a long time in publication, especially some indexing and abstracting journals which take a particularly long time to compile. Other journals may have a tatty appearance but may be very current. Current information is the most difficult to find because of the inadequacy of memory and the delays both in publication and compilation of indexes. Electronic newspapers and the swift updating of some databases available on-line assist with this. Memory usually condenses time or is incomplete, but as indexes are not compiled until some time after events have taken place individual issues of journals may need to be searched for information. *Keesing's contemporary archives* is current and helpful with national events while *Research index*, an index to the daily and weekly press, appears within two weeks of the articles listed.

It is helpful to list the sources to be used to retrieve information in the order in which they are to be consulted. If any are remote or need to be contacted by fax or letter they should be contacted early enough not to cause difficulties and delays later. Books may not be the best place to start if the topic is more likely to have been written about in journals. Use any indexing services available. At this stage try to appreciate any other subject approaches. For example, library science journals and books frequently discuss library buildings and their construction. Similarly, co-gen power stations are likely to be described in power generation literature. Other examples can be cited; computer-aided architectural design is written about not only in its own journal but is indexed in *Architectural periodicals index* (*API* on DIALOG and *APId* on CD-ROM) and also in *Computing and control abstracts*. Historians are interested in vernacular buildings, especially at the local level, and are far better at writing up information than architects. Will information about noise levels at an airport be found with discussions of planning, noise research, aircraft engineering, monitoring instrumentation, with specialist literature on airport construction, or with the literature on pollution?

Terminology varies between subjects, and between indexers. In searching any type of index to a book, journal or abstracting journal, there may be deviations from architectural language, and terminology changes over the years. Usage also changes with time. Colleagues of the 1940s and 1950s might not understand conversations on 'environment', which was once confined in usage to what is now called the habitat of animals. Identify the appropriate terminology for the subject according to the source of the information. For example, the search for information on the environment required for zoo animals will produce articles on 'natural habitat' unless 'conditions for captivity', or something similar, is used in the terminology. One should bear in mind also that modern approaches to this topic are based on the desire to emulate 'natural habitat', thus making the search more difficult. Similarly, the original definition may appear not to be yielding the sort of information required. Terminology should be redefined, either broadening the field of search because little has been found, or narrowing the field because too much was located, some being irrelevant to design.

In the context of searching on-line and CD-ROM databases, full text sources and bibliographies then the use of 'free language' or 'natural language' appears to enhance the possibility of finding the original search term. But different words are still used to describe the same topic – particularly to give an interesting style for readability. 'Key' articles sometimes exist which either crystallize information on a topic or which represent the basis from which other work has developed and from which other articles digest or rehash information. Locating one of these quickly may produce sufficient references or provide a good start. A review may perform a similar function in that it will discuss all literature and information on a subject, summarizing the content, discussing it critically and providing a synthesis. Some publications from The Building Research Establishment (BRE) have done this, e.g. *Wind environment around buildings* by Penwarden and Wise (HMSO, 1975). Subject series entitled 'Advances in . . . .' and 'Progress in . . . .' have been running for many years in some areas of science and technology. In construction such reviews are few.

Journal articles often discuss topics on which no book exists. Indexes and abstracts to journals are discussed at length in Chapters 3 and 4. They will often provide references quickly and have a wide scope. The on-line availability is also discussed and has considerably improved search speed but led to other problems of retrieval and comprehensiveness. Abstracts may provide useful information, but may evaluate and criticize. Articles with numerous references can start the information-snowball, but in architecture this may be rare – many articles do not cite their sources of information as well as those in other disciplines. Key authors may be identified and used in the author indexes of reference tools to locate their other relevant works. Authors may be used in the citation indexes, *Art and humanities citation index, Science citation index* and *Social sciences citation index*. Corporate authors, i.e. companies, practices, used in this way may help to locate a lot more information.

Books may be located via the articles, bibliographies and library catalogues, both printed and on-line. This is covered in Chapter 5. Some databases and abstracting journals include books and government publications as well as journal articles. Publishers' lists can be useful. The on-line and CD-ROM book lists, *Book bank* and *Bookfind* can be useful, although not designed for subject searching. Whenever using books be aware of the effect of changed legislation, standards and advances in technology on the information, as books tend to be older and these aspects change quickly. Throughout a search, check references and cross-references. Read. As you read and digest, so new lines of approach and reference will arise.

Indexes cover in-house company reports, research reports from academic institutions and reports communicating government-funded research results, among others. The most useful of these indexes are the BLLD's monthly *British reports, translations and theses* which superseded the *BLLD announcement bulletin*, and has regular cumulative subject indexes; the abstracts in the journals; the US Department of Commerce, National Technical Information Service (NTIS) database on-line and on CD-ROM. The problems of using and obtaining reports are discussed in greater detail in Auger's *Use of reports literature* (Butterworths, 1975) and in Mildren's *Information sources in engineering* (3rd edn, Bowker- Saur, 1995). It is important to remember that, while books and articles are secondary publications and their content may have been checked for accuracy, reports are the first stage in communicating research and may even contain inaccuracies in their findings.

Conference proceedings are another source of information with a separate indexing system. Most detailed and current are the BLLD's *Index to conference proceedings*, also available on-line, and the ISI service's *Index to scientific and technical proceedings* (ISTP) and *Index to social sciences and humanities proceedings* (ISSHP). These are now available on CD-ROM, but the coverage of the version used should be checked — they are not all as complete as the on-line version. Not all proceedings published contain full papers: some are summaries; others are fully researched and documented. The discussion is rarely recorded in full, and yet for the participants this is often the major benefit.

Reference books are found in most main libraries and are specially designed handbooks, data books, etc., to enable users to find specific information quickly. They are not meant to be read thoroughly.

- Dictionaries give, in alphabetical order, the spelling, pronunciation and definition of words in one or more languages, or of terms in specialist fields.
- Encyclopedias provide an extended summary of all knowledge either generally or on a specific subject, usually in an organized format with an index, cross-references and some suggestions for further reading.
- Directories usually list, in an appropriate order, people, organizations, products research etc., sometimes with brief notes of useful information.
- Handbooks and manuals provide facts and figures which are established and regarded as standard information, frequently needed. The level of background knowledge assumed varies.
- Yearbooks frequently combine directory and handbook

information where this changes frequently and is usually needed in its current form.

Essential reference books include a good dictionary, such as the *Oxford English dictionary* (Oxford University Press, various editions and dates), which takes its definitions from precedent and differs from the *Webster's new international dictionary* which takes definitions from current usage. *Encyclopedia Britannica* is still useful and contains references. Specific encyclopedias are sometimes called dictionaries and vary in quality. Some of the general titles such as the *McGraw-Hill dictionary of scientific and technical terms* (7th edn, 1992) are so large as to cover construction well. *Dictionary of architecture and construction materials* (H Buksch, MacDonald and Evans, 1975-6) was misnamed in that it was a German-English, English-German volume, while the *International dictionary of building construction* (A.C. Schwickers ed., McGraw-Hill, 1972) actually translated between four languages.

Guides and bibliographies

In some instances it is difficult to distinguish between a guide which discusses sources of information and indicates where specific types of query may be answered and a bibliography, especially an annotated bibliography, which is a list of references. An example, cited under official publications is the *Guide to official publications of foreign countries* despite its title is an annotated bibliography rather than a guide, and states this in the introduction. *Information sources in architecture and construction* is far from that type of annotated list as it discusses the types of sources available, non-book sources and others which will be useful.

The first guide in the architecture field was Denison Smith's *How to find out in architecture and building: a guide to sources of information* (Pergamon, 1967). There were many chapters on general formats of encyclopedias, directories, periodicals, etc., with a discussion of library classification and the building profession, as well as bibliographies of architectural history, building types and details. The 1970s and 1980s have seen such an increase in the volume of published material that much of this is now dated. There are also now new formats which were not then known (see Chapters 5 and 12).

There are various series of guides which should be used when searching for information in an unfamiliar field, for example in biology for zoos, education for special schools. The earlier one was the Pergamon *How to find out . . .* series and then the Butterworths series *Information sources in . . .* which is now published by Bowker Saur. Current titles include: *Information sources in agriculture and food science* (G. P. Lilley, 1981); *Information sources in the earth sciences* (D.N. Wood et al., 2nd edn, 1989); *Information sources in economics* (J. Fletcher, 2nd

Figure 1.3: Dewey decimal classification

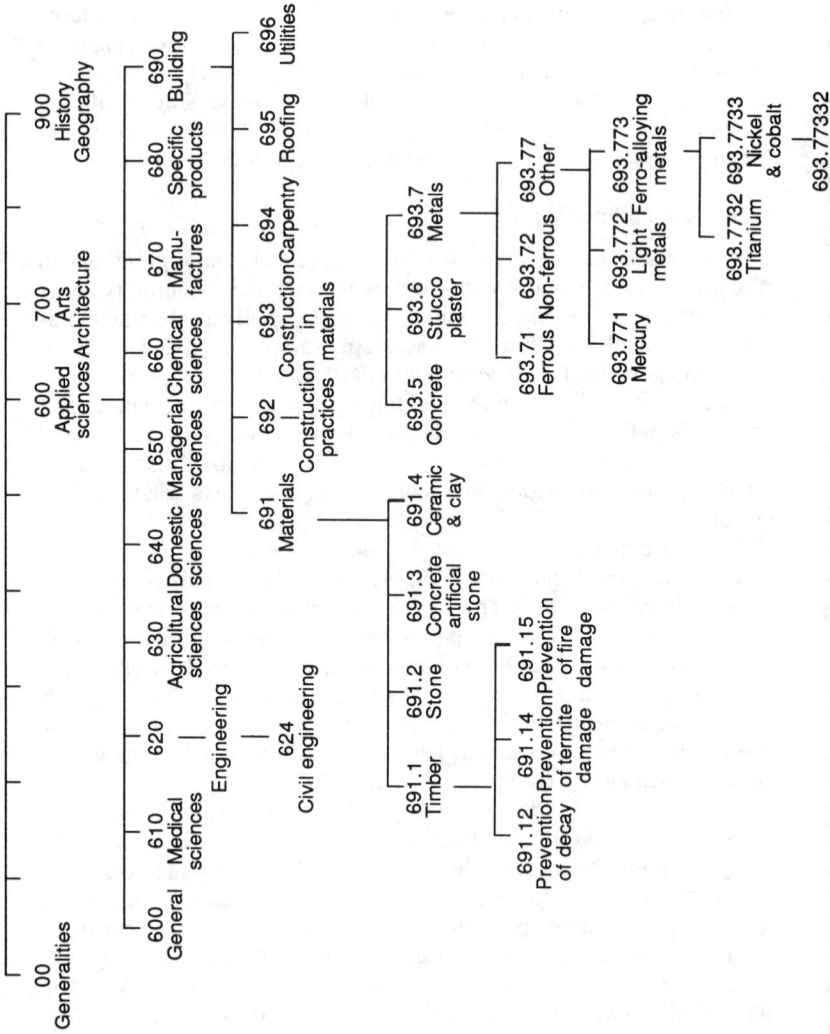

edn, 1984); *Information sources in energy technology* (L.J. Anthony, ed., 1988); *Information sources in environmental protection* (S. Eagle, ed., 1996); and *Information sources in sport and leisure* (M. Shoebridge, ed., 1992). *Information sources in engineering* (K. Mildren and P. Hicks, 3rd edn, 1995) is very much complementary to this book and the chapters on reports, standards, patents, conferences and 'Information and the engineers' complement and expand on information covered here. The chapters on 'Design and ergonomics', 'Environmental engineering', 'Transportation and traffic planning', 'Structural engineering', 'Construction engineering', 'Construction management' and 'Ground engineering' complement guidance given below and also illustrate the different approach taken by the engineer.

Mansell have also published a number of useful bibliographic guides, usually containing a discussion of the topic and sources followed by a bibliography. Useful titles include: *The history of urban and regional planning: an annotated bibliography* (A. Sutcliffe, 1980); *Housing policy in Britain: an information sourcebook* (T. Newson and P. Potter, 1985); *Keyguide to information sources in agricultural engineering* (B. Morgan, 1985); *Keyguide to information sources in archaeology* (P. Woodhead, 1985); *Keyguide to information sources in CAD/CAM* (J. Cox et al., 1988); *Keyguide to information sources in cartography* (A. Hodgkiss and A. Tatham, 1986); and *Keyguide to information sources in online & CD-ROM database searching* (J. Cox, 1991).

Many guides in the art field also cover architecture but there are few which are specific to architecture itself. Sharp's *Sources of modern architecture* (2nd edn, Architectural Press, 1980) discusses design and the work of modern architects, giving lists and bibliographies, but does not develop the theme into the construction of those buildings. It is complemented by Ruth Kamen's *British and Irish architectural history: a bibliography and guide to sources of information* (Architectural Press, 1981). Scarecrow Press has published J.B. Godel's *Sources of construction information* in several volumes from 1977, which covers US practice.

Planning as a topic was covered by one of the first guides which set a standard of excellence: Brenda White's *Sourcebook of planning information* (Bingley, 1971). Unfortunately, this has never appeared in a second edition although it still retains some relevance. Almost unique is Trevor Aldridge's *Directory of registers and records* (5th edn, Longman FT Law & Tax, 1993), which provides reliable, regularly updated indications of and guides to the sources of specific information on births, wills, financial records, property records and professional advice including site plans, maps and rights of way. The most current of these are often to be found in the pages of the journals, but the superb *Architects' journal (AJ)* 'Annual review' and guide to sources of information ceased in the 1980s. Here, the summaries of information related to major building types, hazards, and topics such as practice, law and energy, whilst the second part summarized the availability of those services that could assist with finding information, such as major trade associations, guides and information services.

The *AJ* series of guides and handbooks is familiar to many and these books have always included bibliographies and guidance as well as basic data and techniques. The most familiar is probably the *New metric handbook,* which has been through many editions. The originals were published weekly in *AJ* and then completed as books, for the most part. They included the *AJ Handbook of building enclosure*, the *AJ Handbook of building structure*, the *AJ Handbook of environmental powers* (now heavily superseded by new legislation), the *AJ Handbook of urban landscape*, the *AJ legal handbook* and the *Housing rehabilitation handbook*. Others began in this series and were published under different titles such as Duffy and Worthington's *Planning office space* (Architectural Press, 1976), whose ideas are now sadly dated, and the *Handbook of sports and recreational building design* (4 vols, Architectural Press, 1981), now revised in conjunction with the Sports Council and republished by Butterworth, 1993–4. *Specification* has been at the right hand of architects for a long time and has bibliographies and references in most sections, as does the *Architect's standard catalogue*. Both publications are annual. The Barbour products referred to in Chapter 5 are massive bibliographies but without guidance. Standards are included.

Useful publishers and bookshop lists to have around are those from the RIBA, the Building Bookshop, the British Cement Association, and the Institutes. Libraries may have the comprehensive *British books in print* and *Books in print* covering the United States. Both are now in microform, on-line and in CD-ROM formats as well as in hard copy. *British national bibliography* catalogues most items placed in the British Library under the Copyright Deposit regulations. Most countries have their own national bibliography which varies in coverage. The catalogue of the Library of Congress is more like the printed catalogue of the British Museum library, now known as the British Library. Catalogues of major libraries have long been a source of information for academics, less so for those in professional practice. This source has become of more value as the Internet and, in Britain, the JANET systems have made it possible to search library catalogues from remote locations.

Catalogues and indexes

In any book or directory the contents are listed and indexed to provide a means of retrieval. The mystique often built up around indexes is largely the product of imagination, but the compilation of good indexes does require great skill and many reference texts would be useless without good indexing. Ease-of-use involves a little understanding of techniques which vary according to the purpose: library catalogue, product catalogue in a directory, book index. All that any of these do is to produce a list of, and an index to, the contents of a location. The list is arranged in an easy-to-understand fashion with a clear structure, which may be by topic, by alphabet or otherwise. Styles and formats vary. Essential information is always the topic (item) and the location, whether that is a page number, shelf number or bibliographic reference. Words can become stumbling blocks in themselves, and if the term first thought of is not located then alternatives must be found – synonyms, near synonyms, etc. A dictionary or thesaurus may be necessary.

The arrangement of index terms may be approached in various ways, using a variety of subheading systems, using inversion of terms, or not, and ordering the words according to each letter, regardless of spaces, or by the putting the short words before the long. Problems may arise in using indexes and, in some cases, the distances separating connected terms may be quite considerable according to the method of organization employed. Page layout sometimes becomes very important in identifying subordinate terms.

If the library catalogue – which may be on cards, on computer, on microfiche, in print or in any other format – is seen as an index which is usually organized by author and title as well as by topic, then its mystique may be minimized. With the use of computers the order may be less significant, as searching is more often done on criteria defined by words and groups of words. At this point the order of the actual information becomes less critical as manipulation has become easier. Printouts and listings are possible in various orders.

A subject listing of information is usually presented to users in two ways:

- an alphabetical arrangement of words and phrases representing the topics, which we call an *index*. This is essential if one is to locate any particular term in the text.
- a logical arrangement of the subjects, grouping them together to keep like with like, part with whole and so on. This latter is *classification*.

Classification and indexing are the bases of arrangement in all collections of information, be they books or encyclopedias or libraries, but they may be undertaken according to different principles. It is useful to understand the basics of these. Essentially, classification means putting together things that are alike and separating those that are different. This book is organized in such a way that the general topics come before the specific, and the specific are arranged according to a simple construction model starting with the site and moving through the materials to the completion and then the conservation and history of the full buildings. Chapter numbers, or codes of some type, are assigned merely as a means of swift processing or arrangement. The basic ways of categorizing are:

- by taking general concepts and moving through to specifics in a specific order which may resemble a family tree (see Figure 1.3, excerpt from *Dewey decimal classification*), or may combine with the second method below,
- by listing categories according to the characteristics which they share in such a way that there can be no overlap or uncertainty as to the appropriate position of anything *unless* the item covers two topics. This is the approach taken by CI/SfB. An example is shown below.

Buildings	Structure	Construction form	Materials	Requirements & activities
Factories	Roofs	Section	Brick	Office administration
Health centres	Ceilings	Sheet	Slate	Contract procedure
Houses	Windows	Liquid coating	Glass	Insulation requirements

Evaluation

It is easy to accept information once written as being correct, but is it? Has the printer made an error which proof-reading has failed to correct? If a figure is in error and a calculation is based on it, what could the result be? It is best to be aware of such problems and to 'test' or appraise the information presented. The author may be a well-known authority, an academic with no practical business experience or a journalist who will produce a very chatty account – helpful for background in an unfamiliar area but not always fully reliable. The ability to write is not often as good among those whose technical expertise is excellent. Some authors are biased, even in the presentation of facts. Look for biographical information stating where the author is working, what his qualifications are, his nationality. The title page, introduction or preface may help. Dust-jacket 'blurb' is designed to sell – omission is a favourite ploy.

Gimmicky titles may indicate poor quality within or may be a sales device. Subtitles elaborate the content or tone of the work indicating that a book with a seemingly helpful title is actually irrelevant. The publisher may indicate the tone of the work; some are known for a particular type of publishing. There are scholarly and popular presses and small propagandist private presses. Sweet and Maxwell tend to be law publishers, the university presses are scholarly and, although they usually relate to their country of origin, some US schools, such as Yale, have published British texts, and vice versa.

Date and edition are vital. Not all information needs to be current, but, where law, standards and advances in technology are concerned currency is essential. There is a difference between a revised reprint and a new edition, and a reprint does not imply revision. Check also the date to which the data in the book relate, especially with reference books or handbooks, as it may well be considerably before the publication date. The contents list often indicates the scope of the book, its depth and weighting of various parts. Omissions may be noted either in the introduction or the preface, which should indicate also the aims, limitations and level of the material. In an article this should be done in the opening paragraph.

Check the references. Do they appear reliable and are they up-to-date? Look for authorities, which should be quoted. Is sufficient information given to locate the references? A list in Bowyer's *Vernacular building conservation* (Architectural Press, 1980) omitted dates and lacked any standardization. This does not instil confidence. Enquiries revealed that it had not been compiled by the author. Many architecture books have in the past lacked references. The results of academic work are usually well referenced. An author may be known by local or special libraries to be frequently inaccurate in citing references. For example, Leicestershire Archive Office pointed this out with regard to W.G. Hoskin's *The Midland peasant* (Macmillan, 1965). Bibliographies may not be as current as they should be. A few current references in a handbook may be adequate. More detailed information may require a bibliographic search but not a need for a little basic information.

Indexing also varies in quality. Is there an index at all? If you are locating very specific information check that the index is detailed enough to reflect the content adequately. Indexing is not always done by the author and varies in depth.

In reading, try to distinguish facts from interpretation, skimming the less useful sections and scanning others for information. Be sure that hypotheses are substantiated with good evidence, figures, diagrams and references. Style of writing differs and affects comprehension. If an account is difficult to understand a similar version by another author may be presented in a clearer style. Do not accept every word as true. Look for bias and evaluative or critical treatment. After reading a few items on a topic it should be possible to separate facts from opinion and develop a personal viewpoint.

Organizing information

Apart from the concept of integrating the gathering and organizing of information with the objectives and with the presentation of information, the most important thing to remember is that this stage reflects the way you work and quickly becomes a habit. It is easy to drift into sloppy habits and very difficult to break them. The message in this section is to develop a sound procedure and then stick to it, if at all possible. Some examples of how things go wrong are: a report is required urgently, but in the rush you cannot recall which items in the piles of literature are really relevant, without re-reading everything; you need to retrieve an article, but to whom was that vital article lent?; a conference proceedings arrives two months after it was requested on loan, and you cannot remember why you wanted it; a really useful photocopy of an article contains no details of its source, so can it be quoted?; the substance of that brilliant idea which seemed so vivid has evaporated by the next day when you come to write it down.

Recording

Records are important, and many architects develop personal record systems at an early stage. Nothing is more frustrating than not being able to recall what was said yesterday and the source you were told to check for particular information about a worrying technical problem. When a problem recurs, your records should indicate not only where to find the answer but also the additional hints that were published later. There are two types of record necessary: what was searched and what was found. In recording what was searched, keep a list of sources and check off items, making brief notes of problems in using or finding them and of content. In the case of serial publications such as journal indexes, note the years that have been checked. Notes of references found are best kept on slips or cards, since these can be easily filed or shuffled. Larger cards may be used for notes on the subject content. The computer is now providing considerably improved indexing capabilities for such notes. But the basic information noted is still the same and should be enough to help to locate the items and refer to it in written reports, etc., according to one of the two systems described below. If the item is retrieved it is best to note where it was located, and, if in a library, make a note of the classification number in order to save time should it be needed again.

Experience in teaching architectural and building students has shown that the former tend to begin to develop their own personal reference collection early in their career, frequently with some form of indexing or organization. This often flags later. The latter, in common with many other professionals, collect but do not organize. Scraps of paper, useful addresses and memory tend to get lost or to fail. Organizing does take time but repays that time when it is possible to find the required information quickly and easily at the desk. Methods vary and are described in some texts, the recent ones making the assumption that one has access to a computer, or unlimited funds. Neither may be true for everyone at present but the notebook computer will soon be on everyone's desk.

Presenting a search

The result of a search may be information which is immediately applied to produce a drawing, to ring a manufacturer or to complete a bill of quantities, etc. If it is a list of bibliographical references, this must be organized and presented either as a separate item or as the final part of a report or dissertation. The information to include is set out in BS 5605: 1990 *Recommendations for citing and referencing published material*, in conjunction with BS 1629: 1989 *Recommendations for references to published materials* and BS 6371: 1983 (1990) *Recommendations for citation of unpublished documentation*. There should be a clear order: alphabetical by author or title, by topic, by date as appropriate.

Presenting information

Information should always be considered as having a subject and an aim – information is rarely required for its own sake, or, put another way, it is what you do with the information that counts; or what the information (if you communicate it) can do. Information can help in the short term in a number of ways:

- Stimulation: e.g. to help you to be creative and motivated or interested
- Current awareness: e.g. to keep you up-to-date with the 'competition' and developments
- Methodology: e.g. to tell you how to do something
- Theory: e.g. to predict different or future phenomena
- Data: e.g. to compare your own results or use in calculations
- Solutions: e.g. to show you how other people dealt with similar problems
- Education: e.g. to give background details in a new field or to pass an exam.

Communication

Consider the method to be used to communicate the results of your work, taking into account timing and the means of production in relation to whatever form of communication is used:

- Proposals: e.g. to sell a product or service
- Reports: e.g. to satisfy a client of progress or status
- Talks: e.g. to persuade clients to adopt a design solution
- Plans: e.g. to satisfy authorities that regulations have been obeyed
- Articles: e.g. to demonstrate professional expertise
- Drawings: e.g. to express a design to clients and contractors.

The most important consideration should be your audience. What are their objectives and how are they able and willing to attain them? Are their objectives compatible with yours? Again a process of integration is necessary. The specific points to consider are:

- How do you wish to influence them?
- What level do they understand?
- What will they use the information for?
- How much time will they spare to read it?
- How would they prefer to receive information: a long essay, drawings or brief, clear notes?

Of course, an appreciation of all these considerations should influence literature searching and personal records. To summarize, the key concept is the integration of all aspects of the objectives with the method of achieving those objectives. In particular, knowing exactly who is to be influenced and in what way, imagining their position and deciding what would influence them in the desired way.

Written versus verbal

Normally the choice between written and verbal communication is made for us, but the important thing to remember is that written communication may have a greater impact than verbal communication – for example, the great political speeches – but there is greater control. A mistake when talking to an audience is difficult to correct, even if spotted. When talking, you may suffer from nerves and perhaps lack of experience, and also from the effects of the surroundings, including the audience. With writing and drawing the finished product can normally be corrected before it reaches the client.

Written communication

Written communication usually takes the form of a letter, memorandum, report, design, contract or periodical article. The presentation of drawn information should need no discussion and is ably covered in the following works among others: R.F. Reekie, *Draughtsmanship* (3rd edn, Arnold, 1976), L. Dudley's *Architectural illustration* (Prentice-Hall, 1977) and R.W. Gill's *The Thames and Hudson manual of rendering in pen and ink* (rev. edn, Thames and Hudson, 1990).

Report writing has no rigid procedure, but the notes below coupled with a flexible approach should offer some help. You should check for an organization's instructions on layout, house-style, etc. Prepare a statement of intent as this can prove an invaluable yardstick when deciding whether or not to include items of information. Work out a time schedule. This means fixing or acknowledging a deadline for completion of the report. Then check the availability and speed of production facilities, graphics, reproductions, photography, binding, etc. This will then enable you to work out the time required to compose the report. The production of the report can cause more problems than the writing.

Assemble the information and any other relevant material, bearing in mind the statement of intent. It may help to have a card or folder for each section of the report or for each subject division of the work. Information or ideas can be added to the appropriate collection as they arrive. All ideas and information should be examined with a critical eye, particularly checking for accuracy and comparing results and ideas with previous work. Time spent in simply thinking around the material and how it might be presented is never wasted. It can help to write out a provisional list of headings covering the information. These headings can then be arranged into a logical order, and shown to colleagues for comment. Even at this early stage criticism can be helpful. If there are problems in deciding on the structure of the report then consider the alternatives and take the one that fits best with the objectives. Each heading can be expanded by adding brief notes about the work, ideas and information from other sources which relate to that heading. Use the objectives as a guide to selecting which topics require special emphasis, and try to predict questions that may arise in the minds of the people who will read the report.

Writing the report can best be described by considering its various parts. Reports are usually best written over a short period of time to preserve continuity. Do not wait for perfect sentences to form in your mind, but write whatever comes to mind. This way it is easier to start, and then easier to criticize and correct something on paper, rather than something in the mind. BS 4811: 1972 (1986) *Specification for the presentation of research and development reports* and BS 4821: 1990 *Recommendations for the presentation of theses and dissertations* give advice that can be adapted to differing situations. The various parts of the report are considered below.

Front cover: This should include the following:

- Report number: it may be used for physically storing and retrieving a report, if it is part of a series
- Title: must be descriptive, as it may be used to retrieve the report by subject or it may be used to decide if the report is worth reading
- Author's name
- Name of organization producing the report
- Date when writing was completed
- Security classification if necessary.

Title page: This usually gives the information already given on the front cover, perhaps with a little more detail, such as subtitle, names of sponsoring bodies, contract numbers and acknowledgements. The signature of the writer and his supervisor or senior executive, if required, should always appear here.

Summary page: The summary or abstract of the report is best kept to one page. It should be written as though it might be the only part of the report that a busy executive will have time to read. It must convey the message that the report is trying to communicate. At the very least, the summary is the bridge between the title and the body of the report.

Table of contents: This should list all the principal headings in the report in the order in which they appear, giving appropriate page numbers. The table should allow the reader to see at a glance how the report is laid out and to locate quickly any section which he wishes to read. Contents pages are usually written last because they have to cover the entire contents. However, it helps sometimes to write a draft contents page to see how well the report is 'balanced' in terms of structure and headings. It is usual to number (or letter) sections as well as pages. Sections may be systematically broken down by numbers and letters or by decimals. For example:

Principal section		1	1
Main section	(a)	or	1.1
Sub-section	(i)	or	1.1.1

BS 5848: 1980 (1986) *Specification for numbering of divisions and subdivisions in written documents* lays down guidelines.

Introduction: This should give the reason behind the report, the objectives, terms of reference, background, state-of-the-art, previous works and any appropriate discussion which should justify the work and map out the following content.

The work done: The work done is usually split into two main parts: (1) experimental or investigatory, method and results; (2) discussion and theoretical interpretation. The main body of the report is the vital section when it comes to details and accuracy. Make sure all the influencing variables are covered. Diagrams, pictures, graphs, tables, etc., should be used when they represent the best way of communicating information. If a figure is referred to in detail from the text or it is essential to the understanding of part of the text, that figure should be positioned as near as possible to the corresponding text (preferably not over the page). If the figure is referred to from numerous parts of the text, or the size and number of illustrations would unbalance the text making it difficult to follow, then figures should be placed in an appendix. The text should refer to the figures via numbers or codes and/or page numbers. Codes can be a simple running number right through the report or a compound number made up of chapter number/section number/type of figure, etc., e.g. 'Table 4.12.2' in the text could mean a table in Chapter 4 section 12 paragraph 2, and 'Fig. 45' could simply refer to the 45th 'figure'. The text should make clear reference to a 'figure' making sense to the reader. A figure should emphasize the point made in the text. The writer should ensure that its title, labelling, symbols and units are all crystal clear, well defined, make sense and are in a form that the reader can easily use if he has to. Use footnotes or annotations if necessary to avoid overcrowding a drawing. Lastly, do not forget that drawings and diagrams can cause problems in reproduction – so check first what can or cannot be done.

Conclusions and recommendations: These form the end-product of the work and will hopefully justify the effort. Like the summary, these may be some of the only parts of the report that are actually read by busy managers or customers, so again special care is required.

Appendices: These may include tables, graphs, photographs, drawings, etc. (only when it is not appropriate to include these in the body of the report – see 'The work done').

List of references: This is often a neglected area and as a result causes all sorts of problems. There are two main points to remember: first of all the reason for having these references is for other people to obtain the original documents, and therefore it is vital to be accurate and to give as much information as possible. For example, the title will help them to decide if the original is worth having; the issue date should be included, even if it duplicates volume and issue numbers, as a double-check in case you make a mistake and to give an idea of currency; the complete pagination will give an idea of the length of the item and hence one measure of its usefulness; the complete title of a journal will prevent misinterpretation of abbreviated journal titles. The second point is to check whether there is an imposed house-style for references. Whether or not there is a house-style, references should be consistent (for example, indicate 'volume' by volume, Volume, vol., Vol., v., V., v, V or by underlining or by using bold print, but always be consistent!).

There are two main ways of linking the text of the report with individual references in the list; these are the Harvard System, as used in this book, and the numeric system, as frequently found in journal articles (and see Chapters 22 and 23). Quite a lot of detail may be found in the British Standards quoted above and in the *Chicago manual of style* and in Turabian's guide.

Harvard system: This uses author's surname and the year as the link, e.g. the text may contain inserts such as 'the method used by Jones (1980) was also. . .' or 'the established method (Brown, 1960) was also. . .' In this system the list of references would be in alphabetical and date order and of the following form:

> Brown, J. (1960). Title of the Article. *Journal Name*, **6** (3), 542-584.
> Jones, D. (1980). Title of the Article. *Journal Name*, **28** (6), 33–34.

Numeric system: This uses numbers as the link, e.g. the text may, for example, contain inserts such as 'the article by Jones (4) covers. . .' In this system the references are listed in number order as they first appear in the text, e.g:

> 4.   Jones, D. Title of the Article. *Journal Name*, Vol. 28, No. 6, June 1980. pp. 33-34.
> 5.   Brown, J. Title of the Article. *Journal Name*, Vol. 6, No. 3, March 1960. pp. 542-584.

Both systems have their advantages and disadvantages and, depending on what you are writing, you may find one better than the other or, alternatively you may find a hybrid or extended system the best for your purposes.

Where annotations are used, an appropriate explanatory note should be given at the beginning of the list. If you think it is important that the reader should know who wrote a particular reference and when, as it is referred to in the text, then the Harvard system is best. The Harvard system can be bulky and interrupt reading flow if a number of references are cited close together. Other addenda may include any acknowledgements, a glossary, list of abbreviations and symbols with explanations and a distribution list. It is most important to define clearly any units that are used in the report. If the report is long enough to justify an index, then an index should be included.

Revision is an essential part of report writing. It is a good idea to give the proofs to a colleague for comment, and also to put the report aside for a few days before revising it yourself.

Verbal communication

Unlike written communication, a speaker and his audience are in a live situation where it is essential to take into account the interest (and comfort) of the listeners. If one or two of the audience become restless, this will be communicated to the others. It is important to watch for warning signs and then control the situation by varying the presentation. Any presentation should be varied to keep the audience's attention.

When giving a talk, presentation or any other oral communication, decide exactly what you want to achieve, remembering that only a limited amount of 'new' information can be imparted during the length of an average talk – data is better presented on an accompanying handout than within the presentation. Careful consideration as to the nature of the audience and the reason for the talk will determine the most suitable approach, always bearing in mind their background knowledge on the topic. It is not necessary to waste time covering well-known ground, but the impetus can be lost if the level is pitched so high that the presentation is not understood. In a mixed audience everyone has to be catered for at some point without boring one group or losing another in jargon.

All presentations take far longer to prepare than to give. A rough estimate may be about 10 hours' preparation to one hour of talking, depending on the visual aids to be produced. It is important to remember that visuals take time to produce – especially if photography is involved – and time should be allowed for this in the preparatory stages. Preparation of an outline should show a logical progression of ideas, preferably with a climax. Methods of preparation vary – it is possible to prepare notes to refer to during a talk or to completely draft the whole presentation word for word. However, if the latter is then read from the text it can be very flat, especially if spoken in monotone without sufficient dramatic effect. Confidence in the knowledge of the topic, backed by a sound preparation, makes for an effective presentation. Consideration for those in all locations thoughout the room is also important, making sure that all can hear and see, write if necessary, and so on. Rehearsal is – if artificial at the time – useful, and a tape recorder may help the speaker to evaluate how the talk will come across to the audience. In final preparation, it is helpful to list all of the points to be covered – the equipment needed and its location, the room layout, signposting, etc. Last minute hitches are usual but can be overcome if there is a degree of readiness for them.

The secret of a good presentation technique is self-control coupled with a relaxed approach. Speak clearly, naturally and not too quickly without any 'ums', 'ers', etc., but above all say what you are going to cover and get on with it. Looking up towards the audience and receiving feedback from their expressions will improve the presentation. Reaction can be useful provided the speaker is not thrown by audience participation. The development of good verbal communication is a skill, covering more than just presentation to an audience; effective day-to-day communication with individuals, face-to-face or on the telephone, is an essential basis for the development of that skill. There is no substitute for experience.

Conclusion

There is far more information available on all these topics than has been covered in this short introduction. In the original edition of the text there were three chapters covering the same ground. Here, it is preferred to refer to further text and detail than to go over that ground again in summary, focusing instead on topics for which guidance is not so easily found elsewhere. The following references and bibliography give some guidance on possible further reading. There is far more available than is listed below, and new material within this area is published every year.

References and bibliography

Chappell, D. (1994) *Standard letters in architectural practice.* 2nd edn. Blackwell Scientific Publications.

Day, R.A. (1979) *How to write and publish a scientific paper.* Philadelphia: ISI.

Directory of databases. Annual. Gale Research. (formerly *Cuadra directory of databases*).

Gray, D.E. (1970) *So you have to write a technical report: elements of technical report writing.* Washington, DC: Information Resources Press.

Hamilton, A. (1989) *Writing matters.* RIBA Publications.

Kirkman, J. (1980) *Good style for scientific and engineering writing.* Pitman.

MacDonald, J.W. (1992) *Report writing.* Croner Publications.

Maltha, D. (1976) *Technical literature search and the written report.* Pitman.

Mitchell, J. (1974) *How to write reports.* Fontana.

Mort, S. (1994) *Professional report writing.* Gower.

The Chicago manual of style. (1993) 14th edn. University of Chicago Press.

Sussams, J. (1994) *How to write effective reports.* 2nd edn. Gower.

Turabian, K. (1987) *A manual for writers of term papers, theses and reports.* 5th edn. rev. by B.B. Honigblum. University of Chicago Press. Regularly updated since 1937 and available in various reprints.

Turk, C. and Kirkman, J. (1989) *Effective writing: improving scientific, technical and business communication.* 2nd edn. Spon.

Willis, P. (1983) *RIBA dissertation handbook: a guide to research and writing.* RIBA Publications.

A good dictionary should always be close at hand, the Oxford in England and Webster's in the United States. Additional reference books to help with language are:

Roget's thesaurus of English words and phrases. Now available in various editions.

Fowler's modern English usage. (1965) 2nd edn. Oxford University Press.

The Oxford dictionary of quotations. Oxford University Press. Regularly updated and available also as *The concise Oxford dictionary of quotations* and *The little Oxford dictionary of quotations.*

Organizing information

Dossett, P. (1992) (ed.) *Handbook of special librarianship and information work.* 6th edn. London: Aslib.

Foskett, A.C. (1981) *The subject approach to information.* 4th edn. London: Bingley.

Ray-Jones, A. and Clegg, D. (1976) *CI/SfB construction indexing manual.* 3rd edn. RIBA Publications.

CHAPTER TWO

Associations, organizations and libraries

JEANNE M. BROWN

This chapter highlights the types of materials and services provided by some of the most significant sources of information in architecture and construction: associations, organizations and libraries. Suggestions are given on how to select and contact the appropriate source. The task of the information seeker is to select the most effective starting point amongst a wide variety of institutions, and then to communicate the information need successfully to the institution's representative.

Associations and organizations

Associations and organizations play a key role in both the production and communication of information and where the quality of a building is grounded in the information used to produce it, it is critical that the contributions of such groups be fully recognized and utilized. There are hundreds of professional associations and trade organizations in architecture and construction. Each has a unique niche, whether in the topic-focus of the organization, or in the group to which its services are aimed. Each provides a unique combination of services, some to members only. Although it is not necessary to be an expert on organizations to make use of their offerings, it is worthwhile to be aware of the various types of organizations, and the range of their services.

Groups with a geographic base

The identity and functioning of some groups flow from the geographic location of their primary membership. Examples include the International Union of Architects (UIA), the American Institute of Architects

(AIA), the Royal Institute of British Architects (RIBA), the Royal Australian Institute of Architects (RAIA), and the Royal Architectural Institute of Canada (RAIC). The concerns and interests of such groups tend to be broad, encompassing the professional needs of their members. They may be engaged in research, in lobbying, in providing continuing education, in establishing professional standards, and in many other activities. The RIBA's active role in the development of the Warne Report, *Review of Architects (Registration) Acts 1931–1969* is one example.

Dissemination of information, news and research advances is often a key role. The RIBA's *Architect's reference annual*, edited by Peter Adderley, is only one of many publications through which the RIBA seeks to inform its members. The AIA has recently embarked on a project to supply information on-line to subscribing members: *AIA Online* provides not only information produced by the association, such as its directories, but also product information, publications citations, standards and specifications, and costing information. Additional information continues to be added to the system, which has the potential to put a wealth of information into the architect's office in a format that can be manipulated electronically and thus save the user considerable time.

Groups with a topical focus

The preponderance of the organizations in architecture and construction may be said to fall into the category of groups with a topical focus. Whether you are familiar with the British CI/SfB classification or the American CSI format, you can expect there to be at least one group devoted to most areas of these classification schemes. In fact, there are often several groups addressing an area or sub-area. For example, *The ENR directory of construction information resources*, edited by Joseph A. MacDonald, lists 28 organizations under the topic 'concrete/cement/grout' – and that is in the United States alone! In many cases the name of the organization indicates the area of interest. However, this is not always the case. It is not possible, for instance, to know from its name that the American Architectural Manufacturers Association (AAMA) is in fact specifically concerned with windows and siding. Directories arranged by topic, such as *The ENR directory of construction information resources*, are therefore quite useful in identifying relevant groups.

Even for groups with more descriptive names, it is not possible to determine the scope of their activities from the name alone. The range of differences in activities can be illustrated by a comparison of the American Concrete Institute (ACI) and the Tiles and Architectural Ceramics Society (TACS). The former implements a certification programme for technicians in the field, produces a manual with extensive data on concrete, issues several periodicals, has a publications list of about 300 titles, and creates standards through its many technical com-

mittees. The Tiles and Architectural Ceramics Society is more historically oriented. It produces a journal irregularly, a newsletter, a regular
though small leaflet/magazine, and arranges tours for its members.

Research oriented groups

Data and technical advice are provided by organizations and associations to government bodies, to manufacturers and to practitioners. This
function improves the quality of building, and can also save the individual invaluable time and money (not to mention future legal fees!).
Many of the groups mentioned above conduct research and communicate the results of their research and that of others to the building community. The RIBA, the AIA, the ACI, and the AAMA all conduct or
report research. There are also international bodies focused on research,
such as the International Council for Building Research, Studies and
Documentation (Conseil International du Batiment pour la Recherche,
l'Etude, et la Documentation – CIB). However, research agencies closer
to home are more likely to have an immediate impact, and to be the
source of critically needed information.

It pays, literally, to be familiar with the organizations responsible for
disseminating research, and with the publications through which they
communicate. In the United Kingdom, the Building Research Establishment (BRE), the British Standards Institution (BSI), the Building Services Research and Information Association (BSRIA) and the Construction
Industry Research and Information Association (CIRIA) are key contributors of research information. Additionally there are UK associations concentrating on quite specific areas such as the Timber Research
and Development Association (TRADA).

In the United States, the Construction Specifications Institute (CSI),
the International Conference of Building Officials (ICBO), the American Society for Testing and Materials (ASTM), the American Society
for Heating, Refrigerating and Air-Conditioning Engineers (ASHRAE),
the American National Standards Institute (ANSI), Underwriters Laboratories (UL), and the Environmental Design and Research Association
(EDRA) are primary sources of technical data and information. An example of organizations focusing on specific areas of research is the ACI.

Government agencies are often a source of research information. They
may sponsor research, such as Britain's Department of the Environment
(DoE) or the US Department of Energy (DOE), or they may simply
disseminate the information, as does the National Technical Information Service (NTIS) in the United States.

Virtual associations

The virtual world of on-line computing has spawned many on-line associations, in the informal sense of the word. Most require no 'member-

ship' application or fee. One purpose of these groups is to share information, both published and unpublished. The on-line community can also serve to locate experts in a field. One example of a virtual association is the Cooperative Network for Building Researchers (CNBR), currently hosted on-line by the Royal Melbourne Institute of Technology in Australia. CNBR has more than 200 members in many countries, including the United States and UK, as well as Canada, Israel, Brazil, Poland, the Netherlands, Sri Lanka and others. Fields represented are construction management, construction economics, building surveying, town planning, architecture and building science.

Associations outside architecture and construction

Several fields are closely related to, and interrelated with, architecture. The American Planning Association (APA), the Royal Town Planning Institute (RTPI), the American Society of Interior Designers (ASID), the International Society of Interior Designers (ISID), the American Society of Landscape Architects (ASLA) and the Landscape Institute all represent fields closely intertwined with architecture. They provide information used by architects, and are a fertile source of consultants as well. Associations in more distant fields can also supply valuable information. Legal, business, accounting, management and other groups produce information vitally important to the architect in the conduct of business. In addition, when working on a particular building type, associations representing that field should be consulted. For instance, if a library is to be designed, it would be expedient to consult the American Library Association, which has produced both a directory of library building consultants and a checklist of design considerations.

Association information services

Many services have been mentioned above. However, a more extensive exposition will emphasize the crucial contributions of these groups. Some services are available to members only. Often, though, information is available to non-members, although sometimes for a fee. Services of specific associations are given below for illustrative purposes.

Printed material is a common form of association communication. Whether communicating news of the association itself, or research in the field, this remains, even in the on-line world, an effective means of providing information. Many association publications, even those aimed solely at the membership, are available in libraries. Some material, especially pamphlet-type publications, will be available only from the association. According to *The ENR directory* (p.13), the US antitrust law requires that trade organizations provide to anyone who asks 'any industry information the organization has collected'. *The ENR directory* identifies the following classes of information that may be available, often free, often of high quality: construction information, standards and codes, product and method specifications, statistical data, research and development data, and materials testing results.

On-line information is being provided by many organizations. In some cases the on-line information covers articles or reports, or holdings in the organization's library. Both the Environmental Protection Agency (EPA) and the Lawrence Berkeley Laboratory provide access to their library's on-line catalogue through the Internet. In some cases the information is text or data. The Council on Tall Buildings and Urban Habitat maintains a high-rise building database with such information as building heights and other statistics. The *AIA Online* service advertizes access to 850 databases, both bibliographic and data or full-text. Some agencies routinely post information to discussion groups on the Internet. The National Research Council of Canada's Institute for Research in Construction (IRC) posts announcements of their lighting publications on the Internet discussion list 'Lighting' (subscribe to lighting-request@garnet.nist.gov). News of CIB publications has been found on the list of the Cooperative Network for Building Researchers (CNBR). In addition to information dissemination via discussion groups on the Internet, some organizations, such as the National Institute of Standards and Technology, have set up 'sites' on the Intern. The NIST web site (http://www.nist.gov/welcome.html) provides information on NIST laboratory programmes, including the Materials Science and Engineering Laboratory and the Building and Fire Research Laboratory. The AIA provides selected information through the Internet web site (http://www.aia.org).

Some organizations offer an Advisory Service. Both the BRE and the APA provide fee-based or member-only advisory services. The APA's service is called Planning Advisory Service (PAS). Their brochure describes it as 'a research and information service for public planning agencies, private consulting firms, developers and universities'. The service is by subscription, and includes printed materials as well as advice and searches of its unique database of zoning and subdivision codes. The BRE Advisory Service, available to members, includes library searches and telephone advice on professional areas. Though not labelled an advisory service, the Urban Land Institute (ULI) provides ULI Search ($55/hour for members, $75 for non-members in 1995). This service will compile a packet tailored to your specific question, consisting of readings and data and names of contacts/experts.

Referrals, to other groups or to experts and consultants, are an important information service. As the sheer amount of information that is produced increases to staggering levels, and the potential negative (legal) consequences of inadequate information intensify, an increasing reliance upon experts and consultants has developed. The AIA's *Handbook of professional practice* (section 1.13) lists the following associations as sources of consultant information: AIA, Association of Certified Planners (AICP), APA, ASHRAE, ASID, ASLA, American Society of Mechanical Engineers (ASME), and National Society of Professional Engineers (NSPE). Many other associations provide referral services, or can suggest consultants from their own membership.

The ways associations and organizations provide, communicate and generate information are illustrated in this listing of the benefits of the ASLA: publications (the journal *Landscape architecture*, the newsletter *LAND*), on-line information (*DesigNet*, accessible by modem and, at time of going to press, not limited to members), a library (its Information Resource Centre), meetings and exhibitions (annual), employment referral, committees, awards, community assistance teams, continuing education (seminars and workshops, leadership training), a bookshop, the LAfile, legislative information packs, licensure assistance teams, and national public relations activity.

How to identify associations and organizations

There are many ways to identify associations, depending on the resources at hand and the information with which you start. You may have the name of a group and simply need their address or phone number. You may have the name, but feel you need more information about the group itself in order to determine their mission and services. Or you may have a need for information, but not be aware of the group which might be able to furnish you with what you need. Never forget that libraries have many sources of directory information, and information about associations and organizations. It is often most expeditious to query a library for this type of information, even if you are sure that you have it somewhere in your office, but can't locate it at the moment.

That said, there are some sources that may well be in the office. Both the AIA's *ProFile: the directory of US architectural design firms* and the RIBA's *Architect's reference annual* list useful associations. Neither of these lists is comprehensive; in fact they are not particularly long! They can, however, be a ready source of frequently needed addresses and phone numbers.

Journals and other periodicals may afford convenient access to association information. *Progressive architecture* has an annual information sources issue which lists organizations, including directory information, according to topic. This was issued separately from 1987 to 1992, in mid-October. Since then it has been folded into the December issue. *Architects' journal* in its 'Briefing column' frequently focuses on a particular topic, such as landscape architecture, and lists sources of information in that topic, including associations. The annual *Architecture/research*, established in 1991 by the AIA/ACSA Council on

Architectural Research, is primarily a directory of research projects, although articles are also included. Other journals include information on associations and occasionally organizations. One example is *Building design and construction* which included a 'Directory of professional services' in its December 1992 issue. A clipping file for such information as it appears would be useful, although the information can go out of date quickly.

Specialized directories tailored to architecture/building/construction fields are a good investment, even for the small library. Some of these are regularly revised and updated; some are produced for a few years, and then abandoned as out-of-date. However, since it is often only the directory information (names, phone numbers) that is dated, even the latter category of directory can be useful if it provides information on the mission and services of the organization.

The ENR directory of construction information resources: professional societies, technical associations, manufacturers' organizations, government agencies, construction trades unions, business/technical periodicals (publications) (published in 1993, originally published as the *Directory of construction associations* in 1978, with a third edition under the same title in 1987) covers the United States only. The subtitle certainly gives you an idea of the diversity of groups that are directly involved in architecture and construction. Names, addresses and phone numbers (and fax numbers where available) of more than 1600 groups are given (but no descriptive information is provided). It is organized by topic, according to a modified version of the CSI format. It is therefore extremely useful to those starting with a need for information, but no specific association in mind. The directory also has an alphabetical name index, and a keyword index. In contrast to *The ENR directory*, Hugh Brooks has arranged his *Building & construction resource directory* by type of organization. The categories include trade associations, professional associations, government agencies, colleges and universities, and technical bookstores. For the UK, the *CIRIA UK construction information guide*, (4th edn, compiled by B.G. Richardson) is an equivalent directory. Also of interest is the *Directory of official architecture & planning* (annual).

Directories covering international organizations in architecture and construction are the *CIRIA Guide to European Community and international sources of construction information* (2nd edn, 1991, published every three-four years, according to the entry in the *Encyclopedia of associations*), and CIB's *International directory of building research, information and development organizations* (triennial, according to *Encyclopedia of associations*, although the most recent edition is 1986). *An international directory of building research organizations* was published by the US National Research Council in 1989, but there is apparently no intention of updating it. It does contain a paragraph on the mission and research focus of each organization listed.

For all other associations, or for more extensive information on the major associations in architecture and construction than that provided in the directories above, the following titles should prove helpful: *Encyclopedia of associations, Directory of British associations & associations in Ireland, Trade associations and professional bodies of the United Kingdom: an alphabetical and subject classified guide to over 3600 organizations, Directory of European industrial and trade associations, Directory of European professional and learned societies* and *National trade and professional associations of the United States.*

Those in search of information must recognize that finding the organization that can provide the necessary knowledge may be a sequential task. With luck, even if the organization initially contacted cannot help, it can provide leads to those who can. In fact, referral is a very effective way of identifying the precise association or associations needed. Referrals might be made by a librarian, by a colleague, or by another organization. Clearing houses are periodically formed (and often later disbanded), and these clearing houses can serve as an excellent source of referrals. Design Access in Washington DC, established in 1992, describes itself as 'a national information and resource center for the design disciplines, created under the auspices of the National Endowment for the Arts and the National Building Museum. Design Access offers information on design organizations nationwide that act as non-profit, professional, academic and advocacy resources for assistance in specific topic areas.' It is open to the public, and requests for information can be taken by phone.

Last, but not least, appropriate associations and organizations may be identified, and contact information obtained, by posting a query on one of the architecture and construction-related discussion groups on the Internet. On-line groups such as CNBR, Design-L (listserv@psuvm.psu.edu), Built-Environment (mailbase@mailbase.ac.uk), and alt.architecture (newsgroup) can be an extremely effective way of obtaining information since the query is distributed on-line to hundreds of subscribers simultaneously. This is discussed in more detail in Chapter 11.

Libraries

Libraries as sources of information and ideas have been valued through the ages. Although the on-line age has had prophets predicting the obsolescence of libraries, libraries have not only continued but enhanced their role as information providers. If you can imagine information printed or published, you can imagine it in a library. But libraries have changed and developed dramatically in the last 20 years. They are no longer warehouses of books. Videos, access to their own and other library catalogues on-line, electronic indexes and materials of all sorts, images on CD-ROM – all these aspects and more are included in today's library. Some libraries still have card catalogues, but the odds are that such catalogues contain only cards for older materials.

Libraries, like the associations and organizations described above, vary in focus, in services and in clientele. To make best use of libraries, a basic understanding of the types of libraries, the range of library services, and the possible approaches to locating information within libraries is desirable.

Types of libraries

Academic libraries, located on college and university campuses, are intended to support education and research. Their primary clientele is the faculty, students and staff of their institution. The collection of each academic library varies depending on the curriculum of the institution, since the collection must support that curriculum. Other sources of variance might be budget, years spent collecting in a particular subject, and co-operative arrangements with other institutions. You would not, for instance, expect the same depth in the collection of a university library with a recently established architecture programme as you would in a library whose university has had a premier architecture programme for many years. Representative of the latter is the Avery Library at Columbia University with over 250 000 volumes and 1800 periodical titles. Academic libraries at universities with accredited architecture programmes are probable sources of extensive architecture collections. Those institutions in America can be identified using the Association of Collegiate Schools of Architecture's *Guide to architecture schools*. The ACSA *Guide* also provides a volume count of the library's holdings. The RIBA's *Reference annual* lists schools of architecture, with more complete information being found in their *Schools of architecture recognised by the Royal Institute of British Architects*. Many, but not all, academic libraries are open to the public. Some, such as the Avery, require a registration process if the user is not a university member.

Public libraries also vary widely, ranging from one-room reading libraries, to research libraries such as the New York Public Library. Most public libraries, of medium size or more, will be able to offer a basic collection that should include general reference materials – such as the general directories of associations mentioned above – needed in the course of business. Public libraries are, as the name implies, open to the public, although special collections within the library may have more restrictive policies.

Special libraries exist to support the specific information needs of their clientele. A special library may serve a business, an organization or a government agency. The collection is more likely to emphasize current and much used materials, and information of a technical or specialized nature. Libraries in architecture firms can be classed as special libraries. It is unlikely that such a library would be open to anyone outside the firm or practice. It is possible, however, that the librarian may be able to offer telephone assistance, especially when approached by another librarian. Although many firm libraries consist primarily of manufacturers' catalogues, a company library may be an excellent source of information about the organization itself. One example is the Architects Collaborative Library in Cambridge, MA, which, according to the description in Zakalik's library directory, has 1500 manufacturers' catalogues, 2600 books, 400 internal reports, 80 000 slides of the firm's work, 78 000 construction drawings, 850 reels of microfilm of working drawings, job files, specifications. It is not open to the public.

Association libraries and those serving trade organizations also have specialized collections, focused on the information needs of the association or organization. Access policies vary widely among association libraries. Consider the brief descriptions of a sample of association libraries:

Canada's National Research Council's Institute for Research in Construction, in an article in the RAIC *Update* September/October 1993 (p.7), states that: 'The IRC Information Service manages one of the largest collections of books, journals, magazines, and other publications on buildings in North America.' The service is willing to accept calls from architects and identify the best source of information to answer a question. They are on the Internet and will take queries through e-mail.

The British Architectural Library (BAL) of the Royal Institute of British Architects is described in its brochure as 'the finest library in its field in the UK and one of the most important architecture libraries in the world'. Another brochure says 'the collections and services are available to the public – in person, by post, fax, telephone and, increasingly, by on-line and electronic methods'. The public may purchase annual or daily passes. The collection is obviously worth it: 135 000 books, 700 current serials, drawings, manuscripts, photographs, objects, technical and product information, biographies, audiovisual materials. Questions by phone should be of the quick-answer type. Longer questions can be sent by mail or fax but a charge may be levied for the research service.

The AIA Library, smaller than the BAL, has 30 000 volumes and 450 serials. It is open to the public without charge for reference use only, although the AIA Library, like BAL, sells an annual pass to non-members that allows them to check materials out of the library. A reference service is provided to members and non-members. Research assistance, requiring more time, is billed at differential rates for members and non-members. The AIA Library brochure highlights its resources (books, reports, slides, journals, videos, manuscripts, photographs, drawings) and services. To summarize, 'the library takes advantage of the latest computer technology to make available the information you seek'.

ASLA's Information Resource Center is a source of information for ASLA chapters and members. BSRIA is also for members only, according to Pontin in an article titled 'Information providers'.

Government agency libraries are also a form of special library. Their accessibility depends on the mission of the agency which they serve. Many of these libraries are open to the general public, at least for reference use. For example, the Architectural & Transportation Barriers Compliance Board Technical Library does not circulate materials to the public, but will provide reference service. The BRE and DoE in the UK are not generally open to the public but will usually assist with enquiries which cannot be answered elsewhere.

Library services

Level of service, cost for services, and types of services offered vary from library to library, and sometimes vary also depending on the client type (student, researcher, architect). The most basic service is simple access to the collection, mentioned above. Access to the collection affords the opportunity to browse, presuming the library is entirely on open access. Entry through the library doors may also mean access to licensed indexes and databases. Many libraries now offer searching of selected indexes through their on-line catalogues, or by means of CD-ROM computerized databases. Although the indexes are usually licensed for use by the library's patrons only, they can be accessed in most cases even by users outside of the library's primary clientele, if they are on-site in the library.

Borrowing of library materials is a service more often restricted to the library's patrons. In some cases passes or other special arrangements can be made by checking with the library's administration. If borrowing is not permitted to the public, photocopying small portions can sometimes serve as a substitute.

Reference services can range from answering a short factual question or explaining how to use the library's computers, to compiling bibliographies or providing research assistance. Database searching can be a component of the library's reference service, although a fee may be charged. Many libraries compile bibliographies on popular topics, and guides to the use of the library. These are usually available at the reference desk. Individual library policy dictates the level of reference service offered to various categories of patron, and whether service is provided by phone, mail, e-mail, or in person only. Sometimes a service may be extended to someone who is not part of the library's clientele only if it does not take much time. An answer to a more time-consuming question may be attempted but not given priority attention.

Inter-library Loan (ILL) and document delivery are restricted to the library's registered patrons. Since no library can expect to hold all materials that might be requested, the Inter-library Loan system allows libraries to share their collections on an as-needed basis. ILL is a valuable service, but one which can take many weeks or months as staff search for an item from other libraries. Even though computers have greatly improved the ability of libraries to locate materials, a lending library may report the item is already checked out or that it does not circulate at all. The British Library Document Supply Centre (BLDSC) can often supply books and journal articles by return of post and is used not only in the UK and Europe but also by the rest of the world.

Document delivery services provide photocopies of a report or article, obtained from another library or from a commercial vendor. It is possible to obtain document delivery without going through a library. The Colorado Alliance of Research Libraries (CARL) provides services for a fee to a world-wide clientele. CARL delivers articles by mail or fax with its Uncover service, accessible through the Internet by telnetting to database.carl.org. The Uncover database includes more than 17 000 journals, although not all publishers have agreed to terms permitting document delivery.

Selective dissemination of information (SDI) is a service offered by some libraries, particularly special libraries. It involves identifying and forwarding information needed for ongoing research, based on a profile of a patron's interests. CARL provides an SDI service via the Internet, forwarding by e-mail article citations that respond to the profile of interest input on-line by the user.

More and more libraries find themselves in the position of restricting or charging for services, due to the increasing demands put on their collections and staff, and the often declining budgets with which they are faced. For this reason it may sometimes be more effective to go to the librarian of your own institution, even if you are sure that the library does not have the information you require, and ask your librarian to make the contact with the librarian of another institution. Your degree of urgency, library policies, and other factors will suggest the appropriate course of action.

Choosing the appropriate library

Type of library is one of the clues to be used in choosing the library appropriate to your use and information need. However, it is not an infallible guide. For instance, the BAL and the Avery libraries function similarly as THE architectural collections in their respective countries, though one is technically an association library, and one is an academic library. Trying to distinguish the appropriate library solely based on type is not always effective.

Type and topic of the information needed is another basis for choice. As discussed above, public libraries are good sources for general information including information in areas of business, finance, personnel and management. Information of a more technical or specialized nature may require an academic or special library. The character and strengths of the library's collection are important concerns in choosing the appropriate library. Preliminary evaluation of a library's collection can be based on the type of library, and on such factors as the mission of the institution and how long it has been in existence. However, more information is needed to assess the collection effectively. It is possible to obtain that information before (or without) going to the library, by accessing the library's on-line catalogue remotely, either electronically e.g. through the Internet, or by means of printed catalogues.

Many library catalogues are now accessible through the Internet. Even a few simple subject or keyword searches of an on-line catalogue can convey a sense of the currency and depth of a collection in your area of interest. Some strong US library architecture collections with catalogues accessible through the Internet are the Avery Library (1981 onwards), Harvard University, Carnegie Mellon, Arizona State University and the University of California. In the UK, catalogues for Oxford, Cambridge, the University College of London University and many others are accessible on-line. Access instructions (how to 'telnet' or link to a specific computer) are available by gophering to yaleinfo.yale.edu, then choosing the following from successive gopher menus: Browse YaleInfo, Library Catalogs World-Wide. Yale maintains a list of library catalogues available through the Internet. The list can be searched by location or keyword. Libraries from all over the world are included. Many UK libraries are accessible through the academic network, JANET, which is itself accessible on the Internet.

Before the wide accessibility of on-line catalogues, published library catalogues served to draw attention to outstanding collections. They can still serve that purpose. Though, with the exception of the New York Public Library catalogue, they cannot be considered sources of current holdings: they are a reflection of the historic strengths of a collection. Examples of published library catalogues include the Avery Library catalogue (Columbia University), the New York Public Library Art and Architecture Division catalogue, and the British Architectural Library catalogue. The New York Public Library supplements its *Dictionary catalog of the Art and Architecture Division* with the annual *Bibliographic guide to art and architecture.*

Specialized researchers should consult *Subject collections, a guide to special book collections and subject emphases as reported by university, college, public, and special libraries and museums in the United States and Canada* compiled by Lee Ash and William G. Miller. It is not comprehensive, depending as it does on self-reporting by libraries, but it can identify sources not found easily in any other way. It reports, to give one example, 10 libraries with special collections on Frank Lloyd Wright (although it does not include the sizeable collection on the subject at Arizona State University).

The decision on whether to approach a particular library may be based on its policies regarding access. It is wise to call a library before appearing on its doorstep, to verify access policies and opening hours. Many academic libraries, as well as some libraries of other types, are now supplying this information through the Internet. Often the information section of the opac (library on-line catalogue) will contain access information. For example, Harvard's on-line catalogue, *Hollis* (Harvard OnLine Library Information System), contains information on each of the Harvard libraries, including whether access is restricted for 'outside readers.' Your professional affiliations will of course enter into the choice of a library. If you are a member of an association that has a library, or if you are faculty, student or staff at a university, your choice of library will be guided by your affiliation. Some libraries have reciprocal agreements with other libraries, allowing visiting faculty to have library privileges.

Level of expertise may also be a consideration in choosing a library. Strong architecture collections in academic or association or special libraries will be staffed by librarians who are skilled in providing information to the architecture and building communities and will often have a subject background as well.

Library directories

Directories of libraries exist to assist in determining the appropriate library, and in making contact once that determination is made. Directories often give some indication about the collection; may provide information on access policies and services offered by the library; and contain addresses and phone numbers, and the names of the librarians. In addition to general directories, such as the *World guide to libraries*, the *American library directory* and the *British Library directory*, there are specialist directories published periodically. One such is the *Directory of special libraries and information centers* edited by Joanna Zakalik. It is in three volumes. Volume I is arranged alphabetically by library name, with a subject index. Volume II contains the geographic and personnel indexes, and volume III supplements the first two. Coverage is international. Entries give address, phone, personnel, holdings, services, public access, computerized services, publications. The *Aslib directory* is a source of specialized information for libraries in the UK.

While government agency libraries may be listed in the directories mentioned above, specialist directories of such libraries include the *Guide to libraries and information units in government departments and other organizations* (UK) and the *Directory of federal libraries* (USA).

Mining the library's resources

Consulting a librarian

Asking a librarian is usually a good first step, whether the question is general or technical, quick answer or detailed research. Unless you are extremely familiar with libraries and their resources, you cannot always judge whether a question can be easily and quickly answered. Some types of question usually fit into the category of easy and quick – such as directory-type questions 'What is the address of...?' – but others may or may not. For instance, suppose you are looking for readings on the subject of wayfinding. If the library happens to have compiled a bibliography on this subject, then the question is easy and quick to answer. If not, the legwork will be extensive. The amount of time a librarian can devote to a question depends on many factors, some of which were mentioned above: policy of the library, work load at the time, type of library, etc. However, if the librarian is not able to answer, or to spend the time necessary to answer, a question, he or she will most likely be willing to offer ideas on how to go about finding the answer, or refer the enquirer to another library or association.

The first edition of *Information sources in architecture*, in the chapter on libraries, cited the UK's Department of the Environment publication *How to find out* when giving these seven rules to follow in asking a librarian for information:

1. Ask personally. A question can be completely altered if it has been passed through several people – so ask personally.
2. Say who you are.
3. Say why you need the information.
4. State the urgency. A quick and short answer may be more useful than a week's delay and a more comprehensive answer.
5. Be accurate and concise.
6. Give as many relevant facts as possible.
7. Don't anticipate the answer.

The authors of the chapter, Ruth H. Kamen and Valerie J. Bradfield, go on to offer further advice which stands the test of time:

Communication involves transmitting, understanding and receiving a message. Understanding must be achieved by both parties. Therefore it is important to be able to express a question clearly to get the right answer. Enquirers may expect to be questioned and should explain in detail the question, its origin, and the amount, level and complexity of the information needed. Any names or unusual words should be spelled. It is helpful to know how recent or current that particular information needs to be, what steps have already been taken to locate it and whether foreign-language material is acceptable. It is best to explain as though talking to a colleague without simplifying. If the librarian does not understand then questions will clarify points, but simplification can distort and present the wrong terminology. Alternative words may be sought in an effort to clarify an enquiry or find index terms. Most specialist librarians have a wide understanding of the relevant terminology. Since there may be a delay in providing the answer it is also sensible to indicate where and when to telephone.

Do-It-Yourself

If the question falls into the research category, and you do not have a corporate library to which to refer it, the choices are either to do the research yourself or to hire someone else to do it. If you plan on doing the research yourself, there are publications which can assist you in plotting a course of action. The library itself may have guides to the contents and use of its collection. The guides may suggest databases available in the library, or even outline a research approach to certain popular topics. Books on architectural research often have chapters focusing on library research. These are good introductions, short but covering the key elements of library research. Two examples of this type of guidance are: Chapter 5 of Kathryn H. Anthony's *Design juries on trial*, 'Avoiding guesswork: learning how to research your project and its users'; and Chapter 4 of Robert Wehrli's *Environmental design research: how to do it and how to apply it*, 'Methods of environmental design research: library research.' Lois Jones' *Art information: research methods and resources* also has a chapter on architectural research. Suggestions on doing library research are included, of course, in this book, along with other types of information gathering. In addition, there are many general books explicating the various techniques of library research. The librarian will be able to recommend titles of this sort.

Information brokers

At times, for complex or time-consuming problems, a professional, paid researcher may be the most cost-effective method of conducting library research. The field of information-for-hire has grown three-fold in the last 10 years. An information broker may be an individual 'infopreneur' or a company, library or association. Each information broker offers a unique combination of services and expertise. Types of service include database searching, compiling bibliographies, current awareness, standards and specifications retrieval, translating, patent or trademark searching, legal searches, document delivery and clipping services. Fees also vary! Several directories exist to assist you in choosing an information broker, including the annual *Burwell directory of information brokers*, the Association of Independent Information Professionals' annual directory, and a directory compiled by the Los Angeles County Public Library, *FISCAL Directory of fee-based research & document supply services*. The *Burwell directory* lists nearly 1600 firms from around the world. The UK section is composed of more than a hundred entries, including entries for the editor of this book, and for organizations such as TRADA and BSRIA mentioned in the associations and organizations section above. Listings include address, phone and other means of communication (e.g. fax or Internet address), the professional associations to which the broker belongs, subject expertise, services offered and fees. There are several indexes provided. The subject index is especially useful for those needing specialized information. Architecture, building and construction are all listed as subjects. Not all queries require a specialist, and many of the information brokers indicate that they are prepared to handle all subjects.

Conclusion

Associations, organizations and libraries are all primary sources of information in the field, and all are under-utilized. Whether it is the pressure of deadlines, or, as Wehrli calls it, the 'no-information myth' (i.e. there couldn't be any information available on x topic), buildings are being designed and constructed without benefit of critical or desirable information. By joining key associations to ensure awareness of current developments in the field, and contacting other organizations and libraries at various points in the building process to obtain information as needed, the time lag in incorporating research results into buildings can be effectively shortened. With potential benefits like better buildings and satisfied clients it is worth the effort.

References and bibliography

Adderley, Peter. *Architect's reference annual.* RIBA Publications.
American Institute of Architects. *ProFile: the directory of US architectural design firms.* Washington, DC: American Institute of Architects.
American library directory. Annual. New York: Bowker.
Anthony, Kathryn H. (1991) *Design juries on trial.* New York: Van Nostrand Reinhold.
Ash, L. and Miller, W.G. (1993) *Subject collections, a guide to special book collections and subject emphases as reported by university, college, public, and special libraries and museums in the United States and Canada.* 7th edn. New Jersey: R.R. Bowker.
Aslib (1994) *Aslib directory of information sources in the United Kingdom.* 8th edn. London: Aslib.
Association of Collegiate Schools of Architecture (1994) *Guide to architecture schools.* 5th edn. Washington, DC: ACSA.
Association of Independent Information Professionals. *Annual directory of members.* Annual. New York: AIIP.
Avery Library (1968, enlarged edn., 1972–1980) *Catalog of the Avery Memorial Architectural Library of Columbia University.* Boston: G.K. Hall.*British Library directory.* (1989) London: St. James Press.
British Architectural Library (1865, 1937-38) *Catalogue.* RIBA.

Brooks, Hugh (1992) *Building & construction resource directory*. Newport Beach, CA: HBA Publications.

Burwell, Helen P. (ed.) *The Burwell directory of information brokers*. Annual. Houston, TX: Burwell Enterprises.

Construction Industry Research and Information Association (1991) *CIRIA Guide to European community and international sources of construction information* 2nd edn. London: Construction Industry Research and Information Association.

Conseil International du Bâtiment (1986) *International directory of building research, information and development organizations*. 5th edn. New York: Spon.

Dale, Peter (1994) *Guide to libraries and information units in government departments and other organizations*. 31st edn. London: British Library, Science Reference & Information Service.

Daniels, P.K. and Schwartz, C.A. (1994) (eds.) *Encyclopedia of associations* 28th edn. Detroit: Gale.

Directory of British associations & associations in Ireland. (1994) 12th edn. Beckenham: CBD Research.

Directory of European industrial and trade associations. (1991) 5th edn. Beckenham: CBD Research.

Directory of European professional and learned societies. (1989) 4th edn. Beckenham: CBD Research.

Directory of official architecture & planning. (1993) London: G. Godwin.

Evinger, W.R. (1993) *Directory of federal libraries*. 2nd edn. Phoenix, AZ: Oryx Press.

Haviland, David (ed.) *The architect's handbook of professional practice*. Washington, DC: American Institute of Architects.

Jones, Lois Swan (1990) *Art information: research methods and resources*. Dubuque, IA: Kendall/Hunt Publishing.

Los Angeles County Public Library (1993) *FISCAL Directory of fee-based research & document supply services*. Chicago: ALA Books.

MacDonald, J.A. (1993) *The ENR Directory of construction information resources: professional societies, technical associations, manufacturers' organizations, government agencies, construction trades unions, business/technical periodicals (publications)*. New York: ENR Special Projects.

Millard, P. (1993) *Trade associations and professional bodies of the United Kingdom: an alphabetical and subject classified guide to over 3600 organizations* 11th edn. Detroit: Gale Research.

National trade and professional associations of the United States. Annual. 29th edn. Washington, DC: Columbia Books.

New York Public Library. Art and Architecture Division. *Dictionary catalog of the Art and Architecture Division*. Boston: G.K. Hall.

New York Public Library. Art and Architecture Division. *Bibliographic guide to art and architecture*. Annual. Boston: G.K. Hall.

Pontin, Dorothy (1994) Briefing Column: Information Sources. *Architects' Journal*, **34** 9 March.

Pontin, Dorothy (1994) Briefing Column: Information Providers. *Architects' journal*, **30** 23 March.

Richardson, B.G. (1989) *CIRIA UK construction information guide*. 4th edn. London: Spon.

US National Research Council Building Research Board (1989) *An international directory of building research organizations*. Washington, DC: National Academy Press.

Warne Report (1993) *Review of Architects (Eegistration) Acts 1931–1969*. HMSO.

Wehrli, Robert (1986) *Environmental design research: how to do it and how to apply it*. New York: John Wiley & Sons.

World guide to libraries. (1993) 11th edn. Munich: K.G. Saur.

Zakalik, Joanna M. (ed.) *Directory of special libraries and information centers*. Annual. Detroit: Gale Research.

CHAPTER THREE

Periodicals

KATHARINE R. CHIBNIK

It is little wonder that periodicals are so popular. They are packaged in a convenient format, portable, filled with concise but in-depth information, relatively inexpensive and, sometimes, contain discussions which enliven the mind. With the advent of the Internet, considerable interest and energy is being focused on direct delivery of texts, such as articles, through electronic means. However, for architects and the allied fields, these explorations will only blossom fully when graphics, which are such an integral part of architectural articles, as well as texts, are easily and quickly transferable to home computers.

Periodicals serve a multitude of purposes for a multitude of audiences. Some concentrate on articles for a wide audience, while others contain articles of interest only to a very limited audience. Some focus only on current events, while others devote their pages to subjects of historical interest. Some cover news and events, others intellectual theory, others arcane details and mathematical formulae, while still others only beautiful photographs and few words.

Due to the shorter production time for periodicals than books, periodicals often contain information that is more current. They also have the added advantage of being published at regular intervals so that short items of interest, often vital to a practitioner's knowledge or business, can be included, which would be deemed inappropriate for a book. In addition to being the disseminators of current information, periodicals are vital tools in the development of intellectual discourse within the profession, which then becomes transformed into actual projects in the built environment.

Periodicals are interchangeably referred to as magazines, journals and, less commonly, serials. A periodical is defined as a publication that is issued at regular intervals with the intention of being published indefinitely. Most appear more frequently than annually and less frequently than daily. By far the most common frequencies are monthly and quarterly, although some periodicals appear weekly, fortnightly, annually, biennially, or even irregularly.

In general, as publication frequency decreases, periodical articles become more scholarly and less time-dependent. Thus, weeklies publish short articles covering current events and association news, sources for supplies, price information and advertisements; monthlies publish longer articles covering current trends, new projects, new technology, new products and advertisements; quarterlies cover trends in depth or focus each issue on one subject; and annuals tend to publish review articles and research articles. However, most periodicals contain a combination of these features, consisting of brief notes, longer articles, advertisements, letters to the editor (where lively exchanges may occur) and even book and exhibition reviews.

In the last 10 years, there has been an enormous growth in the number of periodicals of potential interest to architects and allied professionals. Frances C. Gretes, in her *Directory of international periodicals and newsletters on the built environment* (2nd edn, Nostrand, 1992), states that she added more than 500 new titles in the six years between the first and second editions. Each year, however, a surprising number of magazines fold – for reasons of rising costs, lack of subscribers, inadequate advertizing revenue, or just shifts in topical interests.

Luckily for the consumer, the price of architectural periodicals has not reached the heights found in the sciences, where periodicals and pre-prints have taken over the publication market and prices have sky-rocketed. However, due to the need for illustrations (and often colour illustrations) as an integral part of the format, the price of producing an architectural magazine is not inconsiderable.

Clearly no person or firm has the time, inclination, or funds to purchase and read a fraction of the architectural periodicals produced. Firstly, one relies on the information found in the 'glossies'; the popular, commercially produced magazines of the field. Within the sphere of 'glossies', there is an inevitable overlap in the major architectural projects covered. While many architectural periodicals are international in scope and are read by an international audience, which popular periodical is read is largely determined by where one lives. Thus, in Great Britain, one might regularly read *Architects' journal, Architectural review* and *Building*, in the United States, *Progressive architecture, Architectural record* and *Building design & construction*, in France, *Architecture d'aujourd'hui*, in Germany, *Deutsche Bauzeitung* and *D B Z: Deutsche Bauzeitschrift*, in Italy, *Casabella* and *Costruire*, and in Japan, *Shin Kenchiku* and *A & U*.

A second source of professional periodical reading emanates from associations and organizations. Many associations and organizations produce newsletters which are received as part of the membership. The purpose of the newsletter (usually 4-10 pages long) is to keep members informed of association activities and other members' activities. They form a section of the backbone of the professional network with which one interacts and does business.

At the same time, these associations or organizations may be producing or sponsoring (with a commercial publisher) a full-length journal, which becomes 'core' reading for a given professional group. For instance, the American Planning Association publishes the quarterly scholarly journal, *JAPA, Journal of the American Planning Association*, which includes lengthy well-researched articles on urban planning and urban affairs, symposium proceedings, research notes, reports and long book reviews, as well as the more popular monthly *Planning magazine,* which covers news and analysis of city and regional planning issues, and the *JobMart* newsletter whose sole purpose is to list employment opportunities for planners. Similarly, the Royal Institute of British Architects (RIBA) publishes the well-respected periodical, *RIBA journal,* which presents a range of professional news, technical notes and product information, and the American Institute of Architects (AIA) publishes *Architecture: the AIA journal,* which provides in-depth coverage of American design and technological developments as well as news sections on legal issues, awards and new projects, and notes on firms and programmes.

Directories of periodicals

Given the number of architectural periodicals published that might contain articles of interest, how can one decide which periodicals to read? How can one even know which periodicals exist?

Gretes' *Directory of international periodicals and newsletters on the built environment*, mentioned above, is particularly useful. In the 1992 edition, she lists over 1600 titles from 57 countries. Each entry includes the subscription address, number of issues per year, cost, circulation, contents features such as advertisements, book reviews, bibliographies or calendars, types of illustration, such as photographs or drawings, and where the item is indexed or abstracted, plus an annotation by Gretes commenting on the magazine. The listings are arranged in 14 broad subject categories including Architecture, Office practice, Building types, Building and construction, and Interior design. Most of the broad subject areas are further subdivided. Building types is divided into offices, hotels, airports, parking, etc., making it easy to pick out categories of interest. Gretes also includes an alphabetical listing by title, a highly detailed subject index (covering, for example, journals about colour, journals about terracotta, journals about people movers and the like), and an extremely useful geographical index which sorts periodicals by country of publication.

Doris Robinson's *Fine arts periodicals: an international directory of the visual arts* (Peri Press, 1991) is another specialist listing of periodicals. Its scope is wider than Gretes in that it covers the span of the visual arts. It includes useful sections on decorative arts and crafts and on buildings and interiors, as well as including a listing of indexes and abstracts. However, the listings are limited to periodicals published in English or those having either an English language summary or abstract or those which are indexed by at least one of the indexing or abstracting services included. The annotations are descriptive and cover primarily the contents of the journals. Gretes' annotations are more helpful in providing the reader with a sense of the periodical's style and content.

A more general source of periodical listings is *Ulrich's international periodicals directory* (R. R. Bowker), a five-volume set published annually which lists periodicals by broad subject categories. As indicated by its title, the scope of listings is international. The 33rd edition (1994–95) of this immense directory listed 147 000 journals under 967 subject headings. It also listed 9532 titles that were known to have ceased or suspended publication in the last three years. Each entry includes title, publisher and address, editor, price, circulation and other relevant information. An important feature of each entry is the inclusion of which abstracting or indexing services cover articles from the journal. Irregular serials and annuals, which were previously listed in a separate publication, are now included. *Ulrich's* is also available in CD-ROM and on-line formats. Due to the relatively high price of the set, many firms may not wish to purchase *Ulrich's*. It is available for consultation at most mid-size and larger public and academic libraries.

Another useful source for periodical titles is the annual *Encyclopedia of associations* (Gale Research). This is also available as CD-ROM and on-line. The 29th edition (1995) consists of three volumes: national organizations of the USA; geographic and executive indexes; and a supplement. The base volume and supplement list a total of 22 000 non-profit trade and professional associations which consist of voluntary members and are headquartered in the United States. In addition to the US volumes, there is also a two-volume set devoted to international organizations, containing over 11 000 listings. The main volume and the supplement of each set are organized by subjects such as trade, business and commercial organizations, public affairs organizations, social welfare organizations, etc. Each entry contains vital information such as organization address, membership size, description of the group's purpose and activities, committees and its publications along with their circulation size and price. Each set contains a wonderful keyword index to the organizations (the US index lists all the organizations in both sets) which allows one to see quickly what types of organizations exist in a given field. For example, under the keyword Architecture, one finds not only the American Institute of Architects, but also such organizations as the National Institute for Minority Architects, the American Society for Golf Course Architects, and the Frank Lloyd Wright Foundation.

Finding citations

While most practising architects, architectural students and architectural librarians keep abreast of important news and developments by reading or scanning certain periodicals, this method, by its nature, limits the information found to a relatively small universe of the total information published.

Unfortunately, one cannot always remember where one saw a certain piece of crucial information. One remembers the author but not the magazine; the magazine but not the year or the issue; the keywords in the title but not the complete title, etc. Indexes can come to the rescue.

Many periodicals publish an annual index to the year's issues either in the last issue of the year or in the first issue of the next year. Information about if and when the index is produced is usually found along with the subscription information. Entries in *Ulrich's* also note whether an annual index is issued. However, unless one has a fairly good idea of when and where a specific article was published, one must search through each index of each journal. This can be a tedious task. Some journals do produce cumulative indexes covering a range of years, usually at five or ten year intervals, which makes this job considerably easier.

A more efficient way of finding journal articles is to use an indexing or abstracting service. These are reference tools which act as bibliographic pointers to articles in journals. An indexing service cites articles within a given topic listing author, title, journal name, volume and issue number, year and pagination. It may also state the kinds of illustrations included, as well as whether the article includes bibliographic references to other articles or books. An abstracting service is similar to an indexing service but contains an added bonus: a brief synopsis of the contents of the article. This is extremely useful in helping one to determine whether one wants to read the article. Sometimes, the synopses are so extensive that one does not have to read the article to understand its gist!

Evaluating indexing and abstracting services

Often there is overlap in the journals covered by different services, even while they are focusing on a specific aspect of a topic. Therefore, it is important to analyze the periodical coverage of a given service while using it and before purchasing it. This will ensure that it is a service which actually cites articles which are useful to the topic which you are seeking articles. If one is looking for articles on a new product, one must go to an extremely up-to-date index. Likewise, if one is looking for the information on an historic topic, say a Le Corbusier building, one must be prepared to look up information both in current indexes for recent articles and in older indexes for articles written at that time the building was created. Unfortunately, there is no comprehensive index which covers all magazines, or even all magazines in the field of architecture and its allied arts!

When deciding which index or abstracting service to use, there are a number of factors which one should consider:

- Is it an index or an abstract?
- How many periodicals are covered by the service?
- What types of periodicals are indexed – popular, scholarly, technical?
- How far back in time does the index go?
- How up-to-date is the index – what is the time lag between article publication and publication of the citation?
- How often is the index updated – annually, quarterly, continuously, every five years?
- Does it cumulate citations or add supplementary updates?

Print, CD-ROM and on-line formats

Today, most indexes and abstracts are produced through computer technology, that is, the indexing itself is done by subject specialists, but the output, the product, is formatted through computer files. In what format the information is delivered to you, the user, varies. Currently many of these indexing and abstracting services are available in multiple formats, such as print, CD-ROM and on-line databases. Therefore you must not only evaluate the index or abstract itself, but also evaluate and decide upon the format through which you wish to receive the information.

Each format has its own advantages and disadvantages which must be weighed against your needs.

- Print volumes are readily available, multiple entries can be scanned on one page, and they are easily photocopied. However, they take up room on the shelf, usually come out only in annual updates, and have a relatively limited number of ways in which they can be searched.
- CD-ROMs are compact, menu-driven and user-friendly. Searching is much more efficient and certain than when using print versions, and retrieval is quick. However, one must have the hardware, a

computer with a CD-ROM player, in order to access the information.
- On-line databases are often the most up-to-date as data can be fed into them directly. Retrieval of search queries is fast. But, one must learn how to search the database before one can even access the information. Sometimes this is menu-driven, but sometimes one must learn the systems' commands. Moreover, one must pay a relatively hefty fee either to purchase a search subscription or to search by individual item.

One of the significant advantages of computer files, either CD-ROM or on-line, is that all the data available can be searched at once. In print products, each volume covers a time range, say a one-year or a five-year period, and one must look through each volume to ensure that all the citations have been found, which is time-consuming. However, it must be stressed that few indexes and abstracts have put older information into their computer files. The beginning date for computerized index is usually around 1980. Information previous to that time must be hunted for through print indexes.

Indexes and abstracting services

Just as there are numerous periodicals published, there are numerous indexes and abstracting services covering architecture and the allied arts. Gretes in the *Directory of international periodicals and newsletters on the built environment* lists 15 services specifically related to building design and construction and 57 others which offer citations to at least one architectural magazine. Below, a few of the periodicals most useful and pertinent to architecture and building technology periodicals are described. Some are particularly useful due to the wide scope of their coverage, while others offer excellent coverage either of narrow fields of interest or of less common periodicals.

The two indispensable indexing services in the field of architecture are the *Avery index to architectural periodicals* and the *Architectural periodicals index*. The two complement each other. The *Avery index to architectural periodicals*, which is produced in New York, covers more American journals and American projects, while the *Architectural periodicals index*, which is produced in London, covers more British journals and projects. Each routinely indexes between 300 and 400 periodical titles per year. Both aim for international coverage. Both concentrate on architectural articles and its allied arts, including architectural design, history and practice of architecture, landscape architecture, construction technology as reported by the architectural press, urban planning in its practical aspects rather than its theoretical or sociological aspects, and interior design and furniture as related to architecture.

In their print formats, the two are organized differently and each method has advantages depending upon what one is looking for, as described below. Both are relatively expensive for an individual practitioner or office, but each is available through a variety of means, which makes access possible, even if use is relatively infrequent.

The *Avery index to architectural periodicals* is produced at the Avery Architectural and Fine Arts Library, Columbia University, New York, from the periodicals received at that library. The Avery Library is the premier architectural library in the United States and carries an extensive collection of American and international periodicals. The *Avery index* has been an operating program of the Getty Art History Information Program since 1983. The *Index*, which began production in 1934 as a card file within the library, is presently available as:

- an on-line database available by annual subscription through CitaDel, a service of RLG (Research Libraries Group)
- a CD-ROM updated annually (G.K. Hall)
- a printed index with annual updates (G.K. Hall)

The print indexes cover 1934 to the present. The second edition consists of 15 volumes plus supplements (1975, 1977, 1979–1982 and subsequently annually). Up to the 1977 printed supplement, the *Avery index* was photo-reproduced from the cards in the catalogue. Core American architectural periodicals such as *American architect, Architectural forum, Architectural record, Progressive architecture* and *Architectural review* have been back-indexed through their entire runs. Since 1978, the *Avery index* has been produced as a computer database with the print volumes issued as a by-product of the computer file. Each entry includes article title, author, language of text and summaries (if non-English), bibliographic and illustrative information, and journal name and citation (year, volume, issue, pagination). Brief contents summaries are often provided. Book reviews, exhibition reviews and obituaries are indexed.

In the print version of the *Avery index*, one can search directly by topic (multiple topics are given to each article), architect, firm, author and country. Topical subject headings are further divided by styles or time periods, countries, cities, and specific building names. Topical subject headings are derived from the *Art and architecture thesaurus* (Getty Art History Information Program). Topical cross-references, leading the user to the proper subject heading and to more specific subject headings, are included within the text of the *Avery index* itself. Comprehensive articles on the oeuvre of an architect are found directly under name and also under the topical heading (Profession) – (Nationality), e.g. Architects – France. However, in the print version one cannot search directly by city or building name. To search by city, one must look under the country first and then the name of the city, e.g. England –

London. To search by specific site or building, one must search under country, then city, then building type (subject), which is a bit awkward and confusing. For example, the Chrysler Building is listed under United States – New York (New York) – Tall Buildings – Flatiron Building. If the listing for a given country and city is short, one can easily scan for the building name. But if the city listing is long, say New York or London, with many topical subdivisions, one can easily miss finding the building name.

The printed *Avery index* is organized in one alphabetical sequence, with entries under topic, architect, firm, and with article authors repeating completely, so that essential information is immediately available without further searching. This is a distinct advantage to the user. It does mean that each annual print cumulation since 1983 has consisted of four-inch-thick volumes.

The CD-ROM and the on-line database cover 1977 through to the present. In addition to eliminating the need for individual searches in each annual supplement, the database and the CD-ROM offer more search combinations through keyword searching and Boolean operators; direct searching of building names and city names; keyword and phrase searching of article titles; journal title searching; and limiting by features such as language of article, type of illustration and date of publication. The CD-ROM is much less frequently updated than the database itself which is available directly through RLIN, the network of RLG. The CitaDel service through RLIN is a user- friendly menu-driven system which is available through subscription fee.

The *Architectural periodicals index*, popularly known as the *API*, is produced by the British Architectural Library of the Royal Institute of British Architects in London. This is the pre-eminent architectural library in Europe. It is available as a printed index (quarterly with annual cumulations), as a per-search fee database through DIALOG (file 179, the *Architecture database*) and as a CD-ROM, the *APId* (updated quarterly). It began in 1972, replacing the RIBA *Annual review of architectural periodicals* (1965-1972). Previous to 1965, articles were indexed quarterly in the RIBA *Library bulletin* (1946-1972) and the earlier RIBA *Library review of periodicals* (1933-1946). As the *Architecture database* file on DIALOG it contains not only the contents of the *API* from 1978 to the present, but also the British Architectural Library Book catalogue from 1984 to the present.

Like the *Avery index*, each entry consists of article title, author, language of text and summaries (if non-English), bibliographic and illustrative information, and journal name and citation. An English-language translation of the title is given for non-English articles. Each entry is printed under the appropriate topical subject headings with bibliographic and citation information included. Subject headings are further sub-arranged by country, city and name of building. When the work of an architect is featured in general, it is found under the name of profession and then the nationality of practice. The subject headings used in the *API*, along with cross-references, are published separately in *Architectural keywords* (RIBA Publications, 1982). No cross-references are included in the printed volumes themselves.

Unlike the printed *Avery index*, the printed *API* is organized by entries of topical subjects with added indexes at the rear. Each quarterly contains a name index which includes all architects, firms, organizations, and authors. References (a unique letter-number combination) refer the reader back to the main topical section. The advantage of this organization is that the volumes are considerably thinner than the volumes of the *Avery index*. However, the disadvantage is that one cannot tell directly from the name index which building project is being cited. One must look up each reference to see if it is a citation to the project which one seeks. This is particularly labour-intensive for prolific architects who will have numerous cryptic alpha-numeric references after their names. With practice, one can somewhat limit one's searches by guessing what topic the initial alphabetic code stands for, for example, H for Houses or Housing, or O for Office Buildings. In addition to the name index, in the annual cumulation, which takes the place of the fourth quarterly, there is a handy 'Topographical and building names index', in which entries are listed in four different ways: (1) country: subject heading; (2) country: city: subject heading; (3) country: city: building name; and (4) building name: country. The last two are particularly helpful, eliminating the confusions existing in the printed *Avery index*. One can easily scan for articles by city, as long as one remembers to look under country first, for example, United States: New York (New York): Penn Station, or by building name, for example, Pennsylvania Station: United States: New York (New York). Unfortunately, the 'Topographical and building name index' is only available in the annual cumulation.

The *Construction index* (ArchiText) is currently published annually, formerly published quarterly with an annual cumulation (1988-1992), covering the fields of building design. It is particularly useful when one needs information about new products and new technological advances in building structures. It indexes such diverse periodicals as *Progressive architecture, Engineering news-record, Architectural lighting, Concrete repair digest, Glass digest* and *Journal of light construction*. Its specific focus is on the structural aspects of architecture, so for a journal such as *Progressive architecture*, only those articles which pertain to construction and structural information are indexed. It is topically organized, based on the classification structure of the Construction Specification Institute (CSI), *Masterformat — master list of section titles and numbers*, which is also used by Sweet's *Catalog File*, a tool familiar to American architects, builders and engineers. This structure results in a classed listing of articles by topics such as 'conveying systems', and materials such as 'woods and plastics', with very specific subheadings, such as 'moving walks' and 'wooden trusses'. In addition, there is a series of classifications devised by ArchiText to cover broader fields such as 'functional characteristics' (for example, ergonomics, post-operation evaluation), 'sensible characteristics' (such as colour control, visual comfort), 'production issues' (such as CAD, schedules and tables) and the like. Along with the standard entry information (article title, author, journal title and citation data), there is a brief but insightful annotation. Individual projects and firms, including firm's role, such as general contractor or regulatory agency, are listed between the citation and the annotation. Unfortunately there is no index to firms, individuals or projects.

The *Index to historic preservation periodicals* (G.K. Hall), produced by the National Trust for Historic Preservation Library Collection of the University of Maryland at College Park, has been published twice so far – a base volume of 5000 entries covering 1979–1987 and a first supplement covering 1987–1990 with 5000 more entries. The base volume includes references not only to periodical articles but also to clippings and brochures. The *Index* covers several hundred periodicals, primarily American and regional, although there is some coverage of international periodicals. Periodicals included range from the well-known, such as the *Old-house journal* and *Historic preservation,* to the obscure, such as *Quapaw quarter chronicle* and the *Orange Empire Railway Museum gazette.* For well-known journals, those of larger circulation, there is considerable overlap with the *Avery index* and the *API.* The value of this index lies in its narrow focus and its coverage of lesser-known journals, which are only indexed here. The base volume is a photo-reproduction of the Trust's card catalogue file. Only one subject heading is given per article. The supplement was produced from a computer database and each article has been given up to three subject headings plus a geographic heading at either country or country and state level. Sadly there is no index to cities, specific buildings, personal names or organizations. The useful *Thesaurus of subject and geographic headings* attempts to standardize the evolving terminology of the field.

Another useful tool is *Art and archaeology technical abstracts* (AATA) published semi-annually by the Getty Conservation Institute in association with the International Institute for Conservation of Historic and Artistic Works, London. From 1966-1983, the *AATA* was published by the Institute of Fine Arts of New York University for the International Institute. It is available on-line from the Conservation Information Network (Getty Conservation Institute). The on-line database includes citations from the *AATA* and also from the holdings of the International Centre for the Study of the Preservation and Restoration of Cultural Property (ICCROM), the Canadian Conservation Institute, the International Council on Monuments and Sites (ICOMOS), and the

Conservation Analytical Laboratory of the Smithsonian Institution.

As the title indicates, this is an abstracting service with detailed descriptive annotations. What is not evident from the title itself is why this tool is useful to architects and allied practitioners. With so much architectural practice today consisting of renovation and preservation of buildings, this specialized tool contains citations to technical literature which are not easily found through other sources. Not only does it include general subject categories such as 'architectural conservation' and 'conservation practice', but it also has detailed listings by materials with such subheadings as 'stone', 'minerals', and 'related building materials'. There is an author index and a detailed subject index, which also includes sites and organizations, which refer back to the main classified sections.

Many other indexing and abstracting services cover articles that are of interest to architects and those in the building field. Some worth mentioning include: the *Art index* (H.W. Wilson), which indexes approximately 50 popular architecture magazines; the *Engineering index* (Engineering Information) which is available on-line as COMPENDEX and useful for structural and civil engineering information; ICONDA (Information Centre for Regional Planning & Building Construction of the Fraunhofer, Stuttgart) available on CD-ROM through Silverplatter; the *Journal of planning literature* (Sage Publications), published quarterly and covering all the major urban (town) planning periodicals; and the *Design and applied arts index* (Design Documentation) covering subjects ranging from industrial design to design for the disabled.

An interesting new development in 'indexing' is illustrated by UnCover (Denver, Colorado). Through computer technology, this index scans the tables of contents of 17 000 periodicals. While its date coverage is presently very shallow (1988 to the present), the number of journals covered is quite amazing. There is no attempt to provide standardized subject headings, standardized forms of names, or even to deal with variations in titles found between the table of contents and the actual articles. Retrieval is by keyword as found in the article titles listed in the table of contents, the journal title, and the article summary if included in the table of contents. This may cause some problems for architectural research where the architect or the project name may not be found in the article title, but may be the pivotal piece of information known. However, this service offers two important advantages: firstly, while many indexing and abstracting services lag considerably behind the article's original publication date, UnCover updates its database very quickly and secondly, it covers a huge number and range of periodicals in one integrated database so that one can draw on many periodicals without analyzing the contents of the service.

UnCover also offers some interesting services:

- browsing by journal title to allow one to pull up an issue's table of contents

- 'profiling', which allows one to select journals and have their table of contents automatically sent to an electronic mail address, and
- fee-based document delivery, where one can order articles on-line to be sent via fax and billed via credit card.

Obtaining periodicals

After one locates a citation to an article of interest, a major obstacle may be finding the periodical that contains the article. What good is a reference if the article is not available? Few of us can manage individually to maintain a file of major journals, much less files of the lesser-known journals. For the practitioner within a firm, one solution, of course, is the establishment of a firm library. However, most firm libraries do not subscribe to a large variety of periodicals, but rather carry a core selection of periodicals suited to the specialized needs of the firm.

Various mechanisms have been devised to solve this problem. One is the union serial list, which lists which libraries keep which periodicals. Today, these are mostly maintained on-line through library consortia.

In the UK, requests for articles can be made through the British Library Document Supply Centre, which forwards requests to special libraries. Most public and academic libraries in the United States are part of co-operative loan networks and are able to obtain copies of articles through these Inter-library Loan (ILL) services. These services rely on regular mail and fax delivery, although direct delivery through electronic mail will probably become prevalent in the future. Delivery time for ILL can vary considerably, ranging from a few days to four weeks or more if the article must be obtained from another country. Articles obtained through ILL are usually copied by the owning library and forwarded without a direct fee.

Another relatively new development has been the introduction of fee-based document delivery services. Some emanate from the index itself. For instance, the *Construction index* offers a fee-based photocopy service of articles through the American Institute of Architects Library and the BAL offers a fee-based service for all articles indexed in the *API*. Also springing up are commercial document delivery services. *COMPENDEX* and UnCover allow one to order articles on-line, for a fee plus copyright fees, paying by credit card, and then receiving them by mail or fax. These services are usually faster than Inter-library Loan, but of course they cost money.

Future trends

Advances in production technology coupled with the emergence of the Internet as a global means of communication are in the process of transforming both the publishing industry and the object which we commonly call the periodical. The recent development of graphics interfaces on the Internet is crucial to this transformation in fields like architecture which are dependent on both words and images.

On the simplest level, more and more periodicals will be published with accompanying computer disks, CD-ROMs, etc. Inevitably articles on disk will become interactive. It is unclear whether print will remain the primary means for disseminating the information currently available in periodicals. Digital files allow one to send texts and images electronically direct to the reader's computer, in effect bypassing the need for a print run. They also allow the information to be transformed, changed and incorporated into other texts and images.

One can imagine a future in which the concept of the periodical issue, published with a certain set of articles and mailed to a reader at a specified time interval, is no longer the norm. Rather, the reader could 'create' his own periodical by requesting certain files and not others, specifying the format and where the articles are to be sent. But for now, the periodical as we know it is too convenient and too compact, both physically and intellectually, to be consigned to an early interment. Hopefully the new and the old will be able to co-exist.

CHAPTER FOUR

Computerized information retrieval: databases

VALERIE J. NURCOMBE

The increased storage capacity of computers has given the information profession a means of automating some of the more time-consuming processes of information retrieval. A large store with an efficient search mechanism can provide current and retrospective information to the construction industry quickly and accurately. That information may be in the form of bibliographic references, data, figures, diagrams or standards. This chapter will outline the development of services and examine their use to the architect and building profession. It will not discuss the applications of computers to architectural design, structural calculations and project scheduling, etc., which is done elsewhere. Throughout the guide many references will be found to various databases and even to a few traditional paper-based indexing and abstracting journals – not all are yet computerized and not all libraries can yet afford to do all searching on-line. The paper services have their value in presenting an overall view of the service and its style of indexing – the human eye can scan more at once than the computer can show on screen and the benefits of serendipity are ever present.

Development and availability

Advances in technology over the past decade have provided larger storage capacity in smaller devices with simpler procedures for the person in the office utilizing the services of the machine. The specialist programmers and electronics engineers have made the 'chip' useful not just to program the washing machine, to program the heating services for a building or to assist with the production of drawings, but also to store data required for processes that have not yet been mechanized and may never be. The cumulation of monthly or weekly parts of journals into annual issues has also become simple and speedy using a computing or word-processing facility. Although the developments have made it easier for the construction professional to use resources directly without an intermediary, many still prefer to ask for assistance because search expertise can lower costs and improve results.

Once the information is available on the computer it can be reorganized and used in a variety of ways. The initial growth of these databases was slow in the early 1960s. *Biological abstracts* has had an author index on-line since 1957 and a subject index since 1959, and *Chemical abstracts* began the *Chemical titles* database in 1962. The databases created can be made available as machine-readable services on a national and international basis. Researchers experimented in the later 1960s and commercially available services began in the United States, with Lockheed (DIALOG) and Systems Development Corporation (SDC) being the first firms to offer the facility. Europeans were able to use their services when, in 1974, the Tymshare telecommunications network made access available in Europe. Since then the growth has been dramatic and access methods have changed.

'Host', 'supplier' or 'vendor' are names given to a commercial organization which makes databases available on-line to any user with a VDU/terminal 'dialling' in from remote points. Costs are made up of a number of factors. The operator-time is not included and variables include the database used, the type of contract as a subscriber to the supplier and the prints made. The main features are the telecommunications charge while connected to the host computer, the charge for the connect-time into a database, the charge for off-line or on-line prints according to volume and the monthly or annual charge for a password to the system. This latter is often minimal, but if access is to be made available for a number of systems to extend the range of databases available these charges could mount up considerably. Each supplier charges per database as shown in its manual or price list.

Contact is made with the supplier using a password. This means that although many databases are theoretically available it is necessary to contact each host organization separately to register and obtain a password. Some of the largest suppliers offer hundreds of databases to subscribers and, where some databases are only available via one supplier, others, like MEDLINE or COMPENDEX, are available from many. Several European suppliers linked together to form the Euronet DIANE group – Direct Information Access Network for Europe – sponsored by the Commission of the European Communities as a communications network. It was a communications and co-operative network rather than a host organization itself. More recently all the databases reached via Euronet DIANE have been moved to ECHO, which is now the main EU host.

The main British suppliers are the British Library Automated Retrieval System, BLAISE, based at the British Library, and ESA-IRS via Dialtech, based at the British Library Science Reference Information Service (SRIS). Brochures describe their services. All brochures are updated regularly. Subscribers also receive a manual explaining the commands used, the specific search procedures and details of each database available. New subscribers are usually given an allocation of free time to get used to the system in their first month of usage. Training sessions and off-line training discs are also available. BLAISE offers bibliographic databases, databases containing data on research, thesauri to assist with searching and also the British Library catalogue (British Museum) and *United Kingdom official publications from HMSO*, now available as a CD-ROM called UKOP including Chadwyck-Healey's COBOP. Access is made in the usual way on the telephone lines. For users without terminals searches can be made on request to the British Library.

The Dialtech service now operates from SRIS providing a UK help desk for the ESA-IRS service at Frascati, near Rome, using the European Space Agency computer. Full manuals and database search descriptor sheets are available on subscription. More UK-based databases are available here than elsewhere. QUESTEL-ORBIT now offers many of the databases formerly on Pergamon Infoline, which has had a somewhat chequered history.

DIALOG is still the largest and best known host internationally. Originating in 1972 with Lockheed it was bought out by Knight-Ridder and continues to develop not only its databases but also its CD-ROM products. There are over 250 databases available. All are listed in its annual catalogue. Other major hosts include RLIN, referred to elsewhere, STN from the United States, Datastar (purchased by DIALOG in 1994) and many local country-based ones. Assistance can be found in the Gale/Cuadra *Directory of databases,* which also lists hosts.

Brokers

Those without terminals can also use these services through local library information services, and through information brokers. Aslib offers a search service, as does SRIS. Some academic libraries will also offer information services, at a fee, to their local professional community. Brokerage services developed in the United States and there are more there than elsewhere. Most such brokers can be located by contacting the Institute of Information Scientists or the Library Association in the UK, or by consulting *Who's who in the UK information world* (London: TFPL), *Directory of information brokers and consultants* (England: Effective Technology Marketing and Information Marketmakers) and Longman's *CICI Directory of information products and services*. All are regularly updated. Aslib itself operates a brokerage service, as do many research libraries. Also useful is the international *Burwell directory of information brokers* (Houston, Texas: Burwell Enterprises) Many more exist locally and can be traced through the library and information associations of the relevant country (see Chapter 2).

Databases

The reasons for the use of databases in preference to manual abstracting services are covered in the previous chapter. Searches are best if they are very precise – the wider the topic the more references are retrieved and the more difficult it is to search through for the relevant information. At this point it is helpful to have the benefit of abstracts to each item. Although a database such as NTIS, the National Technical Information Service of the United States, covers mainly US reports, it does not exclusively do so and reports from BRE and Road Research Laboratory will be included. It is sometimes useful to see and even learn from experience reflected in information from other countries: in the 1960s, reports in NTIS, from the United States, identified research into the problems experienced in the 1970s in Britain.

Many databases, particularly bibliographic databases, are now international in their coverage regardless of their country of origin. Thus, the first British database covering construction, ACOMPLINE, originally derived from *Urban abstracts*, remains heavily British but still international. Since the demise of the Greater London Council it comes from the London Research Centre and covers all aspects of construction, architecture, planning, housing and administration. There are many references throughout the text to *API, Architectural periodicals index*, available on-line via DIALOG and emanating from the RIBA's British Architectural Library. ICONDA (available from STN and Orbit) contains much from the British research establishments which are part of the Department of the Environment, particularly the PSA, until its demise, and BRIX/FLAIR (available from ESA) which has a technical bias arising from the combined databases of the Building Research and Fire Research Stations. ICONDA is the result of considerable international activity to co-ordinate national construction resources through the International Council for Building Documentation; there are over 300 000 records from 1974. A discussion of its origin will be found in the first edition of this guide. Professional organizations in many countries are contributing to it, and a recent addition is *Construction index* from Architext which indexes 45 US construction journals. RSWB covers journals, monographs and conference proceedings, mainly in German, relating to building, construction and planning.

Although Gale lists 26 databases under 'Architecture' (July 1994), 31 under 'Building construction' with an overlap of only two, and 47 under 'Construction industry' of which one appears under all three headings, in fact four of the latter also appear under architecture and 13 under building. The overlap is not great, but the number of the general titles included under the subject headings is large. Many listed are small or fringe. Language is no barrier. A sample of titles is given:

Applied science and technology index
The architecture database
AUSSTATS
Australian architecture database
Avery architecture database
Banques de Données Macroeconomique
BATIC
BCIS On-line
E.H. Boeckh computerized building cost estimating
BRIX/FLAIR
Building permits: residential and nonresidential
BYGGFO
Canadian standards
CCIDOC
Computerized cost programs
Conservation information network
Construction labor report
Descripcion del patrimonio historic-artistico espanol
Dodge construction analysis scheme
DRI Utility cost forecasting
ICC Keynotes market research
ICONDA
JICST file on science and technology (Japan)
Monitel2
MSA and state housing construction
Publications of the Institute for Research in Construction
Raumordnung, Stadtebau, Wohnungswesen, Bauwesen
Reuter TEXTLINE
Sageret
VROMDOC

The *CD-ROM directory* adds to these from other on-line original databases – no two sources will give the same list for any subject headings. Some think more laterally than others, thus this title adds CITIS from Ireland, covering civil engineering from Ireland, *Bouw-CD* from Holland and a number of product databases including those from Sweet and *System George*, the latter covering specifications, product sources and reviews.

Many general databases include something on the different aspects of architecture and construction. Offerings such as *Art index* and COMPENDEX (the on-line version of *Engineering index*) are prime examples. The latter is also available in various versions on CD-ROM from DIALOG. *Art index* is discussed in the last chapter, *Applied science and technology index* covers a broad range of technical areas and *Business periodicals index* is on the commercial side. All are from H.W. Wilson and available via their own host, Silverplatter CD-ROMs and other on-line hosts. *Current technology index*, on-line and on CD-ROM, is the British equivalent of *Applied science and technology index*, originating from the *British technology index* and Library Association Publishing, but now published by Bowker-Saur. INSPEC is the on-line database of the Institution of Electrical Engineers but its inclusion of topics relating to the application of electronics in other spheres makes it of interest in construction.

As buildings are constructed for different uses so the discussion of buildings in context is often found in less obvious sources: *Agricola, Agris* and *CAB Abstracts* are good on agricultural and related buildings; waterside buildings are referred to in *Aqualine*; library buildings are usually fully discussed and plans mentioned in LISA; schools, colleges and universities will be found in ERIC; and health buildings in *Excerpta medica* and DHSSDATA among others. Climate is covered in *Meteorological and geophysical abstracts* on DIALOG and the *World climate* disk from Chadwyck-Healey containing data from the Climatic Research Unit at the University of East Anglia. LEDA, the Earth Images catalogue on ESA, contains lists of remote sensing images available. *Geomechanics abstracts*, *Georef* and *Geoarchive* cover survey and geology, while the French *Urbamet* and the German RSWB include reference to planning and housing, although not all contributions are in English. Most databases internationally available may be searched in English.

Environment is covered by Chapters 12 and 18. The databases available have grown in line with the public concern and interest. *Enviroline* and *Environment abstracts* have been available for over 10 years and have a US bias. Rather different are offerings like the CD-ROM, *Digests of environmental impact statements* (Microinfo), which includes extensive abstracts of all statements issued by the US federal government. *Earth Summit* (Microinfo) contains all papers and documents, published and unpublished, relating to the summit and Agenda 21, etc., but is not updated. The CD-ROM *Environment library*, also from Microinfo, is a subset of OCLC's full union catalogue database containing 300 000 plus references published over a 100 year span! Only a few titles can be named here, but the scope and content is becoming broader and more diverse every year – no longer are databases only bibliographic references; full text and fact are mixed, especially in the CD-ROM format, in order to provide a cohesive, marketable product. Prices, however, still need to come down and not every organization yet has sufficiently easy access to the equipment.

Chemical abstracts, the first and the 'mother' of all databases, is wider in scope than its name implies in that titles such as *Concrete* and *Construction* (USA) are indexed so many construction problems will be covered: corrosion is a good example. Even if the articles are highly technical the results will be appropriate. The datasheets from the hosts and the manuals available are particularly useful when searching these large databases in order to maximize retrieval of relevant references. *Metadex* (DIALOG on-line and on-disk) will give references to metals in construction use, while *World textiles* includes all types of material from geo-textiles for ground use to roofing textiles for a wide range of uses and interior design textiles. *RAPRA* from the Rubber and Plastics Research Association is a further example, as is *Ceramics abstracts*. The range is endless – this is only a taster.

Various types of technical information come from a wide range of sources. Patent literature can provide useful specifications and references are available from *Chinapats* (Chinese patents), the various CLAIMS databases (US), INPADOC (general), *World patents index* or *Italpat* (Italy) among others. Standards databases are discussed in Chapter 6 and include *Standardline, IHS International standards and specifications* and *Standards and specifications* (US). The guides discussed at the end of the chapter often include brief lists of the main databases by topic, and all the hosts list their databases both alphabetically and by topic.

General databases also include those such as *Conference proceedings index* (also on CD-ROM and on BLAISE) from the British Library and *Current research in Britain* (also on CD-ROM; from Longman Information & Reference) which naturally cover all possible topics, being centred on the medium rather than the subject. ISI's offerings in this sphere, *Index to social sciences and humanities proceedings* (architecture) and *Index to scientific and technical proceedings* (construction), have a wide appeal backed up by their document delivery service. ISI's original fame was in offering a citation index in print and then on-line, *Science citation index* accompanied by social sciences versions, relied upon the fact that most academic articles cite other articles and the volume of citations to any given article can give an indication of its 'value' by its 'popularity'. The print versions needed patience and care if they were to be used successfully, however, this was the ideal candidate for on-line delivery given its complex nature. *Index translationum* covers a wide range of translations to and from English. *CD-thèses* is a French database covering all disciplines (Microinfo distr.). Similarly *NTIS* may have been set up to cover US government research reports but now has international coverage of all technical topics from space to road construction.

Although Whitakers' *British books in print* and *Books in print* have been available on-line and in microfiche (as well as in print) for some time, they are now also on CD-ROM and have been joined by many other similar services. *BookFind-CD* from Bookdata is available in a

full world-wide edition, a compact version of this without the readership details, tables of contents, descriptions, etc. A standard edition
includes non-book material and special editions are being developed
for Australia, South Africa and New Zealand to cover local availability.
Cumulative book index and *Book review digest* on-line and on CD-ROM
(H.W. Wilson and Silverplatter) are wide-ranging. K.G. Saur produces
German books in print and *German books out of print* on CD-ROM
(Microinfo distr.). OCLC's *Firstsearch* includes *Worldcat*, a source of
bibliographic data.

Databanks

The first edition of this guide spent considerable time discussing the
relatively new phenomenon of databanks – the use of computers for the
storage of data which could then be made available nationally or even
internationally was a new concept. The field has changed so drastically
that in the 1990s databanks are considered usual, and they exist on all
the major hosts alongside the bibliographic databases although few are
actually technical. Those that are tend to be 'closed access', i.e. for
subscribers only, using the services of the host as a means of communication. The databases used by companies every day are local databanks
covering their jobs, personnel, finance, background information, etc.
Experience with purchased software for structural and other calculations has led to the retrieval of, for example, load data within the computer system. Plant lists can be developed for one project, re-used,
developed and amended for another, while saving the additions and
information from experience together with the original basic name data
to create a personalized database of experience. Databases and databanks
are no longer only computerized replicas of print products – many are
prepared and published only in non-book formats. The databanks now
offered commercially take several directions:

- experience information related to products and practices
- product literature and data in full text including standards
- company data ranging from addresses and personnel to facts and
  figures on performance
- credit rating
- statistics, e.g. census on CD-ROM or statistics on-line
- telephone and other directories, dictionaries and encyclopaedias
- full text of technical information related to a range of information
  such as health and safety
- newspapers and journals
- texts relating to executive bodies such as Parliament, Congress
  and the EU

- legal cases and law in full text.

While some are only available on-line, many may be available in a variety of ways combining media appropriate to archiving or updating. Thus a CD-ROM or microfiche collection of full text documents may be updated by an on-line service or by a floppy disk once a month. A print volume may be updated by an annual CD-ROM but not actually reprinted for some time – when it is, then it too will also be available electronically. As most print products are now prepared electronically, the by-product – the data from which they are compiled – can be marketed separately as a bonus. In some cases print will disappear when a larger proportion of users have the required equipment, and prices permit. The first two topics above are covered in Chapter 5. It is only a matter of time before the various Barbour and Ti products on microfiche discussed throughout this guide are available as on-line and CD-ROM packages.

Company information, from financial and planning information through to names and addresses and directorships, is available on-line from companies such as Extel, Frost and Sullivan, ICC, Dun & Bradstreet, Kompass, Moodys, Hoppenstedt (Germany) and Predicasts. Some have print offerings as well as electronic. Kompass directories are contacted direct for on-line interrogation (Reedbase), but the new *Kompass CD-book* gives nearly all the information in the print version at a similar price, but with better searching facilities. Unusually it replicates the print format. UK, US and China 'volumes' are available and others may follow. The US *Leadership directories* (Monitor Leadership Directories) covering officials, organizations, associations and companies from commercial, federal, municipal and other spheres are now available on CD-ROM from Chadwyck-Healey. The range is so wide that the many guides to business information data published regularly cannot all be listed here. Credit information from Dun & Bradstreet can be consulted on-line as can *Who owns whom, Who directs what* and Marquis' *Who's who*, among others.

TED, alias *Tenders Electronic Daily*, is one of the most regularly used EC databases. Available on ECHO, subscription is free but use is charged. Each day new tenders, which must be publicly advertized by organizations in member countries to allow free competition, are posted to the database. Searches, based on product codes or other criteria, may be stored and run against the daily updates to ensure early notification of new jobs available for tender. The print equivalent arrives several days later: the daily *Official journal S* supplement.

Statistics from the Central Statistical Office (UK) are now available on-line and those from the Statistical Information Service (USA) have been for a considerable time. Chadwyck-Healey produced the British 1981 census on CD-ROM some time after the event using Australian software already in use for similar purposes and, in 1994, produced the data for the 1991 census, thus making it possible not only to read the information but to re-work and develop it according to the models required for particular projects and to area specifications not already given. In Britain the ESRC Data Archive at the University of Essex was set up in the 1980s to collect, archive and make available electronic statistical information, with an unusual degree of foresight into its future importance, and into related archiving problems. EUROSTAT has made a wide range of its statistics available in various formats and published a handbook describing them.

Telephone directories on-line were pioneered in conjunction with video text in France where the free issue of 'Minitel' terminals ensured their success more quickly than similar offerings elsewhere. The directories of the United States have long been available on microfiche and are available on CD-ROM as *Selectphone*, formerly *Prophone* from Pro CD. This company also makes available *Canadaphone* and *Australiaphone*. The British Telecom directory, *Phonebase*, for the whole country is now available on-line and on CD-ROM although prohibitively priced. (It would appear that the price will come down in the near future.) Similarly, postcode directories from various sources including, in the UK, the Post Office and the Ordnance Survey, have been made available on floppy disk, on CD-ROM and on-line. Their use for mailing purposes has been widely publicized.

Dictionaries, thesauri and other similar works are being made widely available as CD-ROM equivalents to the print versions by publishers such as Oxford University Press and Collins. The CD *Electronic English dictionary and thesaurus* (Harper Collins) combines *Collins English dictionary* and *Collins thesaurus*. The *Oxford English reference shelf* offers various of its print products on CD-ROM on the open market at reasonable prices. There is a similar language dictionary CD-ROM. However, the full version of the *Oxford English dictionary* on CD-ROM is prohibitively priced. *Le Robert electronique* is available on CD-ROM from Chadwyck-Healey and represents the French standard dictionary. In a slightly different trend, Oxford University Press is offering *Art and architecture thesaurus* (2nd edn, 1995) in five volumes or on seven floppy disks with a manual. The 20 volumes of the useful *McGraw-Hill Encyclopedia of science and technology* are available on one CD-ROM for £795 (1995). The search advantages are tremendous for precise topics not covered by a full article. Gale's *Encyclopedia of associations* is available on-line from DIALOG, and on CD. *Ulrich's international periodicals directory* is currently available in print, on CD-ROM, on microfiche, on-line and on tape! The *Standard periodicals directory* is available on CD-ROM from Library Alliance. Aslib's *Information sources in the UK* is not only available in print but on CD-ROM for the first time (March 1995 – based on the 8th edition by K.W. Reynard, 1994), but at

£30 more than the book. DIALOG hosts *American library directory* and *Biography master index.*

Health and safety information has become increasingly important particularly with the obligations of the CPD, and it therefore comes as no surprise to find that much of the chemical information on hazardous materials has been available on-line for a long time via databases such as RTECS and *Chem-bank* (CD-ROM also) and US hazardous materials data and references. Barbour has produced the *Health & safety microfile*, combining microfiche full text of publications with a print index, and HMSO with the Health & Safety Executive has produced OSH-CD which gives full text of various publications, guidance and legislative, on health and safety (available from HMSO). The latter is supplemented by OSH-OFFSHORE for the oil and gas industries. Canadian health and safety literature and legislation is contained in OSH CanData from Microinfo, while OSH-ROM contains US and UN references as well as HSELINE, the UK HSE database. *OHSA Regulations, documents and technical information* covers US Occupational Health and Safety Administration data. There are many others.

The range of full text journals available on-line has grown from the text of the newspapers to academic journals. There is some primary publishing with the beginning of the 'live' journal with contributed papers available on demand. Chapter 11, which covers the Internet, expands on this. Initially the newspapers became available on microfiche, then on-line and now on CD-ROM, both as back files and as an on-going current file. British newspapers, the *Daily Telegraph, The Times, The Independent, The Guardian* and *The Financial Times,* are on-line via ESA and on CD-ROM from Chadwyck-Healey, while *The Washington Post* and *New York Times* are on-line via several hosts and on UMI CD-ROMs. DIALOG offers many more newspapers on-line and on CD-ROM, including the above and the *Los Angeles Times, Boston Globe, Chicago Tribune* and *Washington Times.* Questel-Orbit can add *L'express* and *Les echos,* among others, to these. There are titles from most major countries in most languages.

The legal community has developed a cross between databanks and databases containing both references and facts. LEXIS has been owned by various proprietors but now provides a wide range of legal 'libraries' on-line covering the statute and case law of the major countries of the world, not only English speaking. The European Union's legislation, cases and references to it are covered in *Celex* and *Scad,* which are made available by a number of hosts, and on CD-ROM from Context Ltd (*Scad* is also available from Chadwyck-Healey). They are part of Context's JUSTIS service including other parliamentary resources and the text of the EC *Official journal.* US Congressional databases are many, covering many aspects of its work. There are many more including the House of Commons and House of Lords *Hansard* (see Chapter 7).

Butterworth now offers *Books on screen,* which gives full text of handbooks, stock exchange listings and company law on CD-ROM, and also tailors its company, tax and information packages to client needs, incorporating company manuals and guidance. At present this is a UK package only.

Data protection and copyright

In the UK and most other countries not only does copyright limit the use and dissemination of data retrieved and stored electronically but also by the Data Protection Act or similar local acts. Copyright not only protects the author or designer's interest in a work of art, literary or otherwise, but in the development of software and database design. Data protection applies to the storage on any medium (paper and print were originally omitted from the regulations due to an overwhelming realization and concern for what could be done with the computer) of personal information, and places conditions on its proper use with which all must comply. Those with data on computer must register their holdings with the Registrar. The law is complex and covers a wider range than might initially have been thought. The professional's list of contacts containing telephone numbers and comments about them and their experience, products, etc. is registrable, as is the doctor's list of patients. The library catalogue is also registrable as the details of books against authors' names are deemed to be personal information!

Searching

The guides referred to below give advice in search techniques. The user manuals to the various hosts show how to conduct searches using the various commands available. To facilitate searching by irregular users and novices, menus and Windows interfaces are being designed for many hosts – ESA-IRS and DIALOG, for example. It has already been mentioned that while almost any topic may be searched on-line the more precise the request the more accurate the answers which will be provided.

The first stage in a search, once it has been decided which database(s) are to be used, is to construct a 'search profile' checking the manuals for coverage of the databases and specific search limitations and idiosyncrasies of vocabulary, particularly the usage of UK or US English with the variant spellings. Databases are either interrogated by searching for terms among the whole of the entry, including or excluding the abstract also, or by restricting the search to terms used in the title, the subject keywords, or other part of the entry, with constraints such as language, not before a particular date, etc. The topic must be thought out to ensure that all implications are discovered and all synonyms, etc. identified. Where thesauri exist, they should be used when planning a search. Some databases, such as API, BIOSIS, ERIC and COMPENDEX, have their own thesaurus, while others use the *Construction industry thesaurus* or the British Standards *Glossary of building and civil engineering terms* which is developed from the BSI's more general thesaurus covering all topics. Words which can have several endings (relevant ones) should be contracted to the main stem using the truncation symbol appropriate to the host: for example, '*' representing any number of letters to follow, '?' or '??' representing one or two letters only to follow; thus 'heat*' will retrieve 'heat, heats, heater, heaters, heating, . . .', but 'heat?' will only retrieve 'heat, heats'. 'Alumin+m' may indicate one or more letters missing to allow for the retrieval of aluminium and aluminum.

Planning procedures and strategies in advance saves on-line time – although the present costing trend to charge less for the actual search and retrieval and more for each reference or item displayed no longer places this at such a premium. Some communications systems will store the commands to be sent and permit them to be totally structured in advance and sent with the press of one function key – however, use of these requires great skill in knowing exactly what line will be required by the host. Many programmes will log all keystrokes and responses allowing model searches to be used for training.

When on-line the computer responds to each word input as a search term by indicating how many times that word appears in the database. Terms must then be combined in the most appropriate order to achieve the specification of the search topic. An understanding of basic algebra is useful. For example: a search for the use of heat pumps for domestic hot water installations in Britain might appear initially simply as:

(heat AND pump?) + (house? AND Britain) + (hot AND water AND installation?)

But this is too simple – the alternative terms are missing: house v. domestic, Britain v. UK v. England. The following shows an edited version of the search results for an actual search on COMPENDEX. Each line would have been entered as a command before displaying the result below.

The logic shown in the example illustrates ways in which combining

SEARCH HISTORY

SET	ITEMS	DESCRIPTION	
1	12 260	concrete	
2	9 687	reinforced	
3	2 500	1*2	
4	9 383	defect?	
5	3 199	fault?	
6	6 018	failure?	
7	18 093	4+5+6	
8	274	3*7	
9	14 956	corrosion	
10	65	8*9	(display first few)
11	4	alkali(w)attack	
12	3	sulphate(w)attack	
13	7	11+12	
14	3	9+13	
15	3	8*14	(display)
16	4 822	conversion	
17	706	shrinkage	
18	5 528	16+17	
19	246	3*18	
20	27	high(w)alumina(w)cement	
21	389	7+9+13+20	
22	383	3*21	(display first few)
23	268	22-18	(display first few)

* = and
+ = or
- = but not

thus possible alternative forms of failure which might be differently described should be found. Searches can rarely be sure of finding 100% of all relevant references – the problems are clearly shown by the terms used here and the alternatives not allowed for here where such a complex problem has been simplified

At any time after a * line a set of prints might be requested such as

T8/a/1–4 to show the first four items retrieved so far in the fullest form including abstract

At the end of a search, or when the database in use changes information will be given on the time used, the prints displayed and therefore charged, the session charge if there is one and any other special charges incurred.

terms may be done to allow term *or* term *or* term to be used and added to group of terms *and* group of terms and alternatives tried where too many or too few references result in the second column. Although simplified the concepts are shown – the search had to specify certain types of failure as well as the general terms for failure in order to ensure that all references to defects and failures would be retrieved. It is also possible then to issue the 'deduplicate' command to remove duplicate references from several specified lines in the search. No two searchers will format their strategy in exactly the same manner, and frequently the same enquiry can be structured differently and retrieve different references or data. Similarly, a nil result on a search can mean either the strategy is at fault or that there is no relevant information.

Document delivery

Full text databases or databanks have been discussed – the answer is provided. However, the reference databases are still heavily used and in order to provide a fuller service many now either have their own document delivery service, accessible directly from the search mode, or have linked with other document providers to do both. Thus ESA-IRS offers various means of obtaining any document found, including a direct request quoting the set and item number, to the British Library. DIALOG and others have various services – ISI were one of the first to offer this with their *The genuine article* service. CARL's *UnCover* has already been mentioned in the previous chapters. Blackwell's is the UK agent and help desk. The British Library offers *Inside information*, either on-line or on CD-ROM, and many others are developing. The former offers contents pages from over 10 000 most frequently requested journals backed by delivery either on-line or via the usual forms. *Inside conferences* now offers a similar service from the British Library for conference proceedings. Another recent development with this type of service is OCLC with *Firstsearch*, and others are beginning to offer slightly more expensive, one-off, rates as well as the subscription access for heavy academic and other library users. This is to the benefit of the many company users who may only require such services occasionally, but when they do they require the full text promptly. OCLC has run a union catalogue for a long time and now, via *Firstsearch*, makes some of the expertise available to non-subscribers on a menu-based system on-line. Some of the many databases available are *Worldcat*, COMPENDEX, INSPEC and ERIC. This is supplemented, since November 1994, by *Fastdoc*. Some of the documents and articles that are available in full text may be retrieved via a search and the full item displayed immediately on-line as well as by fax and inter-library loan.

Sources of information

The most current guides will frequently give lists of the most popular relevant databases in each topic area. Recent titles include those by Bradley and Hanson, Convey, and Hartley and others. The methods of searching and designing a search strategy are well covered in these. Orton's guide is perhaps the latest, and is based on experience in running the British Library services.

Directories of databases can be somewhat formidable in size. Cuadra's well-established directory, which was taken over in 1993 by Gale and is now the *Directory of databases,* is available on-line, on disk and in print with regular updates. It covers all types of publicly and privately available databases. The original Gale directory of *Computer readable databases* was merged with the Cuadra *Directory of online databases* and the *Directory of portable databases*. Indexes include geographic, subject and a master name index. The 1990s has seen a reduction in the number of such directories as it has become increasingly difficult to cover all databases in a meaningful way. They have been augmented by many more subject-specific guides, such as the Aslib series listed below and those on building and construction specifically. These need updating on a regular basis, mainly in terms of the detail and the hosts from which they are available rather than any fundamental change as the diversity of the 1980s has stabilized.

The lists of databases from the major hosts present useful guides. Those for Datastar + DIALOG, STN, QUESTEL, ESA-IRS should be obtained for reference. The catalogues from the CD-ROM publishers supplement these. Those from Silverplatter, Learned Information, Chadwyck-Healey, Springer-Verlag and Microinfo are the most detailed. Most list all offerings by title and by topic and give a summary of content. Many stress the different formats available and some are now acting as distributors, e.g. Microinfo. Thus many CD-ROMs are available from several suppliers as well as direct from publishers, although in common with book distributors many of their catalogues do not give the publisher's name.

Some titles manage to combine guidance on search techniques with evaluation of the various databases available. Nicholas and Erbach's work does this and shows the range of information available, as well as the influence on retrieval of different search techniques in different hosts. New offerings include the *CD-ROM handbook* from Sherman.

This chapter does no more than skim the surface of this vast topic, which is rapidly changing as both the Internet and skill with free-text searching develops. Keeping up-to-date requires regular scanning of journals ranging from *Information manager, Online, Database, Journal of the American Society of Information Science, Online and CDnotes* and *Online and CD-ROM review (formerly Online review)*, to *CIIG newsletter, Program* and *UKOLUG newsletter* among others, including those like *AJ* and *Building* which may occasionally notice developments in this field. The annual proceedings of the IOLIM meeting in London each December give useful pointers to developments. Learned Information's newspaper *Information world review* and *Electronic documents* keep users up-to-date, as do Meckler's *CDRom world* and *CDRom review*. *CD-ROM professional* is a new title from Pemberton Press. At present these are expanding and merging as they find their niche in the changing context of electronic information retrieval. News is always given on-line but need not be read on each occasion. In Europe the *I'm guide* and *XIII magazine* are themselves on-line via ECHO, a mainly public host with a few subscription databases, such as TED.

More recently the interest in the Internet has seen the popular computer press publishing articles on other types of on-line searching and the more critical reviewers have noted some of the pitfalls. An error in production can omit key facts. Microsoft's *Encarta* encyclopaedia apparently has errors in the list of Nobel prizewinners 1900-1960, but it looks and feels authoritative to those using it (*PC Magazine*, October 1994, p.103). The same article goes on to point out that when it 'comes to producing relevant search criteria the human researcher is vastly superior to the electronic search engine. Indeed the lack of flexibility in freetext search software makes it positively dangerous to look for data without knowing at least the bare bones of what you're searching for'.

Bibliography

Allcock, S. and Osborne, J. *The online manual*. Oxford: Learned Information (Europe).

Aslib CD-ROM and on-line series:

  Cox, J. (1991) *Building, construction and architecture databases.*

  Cox, J. (1994) *CD-ROM and online environment databases.* 2nd edn.

  English, L. (1994) *CD-ROM and online business and company databases.* 4th edn.

  Parker, N. (1993) *CD-ROM and online management and marketing databases.* 4th edn.

  Pilkington, S. and Rhodes, R. (1992) *Online engineering databases.*

Bradfield, V. J. (1983) (ed.) *Information sources in architecture.* Butterworths. (First edition ed. V.J. Nurcombe.)

Bradley, P. and Hanson, T. (1994) *Going online and CD-ROM.* 9th edn. London: Aslib.

Convey, J. (1992) *Online information retrieval: an introductory manual to principles and practice.* 4th edn. London: Library Association Publishing.

Hartley, R. J. *et al.* (1990) *Online searching: principles and practice.* Bowker-Saur.

Information Access Company *Online user's manual.* Regularly updated.

Large, J.A. and Armstrong, C.J. (1992) *Manual of online search strategies.* 2nd edn. Aldershot: Gower.

Nicholas, D. and Erbach, G. (1989) *Online information sources for business and current affairs: an evaluation of Textline, NEXIS, Profile and DIALOG.* London and New York: Mansell.

Orton, D. and the staff of the British Library Science and Technology Information Service (1995) *Online searching in science and technology: an introductory guide to equipment, databases and search techniques.* London: British Library, sponsored by ESA-IRS.

Sherman, C. (1994) *CD-ROM handbook.* New York: Intertext.

The CD-ROM directory with multimedia CDs. Six monthly. London: TFPL Publishing.

Webber, S. *et al.* (1994) *UKOLUG quick guide to online commands.* 4th edn. London: UK Online User Group.

CHAPTER FIVE

Trade literature and technical information

GILLIAN EDMONDS

Introduction

Since the last edition of this publication there has been a considerable improvement in the standard of trade literature produced by manufacturers in the construction industry. The gap between the level of technical information produced by manufacturers and that from other sources has narrowed considerably. However, this situation is also due to the demise of various agencies such as the PSA, which were previously responsible for technical information of a very high order.

There has also been a change in the relative importance of proprietary products in construction. There is now a strong emphasis on asking manufacturers to act as subcontractors and to provide a design service to the professional. This ensures that the relationship of the individual product or component to the surrounding construction is governed by the manufacturer's specification. There is an increasing reliance on manufacturers to provide technical information, both in print and by producing videos, generic calculations and specification programmes. RIBA Services have been a prime mover in producing standard manufacturers' details on CAD disk with their product, *RIBA-CAD*. In addition, many large manufacturers are producing and distributing their own CAD disks. However, there is still a lot of work to be done in terms of ensuring that the presentation of the information on disk and in hard copy matches the high standards available in trade literature.

Trade literature

It is important to distinguish between truly technical trade literature and a manufacturer's marketing or sales information. For the purposes of this chapter, trade literature refers to technical trade literature, that is, information which allows the construction professional to select and specify products, materials, services or systems.

The description 'trade literature' covers all data sheets, brochures, catalogues, binders and information in any other format which relates to manufactured products or systems and also to services offered by manufacturers or consultants. In addition many manufacturers produce samples of their materials. These are usually provided separately from the literature, but for some products such as fabrics and carpets the sample will be integrated with the technical information.

There are approximately 20 000 manufacturers of building products in the UK (although many are of wider origin), many producing more than one product, so that the range of information which could be kept is vast. It is not surprising, therefore, that the construction professional will only keep information which provides at least some degree of technical guidance to specification. Space in libraries and at the desk is at a premium and no professional can afford to keep information that is not truly germane to the design process.

More and more design offices concentrate on keeping trade literature relating to a specific project, setting up a project library which will eventually hold information relating to the products and systems employed for that contract. The main office library is used to keep a core library of literature from key manufacturers in specific product areas; otherwise information is obtained as and when it is needed.

Finding product information has always been important and becomes increasingly so as manufactured, pre-fabricated products form a larger part of the construction process. A number of directories are published and updated annually which give reliable details of manufacturers and their products, although checks should also be made on the generic specification of a product or material.

BS 4940: the standard for trade literature

Technical trade literature should give the construction professional all of the information required to specify a product or system successfully. Although eventually a discussion may take place with the manufacturer's technical department, designers may initially specify from literature alone. BS 4940: *Technical information on construction products and services* has long been the major source of guidance for the production of technical literature and in 1994 it was considerably revised and re-issued. BS 4940 is now available in 3 parts:

Part 1: Guide for management
Part 2: Guide to content and arrangement
Part 3: Guide to presentation.

The revised standard gives very clear guidance on the type of information which should be included in such publications, lists several generic types of document and details the purpose and scope of each type. An increasing number of construction industry librarians and professionals are asking manufacturers to conform to this standard if they wish literature to be kept within the office library. The first part of the standard helps manufacturers through the process of producing literature while Part 2 details the type of information which should be included. Trade literature should offer a full description of the product covering appearance, size and any information the manufacturer uses to identify it. Any regulations or standards with which the product complies should be listed, as should any limitations on the use of the product. Full technical and performance details should be given and, if appropriate, details of installation and use.

BS 4940 recommends that trade literature should always be dated and refer to any documents which are superseded. Manufacturers are remarkably reluctant to follow this practice, often on the grounds that they do not wish information to look out-of-date if it has not recently needed revision. There is some basis for this concern as it should be common practice for all trade literature to be reviewed every two years. Both legislative and technical change means that any guidance given within the literature could very well be out-of-date after such a period of time. However, as most offices will date incoming literature, the manufacturer may as well date the information themselves. It is also becoming important for both designers and manufacturers to be able to verify that any information given within trade literature was accurate and in line with the legislation and other guidelines current at the time of going to press.

Other media for trade literature

Microfiche and microfilm have been used to store trade literature for many years. There are several major suppliers of systems described below. Barbour Index plc still produce the *Barbour product microfile* which consists of full text trade literature from a number of selected manufacturers across a wide range of product areas. The attraction of this system has always been that Barbour retain control over the manufacturers on the system to ensure that only high-quality information is provided and that the full range of construction products is covered. However, this also means that the system cannot be fully comprehensive and that the subscriber bears the full cost.

The market for this means of storing information has always been limited, partly because microfiche is limited in terms of reproducing literature which works best in full colour. In recent years a number of information providers have begun to see the potential of CD-ROM to store manufacturers' information. Specifiers have always been reluctant to pay for product information in any form and therefore it was only when electronic systems provided technical as well as trade information that the market expanded. More information is given on individual suppliers of microfiche and electronic systems later in this chapter.

Most producers of trade literature have not adapted to the new media available, and the electronic systems usually reproduce literature in the standard A4 format as it was first printed rather than re-designing it visually.

Trade literature in the design process

Construction professionals differ in their use of manufacturers' trade literature and technical information from other sources, but for architects in particular, product information forms a large part of the information resource for any project. Trade literature is considered throughout the design process: right from the very early stages of design when specifiers will be considering the viability of using certain product types and materials; through detailed design when specific information regarding size, appearance and performance is required; to final specification, when the test results must be verified and all requirements confirmed.

It is clear that although information may be gathered on a project-by-project basis there is still a need for generic information relating to product types and for a library of core information.

Storage and retrieval of trade literature

Hard copy libraries

Most practices keep a hard copy collection of manufacturers' information, which is accessible to all members of staff. The collection may be separate from technical information although the same classification system will probably be used for both. Despite a recent growth in the use of electronic media for storing and retrieving product information, the library of hardcopy information continues, and is likely to do so for some time.

The classification system most commonly used is the CI/SfB system, a hierarchical, faceted classification system which has been widely used throughout the construction industry for many years. CI/SfB is composed of five separate tables, each with a different coding system using letters in upper and lower case, numbers and parentheses () to differentiate between tables. The complexity of the system notation poses a challenge for professional specifiers managing without a librarian, as many do, but its complexity is matched by the complexity of the construction process, and the system provides a means of dealing with new concepts, products and materials not offered by other systems.

The *Common arrangement of works sections* (CAWS) is a system developed to deal with specifications and bills of quantity and is used by some practices for dealing with product information. It is, however, weak in terms of dealing with information related to the management and administration of the project or to building design in general.

The Construction Industry Information Group *CIIG Manual* (1994) is a useful source of more detailed information on setting up product and technical libraries and on the implementation of a classification scheme. Further information is given in Chapter 22.

RIBA Services still maintain a product library service and will organize office libraries for clients. Many of the freelance members of CIIG in the UK, and the professional library and information associations in other countries, will also provide a similar service for offices not large enough to warrant their own company librarian. The tradition of company product information libraries serviced once a week, once a month, or as required, is strong in the construction industry for which so much fee-earning time can be wasted trying to locate essential data. The efficient maintenance of such collections and reliance on the services described in this chapter have become essential to the maintenance of quality procedures and to the avoidance of liability issues in the office.

Compendia

Product data from RIBA Services is a collection of A4 data sheets produced to a standard format, using the *CIB master list of properties* as a basis for the way the information is laid out. The data sheets are classified in CI/SfB order and each section is preceded by some general trade and technical information. Manufacturers are included in the system on a fee paying basis but must comply with the standard format. Subscribers to the RIBA Office Library Service receive *Product data* as part of their fee.

The *Barbour compendium* is produced as a single volume and acts a directory of information, providing manufacturers' details under a series of classified headings. The compendium also provides advertizing space on full colour pages which are produced to a standard format, including an illustration of the product and technical details. Manufacturers are encouraged to provide sufficient detail to allow the specifier to make an initial product selection from the information given. The compendium also acts as a directory to a wider range of manufacturers, with listings of company names and addresses and an index to trade names.

The *ASC mini file* from Architects Standard Catalogues is produced as a three volume directory which provides listings of manufacturers and some useful technical information including a list of British Standards classified to CI/SfB. The manufacturers' paid advertizing is in the form of full text product literature, a format which can provide a very high standard of information, depending of course upon the quality of the source material. The ASC has recently been increased in size to A5 which has considerably increased the usefulness of the document.

Microfiche and electronic systems

These two media may seem unlikely bedfellows but in the main those information providers who offered microfiche systems in the past are now moving towards using computers to store and access information on CD-ROM or disk. In the UK both Barbour Index and Technical Indexes offer a product library on microfiche. BCQ from On Demand Information Limited provides a library of full text product literature on CD-ROM (See below).

Finding trade literature and keeping up-to-date

A core library of product information can be built up over time and, once established, manufacturers are likely to continue to send updated information on a regular basis. However, academic and other libraries which are not used by professionals with a specific contract, may need to remind manufacturers of the need to keep them informed, and should check on a regular basis that they are still on the mailing list.

There are a number of ways of obtaining information, and research can be undertaken on the basis of finding information related to a specific product or material, or by finding specific manufacturers or product trade names. The most commonly used tools for this research are directories and the compendia mentioned above, enquiry services and journals. There is no mainstream publicly accessible library of product information and, although there is a need for an archive of product literature, this currently exists only within certain practices, when it relates to products actually specified on projects. Some manufacturers keep copies of all product literature including superseded documents, but many neglect to do this. Barbour Index can supply copies of withdrawn microfiche to subscribers.

The Science Reference library, part of the British Library Science Reference and Information Service, keeps commercial directories, trade literature arranged by company name, market research, journals and individual profiles of companies (including financial information). Many public libraries also keep a wide range of directories (see below). Academic libraries and departments with construction-related courses frequently maintain collections of manufacturers' literature and some of the services discussed below, not only for project use but in order to accustom students to the collections which they should find later within the office environment.

Information professionals

Librarians unfamiliar with construction information may find it helpful to use an information professional with specific construction industry experience to help them build up a trade literature collection or to keep it up-to-date. The CIIG is the body in the UK which represents librarians and other information professionals within this field. Many of the members work full time for practices of all disciplines, but a number of members work on a consultancy basis and are available for regular library maintenance but also for specific research.

Updating can also be carried out using the reply paid services offered by most product journals such as *Building products* and more specialist publications such as *Specifier review*, *DABS* and *Designers data* to which manufacturers subscribe in order to offer this service.

Directories and compendia

Although some directories provide a degree of technical information related to products, generally speaking they are used as sources of reference information to find manufacturers' names and telephone numbers. Some directories also give general technical information and sources of further information about particular product areas while others provide manufacturers with an opportunity to use formatted advertizing space to give more detailed information, for which the manufacturer pays a premium. Many directories are available free to professional practices and to individual members on the RIBA register or similar professional registers.

The *Barbour compendium* mentioned above is one of the most widely used directories listing both manufacturers' names and trade names in classified lists. RIBA Services also produces a three volume directory, the *RIBA Product selector*, which gives comprehensive listings of manufacturers and trade names, using the CI/SfB classification system to arrange the information. Each product grouping is preceded by a list of advisory organizations offering further information and advice, and there is also an alphabetical list of addresses for trade and advisory organizations in the third volume. The directory volumes for RIBA/Ti's construction service provide useful directories complemented by those on civil engineering and other related fields.

There are a number of specialist directories which produce information for specific parts of the construction industry. Some are produced by trade associations on behalf of their members. Unfortunately, many of these specialist directories do not survive after the first year or so as they fail to attract sufficient advertising to support production and very few professionals will purchase the directories, expecting them to be provided without payment. One exception to this is the *Interior designers handbook* (IDH) from Cheerman, which is used by professional interior designers, decorators and architects alike as an invaluable source of information for both products and specialist services. The IDH allows each of the manufacturers in the handbook a paragraph to describe their product or service. It is organized in broad categories, such as materials: paint, contract furniture, fabrics, etc., and then in alphabetical order by supplier, although it is not always easy to find individual manufacturers or very specific products and the volume would benefit from an improved index. Full colour photographic illustrations make it a pleasurable publication to use.

Another successful specialist directory which looks set to stay the course is *External works* (incorporating *Landscape specification*), from Landscape Promotions, which covers a wide range of topics, ranging from technical products such as geosynthetics to planting and street furniture. The products are arranged in broad groupings preceded by an alphabetical subject index. Each section starts with a table of suppliers and products followed by the product sections which may be further sub divided, e.g. 'Natural stone quarries' is divided into 'Sandstone', 'Limestone', etc. Within each section manufacturers or suppliers are listed, giving details of each product or service. In addition to the researched lists there are also pages of full colour formatted advertizing. *Specification*, published annually by EMAP Business Communications in three volumes, is widely used by specifiers as a guide to generic specification, and includes a directory to product information.

Directories covering industry more generally include *Kellys*, the various parts of *Kompass, Sells* and *Dial industry*, all of which are useful for mainstream construction products, and those on the fringe of construction. In the broader spectrum publishers such as Sweet (now part of McGraw-Hill) and Thomas Publishing provide a wide range of directories. Sweet's *Building products for export* is available in a number of editions, including European, and is part of the Sweet's Information Services collection of directories, called 'Catalog files', which contain reproductions of manufacturers' literature in the same way ASC does but without the size reduction. A subject and company name index is provided and the items are organized by the AIA's CIS code with a 'Buyline' number which can be used to contact the hotline service on telephone/fax (+1 (309) 686 4422/3). Some useful titles include *Gen-*

eral building and renovation, Contract interiors, and *Accessible building products.*

Also useful is the Thomas *Register of American manufacturers* produced annually since 1905, in 29 volumes in 1995. This register covers Canada as well as the USA. While not specific to construction, the scope is so wide that it is nevertheless useful, complementing the various versions of *Kompass* serving all continents.

Directory publishing is an expanding field and although the established names have broad coverage rather than being specific to construction they will always be useful where the more specific are not readily available. The basis for inclusion of manufacturers and for the updating of their entries in any of these directories should always be checked to ascertain whether they have to pay for inclusion, or whether inclusion is free and hence coverage more comprehensive. Not all manufacturers are contacted about updating if they do not submit information promptly themselves.

Journals

Reading the construction press is the best way of keeping up-to-date with new products and services from manufacturers. The *Architects' journal* has replaced 'Products in practice' with a new supplement, *AJ Focus* which concentrates on a specific product area in each issue, giving tables of manufacturers and products or services. There is a much higher editorial content than the old 'Products in practice', with articles on new products, technical advances and the impact of changes in legislation, as well as profiles of individual buildings, designers and companies. *Building* magazine and *Building design* also have useful product features or supplements with a related enquiry card service for requests for further information. General product journals, such as *What's new in building,* and those which concentrate on a specific product area, such as *Roofing* and *Blinds and shutters*, are useful sources of product information and in common with other journals offer a readers' request service for further information. Finding product journals related to a specific area is probably not a problem for specifiers as the journal publishers are assiduous in keeping mailing lists up-to-date, however, for others it may not be so easy. Many journals are mentioned in press guides such as *Willings* and *Brad* (available in most reference libraries), and trade associations can often recommend suitable journals and sometimes sponsor their production. Otherwise, consult large publishers of construction journals, such as EMAP, Centaur and Morgan Grampian.

Technical information

While the construction professional relies on product manufacturers to provide good technical data about their specific product or service, this is no substitute for objective, informed technical information which relates to all aspects of the design and construction process. Technical literature consists of information concerning the design and construction of buildings and other structures, which is needed during the design process. It covers: information relating to the building type as a whole; generic information such as space planning or anthropometric data; information relating to materials specification, construction technology and working details; and information on special issues such as environmental topics.

The high cost of producing technical books and the comparatively small market for them has caused commercial publishers to take a cautious view of any proposal from technical authors. The transfer of ownership of the PSA to the private sector saw the loss of a highly valued source of technical information for government agencies and departments; information which once filtered through to the wider profession through experience and practice as well as through direct publication sales.

While the volume and complexity of technical information as a whole has increased, guidance and interpretation from official bodies is less in evidence, largely due to lack of funds. However, many excellent organizations, such as the Building Research Establishment and the Construction Industry Research and Information Association, still produce useful information based on current research. Many of the publications and other sources of technical information used by the construction industry professional are available as full text on microfiche and/or on electronic systems described at the end of this chapter.

Design and construction of building types and structures

Design information includes design guides which highlight the specific requirements of various building types and facilities, as well as examples of building design. In addition, designers need basic anthropometric and space planning data which apply to all buildings. Standard references such as the *New metric handbook* and Neufert are readily available.

Construction information will include all aspects of the construction process; information on generic materials such as glass and timber, other base materials such as bricks, manufactured products and systems – from very basic items such as windows to highly sophisticated elements such as curtain walling systems. As more and more building elements are produced as pre-fabricated, manufactured components and designers have to deal with a sophisticated product technology and, dividing line between information provided by trade and official bodies is becoming more and more blurred. However, standard references include the excellent *Specification*, produced annually by EMAP publications, and *Specification for commercial interiors* gives good basic working details of standard products and fittings as well as generic specification guidance.

Changes in construction and specification methods

A number of factors have radically altered construction techniques and specification methods over the last 5-10 years, notably the growth in the legislation which governs construction. In addition, changes in building design have become more complex and technological. Modern designers have to deal with a sophisticated product technology with many building elements now designed by other specialists or by the manufacturers themselves. The integration of services in buildings is a highly complex, specialist area, with energy and environmental issues playing an increasingly important role. The Building Services Research and Information Association *Publications index* lists publications for the building services industry and includes *Information sources in building services*, edited by their librarian, Stephen Lloyd. Other information relating to building services can be obtained from the Chartered Institution of Building Services Engineers which maintains a library and produces technical publications which are available to non-members.

Specifiers must rely on a wider range of information, based as far as possible on actual experience of construction. Learning from building failures is important, but the consequences of such failures are so great in terms of cost and human health and safety that specifiers need to be able to predict the building's performance as far as possible. Information must therefore also be as up-to-date as possible.

Sterling work has been carried out by a number of organizations and institutions in making building science more exact and predictable. In addition the growth in interest in environmental issues, health and safety and energy usage has made the whole process more complex. The Building Research Establishment produces a series of relevant publications, including BRE *Defect action sheets, Digests, Good building guides, Information papers* and reports, which are now published by Construction Research Communications Limited, part of EMAP Business Communications, and discussed in detail elsewhere.

Storage and retrieval of technical information

Technical information systems

For many years the only serious alternative to keeping hard copy libraries of both trade and technical information was the use of microfiche.

Computer databases and on-line services were mostly used to provide references to publications, journals, reports, etc., rather than to full texts. In addition, while academic libraries and large practices used computers for information retrieval purposes, the specifier was still unused to using a computer for anything other than accounts and word-processing. In recent years, PCs and Apple Macs have become more readily available on the desk top and specifiers have become more familiar with their use.

The development of CD-ROM as a storage medium has probably made the most difference to the professional. CD-ROM is excellent for storing masses of text but images and colour take up lots of space so a number of CDs may be needed. Juke box storage systems are really the best way of dealing with this. Most systems have now developed a means of downloading the results of a search from the CD to a file in order to accumulate information. An essential requirement of any system is that the information is well-organized, is indexed sensibly and has good front-end software in order to access the information easily.

BCQ/ODI

Poulter Communications originally launched Quantarch as a product information system on CD-ROM. Poulter was the first new player to appear in this field for some time, coming from a background of advertizing and marketing rather than of technical information. However, it was soon evident that specifiers would not pay for product information only, however excited they were about CD-ROM, and Poulter revised the system considerably to include technical information. A joint venture with the Building Centre resulted in the product BCQ. This co-operation ceased in Spring 1995 and the service became known by the new company name, On Demand Construction Information. Full text files of product and technical information are stored on CD-ROMs, accessed through software installed on a standard PC. The technical content includes information from HMSO, the Brick Development Association, NHBC, TRADA, BBA, etc. British Standards are available as a separate package but are also sold with the BCQ technical data file. The master database at present holds the following information:

- technical information from HMSO, BDA, NHBC, TRADA, etc.
- BSI Standards related to construction and engineering. (BSI are to launch a new service via this network giving access to users of standards on an annual subscription basis.)
- product information library consisting of full text brochures, from over 1000 manufacturers
- a directory of 5500 product manufacturers
- an architectural directory of information from 500 architectural practices.

In a recent innovation, ODI has launched what it terms an *On-demand information system,* which uses software at the user's local PC to search for the information required; the user is then connected to a master database via a dedicated BT ISDN line. Unlike traditional on-line searching via a standard open telecommunications link, the search process goes on at a local level and the ISDN line is used merely to transfer data. The company quotes 45 seconds for a 12-page British Standard. The information is then downloaded to the user's PC for manipulation. Payment is only for information downloaded, not for search time. The system can be used to warn the user if information in a personal job file has changed when they next come to use it, to avoid working with out-of-date information. The on-line service includes a similar range of information to the CD-ROM service, covering around 3000 brochures from suppliers and text from over 100 technical organizations.

Barbour Index

The 'Construction expert' system from Barbour Index is to be launched in 1995 and provides both product and technical information on CD-ROM with sophisticated database software used to access the information. Its major advantage is the integration of product and technical information related to all aspects of construction. The regulatory and other documents covered have been selected with the assistance of practising architects and engineers, among others. The essentials have been included rather than the extras: these include reference to around 200 organizations and 10 000 manufacturers. Where necessary, reference is made back to text on the microfiche system. Physical and performance data is included in a standard presentation format.

Barbour were the first in the construction industry to offer a microfiche service with the full text of technical documents accompanied by a printed, regularly updated, index volume referring by topic to the appropriate fiche using its number and frame code. Subscribers receive the index volumes and any additional fiche at regular intervals. Obsolete fiche may be removed but only when all references on a fiche have been declared obsolete. For many years this had been done by Ti for engineering but not for construction. (Ti developed their construction microfiche in the late 1970s/early 1980s.) Barbour has since moved on from the basic *Building technical microfile* and *Building product microfile,* to provide engineering technical and product microfiles, a three part health care microfile and microfiles on the topics of planning, health and safety, property and estates management, project management, facilities management. The *Building technical minifile* supplements the above product range by including about one-third of the coverage of the full version at a more realistic price for the smaller practice.

Technical Indexes

Technical Indexes offers both microfiche and CD-ROM systems providing full text of technical and product information, with the CD-ROM library accessed by database software. This is linked with the NBS *Specification manager* to assist with accurate specification. The RIBA/Ti service is available either on CD-ROM, as the *Construction information service*, or in microfiche form, as the *Technical information microfile*. Each of these systems consists of a core of documents relating to construction activities, including standards, legislation and other technical information. This core system is aimed at architects and designers and can be supplemented by the building, engineering and applied engineering files. Product information is available on the *Construction and civil engineering index*, and consists of a 'prime' file of manufacturers who subscribe to the system and a support file adding further manufacturers, including at least one extra from each main product grouping. The microfiche set is supported by a regularly updated index volume. The latter also acts as a useful product/supplier directory.

A range of technical information systems is also available, aimed at contractors and engineers in all branches of engineering. Further information is available on the *RIAI technical microfile* (relevant to Ireland), and the RIBA/Ti *Planning microfile*. Ti offers a number of other services covering all British Standards, US Industry Standards, US Federal and Regulatory documents, International and European Standards, occupational health and safety and other topics. These are available via Ti, or their parent US company, Information Handling Services (IHS) of Colorado. Many of the indexes to these are available from the on-line host services as databases, as well as in the print volumes.

Both the above services are backed up by 'Hotline' services providing information, catalogues and documents not already included in the system. Rapidoc (Ti) supplies publications from BSI, HMSO and others.

Building on-line

This is the only viewdata service to the construction industry available on subscription only. Information is digested and presented in standard videotext screens. Product information is presented with alphabetical and CI/SfB indexes. BLISS is a contract database regularly updated and containing the text of *Building regulations*, with indexes, and the text of the DoE appeals and decisions. BCIS prices and average building costs are also included and updated monthly.

Finding technical information and keeping up-to-date

As the rate of change in legislation, technical advance and management issues increases, so specifiers are more and more wary of committing to hard copy libraries of information, or even to keeping their own databases and other forms of reference. Those companies which offer the provision of technical information and an automatic updating service offer real value in terms of time saving and also are more likely to ensure reliability that information is correct. One of the advantages of subscribing to a packaged information system such as those mentioned above is that the information is automatically kept up-to-date, usually at least every three months. The printed indexes which are produced to accompany these systems would themselves be very useful to many specifiers but the information providers have yet to take commercial advantage of such a service and therefore only market the full system.

A number of companies act as host to on-line services, few of which are aimed specifically at the construction industry, but many offer valuable financial, business and cost information, as discussed in the previous chapter. In theory, on-line services should be of more use to practices than CD-ROM systems, which are higher in capital cost. However, few designers possess the skills to search effectively and efficiently on-line and, as practices possess more and more technology and so many services are available on CD-ROM, the move is in this direction.

Keeping up-to-date is otherwise a matter of looking at individual services from organizations and publishers and obtaining publications such as the *Construction monitor*, published by the DoE in association with *Building*, which is a useful means of keeping up with European initiatives, including legislation. Construction journals are an excellent source of up-to-date technical information of all kinds. The mainstream construction journals, such as the *Architects' journal* and *Building*, produce good technical information in the form of examples of working details, feedback on the performance of materials and products in practice, analyses of current issues and articles on such subjects as energy management, 'green' design, corrosion, condensation, materials technology, construction methods and techniques, and changes in legislation. Many journals feature a number of building studies which look in detail at recently constructed buildings and at the products specified, but also re-visit others which have been in use for some time. Journals may also include building cost analyses, information on building design and technology and standard working details.

Publishers, libraries and bookshops

RIBA Publications is the publishing arm of RIBA Companies and concentrates mainly on producing information relating to contract, practice and management. However, the bookshop at the RIBA in London is an excellent source of text books, biographies, monographs and other works related to design and construction. RIBA Publications offers a subscription service and can provide publications from a number of publishers producing an annual catalogue as well as a list of their own publications. Most publishers keep a mailing list and will send updated catalogues regularly. It is worth ensuring that this information is obtained from the Building Centre bookshop, the BRE and the HSE. The BSI also acts as distributor for publications produced by others and sends listings out with *BSI News*.

The professional institutions have largely been responsible for information related to practice and management although some also produce technical documents relating to their specific subject area. The Royal Institution of Chartered Surveyors (RICS) runs a Library Information Service on subscription from the library at their headquarters in Central London, which also has a bookshop. Most other professional bodies will provide a catalogue of publications on request.

Advisory organizations and institutions

In addition to supplying lists of members, some trade organizations produce guidance on the use and implementation of products in their field. Most trade organizations and associations produce newsletters and publications relating to their subject area; many are very trade-oriented but some are of general interest to specifiers. For example, the Loss Prevention Council produces a range of publications including design guides relating to fire safety, fire prevention and protection, information sheets on building products which are approved by the Council and a range of other publications regarding equipment and security. The National House-Building Council (NHBC) produces its own standards for building and information construction methods and techniques. The Timber Research and Development Association (TRADA) produces a number of publications which are available individually or on subscription and include various design guides, research reports and Wood Information Sheets. Most are included in the services described above.

Conclusion

While the pattern of trade and technical publishing described in this chapter concentrates mainly on the UK, there is a similar pattern in other countries. The communications services described in Chapter 11 will provide an introduction to the main sources in each country. However, the range of manufacturers and technical bodies is so large in each country, and conformity to local, national regulations still so great that for many years to come such services will probably remain mainly national. And yet the largest of the directory services will maintain their importance, particularly for those practices and companies working in the international market still so great.

CHAPTER SIX

Standards and regulations

BARRY H. AND VALERIE J. NURCOMBE

Today there are standards and regulations relating to every aspect of the building and construction industry. Traditionally these regulations have concerned themselves with aspects of building and construction design. Now, however, the architect and designer have to be aware of their increased sphere of responsibility, for example, towards the personnel involved in construction as well as those who are ultimately the end users; the latter is embodied in: *Construction Design and Management (CDM) Regulations* (implementation currently delayed) – reviewed by Sylvester Bone and John Loring *(AJ,* 6 July 1994, pp.23–25): '...they are quite different from the building regulations because there are *no* technical requirements to be satisfied or approvals to be sought. These regulations place a duty on designers to consider the health and safety of people on-site' during and after construction.

The current building standards have developed from the application of standards to housing design in rebuilding London after the Great Fire in 1666. In 1774 they were consolidated into the Building Act, and since then have been augmented by local by-laws, the Public Health Acts of the nineteenth century and, since 1901, co-ordinated and developed by the British Standards Institution. During the twentieth century the process of development and co-ordination of standards has extended in many countries, in different ways, towards the wider approach of the European and International standardization movements. As international professional commitments increase, so also must the architect's and contractor's awareness of other countries' standards, and the co-ordinating and rationalizing work of the standardizing bodies described below.

Standardization can be defined as 'the establishment, by authority, by custom, or by general consent, of rules, disciplines, techniques and other defined conditions which have to be followed to enable a society or particular sections of it to function smoothly and efficiently' (Mildren, 1976). Within the construction industry topics covered by standards include glossaries, dimensions and measurements, definitions and symbols, methods of test, quality, safety, performance and dimensional specifications, and methods of construction. This is a very wide range and all standards should conform to a familiar structure to enable the user to identify parts and content easily. The aims of standardization have been defined by the BSI as follows:

- simplify the group variety of products and procedures in human life
- improve communication
- promote overall economy
- ensure safety, health and the protection of life
- protect consumer and community interest
- eliminate trade barriers. (BS 0: Part 1: 1991).

British Standards

The use of standards was developed to prevent the recurrence of failures (e.g. the Great Fire) and is still seen as a means of at least minimizing failures. But the level of quality specified must be recognized for what it is; a minimum level which architects should study before writing standards into specifications (Vandenburg, 1976). Standards also represent a means of communicating with the professions, a vehicle for transmitting research results into practice (BS 0: Part 3: 1991).

Standards by themselves do not have the force of law, although this is not always recognized. This can, however, be given to them by mention in statutory requirements as, for example, in the case of Statutory Instrument No: 2768: 1991: *Building and buildings. The building regulations 1991* (HMSO, 1991), which came into force on 1 July 1992. This referred to related documents, Approved Document, 1985: D, 1990: F, H, J, L, 1991: A, B, C, G, K, M, R7, *Amendments to the Approved Documents*. (HMSO). *The Amendments 1992 to the Approved Documents* identifies *ENV 1992-1-1* and *ENV 1993-1-1* as appropriate guidance for the design of concrete and steel structures. When the ENV Eurocodes are converted into ENs, it is likely that they will be cited formally in a future revision of *Approved Document A*. Revised Regulation 7 and its Approved Document describe the role of European Standards in meeting requirements for appropriate material and use in a workmanlike manner. The buildings regulations are also discussed in Chapter 7.

The Public Health and Housing Acts, among others, may specify requirements in similar ways; only then does a standard have legal force, and yet standards are very closely related to the regulations and need to provide adequate performance specifications if they are to be effective.

The British Standards Institution (BSI) was the first national standards body in the world. In Britain, it is the main producer of standards and co-ordinates all European and International Standards work in this country. Its work covers all functions outlined above and is outlined in BS 0: *A standard for standards* Part 1: *Guide to the general principles of standardization*; Part 2: *Guide to BSI committee procedures* and Part 3: *A Standard for standards. Guide for drafting and presentation of British Standards* (all 1991 with revision proposed for 1995). This document describes the work of the BSI in standardization and the committee network through which all new standards (approximately 1200 per year) pass from inception and drafting towards final approval and publication. Essential to this work are the standards on drawing practice, alphabetical arrangement and SI units. All are presented in conformity with International Organization for Standardization (ISO) grades, and with the *BSI Recommendations on form and content of British Standards* (1980/10002) now withdrawn and not replaced.

The responsibility for authorizing work on new standards projects, for decisions on the board programme and the relevant priorities lies with the eight sector boards, which include relevant sectors such as: building and civil engineering (including building materials), engineering, electrical/electro-technical and quality management systems. All committees are selected on a basis of expertise in the field and serviced by a secretariat from the institution. Drafts are circulated to the professions for comment before finalization. This process generates publications with the prefix DC, Drafts for Comment, which are available for sale on application to the BSI.

A BRE Design Division team reported to BSI in 1982 on the presentation and use of standards. The survey commented upon the complex language and dull presentation of British Standards, as well as the number of out-of-date copies found in offices. The high prices were cited as a factor decreasing usage. BSI were encouraged to look at the packaging of information, and to implement the recommendations (see *Building*, 23 April 1982). It would appear that BSI took some note of these, with the introduction of the 'PLUS' scheme to update members registered standards at a discount rate.

More recent improvements have been the introduction of the BSI electronic products, CD-ROM services PERINORM Europe, PERINORM International and *NormImage*. PERINORM has replaced the on-line computer database of all current and draft British Standards, *Standardline*.

The main sequence of publications is prefixed BS followed by number, section, date and title. The only exceptions to this practice are the Automobile (AU), Marine (MA) and Aerospace (A,B . . .) series. British Standards prepared under the auspices of CEN and CENELEC and adopted under European harmonization are listed as BS EN. Those not adopted, or those which are European pre-standards, are listed as BS ENV. Therefore, all British Standards publications are immediately recognizable by their unique alphanumeric code – as are those of other countries (see below).

It should also be noted that the CP prefix is being phased out, all new editions being incorporated into the BS series, for example BS 5250: *1989: Code of practice for the control of condensation in buildings.* Unless withdrawn, CP reprints now receive a BS number. (Withdrawn CPs are still available on application.) The *Barbour technical microfile* includes a reference to these remaining CP and new BS numbers in the index, e.g. CP 211 is no longer listed, and the new BS 5492: 1990: *Code of practice for internal plastering* is included. The *BSI Catalogue* also gives the current list of CPs, along with those recently withdrawn (for those it lists the superseding BS), some of which have been updated and amended, e.g. CP 301:1971 (withdrawn) gives BS 8301: 1985. They are also listed at the back of the *Barbour technical microfile* in the organizations section.

All standards are listed in the *BSI Catalogue*, which is updated by a 'pull-out' section entitled 'Update' contained in the monthly issues of *BSI News*, or by annual subscription to the *Supplement*, also issued monthly. Both the *BSI Catalogue* and the *BSI News* are distributed free to members. In 1994 the *Catalogue* was £38 to non-members. The numerical list gives full title, date and a brief description of each standard, which is supplemented by a subject index based mainly on titles. Amendments are noted, giving length and price group, as well as recently withdrawn standards and an indication of those endorsed by other countries. All are available from the BSI Publications Sales Office. Comments regarding the cost inhibiting purchase by industry of the standards required (*Vandenburg 1976*), have been addressed by the BSI setting up schemes such as the Private List Update Service (PLUS), whereby the standards held by members are recorded and automatically updated at the members' discounted price. The various services offered are listed in the *BSI Catalogue*. The scope and staffing of the BSI is described, as well as the quality assurance schemes, the library, information, translation and education services, etc. Availability of standards is important, and the BSI maintains a full library and information service. Official national and international standards are held there, and enquiries can be made by telephone. The *BSI Catalogue* also lists complete reference sets in UK locations. However, the BSI does not hold semi-official or industry standards.

Most architects will also be familiar with the ring bound BS Handbook 3 (1985): *Summaries of British Standards for building, including also Codes of Practice, Drafts for development and other publications* – summaries of some 1500 construction standards with varying degrees of detail, sometimes rendering it unnecessary to purchase the original document. Some 60 per cent of the summaries provide sufficient detail for drawings, specifications and BQs. The rest are more brief, because they are of restricted interest or could not be summarized – this applies to most 'Codes of practice'. The price of the four volumes, including one year's updating service, was £240 to members, non-members £480 in 1994. The Handbook was originally withdrawn by BSI in 1975, and on its reappearance its content and presentation were heavily criticized (*AJ*, 26 July 1978). However, many were content to see the return of a valuable tool, even if there were criticisms on presentation. Indexes indicate summaries added, lost and revised since the 1975 edition (the last in bound format) as well as providing the traditional subject, Ci/Sfb and numerical listings. Other relevant handbooks are now being published which depart from former policy in that their content is not entirely standards, for example, BS Handbook 22: Part 1 (1992): *Quality assurance, Part 2 (1992): Reliability & maintainability.*

The monthly *BSI News* should be used by all professionals to note the new issues and amendment notes. It is the main source of information on the proposals for new standards and drafts for comment. Fortunately for most professionals, many journals also publish selective lists of relevant new standards. *Building* lists new standards regularly, as do *AJ* and other specialist journals. Many also carry reports on significant new standards or amendments. *RIBA Product data* notes new ones, and in *Specification*, in *ASC*, and in the *Barbour technical microfile* lists of standards will be found relevant to any aspect of construction and materials, giving – unlike the *BSI Catalogue* – parts as well as whole standards. These are therefore reliable sources of specific standards information, although it must be remembered that *Specification* and *ASC* are only updated annually. BSI used to list in *Worldwide list of published standards* all new British and overseas standards added to their library. This has ceased. Only those received for sale are now listed in the monthly catalogue supplement.

Performance of products and components is important in any process. Quality characteristics and levels of performance are increasingly being specified in such a way as to allow the use and introduction of more modern techniques, for example, in BS 4873 (1986) *Specification for aluminium alloy windows*, requirements are given for materials, component parts, sizes and tolerances, glazing, security and safety, with specified performance tests to accommodate climatic conditions in various parts of the country.

Testing is also done by the BSI in its laboratories as part of the Quality Assurance Scheme described in the *Buyer's guide* to the Kitemark Scheme. The appearance of the Kitemark symbol or the BSI safety symbol on a product shows that it has been independently tested and approved by the BSI according to the relevant standard and that the quality

| Kitemark | Safety symbol | Shortened BEAB symbol |

of production has been inspected by BSI. All manufacturers are listed in the annual *Buyer's guide* with an alphabetical list of the products licensed to bear the symbols

A similar scheme is operated by the British Electrotechnical Approvals Board (BEAB) and the BEAB symbol also appears on certified and tested products. The shortened BEAB symbol also appears beside any BS summary in *Handbook 3* where it has been awarded. A full list is available from the BEAB. Similar product approval schemes are operated by Underwriters Laboratories Inc. (UL listed) in the USA and CSA in Canada.

Manufacturers able to demonstrate procedures giving a total quality management scheme in accordance with BS: 5750: Parts 1, 2 & 3 (1987) now superseded by ISO 9001, 9002 and 9003, may be accredited by BSI as part of the Quality Accreditation Service.

Quality testing is closely linked to standardization and to the work of the British Board of Agrément (BBA). There are also other testing laboratories in Britain, a number of which are listed in *The CIRIA UK construction information guide* (Spon, 1989) and include the well-established National Physical Laboratory, parts of the DoE, and BRE facilities. There is no national body as in France or Germany, however, the Agrément Board was set up by the government in 1966, and it now operates in close conjunction with the BRE and BSI. Originating from the French system of appraisals, its work is expected to be 'accurate and unbiased in giving an independent assessment of materials, products, components and processes' for their performance in use. In France, all public works contracts must use Agrément-certified products. The system is based on experience and the development of simulative testing with close inspection of manufacturers' quality control. In the UK, the status of the Board is confirmed by its inclusion in the Building Regulations 1985 and 1991. Its certificates contain references to the regulations and satisfy their requirements in certain conditions.

The Agrément Board tests individual products for manufacturers on payment of a fee. Products which fail and which are found to be deficient in some way on first appraisal are usually modified and re-submitted before further marketing. The successful products are awarded a certificate valid for two years, subject to re-testing. These certificates give details of the product, its marketing, its installation and use, the opinion on its assessment, its acceptability under the Building Regulations and a technical description of its handling and performance. It is important to read these certificates to ensure full compliance with the standard being specified. These certificates are listed in the BBA *Supplement to the Approved Documents supporting the Building Regulations 1985 and 1991*, issued quarterly by HMSO, and in the BBA's *Approved products guide*. The BBA *Index of current BBA publications and directory of installers* is revised regularly and updated monthly until each re-publication. A full set of *Leaflets*, freely available, describes the work of the BBA, the procedures and enabling legislation, including the *Construction products regulations 1991*.

The technical background to the certification procedure is set out in MOATS (Methods of Assessment and Technical Specifications) and information sheets, although where the European Union of Agrément (UEAtc) already has approved methods of test and assessment these are used. UEAtc also confirms or re-issues certificates in other countries. This pre-dated the development of the harmonization schemes outlined below and resulted in European Technical Approvals (ETAs). The scheme is described in the Board's leaflet, *The British Board of Agrément and Europe*. A list of assessed products and new certificates is found in *Specification, RIBA Product data, AJ, Building, The architect, What's new in building* and other specialist journals, and in the Agrément Board's own *Newsletter* and publications index volume.

European standards

European standards are derived from several sources: the European Committee for Standardization (CEN), the European Committee for Electrotechnical Standardization (CENELEC), the Electronic Components Committee (CECC), the International Organization for Standardization (ISO) and acceptable national standards (BSI, DIN, etc.). An agreed standard is prefixed EN, and member states are required to publish or endorse it as a national standard within six months. All these EN standards are listed in the *BSI Catalogue* with their respective BS number or notes of equivalents; many relate to building, e.g. EN 63, see BS 2782: Part 10: Method 1005: 1977 (1989) *Determination of flexural properties: three point method* ISO 178, glass reinforced plastics.

In an article published in the R&D series *in Building* (14 March, 1978), George Atkinson surveyed the situation of the British Board of Agrément in the light of European practices at that time. In consideration of the fact that Europe also contributed and conforms at times to the wider net of international standardization, the same journal lamented that there was still very little acceptance 'of other. . .national standards' in the EEC (19 September 1980, p.34) and showed the results of some comparative work with American standards. Since then the EC and EFTA countries belonging to the European Committee for Standardization (CEN) have increased the drive for common standards.

The building and civil engineering sector originally had its roots in the first technical committees of CEN, TC33 *Doors, windows, shutters and building hardware* and TC38 *Durability of wood and derived materials*, both created in 1962. The sector has expanded sporadically from that beginning through the 1970s and early 1980s. It was in response to the emergence of the *Construction Products Directive (CPD)*, December 1988 (originally for implementation by member states by 27 June 1991) [UK: Statutory Instrument No. 1620: *Construction Products Regulations 1991* – implemented 27 December 1991] that the CEN activity increased markedly, showing a 300 per cent growth in the number of harmonized standards available to the industry. This growth still does not fully reflect the more recent increase in committees concerned with further harmonization.

The *CPD* applies to any 'construction product' produced for incorporation in a permanent manner in construction works. The Directive requires that: 'Member States shall take all necessary measures to ensure that the products. . ., which are intended for use in [building and civil engineering] works, may be placed on the market only if they are fit for this intended use, that is to say they have such characteristics that the works in which they are incorporated or installed can, if properly designed and built, satisfy the essential requirements referred to in Article 3. . .'. The 'essential requirements' are set out in Annex 1 to the Directive, as objectives that construction works have to satisfy:

- ID1 mechanical resistance and stability
- ID2 safety in case of fire
- ID3 hygiene, health and the environment
- ID4 safety in use
- ID5 protection against noise
- ID6 energy economy and heat retention.

Under Article 4 (2) it states:

'Member States shall presume that the products are fit for their intended use if they enable works in which they are employed . . .to satisfy the essential requirements. . ., and whose products bear the CE mark. The CE mark shall indicate [among other things]:
(a) that they comply with the national standards transposing the harmonized standards [adopted by CEN, CENELEC or both], references to which have been published in the *Official journal of the European Communities. . .*'

'It is the responsibility of CEN to provide the necessary harmonized standards that fall within its scope of operations . . .' (CEN document *The technical programme* available from BSI). Where there is no harmonized European standard agreed, manufacturers whose products conform to ETAs may affix the CE mark to them and place them on the market in the EC showing that the product allows construction work to meet the six requirements above.

Several journals are monitoring the development of the 'European Products', CE marking and European Technical Approvals (ETAs) which are similar to Agrément Certificates ('Briefing, European products' by Sylvester Bone, (*AJ*, 4th May 1994, p.33). Current progress is also shown in *Construction monitor* and in *UEAtc information* and the European Organisation for Technical Approvals' news sheets and leaflets. *UEAtc information* lists the member institutes with their addresses.

The EC and EFTA have jointly issued five mandates in relation to the *CPD* for specific standards in the following subject areas:

- timber   94 standards
- concrete   41 standards
- masonry   62 standards
- roofing   35 standards
- cement and building limes   4 standards

In addition, the ECs 'Eurocode' programme has been transferred by the Commission to CEN along with a further 54 items of mandated standards work relating to individual parts of each Eurocode. The Eurocode programme began in 1977 with the intention of establishing a set of harmonized technical rules for the design of building and civil engineering works. These Eurocodes were intended as an alternative to the different rules in force in the various member states, and ultimately to supersede them. The adoption of these standards by CEN will not automatically lead to the withdrawal of the various national rules in force. These national standards will co-exist with the Eurocodes for an agreed period determined by the Commission, the member state and CEN.

However, these Eurocode standards were only considered as provisional until the 'interpretive documents' were issued by the Commission. This was some two and a half years later than planned following a complete revision to remove material that was not strictly required to give 'concrete' form to the 'essential requirements'. As a consequence, the first of the Eurocode standards was made available in 1992 with more Eurocodes delayed to follow in 1993/94/95. Initially these were issued as European Pre-standards, ENVs, prior to their acceptance and conversion to full EN standards, e.g: DD ENV 1992: *Eurocode 2: Design of concrete structures;* also DD ENV 1992-1-1: 1992: *General rules for building (together with United Kingdom National Application Document)*, the National Application Document (NAD) enabling the ENV to be used for the design of buildings to be constructed in the UK. From CEN: ENV 1992-1-1 1991, ENV 206. It should be noted that the NADs require the UK loading codes to be used (BS 6399 and CP3 Chapter V, Part 2) until the relevant parts of ENV 1991 (*Basis of design and actions*) are available to give guidance on actions, including loads. Texts are appearing on the use of these, such as Narayanan's *Concrete structures: Eurocode EC2 and BS 8110 compared* (Longman, 1994).

A list of European standards applicable to building and civil engineering is available in section 4 of the *CEN catalogue of European standards*, issued annually. The catalogue also includes Harmonization Documents (HDs), such as HD 1000: 1980 *Service and working scaffolds* and HD 1004: 1992 *Mobile access and working towers*; and CRs such as CR 245:1986 *Thermal insulation – classification of building materials*. All items should be obtained from the national standards office, not CEN.

The recent trend in switching from 'paper' information to 'electronic' sources of information is supported by BSI in its service PERINORM Europe. This CD-ROM contains bibliographic details of British, French, German, Austrian, Swiss, Dutch, European and International Standards such as ISO, IEC, CEN and CENELEC. The CD also contains the French and German technical regulations. BSI has another service, *NormImage*, which CD-ROM provides full text of British, German and French standards, and comes complete with a search database for ease of retrieval. Both of the BSI CD-ROMs are available on subscription.

International Standards

BSI authorizes the use of all the above and ISO standards by publication as British Standards. All are listed in the *BSI catalogue*. The International Organization for Standardization (ISO) was set up in 1947 after a number of years spent working towards international co-operation. The ISO publication, *Compatible technology worldwide,* gives an overview of its membership, objectives and activities. Progress continues to be slow in securing agreement on the range of international standards, however, the growth of multi-national companies in the 1960s, coupled with the growth in overseas work, has increased movement – mainly in engineering. At the end of 1992, little appeared to have been achieved in building and construction by comparison, with only 336 standards published. However, a total of 221 work items, 79 committee drafts and 114 Draft International Standards were reported. These Draft Standards are prepared for discussion among the member institutions, by committee, until agreement is reached. The trend toward internationalization has increased in an effort to unify the many diverse practices, although acceptance is not universal. For example, ISO 6240: 1980 *Recommendations for performance standards in building – contents and presentation* (BS 6019, 4 pages), was criticized as 'confused and limited' (Martin, 1980). Conformity may also be limited.

The BSI CD-ROM PERINORM International contains all the

PERINORM Europe information, plus details of American standards such as ASTM, IEEE, UL and ANSI. *NormImage* also provides full text of International Standards. BSI, as the UK ISO member, also acts as the 'specialized enquiry point' for the ISONET, the ISO information network, a co-operatively developed system providing rapid access to information about standards, technical regulations and testing and certification activities currently used in different parts of the world.

Other countries

A few countries are sufficiently important for their standards work to be briefly described here. A detailed list of countries, giving reference codes and publications will be found in Mildren. A list of ISO members shown in the Appendix to this chapter summarizes this (current in 1994).

United States standards

The American National Standards Institute (ANSI) is not a publisher like BSI but a clearing-house for standards publications, maintaining a library of standards from around 50 other countries and publishing a number of listings of American standards: the annual *Catalog*, with monthly supplements, *Listing of new and revised American National Standards*, a quarterly *Magazine of standards* and a bi-weekly magazine, *Standards action*.

The American Society for Testing and Materials (ASTM) also produces standards which are listed in the *Annual book of ASTM standards* complete with index (70 volumes, 1994). The sheer volume of standards sometimes makes identification difficult. The annual *List of publications* covers all other types of ASTM publication. The bi-monthly *Journal of testing and evaluation* reports research, while the monthly ASTM *Standardization news* lists additional standards.

There are many other societies concerned with the production of standards in the United States, of which the largest is the National Institute of Standards Technology. There are also government standards, mainly defence, which are listed in either the *Guide to specifications and standards of the Federal Government* (1963) with its monthly cumulative supplements, or the Defense Department's *Index of specifications and standards*, also with a cumulative supplement, bi-monthly. In Britain and the USA the most comprehensive listing of these is the microfilm and CD-ROM service from Technical Indexes, known as Information Handling Services (IHS) in the United States, covering all standards from ANSI, ASTM (both of which have construction subgroups), ASCE, ASHRAE, IEEE and NFPA among 28 institutions in the USA. This service also includes other countries but is now rivalled by the newer and smaller ILI service mentioned below.

German standards

The Deutsches Institut für Normung identifies its standards with the letters DIN. These are kept and listed comprehensively at BSI. *Catalogue of DIN Standards* lists them annually with *DIN Mitteilungen* updating it bi-monthly. English translations are listed monthly in the 'Update' section of *BSI News*. VDEs are also German standards and issued by Verband Deutscher Elektrotechniker and usually of lesser interest to those in construction.

French standards

NF standards are issued by the Association Française de Normalisation (AFNOR) and listed in *Catalogues of French Standards*, the monthly *Revue Normalisation*. French standards have been available on-line since 1976, through a service called NORIANE.

Other standards

The majority of the numerous countries producing standards publications are listed briefly in the appendix to this chapter. The range of groupings offered by Technical Indexes (Ti), in addition to the BSI and British Defence Standards, gives an idea of those considered to be of major importance: Japanese, Canadian and German standards (the latter only in English translation) as well as ISO and NATO standards with Euronorms and EEC technical directives and those given above under the United States.

Discussion on the publication of standards will be found in more detail in the publications given below. International Standards, European standards and some other countries' standards may be obtained from the BSI sales office, but not all are held in stock and there may be delays. Delays are also inevitable when purchasing standards direct from the offices of standards institutions abroad. Selective foreign standards are held at some major public libraries and may be consulted there, however, recent financial cutbacks in the UK libraries may mean that the latest amendments or issues are not available. The British Library may also be able to obtain copies once the reference numbers of those required have been identified. The BSI Library has lists to consult for identification purposes. *BSI News* lists new DINs in translation each month, as well as new ISO and IEC standards and drafts, new API, ANSI, IEEE and Underwriters Laboratories standards, among others.

The BSI offers not only advice and help with foreign standards, including translations, but also assistance with correspondence on American and other standards to professionals through the Technical Help to Exporters (THE) service. The service produces several technical publications, including: *Satisfying technical requirements of world markets*, an introduction for exporters to the technical requirements of different markets around the world; and *Mobile construction equipment*, a full set of 39 volumes covering 14 European countries, each covering the regulations, standards and approval requirements relating to equipment used on site.

The standards service offered by IHS now covers the bulk of all standards requirements world-wide. Originally providing an indexing service backed up by full text on microfilm or microfiche, its services are now available on CD-ROM and on-line via DIALOG, although the latter is limited to bibliographic records. The *IHS International standards and specifications* database (file 92) is divided into standards and Milspec sub-files. The former covers 400 US and 40 non-US national and international standards organizations. The *Worldwide Standards Service on CD-ROM* (IHS and Ti) covers bibliographic records for 400 standards organizations which can be located by number and keyword in the title or subject index. The language is shown and the location of the full text on IHS microfilm or the full text service. Of particular interest in this context are the standards from the IEC, ISO, Standards Association of Australia (SAA), Canadian General Standards Board, Canadian Standards Association (CSA), Chinese National Standards (CNS), Japanese Industrial Standards Committee (JISC), Saudi Arabia (SASO), and those from France and Germany.

Most of these services are also available from Technical Indexes (Bracknell, UK). They can also be provided as part of the *RIBA/TI Construction information service on CD-ROM*, with the back up of their *Occupational Health and Safety information service on CD-ROM*, covering many aspects of the construction industry. Technical Indexes' Rapidoc service can supply hard copy of most documents if required.

A similar service is provided by Infonorme London Information, more usually known as ILI, on their *Standards Infodisk*; this covers many American standards, European and International, British, German, Swedish, French, Norwegian, Japanese, Australian and Canadian standards. It gives bibliographic information, a summary and equivalency, translations and address of publisher as well as standards referred to in the text. The service can supply the standards requested, usually within 24 hours, and other technical documents are also available.

Some other guides are mentioned in Chapter 15. This pattern of availability via national standards organizations and national libraries is replicated in many other countries, with variations in detail. Usually the industry or trade desk in embassies and chambers of commerce will be able to help with enquiries.

References

Martin, B. *Standards and building.* RIBA Publications.
Mildren, K. (1976) (ed.) *Use of engineering literature.* Butterworth, pp.105-109. (Updated by C.J. Anthony, 1985). Now in its third edition as: Mildren, K. (ed.) (1996) *Information Sources in Engineering.* London: Bowker-Saur.
Vandenburg, M. (1976) BSI: 75th anniversary. *AJ.* **164** (45), 877–878.
Woodward, C.D. (1972) *The story of standards.* BSI.

Appendix: ISO member bodies

Albania	DSCK	Drejtoria e Stardardizimit dhe Cilesise Keshilli i Ministrave
Algeria	INAPI	Institut algérien de normalisation et de propriété industrielle
Argentina	IRAM	Istituto Argentino de Racionalizatión de Materiales
Australia	SAA	Standards Australia
Austria	ON	Österreiches Normungsinstitut
Bangladesh	BSTI	Bangladesh Standards and Testing Institution
Belgium	IBN	Institut belge de normalisation
Brazil	ABNT	Associaçã Brasileria de Normas Téchnicas
Bulgaria	BDS	Committee for Standardization and Metrology at the Council of Ministers
Canada	SCC	Standards Council of Canada
Chile	INN	Istituto Nacional de Normalización
China	CSBTS	China State Bureau of Technical Supervision
Colombia	INCONTEC	Instituto Colombiano de Normas Téchnicas
Croatia	DZNM	State Office for Standardization and Metrology
Cuba	NC	Comité Estatal de Normalización
Cyprus	CYS	Cyprus Organisation for Standards and Control of Quality
Czech Republic	COSMT	Czech Office for Standards, Metrology and Testing
Denmark	DS	Dansk Standard
Egypt (UAR)	EOS	Egyptian Organisation for Standardization and Quality Control
Ethiopia	ESA	Ethiopian Authority for Standardization
Finland	SFS	Finnish Standards Association
France	AFNOR	Association française de normalisation
Germany	DIN	Deutsches Institut für Normung
Greece	ELOT	Hellenic Organization for Standardization
Hungary	MSZH	Magyar Szabványügyi Hivatal
Iceland	STRÍ	Icelandic Council for Standardization
India	BIS	Bureau of Indian Standards
Indonesia	DSN	Dewan Standardisasi National (Standardization Council of Indonesia)
Islamic Republic of Iran	ISIRI	Institute of Standards and Industrial Research of Iran
Ireland	NSAI	National Standards Authority of Ireland
Israel	SII	Standards Institution of Israel
Italy	UNI	Ente Nazionale Italiano di Unificazione
Jamaica	JBS	Jamaica Bureau of Standards
Japan	JISC	Japanese Industrial Standards Committee

Kenya	KEBS	Kenya Bureau of Standards
Korea (North)	CSK	Committee for Standardization of the Democratic People's Republic of Korea
Korea (South)	KBS	Bureau of Standards
Libyan Arab Jamahiriya	LNCSM	Libyan National Centre for Standardization and Metrology
Malaysia	SIRIM	Standards and Industrial Research Institute of Malaysia
Mexico	DGN	Dirección General de Normas
Mongolia	MISM	Mongolian National Institute for Standardization and Metrology
Morocco	SNIMA	Service de normalisation industrielle marocaine
Netherlands	NNI	Nederlands Normalisatie-Instituut
New Zealand	SNZ	Standards New Zealand
Norway	NSF	Norges Standardizeringsforbund
Pakistan	PSI	Pakistan Standards Institution
Philippines	BPS	Bureau of Product Standards
Poland	PKNMiJ	Polish Committee for Standardization, Measures and Quality Control
Portugal	IPQ	Instituto Português da Qualidade
Romania	IRS	Institutul Român de Standardizare
Russian Federation	GOST R	Committee of the Russian Federation for Standardization, Metrology and Certification
Saudi Arabia	SASO	Saudi Arabian Standards Organisation
Singapore	SISIR	Singapore Institute of Standards and Industrial Research
Slovakia	UNMS	Slovak Office for Standards, Metrology and Testing
Slovenia	SIMS	Standards and Metrology Institute
South Africa	SABS	South African Bureau of Standards
Spain	AENOR	Asociación Española de Normalización y Certificación
Sri Lanka	SLSI	Sri Lanka Standards Institution
Sweden	SIS	Standardizeringskommissionen i Sverige
Switzerland	SNV	Swiss Association for Standardization
Syria	SASMO	Syrian Arab Organisation for Standardization and Metrology
Tanzania	TBS	Tanzania Bureau of Standards
Thailand	TISI	Thai Industrial Standards Institute
Trinidad & Tobago	TTBS	Trinidad and Tobago Bureau of Standards
Tunisia	INNORPI	Institut national de la normalisation et de la propriéte industrielle
Turkey	TSE	Türk Standardlari Enstitüsü
Ukraine	DSTU	Ukrainian Committee for Standardization, Metrology and Certification
UK	BSI	British Standards Institution
Uruguay	UNIT	Instituto Uraguayo de Normas Téchnicas
USA	ANSI	American National Standards Institute
Venezuela	COVENIN	Comisión Venezolana de Normas Industriales
Viet Nam	TCVN	General Department for Standardization, Metrology and Quality
Yugoslavia	SZS	Savezni zavod za standardizaciju
Zimbabwe	SAZ	Standards Association of Zimbabwe

CHAPTER SEVEN

Official publications

MALCOLM GREEN AND VALERIE J. NURCOMBE

The term 'official publications' encompasses the range of publications
emanating from the various levels or tiers of government, its legisla-
tures, departments, ministries and agencies. These vary from country to
country, but as all encompass the law-making bodies, their importance
to every sector of industry cannot be denied. The structure of the government and of its publishing activities varies throughout the world
according to two main factors: the way in which the laws and subsidiary
legal directives are published; and the way in which the official 'publisher', whether agency or department, is constituted and operates. While
concentrating heavily on the UK, this chapter also refers to the styles of
official publishing in other countries.

UK

As one of the older constitutional governments with a continuous history, the pattern of official publishing in Great Britain has influenced
many other countries, particularly those with British roots, including
the present and former countries of the Commonwealth and the United
States.

The Stationery Office (HMSO) was founded in 1786 as a central supply organization but its role of government publisher and bookseller
was not fully assumed until late in the nineteenth century. Its development may be traced in Hugh Barty-King's *Her Majesty's Stationery
Office: the story of the first 200 years 1786–1986* which was written for
the anniversary. The Stationery Office sold but did not publish parliamentary papers until 1882 when it was given full responsibility. Since

then the major role of HMSO has been to act on behalf of parliament and government departments as the central publishing agency for information which those authorities determine should be put on sale to the public.

Although the Stationery Office does not usually commission manuscripts it has, since the 1920s, scrutinized the texts passed to it for printing by government departments for their own use to see if any could be published for sale and thus earn some profit to offset costs. It has always been very aware of the close watch kept on its activities by commercial publishers since its privileged position could permit an unfair advantage to be taken with highly profitable titles. Protests were made when the first volume of *The principles of modern building* was published in 1939 for the Building Research Station, and again the charge was laid by commercial publishers that HMSO was encroaching on their territory when *Flats and houses* was published nearly 20 years later.

The Stationery Office prints and publishes, by direction, whatever is required for the conduct of parliamentary business; it accepts, by agreement, material from government departments for which publication is considered necessary in fulfilment of their obligations and responsibilities to the public. This includes making available information on government policy (departmental circulars, for example), and information required by industry, commerce and the professions that is only available from official sources.

The 1980s saw changes in the pattern of official publishing and in the availability of documents from government departments. HMSO has been less inclined to publish for departments those items judged to be unprofitable, and such items may have been published and sold by the departments themselves. Some departments have developed their own publishing operations and used other commercial publishers on occasion. Also, many publications that were formerly issued free are now priced. Change has continued throughout the 1990s as the moves towards open government, decentralization and deregulation have progressed. It is becoming difficult to define what is meant by 'government publishing' as more and more aspects of government are carried out at arm's length by executive agencies, and further privatization is envisaged.

The Department of the Environment (DoE) is responsible for a large proportion of official publications relating to architecture and construction, but not exclusively so, as other departments retain responsibility for design of buildings within their sphere: e.g. Department for Education for school buildings, Department of Health for hospitals, the Home Office for prisons, the Ministry of Agriculture, Fisheries and Food (MAFF) for agricultural buildings, etc. The Department of the Environment was formed in 1970 by combining the Ministries of Public Building and Works (MoPBW), Housing and Local Government (MoHLG) and Transport (DoT) but now its agencies and divisions are splitting away. The

Property Services Agency (PSA – formerly MoPBW) was moved in 1993 into the private sector, with any remaining central responsibility for construction going to the relevant Department of State, e.g. defence work to the Ministry of Defence. Other departments have had their own design units for many years, e.g. Department for Education's architecture branch, which issues its own *Building bulletins*. Some of these design units have become more prominent as executive agencies, e.g. National Health Estates. Scottish Health Estates has been sold to W.S. Atkins in the private sector. The government-funded research establishments, particularly Building Research Establishment (BRE), now encompassing the Fire Research Station and Forest Research, are all moving nearer the private sector with a slimming down of staff, and of government-sponsored research.

All of the above has had implications on the style and nature of official publishing programmes, with the financial viability of publishing now a factor in its own right. The result of this decentralization is the increased importance of bibliographic control for the practitioner.

Catalogues and lists of official publications

The original attitude of the Stationery Office was that its duty was done if its methods enabled everyone to buy government publications. There was little attempt to attract customers until the 1920s when catalogues began to be produced, although they were woefully inadequate initially. These have improved and are now reliable tools for retrieval with the daily, monthly and annual lists available on subscription, or for consultation at HMSO Bookshops and by telephone, or on-line (see below). Most new construction publications are listed in the professional and trade journals. Details of selected government publications are put up daily on the Prestel viewdata system.

The sectional lists by department, except for No. 61 *Construction*, which used to list all items in print at the time of printing, are now giving way to more lively sales catalogues with titles such as *The environment catalogue* and *The building, housing and planning catalogue*. Some such as *Transport* (No. 22) and *Energy, trade and industry* (No. 3), were revised during October 1994 by HMSO.

More extensive research is possible using the more comprehensive catalogue systems, particularly important as publications may still be valid and still contain current legal requirements although they are out of print and therefore not appearing in sales catalogues. HMSO's bibliographic database has been mounted on the British Library's BLAISE-LINE. It is updated monthly, and covers publications since 1976 including agency publications (those sold but not published by HMSO – particularly from international organizations such as the UN, and the EC). Records include details of names and departments, series and editions as well as titles and the ability to carry out subject searches. Documents that are out of print are indicated and can be obtained from the British Library Document Supply Centre.

There are several sources for details of the publications issued and sold by the departments themselves. An *Annual list* has been produced since 1971 by the combined Departments of Environment and Transport library service, including all available departmental publications issued during the year; this also includes PSA and BRE, and both HMSO and non-HMSO publications. In 1994 the nature of this list changed when Transport split from Environment. The list had earlier ceased to cover the PSA and BRE. At the time of writing, the Environment list is continuing on a monthly basis with annual cumulations, but there is no news as yet of an equivalent Transport list. Most Transport publications are now being distributed by HMSO whether or not they were originally published by HMSO or the Department. The former *PSA in print* annual list still has its uses as libraries have the publications. The *Information directory* is issued each year by BRE, although no longer free, and covers not only leaflets and publications but films, slides and other media presentation formats. Other departmental library and information units provide similar listings although the very detailed one from the Health and Safety Executive may not have a certain future since the publications, free or priced, ceased to be available via the Information Unit or HMSO and were devolved to the new HSE Books as a result of competitive tendering. Such catalogues list the current publications which will be the main concern of the practitioner.

In 1980 Chadwyck-Healey began to list titles published by official departments and other bodies outside the auspices of HMSO in the *Catalogue of British official publications not published by HMSO*. This was well indexed and issued bi-monthly with annual cumulations. Addresses of contributing publishers are listed. In addition, most of the titles covered are available from Chadwyck-Healey in microform. This has presented a very economical and comprehensive source of supply, particularly from outside Britain. A few of the titles listed are not released for publication by the department concerned.

The *Catalogue of United Kingdom official publications* (*UKOP*) is published on CD-ROM and is the first complete catalogue of all official publications, including both HMSO and departmental publications. It is a joint venture between HMSO and Chadwyck-Healey and covers both the HMSO and Chadwyck-Healey databases mentioned above. Quarterly updates and the search facilities make this a very useful title. In addition, lists can be produced of all titles from a department or a division.

Statutes and other legislative information

There are more than 150 Acts of Parliament (excluding Local Acts) con-

cerning such matters as the design and construction of particular building types, arbitration, environment, fire, health, safety, conservation,
insurance, planning, pollution, etc. In addition, there are the official
regulations, orders, circulars, memoranda and guidance relating to the
Acts, as well as the unofficial legal commentaries, explanatory and critical books and journal articles. Many of these will be mentioned in the
appropriate chapter. The language and logic of legislation is not always
easy to follow and recourse to an authoritative explanation and commentary on particular legal matters is to be recommended. The title of
an Act is no guide to its application or relevance.

The processes by which ideas for governing the country become law
can be long and complicated and give rise to a variety of published
documents. Generally speaking, there is a preliminary stage which may
involve publications such as reports of Royal Commissions, Select Committees of Parliament, Departmental, Advisory and Consultative Committees or other groups. These may be published as Command Papers,
House of Commons Papers or House of Lords Papers, or, in some cases,
as non-parliamentary publications. In turn, these may give rise to a paper outlining alternative policies for public discussion (Green Paper)
and/or a paper detailing government policy (White Paper). A piece of
legislation may then be drafted as a Bill, and its numbered provisions
are Clauses which can be amended as the Bill moves through Parliament. After the third reading in Parliament (in the case of an ordinary
government Bill introduced into the Commons first) the Bill is sent to
the House of Lords, where it can be subject to further amendment, and
then returned to the Commons. Finally it receives the Royal Assent. A
Bill which is thus passed then becomes an Act and its clauses become
sections.

There are many guides to the legislative process. Information may be
obtained from the House of Commons Public Information Office, and
current legislation and papers are listed in its *Weekly information bulletin* (weekly when in session). The debates in Parliament are published in
the daily, weekly and sessional *Parliamentary debates (Hansard)*, available from HMSO. *Hansard on CD-ROM* (House of Commons from session 1988/89) and *House of Lords Hansard on CD-ROM* (from 1992/93
session) are available from Chadwyck-Healey. Chadwyck-Healey has
also published microfiche editions of all House of Commons Parliamentary Papers from 1801, with appropriate guides. The most recent
discussion of parliamentary publishing is in the proceedings of a recent
SCOOP seminar *Laws in the making*, while David Butcher's *Official
publications in Britain* is the only current guide to both statutory and
non-statutory official publishing, HMSO and departmental.

Many Acts also give rise to what is known as subordinate or secondary legislation. Under the powers given to them by an Act, Ministers of
the Crown make detailed rules and regulations, not suitable for parlia-

mentary debate, and these are published, in most cases, as Statutory Instruments (SIs), formerly Rules and Orders. Government departments may also send out Circulars to local authorities drawing attention to legislative changes and giving related guidance, interpretation and information. The tendency towards interdependence between Statutory Instruments (and the Acts themselves) and official and quasi-official publications should be noted. The final authority on the interpretation of the law, what is 'reasonable' and 'practicable', for example, are the courts.

HMSO publishes Acts as single titles and in annual bound volumes entitled *Public General Acts and Measures*. The annual *Index to the Statutes* lists all the General Acts in force under subject headings, with detailed subdivisions and cross-references. The companion volume, *Chronological table of the Statutes,* lists all General Acts made since 1235 and shows which have been repealed and the effects of later legislation on those still in force. *Statutes in force* consists of extant General Acts arranged in subject groups in loose-leaf binders. The use of supplements to update these Acts has now been suspended owing to the development of the new *Statute law database* due for availabilty in 1996. This should keep the above works up-to-date for future generations, and although some print volumes will continue, others are, at the time of writing, considerably behind in the publication schedule and unlikely to continue in their present form. There are of course excellent commercial guides to the Statutes, such as the multi-volume *Halsbury's Statutes of England*.

The Statutory Instruments are published individually and in annual volumes. To trace what regulations are in force on a given subject there is the *Index to Government Orders*. The *Table of Government Orders* is a cumulated chronological list of general Statutory Rules and Orders and Statutory Instruments showing which have been revised or amended. Both are published in revised editions every few years by HMSO. Although the SIs are included in the *Daily list of government publications* they are not in the monthly and annual catalogues but have their own separate lists. All of these publications have, however, fallen much behind schedule in the early 1990s and some have been suspended prior to the implementation of the new *Statute law database*. The commercial subject guide is *Halsbury's Statutory Instruments*.

The Building Regulations are the most important statutory provision applied to building design and construction. The *Building Regulations 1985* (England and Wales) (SI 1065) were issued, under the powers mentioned above, as SIs, by virtue of the *Building Act 1984* following a White Paper (Cmnd 8179) in 1981. This made proposals to change the basis of the Building Regulations. In future, detailed standards for buildings would be replaced by 'functional requirements' which would be backed up by technical guidance showing how to meet these functional requirements. Thus, these regulations are now supported by a series of

'Approved Documents' containing the technical guidance. The Approved Document for each part of the regulations shows ways of achieving compliance, but there is also the option of choosing an alternative solution as long as there is evidence that the alternative meets the requirements. The Approved Documents include lists of British Standards which are referred to in the guidance. British Standards and Agrément Certificates are accepted as relevant guidance when they relate to particular aspects of the requirements. The 1985 Building Regulations were a re-cast of the 1976 regulations and a change in presentation and style. There have been subsequent technical reviews and the regulations and guidance in the Approved Documents have been amended. The current legislation for England and Wales is *Building and buildings: the Building Regulations 1991* (SI 2768), as amended in 1992 (SI 1180), 1994 (SI 1850) and in 1995 (SI 1356). These have now been made more accessible by the *Index to the building regulations 1995*, compiled by H. Roberts and S. Bone (HMSO, 1995).

With the abolition of the GLC the intention was to bring the London boroughs under the national legislation, and this was done through the *Building (Inner London) Regulations 1985* (SI 1936) and *1987* (SI 798). Consequently the former *London building byelaws* with their own additional requirements and guidance documents have been superseded.

There are separate regulations for Scotland and Northern Ireland. In Scotland, the *Building Standards (Scotland) Regulations 1990* (SI 2179), as amended 1993 (SI 1457) and 1994 (SI 1266), are in force. The Scottish regulations are supported by a volume of *Technical standards 1990* (amended), which are similar to the Approved Documents, but being loose-leaf are more easily amended. Similarly, in Northern Ireland, *The Building Regulations (Northern Ireland) 1990* (SI 59) apply, as amended, with a series of technical booklets giving guidance on meeting the requirements.

There are numerous guides and commentaries on the Building Regulations. Those in print and up-to-date will be listed in the catalogue of the Building Bookshop and the RIBA *Reference annual* each year. Probably the most widely referred to is *Guide to the Building Regulations 1991 for England and Wales* by Lawrence Davis, with *Knights Building regulations*, in loose-leaf format with text and commentary being the most comprehensive and current. The latest edition of Powell-Smith's *The building regulations explained and illustrated* (9th edn, Blackwell Scientific Publications, 1995) will always provide clear guidance expanding the basic information given in the regulations. Only the most recent citations should be relied upon due to the numerous changes since 1985.

Legislation, regulations and circulars are publicized in the technical press and elsewhere, often with commentaries. Some good general guides to the law as it affects the construction industry include *AJ Legal hand-*

book and *Butterworths construction law manual*. Other aspects of the
law relating to the industry are covered in the series of loose-leaf, regularly updated volumes available on subscription from Sweet & Maxwell.
Titles include *Encyclopaedia of housing law and practice, Encyclopaedia of environmental health law and practice* and *Encyclopaedia
of land development*. Others are mentioned in various chapters and titles are being added every year ranging from topics such as rent and
transport to VAT.

Departmental publications

It is impossible to give here a full account of all the relevant publications produced by government departments, but attention can be drawn
to some important series and a few titles. The various parts of the Department of the Environment are responsible for a large proportion of
official publishing relevant to construction. The Building Research
Establishment (BRE), which comprises the Building Research Station,
the Fire Research Station and the Princes Risborough Laboratory (forest
research), has a publishing programme of interest to all practical designers and builders as well as to researchers, and includes some items geared
to the DIY market. BRE now operates as an executive agency, and is
later to be placed completely in the private sector. Research on the
presentation of technical information for the various construction professionals has resulted in some interesting re-design of series such as
BRE Digests and other technical publications. A full list is available
from their own Bookshop. At the beginning of 1995, BRE announced
its partnership with EMAP Business Communications to establish a
new publishing company – Construction Research Communications Ltd.
BRE will retain responsibility for the technical content of publications,
but the new company should give a wider market for them under the
management of EMAP Architecture, publisher of *AJ*, among other titles.
    The Property Services Agency, formerly a part of the Department of
the Environment, responsible for the provision of buildings and other
construction work for the civil and defence departments of the government, has been sold off but many of its technical publications are still
useful. In the past many of the publications have appeared in series
published by HMSO and remain important even if out of print. The BRE
Digests are now published monthly by BRE and have as their main aim
'to make recommendations in the language of the construction industry
to assist in the application of the findings of research'. A series of *Information papers* was introduced in 1979 with the aim of presenting BRE
research results in a more readily usable and compact form (not exceeding four A4 pages). Another series currently produced is the *Good building guides*, similarly brief documents giving practical information. All
these series are available separately or on subscription from BRE.

Major BRE contributions to construction literature are published as individual BRE *Reports* which, in effect, continue the fine earlier series of *Post-war building studies* and *National building studies*. Most of these reports are of direct value to designers, based on the work of the research stations. Most of the reports are published by the BRE with the odd one still published by HMSO. Information which would formerly have been published in the *Fire Research Notes* and the Forest Products Research Laboratory (FPRL) *Technical notes* and *Timber papers* series now appears in the present BRE series. BRE's Overseas Division issued publications aimed to help the construction activities of developing countries. The *Overseas Building Notes* are prepared principally for housing, building and planning authorities in countries receiving technical assistance from the British government.

Some of the former Property Services Agency publications are still available, but will only be revised if they are economically viable and still have a function in the changed situation. The PSA *Specifications* are being sold under contract by the Department of the Environment, but it is unlikely that any will be maintained by the private sector or commercial publishers. The Department of the Environment no longer produces as many non-parliamentary publications in series although some are still going, for example, the second edition of *Residential roads and footpaths* (HMSO, 1992) still appeared as *Design bulletin 32*, although few others have been issued recently.

The various series produced by the Department of Health over the past 30 years, including *Health building notes*, *Health equipment notes* and *Health technical memoranda* among many others, are being revised and re-issued by National Health Estates as the agency responsible for health establishments. Currently, these documents are published by HMSO. The Architects and Building Branch of the Department for Education still issues publications in the *Building bulletin* series (HMSO) and *Design notes* (departmental). Health and safety has become a major topic for the construction industry with increasing legislation. Regulatory control is maintained through the Health and Safety Executive (HSE), which produces a large number of documents explaining the legislation and giving technical guidance and advice. Publications are listed in a catalogue from the HSE but, following competitive tendering, published and sold mail order by HSE Books, a sales agency appointed by the HSE. However, titles may be sold retail in HMSO and other bookshops. Legislative documents are still published by HMSO as they emanate from Parliament itself and not the HSE.

Statistics

The word 'statistics', as used here, means the collections, both published and unpublished, of facts about the national economy, industry, commerce and social life presented in the form of numerical tables which are periodically kept up-to-date. The importance of statistics is not just that they show what exists in quantitative terms at any one time, but more especially because they can show, by comparison, changes, variations and trends and thus allow for forecasting and planning. It should not be forgotten, however, that statistics are subject to margins of error and that they are open to misuse. Reichmann's *Use and abuse of statistics* (Pelican, 1964) is an extremely readable introduction to the subject.

The major provider of statistics is the Government Statistical Service (GSS), but statistics are also collected by local authorities, public corporations, and professional, trade and other organizations. Statistical information is made available through official and non-official serial publications, and as features, usually regular, in general economic and professional journals. The GSS comprises the statistical divisions of all the main government departments, the Business Statistics Office (BSO), the Office of Population Censuses and Surveys (OPCS) and the Central Statistical Office (CSO). The *Guide to official statistics* is revised periodically by the CSO and published by HMSO. It is the most comprehensive guide to the contents of each statistical publication made accessible through the general classification by which entries are grouped, and augmented by the subject and name indexes. Freely available also from the CSO is the annual *Government statistics: brief guide to sources* which is a detailed handy guide.

The Government Statistical Service publishes through HMSO the *Annual abstract of statistics* and the *Monthly digest of statistics* which cover a wide range of subjects over the whole country, sometimes with regional breakdowns. The annual *Social trends* gives information and articles illustrated by tables and charts on population, income, wealth, education, health, housing, environment and other topics, some of which appear every year, others of which appear only every few years. Similar sources are covered in *Economic trends* (monthly) and *Population trends* (quarterly). *Regional trends* (HMSO) is another annual publication which provides figures for population, social characteristics, housing, education, environment, etc., by standard region.

Of the daunting number of current statistical publications, some should be specifically mentioned. The quarterly *Housing and construction statistics* (HMSO), in two parts, contains tables on construction activity and employment, local authority housing, house building performance, housing, finance and building materials. An annual volume of the same title (HMSO, 1980 onwards) brings together figures for the previous decade. The OPCS publishes a yearly *General household survey* (HMSO) covering such topics as housing, health, education and leisure activities. The Department of the Environment issues press notices on statistics which may up date published serials; information from these is often reported in the periodical press. The DoE also issues *Monthly statistics of building materials and components* (DoE, Construction Market Intelligence Division) and *Construction monitor* (monthly), which follows on from EURONEWS *Construction* and also appears in *Building*. Local figures for towns and regions may be found in the various CIPFA publications. *Digest of data for the construction industry*, first produced by the Department of the Environment in January 1994, is to be a twice-yearly digest (HMSO) covering international comparisons of productivity and costs and a range of other local and national figures including local authority expenditure, vacant urban land and planning data as well as materials and components sales.

Library resources

Most of the publications mentioned in this chapter should be available in large practice libraries; the exceptions would be the large reference works on legislation and the statistical series, collections and guides, most of which should be in the libraries of the professional institutions. The national reference resource for government publications in general is the Official Publications collection of the British Library, London. Government departmental libraries contain most of the official publications relevant to their field of interest. Details of government libraries are to be found in the British Library's *Guide to libraries and information units in government departments and other organisations* (31st edn, British Library, 1994). This is revised regularly. Most departmental libraries allow, by appointment, reference use of their collections by members of the public and they participate in national co-operative schemes. Some departments have special collections, such as the Department of the Environment's collection of local and national plans.

Some of the main libraries of reference to the construction industry have suffered from privatization and financial cut backs. The PSA library is no longer in the public domain and is being restructured by its new owners. Other libraries such as the British Cement Association (formerly the Cement and Concrete Association) have been reduced in size.

Good general collections of statistical publications (and others) are often kept by academic libraries and the large public reference libraries. Many of the former now have special access terms for professionals, varying from access on payment of an annual fee to freedom of access for professionals related to courses in the institution. Although the Department of Trade and Industry's Statistics and Market Intelligence library and the Business Statistics Office library in Newport are no longer as large or as widely available as they were, enquiries can usually be answered. Some statistics not readily available may even be found in the pages of *Hansard* in answer to questions in the House.

With the wide range of publications of relevance to the construction industry, in particular the more essential 'official' documents, especially legislation, it has long been a problem for individuals or firms to keep abreast of new publications and to maintain a collection. Technological developments over the past decade have provided several options, utilizing microfilm and now electronic document imaging and computer searching. Services aim to provide subscribers with the essential documents, which include legislation, standards, publications of the DoE, BRE, etc. This can be an extremely effective method of keeping a collection up-to-date. Details of these services appear elsewhere, for example, RIBA/Ti Technical information on microfilm and CD-ROM, Barbour technical microfile, BCQ Construction industry information system on CD-ROM and on-line. All provide full text.

POLIS, the Parliamentary On-Line Information Service, developed by the House of Commons Library over the last 15 years, has been publicly available under various systems in that time. It is currently accessible through Context, both on-line and on CD-ROM. The indexing in the POLIS database makes it possible to trace legislation, reports, articles and papers on proposed legislation and the stages of legislation through the Houses, linking all together. For a detailed review of this and the *Statute law database* see *Laws in the making*. European Directives and their implementation can also be traced. POLIS was developed as a working tool in the busy library of the House and is used daily by the librarians who developed it to replace ageing and voluminous strip indexes.

Western Europe

It is not possible in such a short chapter to encompass a guide to the official publications of the whole of Western Europe. The guide by Eve Johansson published during the 1980s remains the best introduction country by country. The pattern of publishing varies from the model shown above, in which the official publisher began as a department of the government, even though its present status may be changing, to the model represented by France and Germany and later by the European community (EC), which differs in that all major papers, documents and legislation are published daily in the *Official journal* which, in the case of the EC, is large enough to be split into several daily parts. Other publications may emanate from the departments of the government, via the 'official publisher' or through their own publishing outlets. As with all governments, many may be duplicated and barely 'published' in the accepted sense.

Publications of the EC itself are well covered in Ian Thomson's definitive guide. CIRIA has published a *Guide to European Community and international sources of construction information* (2nd edn, 1991), and there have been a number of guides to construction in different EU countries from CIRIA, RIBA and the ACE which include related government publications. The organizations should be contacted for the latest editions. Ian Thomson also edits *European access* (bi-monthly), which is published by Chadwyck-Healey in association with the UK Office of the European Commission, which 'gives a comprehensive overview . . . of everything that is being published by the EC, and about the EC, and the wider Europe in newspapers, journals and books'. SCAD+CD is the EU official bibliographic database, published by Ellis Publications and distributed by Chadwyck-Healey. CELEX is a similar database covering EU legislation and executive documents.

USA

There are many books written on this topic. However, not all are available readily in other countries. The most useful are Downey and Morehead, supplemented by the many articles in the *Government publications review,* which changed its name in 1994 to *Government information review*, a subtle change of emphasis.

The volume of US official publications, both federal and state, is enormous. The Government Printing Office handles the *Congressional Record,* among others – and the Superintendent of Documents (SuDOC) was established in 1895 to handle efficiently the sale, cataloguing and distribution of publications. The classification codes, SuDOCs, developed to assist this are used by many official publications librarians to organize their collections, referring to the published and on-line listings available from SuDOC. The *Monthly catalog*, although sometimes behind with its cataloguing, includes most titles, but like HMSO there are certain exclusions, either due to block exclusion of patents and maps, or the lack of reporting of departmental publications. The on-line version is widely available. SuDOC does issue some subject bibliographies also.

The pattern of publishing reflects the English pattern of debates of each house: there is a *Congressional record*, less detailed sessional journals and four series of reports or papers – Senate reports, House reports, Senate documents, House documents. Legislation is also published as *Statutes*. Departmental publications and those of the Office of the President are numerous and listed in *Weekly compilation of presidential documents* and *Federal register*, among others. The *United States Government manual* (annual) reflects changes in the government machinery as does the British *Civil Service yearbook*. Any more detailed consideration of these publications is impossible in the short space available here.

The Federal Depository Library System means that nearly 1200 American libraries get free copies of those official publications which they opt to receive – they are no longer obliged to take them all. The use of microforms and CD-ROMs is now assisting both with a more international distribution and with the space problems of these collections. Exchange between national libraries means that many of the above are available in at least one location in many countries. Chadwyck-Healey has published on microfiche and CD-ROM several guides and collections of US government documents.

Since the development of on-line databases and publishing and the Internet there are many more sources both listing US official publications and providing their full text. The volume of research publications has always been sufficient to support the large database run by the National Technical Information Service (NTIS), which covers many topics related to the construction industry, including the reports of the Transport and Road Research Laboratory. NTIS was established as the Publications Board, a federal agency within the Technology Administration of the US Department of Commerce, to assess which scientific and technical information documents could be publicly released after the war. This then became a clearing house in 1970 with the new, current, name. All federal agencies submit public scientific and technical reports to NTIS, which also collects from relevant institutions in other countries thus providing, potentially, the largest source of reports relating to all aspects of construction. This range is particularly wide in that all materials are covered as well as techniques and design aspects. The Departments of Agriculture, Energy and Transportation are included, as well as the Environmental Protection Agency. Database records date from 1964. MicroInfo in the UK also provide an alerting service on specific topic ranges.

Other countries

Guides tend to be few and far between and specific to a small range of countries. However, the *Guide to publications of foreign countries* (1990) is a bibliographic listing under each country of the world aiming to give information about the most important official publications of every country in an abstract to the entry. Published in the early 1980s, the Pergamon series of guides covers Canada, Australia, Japan, Ireland and France.

References

UK

Barty-King, Hugh (1986) *Her Majesty's Stationery Office: the story of the first 200 years 1786-1986.* HMSO.
Butcher, David (1991) *Official publications in Britain.* 2nd edn. Library Association Publishing.

Butterworths construction law manual.(1993) Butterworths.
Davis, Lawrence (1992) *Guide to the Building Regulations 1991 for England and Wales.* Butterworths.
Fitzmaurice, Robert (1939) *The principles of modern building.* HMSO.
HMSO. *The environment catalogue* and *The building, housing and planning catalogue.* Annual from 1993. Free from HMSO, St Crispins, Duke St, Norwich NR3 1PD.
Knights Building Regulations. (updated) London: Chas. Knight.
Ministry of Housing and Local Government (1958) *Flats and houses.* HMSO.
Moorhead, J. (1983) *Introduction to United States public documents.* 3rd edn. Littleton, Col., Libraries Unlimited.
Nurcombe, Valerie J. (1994) (ed.) *Laws in the making: Proceedings of a one day seminar held at the House of Commons 6 September 1993 organized jointly by the House of Commons Public Information Office and SCOOP.* Library Association, Information Services Group.
Speaight, A. and Stone, G. (eds.) (1990) *AJ Legal handbook.* 5th edn. Butterworths.

Other

American Library Association, Government Documents Round Table (1990) *Guide to publications of foreign countries.* Washington, DC: CIS.
Johansson, Eve (1984 & 1988) *Official publications of Western Europe.* 2 vols. Mansell Publishing.
Thomson, Ian (1989) *The documentation of the European Communities: a guide.* Mansell Publishing.

Pergamon Series

Bishop, O. (1981) *Canadian official publications.*
Downey, J.A. (1978) *United States Federal Official Publications.*
Coxon, H. (1980) *Australian official publications.*
Fry, B.M. and Hernon, P. (1981) *Government publications: key papers.*
Kuroki, T. (1981) *An introduction to Japanese government publications.*
Maltby, A. and McKenna, B. (1980) *Irish official publications.*
Pemberton, J.E. (1982) *The bibliographic control of official publications.*
Westfall, G. (1980) *French official publications.*

CHAPTER EIGHT

Maps, drawings and visual information

NANCY PISTORIUS

Introduction

This is an eclectic chapter addressing diverse visual materials relevant
to the study and practice in the field of architecture and also in planning
and landscape architecture. Information sources and techniques considered include: maps, drawings and draughtsmanship; photographs and
photography; slides; and videocassettes.

Since Ptolemy (90-168 A.D.) established the mathematical principles
for map making, the process of refining accuracy and details has been a
continuing quest (1). Modern map makers have at their disposal computers, aerial photography, digital imaging and a wealth of innovative
electronic software and equipment. While this equipment has improved
the documentation of existing land and ocean areas, the historic maps
continue to serve as key sources of information for architects and planners. Various government agencies as well as private companies have
been instrumental in conducting surveys that provide the foundations
for developing maps.

Drawing and drafting are fundamental activities for architects both
during study and training and in professional practice. While computer-
aided design and the use of electronic materials may eventually replace
the application of hand-executed techniques, the manual practice is still
relevant, especially during the training of new architects and in the initial stages of the design process. The materials presented in the section
on drawing and drafting will consist of texts which have set the contemporary standard, as well as supplemental materials useful to laboratory
applications whether during study or in actual practice. Slides, photographs and videotapes are both a product and a resource for the study

and documentation of architecture. Architects often record projects and structures through photographs and/or slides and on videotape. Producing worthy documents and organizing them in a retrievable manner are issues frequently encountered in professional practice. To aid in this process, literature and sources on architectural photography and organizing slides and media materials are identified in the last section of this chapter.

While global coverage would be most desirable, this chapter will primarily focus on the resources of North America and Europe. No attempt is made to provide definitive coverage on the topics presented, but to expose the reader to some of the more important materials and, in certain cases, the most current materials available at the time of publication.

Maps

This section will focus on the types of maps most useful to architects, historians and planners in studying or examining a site, renovating historic structures, or planning a project. Resources for accessing maps and map collections will be presented as well as relevant literature in the field and other factors which make maps useful to architects and planners. A 'Directory' as an appendix to this chapter lists addresses for the principal mapping agencies mentioned in this section.

Sources of information

Before presenting the major map producers and discussing collections of materials, guides to maps, mapping information and map sources will be presented. Brenda White's *Sourcebook of planning information* presents a lengthy chapter, 'Sources of information on maps', which examines all types of land-use maps for the British Isles and indicates where these may be obtained. On an international level, Hodgkiss and Tatham's *Keyguide to information sources in cartography* is an excellent bibliography of sources, books, journals and addresses of mapping agencies, providing world-wide coverage. More current is Perkins and Parry's *Information sources in cartography*, a lengthy bibliography covering various types of maps, articles and books on maps and the mapping process, and addresses of map publishers. The coverage is international in scope and includes more recently published materials than the Hodgkiss publication.

Less detailed is Harold Nichols' chapter in G. Higgens' *Printed reference material* which also covers atlases and international maps. Somewhat comparable publications would be *Walford's guide to reference material* and Eugene Sheehy's *Guide to reference books* and its 1992 supplement edited by Robert Balay. Maps and atlases are discussed in several sections throughout these two publications. As there is considerable overlap between them, having access to both these publications is not critical to acquiring the same information. For those interested not only in information about maps but also in the care, organization and storage of these materials, Nichol's *Map librarianship* and Mary L. Larsgaard's publication *Map librarianship* are considered classic works in the field. The former provides a British viewpoint and the latter an American viewpoint; however, there are many similarities between them. The information provided in the publications cited by Nichols and Larsgaard are further amplified by the chapter on 'Map libraries' by David Ferro in *British librarianship and information work, 1976-1980* which summarizes developments in Britain and North America. Sections in the *Encyclopedia of library and information science* entitled 'Geographical libraries and map collections' and 'Maps, charts, and atlases' review both the history of maps, the mapping process and the development of collections of maps within libraries.

Last issued in 1976, the publication *International maps and atlases in print* continues to serve as a useful identifying tool. Although outdated, it provides insights into the international production of maps by identifying map-producers and maps that have been published on an international level. *GeoKatalog, World map directory* and *World mapping today* have filled the gap left by the demise of the earlier publication. These focus on maps which are current and in print. Along with reviews in journals, the above publications provide an accurate image of the current field of maps, atlases and international mapping projects.

Numerous texts exist on the process of mapping as well as reading maps. Of continuing use are Dury's *Map interpretation* and A.G. Hodgkiss' *Understanding maps,* which briefly covers the history and development of maps and map-making, regional, nautical and Ordnance Survey maps, town plans, and thematic, commercial and private map-making, with a bibliography. Of similar value, but with a North American slant, are J.S. Keates' *Understanding maps,* Miller's *Interpretation of topographic maps* and the more current P.C. and J.O. Muehrcke's *Map use: reading, analysis, and interpretation.* The Keates publication is a brief and direct guide to using maps, while the Muehrcke publication is a longer and very detailed text with emphasis on understanding maps as well as the mapping process. Both are useful and serve needed purposes, especially for assisting the novice map user in understanding the visual information that a map presents. The Miller publication is an excellent guide not only for reading but also for understanding the variables and nuances of topographic maps, and includes an excellent glossary of related terms. Besides the lengthy, and occasionally overwhelming, information available in these and other publications, journals and periodicals also provide valuable and informative articles on maps and mapping tradition.

Journals

Sources of information on new maps and continuing developments in the mapping process are important, since the introduction of automation affects our encounters with visual and graphic information sources. Serial sections in Larsgaard's *Map librarianship* and *Information sources in cartography* list journals, annuals and irregular periodicals related to maps, geography and cartography.

Still of value is Shepherd and Chilton's early (1980) discussion of 'Computer-based enquiries in the map library' (*Cartographic journal*, **17** (2), pp.128-139). *Cartographic journal* is issued twice a year and not only discusses the use of maps but other points of interest to the architect. For example, the discussion of the perception of information on maps suggests interesting ideas on the interpretation of symbols and of information on all plans and drawings. New atlases, maps and similar ventures are reviewed and collections are sometimes discussed. Reviews of maps and of books on maps also appear regularly in both *Geography* and *Geographical journal.*

Several North American journals provide similar coverage. *Geographical review* from the American Geographical Society of New York is international in scope and includes articles on a broad range of topics related to geography including some which would be of interest to architects and planners, such as 'Plaza towns of south Texas' (1992; **82** (1), pp.56–73), which provides local site plans of plaza areas along with discussions of plaza history and development in the region. The *Journal of geography*, produced by the National Council for Geographic Education, contains especially good reviews of new literature and software in the field of geographical education. *Cartographica,* published by the University of Toronto, provides a scholarly approach to the field including reviews of books, map collections, atlases and maps.

Indexing of maps and articles on their use occur in *Geoabstracts, Chemical abstracts, Education index* and *Sage urban studies abstracts.* Of special interest are electronic software tools such as *Earth sciences* (1992) and the *GPO Monthly catalog,* both CD-ROM products that provide current access to maps and mapping services of the major world powers. The former is somewhat broader in its coverage, while the latter focuses exclusively on publications of the United States government. Specifically focusing on architecture are indexes such as the *Architectural periodicals index* (API), also available on CD-ROM, the *Avery index to architectural periodicals,* also available on CD-ROM, and *Architectural index,* which cite maps that have been illustrated and discussed in articles of the journals typically indexed by these sources. In the late 1960s *Architectural design* irregularly published continental town plans showing features of architectural interest. Today, maps of cities at various stages of development or specific street and site plans may be found in the *Journal of the American Planning Association, Storia urbana, RIBA journal, Inland architect* and other current serial publications. Under the auspices of the Council of Planning Librarians' *CPL Bibliography* series, A.G. White published 'Urban cartography: a selected bibliography' (No. 1157, November 1976) which defines the mapping of cities, the inherent factors and areas of concern for cities during the 1970s. The Council of Planning Librarians' new series, *Bibliography,* also sponsored a publication by M.A. Wilson, 'Geographic information systems: a partially annotated bibliography' (No. 268, 1990), which presents the mapping process using computerized digital imagery combined with database information.

National mapping services

This section will examine the government agencies responsible for mapping Great Britain, Canada, Mexico and the United States. The agencies presented are by no means the only government producers of maps but, in each case, are the major map producers and typically responsible for the base maps that are utilized by other governmental agencies as well as private map makers. For information on other countries Bohme's *Inventory of world topographic mapping* is a valuable resource. It identifies the major mapping agencies for countries throughout the world and provides the mapping scales used by each country, map series which exist, and map extracts to demonstrate the mapping products. Useful bibliographies and profiles of the status of mapping coverage of each country are also available.

Britain

The Ordnance Survey and the British Geological Survey (BGS) are primarily responsible for the mapping of Britain. Many countries have no equivalent to the Ordnance Survey and are, therefore, not mapped as systematically or uniformly. The Ordnance Survey, the official surveyor of Britain, not only produces maps but also a wide range of leaflets that describe the agents and sale points of the maps, services available from the Ordnance Survey, and general information on digital mapping, using co-ordinates and levelling, to name just a few of the topics. The full range of maps produced is listed in the annual *Map catalogue*.

The *Map catalogue* contains reduced index sheets for the 1:250 000, 1:50 000 and 1:25 000 scales. The larger scale index sheets must be purchased to provide an accurate location index for sheets on the more detailed scales of 1:10 000, 1:2500 and 1:1250. For the latter two scales the Survey Information in Microform (SIM) service makes information available from the Master Survey drawing after every 50 changes using a microfilm copy of the drawing which is only redrawn to normal standards after 300 units of change. The microfilmed maps, or print-out copies of them, may be purchased at the sales agent's offices which have special copying machines. The Superplan service now permits print-outs to be produced for certain, mainly urban, areas at any scale required from 1:200 to 1:5000 using site-centred plots rather than traditional grid squares. Also available is OS data in digitized format for use with CAD and GIS systems. Arrangements can be made to view the Master Survey drawings at any level of change at local Ordnance Survey offices. Equally useful in verifying the scope of the Survey is *The Ordnance Survey national atlas of Great Britain,* which consists of 1:250 000 maps with complete and updated information on Britain as of 1986.

When using Ordnance Survey maps it is useful to remember that the longer the reference number assigned to a sheet, the larger the scale of the map (i.e. the more detailed the map becomes, although there may not be a published sheet exactly covering that reference number at the larger numbers where Superplan and SIM printouts apply), thus:

TQ 49 SE	refers to 1:10 000
TQ 49	refers to 1:25 000
TQ	refers to 1:50 000

The numbers used to identify sheets in the 'Pathfinder' and 'Landranger' series bear no relationship to these grid reference numbers. An explanation for using the Ordnance Survey maps may be found in the Survey's leaflets and in the publication *Ordnance Survey maps: a descriptive manual* by Harley. It also contains information on the compilation of the maps, the history of the Survey, a description of each series produced by the Survey and a discussion on the accuracy of the maps. Another informative publication is Seymour's *A history of the Ordnance Survey,* which provides an in-depth account on the development of the Survey.

National geological records are the responsibility of the BGS, formerly the Institute of Geological Sciences (IGS), which incorporates the Geological Survey of Great Britain. This is where requests for information on wells, shafts and boreholes may be made, these being based on the appropriate Ordnance Survey map. Maps published include the solid maps showing main strata and maps showing superficial deposits at 1:63 360, replaced by 1:50 000. Six-inch maps at the survey level are available and 1:25 000 maps are published for some parts of the country, new towns and development areas. These and the descriptive *Memoirs* relating to some maps are listed in the BGS catalogue, which is part of the *Ordnance Survey catalogue* but published by HMSO and also available from the BGS. Other records are kept at the BGS and information can be verified through unpublished sources. Soil maps and memoirs at 1:63 360 and 1:25 000 have been published for many areas and are also listed above.

Canada

Several agencies are responsible for the surveying of Canada. The Geological Survey of Canada/Commission Geologique du Canada (GSC) and the Surveys and Mapping Branch of the Department of Energy, Mines and Resources/Direction des Leves et de la Cartographie, Ministere de l'Energie, des Mines et des Ressources and the Canadian Hydrographic Service are the primary mapping agencies.

The GSC publishes an index at the 1:250 000 scale which aids the user in identifying geographic areas of interest. The major topographic series are issued in the scales of :

> 1:500 000
> 1:250 000
> 1:25 000

For specific parts of provinces and cities an additional scale of 1:50 000 exists. There is also a 1:1 000 000 series for the nation. The quadrangle divisions of the Canadian mapping system are thorough and detailed. Bohme's *Inventory of world topographic mapping* provides an excellent example of the organization of the Canadian mapping system.

Maps are available from various locations; however, the Canada Map Office is a reliable source for obtaining topographic, geologic and hydrographic maps. The publication *Maps of Canada: a guide to official Canadian maps, charts, atlases and gazetteers* by Nicholson is a useful tool for identifying Canadian maps and mapping agencies.

Mexico

The primary mapping agency for Mexico is the Secretaria de Programacion y Presupuesto (SPP); however, the Servicio Cartografico of the Departamento Geografico Militar (part of the Secretaria de la Defensa Nacional) also issues maps of select areas of Mexico. Under the SPP, the Direccion General de Geografia del Territorio Nacional (DGGTN) issues a number of topographic and thematic maps within a range of scales, as follows:

> 1:1 000 000
> 1:250 000
> 1:50 000
> 1:10 000.

The country is divided into 2352 areas which average 1000 square kilometres each. The maps are based on these divisions and are both topographical and geological in nature. Some areas are mapped in more detail than others and the mapping survey of the country continues at this time. Atlases continue to serve as the major mapping information sources of Mexico.

USA

The major mapping agency of the USA is the United States Geological Survey (USGS), which is an agency of the US Department of the Interior. Unlike the mapping agencies of many other countries, the USGS is responsible for mapping the topography, geology, hydrology and natural resources of the United States. There are, however, other agencies both within the federal government and in the private sector that do produce maps. The US government agencies include the Defense Mapping Agency (DMA), which is comprised of former military mapping units such as the Army Mapping Service and War Department to name but two; the National Oceanic and Atmospheric Administration (NOAA), which oversees the Coast and Geodetic Survey (USC&GS); the Forest Survey; the Tennessee Valley Authority; and the Mississippi River Commission. Additionally, the US Army Corps of Engineers and the Census Bureau (under the Department of Commerce) continue mapping projects related to their areas. Government agencies tend to use the base maps provided by the USGS and adapt them for thematic purposes to meet the needs of the specific agency.

Access to the USGS maps is through the *Index to topographic and other map coverage* which is issued for each of the states. Its companion publication, the *Catalog of topographic and other published maps*, lists named areas and whether maps are available for them. Ordering information is also provided from regional distribution centres. The *Index* is essentially an 'index map' which grids each state and identifies each part of the grid with a specific name. Where map collections are uncatalogued, this is the most direct access to the maps themselves. In collections of this nature maps are maintained by scale, then state, then alphabetically by name assigned to the grid. The *Index* and *Catalog* also include brief directories of the map dealers within a particular state and the regional depository libraries of the state. The scales typically maintained are:

> 1:250 000
> 1:100 000
> 1:62 500
> 1:25 000 (Alaska only)
> 1:24 000.

Base maps are typically at scales of 1:500 000 and exist for many, if not all, of the states in the US. Currently the production of a new series of 1:500 000 scale maps is in the process of development beginning with states in the Eastern US. For each state a set of three maps is being published. Each set includes a base map containing: identified land features, cities and towns and usually county boundaries; a shaded relief map; and a topographic map of the state. Maps on the 1:1 000 000 scale for each state are common, but not yet available for every state.

Helpful to understanding the history and purpose of the USGS is Mary Rabbitt's *A brief history of the US Geologic Survey*. Her more extensive three volume publication, *Minerals, lands, and geology for the common defense and general welfare: a history of public lands, federal science and mapping policy, and development of mineral resources in the United States* expands considerably on the history of mapping in the United States. Both of these titles serve as descriptions and a history identifying the original charter of the Survey which was to classify public lands, examine geological and mineral resources, and to research the land surfaces of the nation. Thompson's *Maps for America; cartographic products of the US Geological Survey and others* provides very thorough coverage of the variety of maps produced by the USGS and commercial companies. Examples and descriptions of the maps produced are scattered throughout the publication.

USGS maps are also identifiable through means other than the indexes and guide cited earlier. The print version of the *US Monthly catalog* and electronic tools such as *Earth sciences* (OCLC) and the *GPO Monthly catalog*, both available on CD-ROM, are a feasible means for identifying and eventually retrieving the USGS maps. *Earth sciences* is a three-part system consisting of 'Earth Science Data Directory' (ESDD), 'GEOINDEX' and 'USGS Library'. Maps may be found in all of these indexes with the 'GEOINDEX' focusing exclusively on geological maps of the United States and its territories. Maps indexed in this resource may have been published by commercial map companies, universities, professional associations, the USGS, or other governmental agencies. The *GPO Monthly catalog* primarily represents maps either published by or under the auspices of the Government Printing Office (GPO).

Thematic maps

Thematic maps focus on providing information of a specific type or on a single topic. Thematic maps are prepared to demonstrate demographics, identified land, coastal or urban features, environmental elements, weather trends or cultural traits, to name a few of the potential applications. To further understand thematic maps, consulting Dent's *Cartography: thematic map design* would prove useful, as would *Thematic maps: their design and production* by David Cuff. Both publications review the cartography process, types of thematic maps and the thematic map-making process.

British examples of thematic maps include the Department of the Environment (DoE) atlas and small local projects in communities, city governments and academic institutions. The earlier 'Sources of information' section in this chapter contains titles, both books and journals, which list a number of sources containing thematic maps. The size and quality of thematic maps varies. The work of the Experimental Cartography Unit is reported by the Cartography subcommittee of the Royal Society's British National Committee on Geography in many publications such as *Experimental cartography: report on the Oxford symposium October 1963*. Among other publications the unit has produced are *Land use mapping by local authorities in Britain* which shows how local authority databases can be used to create land-use maps.

Land-use maps of the second Land Use Survey of Britain, begun in 1960, are available at the 1:25 000 scale to show agricultural uses at a regional and local level. The maps are sold through Edward Stanford (London) instead of the Ordnance Survey, and are described in the *Land use survey handbook*. Land-use mapping has also been performed at local levels with some results having been published. For example, the University of Sheffield Department of Geography has issued the *Census atlas of South Yorkshire*; the *Atlas of London and the London region* was compiled by Jones and Sinclair; and Patmore's *Merseyside in maps* is also available. Similar publications exist which demonstrate the application of maps in the thematic mapping process.

The major publication from the DoE is the *Atlas of the environment*, which replaces the *Desk atlas of planning maps*, issued in loose-leaf form since 1953 with revised sheets appearing at irregular intervals. Supplements to the *Atlas* are issued as needed and are listed in the DoE *Annual list of publications*. A similar *Atlas* is published by the Welsh Office, and the Scottish Office is also developing a similar publication.

Historical maps range from the Ordnance Survey *Maps of Roman Britain* and *Maps of Monastic Britain* to those preserved in local archive offices and collections which are described in the following text. Lists have been made locally such as the Skelton *County atlas of the British Isles 1579-1850*. Other lists can be traced through the titles listed in the 'Sources of information' section above.

Town plans can be found in a variety of sources: in the Automobile Association's *AA Big atlas of town plans*, the *Directory of town plans in Britain*, the Royal Automobile Club (RAC) Publications book of *UK town plans* and *Street maps of British towns*; and in major road atlases from the British motoring organizations, the Reader's Digest and similar producers. On a larger scale the publications catalogue of Geographia gives a wide range of detailed town plans, metropolitan marketing maps and others, such as the survey of manufacturing industry based on the

1961 Census of Production. Plans for the professional are produced by C.E. Goad of Hatfield, showing the location of amenities, services and traffic flows within urban areas. They were described in a brief article in *Property journal* in 1979 (**1**, pp. 10–11). Several other firms provide such services, for example, Market Location of Leamington, but their plans are aimed mainly at the market research companies and can be expensive if not available in the local library. Published annually, *The municipal yearbook* (London) is an excellent and current resource for identifying local city and county record offices, their addresses and the administrative individuals in charge of those offices. These offices and individuals serve as resources for locating recent local urban and rural maps.

In the USA, thematic maps are typically based on the USGS maps which include maps produced by the National Park Service (NPS), another branch of the US Department of the Interior. Maps issued by the NPS consist of various overall maps of the national parks, mapping guides for those touring through the parks and maps identifying recreational areas, and such as roads and highways to sites in the parks, identification of historical and military sites and monuments, battlefields, national forests and Indian reservations. The NPS also provides guides for each specific park, as well as special maps designed for hikers and climbers consisting of topographical as well as trail and campground information. Within the USGS, special thematic maps are also issued focusing on natural resources. Andriot's *Guide to USGS geologic and hydrologic maps* is the most direct resource for locating USGS maps on minerals, ground water, geology and substrata formations. As with the topographic maps, access is based on site then the geologic or hydrologic element or formation which leads to a map number. These include maps at the 1:1 000 000 scale which identify the underlying coal fields or coal-bearing rock and sediment infrastructures. Other maps are issued on land contours at the 1:125 000 and 1:500 000 scale, including oil, gas and power maps. Additionally, shaded relief maps at the 1:500 000, 1:750 000 and 1:280 000 scales are also issued. Other governmental agencies joining the USGS in the production of thematic maps are the Census Bureau within the Department of Commerce and the independent Central Intelligence Agency, which conducts extensive aerial photographic projects of countries in the Western Hemisphere and especially those bordering the United States.

Non-governmental mapping agencies or companies have historically produced maps which ultimately are thematic in nature. The Sanborn Map Company examined and issued maps for at least 12 000 towns and cities in the United States and some cities in Canada and Mexico between 1867 and 1950. The Sanborn maps, large-scale city maps, were originally developed for fire insurance purposes and continue to be a primary source of information on streets, buildings and public utilities for architects and planners. *Description and utilization of the Sanborn map* is a brief handbook which describes the symbols used on the maps and assists with further interpreting them. Although the Sanborn Map Company stopped updating its maps in the mid-1960s, the maps are still a relevant resource for documenting urban growth and important records for historic preservationists. Using the Sanborn maps in conjunction with city directories, building plans and photographs from the Historic American Buildings Survey and the Historic American Engineering Survey will establish a realistic image of a city, a specific block or an individual building at a specific point in time. There are over 700 000 Sanborn maps, some bound into atlases and many that are unbound. The Geography and Map Division of the Library of Congress is considered to have the largest collection of Sanborn maps. A checklist of the collection is entitled *Fire insurance maps in the Library of Congress*. Many other libraries also have collections of Sanborn maps. Hoehn's *Union list of Sanborn fire insurance maps held by institutions in the United States and Canada* serves as a useful guide to these collections. Although technically they are no longer published, the Sanborn maps are now available in microfilm format from Chadwyck-Healey. The National Map Collection in Ottawa, Canada, also houses a large collection of maps including Sanborn maps. *Fire insurance plans in the National Map Collection* serves as an excellent guide to the maps in this collection, which include those of Charles E. Goad, the Phoenix Assurance Company, the Sanborn Company of New York and the Western Canada Fire Underwriters' Association, all of which participated in the mapping of Canada.

Historic city maps, prior to the Sanborn maps, also serve as an important resource for architects, historic preservationists and urban planners. While they lack the accuracy and detailed information of the Sanborn maps, historic maps provide important information by documenting buildings, streets, and open spaces at earlier points in history. Many of the thematic maps of the historic variety provide broad, somewhat distorted, semi-aerial views of cities. Maps of this type are called panoramic maps. Many US and Canadian map collections contain representative samples of panoramic maps, and the Library of Congress has a large collection. *Panoramic maps of cities in the United States and Canada* lists the maps in the collections at the Library of Congress. Facsimile editions of many panoramic and historic city maps are available for purchase from Historic Urban Plans of Ithaca, New York. Most of the facsimile maps are of engraved or lithographed originals.

Historical city maps are also available in forms other than single sheets or multiple sets. Many are included in a variety of publications from atlases, travel books and histories to journals. Harold Otness' two publications index maps in travel guides and are global in coverage.

These publications are the *Index to nineteenth century city plans appearing in guidebooks* and the *Index to early twentieth century city plans appearing in guidebooks*. Both cite city maps from Baedeker's, Murray's, Black's and Muirhead-Blue's guides, to name a few of the guidebooks indexed. Historical maps and more current maps of all types may be located in the 13 volume *Index to maps in books and periodicals*. This index of the American Geographical Society is international in scope and includes topics which would be of interest to architects and planners. These topics include cities, parks, land use areas, population, recreation, transportation and urban centres. Focusing on America or parts of it are several publications that identify historical maps, including those of cities and towns. The *Research catalog of maps of America to 1860 in the William L. Clements Library* and the *Checklist of printed maps of the middle west to 1900* are multi-volume sets that list sheet maps, map sets and maps in atlases, reports and books. Also included are city and county atlases as well as separate sheet maps relating to urban areas that would be of interest to architects and planners. Historic maps of cities, towns and regions in Mexico and Central and South American countries are listed in *A catalogue of maps of Hispanic America*; however, its companion publication *A catalogue of Latin American flat maps, 1926-1964* excludes city plans. The earlier catalogue covers maps between 1858 and 1923 and includes maps from surveys by travellers and explorers, in published reports, journals and books, and individual sheet maps, map sets and atlases.

For architects and community or regional planners working with the contemporary city, maps from local planning departments or possibly the chamber of commerce might be of value. These departments are typically part of the city or county government structure. Addresses for city governments and officials in charge of the planning department can be found in the *Municipal/County executive directory*. Names of planning departments vary from town to town; however, this publication or The *Municipal year book* provide nearly accurate addresses and managing personnel lists of the departments. One of the best sources of free city maps are the agencies listed in the *World chamber of commerce directory*. This directory contains addresses of chambers of commerce, visitors bureaux and state boards of tourism. Coverage emphasizes cities and towns in the US and Canada but extends to provide global coverage for major cities. City maps are also available from commercial firms. Some of the more prominent firms specialize in road and city maps and include road atlases such as those from the American Automobile Association (AAA), Rand McNally and the EXXON Touring Service.

Aerial photographs

Air photographs, aerial photographs, satellite readings and radar images are a part of twentieth century technological documentation of the topography and geological composition of the earth's surfaces and the land and sea masses of individual countries.

In Britain, the Ordnance Survey prepares or commissions other agencies or commercial companies to perform aerial surveys resulting in maps. Copies are available from the SIM/SUSI, which also issues a price list. Enquiries are typically made to the Ordnance Survey to verify the existence and availability of these photographs. In addition to the Ordnance Survey, the DoE Central Register of Air Photography of England and Wales records details of all maps available and responds to enquiries for surveys of a particular area according to its holdings, referring enquiries to the collections maintaining the photographs which are not held centrally. Occasionally, this will involve contacting the commercial company which performed the initial survey and mapping processes.

The USGS within the United States maintains the primary responsibility among government agencies for aerial photography, through its National Aerial Photography Program (NAPP). The *GPO Monthly catalog* and *Earth sciences* on CD-ROM are again the primary tools for determining the existence of specific aerial photographs. The publication *How to obtain aerial photographs* published by the USGS describes the process for requesting aerial photographs. Images available for purchase may be acquired from one of the National Cartographic Information Centers (NCIC) located throughout the United States. The EROS Data Center is another source of aerial and Landsat images of cities. A visit to a regional depository library to view the photographs and maps may satisfy the information need instead of actually proceeding with the purchasing process. The CIA also performs aerial photography and mapping of countries adjacent to the US, including Mexico, Central America, the West Indies and much of South America.

For architects, planners and landscape architects, understanding aerial photographs may present a challenge. The following three publications, just several among the many available, will aid in interpreting aerial photographs. *A practical guide to aerial photography* by John Ciciarelli describes the process of aerial photography and also the final product, covering the mathematics involved as well as the tools and techniques of the process. Thomas Avery's *Interpretation of aerial photographs* provides more in-depth information on understanding the content of aerial photographs and advances into remote sensing and photogrammetry and the analysis of both in relation to aerial photography. Burnsides's *Mapping from aerial photographs* is a technical explanation of the process and application of utilizing aerial photography in the mapping process.

Collections

Collections vary with regard to type, size and accessibility. To help determine whether and where collections exist and their contents, numerous directories that identify collections and equally numerous guides and catalogues to the collections are available. To determine the best course of action, utilize the sources cited in this section to locate nearby map collections, learn their hours and services, and their ability to accommodate the user's individual needs.

Directories exist at the international level, the national level and, sometimes, regional or local levels. The single source that identifies map collections world-wide is the International Federation of Library Associations (IFLA) publication, *World directory of map collections*. This includes statistics on the size of the collection in its various forms of maps, i.e. printed maps, manuscript maps, globes, atlases, aerial photographs, etc. The directory potentially covers national libraries and archives and all recognized map collections in societies and institutions in countries throughout the world. However, those countries that already publish national directories of map collections are limited to listing only the largest or most important collections. These countries include Britain, Canada, France, Germany and the United States and the national directories for each need to be consulted to gain the best perspective of the map collections available. Directories available for these countries include Watt's *Directory of UK map collections*, the *Directory of Canadian map collections*, the *Repertoire des cartotheques de France*, Cobb's *Guide to US map resources* and *Map collections in the United States and Canada: a directory* by Carrington and Stephenson. These publications are basically organized on the same principle, i.e. by state, province or similar, then by city. The collections covered include government, state, academic, historical society and public library collections. Listings include addresses and telephone numbers, focus and size of the collections, availability to visitors and services.

Before continuing it might be worthwhile to identify the various types of map collections and libraries. These are: large, national research libraries; government agency libraries which are typically thematic in nature; geographical society libraries; large public libraries; academic and university research libraries; historical and antiquarian society libraries; and, state, district, county and city planning agency libraries and collections. See Figure 8.1 for examples.

The British Library maintains a comprehensive on-line file of its various cartographic collections. This file includes current acquisitions and the collections included in the *British Museum catalogue of printed maps, charts and plans*, which in print runs to 15 volumes with a major supplementary volume. Along with the companion publication, the *Catalogue of manuscript maps, charts and plans and of the topographical*

Figure 8.1: Examples of map collections in libraries

	Britain	Canada	France	Germany	Mexico	United States
National/government research libraries:	British Museum	Bibliotheque Nationale du Quebec	Bibliotheque Nationale			Library of Congress
Government agency libraries:	DoE: Ordnance Survey: Scottish Office: Public Record Office	Geological Survey of Canada: Land Registration & Information Service	Bureau des Recherches		Direccion General del Servicio: Meteorologico Nacional	Public Records Office Library: US Army Topographical Library: USGS Library
Geographical society libraries:	Royal Geographical Society		Societe de Geographie de Paris	Gesellschaft fur Erdkunde zu Berlin	Sociedad Mexicana de Geografia y Estadistica	American Geographical Society
Public libraries:	Birmingham Public Library					New York Public Library Boston Public Library: Free Library of Philadelphia
Academic & University research libraries:	Oxford University: University of London: Cambridge University	University of Toronto: McGill University, University of Alberta: Universite de Montreal			Universida d Nacional Autonoma de Mexico	Columbia University: Harvard University: University of Illinois: University of Minnesota: Yale University
Historical societies & archives:	National Maritime Museum	Archives de la Ville du Quebec				American Antiquarian Society: Boston Athenaeum: New York Historical Society
State, district, county and city planning agencies:	Consult the municipal directories presented in the part on 'thematic maps'.					

drawings in the British Museum, it continues to serve as a useful resource regarding the British Museum's collection. This is especially important for researchers lacking immediate access to the on-line file. The catalogue includes manuscript maps and plans, such as estate maps, which have never been printed but were commissioned and used for local private and land-management purposes. J.B. Harley produced a guide to these for local historians, *Maps for the local historian: a guide to British sources.* Local collections often have their own lists as the many brief college guides indicate, as well as those like Birmingham Public Libraries' History and Geography Department's Bibliography No. 1: *Sets of maps and national atlases in the map room.*

Both the Public Record Office and the Scottish Record Office have extensive map collections and both publish guides. These mainly cover the historical part of the collections. The Scottish Record Office published the catalogue of the map library to describe the nature of its collection. Many local libraries have collections relating to the local geographic area and city, and county record offices are also repositories for maps, current and historical. Many published works like P.G.M. Dickinson's *Maps in the county record office, Huntingdon* serve as useful guides to the contents of local collections; however, these become outdated when materials move between and into other collections.

There are several extremely large map collections in North America. The major ones have catalogues listing and describing them. The Library of Congress has one of the largest on the continent and several publications, including *The bibliography of cartography* and *A list of geographical atlases,* identify the extent of this collection which contains not only maps but also books on cartography and the mapping process, atlases and maps in reports, journals, etc. The *Catalogue of the National Map Collection* presents the extensive holdings of this major Canadian collection which also contains maps, as well as journals, books, atlases, reports, etc., in which maps are included. Similar in scope is the *Dictionary catalog of the map division* of the New York Public Library, which is periodically updated by the *Bibliographic guide to maps and atlases.* Typically, these collections are international in scope and include sheet maps, map sets, geographical, thematic, topographical, political and other types of socio-economic maps. The *Index to printed maps* of the Bancroft Library is an example of a published guide to a regional collection. The Bancroft's collection specializes in maps of California and the West, extending north into Canada and south into Mexico. Historical town and city maps are an important part of this collection. Smaller local and regional collections may have in-house guides to their holdings. Contact individual collections to learn of published or unpublished guides to their collections.

Copyright

Both Britain and the United States, as well as Canada and Mexico, have copyright laws that protect materials by acknowledging their creator or producer. Copyright is typically held by the publisher whether it is a government agency or a commercial company. An international copyright agreement, the Bern Convention, exits which maintains copyright agreements between countries thereby protecting copyright on an international level.

The *Copyright Design & Patents Act* of 1988 protects the copying abuse of materials in Britain. Under this, Ordnance Survey maps are copyrighted. An allowance of 700 square centimetres may be copied for study, research or review under the 'Fair Dealing' provision of the Act (2). Any more, or any other uses, require permission and payment of a royalty fee. Leaflets from the Ordnance Survey describe the procedures for 'business and internal use' or 'copyright and other services – publishing'. Similar restrictions will apply to many other maps. These may be amended by European Commission requirements which are under discussion.

In the United States the federal copyright law protects copyrighted works. However, most maps prepared by the federal government or its agencies are not copyrighted and, therefore, are in the public domain and available for copying without limitation. Maps prepared by commercial companies are typically copyrighted. Public Law 94-553, sections 107 and 108, covers 'fair use' and photocopying considerations and exceptions. Under the 'Fair use' provision, the law permits copying of up to10 per cent of a work for educational purposes (3). There are several contingent factors and copying is prohibited if the work will, either separately or as part of a larger work, be used for resale or in commercial publications. Penalties are severe for such cases. Some familiarity with the copyright laws may assist individuals in avoiding any infringement of them. William Strong's *The copyright book: a practical guide* is informative, as are various publications provided by the federal government. Lurie's *Can I copy – ?* specifically focuses on the copying law with regard to legal use within academic environments.

Storage and preservation

Housing and maintaining maps can present problems for architectural firms or small office environments. Therefore a brief section of information on the storage and preservation of these materials will be presented. Due to the often large and unwieldy format of individual maps and also many atlases, storage can present complications for facilities that collect maps on an irregular basis or maintain only a small collection of maps. Traditional map libraries and institutional map collections usually have developed their own resources, equipment and techniques for storing and preserving maps, so the following information is primarily directed toward the small practice or individual collecting maps.

There are several methods for storing maps. These include rolled, hanging and flat storage. Rolled storage usually involves rolling one or more maps together, then housing the rolled collection in a storage tube which is then housed in a vertically or horizontally stacked divided crate. The hanging method requires attaching a special hanging strip to one side of the map and suspending the map in a cabinet specially designed for this purpose. Flat storage is what it implies: maps are slipped into flat files or plan chests that have wide and deep drawers approximately 2½ inches high. For preservation purposes, the last is the preferred means of storage.

Preservation is a major issue regarding any work on paper, and as maps are often published on paper careful handling and storage is essential to prevent deterioration and preserve the maps for long-term use. Housing maps in flat files will contribute greatly to their longevity. They provide a flat surface in each drawer for maps and a protective hood to cover items when the drawer is rolled into its cabinet. As rolled maps age, they become dry and brittle. In this condition they are difficult to unroll and may even disintegrate when unrolling is attempted. While hanging files may be useful, attaching hangers to a map weakens the attached margin and eventually leads to deterioration. Also, since excessive handling is required to refile the map, the probability of damage is increased. In comparison, housing maps in flat files is a fairly simple process requiring minimal handling for retrieval and refiling. Housed in a flat manner, away from the corrosive effects of sunlight, should deterioration still become a problem the maps can be easily enclosed in mylar or another protective, clear material. Torn maps should be mended as soon as possible using strips of Japanese paper affixed with methyl cellulose or another acid-free adhesive. A simpler and easier repair can be made using document repair tape made by Ademco or Filmoplast®. These tapes, available from Light Impressions or University Products as well as from the manufacturers direct, meet archival standards and have the distinct advantage of being reversible (they can be removed using mineral spirits).

Flat files and plan chests are made by various manufacturers. The steel flat files by Safco, Smith System, Mayline and other companies serve several purposes. The steel units provide the most stable environment currently available for maps. Most drawers are supported on sturdy glides or roller systems which facilitate easy access. Flat files are also available in elegant wood or inexpensive fibreboard systems. While these are adequate for temporary storage solutions, using them on a long-term basis will expose maps to the natural acids and gases of the wood or fibreboard, eventually accelerating paper deterioration and creating difficult preservation problems. Typically, maps of the same or similar size are stored together; however, this may not always be possible when organizing a small collection. Flat files are also excellent for storing blueprints and large plans or drawings. But when flat files are stacked and loaded they exert a tremendous weight per square foot on the floor beneath; therefore, the load bearing capacity of the floor and the structure as a whole need to be checked prior to housing a map collection.

Numerous publications exist which include information on the conservation and preservation of maps. Nichols and Larsgaard's books contain information and bibliographies covering storage and preservation. Equally useful is the chapter 'Preservation and storage' in *Information sources in cartography*. Another informative and fairly current publication is DePew's *A library, media, and archival preservation handbook*. Scattered throughout the publication is information applicable to the preservation of maps. Anne Clapp's *Curatorial care of works of art on paper* is a handy manual for laboratory work both in the preventative and problem solving stages. Swartzburg's 'Preservation of library and archival materials' in *Libraries and archives: design and renovation with a preservation perspective* presents concise information and a valuable bibliography, much of which is applicable to the preservation of maps.

Conclusion

It has been the intent of this part of the chapter to present an overview on maps relevant to the needs of architects, landscape architects and community and regional planners. Not presented has been a potentially lengthy discussion on the wide variety of atlases available which contain collections of maps themselves. Since these are more readily available and identifiable than sheet maps and map series, atlases are only briefly mentioned. Although it would be possible to present more details on maps, the focus here is to inform the reader of sources to use to identify maps and to locate nearby collections containing useful material. Consulting the titles discussed will help to familiarize the reader with literature relating to maps. Further advice can be sought from the librarians or curators at various local, regional and national map libraries and collections.

Drawings

The process of drawing is a creative process and in the initial design stages it is primarily a visual and interpretive process. While the basic fundamentals of the drawing process have remained stable for many centuries, translating this creative process into working drawings and fully drafted projects has encountered many transitions, especially during the latter part of this century. For this reason, a brief discussion of the drawing and design processes, selected materials which further the processes, and collected works of drawings and collections will be presented in this section.

Theory and the creative process

The theory of creating and visualizing is a study in itself, based in aesthetics and philosophy. However, this section will focus primarily on materials directly related to the architectural drawing process. Of special interest are some of Le Corbusier's writings. *Towards a new architecture* and *The ideas of Le Corbusier* present his concepts of the creative process and its application for studying or practising architects. In both these publications Le Corbusier presents his theories on the 'spirit' in architecture and the applications of harmony, rhythm and balance during the conceptualization process. Other publications present additional but similar theories on communicating through the drawing and design process. Porter's *How architects visualise* and Lawson's *How designers think* continue to serve as modern standards of design theory for architects and designers. Discussions of creative thinking, philosophies and strategies used in the design process form the basis of both these works. A recent publication, *Envisioning architecture: an analysis of drawings* by Fraser, has the potential to become important in this area as well. It evaluates drawings and presents a fresh approach to the Porter and Lawson information, and includes a selection of different drawing styles and applications by various architects. Laseau's *Graphic thinking for architects and designers* adds a more structured theoretical approach to the drawing process. Crowe's *Visual notes* and Thiel's *Visual awareness and design* present varying approaches, with Crowe's work more directly related to the creative process for architects and planners. Numerous visual images and the processes used to achieve them are presented, including examples from various artists' and architects' journals and notebooks. *Understanding architecture through drawing* by Brian Edwards forms a valuable bridge between the creative concept and the physical application. He stresses the importance of sketching in the design process and its usefulness in developing legitimate drawings which will serve as a basis for a building or project.

The actual drawing process is fostered by the individual's own creativity and personal ability to express that creativity in visual form. Expression of a concept will have different shapes depending on each individual's interpretation. Several publications that may assist with the interpretive process are Ching's *Drawing: a creative process*, Hogarth's *Drawing architecture: a creative approach* and Mendelowitz's *A guide to drawing*. While Mendelowitz approaches drawing as an end in itself,

Ching and Hogarth emphasize the use of sketching and drawing as a part of the design process for architects. However, Mendelowitz presents more basic information on the techniques of drawing which would benefit architects and planners alike. These publications are modern classics for the study and practice of drawing, with Ching and Hogarth's works having greater relationship to architects and planning practitioners. All works present the basics in the use of line, shape and form, creativity, perspective, and representing reality to mention a few of the topics, but Ching's work has a structural focus which is appealing to architects.

Rendering and models

Refining the drawing process leads to the practice of rendering which translates into the presentation drawing process. *Architectural rendering* by Halse continues to serve as a classic work in this area. It provides detailed information on specific renderings to help the reader gain knowledge of the tools (pencils, papers, inks) and techniques used to achieve the details and, ultimately, the final product. Whereas the demonstrations in Halse's book are structured, Kliment's work, *Architectural sketching and rendering,* provides a loose, freehand interpretation to the process. Representative examples of well-known architects' drawings are displayed throughout the work along with brief descriptions of the technical aspects. Philip Crowe's *Architectural rendering* updates many of the ideas of Halse and also demonstrates the use of colour in renderings. Presented is a wide variety of renderings using pen and ink, watercolour, coloured pencil, gouache, etc., with descriptions on applying the medium, the paper used, and any special techniques. Levinson's *Architectural rendering fundamentals* focuses more on using line, curves, perspective, mass, light and figures as elements or part of the whole process. It varies greatly from Burden's *Architectural delineation* which almost exclusively focuses on finished drawings and models. While the process of achieving the renderings is described, it lacks the detail of Crowe's book on the rendering process, but is still useful for demonstration purposes.

Rendered drawings are typically utilized for presentation purposes, and often architects are expected to construct models or maquettes of the rendered, proposed 'building(s)'. *Model graphics* by Koepke and *Building architectural & interior design models fast* by Buckles are excellent, basic workbooks for studio use. Both are well-illustrated and would guide the student or practitioner through the model building process. Cleaver's *Constructing model buildings* is similar and approaches the model from within the presentation process to clients. A long-time standard for constructing architectural models is Taylor's *Model building for architects and engineers*. It is joined by Pattinson's *A guide to professional architectural and industrial scale model building* as the two more advanced and technical texts on architectural models. Both go into lengthy detail about all aspects of the model, from the building to trees and landscaping and various minute exterior and interior details.

Akiko Busch compiled and published *The art of the architectural model,* which illustrates the wide range of design and form that models take. It is well illustrated in colour with models by top architectural firms and some lesser known architects. The models presented include interiors, building complexes, waterfronts and harbour scenes, which represent the potential of architectural models. The materials vary for each of the models but the real focus of this book is on the product, the models themselves, and not on the process of their construction.

Drafting and graphic techniques

When the creative process matures such that an envisioned structure or rendered building needs to acquire the details of design and construction, then architects will proceed to the drawing board or, perhaps, to computer-aided design and drafting (CADD) software to develop designs into working drawings.

Whatever method an architect chooses must be accompanied by acquired knowledge and experience in the detailing process. Numerous publications are available in both Great Britain and North America. Some are extremely detailed and used both in training programmes and in professional practice during the drafting process. Several publications that continue to be classic works in the field are Reekie's *Draughtsmanship: drawing techniques for graphic communication in architecture and building*, Weidhaas' *Architectural drafting and design* as well as his *Architectural drafting and construction*, Hepler's *Architecture: drafting and design*, Falcone's *Architectural drawing and design* and Muller's *Architectural drawing and light construction*. These along with Osamu Wakita's *The professional practice of architectural detailing* and *The professional handbook of architectural working drawings* will provide any student or practising architect with a substantial foundation of design, drafting and construction elements and applications. While these publications do not have exactly the same approach, similar information is provided. They are highly structured and contain numerous working drawings representative of those used in professional practice.

In contrast, Ching's *Architectural graphics* and *Building construction illustrated* are more casual in their presentation yet different from the sketching and initial design style of the works discussed in earlier sections. These, along with Tom Porter's four volumes of the *Manual of graphic techniques*, provide additional examples of the creative potential both during the design phase and also to the more structured draft-

ing phase. Allen's presentation of *Architectural detailing* is more stream-
lined that Wakita's work and really addresses problem solving in a creative and aesthetic manner.

Two areas related to this structured process are the use of signs and
symbols and the importance of entourage. The field of architecture is
full of signs and symbols which shape and interpret the activities of
society and the built environment. Follis' *Architectural signing and
graphics* continues to serve as a standard in the area of signs and symbols in architecture. It is still one of the most complete publications on
this topic. *Symbol signs* focuses exclusively on pedestrian and traffic
symbols. Books of this nature update parts of the Follis publication and
provide expanded information on symbols used by architects, planners
and engineers. Burden's book on *Entourage* has gained wide popularity
among students and architects. Its contents of people, trees, vehicles,
animals, etc., are available for use in projects without the need for copyright concern.

Collections

One of the best ways to understand the process of drawing and its application for architecture is to examine the drawings of various architects.
Numerous books and exhibition catalogues exist which contain representative examples of individuals and groups of architects. These could
be listed at length, but the collections that offer a more encompassing
view of one individual's work are the most worthwhile to pursue. Collections such as those held by the Royal Institute of British Architects
(RIBA) are exceptional and well worth the visit. However, since travel
to various libraries, archives and museums is often not possible, the
published collected works of the drawings of various architects are also
a means to achieve this end. Garland has published the archival drawings of Le Corbusier, Alvar Aalto, Henri Sauvage, R.M. Schindler, Mies
van der Rohe, Walter Gropius, Louis Sullivan and Louis I. Kahn. Many
libraries own these publications and they provide an ideal opportunity
to study the drawings and drawing techniques of some of the world's
most esteemed architects.

The plans, drawings and renderings of contemporary architects are
regularly displayed in monographs and journals. *Process: architecture,
Global architecture* and its various permutations, *A+U (Architecture
and urbanism), El Croquis, Architectural design* and the classic standards of the profession, i.e. *Progressive architecture,* the *Architectural
record,* and *Architecture,* continue to serve as excellent resources for
study and examination of the contemporary process of architectural
drawing.

Visual information

This section will address the value of slides, videotapes and photographs and their importance in both the architectural practice and the academic environment. For the former they are a means for documenting firm projects and for the latter the purpose is most relevant for the study of the history of architecture. The organization of these collections will differ depending on the needs and uses of a firm in contrast to the needs and uses within an academic environment. In either facility, materials of this nature tend to accumulate and require organization to facilitate future retrieval and to assure long-term availability. This section will examine literature relevant to the acquisition, organization and storage of these materials.

Slides

Developing a slide collection, within an architectural firm will differ greatly from an academic slide collection, as the requirements and purposes of these types of collections differ. Academic collections often have networks of contacts with peer institutions which are available to provide current information on cataloguing and processing slides as well as the current trend in automating slide collections. Architectural firms often encounter the problem of organizing these materials into a feasible and retrievable collection. Organizing materials using the detailed systems utilized by academic libraries would result in labour-intensive activities that are usually uneconomical for firms and, thus, beyond their consideration. However, there are organizational techniques and storage information used by academic collections that would serve well in the firm environment.

Sources of information

Although *Slide libraries* by Irvine is somewhat dated, much of the basic information remains applicable for various types of slide collections. Chapters on 'Administration and staffing', 'Classification and cataloguing', 'Acquisition, production methods, and equipment', and 'Storage and access systems' contain much information which will assist a new collection towards positive development. It also has the best bibliography of resources and readings for its time. Articles appearing in the journals mentioned below, as well as in other professional publications, will update the Irvine bibliography. Likewise, Pacey's chapter on 'Slides and filmstrips' in the *Art library manual* also provides standard basic information for handling and organizing slides. A more recent publication containing useful information which addresses the physical environment and staffing needs is *Facilities standards for art libraries and visual resources collections*, also by Irvine and produced in co-operation with the Art Libraries Society of North America (ARLIS/NA). A reasonable companion work would be Schuller's *Management for visual resources collections,* which focuses primarily on management principles and policies but it also contains brief but useful information for organizing slide facilities and collections.

Journals

Due to the continued currency of topics in slide curatorship and issues encountered in visual resource collections, much of the most relevant and timely information will be found in periodicals and journals which focus directly on this topic. A publication which focuses directly on managing slide collections and facilities is the Visual Resources Association (VRA) *Bulletin* (University of Michigan, History of Art Department), which regularly profiles slide collections in museums, academic environments and private collections. This valuable resource includes articles of specific interest such as 'Cataloging architecture slides at the University of Nebraska-Lincoln' and 'Trouble spots cataloging architecture slides' (in the 1993 Fall and Winter issues respectively). The former article addresses the use of AACR2 for cataloguing slides and developing MARC records, while the latter addresses problems encountered in the cataloguing process with regard to identifying images. Likewise, the quarterly publication *Visual resources, an international journal of documentation* provides a scholarly approach to the various forms of visual information in a broader context than slides alone, as well as discussing contemporary approaches to organizing and accessing visual materials. Occasionally, *Art documentation*, the journal of ARLIS/NA, and the *Art libraries journal*, published under the auspices of the Art Libraries Society of the United Kingdom (ARLIS/UK and Ireland), contain articles relevant to the organization, management and care of slides and the profession of slide or visual resources curatorship. While other journals in the field of librarianship and related professions also address issues for non-print materials, the above titles focus directly on topics related to slide and visual resource collections. Of equally informative value would be access to the electronically based Listservers sponsored by the VRA and ARLIS/NA. These include current information and topics of concern both to the profession of visual resource curatorship and issues encountered in visual resource collections.

Slide collections and libraries

Most architectural firm collections are not available to the public or other professionals except as clients or friends of the firm, but many of the collections belonging to university and college schools of architecture or libraries, and community college and public libraries may be used by local professionals. These collections are identified in several directories and handbooks. Sources of academic, museum and public library collections are McKeown's *National directory of slide collections* for Great Britain and Hoffberg and Hess' *Directory of art libraries and visual resource collections in North America*. The VRA is currently developing a 'Directory of visual resources collections in the United States and Canada' which will update the visual resource information of the Hoffberg and Hess publication. Also of value for identifying collections on an international level are the International Federation of Library Associations' *IFLA directory of art libraries* and Evans' *Picture researchers' handbook: an international guide to picture sources and how to use them*. Both describe the nature of the collections, their size and terms of access to the materials.

Within Britain, there are several collections accessible to the public that are worthy of note. These include the RIBA's British Architectural Library, the V and A slide collection, which has a good architectural section, and the collection belonging to the Audio-Visual Department of Birmingham Public Libraries, which is considered extensive. The Architectural Association (AA) collections are only available to members. The AA has recently revised its already large collection which is available for loan. The Courtauld Institute in London also has a good collection with many architecture slides, but permission must be sought to use it. Another guide to collections for the architect is Ruth Kamen's *British and Irish architectural bibliography: a bibliography and guide to sources of information*.

While both the United States and Canada have many visual resource collections that are accessible to the public, most of the larger ones require an appointment, may charge a fee, and do not always circulate their slides. The *Directory of art libraries and visual resource collections in North America* referred to above is a useful tool for learning the various access and lending policies of the collections. The Metropolitan Museum of Art in New York has an extensive slide collection available to the public as a fee-based service. In Washington, DC, the Freer Gallery of Art and the National Archives and Records Administration have public circulating collections which have extensive architectural holdings. These are just a sample of the many North American collections. Borrowing and use practices change, so it is advisable to telephone or write to verify availability and loan policies prior to visiting these or any collections.

Organization of slides

Establishing a new slide collection or reorganizing an existing one requires intellectual as well as physical strategies for organization. The intellectual organization includes identifying images, providing descriptive yet brief information, establishing a logical system for filing and retrieving slides and, possibly, a classification code which is related to the subject of the slide's image. Physical organization includes the purchase, recording, remounting, storing and viewing of the materials or the physical 'presentation' of the results of the intellectual organizational activities. Most of the following discussion and information will address organizing 35 mm slides, however, some of the information is applicable to other forms of transparency.

Before a slide collection is established, especially in a professional firm, the company or institution must evaluate the reasons for which such a collection would be used. If the collection would be primarily used to promote the works of the firm, then it would be more economical for the firm to generate slides as they are needed instead of investing staff time in establishing and maintaining a slide collection. Given the existing and emerging computer technologies and the developments in computer-aided design and drafting (CADD), the possibilities for these systems to generate slides based on project files retained in CADD software is not impossible. Additionally, computer systems and software are always being enhanced and if a system is compatible with an analog program that stores visual images then a firm's projects could be stored, retrieved and generated by the system, although at this time, analog programs are being replaced by advanced digital imaging software. An example is the Kodak Shoebox Photo CD Manager (4), which not only stores and organizes images but also indexes and catalogues them allowing information export to a printer or alternative display format.

If the desire is to establish an image collection of both historical and contemporary structures by various firms and architects, then coordinating and maintaining an actual collection will be necessary. This is the reason many institutional collections have developed and also where some difficulty begins. The difficulty for visual materials and slides in particular is that there is no uniform organizational system for these items. The lack of one or two standardized systems has resulted in a proliferation of schemes, and for this reason no specific manual or guide for describing the intellectual process is available for newcomers to the field. Most visual resource collections develop their own manual, which is essentially an internal document serving as an established organizational plan for the collection. Irvine's chapter 'Classification and cataloguing' (*Slide libraries*, 1979) includes characteristics and factors that 10 different slide collections have used in the intellectual organization of their slides. Just as these 10 collections have unique organizational systems, other institutions have different systems as well.

Several software programs for cataloguing slides are available commercially. These utilize the product of the intellectual process by facilitating the production of slide labels, accession lists and back-up or marker cards. Several systems also strive to serve as a catalogue or retrieval tool for identifying slides using keyword, architects' names, building, etc., to assist in locating where a slide is located in a collection. These systems include: the Michigan Image Cataloging System (MICS), which is in use at the University of Michigan's Ann Arbor campus; Thumbs-Up™, designed for Duke University's Department of Art and Art History; and the Visual Resource Management System (VRMS) developed for the Art Slide Library at Brown University. Another system applicable for a small slide collection of 50 000 slides or less is the LABELbase™ system, which provides information retrieval by project number, architect, keyword, classification number and building name or type.

Intellectual organization

This applies to various aspects known as classification and cataloguing or establishing consistently applied identifiers that will best describe a slide and also serve as the logical system for both filing and retrieving slides. At a practical level and using more familiar terminology these activities are known as identification, description and retrieval. Identification will vary with the client needs or purpose of the facility where the collection will be used. The system applied must be related to both the image and its location in the collection. Complex alpha-numeric and mnemonical coding systems have been devised for this purpose. Irvine's chapter on 'Classification and cataloging' (see above) describes in greater detail how several alpha-numeric systems work and Green's *The classification of pictures and slides* provides another applicable system which might be useful in some collections. Establishing uniform entries can be further assisted by terminology and categories established in the *Art and architecture thesaurus* and by utilizing Schuller's *Standard abbreviations for image descriptions for use in fine arts visual resources collections*. Other potential systems are presented by Harvard-Williams and Bradfield. As mentioned earlier, no single system exists for slide collections, so what works locally will need to be identified and implemented consistently throughout an entire collection. The coding system will be part of the slide label which will facilitate access, retrieval and re-filing of the slide. This system will also be part of a catalogue, list or software program which will help those using the collection to locate specific slides. Access may be by architect, building, building features, location, building type, project or job number or name. An automated management system will provide multiple access points, whereas a manual system usually requires a catalogue or list.

Another factor in the organizational structure of a slide collection includes the description of the slide, or rather the image on the slide. Essential descriptive information includes identifying the building, its location, architect(s) and date of construction. Additional information would include the view, angle or side of the building displayed and any detail or close-up images of special features of the building. This information would be included on any labels attached to the slide. Access to an image and the ultimate retrieval of a slide are the result of the identification and description process. Addressing issues such as how the slides will be used prior to the identification process aids in that process and ultimately in the retrieval process.

Physical organization

This organizational form includes the acquisition, accessioning, mounting or remounting, storage and viewing of slides. Acquisition essentially means acquiring slides. There are two primary ways of acquiring slides. One is to purchase them from commercial slide producers or distributors, and the other is to produce them locally or photograph the images from illustrated sources. In North America, major vendors of architectural slides are ArchiCenter, Art on File International, Saskia, Scholastic Slide Services, Architectural Color Slides, Frieze Frame Images, Honart Slides, Johnson Architectural Images, Landslides, Streetscape Slides, Universal Color Slide Company and Visual Education. These are only a few of the many companies that distribute slides. The Directory at the end of this chapter lists numerous but not all vendors of architectural slides. The *Slide buyers' guide* and the *VRA bulletin* are the best sources for locating slide producers and distributors. Producing slides locally consists of locating good images and learning the use of a camera, the appropriate slide film and the corresponding lamps.

Once the slides are ready for processing many collections assign an accession number and list the slide in an accession file or folder. The accession information describes the source of the slide instead of the image on the slide. This information identifies the company which produced the slide, any company-assigned code, the date the slide arrived or was produced, the subject and the photographer. The accession number is connected to the slide through a catalogue 'list' or the automated management system of the collection in the event another copy or replacement is needed.

To protect slides from moisture and oils from fingerprints it is advisable to remount slides under glass or use plastic and glass mounts. Two successful brands of mounts containing glass are Gepe and Wess Plastics. Both brands come in glass or glassless varieties and in various sizes. Wess produces both a general purpose mount and an archival slide mount. Gepe slide mounts are of archival quality. Both brands of mount are reusable, they maintain the stability of the image during projection and are sufficiently thin to avoid jamming in a projector. Anti-Newton ring glass is recommended for these mounts. Newton rings develop as a result of moisture and bacteria which distorts the emulsion of the slide. In turn, this destroys the visual information rendering the slide useless. Irvine's book contains information on the slide-mounting process. White's survey *Slide collections* also addresses why and when remounting slides into mounts containing glass is recommended. Schrock and Sundt's chapter 'Slides' in *Conservation in the library* and Sundt's publication *Conservation practices for slide and photograph collections* are informative writings both from the viewpoint of the physical processing of slides and the preservation measures. If the advice in these publications is followed, a collection will enjoy greater image stability and increased physical longevity. To complete the processing function, the descriptive information and any assigned code resulting from the identification of the image should be written on the slide mount or written on a label attached to the mount.

The equipment used for storing processed slides also has an important effect as regards preservation of the transparencies. Storage equipment systems vary from cabinets holding files of slides, to 'hanging gardens' (vertical holding frames) and slide sleeves stored in folders or files. Any of these systems are acceptable for storage and preservation purposes providing the proper equipment is used and the storage system meets the needs of both those processing the slides and those using the collection. For large collections, slide cabinets which hold between 500 and 5000 slides in a relatively small space are recommended. Cabinets should also be made of metal rather than wood. Over time, wood emits gases which adversely affect slide images. Metal cabinets, such as those manufactured by Neumade, serve remarkably well; they are stackable, and are available in two-to-five-drawer units and with individual or group filing systems. Slide storage boxes which function in much the same way as the Neumade cabinets are more appropriate for storing small numbers of slides. Typically, they hold approximately 500 35 mm slides and afford easy mobility within various office spaces. 'Hanging gardens' — sliding holding frames in large cabinets — store slides vertically and usually have a light viewer at one end of the cabinet. This illuminates the slides from the back enabling the user to view all the slides on the frame. Luxor Slide-Bank™ is a brand of this type of slide storage system. Each slide holding frame holds about 63 35 mm slides, with the cabinets containing 28 to 35 slide holding frames. Slide storage sleeves typically hold 20 slides per sleeve. Sleeves made of polypropylene instead of commercial plastic provide the most stable environment for preserving slides. The Perma-Saf® and SlideGuard® storage systems offer two similar forms of this type of slide storage. Sleeves containing slides may be stored in ring-binders or suspended on hanging rods and stored in file cabinets or special boxes with hanging systems. The sleeves protect the slides from excessive handling and enable a group of slides to be viewed at one time, as with the 'hanging gardens'. The disadvantage is that removing and refiling the individual slides is cumbersome and requires additional time in comparison to the other two types of slide storage system mentioned. Again, Irvine's book evaluates the pros and cons of these types of systems and Calderhead's *Libraries for professional practice* also discusses equipment.

Viewing slides may be accomplished with several types of equipment: individual slide viewers, projectors and light boxes. Each of these is preferable to holding a slide up to the light and each serves a specific need for viewing slides. When organizing a group of slides for a presentation the pros and cons of each become more evident. Slide viewers are cumbersome and time consuming to use, as are projectors. Light boxes or light tables greatly facilitate the viewing of single slides or groups of slides contained in slide sleeves. Commercial light boxes, such as Luxor's Pro-View™ slide viewer system, are constructed much in the same manner, with an opaque glass working surface with a light source underneath.

Videotapes

Videotapes on architects and architecture are available from a variety of sources which include commercial companies, government agencies and academic institutions. Some distribute the same titles while others produce or sponsor their own products. It is worth noting that several companies that produce slides also produce videotapes. All of these products are protected by copyright laws which prohibit duplication and also prohibit altering the information to a different format. The only exceptions are those covered by the 'fair use' or 'fair dealing' parts of the laws. The 'Directory' section at the end of this chapter lists some representative companies from which videotapes on architecture are available.

Sources of information

Professional publications, both in the field of librarianship and in the field of architecture, regularly cite videotapes relevant to the study of the history and the professional practice of architecture. However, there are several publications of a much broader nature which are often forgotten but are equally important to the overall existence of media materials, not only of the video format but other audio-visual formats as well.

The Bowker publication *AV market place* serves an important purpose to any collection utilizing media materials. It is published annually and is the most current source of addresses for distributors and producers in the United States and Canada. It includes companies responsible for a variety of media products ranging from media items, to equipment for displaying or viewing, to storage facilities. The media formats covered include audio programmes, audio-visual, i.e. slide-tape programmes, videocassettes, over-head educational materials and slides.

Specifically focusing on videos in architecture is the G.K. Hall publication *Architecture on screen: films and videos on architecture, land-scape architecture, historic preservation, city and regional planning.* This publication also includes 35 mm and 16 mm films, videodisks and laserdisks. The films discussed are primarily documentaries produced between 1927 and 1992. The publication is international in scope and is essentially a filmography pertaining to architecture. Some of these materials may be out of print and, therefore, no longer available for purchase.

Journals focusing exclusively on identifying new videotapes for architecture and/or planning are rare. *Media review digest* serves a useful purpose in reviewing media products issued each year. It is published semi-annually and provides world-wide coverage. Using the subject index and the architecture heading, reviews of media products of the previous two or three years are identified. The bi-monthly *Films in review* includes reviews of new movies, films for television and videotapes. When it comes to architecture, the forthcoming publication *Design books & media review*, scheduled to appear monthly, will review books, videotapes, CD-ROM, CADD and software on architecture and design history and technology.

Organization and preservation

Most traditional libraries and collections fully process videotapes using traditional cataloguing and classification rules. These vary between Britain and the United States but, none-the-less, organization along these lines is consistent and such that the videotapes may be located in either on-line or card catalogues at the institutional and local level. Within a professional practice, organizing videos may simply consist of shelving videotapes in alphabetical order by title or of grouping them by subject matter.

Videotapes will have a longer life if several basic rules are usually followed. The first is that videotapes should always be stored vertically, i.e. on one of the long edges. Another is that videotapes must be protected from extremes of temperature, especially heat or sunlight. If the tape is unusually cold or hot, it should be allowed to achieve a normal room temperature before it is played. Authorities determine that the optimum temperature for housing videotapes is 68° F or 20° C with a relative humidity not exceeding 55 per cent (5). Also, if a tape has not been viewed during a period of six months, it should be played on forward and reverse several times through a video player or rewinder to 'recharge' the image. Images tend to migrate on a tape that is not used. Rrunning the tape several times supposedly restores the image to its original viewing quality. Regularly cleaning the heads of video playing equipment will also lengthen the life of videotapes. To prevent accidentally erasing the image, protecting the tapes from magnetic surfaces and electric fields is advised. Various publications containing additional useful information on storing and preserving videotape collections include Swartzburg's two publications, *Preserving library materials* and *Conservation in the library*. Also of value is DePew's *A library, media and archival preservation handbook,* which addresses not only the preservation of paper but also of various audio-visual formats including videotapes.

Photographs

Photographs often form part of the visual materials collected both by architectural firms to document projects and by library and archival collections for use in study and research. This section will examine the process of photography, its application to the documentation of architecture and the value of photographs in the research and study of architecture.

The process of photography

Learning the practice of photography follows a number of basic principles and applications which take into consideration advances in cameras and electronic apparatus and chemical processes. There are several classic texts which are frequently updated. These include Phil Davis' *Photography*, Bruce Warren's *Photography*, London and Upton's *Photography* and Seeley's *High contrast*. The first three, with the same title, are basic technical manuals on cameras, lenses, film and film processes. They also discuss the use of light and visual elements of good photography. Most of the information applies to black and white photography, but colour is included. *High contrast* serves as an excellent resource for using black and white images to convey information. Several architectural photographers have successfully used high-contrast photography to document buildings. To supplement these texts there are several reference tools which are also standards for the practice of photography. The *Focal encyclopedia of photography*, the *Focal dictionary of photographic technologies*, and *The photographer's dictionary* continue to serve as basic reference tools regarding photography.

Documenting architectural projects

Photography continues to be a successful medium for recording buildings and documenting architectural and urban projects. Several publications specifically directed towards photographing works of architecture are Abraben's *Point of view: the art of architectural photography*, Dean's *Architectural photography: techniques for architects, preservationists, historians, photographers, and urban planners* and Kopelow's *How to photograph buildings and interiors*. Abraben's and Kopelow's publications are more current and focus on using various contemporary equipment and photo techniques as applied to buildings and sites. Both discuss composition, the use of light and, in general, photographic techniques to result in successful final images. Many good examples are presented. While Dean's book is somewhat dated with regard to equipment and film, it is still useful for those learning the various elements of architectural photography. Less a discussion on equipment and more on methods is McGrath's *Photographing buildings inside and out*, which includes almost exclusively addresses using colour film and provides useful insights on photographing various types of interiors, i.e. offices, apartments, etc., and the exteriors of buildings to their best advantage.

Julius Shulman published a book entitled *Photographing architecture and interiors* which is also about architectural photographic technique. Shulman is considered one of the top photographers of buildings and architectural settings and essentially set the standard for photographing architecture. Keeping this in mind, his publications essentially present his work, which is remarkable, and in some cases demonstrate the application of high-contrast photography. Another book, *The photography of architecture and design: photographing buildings, interiors, and the visual arts,* also documents both Shulman's photographic process and accomplishments. A retrospective of Shulman's professional work is documented in Rosa's *A constructed view: the architectural photography of Julius Shulman,* which is an excellent companion to Shulman's own publications.

Another publication on photographing architectural works is *The architectural photography of Hedrich-Blessing,* which documents the works of this Chicago-based firm specializing in photography of modern American architecture. Several other publications present the work of various photographers. Both *The photography of architecture: twelve views* and *The American architectural photographer: profiles of the top talent in architectural photography* show contemporary architectural photographers at work and how buildings and sites were documented in the late 1980s through to the 1990s. There are several publications that document the history of architectural photography which was initially intended for the purpose of documenting historical buildings. Robinson's *Architecture transformed: a history of the photography of buildings from 1939 to the present* and *Photography and architecture, 1839-1939* best present this perspective which demonstrates the progress of architectural photography since its invention.

Study and research

World-wide there are numerous architectural photographic collections in libraries, archives and historical societies. Guides and handbooks to collections are a valuable resource for locating specific collections, identifying their focus and discerning their primary clientele. Bradshaw's *World photography sources* is somewhat dated but still serves as an informative publication. It encompasses a broader area than the more current *European photography guide 5,* which covers only Europe, and the *USA photography guide,* which covers only the United States. While Bradshaw's is international in scope, the latter two publications not only include information on collections but also on publishers, galleries, museums, schools and, sometimes, grants and fellowships. Mentioned earlier was Evans' *Picture researcher's handbook,* which is more current than the Bradshaw publication and is also international in scope.

Several catalogues and indexes exist which aid researchers in finding the sites of specific photographers' collections. The *Directory of British photographic collections* by Wall continues to be useful in identifying collections throughout Great Britain. Details such as the subjects of the collection and the photographers primarily featured are included. Collections of all types are represented: anthropology, agriculture, art, transportation and history, to list a few. Additionally, information on the size of the collection, availability of other visual formats in addition to photographs, ability to serve patrons and copying fees are provided. The *Guide to Canadian photographic archives/Guide des archives photographiques Canadiennes* works somewhat differently in that it lists images and identifies the archive where the image is held. The *Index to American photographic collections* is a major resource tool which also identifies photograph collections, photographers and photographs in US collections. Information is very thorough regarding the collections and facilities index. The Smithsonian Institution publishes a multi-volume set, *Guide to photographic collections at the Smithsonian Institution*, describing its collections which range broadly from natural history to art, architecture, cityscapes and related topics. This set of guides includes holdings of slides, photographs and other forms of transparencies in the collections of the Institution.

Conclusion

Considering the wide range of visual information available, the topics covered in this section represent but a small portion. Continuing developments in the areas of digital imaging and laser disk technology will undoubtedly have an impact on the future of storing and managing visual images. Commercial firms involved in producing slides, videotapes, laser disks, software, etc. have copyrighted their products. Duplicating or altering these products could constitute a violation of copyright, so care must be exercised to avoid any form of infringement.

Although some preservation issues were addressed in the slide and videotape sections, additional resources must be mentioned before the close of this chapter. Publications which specifically pertain to the conservation of photographs are Eaton's *Conservation of photographs*, Rempel's *Care of photographs* and Wilhelm's *The permanence and care of color photographs*. Eaton presents a general survey of problems and solutions in photographic restoration of black and white and colour images. Rempel's books is a useful laboratory manual of basics for cleaning, stabilizing, and housing photographs. Conservation techniques and preservation strategies are emphasized in all these publications, with Wilhelm providing a more in-depth and detailed study and analysis of preservation factors for a variety of visual media which includes digital colour prints, colour negatives, slides, and motion picture resources. Numerous other publications are available and as new research and developments in film and film processing occur, changes in the conservation and preservation of visual resources will inevitably result.

References

1. Modelski, A.M. (1977) Maps, charts, and atlases. In *Encyclopedia of library and information science*, **20**, p.119.
2. Hodgkiss, A.G. and Tatham, A.F. (1986) *Keyguide to information sources in cartography*. New York: Facts on File, p.67.
3. Reed, M.H. (1987) *The copyright primer for librarians and educators*. Chicago and London: American Library Association and Washington, DC: National Education Association, p.15.
4. Available from Kodak, SAX Visual Resources, and other distributors of visual media.
5. Swartzburg, S.G. (1980) *Preserving library materials: a manual*. Scarecrow Press, p.103.

Bibliography

Abraben, E. (1994) *Point of view: the art of architectural photography*. New York: Van Nostrand Reinhold.

Adams, I.H. (1966, 1970, 1974, 1988) (ed.) *Descriptive list of plans in the Scottish Record Office*, 4 vols. Edinburgh: Scottish Record Office.

Allen, E. (1993) *Architectural detailing: function, constructibility, aesthetics*. New York: Wiley.

American Geographical Society of New York (1933) *A catalogue of maps of Hispanic America, including maps in scientific periodicals and books, and sheet and atlas maps, with articles on the cartography of the several countries, and maps showing the extent and character of existing surveys*. 4 vols. New York: The Society.

American Geographical Society of New York, Map Department (1968) *Index to maps in books and periodicals*. 10 vols & supplements. Boston: G.K. Hall.

American Institute of Graphic Arts (1993) *Symbol signs: the complete study of passenger/pedestrian-oriented symbols*. New York: The Institute.

Andriot, L. (1994) *Guide to the USGS geologic and hydrologic maps*. McLean, VA: Documents Index.

Architectural Index. (1951-) Boulder, CO: Architectural Index.

Architectural periodical index. (1973-) RIBA Publications.
Automobile Association (1989) *AA Big atlas of town plans.* 2nd edn. Basingstoke: Automobile Association.
AV market place. (1989-) Annual. New York: R.R. Bowker.
Avery index to architectural periodicals. (1963-) New York: G.K. Hall.
Avery, T.E. (1987) *Interpretation of aerial photographs.* 4th edn. New York: Macmillan.
Balay, R. (1992) (ed.) *Guide to reference books: covering materials from 1985-1990.* Chicago & London: American Library Association.
Bancroft Library (1964) *Index to printed maps.* Boston: G.K. Hall.
Birmingham Public Libraries (1979) *Sets of maps and national atlases in the map room.* Birmingham Public Libraries.
Bohme, R. (1989, 1991, 1993) *Inventory of world topographic mapping.* 3 vols. London: Elsevier Applied Science in co-operation with the International Cartographic Association.
Bradfield, V.J. (1976) *Slide collections: a user requirement survey.* British Library (R&D report 5309).
Bradshaw, D.N. and Hahn, C. (1982) (eds.) *World photography sources.* New York: Directories.
Briend, A.M. and Croyere, C. (1991) *Repertoire des cartotheques de France.* Paris: Centre national de la recherche scientifique, Laboratoire de communication et d'information en geographie.
British Library (1844-61, reprinted 1962) *Catalogue of manuscript maps, charts and plans and of the topographical drawings in the British Museum.* 3 vols. British Library.
British Library (1967) *Catalogue of printed maps, charts and plans.* 15 vols. (*Ten-year supplement, 1965-74.*) British Library.
British librarianship and information work, 1976-1980. (1982) 2 vols. London: Library Association.
Buckles, G.M. (1991) *Building architectural & interior design models fast!* Cucamonga, CA: Belpine Publishing.
Burden, E. (1992) *Architectural delineation: a photographic approach to presentation.* 3rd edn. New York: McGraw-Hill.
Burden, E. (1991) *Entourage: a tracing file for architecture and interior design drawing* 2nd edn. New York: McGraw-Hill.
Burnside, C.D. (1985) *Mapping from aerial photographs.* 2nd edn. New York: Wiley.
Busch, A. (1991) *The art of the architectural model.* New York: Design Press.
Busch, A. (1987) *The photography of architecture: twelve views.* New York: Van Nostrand Reinhold.
Calderhead, P. (1972) *Libraries for professional practice.* London: Architectural Press.
Canadian Centre for Architecture (1982) *Photography and architecture, 1839-1939.* Montreal: Centre Canadien d'Architecture/Canadian Centre for Architecture; New York: Callaway Editions.
Carrington, D.K. and Stephenson, R.W. (1985) *Map collections in the United States and Canada, a directory.* 4th edn. New York: Special Libraries Association.
Cashman, N.D. (1990) *Slide buyers' guide: an international directory of slide sources for art and architecture.* 6th edn. Englewood, CO: Libraries Unlimited.
[State]: Catalog of topographic and other published maps. (various dates) Reston, VA: US Geological Survey, National Mapping Program.
Ching, F.D.K. (1985) *Architectural graphics.* 2nd edn. New York: Van Nostrand Reinhold.
Ching, F.D.K. (1975) *Building construction illustrated.* New York: Van Nostrand Reinhold.
Ching, F.D.K.. (1990) *Drawing: a creative process.* New York: Van Nostrand Reinhold.

Ciciarelli, J.A. (1991) *A practical guide to aerial photography*. New York: Van Nostrand Reinhold.

Clapp, A.F. (1987) *Curatorial care of works of art on paper: basic procedures for paper preservation*. New York: Nick Lyons Books.

Clavet, A. (1979-) *Guide to Canadian photographic archives. Guide des archives photographiques Canadiennes*. Ottawa: Public Archives Canada.

Cleaver, J. (1973) *Constructing model buildings*. London: Academy Editions; New York: St. Martins.

Cobb, D.A. (1990) *Guide to US map resources*. Chicago: American Library Association.

Council of Planning Librarians (1979-) *CPL Bibliography*. Monticello, IL: Council of Planning Librarians.

Covert, N. and Wick, V. (1993) (eds.) *Architecture on screen: films and videos on architecture, landscape architecture, historic preservation, city and regional planning*. New York: G.K. Hall.

Crowe, N. and Laseau, P. (1984) *Visual notes for architects and designers*. New York: Van Nostrand Reinhold.

Crowe, P. (1991) *Architectural rendering*. New York: McGraw-Hill.

Cuff, D.J. (1989) *Thematic maps: their design and production*. New York & London: Routledge.

Davis, P. (1994) *Photography*. 7th edn. Madison, WI: Brown & Benchmark.

Dean, J. (1981) *Architectural photography: techniques for architects, preservationists, historians, photographers, and urban planners*. Nashville, TN: American Association for State and Local History.

Dent, B.D. (1990) *Cartography: thematic map design*. 2nd edn. Dubuque, IA: Wm. C. Brown.

DePew, John N. (1991) *A library, media, and archival preservation handbook*. Santa Barbara, CA: ABC-CLIO.

Dickinson, P.G.M. (1968) *Maps in the county record office, Huntingdon*. Huntingdon: Imray Laurie Norie; Wilson.

Directory of town plans in Britain. (1985) Basingstoke: Automobile Association.

Dury, G.H. (1967) *Map interpretation*. 3rd edn. London: Pitman.

Eaton, G.T. (1985) *Conservation of photographs*. Rochester, NY: Eastman Kodak.

Edwards, B. (1994) *Understanding architecture through drawing*. London & New York: Spon.

Eskind, A.H., Drake, G. and McQuaid, J. (1990) *Index to American photographic collections: compiled at the International Museum of Photography at George Eastman House*. 2nd edn. Boston: G.K. Hall.

Evans, H. (1989) *Picture researcher's handbook: an international guide to picture sources, and how to use them*. London: Van Nostrand Reinhold (International).

Falcone, J.D. (1990) *Architectural drawing and design: principles and practices*. Englewood Cliffs, NJ: Prentice Hall.

Follis, J. (1979) *Architectural signing and graphics*. New York: Whitney Library of Design.

Furst, A. (1994) *The American architectural photographer: profiles of the top talent in architectural photography*. Rockport, MA: Rockport Pub.; Natick, MA: Resource World Pub.

GeoKatalog. Annual. Stuttgart: Geo Center.

Getty Art History Information Program (1994) *Art and architecture thesaurus: guide to indexing and cataloging*. 5 vols. 2nd edn. Oxford & New York: Oxford University Press.

GPO on Silverplatter. (1988-) Norwood, MA: Silver Platter (machine-readable data files).

Green, S. J. (1984) *The classification of pictures and slides*. Denver, CO: Little Books.

Guiton, J. (1981) *(ed.) The ideas of Le Corbusier on architecture and urban planning*, trans. M. Guiton. New York: George Braziller.

Halse, A.O. (1988) *Architectural rendering: the techniques of contemporary presentation.* 3rd edn. New York: McGraw-Hill.

Harley, J.B. (1972) *Maps for the local historian: a guide to British sources.* London: National Council of Social Service for the Standing Conference for Local History.

Harley, J.B. (1975) *Ordnance Survey maps: a descriptive manual.* Southampton Ordnance Survey.

Harvard-Williams, P. and Karling, S.A. (n.d.) *Rules for the cataloguing of slides in the Liverpool School of Architecture.* mimeo.

Hayward, R.J. (1977) *Fire insurance plans in the National Map Collection/Plans d'assurance-incendie de la collection nationale de cartes et plans.* Ottawa: National Map Collection.

Hepler, D.E. (1987) *Architecture: drafting and design.* New York: Gregg Division, McGraw-Hill.

Herbert, J.R. (1984) (ed.) *Panoramic maps of cities in the United States and Canada: a checklist of maps in the collections of the Library of Congress, Geography and Map Division.* Library of Congress.

Higgens, G. (1984) *Printed reference material.* 2nd edn. London: Library Association.

Hodgkiss, A.G. and Tatham, A.F. (1986) *Keyguide to information sources in cartography.* New York: Facts on File.

Hodgkiss, A.G. (1981) *Understanding maps: a systematic history of their use and development.* Folkestone, England: Wm. Dawson & Son.

Hoehn, R.P. (1976 & 1977) *Union list of Sanborn fire insurance maps held by institutions in the United States and Canada.* 2 vols. Santa Cruz, CA: Western Association of Map Libraries.

Hoffberg, J.A. and Hess, S.W. (1978) *Directory of art libraries and visual resource collections in North America.* New York: Neal-Schuman.

Hogarth, P. (1979) *Drawing architecture: a creative approach.* New York: Watson-Gupthill.

How to obtain aerial photographs. (1984) Reston, VA: Geological Survey, National Cartographic Information Center.

[State]: Index to topographic and other map coverage. (various dates) Reston, VA: US Geological Survey, National Mapping Program.

International Federation of Library Associations (1993) *World directory of map collections.* 3rd edn. Munich & New York: K.G. Saur.

Irvine, B.J. (1991) *Facilities standards for art libraries and visual resources collections.* Englewood, CO: Libraries Unlimited.

Irvine, B.J. (1979) *Slide libraries: a guide for academic institutions, museums and special collections* 2nd edn. Littleton, CO: Libraries Unlimited.

Jay, B. and Linhoff, A.J. (1993) *USA photography guide.* Munich: Nazraeli Press.

Jones, E. and Sinclair, D.J. (1968) (ed.) *Atlas of London and the London region.* Oxford & New York: Pergamon.

Kamen, R. (1981) *British and Irish architectural history: a bibliography and guide to sources of information.* London: Architectural Press.

Karrow, Jr., R.W. (1981) (ed.) *Checklist of printed maps of the Middle West to 1900.* 13 vols. Boston: G.K. Hall.

Keates, J.S. (1982) *Understanding maps.* London & New York: Longman.

Kliment, S. (1984) *Architectural sketching and rendering: techniques for designers and artists.* New York: Whitney Library of Design.

Koepke, M.L. (1988) *Model graphics: building and using study models.* New York: Van Nostrand Reinhold.

Kopelow, G. (1993) *How to photograph buildings and interiors.* New York: Princeton Architectural Press.

Larsgaard, M.L. (1987) *Map librarianship: an introduction.* 2nd edn. Littleton,

CO: Libraries Unlimited.

Laseau, P. (1980) *Graphic thinking for architects and designers.* New York: Van Nostrand Reinhold.

Lawson, B. (1980) *How designers think.* London: Architectural Press.

Le Corbusier (1927, 1946) *Towards a new architecture.* London: Architectural Press.

Levinson, E.D. (1983) *Architectural rendering fundamentals.* New York: McGraw-Hill.

Library of Congress, Geography and Map Division (1973) *The bibliography of cartography.* 5 vols and supplements. Boston: G.K. Hall.

Library of Congress. Geography and Map Division (1909-1974) *A list of geographical atlases in the Library of Congress, with bibliographical notes.* 9 vols. Washington, DC: Government Printing Office.

Library of Congress, Geography and Map Division. (1984) *Panoramic maps of cities in the United States and Canada, checklist of maps in the collections of the Library of Congress, Geography and Map Division.* Library of Congress.

Library of Congress, Geography and Map Division, Reference and Bibliography Section (1981) *Fire insurance maps in the Library of Congress: plans of North American cities and towns produced by the Sanborn Map Company: a checklist.* Library of Congress.

London, B. and Upton, J. (1994) *Photography.* 5th edn. New York: HarperCollins College Pub.

Lurie, H.R. (1982) *Can I copy – ?: a practical guide to reproduction rights under the copyright law for university and college faculty and staff.* Villanova, PA: Villanova University Press.

Maizlish, A. and Tefft, W. (1992) *World map directory, 1992-1993: a practical guide to United States and international maps.* Santa Barbara, CA: Map Link.

Makower, J., Poff, C. and Bergheim, L. (1990) *The map catalog: every kind of map and chart on earth and even some above it.* 2nd edn. New York: Random House.

McGrath, N. (1993) *Photographing buildings inside and out.* 2nd edn. New York: Whitney Library of Design.

McKeown, R. (1990) *National directory of slide collections.* British Library.

Media review digest. Semi-annual. Ann Arbor, MI: Pierian Press.

Mendelowitz, D.M. (1993) *A guide to drawing.* 5th edn. New York: Harcourt Brace Jovanovich.

Miller, V.L. (1989) *Interpretation of topographic maps.* Columbus, OH: Merrill Pub.

Modelski, A.M. (1977) Maps, charts, and atlases. In *Encyclopedia of library and information science,* pp.117-162. New York: Dekker.

Monteiro, Palmyra V.M. (1967-69) *A catalogue of Latin American flat maps, 1926-1964.* 2 vols. Austin, TX: Institute of Latin American Studies, University of Texas.

Muehrcke, P.C. and J.O. (1992) *Map use: reading, analysis, and interpretation.* 3rd edn. Madison, WI: J.P. Publications.

Muller, E.J. (1992) *Architectural drawing and light construction.* 4th edn. Englewood Cliffs, NJ: Prentice-Hall.

Municipal/County executive directory. Annual. Washington, DC: Carroll Pub.

The Municipal year book. Annual. Chicago: International City Manager's Association.

The Municipal yearbook. Annual. London: Municipal Publications.

National Archives of Canada (1976) *Catalogue of the National Map Collection* 16 vols. Boston: G.K. Hall.

Neubauer, B. (1994) *European photography guide five.* 5th edn. Gottingen: European Photography.

New York Public Library, Map Division (1979-) *Bibliographic guide to maps and atlases.* Boston: G.K. Hall.

New York Public Library, Map Division. (1971) *Dictionary catalog of the map division of the New York Public Library* 10 vols. Boston: G.K. Hall.

Nichols, H. (1982) *Map librarianship.* 2nd edn. London: Bingley.

Nicholson, N.L. (1981) *The maps of Canada: a guide to official Canadian maps, charts, atlases and gazetteers.* Folkestone, England: Wm. Dawson; Hamden, CT: Archon Books.

O'Connor, D.V. (1989) *Guide to photographic collections at the Smithsonian Institution* 3 vols. Washington, DC: Smithsonian Institution Press.

Otness, H.M. (1980) *Index to nineteenth century city plans appearing in guidebooks: Baedeker, Murray, Joanne, Black, Appleton, Meyer, plus selected other works to provide coverage of over 1,800 plans to nearly 600 communities, found in 164 guidebooks.* Santa Cruz, CA: Western Association of Map Libraries.

Otness, H.M. (1978) *Index to twentieth century city plans appearing in guidebooks, Baedeker, Muirhead-Blue guides, Murray, IJGR, etc., plus selected other works to provide worldwide coverage of over 2,000 plans to over 1,200 communities, found in 74 guidebooks.* Santa Cruz, CA: Western Association of Map Libraries.

Ordnance Survey (1990) *Ordnance Survey map catalogue: maps, atlases, guides and services.* Southampton: Ordnance Survey.Pacey, P. (1977) *Art libraries manual; a guide to resources and practice.* London & New York: Bowker in association with the Art Libraries Society.

Patmore, J.A. (1970) *Merseyside in maps.* Harlow, England: Longman.

Pattinson, G.D. (1982) *A guide to professional architectural and industrial scale model building.* Englewood Cliffs, NJ: Prentice-Hall.

Perkins, C.R. and Parry, R.B. (1990) (eds.) *Information sources in cartography.* London & New York: Bowker-Saur.

Perkins, C.R. and Parry, R.B. (1987) *World mapping today.* London & Boston: Butterworths.

Pinkard, B. (1982) *The photographer's dictionary.* London: BT Batsford.

Porter, T. (1980) *How architects visualize.* London: Architectural Press; Westfield, NJ: Eastview Editions.

Porter, T. and Goodman, S. (1980-85) *Manual of graphic techniques for architects, graphic designers, and artists* 4 vols. New York: Scribner's Sons.

Rabbitt, M. (1984) *A brief history of the US Geological Survey.* Alexandria, VA: US Geological Survey.

Rabbitt, M. (1979-) *Minerals, lands, and geology for the common defense and general welfare: a history of public lands, federal science and mapping policy.* 3 vols. Reston, VA: Dept. of the Interior, US Geological Survey.

Reed, M.H. (1987) *The copyright primer for librarians and educators.* Chicago: American Library Association; Washington, DC: National Education Association.

Reekie, R.F. (1976) *Draughtsmanship: drawing techniques for graphic communication in architecture and building.* 3rd edn. London: Arnold.

Rempel, S. (1987) *The care of photographs.* New York: N. Lyons Books.

Robinson, C. (1987) *Architecture transformed: a history of the photography of buildings from 1939 to the present.* New York: Architectural League of New York; Cambridge, MA: MIT Press.

Rosa, J. (1994) *A constructed view: the architectural photography of Julius Shulman.* New York: Rizzoli.

Ross, T. (1992) (ed.) *Directory of Canadian map collections.* 6th edn. Ottawa: Association of Canadian Map Libraries and Archives.

Sanborn Map Company (1940) *Description and utilization of the Sanborn map.* New York: Sanborn Map Company.

Schuller, N.S. (1989) *Management of visual resource collections.* 2nd edn. Englewood, CO: Libraries Unlimited.

Schuller, N.S. (1988) *Standard abbreviations for image descriptions for use in fine arts visual resources collections.* Austin, TX: N S. Schuller (VRA Special Bulletin No. 2).

Seeley, J. (1992) *High contrast.* 2nd edn. Newton, MA: Butterworth-Heinemann.

Seymour, W.A. (1980) (ed.) *A history of the Ordnance Survey.* Folkestone, England: Wm. Dawson & Son.

Sheehy, E.P. (1986) *Guide to reference books.* 10th edn. Chicago & London: American Library Association.

Shulman, J. (1962) *Photographing architecture and interiors.* New York: Whitney Library of Design.

Shulman, J. (1977) *The photography of architecture and design: photographing buildings, interiors, and the visual arts.* New York: Whitney Library of Design.

'Slide market news: a running update to the *Slide buyers' guide*' regular section in *VRA Bulletin*, quarterly.

Smithsonian Institution (1989) *Guide to photographic collections at the Smithsonian Institution.* 3 vols. Washington, DC: Smithsonian Institution Press.

Sobieszek, R.A. (1984) *The architectural photography of Hedrich-Blessing.* New York: Holt, Rinehart and Winston.

Spencer, D.A. (1973) *The Focal dictionary of photographic technologies.* Englewood Cliffs, NJ: Prentice-Hall.

Street atlas USA (computer file): with Xmap system software. (1991) Freeport, ME: DeLorme Mapping.

Street maps of British towns. (1987) London: British Telecommunications.

Stroebel, L.D. and Zakia, R.D. (1993) *The Focal encyclopedia of photography* 3rd edn. Boston: Focal Press.

Strong, W.S. (1992) *The copyright book: a practical guide.* 4th edn. Cambridge, MA: MIT Press.

Sundt, C.L. (1989) *Conservation practices for slide and photograph collections.* Ann Arbor, MI: Visual Resources Association (VRA Special Bulletin No. 3).

Swartzburg, S.G. (1983) *Conservation in the library: a handbook of use and care of traditional and nontraditional materials.* Westport, CT: Greenwood Press.

Swartzburg, S.G. (1980) *Preserving library materials: a manual.* Metuchen, NJ & London: Scarecrow Press.

Swartzburg, S.G. and Bussey, H. (1991) *Libraries and archives: design and renovation with a preservation perspective.* Metuchen, NJ & London: Scarecrow Press.

Taylor, J.R. (1971) *Model building for architects and engineers.* New York: Mc-Graw-Hill.

Thiel, P. (1981) *Visual awareness and design: an introductory program in conceptual awareness, perceptual sensitivity, and basic design skills.* Seattle & London: University of Washington Press.

Thompson, M.M. (1987) *Maps for America: cartographic products of the US Geological Survey and others* 3rd edn. Reston, VA: US Geological Survey.

Viaux, J. (1985) *IFLA Directory of art libraries/Répertoire de bibliotheques d'art de l'IFLA/Addressbuch der kunstbibliotheken von IFLA/Directorio de bibliotecas de arte de la IFLA.* New York: Garland Pub.

Wakita, O.A. (1984) *The professional handbook of architectural working drawings.* New York: Wiley.

Wakita, O.A. (1987) *The professional practice of architectural detailing.* 2nd edn. New York: Wiley.

Wakita, O.A. (1994) *The professional practice of architectural working drawings.* 2nd edn/student edn. New York: Wiley.

Walford, A.J. (1993-95) (ed.) *Walford's guide to reference material.* 3 vols. 5th edn. London: The Library Association.

Wall, J. (1977) *Directory of British photographic collections.* London: Heinemann.

Warren, B. (1993) *Photography.* Minneapolis/St. Paul: West Pub.

Watt, I. (1985) *A directory of UK. map collections.* 2nd edn. Kingston-upon-Thames, Surrey: British Cartographic Society.

Weidhaas, E.R. (1989) *Architectural drafting and construction.* 4th edn. Englewood Cliffs, NJ: Prentice-Hall.

Weidhaas, E.R. (1989) *Architectural drafting and design.* 6th edn. Englewood Cliffs, NJ: Prentice-Hall.

White, B. (1967) *Slide collections: a survey of their organisation in libraries in the fields of architecture, building and planning.* Edinburgh: The Author.

White, B. (1971) *Sourcebook of planning information: a discussion of sources of information for use in urban and regional planning, and in allied fields.* London: Bingley and Hamden, CT: Linnet Books.

Wilhelm, H.G. (1993) *The permanence and care of color photographs: traditional and digital color prints, color negatives, slides, and motion pictures.* Grinnell, IA: Preservation Pub.

William L. Clements Library (1972) *Research catalog of maps of America to 1860 in the William L. Clements Library, University of Michigan.* 4 vols. Boston: G.K. Hall.

Winch, K.L. (1976) *International maps and atlases in print.* 2nd edn. London & New York: Bowker.

Wolter, J.A., Grim, R.E. and Carrington, D.K. (1986) (eds.) *World directory of map collections.* 2nd edn. Munich & New York: K.G. Saur.

Directory of contacts and resources

Addresses for resources listed in this directory are related to companies or institutions cited and/or discussed in this chapter. All addresses are in the USA unless otherwise stated.

CD-ROM products

DeLorme Mapping, Lower Main St., P.O. Box 298, Freeport, ME 04032
  Tel: (207) 865-1234.
Silver Platter, 100 River Ridge Dr., Norwood, MA 02062-5043
  Tel: (617) 769-2599, Fax: (617) 769-8763.

Equipment publishers and suppliers

Chadwyck-Healey Inc., 1101 King St., Alexandria, VA 22314-9455
  Tel: (703) 683-4890, (800) 752-0515, Fax: (703) 683-2176 Chadwyck-Healey Ltd., The Quorum, Barnwell Road, Cambridge CB5 8SW, UK
  Tel: (01223) 215512, Fax: (01223) 215514.
Filmoplast®, Neschen International, Hans Neschen Gmbtt & Co. KG, D-3062 Buckeburg, Germany [Source of archival quality repair tape for paper documents].
Gepe slide mounts are available from Light Impressions, University Products Inc., or local photo supply stores.
Highsmith® Inc., W5527 Hwy 106, PO Box 800, Fort Atkinson, WI 53538-0800
  Tel: (800) 558-2110, Fax: (800) 835-2329.
Kodak Photo Inc., PO Box 3618, Carolina, PR 00984-3618
  Tel: (809) 757-5500, Fax: (809) 757-5011.
Light Impressions, 439 Monroe Ave., PO Box 940, Rochester, NY 14603-0940
  Tel: (800) 828-6216, Fax: (800) 828-5530, Customer Service: (800) 828-9859 [Offers a variety of slide storage systems including Neumade cabinets, slide mounts, plastic sleeves, and other slide mounting and filing systems].
Luxor Corporation, Box 830, 2245 Delany Rd., Waukegan, IL 60097
  Tel: (708) 244-1800, (800) 323-4656, Fax: (800) 327-1698.
Neumade Products Corporation, Box 5001 Connecticut Ave., Norwalk, CT 06856
  Tel: (203) 866-7600, Fax: (203) 866-7522 [Manufacturer of metal slide storage cabinets for housing large collections of slides].
Safco Flat Files are available from Highsmith. Safco manufactures wood and steel

flat files and wire roll and mobile roll files for storing maps or other oversize sheets of paper in either a flat or rolled manner.]

Smith System Manufacturing Co., Box 64515, St. Paul, MN 55164
Tel: (612) 482-0260, (800) 328-1061, Fax: (612) 482-0053 [Manufacturer of steel flat files for storing maps, plans, and/or drawings].

SAX Visual Art Resources, PO Box 51710, New Berlin, WI 53151
Tel: (414) 784-6880, (800) 558-6696, Fax: (414) 784-1176.

University Products, Inc., 517 Main St., PO Box 101, Holyoke, MA 01041-0101
Tel: (800) 628-1912, Fax: (800) 532-9281, Customer Service: (800) 762-1165, (413) 532-9431 [Source of archival materials, slide mounts, slide storage and viewing systems, flat files and LabelbaseÔ software].

Wess Plastic Inc., 70 Commerce Dr., Hauppauge, NY 11788-3936
Tel: (516) 231-6300, (800) 487-9377, Fax: (516) 231-0608 [Source of slide mounts].

Internet lists

ARLIS-L: To subscribe send an e-mail message to: LISTSERV@UKCC.UKY.EDU with the message SUB ARLIS-L followed by your name.

VRA-L: To subscribe send an e-mail message to: LISTSERV@UAFSYSB.BITNET with the message SUBSCRIBE VRA-L followed by your e-mail address and first name then last name.

MAP-L: To subscribe send an e-mail message to: LISTSERV@UGA.CC.UGA.EDU with the message SET MAPS-L followed by your e-mail address and name.

Maps

The following is a brief list of addresses for map distributors and governmental agencies involved in the mapping process. For a more complete list of both governmental agencies and commercial map publishers see Makower's *The map catalog.*

Great Britain

British Geological Survey, Information Systems Group, Keyworth, Nottingham NG12 5GG Tel: (01602) 363241.

Directorate of Military Survey, Ministry of Defence, Elmwood Ave., Feltham, Middlesex TW13 7AE Tel: 0181-890 3622.

Map Productions Ltd., Olwen House, Quarry Hill Rd, Tonbridge TN9 2RH.

Ordnance Survey, Ramsey Road, Maybush, Southampton SO9 4DH
Tel: (01703) 79200.

Canada

Allmaps Canada, 390 Steelcase Rd. E., Markham, Ontario L3R 1G2
Tel: (416) 477-8480.

Canada Map Office, Surveys and Mapping Branch, Energy, Mines and Resources, 615 Booth St., Ottawa, Ontario K1A OE9 Tel: (613) 952-7000.

Canadian Hydrographic Service, Hydrographic Chart Distribution Office, 1675 Russell Rd., PO Box 8080, Ottawa, Ontario K1G 3H6 Tel: (613) 998-4931.

Public Archives of Canadian National Map Collection, 395 Wellington St., Ottawa, Ontario K1A 0N3 Tel: (613) 995-1077, (613) 992-0468.

Mexico

Departamento Geografico Militar, Servicio Cartografico, Secretaria de la Defensa Nacional, Lomas de Sotelo, Mexico 10, D.F.

Guia Roji, Republica de Columbia No. 23, Col. Centro, Delegacion Cuahtemoc, 06020 Mexico D.F.

Instituto de Geologia, Universidad Nacional Autonoma de Mexico, Postal 70-296, Ciudad Universitaria, Mexico 20, D.F.

Secretaria de Programacion y Presupuesto (SPP), Direccion General de Geografia del Territorio Nacional, San Antonio Abad No. 124, Mexico 8, D.F.

USA

Central Intelligence Agency, Public Affairs, Washington, DC 20505.

Defense Mapping Agency, Office of Distribution Services, Attn. DOA, Washington, DC 20315-0010.

Earth Science Information Center, Washington, DC, US Department of the Interior, 1849 C Street NW., Rm., 2650, Washington, DC 20240 Tel: (202) 208-4047, Fax: (202) 208-6097, TDD (202) 219-1510, (800) USA-MAPS.

EROS Data Center, US Geological Survey, Sioux Falls, SD 57198 Tel: (605) 594-6507.

Historic Urban Plans, PO Box 276, Ithaca, NY 14850 Tel: (607) 273-4695.

Library of Congress, Geography and Map Division, Washington, DC 20541 Tel: (202) 707-6277.

Library of Congress, Photoduplication Service, Washington, DC 20540 Tel: (202) 287-5650.

Map Link, 529 State St., Santa Barbara, CA 93101 Tel: (805) 965-4402, Fax: (805) 962-0884.

National Archives, Cartographic and Architectural Branch, 841 S. Pickett St., Alexandria, VA 22304 Tel: (703) 756-6700.

National Park Service, Office of Public Inquiries, Rm. 1013, Washington, DC 20240 Tel: (202) 343-4747.

Sanborn Map Company, 659 Fifth St., Pelham, NY 10803.

US Forest Service, Public Affairs Office, Rm. 3107, South Building, PO Box 96090, Washington, DC 20090 Tel: (202) 447-3957.

US Geological Survey, 119 National Center, Reston, VA 22092 Tel: (703) 648-400, Fax: (703) 648-5427.

US Geological Survey, Map Distribution, Federal Center, Box 25286, Denver, CO 80225 Tel: (303) 236-7477.

Slide collection automation

The following software is available for purchase and application for automating slide collections. These systems may be used for cataloguing slides, labelling slides and, possibly, to provide automated management for visual resource collections. Other systems exist but are not yet available for commercial distribution. Contact the individual vendors for information.

Michigan Image Cataloging System Software (MICS): Contact: Technology Management Office, University of Michigan, Ann Arbor, MI 48109.

Thumbs-Up™ Contact: Graphic Detail, Inc., Westchase One, Suite 500, 4020 Westchase Blvd., Raleigh, NC 27607 Tel: (919) 833-3366, (800) 234-8635.

Visual Resource Management System (VRMS) Contact: Slideware, PO Box 194, Sausalito, CA 94966.

Slide vendors (Britain, Canada and the USA)

This is a representative list of commercial vendors who focus on producing quality architectural slides. See the *Slide buyers' guide* for a complete list of international slide vendors.

American Library Color Slide Company, Inc., American Archives of World Art, P.O. Box 4414, Grand Central Station, New York, NY 10163-4414 Tel: (212) 255-5356, (800) 633-3307, Fax: (212) 691-8592 [Slides on architecture cover prehistoric times to the present. Geographical emphasis is Western Europe and North and Central America with limited availability of slides of Russian structures. One of the few slide vendors which provides the option of purchasing slides already mounted in Gepe mounts and fully labelled].

Architectural Color Slides, 187 Grant Street, Lexington, MA 02173 Tel: (617) 862-9431 [Provides world-wide coverage of slides on architecture].

Architecture of the World, 37 East 19th St., 2nd floor, New York, NY 10003 Tel: (212) 529-1630 [Coverage is architecture from ancient to modern times with an emphasis on buildings of North and South America].

Archvision, 5 Concorde Pl., Unit 1606, Toronto, Ontario, M3C 3M8 Canada Tel: (416) 391-2272, Fax: (416) 391-2616 [Produces architectural slides of historic and current buildings in Ottawa, Montreal and Paris].

Art Color Slides, Inc., 235 East 50th St. #12, New York, NY 10022 Tel: (212) 753-0053 [Architectural slides included in this vendor's collection provide world-wide coverage and broadly represents all historical time periods].

Art on File International, 1837 East Shelby, Seattle, WA 98112 Tel: (206) 322-2638, Fax: (206) 329-1928 [Slides in this collection emphasize architecture, landscape architecture, and historical preservation].

Art Resource, Inc., 65 Bleecker St., New York, NY 10012 Tel: (212) 505-8700, Fax: (212) 420-9286, Telex: 237053 [As the US distributor for Scala Fine Arts, Slides of Florence, Italy, the architecture slides represented include structures from all time periods with a special emphasis on Italian buildings].

Biblical Archaeology Society, Merchandise Department, 4710 41st St., NW, Washington, DC 20016 Tel: (800) 221-4644, Fax: (202) 483-3423 [Distributes slides of historical structures related to biblical times of the Middle East and Egypt].

Bicostal Productions, 830 Cemetery Lane, Aspen, CO 81611-1012 Tel: (303) 920-3328 [The architecture of China and Japan are the emphasis of this company. Historic, vernacular and contemporary structures including gardens are documented in slide form].

Haesler Art Publishers, PO Drawer 1518, Lafayette, CA 94549 Tel: (415) 932-1143 [Emphasis is on architecture of France, Spain and Italy including early Christian and medieval].

Hart Slides World Wide, 224-A Alhambra, San Francisco, CA 94123 Tel: (415) 921-8549 [Architecture and urban settlement sites in Mediterranean countries, South Asia, Japan and Latin America are the emphasis of this company].

Hartill Art Associates, 'Prospect Place', R R.#6, St. Marys, Ontario N4X 1C8, Canada Tel: (591) 229-8752, Fax: (519) 284-4060 [Emphasis of the collection is architectural sites in North America, major South American countries, Southern Europe and Southeast Asia].

Icarus UK, 158 Boundaries Rd., London SW12 8HG, UK Tel: 0181-682 0900 [Emphasis of this dealer's collection is European architecture].

International Structural Slides, PO Box 466, Berkeley, CA 94701-0466 [The focus of this collection is toward modern and contemporary structures, structural factors and architectural engineering principles].

Islamic Perspectives, 42 Monument St., West Medford, MA 02155 Tel: (617) 354-1229 [Focus of this company is Islamic architecture in cities and villages of

Iran, Turkey, India and Spain].

Jericho World Images, PO Box 93, Free Union, VA 22940 Tel: (804) 973-6253 [This firm emphasizes Spanish Colonial and Islamic architecture].

Johnson Architectural Images, PO Box 9712, Madison, WI 53715 Tel: (608) 835-9187. [Slides of buildings dating from 500 B.C. to the present. The collection also emphasizes several 19th and 20th century architects and Chicago architecture].

Landslides, 25 Bay State Rd., Boston, MA 02215 Tel: (617) 536-6261 [Architecture and urban planning of the United States as presented through aerial views are the emphasis of this company].

Media for the Arts, 360 Thames St., PO Box 1101, Newport, RI 02840 Tel: (800) 554-6008, Fax: (401) 846-6580 [Slides emphasize 'Great American Architects' and periods in American architecture. Slides are sold in sets. Additional architectural slide sets examine various periods of architecture or of a country's history, e.g. Byzantine architecture in Greece, Dutch architecture, Egyptian architecture, etc.].

Mini-Aids, 177 Webster St., Box A261, Monterey, CA 93940 Tel: (408) 373-7018, Fax: (408) 373-2533 [Focus of this company's slides is on European architecture. Also, represents slide producers from Europe].

Moorhead/Schmidt Slide Collection, 3400 Montrose Boulevard, No. 302, Houston, TX 77006-4334 Tel: (713) 529-6905 [Produces and distributes architectural slides from all time periods].

H.L. Murvin/Architectural Books, Slides & Seminars, 500 Vernon Street, Oakland, CA 94610 Tel: (415) 658-7517 [Emphasis of this collection is Pre-Columbian, European, North and South American architecture].

Pictures of Record, Inc., 119 Kettle Creek Rd., Weston, CT 06883 Tel: (203) 227-3387, Fax: (203) 222-9673 [Slides of the architecture of archaeological sites in North and South America and the Near East are the focus of this vendor].

Rosenthal Art Slides, 5456 South Ridgewood Court, Chicago, IL 60615-5392 Tel: (312) 324-3367 [This company produces and distributes slides of architecture from all time periods and all geographical areas].

Sandak Visual Documents (Division of G.K. Hall & Co.), 180 Harvard Ave., Stamford, CT 06920 Tel: (203) 969-0442, Fax: (203) 967-2745 [Produces and distributes slides of art and architecture representing all time periods].

Saskia Cultural Documentation, Ltd., 2721 NW Cannon Way, Portland, OR 97229 Tel: (503) 520-8855, Fax: (503) 626-1162 [Vendor of high-quality slides which include extensive holdings of the architecture of Western Europe from ancient Greece to the 19th century].

Scholastic Slide Services, 605 Blair Road, Ottawa, Ontario K1J 7M3, Canada Tel: (613) 749-0862 [Emphasis of this vendor is Canadian architecture. Some European and US structures are also available].

Slides for Education, 22500 Rio Vista, St. Clair Shores, MI 48081 Tel: (313) 733-5815 [The focus of this collection is architecture and public art and the coverage is international in scope].

Streetscape Slides (Division of Image Management Corp.), PO Box 10862, Denver, CO 80210 Tel: (800) 728-8521, (303) 692-9261 [The architecture of northern Europe, the United States and Mexico is the focus of the slides from this vendor].

Taurgo Slides, 154 East 82nd St., New York, NY 10028 Tel: (212) 879-8555 [Slides of architecture from ancient Greece to the eighteenth century are produced by this vendor].

Tektoica Slides, 87 Howard St., Cambridge, MA 02139 Tel: (617) 266-0584 [Construction details and the architecture of North America, Europe, Japan and India are emphasized in the slides of the company].

Universal Color Slide Co., 8450 South Tamiami Trail, Sarasota, FL 34238-2936 Tel: (800) 326-1367, Fax: (800) 487-0250 [Produces both individual slides and slide sets of architectural content. Covers historical time periods from prehistoric to contemporary with a focus on Western Europe, North Africa and North America. Also produces video and filmstrip programmes which are historical surveys of architecture].

Visual Education, 133 Smart Ct., Encinitas, CA 92024 Tel: (619) 942-8405 [Provides and distributes sets of architectural slides focusing on Western art and architecture. Will also mount slides in glass mounts upon request].

Video producers and distributors

This is a brief sample of commercial firms which produce videos on architects and architecture.

ArtsAmerica, Art on Video, 9 Benedict Place, Greenwich, CT 06830.

Facets Video, 1517 West Fullerton Ave., Chicago, IL 60614 Tel: (800) 331-6197.

Insight Media, 2161 Broadway, New York, NY 10024.

Library Video Company, PO Box 1110/Dept. M-32, Bala Cynwyd, PA 19004

The Roland Collection, 22-D Hollywood Ave., Ho-Ho-Kus, NJ 07423
    Tel: (201) 251-8200, (800) 597-6526, (800) 59 ROLAND, Fax: (201) 251-8788
    or Peasmarch, East Sussex TN31 6XJ, UK Tel: +44 1797 230421, +44 1797 230677, Fax: +44 1797 230677.

Viewfinders, Inc., Uncommon Video!!, PO Box 1665, Evanston, IL 60204-1665.

Universal Color Slide Co. (see the entry under the slide section)

Weiner Video, Frederic H. Weiner Inc., 1325 2nd Ave., New Hyde Park, NY 11040.

World Microfilms Publications, Microworld House, 2-6 Foscote Mews, London W9 2HH, UK Tel: +44 171-266 2202, Fax: +44 171-266 2314 [Besides its own products, this company also distributes slides, tape-slide programmes, videotapes and microforms for Pidgeon Audio-Visual, Sussex Video, Lecon Arts. Slides focus on 'Masters of Architecture', British architects and specific buildings or architectural periods. Videos and tape-slide programmes follow a similar structure, emphasizing individual architects and/or specific works of individual architects].

CHAPTER NINE

IT: Geographic information systems

ROBIN WATERS

What is a GIS ?

Geographic information is a term normally used to describe information that has a spatial component relative to the earth's surface. Conventional maps and plans of various types have been used to depict such information in the past with varying degrees of success depending on the complexity of the information to be displayed. National atlases will often have tens or even hundreds of maps of the same area and at the same scale but each depicting a different set of data – topography, soil, geology, population, weather, vegetation, etc.

A geographic information system (GIS) enables data of this kind to be stored and organized in such a way that it can be retrieved, manipulated and presented in many different ways depending on the application being addressed. In the above example of a national atlas an agricultural advisor might ask where there is land that has a certain type of soil, is at a particular height above sea level and has a certain rainfall. A civil engineer might ask for the details of soil, geology and rainfall in a particular catchment area for a new dam — the catchment area could be automatically delineated by using the height (or terrain) model stored in the GIS.

In the late 1960s, computer-aided design (CAD) was developed and given a huge boost by the American space programme. These systems were intended to replace the drawing board and generally assumed that a designer started with a clean sheet. Most of the early applications were for mechanical and electrical design with relatively straightforward geometry but including varying degrees of three dimensional (3D) design and/or viewing capability. In the 1970s, digital mapping systems were developed, often from existing CAD systems. These were usually two dimensional, and were most useful in dealing with large scale maps (e.g. Ordnance Survey 1:1250 and 1:2500 maps) familiar to the construction industry. At the same time some of the CAD facilities were extended into civil engineering with design capability for roads, earthworks and large buildings.

At the beginning of the 1980s the term GIS was invented to describe the computer programs being used to analyze digital maps in ways which extended their use into many other fields. In particular, GIS were designed to answer questions such as: What features lie within a radius of five miles of this point? What features lie within a distance of one mile either side of this road? What areas have a certain soil and a certain rainfall and are less than 10 miles from a railway line? Academically, GIS tended to be the domain of the geographer rather than the engineer, or of computer departments. As a result it developed strongly in the 'small scale' and 'thematic' mapping applications such as human and environmental geography. A separate, but very well funded, set of applications was developed for military purposes and these revolved around digital terrain models for simulation, navigation and command and control functions.

Nevertheless, most of the applications for which GIS is now used were already described and were often being implemented in military research establishments or in the better equipped universities. Now, in the 1990s, GIS has come of age and is being integrated into any application with elements of spatial data. In fact it is sometimes said that in five years' time there will be few GIS systems as such; but that many other systems will have GIS technology embedded within them and will be known by different, application-oriented names.

Applications in construction

Site selection

Any planner or consulting engineer may now use a GIS to help select the site for a construction project. A major shopping centre must be placed where it will attract the maximum number of customers depending on the whereabouts of competing shops, on the distribution and wealth of the local population and on the geography and capacity of the local road network. These variables can now be modelled very successfully with GIS, and reliable datasets for this application are now being made available by public and private sector organizations, e.g. census, demographic profiles, roads. Similarly the selection of a dam site would use a GIS with terrain models of a catchment area, meteorological data, soil and land cover data, for example, using digital terrain models (DTMs), and meteorological, soil and environmental data. These are fed to a computer model with graphical output which is best displayed and analyzed with the GIS.

Site surveys

The normal format for delivery of site surveys from surveyors to the engineers or architects is now on floppy disk or other magnetic media. Before long it will routinely be sent by telephone line. It is arguable as to whether the computer systems used by the surveyor should be described as 'surveying', 'digital mapping' or 'GIS' systems. Those used by the architect or engineer will be CAD systems but may have GIS capabilities. The data may be put into specialized GIS systems for particular purposes. For efficient transfer of data, the survey system must be able to produce, and the CAD system must be able to read, a common format, such as those issued and used by the Ordnance Survey (OS), the various National Geographic Institutes (NGIs), the survey companies and professional institutions.

Design

A designer's work is made much more effective if relevant data are made available in the CAD system where they can be used at all stages of the design. Ideally this might include the geology, soils, topography, buildings, vegetation, etc. This information may come from different sources and some may need converting from an existing map or plan to add to a modern digital survey. All of these data, integrated into a common database, form the essential backdrop to the designer's work.

Visualization

The power of modern computers really comes into its own with the modern visualization packages that are available with both CAD and GIS software. With every development having to be fully investigated before planning permission or financial backing is forthcoming there is a need for accurate and sophisticated visualization to back up the environmental impact analysis which must be carried out. These may include complete computer generated models with background mapping information from a national database. Additionally, or alternatively, site or panoramic photographs can be incorporated into the models in order to add even more realism. Different weather or seasonal conditions (sun angle, fog, rain, leafless trees, etc.) may be built into the model and views generated for any sensible combination of these. Sources are the OS, the NGIs and survey companies.

As built surveys

When construction is complete there are often surveys carried out on behalf of the client to establish that buildings have been constructed to the correct specification and in the correct position. These can form the basis of a computerized database for subsequent management of the buildings and infrastructure if they are delivered in a compatible format. In the UK, the Ordnance Survey will wish to carry out a survey for the large scale database as soon as above ground structures are finalized. In theory these two functions could be carried out by the same team of surveyors with some savings to both. Practically, however, it is difficult to co-ordinate the timing and specification of the two surveys. Recent experiments in Scotland and Yorkshire are promising and it is to be hoped that the OS will be able to use a lot more data collected by other surveyors working for survey companies and the Land Registry (LR).

Asset recording

The first and arguably still the largest use of GIS technology is for the recording and management of the assets of large utility companies and local authorities who have very large investments in fixed pipes, cables and other structures. Historically these assets were recorded on large scale maps, a task which has become very expensive and labour intensive and one that could economically justify some of the earliest digital mapping and GIS systems.

Asset management

Once the assets are recorded on a database and kept up-to-date on a regular basis, the management of those assets can be aided by facilities available from the GIS technology. In utility companies these tasks might include the management of a related customer database which is linked to the distribution network to determine who has which services and who might be affected by an emergency. The engineering department can carry out network analysis and planning functions while the field crews can have large scale, up-to-date plots (or even on-line screens) for finding their own company's services and for avoiding other utility assets. The exchange of data between utilities and other interested parties (e.g. local authorities) has been a catalyst for the development of several systems in different countries. Accurate knowledge of the location of utilities' own plant and of the relative location of other underground services can provide not only savings in monetary terms but also a much improved safety record. It is particularly important to avoid damaging electricity and gas mains (if only for the safety of the workers) and telecoms failures will become less and less acceptable as the information superhighway becomes essential to every business.

GIS techniques

Data capture

Any GIS will only be as useful as the data with which it is built. In many of the utility systems mentioned above it was often suggested that the cost of data capture was between 50 per cent and 80 per cent of the total investment that must be made in a GIS. This may still be true for many systems. As the cost of hardware and software has come down, so the efficiency of data capture has improved and the availability of many other ('third party') datasets has increased. Even where off the shelf datasets are now available, there is still a large investment to be made in capturing the user's own information. This section deals with the different methods by which GIS can be populated with useful data. Ideally it might be considered that new data collected direct from the field or from various forms of remote sensing would always be preferred to the digitizing of existing maps and plans which must inevitably be out-of-date. However, the investment already made in the interpretation of the 'real world' into a map based 'model' may already be considerable - the more so if there are many extra notes and diagrams scribbled on the records. Underground plant may be more reliably recorded on existing plans than it can be traced by pipe detectors. Expensive, experienced employees might be needed to visit many locations on the ground when they might be better employed interpreting old plans or new photographs in the office. Advice may be found from organizations such as the Association of Geographic Information (AGI) and Construction Industry Computing Association (CICA), among others.

Field survey

Construction applications depend crucially on up-to-date field survey for their primary input. In some cases this might take the form of the updating and enhancement of existing mapping (e.g. OS plans/data) and will almost always now be carried out with digital recording field instruments such as the so called 'total-stations' which combine theodolite and laser distance measuring devices. It is now also possible to use the Global Positioning System (GPS) satellites for surveying down to centimetre accuracy in some circumstances, with output recorded in digital form. Whichever survey measurement systems are used it is vital that 'attribute' information is also added to the geometry of the 'map'. Specification of how much attribute information is to be included is a very important task for the commissioning engineer. There can be very large differences in the costing of data capture projects depending on the comprehensiveness and accuracy with which attributes are specified. The location of underground plant is crucial in order to avoid expensive disruption of networks and even danger to employees. Specialist organizations providing information on these include the Land & Hydrographic Survey Association (TSA), the Royal Institution of Chartered Surveyors (RICS) and the Institute of Civil Engineering Surveyors (ICES).

Remote sensing

Remote sensing from space was overhyped in the 1970s and early 1980s with very few satellites in orbit and relatively crude images being sent back to earth. These were useful for synoptic exploration and for building an environmental change database. For construction projects their use was limited to very large projects (e.g. dams and roads) in un-mapped areas where no other information was available. In the 1990s there are a range of satellites in orbit producing very high resolution images which can be ordered in advance from government agencies in several countries. The end of the cold war has enabled the military technology from east and west to be made available for civilian purposes and this is leading to an acceptance of remote sensed imagery as a source comparable, in some cases, to conventional aerial photographs. Because the imagery is in digital form as soon as it is collected, it can be processed easily in digital systems. Also, because of the height from which the imagery is collected, it suffers from less distortion due to variable topography in hilly or mountainous areas. The major sources of this type of information are the National Remote Sensing Centre (NRSC) in the UK, SPOT Image in France and NASA in the USA.

Aerial photography

It is not often realized what a large role aerial photography plays in the surveying and mapping tasks carried out for the construction industry. The tools available for the processing of aerial photographs have kept up with the digital computer revolution and there is now intense competition in the production of semi-automatic systems which use an overlapping pair of photographs (or scanned images of photographs) to produce 3D models, line maps or image maps in a very cost-effective manner. Colour photography is almost invariably used and this enables skilled interpreters to deduce valuable information about structures, vegetation, land use, etc. as well as helping the photogrammetrist to make more accurate measurements more consistently than with the old black and white photographs. Even where conventional paper plans are to be produced, the photogrammetric processes will now be carried out digitally and therefore datasets are produced which can be stored for the future. The measurement of areas and distances from aerial photographs requires an understanding of the geometry of the images and in anything but the flattest terrain it requires specialist equipment and/or software. (Consult TSA and RICS.)

Digitizing of existing maps and plans

Where existing maps and plans are sufficiently up-to-date or where it is necessary to have historical information included in a model, digitizing will be required. For 20 years or so the most popular form of digitizing was the tracing of points and lines with a hand-held cursor on a digitizing table or tablet. This method could cope with virtually any graphic on almost any material and, provided that the operator could see the features that were to be traced, the process was reasonably foolproof. It also produces a vector representation of features well suited to the majority of digital mapping, CAD and GIS software. However, it requires very stringent quality control and is very time-consuming. Today, more and more digitizing is carried out by scanning of the original documents into a raster image file which can either be used directly or subsequently traced (with more or less human input depending on the type of map involved) into a vector, feature-oriented format. Scanners and sufficiently powerful PCs can now be cost justified for virtually all digitizing work and enable the conversion process to be carried out with more 'on-line' quality control which leads to significantly more cost effective digitizing work. (Consult AGI.)

Data structuring

Data structuring begins as the maps are being digitized and is an essential prelude to the use of data in a speedy and fully integrated way. Many GIS now have several acceptable data structures, from simple 'spaghetti' vectors that might be hand digitized in a hurry, through topologically structured line segments which form junctions and polygons with links between them, to complex 3D structures with intersecting surfaces. For many purposes it is necessary to be able to view vector information overlaid on raster images (line maps over scanned aerial photographs) or images on 3D surfaces (satellite images draped on terrain models). The GIS plays a significant role in ensuring that all of these different datasets are structured correctly so that they are in the same co-ordinate system and at sensible resolutions. For further information contact AGI and/or CICA.

Quality control

Ensuring that data is captured (or checked) to a particular specification required for an application is not a trivial process. Neglect of sufficient quality control in many early GIS led to extra expense, reduced functionality or total failure. In the early stages of implementation it is very often the case that a GIS is being compared with a pre-existing manual system and users or managers will be hypercritical of the output quality compared to the plots with which they are familiar. Techniques for quality control include: the overlay of output plots with input documents (for completeness and accuracy); the checking of links between different bits of geometry (such as closed polygons, fully matched junctions, etc.) for topological consistency; the completeness and validity of attributes (that all houses have numbers, that all spot heights have a valid height); and the mundane spelling checks on names and text annotation. Some checking can be fully automatic whereas other checks may require interpretation of displays on colour screens or the production of various types of plots. It should always be remembered that topographical maps and plans are usually depicting a fairly random landscape! Unlike engineering drawings with their straight lines and mathematical curves, maps deal in random curves and arbitrarily placed features. This makes completely automatic checking impossible and calls for the application of the normal industrial quality control procedures with random checks and realistic error budgets. (See AGI and RICS.)

Databases in GIS

A GIS with a dataset loaded fulfils most of the criteria defining a database. It has meaningful data, methods for finding particular elements of the data and tools for extracting, processing and outputting the resulting information. However, it is very often the case, perhaps as a hangover from the days of simpler CAD type digital mapping, that the 'map' or 'graphic' in a GIS is referred to separately from the attribute 'database'. In fact many GIS enable typical desktop databases to link to their essentially geographical data. Simple route finding systems will often enable the user to link an address file by 'look- up' via a gazetteer or table of postcodes which have 'been 'geo-referenced'. Many GIS still handle the graphics and attribute data in different data structures because of the nature of the data types involved. Digital maps are often very large files with variable length records and the peculiarities of 2D or 3D co-ordinates. Attribute data can be straightforward, simple, alphanumeric, fixed length records which fit easily in conventional databases, relational or otherwise. Most databases are listed by AGI or the British Computer Society (B CompS).

Spatial analysis

Spatial analysis is the essence of GIS. Without this analytical functionality, GIS would just be digital mapping with an associated database. With spatial analysis, GIS becomes a uniquely powerful tool for any application in which the distribution of variables in a 2D or 3D space is significant. Although certain spatial operators were associated with different data structures in the early days of GIS, it is now the case that the majority of GIS provide similar functionality whether they have raster, vector or mixed data structures. Typical spatial operators are:

- network analysis (e.g. travel planning, utility planning)
- distances and timings across country (e.g. military planning)
- visibility analysis (e.g. environmental impact, cellular radio)
- overlay analysis (e.g. agricultural planning, impact analysis)
- spatial correlation (e.g. pollution tracing, epidemiology)
- spatial aggregation (e.g. electoral planning, disaster relief)
- spatial disaggregation (e.g. sub-divisions for housing).

Presentation and output

The majority of future 'users' of a GIS will never see the computer or even the screen used by the operator. They will be the managers, planners, engineers or the general public who will see only the end results of the GIS processing. They may only see a single printed map or a list or even a single name that is the answer to the question that they posed and to which a GIS has provided the answer. It follows therefore that the GIS presentation and output functions are absolutely vital to the success of the system. It is still important that the screen-based user interface is tuned to the needs of the operator and that the local plotter or hard copy device is sufficiently fast or of high enough resolution. However, the success or failure of a GIS will ultimately depend on whether the directors or the chief executives perceive that they, or their customers, are getting value for money. The output of the GIS (either directly or via downstream systems) must provide better information, more timely information or lower cost information if it is to justify itself. The plots must be fit for purpose, produced on time and as economically as possible. A simple map with a simple message will be much better in many cases than a very complex map with a lot of irrelevant features and too many colours. A single value with a reliability guide (e.g. time and distance from A to B) may be all that the end user requires. A map is probably only needed as an option. Presentation standards are available from AGI and the British Cartographic Society (BCartS).

Data exchange

Very few GIS exist in isolation. They need to receive data from other systems (GIS or others) and also to transmit data. The formats and protocols for transferring GIS data are still being developed. In lieu of 'official' world, national or even industry standards there are many different one-off or de facto 'standards' being used for data exchange. Various standards from particular industries are used where appropriate (AGI, CICA, BCompS, RICS), for example:

- **dxf** - the drawing exchange standard (originally from AutoCAD) is widely used for simple vector digital mapping and the graphics of some GIS.

- dBase ASCII format is used for various statistical data associated with GIS.
- **pcx** or **tiff** formats are popular for raster image files.
- various GIS software vendors have proprietary exchange formats which have been adopted by other systems out of necessity. (ESRI Arclnfo Export, Intergraph SIF are two examples)
- industry standards have developed for exchange of data for oil exploration, for construction, for navigation and for environmental projects.
- National Standards include the National Transfer Format (NTF) used in the UK, particularly by the Ordnance Survey for sales of its digital map data.

Hardware

GIS development was initiated in the age of the 'mini-computer' and was not seen as a 'business' application. The main developments took place in (or for) governments (particularly the military), public utilities and academia. The data handling requirements were large for their time and peripherals were specialist and expensive. All of these factors led from mini-computers to work stations and hence to operating systems such as VMS and the various versions of UNIX. Furthermore, partly because of the size of the datasets, and partly because of the nature of the applications, it was essential that data could be shared over networks and that its use and security should be centrally controlled.

In the late 1980s developments began to favour increasing use of PCs for GIS with the increasing power and decreasing cost of the platforms themselves and the increasing availability of useful data from governments and commerce at a reasonable price and in PC readable formats. With the development of business applications of GIS and the proliferation of PCs in academia and commerce, GIS systems are now available for both IBM compatibles (predominantly under DOS or Windows) and Macs, although the former dominate the market. The choice of platform for a new GIS user is now more likely to be determined by existing hardware to which access is available than by an 'objective' study. However, there are many GIS systems which, while available in PC versions for small datasets, still need work station power for operational requirements. Many GIS have both UNIX and Windows versions (for example) and a large configuration can include both, networked together, in order to get the best of both worlds. Sharing of rapidly changing data in applications such as utility asset management and military command and control still require central control of the databases involved.

Digitizing tablets have been the mainstay of the data capture industry for many years and are still the lowest cost input device for small volumes and/or varied types of graphics documents if vector data structures are required. The tablet may be solid or back lit and of varying sizes with a hand-held cursor featuring a pointing mark (dot, circle and/or cross hairs) and several buttons. Point and click to record the table coordinates of a point, repeat the process to capture a line. Extra buttons when operating with appropriate software enable the operator to snap lines together, close polygons, associate certain attributes and values or carry out some editing functions. Extra menus can be added for further feature coding, editing, etc. Virtually all GIS software supports digitizing tablets as input devices.

For large maps or graphics to be captured very speedily into digital image (raster) formats, scanners may be used. Typically these feed the document (A2 to A0 or larger) between two rollers and the image is passed over a scanning head. More accurate scanners use either a revolving drum on which the map is stuck down, or a large flatbed over which the scanning head moves. Smaller documents (typically up to A3 size) can be scanned on desktop page scanners. The result of the scanning process is a black and white (1 bit), grey scale (2-8 bit) or colour (8-32 bit) image file on the computer disk. For GIS purposes this image must be registered by reference to known points on the image such as corner marks or grid intersections and then stored in the relevant GIS format. It will be appreciated that whereas a black and white raster image of a line map can be compressed to volumes comparable with the vector equivalent, a full colour file representing an A0 printed map requires tens of megabytes and if the document was a photograph it will be even bigger! These images are of course completely 'unintelligent'. Colours on them will be colours (not vegetation or soil types), line 'features' will not exist as such but merely as changes in the whole image and text will also be completely unrecognized. Raster images may be useful as 'backdrops' with no further processing or they may be the first stage in a digitizing process aimed at providing attributed vector information identical to that captured from a digitizing table.

Extraction of intelligent vector information from a raster image can be approached in several ways and the most appropriate will be determined by the volume of information required, its complexity and the quality and resolution of the original image.

- Image processing. Various automatic processes can be applied to a scanned image in order to clean it up, enhance certain types of feature and separate out different colours. Some of these can be run during the scanning process itself which can speed up the overall result and reduce the size of the data files finally stored. Typical operations would be the removal of speckles (less than a certain number of pixels), edge enhancement on a grey scale image (to pick out lines) and selection of particular features by their

colour (e.g. contour lines, black text, etc.).
- Heads-up digitizing. This process requires an operator to carry out the same operations on the raster image on the screen (with the screen cursor controlled by a mouse) as would have been required on the map on the digitizing table. This would typically be the point-by-point tracing of lines from the image with appropriate input of attributes and topology. However, the big advantage is that the vector drawing immediately appears overlaid on the raster image enabling the operator to check accuracy and progress using the normal pan and zoom commands.
- Computer-assisted feature recognition. Given an image with sufficient resolution and clarity, it is possible for some software to follow lines through the image automatically and even to recognize junctions, right angles, small symbols and words or blocks of text. The operator directs this process and is able to intervene wherever it fails or gets confused. As with heads-up digitizing, the operator can follow progress and ensure the completeness and accuracy of the digitizing.
- Automatic feature recognition and raster/vector conversion. The holy grail of the digitizing world has always been the fully automatic conversion of raster images of maps into intelligent vector datafiles. Progress has been relatively slow! The process works best for good quality line work of a relatively simple nature. Contours (which should never touch or cross each other) are one example, but even where the contour colour separation (with no other features) is available, it is often found that lines do touch in steep areas and numbering of contours interrupts the smooth lines as well as breaks for other reasons. Similarly the polygon maps used to represent soils, land use, geology and other natural or artificial boundary features can provide logical checks for automatic digitizing to achieve good results. In general it has been found that this type of software needs considerable tuning to produce acceptable results and it therefore requires tens or even hundreds of similar specification maps to justify the costs of the tuning process.
- There is also a market for the 'spaghetti' vectorizing of a line drawing where the end result only needs to be a 'vector image' with no intelligence and where the number of disconnected small vectors making up a feature or a piece of text is of no consequence. This simply enables GIS (or CAD) software with no raster background capability to achieve a similar result.

The impact of the Global Positioning System (GPS) on the world of GIS is appropriately mentioned here. Small portable receivers using signals from a constellation of 24 satellites, and requiring very little operator training, can now determine position on the earth's surface to the accuracy required by the majority of GIS. The implication is that 'digitizing' of point features (electricity poles, manhole covers, etc.) and linear features (roads, pipelines, rivers, etc.) is now economically feasible when they are visited by engineers and maintenance crews for any reason. In many cases this may be a way of revising, correcting or even replacing the conventional digital data collected from maps which may often have been inaccurate and out-of-date. However, it must be appreciated that relative positions of adjacent features on maps are usually quite accurate whereas superimposition of 'new' satellite co-ordinates on 'old' (and often less accurate) map co-ordinate systems may cause more confusion than it solves. National mapping agencies such as the Ordnance Survey will provide a service to correct GPS positions to the national grid and should certainly be consulted if this method of data capture is likely to be followed. (See also RICS, TSA and ICES.)

Given the visual nature of much of the output of GIS for most applications, the display processing and screen resolution and colours must be able to cope with large, high resolution colour images. Multicoloured pen (line drawing) or inkjet (continuous colour image) A0 plotting devices can now be obtained for between £5000 and £10 000. Higher throughput electrostatic plotters can be up to five times more expensive. Since many users will judge the performance of the whole GIS by the appearance of its output, it is vital to get as good a plotter as can be afforded. Not all GIS support (or fully support) all plotters directly. It is sometimes therefore necessary to use intermediate plot processing software and this may be even more useful if the plotter is supporting more than one application. Laser or inkjet printers are perfectly adequate for GIS output on smaller formats.

Data sources

Metadata and directories

There are few comprehensive directories of digital data for GIS systems anywhere in the world. Each GIS vendor usually provides some basic data or has a list of potential suppliers for applications already covered. Even when datasets are located it is very difficult to assess their relevance for a new application. Standards for metadata are only just being promulgated and this is more likely to lead to action in the USA where a presidential directive has recently mandated federal bodies to make metadata available in a standard format. In Europe there is some activity by CERCO (Comité Européen de Responsable Cartographie Officielle), the organization representing all of the National Geographic Institutes and they are co-operating with a commercial project (OMEGA,

GeoInformation International) aimed at providing metadata for both conventional maps and digital data. In the UK, after a very slow start there are now several initiatives aimed at providing comprehensive directories for digital geographical data. These include the SINES service from the Ordnance Survey, which deals with government data sources, a directory produced by Oxford Brookes University and a longer term initiative by a team at Manchester University. There is also the annual *International GIS sourcebook*, published by GIS World, which covers data sources in the USA in particular detail.

National mapping agencies (Geographical Institutes)

Official mapping is organized differently from country to country. The UK and Ireland have Ordnance Surveys (separate for Great Britain, Northern Ireland and Ireland) while many other European countries have Geographical Institutes or military mapping agencies for medium and small scale mapping. Larger scale maps and plans are usually the responsibility of local authorities and/or the national cadastral offices. Most of the official mapping agencies of Europe support CERCO and their addresses are listed in Table 1 below. The extent to which official mapping is available in digital form varies from country to country. There is no European Union body charged with a topographic mapping responsibility although Eurostat in Luxembourg has built a small scale GIS called GISCO from which 1:1M and smaller scale datasets are available.

The Ordnance Survey (GB) is the largest supplier of digital mapping information for Great Britain. Vector versions of all 1:1250 (towns and cities) and 1:2500 (remaining developed land) scale maps are now available and are regularly updated. Raster versions of the 1:10 000 (b/w) and 1:50 000 (colour) are available for the whole of Great Britain. The 1:250 000 and 1:625 000 maps are also available as digital vector files. This comprehensive coverage makes Great Britain by far the most advanced country (of its size) anywhere in the world for publicly available digital mapping. However, for construction purposes it may often be necessary to update and upgrade the OS map data, not least because at the 1:1250 and 1:2500 scales it has no contour or height information other than a few spot heights and benchmarks. However, there is a comprehensive terrain model with a horizontal resolution of 50 metres which may be useful for line of sight, radio planning and environmental impact visualization studies. OS also provides, with Supermap, a very good service for up-to-date large scale maps, printed on demand and to the user's specification. Unfortunately it is not yet possible to get the same service for digital data though it cannot be far away.

In North America the United States Geological Survey (USGS) has federal responsibility for national mapping at scales of 1:25 000 and smaller, while states and municipalities have responsibility for larger scale mapping. USGS has a large quantity of its 'quad-sheets' now becoming available in digital form. In Canada the Energy, Mines and Resources Ministry produces federal mapping in digital form. The provinces have their own mapping organizations.

Geological, soil and land use/land cover surveys

Geological conditions are of great concern to the construction industry and national, government-funded bodies have developed over the last 150 years to address this need. In the UK the British Geological Survey (BGS) carries out fieldwork and research, compiles maps and databases and publishes the results in a variety of forms. Most of its work is now carried out with a view to storing, manipulating and presenting the information in digital form. BGS has invested in GIS and is a major source of information for the construction industry. In addition to surface and solid geology, the survey provides an index of boreholes, specially detailed maps of the availability of aggregates and the geochemical analysis of rivers and streams throughout the country. A joint publication with Wimpey Environmental includes digital datasets of various construction related conditions such as susceptibility to frost. Arup GeoTechnic is responsible for a DoE sponsored database of abandoned mining operations and British Coal also maintains extensive records of its pits.

Official soil and land cover surveys of Great Britain are carried out by the Soil Survey and Land Research Centre and the Institute of Terrestrial Ecology for England and Wales, and by the Macaulay Land Use Research Institute for Scotland. Rendel Geotechnics maintains a Landslide Databank for Great Britain which was originally sponsored by the DoE. The Institute of Hydrology has a Water Information System which holds a comprehensive model of the British topography with derived drainage and run-off characteristics for calculating the effect of rainfall and floods.

In the rest of Europe, similar agencies exist though none appear to be as far advanced in promoting their products and services to potential users. In the USA the US Geological Survey combines the functions of geology and topography which in the UK are divided between the BGS and the OS. Individual states have their own geological surveys operating at a more detailed level. The Federal Soil Conservation Service has been providing digital datasets for many years.

Environmental agencies

National governments have a range of environmental research agencies which collect and analyze information of use to the construction industry. In the UK the Natural Environment Research Council (NERC) runs several different operations, such as the Institute of Terrestrial Ecology (which produces land use statistics and datasets) and the Institute of

Hydrology (river and ground water research). All of these use GIS and can produce datasets for other GIS users. The National Rivers Authority has responsibility for the management of the UK's rivers and is implementing a very large GIS in order to integrate all of the topographical, meteorological and surface related information required to predict flooding, detect pollution sources and monitor any plans that affect rivers directly or indirectly. The Meteorological Office has digital data back to 1960 and the National Environmental Technology Centre (Air Quality Section) has information relating to various pollutants in the atmosphere also dating back to 1960.

The US Federal Emergency Management Agency (FEMA) produces flood plain data, for example, and the Environmental Protection Agency (EPA) maps natural and man-made environmental hazards. International institutions operate at regional, continental and global scales to monitor the environment and to carry out research on the causes and effects of changes to the environment. Regional operations typically concern themselves with river basin management, animal and bird migration and the local effects of atmospheric pollution. GIS is used for all of these purposes and the data may be available. Continental operations, such as the European Environment Agency, recently established in Copenhagen, will have a wider brief but may also directly affect legislation for many nations. The EU CORINE programme aims to generate a grid based dataset for the whole of Europe which will enable the effects of pollution to be monitored in the long term. The United Nations Environment Programme has a global GIS that aims to provide advanced warning of phenomena such as global warming and desertification.

Satellite images

Remotely sensed images of the earth's surface derived from satellite based scanners have been used for synoptic views of large areas for many years. They have been supplied, in the main, by the Landsat series of satellites orbited by NASA in the USA and the SPOT series launched and operated by the SPOT Image company in France. Latterly the Russian space programme has been allowed to market imagery in the West and some of this is of much higher resolution than had been available from Western sources. This in turn has had the effect of opening some previously secret western technology to the commercial world. Both Russian and SPOT images can be ordered for particular areas at particular times, though weather conditions mean that 100% success is not always achievable or may be delayed. The images may be directly scanned in space and transmitted to ground stations for further processing as in the case of SPOT and Landsat or they may be scanned on the ground from conventional photographs taken in space and returned to earth for development. This latter process is used for some of the Russian imagery and is one reason why it may have a higher resolution. In the UK the main source of satellite imagery is the NRSC which acts as an agent for most primary producers of remote sensing data. Many GIS can now accept these images directly, though they require geo-referencing and transforming to the GIS co-ordinate system. This may be performed by the image provider, by a value added processor, or may be left to the end-user. Various types of image processing may also be employed to enhance the image, either to extract particular types of information or to compare more up-to-date images with their predecessors.

Aerial photographs

Air photographs can provide a wealth of information for construction projects. They may be used as an input for the digital mapping process using photogrammetric techniques, usually by specialist firms. They may also be used as a source of qualitative information about the vegetation, land use or building types which can be added to a GIS. More recently it has become possible to put scanned aerial photographs into GIS that have the necessary coloured image background facilities. In the latter case care must be taken to rectify the image to the GIS co-ordinate system and it must be understood that positional and measurement errors in the image may be present in areas with considerable height differences across a single photograph. Specialized and sophisticated orthophotographical software may be able to take care of such distortions but will considerably increase the cost of the image.

New aerial photography can be commissioned from many organizations and reasonable notice should be given to allow for suitable weather and lighting conditions. If leaves or crops are likely to obscure features or cause difficult measuring conditions it is even more important to commission the photography well in advance. Existing libraries of air photographs may often contain sufficient photography for contouring or general reconnaissance and these can be found in a variety of companies and institutions. In the UK, the National Association of Aerial Photographic Libraries (NAPLIB), publishes (through ASLIB) a very comprehensive directory of sources of air photography (current and historical, UK and world-wide) and the Ordnance Survey runs an enquiry service for up-to-date coverage. Older photography can be very valuable in researching previous land uses and original topography before more recent earthworks, tips, etc.

Geo-demographic data and commercial 'value added' suppliers

Geo-demographic data are based on the information gathered by national statistical offices for various purposes. While obviously vital for national and local government planning, these data are now being used for a variety of commercial purposes. When combined with the bounda-ries of the census areas themselves and with a variety of other adminis-trative or postcode boundaries the resulting analyses can be very powerful tools for direct marketing and site selection. In England and Wales the Office of Population Censuses and Surveys (OPCS) sells data directly and through several accredited census 'agencies'. The equivalent in Scotland is the General Register Office (GRO). The European Commis-sion has a statistical office (Eurostat) which attempts to harmonize the statistics from each member country and has developed a GIS capability to help. GISCO, as it is known, is now being marketed.

In addition to the data sources mentioned above, there are now a grow-ing number of organizations offering value added datasets for use in GIS. These are often repackaging of government data in formats or structures which better match particular systems or applications than the standard formats normally supplied. This growth industry has taken off much more quickly and profitably in the USA, where the government data is not copyright and can be bought for the marginal cost of copying it. In Eu-rope the copyright on government data is strictly enforced and charges are often set to recover much of the cost of the data collection as well as the cost of dissemination. The contrasting results of these different phi-losophies are argued about fiercely in the GIS press and there are good cases to be made for both sides. Although the OS is frequently attacked for unimaginative and restrictive practices as well as high cost of data, it is the world leader in the detail and coverage of its digital database. Major commercial publishers of GIS data in the UK are the Automobile Associa-tion (through Kingswood), Bartholomew/Times, The Data Consultancy, GisDATA, GeoInformation International and MR Datagraphics.

Land ownership and the other charges that might exist on a piece of development land must be investigated at the planning stage. H.M. Land Registry is the source of information on registered land for Eng-land and Wales (though there is still much land unregistered in the UK) and there are equivalent bodies in Scotland and Northern Ireland. There is now an on-line database available to carry out searches on non-confi-dential information though there is as yet no digital access to the plans. However, LR is taking the lead in the experiments now taking place with a view to setting up a National Land Information System based on OS large scale data and including information from the Registry, the Valuation Office and from local authorities. Local authorities may have digital data available from their land charges departments but these have not been in the forefront of GIS implementations.

Archaeological sites and the various boundaries of national parks, nature reserves and sites of special scientific interest are all available in digital form for use in GIS, the former from English Heritage and the latter from English Nature (via MR Datagraphics). Finally, there is a useful set of data held in the Highways Agency in Leeds which catalogues the transport and road traffic issues familiar to all. Data includes roads in digital form, accident statistics and traffic flows.

Systems

It is not the place of this chapter to try and list all GIS vendors or even those with a special construction-oriented bias. Many CAD systems, on their own or with suitable 'add-ons', will carry out GIS tasks adequately. AutoCAD by AutoDesk is by far the most popular CAD system in the world and now has several GIS capabilities itself, has many GIS value added packages and exchanges data very readily with specialist GIS software. If engineers or architects are already using an AutoCAD system it may pay to use it for GIS initially.

Microstation by Intergraph has a pedigree that includes all types of work station-based CAD applications and now integrates with the Modular GIS Environment (MGE) which provides a full range of GIS capabilities on PC platforms. Intergraph systems have been particularly strong in utility and military applications but have a complete range of functionality.

PC ArcInfo from the Environmental Systems Research Institute (ESRI) is probably the best known GIS in the world. For users with existing or bought-in datasets, not requiring data capture facilities, ArcView provides a very cost-effective GIS capability. ESRI, as its name suggests, started off in the environmental application area and has maintained a lead in that area. For more thematic-oriented GIS (for site selection, route finding, geo-demographic analysis, etc.) the leading desktop packages are MapInfo (MapInfo Corp.), Atlas (Strategic Mapping), SPANS (Tydac) and Tactician (Tactics International). These GIS started on PC platforms and have no work station antecedents to limit them - on the other hand they may have limitations when seeking to handle very large datasets or carry out complex processing.

Terminology

For the real beginner there is a free *Rough guide to GIS* available from GeoInformation International (GI), the publishers of *GIS Europe* and *Mapping Awareness*. This might be suitable for handing out to the board of directors or for members of staff who do not use GIS directly but ought to have some knowledge of the subject. GIS Tutor 2 is a PC or Mac-based introduction to GIS also available from GI.

AGI produces a *Dictionary of GIS* which explains most of the terms which a user of GIS will come across. This has an British English bias so the glossary in the *GIS World sourcebook* may be more useful to those in the Americas.

Conferences and exhibitions

Conferences, exhibitions, seminars and meetings are the best way of keeping up-to-date and are well covered in the relevant journals, particularly:

UK	*Mapping awareness*	GeoInformation International, UK
Europe	*GIS Europe*	GeoInformation International, UK
	Surveying world	GITC, Netherlands
USA	*GIS World*	GIS World, USA
	Business geographics	GIS World, USA
	GeoInfo systems	Advanstar Publications, USA
Australia	*GIS User*	S. Pacific Science Press, Australia

Table 1: CERCO member agencies March 1994

Country	Address	Phone and Fax Nos.
Austria*	Austrian Federal Office of Metrology and Surveying Schiffamtsgasse 1-3, A 1025 Vienna	+43 222 211 76/3602 +43 222 216 10 62
Belgium*	Institut Geographique National Abbaye de la Cambre 13, 1050 Bruxelles	+32 2 648 64 80 +32 2 646 25 42
Croatia	Geodetski Fakultet Kaciceva 26, Zagreb	+38 49 442600 +38 49 519305
Cyprus	Cyprus Dept. of Lands and Surveys 29 Michalakopoulo Street, Nicosia	+357 2 302929 +357 2 366171
Denmark*	Kort-og Mabrikelstyrelsen Reutemestervej 8, 2400 Copenhagen	+45 3587 5050 +45 3587 5059
Estonia	Estonian State Land Department Mustamae Strasse 51, PO Box 1635, Talliuv EE0006	+372 142 528202 +372 142 528401
Finland*	National Board of Survey PO Box 84, SF-00521 Helsinki	+358 0 154 5003 +358 0 154 5005
France*	Institut Geographique National Av. Pasteur 2, 94160 Saint-Mande	+33 1 439 88273 +33 1 439 88445
Germany*	I fAG Richard-Strauss Allee 11, D-6000 Frankfurt A.M.	+49 69 633 33 71 +49 69 633 34 25
Greece*	Hellenic Military Geographical Service 4 Evelpidon Strasse 11362, Pedion Areos, Athens	+30 1 884281216 +30 1 8817376
Hungary	Department of Lands and Mapping Ministry of Agriculture H-1860 Budapest 55, PO Box 1 Hungary	+36 1 131 4130 +36 1 111 2021 or +36 1 153 0518
Iceland	Landmelingar Islands (Iceland Geodetic Survey) Laugavegi 178 Box 5060, 125 Reykjavik	+354 1 681611 +354 1 680614
Ireland*	Ordnance Survey Phoenix Park, Dublin 8	+353 1 8206100 +353 1 8204156

Table 1: Continued.

Country	Address	Phone and Fax Nos.
Italy*	Capo Sazione Relazioni Internazionali	+39 55 12775 - 267
	Istituto Geografico Militara Italiano	+39 55 282172
	Via Cesare Battisti 10, 50100-Firenze	
Latvia	Dept. of Geodesy and Cartography	+371 0132 211263
	11 Novembra krasamala 31, IV-1484 Riga	+371 0123 225039
Lithuania	Lithuania State Dept. of Surveying and	+370 0122 62 71 05
	Mapping	+370 0122 62 76 18
	A Jaksto 9, 2600 Vilnius	
Luxembourg*	Administration du Cadastre et de la	+352 449 01266
	Topographie	+352 449 01333
	BP 1761, L-1017 Luxembourg	
Netherlands*	Topografische dienst	+31 5910 96201
	PO Box 115, 7800 AC Emmen	+31 5910 96296
Norway	Statens Kartverk	+47 67 19000
	N-3300 Honefoss	+47 67 18001
Poland	Ministry of Physical Planning and	+48 2 628 73 64
	Construction	
	Department of Geodesy, Cartography	+48 2 628 58 87
	and Land Management	
	Wspolna 2, PL - 00926 Warsaw	
Portugal*	Instituto Geographico e Cadastral	+351 1 609925
	Prays Da Esbrela, 1200 Lisboa	+351 1 3970248
Slovak	Geodesy, Cartography and Cadastre	+42 7 492002
Republic	Authority	+42 7 497573
	Hlboke Road 2, 813 23 Bratislava	
Slovenia	Republiska geodetska uprava	+386 1 312315
	Kristanova 1, 61000 Ljubljana	+386 1 122021
Spain*	Centro Nacional de Informacion	+34 1 554 16 45
	Geografico	+34 1 553 29 13
	C/General Ibanez de Ibero 3,	
	28003 Madrid	
Sweden*	National Land Survey of Sweden	+46 26 153423
	S-801 82 Galve	+46 26 653160
Switzerland	Office Federal de Topographie	+41 31 9632111
	Seftigenstrasse 264, CH-3084 Wabern	+41 31 9632459
Turkey	General Command of Mapping	+90 4 3197740
	TR 06100 Cebeci, Ankara	+90 4 3201495
UK*	Ordnance Survey	+44 1703 792 052
	Southampton SO9 4DH	+44 1703 792 660
UK*	Ordnance Survey of Northern Ireland	+44 1232 661244
	Stranmillis Court, Belfast BT9 5BJ	+44 1232 683211

*Members of the European Union at January 1995

Table 2: Different organization of mapping responsibilities in European Union

Country	Maps > 1:10k	1:10k to 1:100k	Civ/Mil/Loc
UK, Ireland	Ordnance Survey	Ordnance Survey	Civil Gov. Agency
France, Belgium, Denmark, Luxembourg, Spain, Portugal, Italy	Local Authority Institute Cadastres	National Geographic	Civil Gov. Agency
Greece, Netherlands	Local Authority	Military Survey	Military
Germany	Lander (States)	Lander (States)	Civil

Table 3: Magazines, journals and yearbooks

Title	Freq	Publisher
Geographic information - the yearbook of the Association for Geographic Information	annual	Taylor & Francis, UK
International GIS sourcebook	annual	GIS World, USA
Mapping awareness	10 p.a.	GeoInformation International, UK
GIS Europe	10 p.a.	GeoInformation International, UK
GIS World	10 p.a.	GIS World, USA
Business geographics	6 p.a.	GIS World, USA
Geodetical info magazine (GIM)	12 p.a.	GITC, Netherlands
Surveying world (SW)	6 p.a.	GITC, Netherlands
International journal of geographic information systems	n.k.	Taylor & Francis, UK
The photogrammetric record	2 p.a.	The Photo - grammetric Society, UK
Cartographic journal	2 p.a.	British Cartographic Society, UK

References and bibliography

Selected works of general interest and those with particular relevance to the architectural and construction industry are included here. Not all are referred to in the text. They give a useful current guide to texts in this field.

American Society for Photogrammetry & Remote Sensing (1991) *Integration of remote sensing and geographic information systems.* American Society for Photogrammetry & Remote Sensing.
Anson, R.W. and Ormeling, F.J. (1993) *Basic cartography.* vol. I. 2nd edn. Elsevier Applied Science.
Avery, Thomas Eugene (1992) *Fundamentals of remote sensing and airphoto interpretation.* 5th ed. Macmillan USA (Maxwell Macmillan International).

Belward, Alan S. and Valenzuela, Carlos R. (1991) *(eds.) Remote sensing and geographical information systems for resource management in developing countries.* Kluwer Academic Publishers.

Birkin, M. (1995) *Intelligent GIS: location decisions and strategic planning.* Longman Scientific & Technical.

Boehme, R. (1993) (ed.) *Inventory of world topographic mapping.* vol. 1: Western Europe, North America and Australasia. vol. 2: South America, Central America and Africa. vol. 3: Eastern Europe, Asia, Oceania and Antarctica. Pergamon.

Boxall, S.R. *et al.* (1993) *Airborne remote sensing of coastal waters.* HMSO in association with National Rivers Authority.

Buiten, Henk J. and Clevers, Jan G.P.W. (1994) *Land observation by remote sensing: theory and applications.* Gordon and Breach.

Cassettari, Seppe (1993) *Introduction to integrated geo-information management.* Chapman & Hall.

Cracknell, A.R. and Hayes, L.W.B. (1990) (eds.) *Remote sensing yearbook 1990.* 3rd edn. Taylor & Francis.

Craglia, Massimo (1991) *GIS in Italian urban planning.* Sheffield: University of Sheffield, Department of Town & Regional Planning.

Drury, S.A. (1990) *A guide to remote sensing: interpreting images of the earth.* Oxford University Press.

European GIS yearbook. (1994) Miles Arnold and Blackwell NCC in association with *Mapping Awareness.*

GIS World (1994) *International GIS sourcebook.* 5th edn. GIS World.

Green, D.R., Rix, D. and Cadoux-Hudson, J. (1993) (eds.) *Geographic information 1994: the source book for GIS.* Taylor & Francis.

Gunston, M. (1993) *Geographic information systems: a buyer's guide.* HMSO.

Gurney, R.J., Foster, J. and Parkinson, C. (1993) (eds.) *Atlas of satellite observations related to global change.* Cambridge University Press.

Lawrence, G.R.P. (1992) (ed.) *Qualifications: survey and mapping qualifications for the 1990s.* British Cartographic Society.

Lilles, Thomas M. and Kiefer, Ralph W. (1994) *Remote sensing and image interpretation.* 3rd edn. John Wiley and Sons.

McDonnell, P.W. (1990) *Introduction to map projections.* 2nd edn. London: RICS Landmark Enterprises.

Maguire, D.J., Goodchild, M.F. and Rhind, D. (1991) *Geographical information systems: principles and applications.* Longman.

Maling, D.H. (1992) *Co-ordinate systems and map projections.* 2nd ed. Pergamon.

Marble, D F. (1994) *GIS in development planning.* Taylor & Francis.

Neumann, J. (1994) (ed.) *Multilingual dictionary of technical terms in cartography.* 2nd edn. K.G. Saur.

Parry, R.B. and Perkins, C.R. (1993) *Mapping in the UK: maps and spatial data for the 1990s.* Bowker-Saur.

Paulsson, Bengt (1992) *Urban applications of satellite remote sensing and GIS analysis.* USA: World Bank.

Rhind, David and Mounsey, Helen (1994) *Understanding GIS.* Taylor & Francis.

Richards, J.A. (1993) *Remote sensing digital image analysis: an introduction.* 2nd edn. Springer-Verlag.

Royal Institution of Chartered Surveyors (1994) *Data specification guidelines for the interchange of survey information.* London: RICS Landmark Enterprises.

Royal Town Planning Institute (1992) *Geographic information systems (GIS): a planner's introductory guide.* London: Royal Town Planning Institute.

Royal Town Planning Institute (1993) *GIS: potential and applications.* London: Royal Town Planning Institute.

Snyder, John P. (1993) *Flattening the earth: two thousand years of map projections.* University of Chicago Press.

Winterkorn, Erik (1993) *CICA Survey of local authorities GIS usage.* Cambridge: Construction Industry Computing Association.

CHAPTER TEN

IT: Computer-aided design

ERIK WINTERKORN

CAD is generally taken to stand for computer-aided design, which in its
broadest sense is the application of computing technology to the design of a product or the process of design generally. Like an enormous
hydra, CAD has a head which is the computing science that permits the
definition and manipulation of graphic entities, but its tentacles reach
deep into the ocean of information technology which embraces all computing and telecommunications technology plus most of consumer electronics and broadcasting. Unlike a hydra, any definition of the limits of
CAD would be arbitrary. Although the technologies that combine to produce the CAD tools used by the construction industry are unfamiliar to
many construction industry professionals, their use in the industry is
well established, and one finds information on CAD in many magazines
and books.

The term 'computer-aided architectural design' (CAAD) is commonly
used in conjunction with architectural applications, but in the United
States architectural uses of CAD are frequently classed with other engineering and construction applications and referred to as the AEC market
sector. Although perhaps not directly applicable to architectural uses of
CAD, information relevant to the construction industry use of CAD can
be found associated with keywords such as computer graphics, computer-aided drafting (also CAD), computer-aided design and drafting
(CADD), computer-aided design and computer-aided manufacture
(CADCAM or CAD/CAM), computer-aided engineering (CAE), computer aided facilities management (CAFM), computer integrated manufacturing (CIM), engineering data management (EDM), imaging,
mapping, terrain modelling, visualization, rendering, multimedia and
many more. A researcher interested in future architectural or construc-

tion industry applications of CAD would be wise to investigate its use in other industrial sectors.

Although widely used, computer graphics technology is still relatively new. Ivan Sutherland is usually cited as devising the first successful interactive graphics system at the MIT in the early 1960s. The first commercially viable CAD systems for architectural design which ran on mini-computers entered the marketplace in the early to mid-1980s. Researchers into architectural uses of CAD will not find a large number of good authoritative textbooks on the subject, but relevant articles on architectural uses of CAD (rarely of great scope or depth of insight) appear in many general construction industry publications. Many names of CAD pioneers show up in conference proceedings and the more prestigious CAD journals. For those wishing to obtain a specific piece of information, or an informed view on some aspect of CAD or CAAD, e-mailing or telephoning people may prove more effective than sifting through copious amounts of published material which dates rapidly. Computing associations and academia are good places to start when looking for the right persons to contact, but CAD system user groups, and the development and support personnel within software development organizations, may also be helpful.

Over the last 10 years, I have been asked many questions by architecture professionals, but I cannot remember any who asked about the philosophy of using CAD for the purposes of architectural design. Most wanted to know how many other firms were using the technology, what CAD systems do, which ones were the 'best', how much CAD costs, and (only as an afterthought) how to manage its use. Most of the information that was drawn upon to answer such questions came from system vendors and users, not academic theorists.

Information from vendors

The following comments may not seem particularly germane to architecture, but a large architectural practice that has invested heavily in CAD will have staff that spend a considerable amount of their time seeking information from the specialist vendors of the CAD technology they use.

CAD system vendors produce not only sales literature, user manuals and training manuals, but also much other material for internal use. When seeking anything but pricing information, it is usually most fruitful to approach development and support personnel. Sometimes the people best equipped to answer a detailed technical question about a CAD program are not employed by the marketing company. It is not uncommon to find core software from a separate source being customized, rebadged and sold by a number of competing vendors.

Vendor sales literature

The information content of most CAD system promotional literature is low. Although the Construction Industry Computing Association (CICA) has a library full of such material, it dates so quickly it is hardly worth collecting, except as a record of system development. Newsletters are mostly promotional, but vendors' in-house magazines sometimes contain articles by the heads of software development sections which reveal more than was perhaps intended. Press releases are usually not worth saving, except as milestones, and are often misleading. Vendors keep press clippings and reviews of their products. They also produce promotional slides (for seminars and lectures) and videos. Although most of the videos currently produced tend to emphasize corporate image, some of the earlier ones were prepared to educate prospective clients about the uses of CAD. Vendors also collect project data (drawings, models and high quality rendered images) produced by users (who retain copyright).

Vendor technical summaries

Some software vendors freely distribute surprisingly good technical descriptions. Whether or not they normally release them, vendors produce technical summaries for internal briefing purposes. Product summaries are most common, but larger firms often prepare documents on issues such as the performance of their programs on different hardware platforms, communication protocols, data exchange and many other subjects.

Vendor catalogues of third-party products

Vendors of general purpose CAD drawing and modelling software seek to promote their systems as platforms supporting specialist applications developed by other, third-party, commercial software developers. By promoting sales of these third-party products, they promote sales of their own systems. Hence they publish catalogues of third-party products which usually also list their own applications. These can be good sources of brief software descriptions that often state which other software modules are required for running each specialist application. The descriptions of the publisher's own products are often surprisingly accurate (although the trend is for less information to be divulged).

Vendor program documentation

User and training manuals are of obvious value, and although generally made available only to users, they can be obtained by system reviewers and legitimate researchers. Unfortunately, when describing functionality to users, the authors of manuals frequently employ non-standard computing terminology. They seek to explain what a program does, but not how it does it, or what the program is really for, and they usually deal inadequately with functional limitations. Many CAD systems now offer program tools which permit direct access to programme code. For researchers interested in detailed computing issues, manuals which explain how a system can be customized can be very informative.

Vendor QA documentation

An increasing number of UK software development firms are seeking certification for their quality assurance systems to BS 5750 Part 1 (ISO 9001) under the TickIT initiative. Many more are instituting QA procedures, but holding off on formal certification. There is now world-wide recognition of the importance of software quality assurance, and quality assurance generates vendor documents such as product development plans, test procedures and test results, logs of user complaints and remedial action, lists of known software bugs, etc. Under special circumstances a software developer may make such documentation available to users and important prospective customers.

Vendor information on users

For marketing and many other purposes, vendors collect information about the users of their products. Some vendors carry out user-satisfaction surveys on a regular basis but rarely, if ever, release the results of such surveys. Vendors support user groups for commercial reasons and as sources of feedback. The vendors of lower cost packages often do not know all the firms using their products, but they will generally identify reference sites for prospective customers and cannot help but divulge the names of user group chairmen. Most vendors never release complete lists of their users, but some do.

Demonstration copies

As the cost of CAD software falls, and with the advent of data compression and optical disk technology, even vendors of large complex programs can afford to give (or sell at a modest price) demonstration disks to potential customers. Sometimes, with the exception of file saving and printing capabilities, these are fully functional copies. In some cases they are distributed on compact discs as part of collections of software that can be unlocked (made fully functional) with a code revealed on payment of a fee by credit card. If complete and fully functional, the documentation/help systems available with demonstration programs can be quite informative.

Vendor mailboxes

Increasingly, software houses are establishing mailboxes to disseminate information to their customers. They sometimes post lists of software bugs and provide 'work-arounds' or fixes that can be downloaded. Some vendors also host user forums (see Chapter 11).

Information from users

Information from user firms

Users of individual CAD systems can be found via user groups and computing associations. Users are one of the best sources of information on many subjects, including:

- CAD systems' capabilities and limitations
- system/software reliability and bugs
- approaches to structuring CAD data
- CAD system management
- methods of backing up CAD data
- the economics of system usage
- experience of data exchange
- gossip about the system vendors and the rate of development and positioning of their products
- terms and conditions of vendor supply and maintenance contracts
- quality of vendor support and maintenance.

The easiest way of finding architectural users of a particular system is to ask the system vendor for reference sites and the names of any user group chairmen. When asked for reference sites, vendors usually respond with the names of satisfied users. This is not necessarily bad: frequently a user's dissatisfaction has more to do with the user than the system being used, and most users do not love their CAD vendor. Researchers are advised to seek firms that have at least two years' experience of system use. If the firm that controls the distribution rights to a product is too distant from its users, try contacting specialist dealers and whoever provides the main customer support service and help line.

A researcher seeking information directly from an architectural firm may encounter a range of staff with different levels and types of CAD knowledge and expertise. In a large architectural practice the following staff roles may be encountered:

- a partner or director with overall responsibility for IT, but perhaps little detailed technical knowledge about CAD
- an IT manager dealing with all the firm's computing and communication systems, who liaises with others regarding the

use of these systems, negotiates contracts with suppliers of hardware, software and training, and ensures that the firm's systems remain operational without data loss
- one or more CAD managers who monitor the provision and utilization of CAD resources on projects across the organization, set and enforce CAD standards, arrange CAD training, disseminate information, chair internal user groups, liaise with other organizations on CAD data exchanges, and have direct responsibility for guarding against CAD data loss
- CAD co-ordinators who co-ordinate the way CAD is used on specific projects
- super users, who are very proficient in the use of particular CAD systems or aspects of a single CAD system's operation and programming
- ordinary system users, some full-time, some only occasional.

The above descriptions are very broad; in very large firms there are staff that do little else but keep networks and plotters running; in smaller firms all the management roles may devolve to a single person.

Researchers should consider the following issues when seeking information from users:

- CAD programs tend to be rich and complex; different firms may use them in very different ways, and be unaware of the full capabilities of new releases of the systems they have used for many years.
- a user's system may have been customized to add functionality not present in the raw software purchased from the vendor. Some specialized architectural users have customized their systems so extensively that the original developers would not recognize them.
- having mastered a particularly arcane and difficult CAD system, users often fall in love with it – almost without exception, users are biased.
- mastery of CAD is now one criterion used by clients to discriminate between architectural design firms – architectural firms are sensitive to this.

CAD system user groups

When asked about the type of information user groups can provide, one user group chairman replied: 'Ultimately most information about a CAD system software is held by the vendor, often users don't know what information exists or what they are looking for. User groups are a good way of exchanging information about what information the vendor has, and how to get it.' Almost every CAD system eventually spawns a user group. In their early days some such groups were financially supported by the vendor. Mature groups tend to be independent and may adopt a somewhat adversarial position vis-a-vis the software vendor. User groups for systems like AutoCAD and MicroStation will contain construction industry specific sub-groups representing different professional disciplines and groups interested in specific software modules.

User groups publish newsletters containing information on how different firms use their systems, the action being taken on software development requests (sometimes), software bugs and work-arounds, comments on new software releases, ways of improving different aspects of system performance and programs to automate activities such as backing up data, plotting and other chores. Some user groups now also support on-line bulletin boards. However, much of the CAD knowledge available through user groups is exchanged at sub-group meetings and never formally documented.

User groups often co-ordinate requests for improvements in and extensions of system functionality that are relayed to the software developers in the form of development 'wish lists'. Vendors usually ask that these lists be prioritized. Such lists therefore indicate the features that systems lack and how important those features are to the users. Perhaps most importantly, user groups must maintain mailing lists and lists of the chairmen and secretaries of any sub-groups. Sub-group chairmen usually know which group members possess particular expertise in different areas.

Guides to sources of information

There are few good general guides to sources of information on the use of CAD in construction. The annual *ACM Guide to computing literature* may be the best guide to books, but each year is dealt with separately and researchers must consult back issues to avoid missing useful titles. It contains bibliographic lists and useful author, keyword, category, subject, review and source indexes. However, sources of construction industry information are regularly reviewed in the pages of the newsletter produced by the Construction Industry Information Group. Researchers may also wish to contact ARCLIB, the Association of Librarians in Schools of Architecture, an unattached co-operative group serving architecture courses in higher education establishments in the UK and Ireland. Inquiries can be directed to the Architecture Library at the Edinburgh College of Art.

General guides to organizations that keep or produce construction information, such as the *CIRIA Guide to European Community and international sources of construction information,* give little (almost no) indication of the CAD-related activities of the organizations they list. General computing guides such as the UK's *Computer users yearbook* and *Software users yearbook* taken together list many of the computing conferences and magazines that deal with CAD, but their listings of CAD system suppliers and software are far from complete.

CICA sells sections of its *Software directory* which contain a fairly comprehensive list of the main (it does not attempt to exhaustively list third-party products) construction industry CAD drafting and modelling systems sold in the UK and the names and addresses of UK CAD vendors (but little descriptive information). The information on CAD is derived largely from an annual survey of CAD system vendors which started in 1984 and solicits data on numbers of UK construction industry user firms of different types, total numbers of UK, European and world users, plus suppliers' details, general information on software functionality, typical hardware configurations, costs, etc. Until 1992, the information gathered was published in an annual report entitled *CICA's Annual CAD systems sales survey* but the data collected from more recent surveys were only published in summary. The *CAD ratings guide* by W. Bradley Holtz is excellent. It includes detailed information about a wide range of CAD systems, together with user comment on the systems. There are about three general on-line guides to microcomputer software available via DIALOG, but CICA rarely refers to them.

Texts

Texts on the more popular CAD systems can be found on the shelves of most book shops, but the best places to find books on CAD are the libraries located at major universities with schools of architecture and engineering. One can access the on-line catalogues of the libraries of UK universities via JANET.

The following general books cover CAD, its use for architectural purposes, and some more advanced topics such as knowledge-based systems and the limitations of computer approaches to design. Allowing for the fact that the software reviews contained in CICA's publication, *MicroCAD software evaluated*, are now dated, the lessons this book offers about what is important and how to classify and describe CAD software are very valuable. *Computers in architecture* edited by Francois Penz is a collection of papers delivered at an architectural computing conference sponsored by Apple computers.

Bijl, A. (1989) *Computer and design practice.* Edinburgh University Press
Dreyfus, H.L. (1992) *What computers still can't do: a critique of artificial reason.* MIT Press.
Dreyfus, H.L. and Dreyfus, S.E. (1988) *Mind over machine: the power of human intuition and expertise in the era of the computer.* The Free Press.
Dym, C.L. and Levitt, R. E. (1991) *Knowledge-based system in engineering.* McGraw Hill.

Flores, T. and F. (1986) *Understanding computers and cognition: a new foundation for design.* Addison Wesley.

Foley, J.D. et al. (1990) *Computer graphics: principles and practice.* 2nd edn. Addison Wesley.

Mitchell, W. J. (1990) *The logic of architecture.* MIT Press.

Penz, Francois (ed.) (1992) *Computers in architecture: tools for design.* Longman.

Richens, P. (1990) *MicroCAD software evaluated.* CICA.

Rooney, J. and Steadman, P. (1987) (eds.) *Principles of computer aided design.* Pitman/Open University (This is a good general introduction to CAD).

Schmitt, G. (1988) *Microcomputer aided design for architects and designers.* Wiley.

Schon, D. (1983) *The reflective practitioner: how professionals think in action.* Winograd: Basic Books.

The following texts deal with subjects such as multimedia, visualization, and image manipulation:

Mitchell, W. (1992) *The reconfigured eye.* MIT Press (on manipulation of photographs).

Mitchell, W. and McCullough, M. (1991) *Digital design media.* Van Nostrand Reinhold.

Yager, T. (1993) *The multimedia production handbook.* Academic Press.

The last two books contain information on CAD management, but the authors listed below address wider issues:

Jones, Peter (1992) *CAD/CAM: Features, applications and management.* Macmillan.

Port, S. (1989) *The management of CAD for construction.* BSP Professional Books.

The best CAD systems management manual available is Ove Arup & Partners' *Arup CAD good practice guide* (1994). Although oriented toward AutoCAD the guide is an excellent example of the standards necessary in a professional practice.

Periodicals

CAD is just another set of related computing technologies that different sectors of the construction industry use in different ways. Consequently some articles relating to CAD appear in most of the general construction industry professional magazines, such as *Architecture* (the American Institute of Architects journal), *RIBA Journal*, the *Architects' journal*, *Building design*, *New civil engineer* and *Building*, on a fairly regular basis. The same is true of similar professional publications in other countries.

The United Kingdom is graced with a large number of weekly tabloid newspapers on computing. These usually have little direct information on CAD systems and less on architectural uses of CAD, but as CAD is affected by most computing developments and is an important sector of computing in its own right, general tabloids such as *Computing, Computer weekly* and *MicroScope* offer good background reading for general market news, disputes, take-overs of companies and products, stock quotations in different markets, quarterly and year-end results, articles on research (rarely construction CAD specific), sections on events and people, and advertizements giving salary figures. They often contain useful general survey data on computing topics of general interest. Since the UK computing industry is heavily influenced by the activities of a relatively small number of large international companies, the percentage of international news coverage is actually quite high. Similar publications, although not necessarily in the tabloid format, exist in most industrialized countries.

CADD is probably the UK's best known monthly CAD tabloid, probably because so many people receive free copies. Some accuse it of bias because every three months it is published with a copy of *MicroStation user Europe*. It serves as a monthly log of press release information covering all CAD industry sectors, and architectural applications receive some coverage. Some articles, technology reviews and software reviews are written by authors from the vendor community and are clearly biased (but still interesting), others are surprisingly fair.

Learned magazines with an international readership include *Automation in construction*, a relatively new international quarterly journal which publishes original papers on the use of IT in architecture, engineering and construction (AEC), including the maintenance and management of construction facilities. It has a good internationally representative editorial board and features articles on CAD, CAE, product modelling, expert systems, standards, data exchange, simulation models, graphics, facilities management, management control systems, robotics and a wide range of other subjects.

Computer-aided design is one of the oldest (25 years) international learned CAD journals. It also has an editorial board of CAD luminaries, but covers a broader range of CAD/CAM applications, with articles on subjects such as molecular design, as well as mechanical and electrical engineering, architecture and building design, and many other areas of CAD. It is published 10 times a year.

Both the above should be included in a good construction CAD library, but are academically biased. The references cited with the learned papers are good guides to other sources and conference proceedings. Both have good future events calendars. *Computer-aided design* reviews conferences and new CAD publications on a regular basis.

Although not focused on architectural design, *Design studies* (Butterworth-Heinemann), a rather expensive quarterly distributed in the UK and Europe, covers design and design management innovation in industry and is particularly good on the theoretical aspects of applying information technology to design problems.

Again not focused on the construction industry or architectural issues, *Computer graphics and applications* (a journal published by the IEEE Computer Society which is a member society of the US Institution of Electrical and Electronic Engineers), which is very good on reporting precompetitive stage research, and *Computer graphics forum* (the EUROGRAPHICS journal) are good for papers on graphics technology, but these are really not for the average construction industry professional.

Popular magazines

The US magazine *Architectural & engineering systems* (from Mediacom of Fort Collins, CO) is in the right subject area, but has little meat to it. *Design net* (formerly MCN Microcad News), a magazine concerned with the use of CAD in AEC and manufacturing, is distributed in the United States, Canada and Europe. Each issue has a 'Focus' section dedicated to a series of articles on a particular aspect of CAD-related technology.

CADCAM, which bills itself as 'the complete guide to computer-aided design', is probably the best known UK CAD monthly. It offers product release news, case studies, software and technology reviews, buyers' guides and seminar listings. There are equivalents of *CADCAM* in most industrialized countries.

Other magazines that are worth reading include: *Computer-aided engineering, Computer graphics world, Cadence* and the numerous AutoCAD-oriented publications such as *CAD user* and *Caddesk*.

Newsletters

There are lots of newsletters that are seldom heard of, such as *Document management technology*, a short newsletter billed as a management report on scanning, CAD data conversion and drawing and technical document management, which has separate European/UK and US editions. Some newsletters like the *Engineering data newsletter* published by Datamation of Cambridge (UK) have very high quality coverage of matters relating to data exchange. *Engineering automation report* is billed as the monthly newsletter for engineering management and presents industry news, company news and analyses of vendor strategies and profits, product developments, news of contract awards, book reviews and upcoming events. *A-E-C Automation newsletter* is high quality CADCAM gossip.

Abstracts and indexes, databases and research information

There are many print, on-line and CD sources of such information, but a day spent checking the references listed in back issues of *Automation in construction* will probably identify most of the important authors on architectural CAD applications, and which conferences in the past have attracted the largest collections of interesting papers in different subjects areas.

It is more common to find articles on construction industry and architectural CAD applications in construction industry publications, so it is worth looking in ICONDA and consulting *API*. The RIBA British Architectural Library's integrated database of bibliographic information is available on-line via DIALOG and as a CD-ROM (see Chapter 4).

The Association for Computing Machines (ACM) SIGGRAPH *Bibliography* is available on-line, and abstracts of the US IEEE publications are important in order to sift out the information of interest to construction industry professionals. However painful, if you want to be thorough it is worth consulting general indexes of scientific and technical literature, such as those prepared by ISI (Institute for Scientific Information).

Microcomputer abstracts (formerly *Microcomputer index*), a bibliographic subject and abstract guide to magazine articles from 50 microcomputer journals, can be accessed via DIALOG. Other guides on DIALOG include the *Microcomputer software guide,* providing current coverage of bibliographic data which is updated monthly by R.R. Bowker, and the *Buyer's guide to micro software*, a monthly updated directory of business and professional microcomputer software available in the United States compiled by Online of Weston, CT.

In the UK, *ImpacT*, a new information technology newsletter produced by the UK Engineering and Physical Sciences Research Council (EPSRC), provides information of interest to IT researchers and business. Coverage includes research programmes, policy and results, European news items from the UK Department of Trade and Industry, and exchange of readers' news and views. CORDIS, Community Research and Development Information Service, is a collection of eight on-line databases covering EC-funded research and technological development programmes, projects, potential partners for collaboration and the latest calls for proposals and tenders. It is a free service available via the ECHO database host using a PC and modem or through networks such as JANET or the Internet and has recently also become available on CD-ROM.

Information sources that may be contacted via the Internet include: *The virtual reference desk,* which is hosted by the University of California at Irvine and which gives access to Library indexes, US government publications, and other sources of information; *Sources in architecture and building,* hosted by the University of Michigan, which lists many references to image banks, academic papers, etc.; and *Design net*, hosted by the Stanford Center for Design Research, which maintains *Design Net*, a directory of design research services. The publications and data of design research laboratories such as the Key Center of Design Computing at Sidney and the MIT Department of Mechanical Engineering Design Division can be obtained via the Internet.

Conferences and exhibitions

The most important UK exhibitions are the RIBA's Construction Industry Computing Exhibition (to be called Construct IT in future), which is now staged, together with Compubuild, and the ICAT Exhibition organized by EMAP. However, the A/E/C Systems show in the United States is the mother of all construction industry computing exhibitions.

SIGGRAPH conferences are important, as are those held by CADFutures, EUROGRAPHICS and CEBIT. There are so many conferences now that many people only attend the ones at which they present papers. The *Proceedings of the SIGGRAPH 1993 conference* in the computer graphics annual series was published by SIGGRAPH in New York and is also available on CD-ROM. There is a cumulative index with it for the papers of all the conferences since 1984.

Each year, Daratech, a well-known source of market intelligence, invites the top CEOs from CAD/CAM/CAE industry to describe their strategies to an audience of about 420 people. Recently these meetings have revolved around topics such as virtual reality, new 3D modelling technologies, object-oriented databases and programming, STEP (1) and other aspects of engineering and product data modelling (EDM and PDM). Other sources of CAD/CAM market intelligence include the reports prepared by members of CATN(Computer Aided Technologies Network), the Anderson Report and Daratech reports.

Associations

Many professional institutions have computing panels, but expect to be referred elsewhere for advice on CAD. In the UK, computing enquiries received by the Chartered Institute of Building, Construction Industry Computer Users Group, the Federation of Master Builders, the Royal Institute of British Architects and the Royal Institution of Chartered Surveyors will probably, by commercial arrangement, be redirected to the CICA.

The CICA acts as the secretariat for the Construction Industry Technology Forum (CITF), which acts on behalf of the Construction Industry Council, Building Centre Trust, Building Research Establishment, CICA itself, the Construction Industry Training Board and Construction Industry Research and Information Association. The Forum is supported by the UK Departments of the Environment and of Trade and Industry, and the Building Materials Producers (BMP). The CICA also has an Advisory Committee composed of representatives of most of the UK construction industry professional organizations. CICA has published a number of CAD evaluation reports and most issues of its quarterly, *CICA Bulletin,* contain information on new releases of CAD system software or CAD use. CICA's sister association in Australia is ACADS.

The Architectural Schools Computing Association (ASCA) is a forum for the exchange of information on IT and education among UK schools of architecture. The Royal Institute of British Architects (RIBA) used to maintain a central computing committee, but after a restructuring exercise responsibility in this area devolved to a RIBA computing group chaired by Jaki Howes of the Leeds Metropolitan University. This group disseminates information on architectural computing matters and gathers data from the RIBA regions on computer use. The RIBA British Architectural Library contains an interesting, but not extensive, collection of books on CAD and its Drawings collection includes drawings which were winners in the three categories of the annual CICA CAD Drawing Award competition.

The Computer Graphics Suppliers Association (CGSA) is a trade association for the UK CAD/CAM, imaging and document management industry. It acts as a forum for communications between vendors and a channel for the exchange of confidential information (i.e. which exhibitions are worth attending each year). It sponsors promotional events and runs a salary tracking and reporting service. Members are sent advice on local and international legal, corporate and technical regulations in the form of a monthly magazine and other publications. However, it does not exist to serve the public directly.

The British Computer Society (BCS) has a sub-group called the BCS Computer Aided Design/Engineering Group which meets in the evenings. The aim of the sub-group is to promote CAD awareness and to act as a bridge between specialists and industry. There is also a BCS Computer Graphics and Display Group.

The Building Environmental Performance Analysis Club (BEPAC), as its name suggests, is primarily interested in computing tools for modelling and analysing the environmental performance of buildings. Such tools fall within the scope of CAD, and increasingly are being linked to general building modelling systems. This is an important area and BEPAC serves as the UK gateway to an international network of groups active in this area. The CAD Centre in Cambridge is not particularly concerned with architectural computing, but is a source of expertise in other areas, particularly process plant and petrochemical applications of CAD.

Electronic Data Interchange (Construction) (EDICON) is dedicated to promoting the use of electronic data interchange in the UK construction industry. An affiliate of UN/EDIFACT (United Nations Electronic Data Interchange for Administrations, Commerce and Transport), this group works with the MD5 Construction Message Development Group of Western Europe/EDIFACT group. Among other types of messages, MD5 is working on messages for construction drawing administration and drawing organization.

The Eurographics Association has its secretariat in Switzerland, but can be contacted through the computing centre at Loughborough University of Technology. It has 1000 members, who are interested in computer graphics and areas such as CAD, CAM, CIM, visualization, human computer interfaces, image processing and machine vision. Most of the association's activities centre around its annual conference and the smaller seminars its various branches organize. These deal mainly with new developments in the world of graphics research rather than applications.

The IEEE Computer Society is concerned with advances in the theory and practice of computer science and engineering, and promotes the exchange of information among its world-wide 100 000-strong membership. The Society organizes conferences and, in addition to *Computer graphics and applications*, publishes a monthly called *Computer*, four other magazines, conference proceedings and research transactions.

A UK Multimedia Special Interest Group was formed in April 1994 at a meeting hosted by the DTI. The prime objective of the group is to provide a forum for the exchange of information with a view to promoting the development and application of multimedia technologies in the UK by providing a focus point for discussion, supporting collaborative development of multimedia technologies and methods for future applications, and collating, documenting and distributing the views of industry.

Information on CAD data exchange standards

The most widely used de facto standard for the transfer of vector data is AutoCAD's Data Exchange Format (DXF), a subset of AutoCAD's Drawing Interchange File format. However, there are numerous other standards for the exchange of different raster and vector drawing and map data. Details of DXF are published in the AutoCAD user manuals and numerous other books on AutoCAD, but one would contact other vendors for information on their DXF and other translators.

IGES (Initial Graphic Exchange Specification) is the most widely used formal international standard for the exchange of vector data; in time it will be superseded by STEP, the ISO 10303 series of product information exchange standards. There are many people involved with and working on product data exchange standards, but probably the best UK sources to contact initially for information on formal standards for CAD and construction industry product data exchange are the British Standards Institute, CADDETC (CADCAM Data Exchange Technical Centre) and the CICA. The CICA is funded by the DoE to report on developments in STEP relevant to the construction industry. CADDETC is a good source of STEP, IGES and other data standards.

The US National Institute of Standards and Technology hosts the SOLIS collection of ISO 10303 STEP documents and related information. Other sources include the PDES, US Product Data Association, Association GOSET, The Netherlands Organization for Applied Scientific Research (TNO) and the Ministry for Building in Germany.

Recommendations for structuring CAD data

BS 1192 *Construction drawing practice: Part 5: Guide for graphic representation by computer*, drafted by a BSI committee headed by CICA's general manager, contains information on the way CAD systems typically structure data and makes recommendations on how construction industry users should allocate drawing layers.

Layer naming convention for CAD in the construction industry Version 2, prepared by the AutoCAD User Group and Autodesk Limited contains detailed recommendations on how CAD data should be structured to comply with the more general recommendations of BS 1192: Part 5.

Many building product suppliers now distribute graphic representations of their products for incorporation into the CAD drawings prepared by construction industry professionals. RIBA Information Services' RIBACAD is the best known collection of this type of data. Sheffield Hallam University's School of Leisure and Food Management supply sets of catering equipment symbols.

Conclusions

This paper has covered the main sources of information on architectural and construction CAD of which CICA is aware. However, it is far from definitive and some sources of information have been omitted as unlikely to be of interest to most researchers. Perhaps too much attention has been drawn to the types of information available from vendor organizations and user groups – these sources can be very helpful if approached in the right way, but are unlikely to respond to postal enquiries or crude requests for what may be deemed commercially sensitive information. Organizations like CICA are very experienced at obtaining information from these sources; other researchers may experience difficulty. Despite the now widespread use of CAD in the construction industry, it is a sad fact that little high quality information exists about the real impact which CAD, in its many forms, has had on the construction industry.

References

STEP—STandard for the Exchange of Product model data (its official designation is ISO 10303) is one of the aims of a range of activities being undertaken by Subcommittee 4 (Manufacturing Data and Languages) of Technical Committee 184 (Industrial Automation) of the International Organization for Standardization.

CHAPTER ELEVEN

IT: Communications

JEANNE M. BROWN

Networking is one of the communication advances revolutionizing the ways in which we interrelate. Alan Flatman in *The responsible workplace*, edited by Francis Duffy et al., identifies the following as having an impact in the near future: pocket phones, voice recognition phones, document scanning, increasing application of video technology, networking developments and video conferencing. Video conferencing in particular, with the capability of displaying and modifying design drawings in concert with project members in other locations, even other countries, offers significant advantages. Flatman notes that as the technology becomes both more sophisticated and cheaper it could become a standard facility of the personal — not just corporate — work station. In this chapter, the resources of the Internet for architecture and construction information, as well as its potential use as a communications tool, will be discussed and other manifestations of advances in communications technology will be touched upon.

Whether it benefits the architect working on an international project, or the team member working on-site who needs to access files in the office or document problems on-site, on-line communications can and are facilitating effective team-work. On-line collaboration is the subject of a short article in *Architecture*, the AIA journal, by B.J. Novitski, who mentions several ways architects are currently collaborating on joint projects using fax, video conferencing and e-mail. Networking success stories are related by O.R. Witte in his article, 'Pooling resources'.

These developments are not yet ubiquitous. Many are cutting-edge technology, and/or too expensive to be implemented by more than a few, although the predictors see them as near, not distant, future developments. The most difficult hurdle in implementation may not be technological at all. Discussions on the Internet groups have mentioned technophobia in the architecture profession. Robin Baker's *Designing the future: the computer in architecture and design* expresses the idea that the field itself will have to change to make use of this technology: both to a 'view of information as a commodity' and to an acceptance of 'interrelationships that form the basis of the new electronic design office'.

Communications technology

Advances in communications technology are proceeding rapidly. Networking is one aspect of that technology that has had a substantial impact on the distribution and availability of information. Networking applications in the form of LANs (Local Area Networks) and WANs (Wide Area Networks) are found in many office environments. The most striking embodiment of networking is the Internet. Known to many as the information superhighway, the Internet has become a form of mass communication in just a few years. At the same time, it functions as an on-line library of staggering proportions.

The Internet

The Internet is most often described as a 'network of networks'. It evolved from a network set up by the US Defense Department. Those interested in the history of the Internet are referred to the many books on the Internet being published, such as Rheingold's *The virtual community*, for further reading. Suffice it to say that there is no central organization of the information available on the Internet. It has grown in fits and starts, and in whatever directions individuals or groups cared to take it. The Internet is a global communication network; it is a repository of knowledge and data; and it is a public forum. Through the Internet travel sound, text, data, video, images and computer files including software.

The Internet links millions of computers world-wide, that is, it allows millions of computers to talk to each other. The growth of the Internet in the last several years has been phenomenal. Hobbes' *Internet Timeline* (June 20, 1994 version, posted to the Internic gopher) charts the milestones and the growth of the Internet since 1967, when a plan was presented for a packet-switching network. In 1971 there were 23 host computers. The number of hosts exceeded 10 000 in 1987, 100 000 in 1989, and 1 000 000 in 1992. The figure for January 1994 is 2 217 000 hosts. Each host represents multiple users. *Matrix news* in March 1993 estimated that there were 9 850 000 Internet users. One year later, *Fortune* estimated the number of users at 20 million.

The development of network capabilities is increasing rapidly as well: an e-mail (electronic mail) programme was invented in 1972; gopher was released in 1991; and the World Wide Web (WWW) software was released in 1992. In 1993 the rate of gopher traffic was up 997 per cent over 1992; the rate of web traffic was up 341 634 per cent!

Many factors could be said to account for this sudden growth: the achieving of a critical mass of participants and of resources; improved means of access; improved and extended telecommunications facilities in various countries; and the coverage provided by the popular press. Hobbes' *Timeline* identifies 1993 as the year when businesses and the media really started taking notice of the Internet. Tetzeli, in his 1994 article, quotes Anthony Rutkowski of the Internet Society as saying that 63 per cent of the networks registered world-wide 'belong to businesses or their research labs'.

The Internet as an information repository

The Internet links millions of computers. Through these links, the information available at any one computer can be made accessible to the millions of people accessing the Internet. Although any attempt to provide a comprehensive list here would be useless, both because of the quantity of information and the ever-changing nature of the 'net', it is possible to outline some of the types of information you will find. Because even addresses change with regularity, specific addresses will generally not be indicated below. To find the sources mentioned, you can use Internet search tools such as Veronica and Archie, go through the master gopher hierarchy to reach gopher sites, or consult the most recent revision of the guide *Architecture and Building: Net resources*, compiled by Jeanne M. Brown, posted to the gopher at the University of Michigan Clearinghouse for Subject-Oriented Resource Guides. ('Gopher' can be thought of as a space on the net; or as a means of organizing information using a hierarchy of menus which allows browsing through a series of information offerings.) The current address for the University of Michigan Clearinghouse is URL: gopher://una.hh.lib.umich.edu/70/00/inetdirsstacks. A hypertext version of the guide is available at http://www.unlv.edu/library.

Library catalogues

There are currently over 600 library catalogues from all over the world searchable through the Internet. More than 60 per cent of the schools of architecture recognized by the RIBA, and most of the architecture schools accredited by the Association of Collegiate Schools of Architecture, make their library catalogues accessible through the Internet. Because the Internet has been a network for research and scholarly institutions until recently, the library collections represented are primarily those of academic libraries. Government libraries are also present, such as that of the Environmental Protection Agency, and the library of the Lawrence

Berkeley Laboratory. The Library of Congress catalogue can also be accessed, as can the British Library catalogue, although registration is required for the latter.

Yale University maintains a list of library catalogues accessible via the Internet at its gopher site. Yale's list is arranged in menus that lead one through a series of geographical choices: continent, country, state, institution. The list is also keyword searchable, so if you know the name of the library or university, you need not go through the sequence of menus to find the entry. Most libraries have two entries: one provides directions – telnet instructions – on how to access the library's catalogue; the other entry is really not an 'entry' so much as an option to instruct Yale's computer to make the telnet connection for you. If you choose this type of entry (which has the designation <telnet> at the end of it), you will be taken to the remote library catalogue. To get to Yale's gopher, gopher to yaleinfo.yale.edu. To get to the library list, choose 'Browse YaleInfo' and 'Library Catalogs World-Wide' from successive menus.

Indexes and bibliographies

Specialized indexes covering a range of topics are available on the Internet. The ACM SIGGRAPH bibliography can be searched by keyword. Arizona State University's *Solar energy index* makes citations to journal articles, patents, technical reports, and pamphlets on alternative energy sources obtainable. *Quakeline*, a project of the National Center for Earthquake Engineering Research, supplies bibliographic information for print and non-print materials on earthquakes and related topics. The NISS (National Information on Services and Systems) Bulletin board, accessible on Britain's network JANET (Joint Academic Network), provides a home for the index to the journal *Building research and information*. Other indexes are currently on-line, and projects to develop additional ones have been announced. The *Avery index to architectural periodicals* is temporarily available on the net for free searching as part of the Getty Art History Information Program research into database retrieval.

General indexes and databases are also available, sometimes for a fee. Fee-based databases accessible through the Internet include DIALOG, OCLC and RLIN. Uncover, an index to 17 000 journals including many in architecture and construction, is free. Operated by CARL (Colorado Alliance of Research Libraries), this table of contents index provides keyword access to authors, words in article titles, and summaries if the summaries are in the table of contents. Within 48 hours of receipt of a journal issue, the indexing is on-line. Document delivery by mail or fax can also be requested on-line; there is a fee for the delivery service.

Journals

Electronic journals are being published over the Internet, and archives of back issues established. Architecture's first electronic journal was *Architronic*, produced by the Kent State University Department of Architecture and Environmental Design. Other early experiments with electronic journal publishing are taking place, not necessarily over the Internet. One example of this latter category is Princeton University Press' *Architecture on line*, which is both an electronic journal and an on-line discussion forum.

Gophers and web sites

The World Wide Web (WWW) is the hypermedia space of the Internet. Sounds, images, video, text – all can be combined at a web site into one document. As you make your way through the document, highlighted portions can be selected to transport you to another document or site, or to view the graphic or hear the audio component of the document if such has been provided. Gopher and web sites containing a wide range of information have been set up on computers in many countries – all accessible through the Internet. Information can be found on ecologically sensitive design, building engineering, standards organizations, industrial design, manufactured products, architecture instruction, digitizing projects, examples and tutorials on computing in architecture, design for accessibility, housing – and on many specific sites, locations, building types and architects. Some architects are effectively using the net to publicize their work. The Centre for Design at the Royal Melbourne Institute of Technology in Australia makes full text research papers available, as well as information about the Centre and a database of members of the Cooperative Network of Building Researchers. The University of California at Berkeley's Environmental Design Library provides library guides and bibliographies, as well as links to on-line archives of *Cadalyst* and *computer world* magazine. ArchiGopher, at the University of Michigan, has mounted a display of architectural images from Palladio to lunar architecture. ICARIS (Integrated CAD in AEC Research Information Server) in Slovenia is making available information on computer integrated construction. The US Environmental Protection Agency uses the Internet to publish its standards and rules, as does the US Occupational Safety and Health Administration.

Web sites have been set up by the UK BRE, Canada's IRG, the Australian National University Institute of Arts, the University of Virginia Digital Image Center of the Fiske Kimball Fine Arts Library, the University of Toronto Center for Landscape Research, and the Solar Energy and Building Physics Laboratory in Switzerland – to name but a few of the universities, associations, research centres and other institutions with a web presence.

FTP files

The Internet has countless files available for transfer to your computer. They are sent using a protocol called file transfer protocol (FTP) and hence are often referred to as ftp files. Files can be text, images, software programs – anything a computer can store. Many gophers and web sites list ftp files, and may allow a transparent transfer if the entry for that file is selected. Files can be located through the Internet search tool, Archie.

Types of information

The range of information needed by professionals in architecture and construction is constantly expanding. Legal, business, governmental, financial and legislative information can all be required. Vast amounts of this type of information are being added to the Internet, making it accessible to the individual work station. General information such as addresses, dictionaries and thesauri – even weather reports – can be found. As with the architecture and construction information discussed above, much of this can be found at gopher and web sites on the net.

Finding information

Specific information is not always easy to find. Exploring the Internet can be fun, but time-consuming. The University of Michigan Clearinghouse for Subject-Oriented Resource Guides mentioned earlier is an excellent place to start, with guides compiled for many subjects. There are also search engines available to identify net resources, such as World-Wide Web worm, Veronica and Archie, with more under development. In addition, there are companies which will search the Internet for a fee. Some of the information brokers mentioned in the chapter on associations have made searches of the Internet their speciality.

The Internet as a communications channel

Electronic mail (e-mail) is a staple of the Internet. In fact, e-mail is the most used net function. Even those not interested in learning anything else about the Internet are usually eager to master and use e-mail. It has obvious advantages for person-to-person communication: it eliminates phone tag and it is quick, cheap, easy and convenient, and informal. It can substitute for both phone and postal services, but it is more than a mere substitute. Its ease of use actually generates communication. A comment that would seem too inconsequential to be mailed or even phoned, can be sent by e-mail without a second thought. *Investor's business daily* (14 April 1994, p.4) quotes Mark Gibbs, co-author of *Navigating the Internet*, as saying 'the Internet will become the world's primary means of communication and will soon carry more mail than the entire postal services world-wide. . . the Internet now connects more people, resources and services than any other communications system except for the telephone system'. Setting aside the issue of who pays for network traffic, government, institution or individual, it is less expensive to communicate using the Internet. *The New York Times* (19 April 1994, C3) reports: 'ANS (Advanced Network Services) says that a one page e-mail message sent by network costs less than 2 cents, compared to 29 cents for a letter sent by mail and an even higher cost for a fax message'. You can, by the way, send faxes through the Internet as well.

In the global environment of joint projects and international teams, speedy, inexpensive communication is, or soon will be, a requirement of business. The European Community, a single European Market, is just one aspect of this trend toward globalization. Time zones need no longer control the pace of work. On-line communication eases and speeds the flow of project information back and forth, between architect and client, between architect and consultants. Comments and revisions can be expeditiously noted and incorporated. Changes can be shared with many others quickly, and consensus reached. Short deadlines can more easily be met. For many businesses, the e-mail capacity of the Internet is reason enough to get connected.

The Internet as a public forum

E-mail is not just a person-to-person communication mode. The e-mail function is used to effect public forums. The two most widespread forms of public forums are the listserv or discussion group, and the newsgroup. Messages addressed to a particular listserv forum can be sent to all the 'subscribers' of the forum simultaneously; messages sent to a newsgroup are 'posted', as messages are posted to a bulletin board.

Discussion groups or listservs are organized around subject interests. Lists of listservs/discussion groups are available at many sites on the net. There are hundreds of discussion groups in practically every field imaginable. In architecture and construction, there are lists for landscape architects (LARCH-L), urban historians (H-URBAN), construction researchers (CNBR-L, ICARIS, IRMA), architecture librarians (ARLIS-L and AASL-L), lighting professionals (LIGHTING), construction practitioners (BUILT-ENVIRONMENT), etc. The introductory message from the Cooperative Network for Building Researchers (CNBR) stresses the communications aspect of the group: 'The objective of the network is to utilise the advantages of modern electronic communications technology in order to provide researchers with a means of rapid and flexible communication, on a national and international basis.' Participation is not limited, in most discussion groups, to professionals in a particular field. In fact most groups are a mixture of experts and neophytes. Since we are all neophytes in some area, we can by turns be the requester and supplier of information. It is this sharing of expertise that makes the Internet not just a communications system, or a giant computer database, but a social phenomenon.

Newsgroups are more chatty, less scholarly discussion groups, also organized around subject interests. Some of the newsgroups in the field are alt.architecture (the 'alt' indicates it is a newsgroup in the 'alternative' hierarchy of groups, as opposed to the biz – business, comp – computers, ieee – Institute of Electrical and Electronics Engineers, sci – science, ddn – Defense Data Network or other hierarchies), alt.housing.nontraditional, alt.architecture.alternative, alt.architecture.int-design, alt.cad, alt.planning.urban and sci.engr.lighting.

Discussions in these forums can cover any topic its members or subscribers wish to raise. Technical questions, philosophical or professional issues, even what have in the past been thought of as 'library' questions such as help on completing a bibliographic citation, have all been considered. 'Discussion' is not all that happens in a discussion group. Jobs are posted, conferences and competitions announced, books are reviewed, tables of contents for journal issues are shared. The number of participants or subscribers to a discussion group varies. It could be less than 100 or more than 1000. Amongst the group, the chances of someone having the information requested, or an insight into the problem raised, is good. The group is often helpful, too, in referring to an expert who may or may not be on-line.

The potential of the Internet, with its millions of on-line users, for commercial marketing is not insignificant. Although at first the Internet was strictly non-commercial, recently businesses have been getting on the Internet in large numbers. Many are doing so merely or primarily to facilitate communications, even in-house communication. Many others are setting up shop, realizing that the communication (call it advertizing!) potential with clients is tremendous. There are also companies which are ready to help businesses or firms set up an Internet 'presence' such as a listing in the Internet yellow pages, or a virtual site with samples of past work and firm specialities outlined. Such a presence is acceptable to Internet users, who see it as additional information. On the other hand, a mass e-mailing of advertizing or junk mail has been reacted to quite negatively by the recipients. An example of marketing in the architecture/construction field is TNO (The Netherlands Organization for Applied Scientific Research) which has a site on the net with information about the R&D company and its divisions.

Internet summary

The world seems to move faster every day. The shelf-life, and half-life, of information is shortening, making it harder to keep up with advances, while at the same time it is more and more critical to do so. Speedy and convenient communication of information has become an essential condition of doing business. A system such as the Internet addresses this need. Journals have in the past been the premier sources of current information, but journals have lead times and space constraints. The Internet has neither. Using the Internet, it is possible to communicate with data sites, access library catalogues, download critical information in electronic format, and obtain needed documents. Most importantly, the Internet allows communication of the individual with the expert, the individual with a colleague, and the individual with groups of other individuals interested in the same topic. Although there is much that needs to be done in terms of organization of information and creation of access/finding tools, the Internet is an exciting mode of communication, and a valuable source of exponentially increasing resources.

AIA Online and DesigNet

In addition to the Internet, other initiatives are underway to provide information and communication with colleagues in an online context. Two such initiatives are the American Institute of Architects' *AIA Online* service, and *DesigNet*, offered by the American Society of Landscape Architects. The *AIA Online* service in many ways parallels the functions of the Internet. Electronic mail, group discussions and access to information and databases are all part of the service. The advantages are that it contains materials not available on the Internet (often commercially produced, including materials produced by the AIA itself, such as its directory), and it is highly focused on information needed by the profession, making information easier to find. The disadvantages are the per-minute access fee and the need for special software. *DesigNet* is not currently charging an access fee (though area code 202 means a long-distance charge for most); nor does it require special software. Anyone with a modem can dial in. It too has electronic mail and conference/forum functions, as well as databases and publications. Integration of *DesigNet* with the ASLA journal *Landscape architecture* occurs to the extent that print articles with online information available on *DesigNet* are indicated with a special symbol at the end of the article. Plans to have the discussions sections of *DesigNet* accessible from the Internet have been mentioned on LARCH-L (the landscape architecture Internet discussion group).

Conclusion

Computers linked with communications technology can be the key both to building in-house databases in which the lessons of past projects can be incorporated into future ones, and to accessing the growing number of databases available through the Internet and other networks. It can also be a tool in bringing about collaboration as a work mode norm. Increasing collaboration on the one hand, and active acknowledgement of the individual's contribution on the other, can form the basis of incorporating the virtual world into the 'real' one of the building business.

References

Baker, R. (1993) *Designing the future: the computer in architecture and design.* New York: Thames and Hudson.

Laing, Andrew and Crisp, Vic (1993) (eds.) *The responsible workplace: the redesign of work and offices.* Oxford: Butterworths Architecture in association with *Estates gazette.*

Novitski, B.J. (1994) Designing by long distance. *Architecture*, February, 117-119.

Rheingold, Howard (1993) *The virtual community.* Reading, MA: Addison-Wesley.

Tetzeli, Rick (1994) The Internet and your business. *Fortune*, 7 March, 86-96.

Witte, Oliver R. (1990) Pooling resources. *Architecture*, September, 117-121.

CHAPTER TWELVE

Urban and land use planning

JOHN BARRICK

The system of town and country planning is concerned with balancing the various and competing uses of land resources for the benefit of the community. This section contains references to texts on the evolution and working of the planning system, as well as to changes that have taken place since the first edition of this book. It includes also references to law, government advice and policy, planning obligations, environmental impact assessment, urban renewal and regeneration, Europe, town centres, retail planning, economic development, sustainable development, race and ethnic minorities, conservation areas, green belt and public and community participation.

General texts and overviews, government advice and policy

Town and country planning in Britain by J.B. Cullingworth and Vincent Nadin, which is now in its 11th edition (Routledge, 1994), provides a useful reference and guide to the British planning system. An examination of government policy is given in *Assessing the impact of urban policy* from the Department of the Environment, Inner Cities Research Programme (HMSO, 1994) which includes consideration of partnerships, urban programmes, Action for Cities and Urban Priority Areas. An overview of public policy since the war is provided in Rob Atkinson and Graham Moon's *Urban policy in Britain: the city, the state and the market* (Macmillan, 1994). This is an examination of the new pressures on public policy-making. Part one of *British urban policy and the Urban Development Corporations*, edited by Rob Imrie and Huw Thomas (London: Paul Chapman Publishing, 1993) consists of a review of Urban Development Corporations in context. The purpose of the study by the Department of the Environment (DoE), *The costs of determining planning applications and the development control service* (HMSO, 1994), was to assist in improving the data available on which future decisions on the level of fees for planning applications would be made.

Government views on various matters relating to the planning system are set out in the following publication: Department of the Environment, *Development plans: a good practice guide,* prepared by Arup Economics and Planning and CR Planning (HMSO, 1992). The Department of the Environment's *Countryside survey 1990: main report* (DoE, 1993) covers the following subjects: countryside, rural land cover, boundary features, vegetation, freshwater studies and soil surveys. Another DoE publication, *The UK environment* edited by Alan Brown (HMSO, 1992), covers a wide range of environmental matters including climate, air quality, pollution, global atmosphere, soil, land use, land cover, inland water resources, water quality, water pollution, marine environment, coast, wildlife, waste, recycling, noise, radioactivity, health, public attitudes and expenditure. The Department of the Environment *Environmental appraisal of development plans: a good practice guide* was prepared by Baker Associates and the University of the West of England, Bristol (HMSO 1993) and covers environmental appraisal, environmental impact assessment (EIA), development plans and sustainable development.

Directories

Contact is often necessary with officials at local and national levels, or with relevant professional consultants. There are various reference books available to assist in identifying the names and addresses of relevant contacts. *Municipal yearbook* (Municipal Publications) is issued annually in two volumes. Volume I is entitled 'Functions and officers' and includes sections on architecture and building and planning. The section on planning covers organizations concerned with town and country planning administration, planning officers, regional organizations of local planning authorities and the Royal Town Planning Institute. Volume II is entitled 'Authorities and members' and lists all local authorities and officers. *Directory of official architecture and planning* (Longman) is issued annually and lists local authority associations, local government in England and Wales, London, Scotland and the Isles, Northern Ireland, development and planning bodies, public services and statutory authorities, parks and tourist boards, professional and training bodies, sources of professional information and related organizations. The *Planning directory* (6th edn. Royal Town Planning Institute with Hillier Parker) lists contacts for central government, Development Corporations, National Parks and local authorities. It also contains *Hillier Parker's guide to the Use Classes Order and Permitted Changes of Use (England* and *Wales) and Hillier Parker's guide to the 1989 Use Classes Order (Scotland).* The *Directory of planning consultants,* issued by the Royal Town Planning Institute, is a directory of firms offering the services of Chartered Town Planners and legal members of the Royal Town Planning Institute.

Planning journals and abstracting publications

Planning journals cover the subject from various perspectives ranging from the weekly news-based publications to quarterly academic journals. The subject coverage they provide varies also, ranging from the system in general to a focus on particular subject areas. *Planning week,* formerly *The Planner,* is the official journal of the Royal Town Planning Institute and covers all aspects of current planning issues, news and information about its work. *Planning for the natural and built environment* from Ambit Publications is also weekly with news coverage and general articles. Journals providing a more academic coverage include *Town planning review, Urban studies, Regional studies, Planning practice and research, Journal of property research, Journal of environmental planning and management, Journal of environmental law* and *Built environment.* In the European context, *European planning studies* and *European environment* provide much useful material. Although it is not, strictly speaking, a planning journal, *Project appraisal* does contain useful articles in its coverage of cost-benefit, impact assessment, risk analysis and technology assessment.

The London Research Centre produces a range of relevant abstracting publications. This includes *Environment news* (weekly), *Local Europe* (monthly) on European matters affecting local government, *Planning and transport news* (fortnightly) and *Urban abstracts* (monthly). Details of further publications and prices may be obtained from the London Research Centre.

Planning law

For the non-specialist coming into contact with the planning system, planning law can seem daunting but use of the following basic materials should help provide a background understanding. There are many reference volumes, including Sweet & Maxwell's *Encyclopaedia of planning law and practice.* These six loose-leaf volumes cover Acts of Parliament, Statutory Instruments, circulars and other guidance material including Planning Policy Guidance notes (PPGs). It is updated quarterly. Butterworth's *Planning law service* is a two volume loose-leaf commentary organized on a subject basis and includes material on authorities, policies and plans, the need for and obtaining of planning permission, additional controls and powers, redevelopment and regeneration, enforcement, appeals and compensation. Each of these sections is followed by a sub-section on precedents (Butterworths, updated quarterly). Gordon Holt et al., *Development control practice*, consists of three loose-leaf volumes providing a commentary on the factors involved in seeking and making decisions on planning cases. It is organized on a subject basis with reference to cases in the text (Ambit Publications, updated quarterly).

The Barbour Index *Barbour microfile planning* consists of a set of microfiche covering the full text of official publications, journal articles, reports from organizations and other materials with good coverage of planning decisions and case law. Sweet & Maxwell's *Planning law practice and precedent,* edited by Stephen Tromans and Robert Turrall-Clarke, is a collection, in one loose-leaf volume, with a paperback volume of precedents, covering the law likely to be of most interest to the practitioner. It refers to the Acts themselves, Statutory Instruments, decided cases, circulars, policy guidance and published appeals (Sweet & Maxwell, updated quarterly). *The planning factbook,* with executive editor, Pat Thomas (London: Professional Publishing, 183 Marsh Wall, E14 PFS) is a single volume loose-leaf publication, updated quarterly, covering the following subjects: control of development, planning policies, permissions required, the planning application, enforcement, blight, compulsory purchase, compensation. There is also a directory with further information. The information contained here will be particularly useful for those less well-versed in the intricacies of the system, but could be useful also for those seeking background information. A J. Little's *Planning controls and their enforcement*, a one volume, loose-leaf edition, is intended to provide a simple and concise guide to the state of the law about the enforcement of planning control (Shaw & Sons, updated quarterly).

Texts are useful in providing the outline to the planning system but must be used in their latest edition and in conjunction with the reference material above: Heap's *An outline of planning law* is now in its 10th edition, while Telling's *Planning law and procedure* is regularly published in new editions. *Butterworths planning law handbook* and Moore's *Practical approach to planning law* are both in their second editions. Malcolm Grant has published several authoritative texts, including *Urban planning law* and *Permitted development. Blundell and Dobry's Planning appeals and inquiries,* now in its fourth edition, by Carnwath et al., is useful when used with Purdue and Fraser's *Planning decisions digest*, while in specific areas there are texts such as Charles

Mynors' *Planning control and the display of advertisements* and Felix Bourne's *Enforcement of planning control*. *Journal of planning and environment law* (monthly) and *Planning appeal decisions* (bi-monthly), both from Sweet & Maxwell, are very useful to update these.

It is vital to be aware of planning law, but awareness of advice from the Department of the Environment is important too and this is set out in Circulars, Statutory Instruments and PPGs. These are collected in the encyclopaedias mentioned, but are also available from HMSO. PPGs set out the government's policies on different aspects of planning. These must be taken into account by planning authorities and may be material to planning decisions.

Planning gain/agreements/obligations

A recent and important text on this subject is *Gains from planning? Dealing with the impacts of development* by Patsy Healey et al. The following series of articles by Edwards and Martin is useful: 'Decisions: a sufficient interest', on the importance of distinguishing between the general interest of the public in seeing the law obeyed and of the person who has a particular interest in the matter above the generality; 'Section 106 and planning gain – clarification or confusion?' and 'Section 106 and planning obligations', which gives further consideration of the legality of local authority demands and the problems attendant on planning gain following from the previous article. *The economics of planning gain: a re-appraisal* by John Bowers asks whether the introduction of planning gain into the planning process is likely to enhance consumer welfare, as do N. Lichfield in *From planning obligations to community benefit* and Nigel Moor in *Planning gain: an A-Z of advice*. The uncertainty in the law and practice in this area is examined in two articles by Andrew Gilbart and Stephen Ashworth in *Journal of planning and environment law*.

Environmental Impact Assessment

The use of EIA has become increasingly important and the following publications are all worth consideration. *The impact of environmental assessment on local planning authorities*, by Christopher Wood and Carys Jones, discusses studies of two samples of 24 local authorities which were undertaken to determine the effect of environmental assessment regulations on planning practice. It covers environmental statement (ES) procedures, deciding on the environmental assessment (EA) coverage, preparing and reviewing the environmental statement, consultation and participation, and decision-making. The response to the survey was that

EA was a 'useful exercise and a positive contribution to informed decision-making in the planning process'. Strategic environmental assessment (SEA) – see the book of the same name by Riki Therivel et al. – is
used to assess the consequences of policies, plans and programmes at
earlier stages of decision-making. Two articles consider the quality of
EIAs: C. Wood, N. Lee and C.E. Jones' 'Environmental statements in the
UK: the initial experience' examines the distribution of environmental
statements by type of regulation and by the type of project for which
they were prepared; Norman Lee and David Brown's 'Quality control on
environmental assessment' discusses the quality of the 200-250 ESs
produced each year in the UK and finds that it has improved since 1988.
Monitoring environmental assessment and planning from the Department of the Environment is also important. *Project appraisal* (September 1992) is a special issue on strategic environmental assessment and
consists of papers by N. Lee and F. Walsh, 'Strategic environmental
assessment: an overview', Graham Pinfield, 'Strategic environmental
assessment and land-use planning,' John Gardiner, 'Strategic environmental assessment and the water environment' and W.R. Sheate, 'Strategic environmental assessment in the transport sector'. *Environmental
assessment: a guide to the procedures* from the DoE gives general guidance to developers on the nature of environmental impact assessment
and practical aspects of preparing an environmental statement. It explains the procedures that apply to projects falling within the scope of
EEC Directive 85-3337-EEC requiring planning permission in England
and Wales. Projects, such as motorways, harbour works and long-distance pipelines, not requiring planning consent but also falling within
the scope of the Directive, are covered, along with a brief description of
procedures in Scotland and Northern Ireland.

Minerals extraction and contaminated land

Tom Cairney's *Contaminated land: problems and solutions* gives background but government guidance is of particular importance here and
the series of *Minerals planning guidance notes* must be consulted, especially as they cover general considerations and the development plan
system (MPG 1), specific topics such as coal mining and colliery spoil
disposal (MPG 3), minerals planning and the General Development Order (MPG 5), guidelines for aggregates provision in England and Wales
(MPG 6, 2nd edn, 1994) and the control of noise at surface mineral
workings (MPG 11).

Urban renewal and regeneration

Urban regeneration: property investment and development, edited by Jim Berry, Stanley McGreal and Bill Deddis, seeks to 'evaluate linkages between urban regeneration, investment strategies and the development process'. Richard H. Williams and Barry Wood's *Urban land and property markets in the United Kingdom* is number four in a series on the different national urban land and property markets of Europe. The others in the series are (1) *The Netherlands,* (2) *Germany,* (3) *France,* (5) *Italy* and (6) *Sweden.* Hedley Smyth's *Marketing the city: the role of flagship developments in urban regeneration* is an exploration of the concept and practical application of marketing cities and large towns particularly with reference to flagship developments as a contribution to urban regeneration. Flagship developments are defined as developments in their own right, which may or may not be self-sustaining, marshalling points for further investment, or marketing tools for an area or city.

New settlements

The establishment of new settlements, as opposed to the already established new towns, has been a subject of much discussion and the following report provides a useful history and review of the subject: the Department of the Environment, Planning Research Programme's *Alternative development patterns: new settlements.* It is worthwhile also consulting Chris Owen's article, 'Over to local processes' (*Town & country planning*), which consists of an introduction followed by a directory of new settlement proposals prepared by the New Settlements Research Group at Loughborough University. Colin Ward's *New town, home town: the lessons of experience* traces the history and development of new towns and looks at sustainable developments and new communities.

Town centres

There has been a debate about the future of town centres since the first edition of this book and the publications mentioned here should give some idea of the arguments and ideas that have been put forward. The Civic Trust's *Liveable towns and cities* is a consultation document prepared by the European Institute for Urban Affairs, Liverpool John Moores University. This discusses the idea of liveability and goes on to consider transportation systems and needs, greening the city, town centres and the retailing revolution, urban design, housing, safer town centres, arts and culture, telecommunications and new technologies, and managing and maintaining town centres. Also important are the Department of the Environment's two studies, *Planning policy guidance: town centres and retail developments* (PPG 6, revised) and *Vital and viable town centres: meeting the challenge.*

Retail planning

The most important area of interest in retail planning has been the effect of out-of-town shopping developments on high street shopping and shops. The two following books consider this and other issues in retail planning: *Retail change: contemporary issues,* edited by Rosemary Bromley and Colin Thomas, which focuses on the economic, social and environmental implications of recent changes in retailing activity; and Clifford Guy's *The retail development process: location, property and planning.* Government guidance on retail issues is set out in PPG 6 (above). The impact of such centres is discussed by Mary Davidson and Colin Bell in 'Out-of-town or town-centre?' in *Estates gazette,* which examines the issues involved in the discouraging of new retail development on green field sites. Two studies that consider the impact of particularly large developments are: the Department of the Environment's *Merry Hill impact study: final report for West Midlands Planning and Transportation Sub-Committee CENTRO, Wyre Forest District Council* by Roger Tym and Partners with Colquhon Transportation Planning, which describes Merry Hill and goes on to consider its accessibility and catchment area, employment and the appraisal of affected centres; and E. Howard's 'Assessing the impact of shopping-centre development: the Meadowhall case' in *Journal of property research,* which describes the design of the new centre and gives information about catchment and customers. Peter Stonham's 'Limited Shelf-life for town centre retailing?' in *The urban street environment* assesses the problems that out-of-town centres cause for town centres. References which also deal with other developments in retail planning, including warehouse shopping and factory outlets and the consequences of planning guidance, are Kate Hall's 'Warehouse clubs and planning control' in *Journal of planning and environment law,* Peter Jones and Claudio Vignali's 'Factory outlet shopping centres' in *Town and country planning* and, by the same authors, 'Factory outlet shopping centres – developments and planning issues' in *Housing and planning review.* Anna Minton's 'Shopping around' in *Planning week* considers predictions about the retail revolution with reference to club warehousing, factory outlets and television shopping. David Nicholson-Lord in 'Store wars' asks whether public opinion can stop the 'tide of car-borne consumerism' and stop superstores eating the heart out of the high street. Both S. Norris and P. Jones' 'Planning: retail impact assessment – the future?' in *Estates ga-*

zette and David Parsons and Paul Sherman's 'Counter-revolution' in *Planning week* assess the prospects for a move back towards traditional forms of shopping in the light of the development of the retail industry. Brian Raggett's 'Acting in the interests of the public realm' in *Planning week* examines research confirming the threat to town centres from out-of-town regional shopping centres.

Economic development

The involvement by local authorities in promoting economic development has increased since the previous edition of this book and the following references indicate current thinking and practice: Robert J. Bennett and Gunter Krebs' 'Local economic development partnerships: an analysis of policy networks in EC-LEDA local employment development strategies' in *Regional Studies*; and Tony Bovaird's 'Analysing urban economic development' and 'Managing urban economic development: learning to change or the marketing of failure?', both in *Urban studies*. This last article examines the different ways in which urban economic development policy has been managed and compares the experiences of Britain, the United States and Germany. Other studies of local economics are: Chris Collinge's 'The dynamics of local economic intervention: economic development and the theory of local government' in *Urban studies*; Aram Eisenschitz and Jamie Gough's *The politics of local economic policy: the problems and possibilities of local initiative*; and Graham Haughton's *The local provision of small and medium enterprise (SME) advice services*. Keith Hoggart's 'Political parties and district council economic policies: 1978-90' in *Urban studies* assesses whether strong political party effects can be found in the local economic policies of the 333 non-metropolitan district councils in England and Wales. Also useful are Andrew A. McArthur's 'Community business and urban regeneration' in *Urban studies*; and Angela Monagha's 'The life and times of Community Development Trusts' and John Pearce's 'Enterprise with social purpose' both in *Town & country planning*.

Race/ethnic minorities

The relationship between the planning system and ethnic minorities has been a subject of some concern and the following studies should be consulted: the Royal Town Planning Institute's *Ethnic minorities and the planning system*, a study commissioned from Vijay Krishnararyan and Huw Thomas; and *Race, equality and planning: policies and procedures* by the same authors. A useful chapter in Rob Atkinson and

Graham Moon's *Urban policy in Britain: the city, the state and the market* is Chapter 10, entitled 'Race, urban problems and urban initiatives'. It covers the development of the 'race problem', urban initiatives and race since 1968, race and urban local government, employment and housing. Also useful is Ian Munt's 'Race, urban policy and urban problems: a critique on current UK practice' in *Urban studies*.

Women and planning

A very useful study is *Women and planning* by Clara Greed, which consists of a history and analysis of women and planning. Also very useful are *Women and development plans* (Working Paper No. 27) from Nick Calder et al. at the Department of Town and Country Planning, University of Newcastle upon Tyne, and Jo Little's *Gender, planning and the policy process*.

Conservation Areas

Town planning review, October 1993, contained a series of useful articles on aspects of conservation: Heather Barrett, 'Investigating townscape change and management in urban conservation areas: the importance of detailed monitoring of planned alterations'; John Hendry, 'Conservation Areas in Northern Ireland: an alternative approach'; Malcolm Horne, 'The listing process in Scotland and the statutory protection of vernacular building types'; Philip J. Hubbard, 'The value of conservation: a critical review of behavioural research'; and Peter J. Larkham, 'Conservation in action: evaluating policy and practice in the United Kingdom'. Peter J. Larkham and Andrew N. Jones' 'The character of Conservation Areas in Great Britain: a study' (*Town planning review*) and *The character of Conservation Areas: a study,* commissioned by the Royal Town Planning Institute from Chesterton Consulting and the University of Central England, are important current works. Other useful sources are Penny Jewkes' 'Protecting the historic built environment' in *Journal of planning and environment law*; Peter Larkham's 'Conservation Areas and plan-led planning: how far can we go?' in *Journal of planning and environment law*; Charles Mynors' 'Conservation law' in *Town and country planning summer school, 1993*, held at the University of Lancaster; Norton and Ayers' 'Conservation Areas in an era of plan-led planning', also in *Journal of planning and environment law*; and G. Pearce's 'Conservation as a component of urban regeneration' in *Regional studies*.

Green Belt

There has been considerable discussion about the use of Green Belts land in recent years and, at the time of writing, a revision of PPG 2 on *Green Belts* is expected. The most comprehensive review of the use of the concept is to be found in the DoE's *The effectiveness of Green Belts*, a report prepared by Martin Elson et al., the purpose of which was to review the effectiveness of Green Belt policy and how it might be improved. The most useful history of the growth and development is Martin Elson's *Green Belts: conflict mediation in the urban fringe*. Particular aspects of Green Belts are examined in the following references: Martin Elson and Amand Ford's 'Green Belts and very special circumstances' in *Journal of planning and environment law* and which considers Green Belts and new development; and, in *Town and country planning,* Martin Elson's 'A move towards sustainable development?', Adrian Smith's 'The Green Belt – agent for regeneration or stagnation?' and John Delafons' 'Green Belt and braces' which looks at the draft revision of PPG 2 and suggests that the Green Belt concept would be better applied if accompanied by more rational and sustainable policies for future development. Denzil Millichap in *A flexible friend or capricious mistress?* examines the revisions proposed in the latest consultation paper on Green Belts and also the problems of incremental change of this nature. Robertson in *Battling against the odds* looks at the lessons to be drawn from past Green Belt developments and recent government guidance and examines how the prospects for commercial schemes can be enhanced. Nigel Moor and Frederick Stafford's *Planning policy in Green Belts* asks whether Green Belts are an efficient use of land and do they lead to over-development in urban areas? Paul Longley et al. 'Do green belts change the shape of urban areas? a preliminary analysis of the settlement geography of South East England', in *Regional studies* speaks for itself. A review of recent UK work in the evaluation of environmental costs and benefits is Nick Hanley and Jacqui Knight's *Valuing the environment: recent UK experience and an application to Green Belt land.* It begins with a brief review of available methods such as travel cost approach (TC), contingent valuation (CV), willingness-to-pay (WTP), willingness-to-accept-compensation (WTAC) and hedonic price studies (HP), and goes on to consider whether stated bids overstate or understate true WTP/WTAC methods, examining the design and results of CV survey with reference to the Chester Green Belt. Gordon Cherry in *Green Belt and the emergent city* suggests a two tier land reservation policy rather than a 'blanket' Green Belt. These are Class 1 'fully protected' and Class 2 'provisionally protected'.

Public and community participation

Public participation is a significant element in the planning process and the following references give an idea of some current views on the subject: Colin Rallings, Michael Temple and Michael Thrasher's *Community identity and participation in local democracy*; Tim Edmundson's 'Public participation in development control' in *Town and country planning summer school, 1993*; and Bob Evans' 'Planning, sustainability and the chimera of community' in *Town & country planning*. The last is particularly interesting on the idea of community as an ideological concept. Jill Grant's 'On some public uses of planning "theory": rhetoric and expertise in community planning disputes' in *Town planning review* is interesting, while David Wilcox in *The guide to effective participation* sets out guidelines on how participation may be carried out. See also his article 'Participation – sham or shambles?'.

Europe

The operation of planning systems in other European countries as well as decisions made in Europe and the consequences for land use in the UK are covered in the following studies: H.W.E. Davies', 'Europe and the future of planning' in *Town planning review*; and the Department of the Environment, Planning Research Programme's *Integrated planning and the granting of permits in the EC* by GMA Planning in association with PE International, Jaques and Lewis. This report examines the operation in practice of development-related forward planning and consent granting systems in France, Germany, the Netherlands and Spain and compares these to the systems in England and Wales. An introduction is followed by chapters covering forward planning systems and granting of consents and integration; the significance of forward planning and consent granting systems in corporate location decision-making; and, finally, efficiency and effectiveness. Useful comparative material can be found in Peter Hall's 'Forces shaping urban Europe' and in Patsy Healey and Richard Williams' 'European planning systems: diversity and convergence', both in *Urban studies*. A study which focuses on the consequences of EC decisions is the Royal Town Planning Institute's *The impact of the European Community on land use planning in the United Kingdom: commissioned study* and its volume of *Supporting information*. There are two journals of particular interest within the European context: *European planning studies* had its first issue in 1993 and contains articles on planning and related matters at both European and specific country levels. *European environment* focuses more on strictly environmental considerations such as waste, recycling and pollution.

Sustainable development

Following the Rio Conference, sustainable development has become an area of increasing concern in recent years and the following publications provide useful reading. The Rio proceedings are contained within the United Nations Conference on Environment and Development's *The Earth Summit: introduction and commentary* by Stanley P. Johnson, and the United Nations' *The global partnership for environment and development: a guide to Agenda 21: post Rio edition*. Post Rio the following DoE publications are all useful: *Biodiversity: the UK action plan* (Cm 2428); *Sustainable forestry: the UK programme* (Cm 2429); *Climate change: the UK programme*, (Cm 2427); and *Sustainable development: the UK strategy* (Cm 2426). *Transport, the environment and sustainable development*, edited by David Banister and Kenneth Button, is an examination of the relationship between transport, urban structure and environmental degradation. Andrew Blowers examines 'Environmental quality' in *Urban studies*. Also useful are: David Gibbs' 'Towards the sustainable city: greening the local economy' in *Town planning review*; Patsy Healey and Tim Shaw's 'Planners, plans and sustainable development' in *Regional studies*; S.J. Marvin's 'Towards sustainable urban environments: the potential for least-cost planning approaches' in *Journal of environmental planning and management;* Denzil Millichap's 'Sustainability: a long-established concern of planning' in *Journal of planning and environment law*; Janice Morphet and Tony Hams' 'Agenda 21 and towards sustainability: the EU approach to Rio' in *European information service*; Petter Naess' 'Can urban development be made environmentally sound?' in *Journal of environmental planning and management*; David Pearce et al.'s *Blueprint 3: measuring sustainable development*; and R. Kerry Turner's *Sustainable environmental economics and management: principles and practice*.

Research

The results of research can be helpful. The Royal Town Planning Institute has produced two volumes of research carried out in accredited planning schools. The *Register of research* was produced in 1990 with a supplement in 1992. Each entry indicates the title of project, name of planning school, name of researchers, sponsorship, a brief description of the project and resultant publications. There are subject and researcher indexes. Many of the academic Schools of Land Use and of Planning publish results of research in various series of Working Papers, Research notes or similar. Some of these useful local studies may not otherwise be published.

On-line and CD-ROM systems

The London Research Centre provides three on-line databases in this subject area. ACOMPLINE contains abstracts of books, journal articles, reports and other material with bibliographical details and added keywords. URBALINE is updated daily and contains short abstracts of press reports from the national press, press notices and news items from journals. RESLINE, the most recent, covers local authority commissioned research. ACOMPLINE and URBALINE are also available in CD-ROM format on URBADISC which has, in addition, references from French, Spanish and Italian databases.

References

Ashworth, Stephen (1993) Plymouth and after (II). *Journal of planning and environment law*, December, 1105-1111.

Atkinson, Rob and Moon, Graham (1994) *Urban policy in Britain: the city, the state and the market.* Macmillan.

Banister, David and Button, Kenneth (1993) (eds.) *Transport, the environment and sustainable development.* London: Spon.

Barrett, Heather (1993) Investigating townscape change and management in urban Conservation Areas: the importance of detailed monitoring of planned alterations. *Town planning review,* **64** (4), 435-456.

Bennett, Robert J. and Krebs, Gunter (1994) Local Economic Development Partnerships: an analysis of policy networks in EC-LEDA Local Employment Development Strategies. *Regional studies,* **28** (2), 119-140.

Berry, Jim, McGreal, Stanley and Deddis, Bill (1993) (eds.) *Urban regeneration: property investment and development.* London: Spon.

Blowers, Andrew (1993) Environmental quality: the quest for sustainable development. *Urban studies,* **30** (4/5), 775-825.

Bourne, Felix (1992) *Enforcement of planning control.* 2nd edn. Sweet & Maxwell.

Bovaird, Tony (1993) Analysing urban economic development. *Urban studies,* **30** (4/5), 631-658.

Bovaird, Tony (1994) Managing urban economic development: learning to change or the marketing of failure? *Urban studies,* **31** (4/5), 573-603.

Bowers, John (1992) The economics of planning gain: a re-appraisal. *Urban Studies,* **29** (8), 1329-139.

Bromley, Rosemary and Thomas, Colin (1993) (eds.) *Retail change: contemporary issues.* London: UCL Press.

Cairney, Tom (1992) (ed.) *Contaminated land: problems and solutions.* Blackie Academic and Professional, Chapman & Hall.

Calder, Nick et al. (1994) *Women and development plans.* (Working Paper No. 27) University of Newcastle upon Tyne, Department of Town and Country Planning.

Carnwath, Robert et al. (1990) *Blundell and Dobry's planning appeals and inquiries.* 4th edn. Sweet & Maxwell.

Cherry, Gordon (1992) Green Belt and the emergent city. *Property review,* **1** (3), 97-101.

Civic Trust (1994) *Liveable towns and cities.* London: Civic Trust.

Collinge, Chris (1992) The dynamics of local economic intervention: economic development and the theory of local government. *Urban studies,* **29** (1), 57-75.

Cullingworth, J. Barry and Nadin, Vincent (1994) *Town and country planning in Britain*. 11th edn. Routledge.

Davidson, Mary and Bell, Colin (1994) Out-of-town or town-centre? *Estates gazette*, **9409**, 170-171.

Davies, H.W.E. (1993) Europe and the future of planning. *Town planning review*, **64** (3), 235-249.

Delafons, John (1994) Green Belt and Braces. *Town and country planning*, **63** (4), 99-100.

Department of the Environment et al. (1994) *Biodiversity: the UK action plan* (Cm 2428); *Sustainable forestry: the UK programme* (Cm 2429); *Climate change: the UK programme* (Cm 2427); *Sustainable development: the UK strategy* (Cm 2426). HMSO.

Department of the Environment (1993) *The effectiveness of Green Belts*. Report prepared by Martin Elson, Stephen Walker, Roderick Macdonald and Jeremy Edge. HMSO.

Department of the Environment (1993) *Merry Hill impact study. final report for West Midlands Planning and Transportation Sub-Committee CENTRO, Wyre Forest District Council.* by Roger Tym and Partners with Colquhon Transportation Planning. HMSO.

Department of the Environment (1994) *Vital and viable town centres: meeting the challenge*. HMSO.

Department of the Environment/Welsh Office (1989) *Environmental assessment: a guide to the procedures*. HMSO.

Department of the Environment/Welsh Office (1993) *Planning policy guidance: town centres and retail developments* (PPG 6 (rev.)) HMSO.

Department of the Environment, Planning Research Programme (1993) *Alternative development patterns: new settlements*, by Michael Breheny, Tim Gent and David Lock. HMSO.

Department of the Environment, Planning Research Programme (1993) *Integrated planning and the granting of permits in the EC*, by GMA Planning in association with PE International, Jaques & Lewis. HMSO.

Department of the Environment, Planning Research Programme (1991) *Monitoring environmental assessment and planning*, by Christopher Wood and Carys Jones of the EIA Centre, Department of Planning and Landscape, University of Manchester. HMSO.

Edmundson, Tim (1993) Public participation in development control. In proceedings of *Town and country planning summer school, 1993*, pp. 59-62, University of Lancaster.

Edwards, Martin and Martin, John (1994) Decisions: a sufficient interest. *Estates gazette*, **9403**, 126-127.

Edwards, Martin and Martin, John (1994) Section 106 and planning gain – clarification or confusion? *Estates gazette*, **9404**, 129-132.

Edwards, Martin and Martin, John (1994) Section 106 and planning obligations. *Estates gazette*, **9407**, 177-181.

Eisenschitz, Aram and Gough, Jamie (1993) *The politics of local economic policy: the problems and possibilities of local initiative*. Macmillan.

Elson, Martin (1986) *Green Belts: conflict mediation in the urban fringe*. Heinemann.

Elson, Martin (1994) A move towards sustainable development? *Town & country planning*, **63** (5), 154-156.

Elson, Martin J. and Ford, Amanda (1994) Green belts and very special circumstances. *Journal of planning and environment law*, July, 594-601.

Evans, Bob (1994) Planning, sustainability and the chimera of community. *Town & country planning*, **63** (4), 106-108.

Gardiner, John (1992) Strategic environmental assessment and the water environment. *Project appraisal*, **7** (3), 165-169.

Gibbs, David (1992) Towards the sustainable city: greening the local economy. *Town planning review*, **65** (1), January 99-109.

Gilbart, Andrew Q.C. (1993) Plymouth and after (I). *Journal of planning and environment law*, December, 1099-1104.

Grant, Jill (1994) On some public uses of planning 'theory'. Rhetoric and expertise in community planning disputes. *Town planning review*, **65** (1), January, 59-76.

Grant, Malcolm (1989) *Permitted development: the Use Classes Order 1987 and the General Development Order 1988.* Sweet & Maxwell.

Grant, Malcolm (1982) *Urban planning law.* Updated. Sweet & Maxwell.

Greed, Clara (1993) *Women and planning.* Routledge.

Greenwood, Brian (1990) *Butterworths planning law handbook.* 2nd edn. Butterworths.

Guy, Clifford (1994) *The retail development process: location, property and planning.* Routledge.

Hall, Kate (1994) Warehouse clubs and planning control. *Journal of planning and environment law*, May, 408-411.

Hall, Peter (1993) Forces shaping urban Europe. *Urban studies*, **30** (6), June, 883-898.

Hanley, Nick and Knight, Jacqui (1992) Valuing the environment: recent UK experience and an application to Green Belt land. *Environmental planning and management*, **35** (2), 145-160.

Haughton, Graham (1991) *The local provision of small and medium enterprise (SME) advice services* (CUDEM Working Paper Series No. 10) Leeds Metropolitan University.

Healey, Patsy and Shaw, Tim (1993) Planners, plans and sustainable development. *Regional studies*, **27** (8), 769-776.

Healey, Patsy, Purdue, Michael and Ennis, Frank (1993) *Gains from planning? Dealing with the impacts of development.* Joseph Rowntree Foundation (The Homestead, 40 Water End, York YO3 6LP).

Healey, Patsy and Williams, Richard (1993) European planning systems: diversity and convergence. *Urban studies*, **30** (4/5), 701-720.

Heap, Desmond (1993) *An outline of planning law* 10th edn. Sweet & Maxwell.

Hendry, John (1993) Conservation Areas in Northern Ireland: an alternative approach. *Town planning review*, **64** (4), 415-433.

Hoggart, Keith (1994) Political parties and district council economic policies, 1978-90. *Urban studies*, **31** (1), 59-77.

Horne, Malcolm (1993) The listing process in Scotland and the statutory protection of vernacular building types. *Town planning review*, **64** (4), 375-393.

Howard, E. (1993) Assessing the impact of shopping-centre development: the Meadowhall case. *Journal of property research*, **10** (2), 97-119.

Hubbard, Philip J. (1993) The value of conservation: a critical review of behavioural research. *Town planning review*, **64** (4), 359-373.

Jewkes, Penny (1993) Protecting the historic built environment. *Journal of planning and environment law*, May, 417-422.

Jones, Peter and Vignali, Claudio (1993) Factory outlet shopping centres. *Town & country planning*, **62** (9), 240-241.

Jones, Peter and Vignali, Claudio (1994) Factory outlet shopping centres – developments and planning issues. *Housing and planning review*, **49** (1), 9-10.

Larkham, Peter J. (1993) Conservation in action: evaluating policy and practice in the United Kingdom. *Town planning review*, **64** (4), 395-413.

Larkham, Peter J. (1994) Conservation Areas and plan-led planning: how far can we go? *Journal of planning and environment law*, January, 8-12.

Larkham, Peter J. and Jones, Andrew N. (1993) The character of Conservation Areas in Great Britain: a study. *Town planning review*, **64** (4), 395-413.

Lee, Norman and Brown, David (1992) Quality control on environmental assessment. *Project appraisal*, **7** (1), 41-45.

Lee, N. and Walsh, F. (1992) Strategic environmental assessment: an overview. *Project appraisal*, **7** (3), 126-136.

Lichfield, N. (1992) From planning obligations to community benefit. *Journal of planning and environment law*, December, 1103-1118.

Little, Jo (1994) *Gender, planning and the policy process*. Pergamon.

Longley, Paul et al. (1992) Do Green Belts change the shape of urban areas? a preliminary analysis of the settlement geography of South East England. *Regional studies*, **26** (5), 437-452.

McArthur, Andrew A. (1993) Community business and urban regeneration. *Urban studies*, **30** (4/5), 849-873.

Marvin, S.J. (1992) Towards sustainable urban environments: the potential for least cost planning approaches. *Journal of environmental planning and management*, **35** (2), 193-200.

Millichap, Denzil (1994) A flexible friend or capricious mistress? *Estates gazette*, **9416**, 138-139.

Millichap, Denzil (1993) Sustainability: a long-established concern of planning. *Journal of planning and environment law*, December, 1111-1119.

Minton, Anna (1994) Shopping around. *Planning week*, **2** (10), 10.

Moor, Nigel (1993) Planning gain: an A-Z of advice. *House builder*, **52** (5), 32-33.

Moore, Victor (1990) *A practical approach to planning law*. 2nd edn. Blackstone Press.

Monaghan, Angela (1994) The life and times of Community Development Trusts. *Town & country planning*, **63** (3), 88-90.

Morphet, Janice and Hams, Tony (1994) Agenda 21 and towards sustainability: the EU approach to Rio. *European information service*, **147**, 3-7.

Munt, Ian Race (1991) Urban policy and urban problems: a critique on current UK practice. *Urban studies*, **28** (2), 183-203.

Mynors, Charles (1993) Conservation law. In proceedings of *Town and country planning summer school, 1993*, pp.6-10, University of Lancaster.

Mynors, Charles (1992) *Planning control and the display of advertisements*. Sweet & Maxwell.

Naess, Petter (1993) Can urban development be made environmentally sound? *Journal of environmental planning and management*, **36** (3), 309-333.

Nicholson-Lord, David (1994) Store wars. *Perspectives on architecture*, **1** (2), 28-31.

Norris, S. and Jones, P. (1993) Planning: retail impact assessment – the future? *Estates gazette*, **9304**, 84-85,88.

Norton, David M. and Ayers, John H. (1993) Conservation Areas in an era of plan led planning. *Journal of planning and environment law*, March, 211-213.

Owen, Chris (1993) Over to local processes *Town & country planning*, **62** (11), 305-309.

Parsons, David and Sherman, Paul (1994) Counter-revolution. *Planning week*, **2** (9), 18-19.

Pearce, David et al. (1993) *Blueprint 3: Measuring sustainable development*. Earthscan.

Pearce, G. (1994) Conservation as a component of urban regeneration. *Regional studies*, **28** (1), 88-93.

Pearce, John (1994) Enterprise with social purpose. *Town & country planning*, **63** (3), March, 84-85.

Pinfield, Graham (1992) Strategic environmental assessment and land-use planning. *Project appraisal*, **7** (3), 157-164.

Purdue, Michael and Fraser, Vincent (1992) *Planning decisions digest*. 2nd edn. Sweet & Maxwell.

Raggett, Brian (1994) Acting in the interests of the public realm. *Planning week*, **2** (18), 10-11.

Rallings, Colin, Temple, Michael and Thrasher, Michael (1994) *Community identity and participation in local democracy.* Commission for Local Democracy, Glen House, 200-208 Tottenham Court Road, London W1P 9LA.

Robertson, John (1994) Battling against the odds. *Estates gazette,* **9416,** 135-137.

Moor, Nigel and Stafford, Frederick (1994) Planning policy in Green Belts. *Architects' journal,* **199** (6), 22-24.

Royal Town Planning Institute (1993) *The character of Conservation Areas,* a study commissioned from Chesterton Consulting and the University of Central England. London: Royal Town Planning Institute.

Royal Town Planning Institute (1993) *Ethnic minorities and the planning system,* a study commissioned from Vijay Krishnararyan and Huw Thomas. London: Royal Town Planning Institute.

Royal Town Planning Institute (1994) *The impact of the European Community on land use planning in the United Kingdom,* commissioned study. London: Royal Town Planning Institute.

Royal Town Planning Institute (1994) *The impact of the European Community on land use planning in the United Kingdom,* commissioned study, *supporting information.* London: Royal Town Planning Institute.

Sheate, W.R. (1992) Strategic environmental assessment in the transport sector. *Project appraisal,* **7** (3), 170-174.

Smith, Adrian (1994) The Green Belt — agent for regeneration or stagnation? *Town & country planning,* **63,** (5), 156-175.

Smyth, Hedley (1993) *Marketing the city: the role of flagship developments in urban regeneration.* Spon.

Stonham, Peter (1993) Limited shelf-life for town centre retailing? *The urban street environment,* **10,** 10-17.

Telling, A (1993) *Planning law and procedure.* 9th edn. Butterworths.

Therivel, Riki et al. (1993) *Strategic environmental assessment.* London: Earthscan.

Thomas, Huw and Krishnarayan, Vijay (1994) *Race, equality and planning: policies and procedures.* Avebury.

Turner, R. Kerry (1993) *Sustainable environmental economics and management: principles and practice.* Belhaven Press.

United Nations Conference on Environment and Development (1993) *The Earth Summit: introduction and commentary* by Stanley P. Johnson. Graham & Trotman.

United Nations (1993) *The global partnership for environment and development: a guide to Agenda 21: post Rio edition.* HMSO.

Ward, Colin (1993) *New town, home town: the lessons of experience.* Calouste Gulbenkian Foundation.

Wilcox, David (1994) *The guide to effective participation.* Brighton: Partnership Books.

Wilcox, David (1994) Participation — sham or shambles? *Planning,* **1074,** 7.

Williams, Richard H. and Wood, Barry (1994) *Urban land and property markets in the United Kingdom.* London: UCL Press.

Wood, C. and Jones, C. (1992) The impact of environmental assessment on local planning authorities. *Environmental planning and management,* **35** (2), 115-127.

Wood, C., Lee, N. and Jones, C.E. (1991) Environmental statements in the UK: the initial experience. *Project appraisal,* **6** (4), 187-194.

CHAPTER THIRTEEN

Site survey, specifications and costing

MALCOLM GREEN

Site survey

This section is concerned with the physical measurement of the surface area on which a structure is to be set and not site investigation, which involves the examination of the conditions below the surface, i.e. the soil and geological conditions which will influence the actual construction and its design. The latter is covered in the companion volume to this one edited by Mildren, *Sources of information in engineering* (1995). The surveyor uses various techniques and instruments to measure distance and angles: the architect may wish to carry out a simple survey himself or be able to interpret the report from the professional surveyor. Developments in computing have made complex calculations a thing of the past and electronic distance measurement and data logging greatly simplify the task.

Mapping

A first look at a site may be obtained from large scale mapping: Ordnance Survey (OS) maps have long been available at 1:2500 or 1:1250 covering any location in the UK where construction is likely to take place. However, conversion of OS map data to electronic storage enables a site-centred map to be produced for any site in question, which can be enlarged to 1:200 if required. For larger areas photogrammetric surveys may be undertaken. Photogrammetry is a scientific method of obtaining accurate measurements from ground or airborne imagery in order to produce a precise representation of the feature of interest. The

American Society of Photogrammetry's *Manual of photogrammetry* is the established handbook, which sets out procedures, theory and instrumentation.

For construction specialists wishing to commission a survey, the RICS has published a *Specification for mapping 1:100 to 1:10 000* (1988) and, taking account of the developments in data transfer, has also published *Data specification guidelines for the interchange of survey information* (1994). A suitable professional firm to undertake a survey commission may be selected from the Land and Hydrographic Survey division of the RICS whose directory, *Land survey, hydrographic survey, geographic information management: directory of UK professional services* was available in a sixth edition in 1993. There is also a UK Land and Hydrographic Survey Association whose directory lists members who specialize in land surveying, photogrammetry, aerial and hydrographic surveying.

Textbooks

For an understanding of the traditional methods of surveying and the work of the professional surveyor, Bannister's *Surveying* is an established work now in its sixth edition by A. Bannister, S. Raymond and R. Baker (Longman and Wiley, 1992) taking account of electronic developments. More recent publications have taken account of the changes in practical surveying: R. Brinker and R. Minnick, *The surveying handbook* (2nd edn, Chapman and Hall, 1994), is a comprehensive volume giving guidance on every technique of concern to the surveyor. S.V. Estopinal's *A guide to understanding land surveys* (2nd edn, Wiley, 1993) is a more readable guide to surveying practice and procedures while A.L. Allan in *Practical surveying and computations* (2nd edn, Butterworth-Heinemann, 1993) covers the major changes brought about by technological developments. C.D. Burnside's *Electromagnetic distance measurement* (3rd edn, Oxford: BSP Professional, 1991) explains the principles and practice of the latest techniques, including electromagnetic position fixing and satellite methods.

For information on the use of traditional equipment, M. Cooper's *Modern theodolites and levels* (2nd edn, London: Collins Professional, 1987) is a helpful book and BRE Digest 202 *Site use of the theodolite and surveyor's level* provides a brief basic guide for the non-specialist. Information on equipment can be obtained from manufacturers' catalogues.

Setting out on-site

Once a construction project gets onto the actual site, the role of the surveyor may involve the actual control of setting out and the subsequent monitoring of the development. The basic principles of setting out are described in: B. Sadgrove's *Setting out procedures* (Butterworths/

CIRIA, 1988), S.G. Brighty and D.M. Stirling's *Setting out guide for site engineers* (2nd edn, Oxford: BSP Professional, 1988) and J. Muskett's *Site surveying* (Oxford: BSP Professional, 1988). All of these books explain the use of equipment and provide concise guidance for setting out construction work using modern equipment and methods.

Specification

The specification is the written description of the design process to enable the various parties involved in construction to inform each other of the requirements. Specification information is developed at all stages of design to record the requirements from a client on design drawings and documents, and is ultimately formalized into a project specification which will form part of the contract documents from which a contractor will tender for the construction of the project.

Specification writing has advanced considerably in the past 20 years: the development of standard clauses, as in Fletcher and Moore's *Standard phraseology for bills of quantities* and Monk and Dunstone's *Standard library of descriptions of building works*, enabled the specifier to move away from the last-minute, ill-conceived document it always appeared to be. However, the real breakthrough was achieved by the development of the *National building specification (NBS)*, first introduced in 1973, developed by a service company of RIBA. *NBS* is developed by NBS Services and is available on subscription in three versions, broadly relating to the size of project (the form of contract used), i.e. Standard, Intermediate and Minor. The text has been developed over the years and is continually updated. The *NBS* uses the Common Arrangement of Work as developed by the Co-ordinating Committee for Project Information (CCPI) and provides a set of clauses linked to technical advice so that specifiers can prepare their own tailor-made specification to a consistently high standard. The text throughout is accompanied by guidance notes and references to standards and other important aspects. From 1995 a full reference list of documents, standards and legislation referred to is provided. *NBS* is also available on disk for most word-processing software, and *Specification manager* is designed to facilitate the production of a project specification, to incorporate office guidance and provide access to project and standard data. Links are provided to other software such as CAD and CD-ROM full-text databases of standards and legislation.

The other development that has progressed standardization in the presentation of design information resulted from the work of the Co-ordinating Committee for Building Information. Set up by industry as a continuation of the government sponsored committees of the 1970s, which sought to progress the improvement and co-operation of the various parties involved in the construction process, the initiative sought to develop and clarify the conventions used in the communication of information between designers and contractors. The primary working tool to emerge from the CCPI was the *Common arrangement of works sections* (CAWS), which replaced the traditional arrangement of specifications and bills of quantities, the so-called 'trade' sections. The object was to enable those parts of documents which relate to each other to be more easily identified, thus enabling information for sub-contractors and suppliers to be transferred without further processing, thereby eliminating possible errors. This order of description was incorporated in a revised edition of the *Standard method of measurement* (7th edn), developed by the RICS.

Other specifications have been developed; the *PSA general specification* for public sector work is currently available from the BRE Bookshop in its last edition of 1991. It provides the basis for specification on major government projects, again following CAWS and including guidance notes. With the privatization of the PSA, its future is uncertain. It is also available in a Minor works version and on disk for IBM compatible PCs. The *National engineering specification* for mechanical and electrical work is produced by a wholly-owned subsidiary of the Chartered Institution of Building Services Engineers and developed through the initiative of a group of professional practices, with the support of various professional bodies. It provides a standard set of clauses for work in the services engineering sector, also structured in accordance with CAWS and fully integrated with CCPI principles. It is available on subscription.

There is also the Department of Transport's *Specification for highway works* (now Highways Agency). More specialist specifications have been published, such as the Institution of Civil Engineers' *Specification for ground investigation* (1993) which is particularly important given that all construction begins in the ground and any early problems with constructing foundations could be attributed to inadequate site investigation. This publication is intended for general application and sets out in detail the procedures to be adopted with schedules to establish the scope of the investigation. It provides for bills of quantities to detail the items corresponding to the specification and is issued as part of a group of four publications which aim to improve the quality of site investigations and, as a result, improve the whole construction process. The Water Authorities Association has produced a *Civil engineering specification for the water industry* (4th edn, 1995). Since the first issue in 1984 this has become the standard document for civil engineering contracts let by the water companies and also by local authorities. There is also the *National structural steelwork specification* (3rd edn, 1994) from the British Constructional Steel Association with the Steel Construction Institute.

In all of these, the long-standing publication *Specification* has been rather over-shadowed. First published over 90 years ago, this annual publication from EMAP Architecture is now produced in three volumes – technical, product and clauses – designed as a desk top reference tool as well as a source of standard clauses. The presentation still follows the traditional trade sequence. Clauses are also available on disk, if required.

With the development of computer technology the writing of specifications can be greatly assisted and information can of course be exchanged in electronic, rather than written, format. Both NBS and PSA specifications are available on disk. NBS' *Specification manager* is an interactive program that enables tailor-made project specifications to be produced. With the on-going development of technology it will be possible to relate CAD produced drawings to the specification, thus enabling the full co-ordination envisaged by CCPI to be realized.

There are of course various publications that provide guidance on and assistance with the currently recommended techniques and procedures for the specification process, as well as the standard text books. Some of these are cited below, but others may be found in the professional bookshops or by reference to their catalogues (Building Bookshop, Surveyor's Bookshop, RIBA Bookshop in London).

CCPI publications

Project specification: a code of procedure for building works seeks to set down concisely the principles of specification and gives recommendations on how specifications can be properly co-ordinated with drawings and bills of quantities. *Standard method of measurement (SMM7)* (RICS with Building Employers' Federation, 1988) was brought into line with the drawings and specification codes. *Measurement: a code of practice* provides a practice manual for *SMM7*. *SMM7 library of standard descriptions* complements the above. *Common arrangement of works sections for building works* (Building Project Information Committee, 1987) provides a generally acceptable arrangement for specifications and bills of quantities for building projects. *Production drawings* is a code of procedure for building works which encourages the production of drawings so that the necessary information can be effectively provided.

Texts

C.J. Willis and J.Willis' *Specification writing for architects and quantity surveyors* is now in its 10th edition (Oxford: BSP Professional, 1991) and has become a standard, revised to take into account developments in specification writing and the use of standard clauses and computer-based editing. More recent titles include Cox's *Writing specifications for construction* (McGraw-Hill, 1993), which provides a straightforward guide, and W. Lohmann's *Construction specifications*

(Butterworths Architecture, 1992), which gives a more in-depth approach to project documents with checklists based on standard practice.

Costs

In the United Kingdom the quantity surveyor is the traditional professional concerned with construction costs, but the architect and engineer must be aware of costing practice in order to prepare designs to meet a client's requirements. In the economic climate that has prevailed beyond the 1980s cost information assumes even greater importance and a project may involve a cost consultant in a far more exacting role than that of the quantity surveyor.

Cost information may be obtained from several sources. The most common are 'price books' which quote standard or average prices of materials and components and rates for work, and the evidence that can be gleaned from cost analyses of individual buildings, published in the technical press and through commercial cost databases. Developments through the 1980s have placed increasing emphasis on determining the life-cycle costs of buildings, as an extension of the more simple maintenance costs for which data has been collected for some time.

Price books

The standard 'building price books' that have been produced over many years (over 100 in some cases) broadly follow the same principles and usually appear annually. The long-standing publications by Spon, Laxton, Griffiths and Hutchings all contain prices of materials, measured rates, daywork and fees, presented in a standard format. Each has its followers either by total preference or for particular areas of information.

In the 1980s a new publisher, Wessex, came on the scene with volumes covering building and civil engineering, the latter now taken over by Thomas Telford, the publishing imprint of the Institution of Civil Engineers. These publications took advantage of computer technology from the outset, and are available on disk to enable in-house manipulation of data for the production of cost estimates.

Spon in particular has diversified and produced more specialist price books for different sectors of the construction industry. There are *Architects & builders price book* and *Mechanical and electrical services,* both edited by Davis Langdon and Everest, and *Landscape & external works* edited by Derek Lovejoy Partnership and Davis Langdon and Everest, all of which are now annual. There is also *Spon's building cost guide for educational premises* edited by Tweeds Chartered Quantity surveyors, cost engineers, construction economists. Bryan Spain is a consultant to Tweeds and author of *Spon's contractors handbook series* and Spon's *Home improvement price guide.* An *International construction costs handbook* was published in 1987 but has not since been revised although followed by a *European construction costs handbook* (1992 with a new edition in preparation), covering the ex-iron curtain countries as well as the United States and Japan for comparative values, and an *Asian and Pacific rim construction costs handbook* (1993). There are also, from the same organization, *Spon's plant and equipment price guide* with *Spon's serial number guide* which lists the serial numbers used for plant and equipment, identifying the year of manufacture and first sale over the last 25 years.

Also in this category are *Griffiths landscape and gardens price book* (1994/5) (available from the Building Bookshop) and the price guides from Building Materials Market Research: *The green book*, plants and landscape materials price guide; *The blue book*, heating and plumbing, lightside building materials price guide; *The buff book*, heavyside building materials price guide; *The cement supplement*; and *The yellow book*, electrical materials price guide. All are regularly updated and available on subscription.

The Property Services Agency *Schedule of rates for building works* was prepared for use on public sector work, but is still relevant to other work. This was last issued in 1990, listing some 20 000 rates covering all aspects of building and construction works. Now that the PSA no longer operates in the public sector itself, the revision of this seems unsure. Similar PSA schedule of rates volumes also exist for electrical services, mechanical services and landscape management. Current versions and updates can be located via the Building Bookshop *Catalogue*. With the change to tendering even for professional consulting services, early accurate cost information has become increasingly important and *Spon's budget estimating handbook* (2nd edn, 1994), edited by Bryan Spain of Spain and Partners, has filled a need here.

Building Cost Information Service (BCIS)

The BCIS was inaugurated in 1962 on a restricted basis as a service through the RICS. By 1972 all construction professionals who were able to contribute data to the service were able to participate. Essentially, the service is a collaborative venture for the exchange of cost information from actual projects. The information is held on computer which also enables an on-line service to be provided. The print subscription service provides cost analysis data sheets covering materials, labour, regional trends, cost studies and detailed cost analyses, via its bulletin service and *Quarterly review of building prices. BCIS on-line* allows use of the same data for personal searching, and provides faster access to the most recent information; data can be downloaded and, using BCIS software, can be manipulated to provide in-house cost estimates. BCIS is mainly a subscription service.

The Building Maintenance Cost Information Service started in 1971 in direct response to government pressure for independent information on property management, maintenance and refurbishment. It is also a subscription service, providing a series of bulletins and cost briefings and the *Price book for building maintenance*. There are also one-off studies of related topics, many of which are still in print. The service or the publications are available from BMI at the same address as BCIS.

Textbooks

Whilst some favourite book may be out of print currently, if a publication has stood the test of time it will be revised from time to time and be published in successive editions. However, the passage of time, and the changes brought about by technology mean new ideas and methods of working. The current catalogues from the Building Bookshop and RICS Books should be consulted to take account of new texts. *Cost planning of buildings* (Oxford: BSP Professional, 1991) by D. Ferry and P. Brandon has now reached its sixth edition, thus demonstrating its position as a standard work. It discusses the design process and cost implications and looks at cost planning techniques.

Two recent books consider current aspects of building economics: A. Ashworth's *Cost studies of buildings: investigations and methods for forecasting and controlling costs of new building works* (2nd edn, Longman Scientific & Technical, 1994) and R. Pilcher's *Project cost control in construction* (2nd edn, Oxford: Blackwell Scientific Publications, 1994) examine aspects of cost control feasibility thorough to design and on-site construction.

Traditional quantity surveying is explained in the long-standing book by C.J. Willis and D.E. Newman, *Elements of quantity surveying* (8th edn, Oxford: BSP Professional, 1988). *Practice and procedure for the quantity surveyor* by A. Willis (Oxford: Blackwell Scientific Publications, 1994), now in its 10th edition, reflects the fast changing role of the quantity surveyor with sections on cost control and project management.

Cost indices

The most commonly known index is the Retail Price Index which provides a measure of the change in prices over the years. More detailed figures are needed to identify the specific price levels in a particular industry; these are available from the mass of statistics published in the UK by the Central Statistical Office and presented in a more manageable form for the construction industry by various publishing sources.

A 'Building cost and tender index' appears in the Spon price books and the RICS *Building cost information service* compiles indexes of the data from the prices and the tenders it receives (see above). *Spon's con-*

struction costs handbooks and price indices brings together in one volume all of the major series which measure change in construction costs and prices in the UK, including historical data. Information is presented in tabular and graphical form (see above). Spon are also now producing *Construction economics in the single European market* from 1995. Spon's wide range of cost handbooks has been discussed earlier.

A new publication from the Department of the Environment, *Quarterly building price and cost indices: public sector works*, published by the Building Research Establishment, contains details of price and cost indices for building tenders, house building, road construction, output prices, and a location and function table to enable the costs for a project to be calculated. The *Monthly bulletin of indices for use with the price adjustment formula* (HMSO) was first published in 1969 to enable variations of resource costs in building and civil engineering to be allowed for in calculations.

Current awareness

In addition to the cost analyses of recent buildings which are covered by the Building Cost Information Service, detailed building studies are published from time to time in the technical press, and may include a cost analysis. Such studies appear in *Architect's journal* and *Building* regularly. These have also published various features on costing. The *Architects' journal* started an occasional series on 'Initial cost estimates' in 1986, dealing with different building types, and in 1994 launched a series on 'Plan shape' which looks at the effect of design decisions on building costs. *Building* started an occasional series in 1993 entitled 'Cost models' which also deals with different building types and in 1994 launched a monthly supplement to the main magazine, *Building economist*, which includes news articles and statistics of relevance to the cost and price specialist. This replaces the *Chartered quantity surveyor* but is not the official journal of the RICS Quantity Surveyors Division.

The only printed current awareness service for the construction industry is that produced by the RICS Information Service from the RICS library holdings. The monthly *Abstracts & reviews* contains features as well as bibliographies and references, and the *Weekly briefing* is a concise summary of the news each week as referred to in the popular and the technical press. There are interesting references for the cost specialist from time to time. More detailed articles also appear in the *Chartered surveyor monthly*, the monthly professional journal of the RICS, for example, 'Recession: a comparison of the 1980s and 1990s' (March 1994) and 'Construction material prices' (June 1994).

CHAPTER FOURTEEN

Design data

JACQUELINE PUGSLEY

This chapter offers guidance on the information sources available for designing a new type of project. When tackling a new design, user needs must be investigated and new data assembled. One may also be concerned to bring oneself up-to-date with new techniques as they develop. New influences, issues and equipment need to be included in the design process and integrated into the design.

In *Inquiry by design*, John Zeisel suggests that there are two types of information needs for the designer. The first is the need for information as a catalyst for design solutions and possibilities. In this part of the design process, the designer requires information on examples of building types and often uses this as a starting point for interpreting the design implications of the project. The second information need is the body of knowledge for testing the design images. There are four aspects of design data:

Information catalyst:
1. The precedent study
2. The user study (i.e. the study of users and their normal activities)
Image testing and standards:
3. Special requirements of equipment, users, structures
4. Standard technical product and systems information

The precedent study usually requires reference to architectural periodicals, the analyses of buildings therein and studies of modern architecture. The *Architects' journal* and *Building* will contain building studies and this sort of material can be located using the *Architectural periodicals index* among others.

Information on building types is frequently found in the written material of the related subject. Thus for schools and their changing needs, books and journals on education should be used. For crown courts, look at law journals. Computer-user needs will be discussed in the literature of management and computers. One can easily identify journals for particular areas of work through either *Willing's press guide* or *Benn's media directory*. Both of these are widely available and easy to use. Indexing and abstracting services are always the quickest source to background information because they distil into one publication the references from several different titles and thereby provide an immediate survey of the information available. Abstracts and indexes can be located fairly easily in major educational or institutional libraries. Most subject areas have at least one relevant service. Many have a related database, which can speed the search considerably.

This chapter will investigate the resources providing information at the start of a project. The basic resources will be outlined and, hopefully, this will point the way to the more obscure lines of enquiry. This will mean discussing the texts and reference books available, before noting some of the most helpful journals, indexes and abstracts, and associations.

Starting points

There are a number of basic texts that can be used as starting points in the design process. A general source is *Project management for the design professional: a handbook for architects, engineers and interior designers* by David Burstein and Frank Stasiowski, now in its second revised edition. Roger Clark and Michael Pause have produced *Precedents in architecture* which investigates many different methods of representing existing buildings such as 'additive and subtractive' or, 'repetitive to unique'. This is undertaken in order that designers of future buildings may use these ideas 'to organize decisions, to provide order and to consciously generate form' (p.139). The first half of the book is a discussion of the work of a wide variety of architects and the second half is dedicated to investigating formative ideas. Van Nostrand Reinhold are also the publishers of Sanford Hohauser's *Architectural and interior models: design and construction*. A further, more generally useful title from this publisher is *Building construction and design* by James Ambrose. Strike, in *Construction into design: the influence of new methods of construction on architectural design, 1690-1990*, takes a historical view. Giedion's *Space, time and architecture: the growth of a new tradition* is a classic text. Also indispensable is the *Encyclopaedia of architecture: design, engineering and construction*, a five volume collection edited by Wilkes and Packard. Michael Brawne's *From idea to building* provides a comprehensive review of building types, including many of his own projects.

There are also examples of the kind of valuable extras that can offer a new perspective on the design process in *Better building: your money's worth in design, construction and maintenance* by R.S. Beri and in Stephen Curwell's *Buildings and health: the Rosehaugh guide to the design, construction, use and management of buildings*.

For the basic building types, the *AJ Annual review* established a bibliography with notes on new pamphlets and articles and a review of the year's work and developments. Unfortunately, publication of this title ceased in the 1980s. For current information, surveys of building types require a reading of any of the well-established handbooks or use of an in-house current awareness collection or use of the abstracts and indexes already mentioned. The *Architects' journal* continues to publish profiles of buildings in its series of AJ Building Studies. The Architectural Association has a series on building types which aims to provide an in-depth, highly descriptive evocation of building types of particular interest during a given period. For example, two titles in the series are: *Osaka follies*, which records the follies designed for the Osaka Expo of 1990; and *Cities of childhood: Italian colonies of the 1930s*, which tells of the history and role of this phenomenon. Longman publish a series of building studies and several titles from the series are noted below.

Handbooks

The usual starting point for information is the desk reference handbook which is generally intended to act as a 'one stop' reference tool for the professional providing all the basics for the early stages of a project. At least one of the following should be readily available to every designer. Although it may prove more expensive to keep the latest editions of two of the handbooks, the advantage of this strategy is that the titles chosen will, if selected with care, complement each other.

Some of the articles at the front of *Specification* will prove helpful. It is usually published in three parts: Products, Technical, Clauses. In Britain, the standard handbooks are either Mills' *Planning* or Neufert's *Architects data* or the *New Metric handbook*. This last is one of a number of resources that have been loaded in full text onto the Construction Information Service of the TI/RIBA CD-ROM service. The *New metric handbook* replaced the *AJ Metric handbook* (Architectural Press, 1969) some time ago. This source provides basic data on a wide range of building types. Also covered are environmental and structural design topics, such as thermal comfort, lighting, sound, security, transport interchanges and others. Treatment of most subjects is fairly brief but the publication offers adequate basic information. References to further reading are given at the end of most chapters, but these are limited in number. The core of the book is the anthropometric and ergonomic data. Contributors include Selwyn Goldsmith, Jolyon Drury and Fred Lawson. By a happy coincidence, the buildings covered in *New metric handbook* complement rather than duplicate the coverage of Mills or Neufert.

Neufert's *Architects data* was originally published in German in 1936. A revised edition, in English, was published in 1970 and the latest available edition at present is the third edition of 1987, which was reprinted in 1993. This edition is more international than its predecessors. There are 28 sections that follow a logical sequence from 'habitat' to 'community' through to 'leisure'. However, data are given without reference to the country of origin. The bibliography covers British and American publications, statutes and standards in one sequence, which is referred to by numbers in the text. It is therefore not easy to follow references on one type of building. This may not present an insurmountable problem when there are so many ways of identifying standards, such as, for instance, the *Worldwide Standards* service on CD-ROM (IHS and Ti). However, the cost of this publication reflects its status as a standard reference work and one hopes to find most of what is sought without being frustrated by the indexing.

Planning by Edward Mills used to be one large volume of basic design data relating both to general needs for circulation, work and design and to specific building types, but in the ninth edition of 1977 it comprised five volumes. The first volume covers general data on circulation, fittings, anthropometrics and conversion tables. Each of the other volumes deals with groups of building types: *Planning: buildings for education, culture and science*; *Planning: buildings for health, welfare and religion*; *Planning: buildings for administration, entertainment and recreation*; *Planning: buildings for habitation, commerce and industry*. Each volume discusses the range of buildings within its scope and provides reference drawings and data as well as lists of significant buildings, references to articles, texts, standards and legislation. The volume of references varies but careful reading of the text will often reveal more leads than those listed in the basic bibliography at the end of each section.

Also useful are two volumes of data similar to the titles listed above but originating in the United States: *Time-saver standards for building types* by De Chiara and Ramsey and Sleeper's *Architectural graphic standards*, now edited by J.R. Hoke Jr. The latter title has a long history and is prepared in association with the American Institute of Architects. It is a compilation of information from a large number of contributors, mainly firms. This concentrates more on technical data than the other volumes above, but it also includes anthropometric and design data. There is also a series of Architects data sheets published by Architecture Design and Technology Press. The titles in this series include: *Food preparation spaces* and *Dining spaces*, both by James Dartford; and *Office spaces* and *Indoor sport systems*, which are both by Robert Crane and Malcolm Dixon. For an in-depth discussion of computer graphics hardware and software, as well as basic operating procedures for computer-aided design, *Architectural working drawings* by W.P. Spence is recommended. The book also includes a technical vocabulary.

Specific building types

A broad range of building types are covered in Ouden and Steemers' *Building 2000*. Volume I covers schools, laboratories and universities, sports and educational centres. Office buildings, public buildings, hotels and holiday complexes are included in Volume II. One enlightening text that takes a particular perspective on the idea of modern building types is *Buildings and power: freedom and control in the origin of modern building types* (Markus).

For factories, offices and other workplace environments the journal *Facilities design and management* is concise and carries a regular supplement entitled *Management guide*. Supplement number three, published in June 1994, offered a design guide for the provision of company restaurants, and supplement number two, appearing in April 1994, was concerned with 'green' workplaces.

Housing

This is an extremely well-documented area with several established publishers in the field. The Building Research Establishment has produced the *BRE housing design handbook: energy and internal layout*. Iain Colquhoun and Peter Fauset are authors of *Housing design in practice*. On a professional level, two journals may prove useful. The first of these is *Architectural record*, which has the virtue of including supplements on interiors and houses. The second is *Domus*, which is brilliantly illustrated.

There are a number of periodicals that publish house plans. *Architectural designs* is a United States journal which includes designer home plans. Garlinghouse, also of the United States, publish a few titles on this theme, for example, *Owner built home plans*. There are some other titles worth mentioning: *American classic house plans: custom homes book of plans* from Glendower holdings. There is also the *Daily Mail book of home plans*. Popular curiosity and owner design and building contribute to the number of titles in this area. Eighteenth century books of house plans will be found in the historic collections of the RIBA and others. Ideas expressed there might inspire innovations at early stages in the design process.

There are many 'do-it-yourself' style publications relating to housing, some of which may be useful. Peter Cowman's *Be your own architect: handbook of house design and construction* is still a helpful publication. On a more professional footing, there is *Residential kitchen design: a research based approach* by Koontz and Dagwell. Also available is *Kitchen planning and management* by John Fuller and David Kirk. Forthcoming, at the time of writing, is *Bathrooms: planning and remodelling* from Sunset Books; *Kitchens and bathrooms* was published previously in the same series. Ward Lock have also started a series of books in this area under the general title of *Creating a home*. Finally, Conran Octopus are publishers of Nonie Niesewand's *Creative home design: bathrooms and bedrooms* (1986). Perhaps the design pedigree associated with this particular publishing house lifts the book above the level of the coffee table, onto the professional's workbench.

Strong themes have emerged in the literature of houses. One such is the concept of design for security. The theory being, according to one reviewer, that careful design of housing could 'eliminate residential crime'. Two texts which cover this area are Stollard's *Crime prevention through housing design*, and *Crime free housing* by Poyner and Webb. The Home Office research study which appeared in July 1993, *Housing, community and crime, the impact of the priority estates project*, is particularly important. Another theme of growing significance is housing for health. This idea is promoted by the World Health Organisation's objective of healthy housing for all by the year 2000. Ranson's *Healthy housing: a practical guide* addresses this issue by offering solutions to health-related housing problems. From the Audit Commission for Local Authorities in conjunction with the National Health Service there is *Healthy housing: the role of the environmental health services*. The Department of the Environment *Design guides* are still useful. These are particularly good for planning space requirements in the home. These documents are available from the department or HMSO and are included in the *Barbour building technical microfile*.

Libraries

There is an enormous amount of material about library construction, a great deal of which originates in the United States. However, this material is largely transferable as it contains much that is useful to all situations or locations. For a fuller review of the literature of this topic refer to *Planning library facilities: selected annotated bibliography* edited by Mary Sue Stephenson. From the same publisher there are two other useful titles available: *Planning library buildings and facilities: from concept to completion* by Raymond Holt and Heather Edwards' more specific *University library building planning*. The third revised edition of *Planning and design of library building* by Godfrey Thompson is already established as a standard text for architects and librarians alike. A title which elucidates one of the key interests of those who work in libraries, and may therefore be of special interest, is Kirby's *Creating the library identity: a manual of design.*

Of course, one of the best informed sources for data on library buildings will be the professional library association for the country in which the project is undertaken. The International Federation of Library Associations has produced *Library buildings: preparation for planning,* edited by Michael Dewe. Many professional associations have affiliated groups that cover special interests and the publishing pattern of these groups may be small and infrequent but, nevertheless, highly valuable to one following through a special interest. For an example of this pattern, see one of the occasional papers of the Colleges of Further and Higher Education group of the UK Library Association, *Library design: principles and practice for the college library.* The American Library Association has published *Planning academic and research library buildings* edited by Metcalf and Weber. Also available is *Design and evaluation of public buildings* by Lushington and Kusak. A text with a title that gets straight to the point is *Library space planning: a how-to-do-it manual for assessing, allocating and reorganising collections, resources and facilities* by Ruth Fraley and Carol Lee Anderson. For more specific design challenges one might try *Planning school library media facilities* (Anderson) or *Creative planning of special library facilities* (Mount), as appropriate.

Healthcare buildings

There is an excellent source in the Longman Building Studies series by Paul James and Tony Noakes: *Hospital architecture.* This has a short bibliography and an index which will assist in identifying particular examples of the building type. The Department of Health has produced *General medical practice premises for the provision of primary healthcare services.* This is published in the Health Building Notes series which covers a wide range of buildings. NHS Estates now publishes some texts itself as well as through HMSO. Bush-Brown and Davis are the authors of *Hospitable design for healthcare in senior communities.* Butterworths Architecture have published Cox and Groves' *Hospital and healthcare facilities: design and development guide* which replaces the much earlier volume by the same authors, *Designing for healthcare.* Jain Malkin is the author of *Hospital interior architecture: creating healing environments for special patient populations.*

Retail buildings

There is much material relating to shop design and the layout of specific function areas within the retail development e.g. point-of-sale. The Institute of Grocery Distribution has a library which includes a special slide illustrations collection dedicated to shopfront design and shop layouts. Loans of up to two weeks are available for non-members of the Institute.

In terms of bibliographic sources, *Retail store: design and construction* (1991) by W.R. Green is now available in a second revised edition from Van Nostrand Reinhold. Butterworths has produced *Designing and planning for retail systems* by Gosling and Maitland. *Nikkei store design* is a journal specifically dedicated to shopfront design. As this topic is directly relevant to sales success, it is also worth using the indexing services from the fields of management and marketing. *Management and marketing abstracts* and *Anbar* will both contain references of interest. *Marketing strategies for industry* can help to identify market research reports produced commercially on the topic and this will lead to a wide range of publishers and authors. Some specialist journals contain regular market research reports; one example is *Retail intelligence* from Mintel.

Hotels

One of the key authors in this field is Fred Lawson, who contributed a chapter to the *New metric handbook*. There are two forthcoming volumes from Lawson: *Hotels and resorts: planning, design and refurbishment* and *Restaurants, clubs and bars: planning, design and investment in food service facilities* (1994). The latter is a revision of the 1991 edition and is considerably less expensive. These titles are part of Butterworth Architecture's series entitled 'Library of planning and design'. Alan Phillips has edited *The best in lobby design: hotels and offices*. Information is also included in the series of Architects data sheets cited above. There is also a specialist journal, *Hotel specification international*.

Designing office environments

Building 2000, noted above, includes coverage of offices. The Steel Construction Institute has produced *Design and construction methods for multi-story office buildings in North America*. Not surprisingly, given the economic factors involved, there is plenty of material on the refurbishment of existing buildings. The Building Research Establishment and the Energy Technology Support Unit are publishing in this area: *Environmental methods for existing office buildings* by P. Bartlett et al. is part of a series of reports on 'green issues' from the Building Research Establishment. The Energy Technology Support Unit has published *Refurbishment potential in office buildings* in its series of Energy Publications. Alan Phillips is the editor of a number of texts published by Batsford: *The best in industrial architecture, The best in science, office and business park design, The best in office interiors.* Another useful text is *Responsible workplace: redesign of work and offices* by A. Laing and V. Crisp.

There has been an increase in interest in design data for office planning which is largely due to two recent phenomena. The first is the ubiquity of the visual display unit (VDU), and the consequent changes to working patterns and comfort requirements. The second is the success of claims for compensation for repetitive strain injury. Patricia Leighton explains the obligations of the designer in this context in *The work environment: the law on health, safety and welfare.*

The European Computer Manufacturers Association publishes standards in this area and its publication, *ECMA 136 Ergonomics: requirements for non-CRT visual display units,* appeared in 1989. Also of interest, although dated, is *Visual display unit workplaces: emerging trends and problems* from the European Foundation for the Improvement of Living and Working Conditions. One can trace publications from this organization through the Luxembourg office of the Office of Official Publications of the European Commission, or through HMSO, the UK distribution agents. The UK Health and Safety Executive issues regulations for this area. Its *Display screen equipment at work: health and safety (display screen equipment) regulations 1992 guidance on regulations* was originally published under the title *Work with display screen equipment: a guide to the health and safety (display screen equipment) regulations.* There are a few books for workers such as Bentham and Huw. Croners' loose-leaf binder, *Croners' display screen equipment* gives a different point of view and has the advantage of being easily updated. It appears as part of a series on health and safety in practice. All of the above relate to the European Commission Council Directive of 12 June 1989 on the introduction of measures to encourage improvements in the safety and health of workers at work (89/391/EEC). This is reported in full in the *Official journal* of the Commission, in the Legislation series (183 29/06/89). Case studies and management policies are presented in *Promoting health and productivity in the computerised office: models of successful ergonomic inventions* (Sauter).

On repetitive strain injury, one description of failure to design effectively for work in office environments is offered in *RSI: repetitive strain injury, carpel tunnel syndrome and other conditions* by Wendy Chalmers Mill. Another example is *RSI* by E.C. Huskisson. This is a topic which has been very well reported in the national press and it will require only a speedy search of the major indexes to discover more detailed articles. The key words to use for searching should include 'rsi' or 'repetitive strain injury' or 'musculoskeletal disorder' or 'upper limb disorder'. But when searching for information on complex topics spelling can vary, e.g. in carpel tunnel syndrome, 'carpel' may also be spelled 'carpal'.

Building for recreation

Alan Phillips is the editor of *The best in leisure architecture*. A revised edition of *Handbook of sport and recreational building design* was published recently in conjunction with the Sports Council. The editors of this title, which has become a standard, are J. Geraint and K. Campbell. One of the key changes in architecture for recreation is in the way that design allows for multiple use by occupants and users. Another useful title in the Longman Building Studies series is *Theme parks, leisure centres, zoos and aquaria* by Anthony and Patricia Wylson. *Amusement facilities, karaoke rooms, game parks, amusement complexes* is another title which reflects contemporary multiplicity of use.

Pritchard's recent article in *Planning week* highlighted the current interest in planning for sports stadia and draws parallels with the lessons learned during the golf course boom of a few years ago. The design of football stadia has been radically altered in the UK following the report of Lord Taylor after the events at Hillsborough: for instance, seated fans take up more room than standing fans; and crowd controlling designs can be intrusive.

Others

Some basic data will be better located in an engineering handbook such as *Kempe's engineers yearbook*. In addition, the *Barbour building technical microfile* has in some ways cut out the need for intermediary handbooks. Several building types are covered in this source, e.g. agricultural, office, health, recreational and sport. There are also many references that relate to specific buildings, like hospitals or junior schools, under specific structural problems and materials. At other times, an association should be contacted. There are many useful suggestions in the Barbour microfile. The Department of the Environment has issued a booklet called *Guidelines for the design of government buildings*. R. Dober's *Campus design* is a landmark volume and, while originating in the United States, it contains many examples from around the world. Other building types of current interest are covered in volumes such as *Supersheds: the architecture of long-span large volume buildings* by C. Wilkinson and *The atrium comes of age* by Saxon.

Anthropometrics

People use buildings, people complain about buildings designed for non-humans by architects who are human. As a result, much work has been done on the science of anthropometry. This is defined as 'the branch of science that deals with the measurement and proportions of the human body and their variation' (*Oxford shorter English dictionary*). The definition goes on to note that the term is used especially for the process of designing furniture and machinery and this is the sense in which it is used here. It may seem incredible that design texts can give different data for the average human reach, but it is possible. In fact, there are several versions of the 'average person'. The attempts of Le Corbusier to address this issue in *Le modulor* are discussed in the opening pages of Neufert's *Architects data*. MIT's *Humanscale* by Niels comprises nine volumes including cards, calculators, charts and drawings to give basic data and means for calculating varying human dimensional needs in a novel way, likely to appeal to many architects. Studies of the space needs in buildings are not numerous. H. Dreyfuss Associates' *Measure of man and woman: human factors in design* remains one of the standard texts. This latest edition has been expanded to include womankind as well as men, as reflected in the new title.

The Land Use and Built Form study group at the University of Cambridge School of Architecture has produced many useful studies both in its former name and under its new name as the Martin Centre for Architectural and Urban Studies. Panero and Zelnik's *Human dimension and interior space* is a unique source book of standards for designers with anthropometric tables relating to different types of persons and activities and also to the ways in which needs affect interior design. The elderly and people with disabilities are also included. There is also Miller and Schlitt's *Interior space: design concepts for personal needs*.

Ergonomics

Complementary to anthropometrics is the study of the efficiency of persons in their environment, whether at work or play. The dictionary definition of ergonomics is 'the field of study that deals with the relationship between people and their working environment as it affects efficiency, safety and ease of action'; in other words, how they perform tasks and the best ways in which to provide for effective task performance. Hence, for the designer, thought is required not only about human dimensions but also about the best layout for various purposes. Although many people prefer personally designed spaces to work in, there are recommendations which can be followed in numerous different situations. Works like Inchbald's *Bedrooms* and Kira's *The bathroom* should be referred to. Unfortunately, some sources for this topic will only be identified by consulting bibliographies, handbooks and the *Architectural periodicals index*.

There is an excellent introduction to the topic provided by *Ergonomics for beginners: a quick reference guide*. This text is the new and fully revised edition of *Vademecum ergonomie*, which is an established Dutch classic. A summary checklist is included as well as specifications for comfortable sitting and standing postures. *Contemporary ergonomics:*

ergonomics for industry is an annual publication which includes the proceedings of the annual conference of the Ergonomics Society. The latest edition is 1994 edited by Sandy Robertson of University College London. The same publisher (Taylor and Francis) produces international reviews of ergonomics: *Current trends in human factors research and practice* is a two volume work edited by D.J. Oborne. There are many other useful texts available through this specialist publisher, such as *Person-centred ergonomics: a Brantonian view of human factors,* which is also edited by Oborne, Stephen Pheasant's *Bodyspace: anthropometry, ergonomics and design* and *The worker at work: a textbook concerned with men and women in the workplace.* There are other publishers in the field. Huchinson's *New horizons for human factors in design* includes coverage of design of the industrial workplace; of environmental factors such as noise, temperature, atmosphere, vibration and acceleration; and also of human factors in expanding technology. John Harrigans's *Human factors research: methods and applications for architects and interior designers* is part of a series called Advances in Human Factors/ Ergonomics published by Elsevier. Carl Hoyos and Bernard Zimolong's *Occupational safety and accident prevention: behavioural strategies and methods* is part of the same series.

British Standards sometimes provide this sort of data, for example, BS 5940: Part 1: 1980 *Office furniture: Part 1: Design and dimensions of office workstations, desks, tables and chairs* or BS 3044: 1990 *Ergonomic principles in the design and selection of office furniture.* Those interested in this area of investigation should be aware of the work of the Ergonomics Information Analysis Centre at the University of Birmingham School of Manufacturing and Mechanical Engineering. This group has been gathering information since 1959. Enquiries can be answered and bibliographies are available. If there is no bibliography on a specific topic, a tailor-made reading list can be compiled. The group publishes *Ergonomics abstracts,* which regularly indexes a wide range of journals from the arts, life sciences, technology and management fields. This source is scheduled to become available in CD-ROM format; Taylor and Francis will continue as publishers. Other sources for abstracts on ergonomics include *Psychological abstracts,* also available as PsycLIT on CD-ROM and PsycINFO on-line, and *Design and applied arts index,* which recently became available on CD-ROM, however, at the time of writing, only using Macintosh technology.

Barrier-free and accessible environments for elderly or disabled people

Although not necessarily grouped together, modern society continues to show concern for these two groups of persons and the legislative requirements for access to buildings and circulation within buildings often apply equally to both groups. Now in its third edition, Selwyn Goldsmith's *Designing for the disabled* remains a classic basic text. This volume contains a wealth of data and an extensive bibliography, relating not just to purpose-built buildings but also to needs in other buildings. The text has been loaded in full onto the TI/RIBA *Construction information system*. The Centre for Accessible Environments produces many notes and leaflets giving data for use in specific instances as well as a bibliography/information sheet series which includes *The good loo design guide: advice on WC provision for disabled people in public buildings* by Stephen Thorpe. The Centre has also published a paper on assessing the success of designs for disability called *Access audits: a guide and checklists for appraising accessibility of buildings for disabled users* (D. Fearns), which is also available on the Barbour microfile.

The concentration on housing is reflected in the numerous *AJ* analyses of new homes and in volumes such as B.B. Raschko's *Housing interiors for the disabled and elderly*. The prevalence of texts in this area, covering needs for housing is also demonstrated by two US publications: M. Wylde's *Building for a lifetime: design and construction of fully accessible homes* and Branson's *Complete guide to barrier-free housing: convenient living for the elderly and the physically handicapped*. Batsford have also produced texts in this area, including both *Housing the elderly: options and designs* by the Weals and *Retirement facilities* by Goodman and Smith.

As well as texts, there are standards to consider: BS 4467: 1980: *Anthropometric and ergonomic recommendations for dimensions for designing for the elderly*. There are other types of recommendation as well. The Property Services Agency has produced *Facilities for the disabled: a PSA building design guide*, which includes statutory and advisory elements and a good checklist. As an example of the very specific material in this area, there is *Housing the disabled* (1980) from Torfaen Borough Council and Cwmbran Development Corporation by John Hunt and Lesley Hoyes. One can often find this sort of data very inexpensively. A very different building type is discussed in *Building design for handicapped and aged persons* issued in a series called Tall Buildings and the Urban Environment published by McGraw-Hill. Some writers take a holistic view of design for these user groups as is reflected in the title of Raymond Lifchez' *Rethinking architecture: design students and physically disabled people*. Forthcoming is a volume by Ian McKee, *Disabled people and buildings*.

There are other related areas and functions to take into account in the design of barrier-free environments and *Landscape design for elderly and disabled people* (Stoneham) points to some of the issues to be taken into consideration during the design process. *Caring environments for frail and elderly people* by Geoffrey Salmon is an excellent and well-illustrated source that is very good on the aspects of frailty which may remain obscure to the able-bodied. There is a specialist journal in this area from the United States, *An approach to barrier free design*, produced by A Positive Approach Inc.

Designing in existing buildings

Although this is obviously a specialist area of activity which places special demands on the designer, there are two texts worth mentioning: Peter Smeallie and Peter Smith are authors of *New construction for older buildings: a design sourcebook for architects and preservationists*; and there is also *Construction refurbishment and design* by Robert Headlam.

Abstracts and indexes/databases

So much has been published in this area that the periodical indexes and abstracts are essential resources. Material published for architects and designers will be found in the two most important indexes for this subject: the *Avery index to architectural periodicals* and the RIBA's *Architectural periodicals index* both also available on CD-ROM. *Avery* has been published since 1963, by G.K. Hall, Boston, which also produces *Bibliographic guide to art and architecture*. It will also be worthwhile to consult the *British humanities index, Social service abstracts, Applied social sciences index & abstracts, Current technology index* and the *Arts and humanities citation index*. Another source is the Chartered Institute of Building, whose Technical Information Service used to provide TIS papers and which has merged with the *Construction information digest*, formerly *Building management abstracts*, and the Estimating Information Service to form a subscription service called the *TIS File*. The Information Resources Centre handles enquiries for members only. *Current technology index* has a number of references to anthropometrics and ergonomics in buildings. *Psychological abstracts* will also prove useful for detailed study, although it can be more difficult to use. A few references will be found to specific situations in *International building services abstracts* compiled since 1966 by BSRIA.

Information from the people using the buildings will come from their own journals and these will be indexed in services like Medline (available on CD-ROM and on-line), *Abstracts of healthcare management, CINAHL, British education index* and ERIC (on CD-ROM). *Library and information science abstracts* is an excellent source for information on library design implications and it is available on CD-ROM or in hard copy. Predictions that this sort of data would become available on databases which could be run by even small practice libraries are coming true, thanks to on-line and CD-ROM technology. Many academic libraries operate CD-ROM networks. Some of the more important ones for this subject area are *Worldwide Standards* (which can be included in a subscription to the TI/RIBA system) and ILI's *Standards Infodisk*. For most other aspects of the subject *Art index* and the *British humanities index* are both excellent.

On-line systems remain a vital source, especially the RIBA's *Architecture database*. There are also one or two files available through IRS-Dialtech, for example ACOMPLINE/URBALINE. There is some very useful information on social issues on *GreenNet*, available through the Association of Progressive Communications on the Internet. There is a wealth of (largely) untapped data accessible through this link but learning sources is a personal matter and although this is exciting (and cheap) to use, coverage can be capricious.

Key journals

Building design, Architects' journal and *Architectural design* are essential. *Architectural review* is indexed in the *Arts and humanities citation index*. *Architecture and behaviour* appears in English and French and is indexed in *Psychological abstracts*. *World architecture* and *Architecture today* are good general sources. *Building* is abstracted in *Abstracts of healthcare management* and also in *Building management abstracts*.

There are a number of magazines for the area of design in general. Some of those more relevant to architectural design are *Design studies, ID International design magazine* and *Blueprint*. *Blueprint extras* are large format monographs and are available through the Architectural Association. One or two other journals may prove to be of interest to the specialist: *Energy design update, Environmental building news* and *Lighting dimensions*. A new journal, *Environments by design*, is to be published by Kingston University. This research journal comes jointly from the Faculties of Design and of Architecture.

Organizations and associations, enquiries

Among the wide variety of organizations and associations able to answer enquiries relating to design, the most important is the British Architectural Library at RIBA. There are also a number of special interest groups that may be in a position to offer an insight into the needs of specific groups of people. Pressure groups, and special interest groups, may publish leaflets and guide notes. For example, the Centre for Accessible Environments has an extensive publishing programme, which includes seminar reports on a wide spectrum, e.g. *Football stadia facilities for people with disabilities*. This organization also offers free technical information and advice. An 'access appraisal' service is offered for a fee. Talking to a representative of such a group can add colour and insight to the data sources. Special interest groups of all kinds can be found in the indispensable *Directory of British Associations* or Millard's *Trade associations and professional bodies of the United Kingdom*.

One of the advantages of contacting organizations is that the information provided will often reflect the current scene and will therefore, to some extent, update the finer points of the information found in texts. This is especially important in terms of standards or legal requirements, but it is also useful to make oneself aware of the 'hot topics' in a given area. Examples of specialist organizations in areas of particular interest currently are the Federation of Environmental Trade associations and the National League of Blind and Disabled. Documents from some organizations appear in the Barbour microfile collection. Indeed, many associations can be identified through its index.

One needs to keep aware of changes within the organizations themselves. It has recently been proposed that the Design Council be reorganized on a regional basis and provide a consultancy service to local firms through the Business Link network which has recently been established by the Department of Trade and Industry (see Weale). The reorganization should also see the relaunch of the magazine *Design*. Contacting the right part of the right government department in the UK is greatly aided by use of the *Civil service yearbook*, which includes addresses and telephone numbers of all parts of departments. The best way to tap into the range of constantly changing services offered by the Business Link set-up and all the other services and assistance offered by the Department of Trade and Industry, is to contact the local regional office. Some organizations are information suppliers in the formal sense of publishing, either books/pamphlets/journals or standards and codes of practice. The European Computer Manufacturer Association is a good contact to be aware of for this reason. The British Constructional Steelwork Association are publishers of some texts mentioned earlier in this chapter. Some organizations are well-established as authorities in their subject area, e.g. the Sports Council; the National Playing Fields Association. The Society of Motor Manufacturers and Traders publishes guidance on design data relating to transport and traffic around buildings.

The most convenient type of organization to use is one which has a formal enquiry service. The British Standards Institute offers a Technical Help for Exporters service. The Industrial Society, as well as running an extensive publishing programme, also has a library. It is advisable to book in advance if you wish to visit. There is also a members-only enquiry service. The same sort of arrangements apply for the Institute of

Management's Management Information Centre at Corby. This organization is able to supply reading lists from a pre-printed range covering over 100 topics. The database of abstracts of library holdings is available on CD-ROM. Universities and colleges are sometimes willing to provide information as the two examples already cited of the University of Cambridge and the University of Birmingham adequately illustrate.

In the event that the topic under research is so obscure that there are no published data available and an information broker is unable to assist, the last resort is to undertake original research. John Zeisel's *Inquiry by design: tools for environment behaviour research* is an excellent source for formulating your own questions to users. The chapter on observing the physical traces of behaviours is particularly enlightening. Along the same lines, although more explicitly aimed at professionals in the building industry, is Bentley, Murrain and Smith's *Responsive environments: a manual for designers*. This valuable and stimulating source was first published by Architectural Press in 1985. The latest edition is 1994. As a guide to getting users involved in design, *User participation in building design and management: a generic approach to building evaluation* is invaluable. After all that, in order to check on how well you have performed, try Taylor Hosker's *Quality assurance for building design*, which shows how a building design team can develop, and implement, a quality assurance system.

Appendix: Butterworth titles available in full text format on TI/RIBA as at July 1994

AJ handbook of building enclosures
AJ legal handbook the law for architects
Building envelope
Building failures: a guide to diagnosis, remedy and prevention
Building legislation and historic building
Detailing for acoustics
Everyday details
Foundation design
Guide to the building regulations
Handbook for Clerk of Works
Housing for elderly people: a guide for architects and clients
Landscape detailing
Legal reminders for architects
New metric handbook
Working drawings handbook

References and bibliography

Ambrose, James (1992) *Building construction and design.* Van Nostrand Reinhold.

Amusement facilities, karaoke rooms, game parks amusement complexes. (1993) Tokyo: Shotenku Chiku-sha.

Anderson, P. (1990) *Planning school library media facilities.* Hamden, CT: Library of Professional Publications.

Architectural Association (1988) *Cities of childhood: Italian colonies of the 1930s.* Architectural Association.

Audit Commission for Local Authorities and National Health Service (1991) *Healthy housing: the role of the Environmental Health Services.* HMSO.

Bartlett, Paul (1993) *BREEAM/Existing offices: environmental method for existing office buildings.* Building Research Establishment.

Bathrooms: planning and remodelling. (1994) USA: Sunset Books.

Benn's media directory. Annual. Benns Business Information Services.

Bentham, Peggy (1991) *Visual display unit terminal sickness: computer health risks and how to protect yourself.* Green Print.

Bentley, I. et al. (1992) *Responsive environments: a manual for designers.* Butterworths Architecture.

Beri, R.S. (1990) *Better building: your money's worth in design, construction and maintenance.* India: Sangam Books.

Branson, G.D. (1991) *Complete guide to barrier-free housing: convenient living for the elderly and the physically handicapped.* Whitehall, VA: Betterway Publications.

Brawne, Michael (1992) *From idea to building.* Butterworths Architecture.

Building Research Establishment (1993) *BRE Housing design handbook: energy and internal layout.* Building Research Establishment.

Burstein, David and Stasiowski, Frank (1991) *Project management for the design professional: a handbook for architects, engineers and interior designers.* 2nd edn. New York: Whitney Library of Design.

Bush-Brown, A. and Davis, D. (1991) *Hospitable design for healthcare in senior communities.* New York: Van Nostrand Reinhold.

Civil service yearbook. Annual. HMSO (also on CD-ROM).

Clark, Roger and Pause, Michael (1985) *Precedents in architecture.* New York: Van Nostrand Reinhold.

Colquhoun, Iain and Fauset, Peter (1991) *Housing design in practice.* Longman.

Contemporary ergonomics: ergonomics for industry. Annual. Taylor & Francis.

Cowman, Peter (1992) *Be your own architect: handbook of house design and construction.* Skibbereen, Co. Cork, Ireland: Peter Cowman.

Cox and Groves (1994) *Hospital and healthcare facilities: design and development guide.* Butterworths Architecture.

Crane, Robert and Dixon, Malcolm (1991) *Office spaces.* Architecture Design & Technology Press (Architects data sheets vol. 3).

Crane, Robert and Dixon, Malcolm (1991) *Indoor sport systems.* Architecture Design & Technology Press (Architects data sheets vol. 4).

Croners' display screen equipment. (1992) Croners' series on health and safety in practice.

Curwell, Stephen (1990) *Buildings and health: the Rosehaugh guide to the design, construction, use and management of buildings.* RIBA Publications.

Dartford, James (1990) *Food preparation spaces.* Architecture Design & Technology Press (Architects data sheets vol. 1).

Dartford, James (1990) *Dining spaces.* Architecture Design & Technology Press (Architects data sheets vol. 2).

De Chiara, J. (1990) *Time-saver standards for building types.* 3rd edn. McGraw.

Department of the Environment (1991) *Guidelines for the design of government buildings.* HMSO.

Dewe, Michael (1989) (ed.) *Library buildings: preparation for planning*. K.G. Saur Verlag.

Diffrient, Niels et al. (1981) *Humanscale*. Boston: MIT.

Dober, R. (1992) *Campus design*. Wiley.

Dul, J. (1993) *Ergonomics for beginners: a quick reference guide*. Taylor & Francis.

ECMA 136 Ergonomics: requirements for non-CRT visual display units. (1989) European Computer Manufacturers Association.

Edwards, Heather (1990) *University library building planning*. Scarecrow Press.

European Foundation for the Improvement of Living and Working Conditions (1987) *Visual display unit workplaces: emerging trends and problems*. HMSO.

Fearns, A. (n d) *Access audits: a guide and checklists for appraising accessibility of buildings for disabled users*. Centre for Accessible Environments.

Football stadia: facilities for people with disabilities. (n d) Centre for Accessible Environments.

Foster, Janet et al. (1993) *Housing, community and crime, the impact of the priority estates project*. Home Office.

Fraley, Ruth and Anderson, Carol Lee (1990) *Library space planning: a how-to-do-it manual for assessing, allocating and reorganising collections, resources and facilities*. 2nd edn. New York: Neal-Schuman Publishers.

Fuller, John and Kirk, David (1991) *Kitchen planning and management*. Butterworth-Heinemann.

Geraint, J. and Campbell, K. (1993) *Handbook of sport and recreational building design*. Butterworth-Heinemann.

Giedion, S. (1967) *Space, time and architecture: the growth of a new tradition*. 5th rev. and enl. edn. Cambridge, MA: Harvard University Press.

Goldsmith, Selwyn (1976) *Designing for the disabled*. RIBA.

Goodman, Raymond and Smith, Douglas (1992) *Retirement facilities*. Batsford.

Gosling, D. and Maitland, B. (1976) *Designing and planning for retail systems*. Butterworths.

Green, W.R. (1991) *Retail store: design and construction*. Van Nostrand Reinhold.

H. Dreyfuss Associates (1993) *Measure of man and woman: human factors in design*. New York: Whitney Library of Design.

Haber, G.M. and Blank, T.O. (1991) *Building design for handicapped and aged persons*. McGraw (Council on Tall Buildings and Urban Habitat).

Harrigan, John (1987) *Human factors research: methods and applications for architects and interior designers*. Elsevier (Advances in Human Factors/Ergonomics).

Headlam, R. (1987) *Construction refurbishment and design*. London: Estates gazette.

Health and Safety Executive (1992) *Display screen equipment at work: Health and Safety (display screen equipment) Regulations 1992: guidance on regulations*. HMSO.

Hohauser, Sanford (1985) *Architectural and interior models: design and construction*. 2nd edn. Van Nostrand Reinhold.

Holt, Raymond (1990) *Planning library buildings and facilities: from concept to completion*. Scarecrow Press.

Hoyos, Carl and Zimolong, Bernard (1988) *Occupational safety and accident prevention: behavioural strategies and methods*. Elsevier (Advances in Human Factors/Ergonomics).

Hunt, J. and Hoyes, L. (1980) *Housing the disabled*. Wales: Torfaen Borough Council and Cwmbran District Council.

Huchingson, R. (1981) *New horizons for human factors in design*. McGraw.

Huskisson, E.C. (1992) *RSI: the keyboard disease*. London: Charterhouse Conference & Communication Company.

Huw, Ursula (1987) *Visual display unit hazards handbook: a workers guide to the effects of new technology*. London Hazards Centre Trust.

Inchbald, J. (1969) *Bedrooms*. Studio Vista.

James, Paul and Noakes, Tony (1994) *Hospital architecture*. Longman Building Studies series.

Kempe's engineers yearbook. Annual. Morgan Grampian.

Kernohan, D. (1992) *User participation in building design and management: a generic approach to building evaluation*. Butterworths Architecture.

Kira, A. (1976) *The bathroom*. New rev. edn. Penguin.

Kirby, J. (1985) *Creating the library identity: a manual of design*. Aldershot: Gower.

Kitchens and bathrooms. (1991) USA: Sunset Books.

Koontz, T. and Dagwell, C.V. (1993) *Residential kitchen design: a research based approach*. New York: Van Nostrand Reinhold.

Laing, A. and Crisp, V. (1993) *The responsible workplace: the redesign of work and offices*. Butterworth Architecture in association with *Estates Gazette* (Duffy, F. series ed. for DEGW with BRE).

Lawson, Fred (1994) *Hotels and resorts: planning, design and refurbishment*. Butterworths Architecture (Library of Planning and Design).

Lawson, Fred (1994) *Restaurants, clubs and bars: planning, design and investment in food service facilities*. Butterworths Architecture (Library of Planning and Design).

Leighton, Patricia (1991) *The work environment: the law on health, safety and welfare*. Industrial Society.

Lifchez, R. (1987) *Rethinking architecture: design students and physically disabled people*. University of California Press.

Lushington, N. and Kusak, J.M. (1991) *Design and evaluation of public buildings*. Hamden, CT: Library Professional Publications.

McKee, I. (Dec. 1995) *Disabled people and buildings*. J.Kingsley Publishers.

Malkin, Jain (1992) *Hospital interior architecture: creating healing environments for special patient populations*. New York: Van Nostrand Reinhold.

Markus, T.A. (1993) *Buildings and power: freedom and control in the origin of modern building types*. London & New York: Routledge.

Metcalf, Keyes De Witt and Weber, David (1986) (eds.) *Planning academic and research library buildings*. American Library Association.

Mill, Wendy Chalmers (1994) *RSI: repetitive strain injury, carpel tunnel syndrome and other conditions*. London: Thorsons.

Millard, P. (1993) *Trade associations and professional bodies of the United Kingdom*. 12th edn. London: Gale Research.

Miller, Stuart and Schlitt, Judith (1987) *Interior space: design concepts for personal needs*. Praeger.

Mills, E. (1977) *Planning*. Butterworths.

Mills, E. (1977) *Planning: buildings for administration, entertainment and recreation*. Butterworths.

Mills, E. (1977) *Planning: buildings for education, culture and science*. Butterworths.

Mills, E. (1977) *Planning: buildings for habitation, commerce and industry*. Butterworths.

Mills, E. (1977) *Planning: buildings for health, welfare and religion*. Butterworths.

Mitchell, Donald (1992) *Library design: principles and practice for the college library*. Occasional papers of the Colleges of Further and Higher Education group of the UK Library Association No. 10. Library Association.

Mount, E. (1988) *Creative planning of special library facilities*. New York: Haworth. (Haworth series in special librarianship).

Neufert, Ernst (1987) *Architects data*. Blackwell Scientific Publications.

Tutt, P. and Adler, D. (1988) (eds.) *New metric handbook*. Butterworths Architecture.

NHS Estates (1992) *General medical practice premises for the provision of primary healthcare services*. HMSO (Health Building Notes series).

Niesewand, Nonie (1986) *Creative home design: bathrooms and bedrooms*. Conran Octopus.

Oborne, D.J. (1987) *Current trends in human factors research and practice* 2 vols. Taylor & Francis.

Oborne, D. J. (1993) *Person-centred ergonomics: a Brantonian view of human factors*. Taylor & Francis.

Osaka follies. (1990) Architectural Association.

Ouden, C. den and Steemers, T.C. (1991) *Building 2000*. Commission of the European Communities. Dordrecht & Boston: Kluwer.

Panero, Julius and Zelnik, Martin (1992) *Human dimension and interior space*. Architectural Press.

Pheasant, Stephen (1986) *Bodyspace: anthropometry, ergonomics and design*. Taylor & Francis.

Phillips, Alan (1993) (ed.) *The best in industrial architecture*. Batsford.

Phillips, Alan (1992) (ed.) *The best in leisure architecture*. Batsford.

Phillips, Alan (1991) (ed.) *The best in lobby design: hotels and offices*. Batsford.

Phillips, Alan (1992) (ed.) *The best in office interiors*. Batsford.

Phillips, Alan (1993) (ed.) *The best in science, office and business park design*. Batsford.

Poyner, B. and Webb, B. (1991) *Crime free housing*. Butterworths Architecture.

Pritchard, Stephen (1994) Sporting strategies. *Planning week*, 28 July, 16-17.

Property Services Agency (1989) *Facilities for the disabled persons in government buildings: design requirements and guidance information*. PSA.

Hoke Jr., J.R. (1994) (ed.) *Ramsey and Sleeper architectural graphic standards*. Wiley.

Ranson, R. (1991) *Healthy housing: a practical guide*. Spon.

Raschko, B.B. (1992) *Housing interiors for the disabled and elderly*. New York: Van Nostrand Reinhold.

Refurbishment potential in office buildings. (1986) Energy Technology Support Unit.

Salmon, G. (1993) *Caring environments for frail and elderly people*. Harlow, Essex: Longman Scientific; New York: Wiley.

Sauter, S.L. (1990) *Promoting health and productivity in the computerised office: models of successful ergonomic inventions*. Taylor & Francis.

Saxon, R. (1994) *The atrium comes of age*. Harlow: Longman.

Smeallie, P. and Smith, P. (1993) *New construction for older buildings: a design sourcebook for architects and preservationists*. Wiley.

Specification. Annual. EMAP Business Publications.

Spence, W.P. (1993) *Architectural working drawings*. New York: Wiley.

Steel Construction Institute (1986) *Design and construction methods for multi-story office buildings in North America*. Steel Construction Institute.

Stephenson, Mary Sue (1990) *Planning library facilities: selected annotated bibliography*. Scarecrow Press.

Stollard, P. (1991) *Crime prevention through housing design*. Spon.

Stoneham, J. (1994) *Landscape design for elderly and disabled people*. Chichester: Packard.

Strike, J. (1991) *Construction into design: the influence of new methods of construction architectural design, 1690-1990*. Butterworths Architecture.

Taylor, M. and Hosker, H. (1992) *Quality assurance for building design*. Harlow, Essex: Longman Scientific and Technical.

The worker at work: a textbook concerned with men and women in the workplace. (1989) Taylor & Francis.

Thompson, Godfrey (1992) *Planning and design of library building*. Butterworths Architecture.

Thorpe, Stephen (1988) *The good loo design guide: advice on WC provision for disabled people in public buildings*. Centre for Accessible Environments.

Weal, Francis and Francesca (1988) *Housing the elderly: options and designs*. Batsford.

Weale, Sally (1994) Revamp of Design Council leads to closure of London HQ. In *The Guardian*, 5 August, 3.

Wilkes, Joseph and Packard, Robert (1990) *Encyclopaedia of architecture: design, engineering and construction*. Wiley.

Wilkinson, C. (1991) *Supersheds: the architecture of long-span large volume buildings*. Butterworths Architecture.

Willing's press guide. Annual. Reed Information Services.

Wylde, M. (1990) *Building for a lifetime: design and construction of fully accessible homes*. Taunton Press.

Wylson, Anthony and Patricia (1994) *Theme parks, leisure centres, zoos and aquaria*. Longman.

Zeisel, John (1985) *Inquiry by design*. Cambridge University Press.

CHAPTER FIFTEEN

Executing the design: materials, structures, construction

PETER ADDERLEY

Introduction

A major part of the professional's time is spent at this stage of a project. The design has to be developed, detailed decisions made and precise specifications drawn up. However brilliant the design concept, structurally and aesthetically, successful execution depends on appropriate choice of materials and properly designed construction. A wide range of documents needs to be consulted and a major part of an office library is likely to be devoted to them. Because trade literature is constantly in use and is free, there may be a temptation to rely on it too much. This would be a false economy. It should be backed up by a reasonable collection of definitive, authoritative texts. Books and handbooks can save much research time and reduce the risk of mistakes, and there must be ready access to the regulations and standards with which both procedures and buildings have to comply.

Scope

Various levels of detail are involved. They include, from general to particular:

- complete structures and structural design
- building construction of individual structural elements
- non-structural elements and finishes
- manufactured products, which can range from loose substances and small components to complete assemblies
- materials used in the above
- properties of materials and constructions

- abstract and theoretical considerations.

Design factors include structural stability, protection from weather, protection from fire and other hazards, and environmental considerations. There is no clear dividing line between these subjects, and there is much overlapping between the various sections of this chapter. In particular, many of the references mentioned in the section on materials will also be relevant to the later sections.

The technical subjects dealt with here have spawned an enormous number of new and revised publications of all kinds in the last decade. Only a selection can be given. While some of the publications mentioned in the first edition are out-of-date or have been superseded, many are still valid and in popular use. Here too, however, only a selection of the older ones can be mentioned. Note also that some familiar titles now come from different publishers – changes occur in the field of publishing as in any other. The subject matter of this chapter is closely related to that of the chapters on trade and technical literature, on standards and regulations, on specification and on conservation. Building services are covered in Chapter 16.

Information needs

The design professional should have a thorough understanding of the materials and products available and how they are put together. This will come from his initial training, subsequent experience and a study of current literature. Training will have included an introduction to materials and construction and the use of a number of textbooks. However, where he continues to use his college texts he should be aware that lecturers have their biases and preferences; sometimes their own knowledge of what is available may not be complete; they may also rely on their colleagues' works. In any case, he cannot rely on these texts to solve all problems for the next 40 years. He must keep abreast of developments. While book knowledge is necessary, seeing and handling the materials is also important. If a picture is worth a thousand words, a sample is worth a thousand pictures. A samples collection is an important part of any library. Experiencing materials and products in workshops and on site is perhaps even more important for a full appreciation of their characteristics.

Change and development

Methods change – to cut costs, to solve problems or to meet the requirements of more stringent regulations and standards; products change – to cut manufacturing costs, to cope with the shortage of raw materials or to find alternatives to hazardous materials; new products appear – to meet known needs or to exploit new discoveries. A great deal of research has been carried out in recent decades into different types of failures and their causes – problem areas such as flat roofs, high alumina cement and wall-tie corrosion. This has shown that much of the necessary information was already known and available, but was either not sufficiently widely disseminated or just unheeded. These matters are now widely reported in the press and set out in official publications, notably from the BRE, as well as in publications of the relevant trade associations. There are also several books devoted to failures and hazards (see the heading 'Specific topics' below).

The problem is to be aware of these publications, to learn the lessons and to absorb them into the practice's procedures and documentation. It will always be useful to maintain a collection of the annual publications lists from publishers, bookshops and professional and trade associations. Note particularly the *BRE Bookshop catalogue*, the *Building Bookshop catalogue*, the *RIBA Bookshop catalogue* and the *RIBA List of recommended books* (now incorporated in the *Architect's reference annual* from RIBA Publications). Publishers with a useful range of technical books include Butterworth-Heinemann, Gower, Longman, Macmillan and Spon (Chapman Hall). Developments are often first published in conference proceedings. These should not be overlooked; they may often be in greater detail than the original presentation, and provide useful reviews of current knowledge and practice as well as looking ahead. Look out for announcements from professional associations, research bodies and publishers.

Keeping up-to-date

A professional is expected to be knowledgeable as to the current state of the art, and a conscious and continuous effort to keep up-to-date is therefore essential. There are two kinds of activity involved – browsing and detailed study. Browsing and skimming should be a regular discipline to note what is new in general terms. Detailed reading up on specific topics may be needed for a particular project or to develop expertise in a new subject area, or just out of interest. This could entail both general scanning to locate items of relevance and the reading of specialized publications on the topic, depending on whether the intention is to immerse oneself in the subject or just to locate specific required data. A procedure is necessary for effective current awareness – standing orders for official publications, scanning the journals, informing staff.

Sources of information

Sources of information on materials and construction include:

- the Building Centre and other permanent exhibitions, displays and showrooms
- the Building Exhibition and the many specialist and trade exhibitions

- CPD material from professional institutions and publishers, including open-learning packages and videos.

The DoE is the government department responsible for construction, including the Building Regulations and the effects of UK membership of the European Union. Technical information, though, comes largely from the Building Research Establishment (BRE) – perhaps one of the most important sources of all. (The Property Services Agency (PSA) was formerly very important, but its future role under privatization is not yet clear.)

Trade associations form a very important class. They have expert technical knowledge, and many of them produce literature of a high quality. Professional institutions play an important role in keeping their members informed, but the effectiveness of this depends very much on the resources available. Obtain the publications catalogues of all the main organizations – the listings form a salutary reminder of the wealth of information published.

Manufacturers' catalogues will be needed for day-to-day consideration of available products and detailed specification. In addition to product information, however, some catalogues contain much technical information and act as very effective textbooks. Provided that the user ensures that the latest versions are obtained from the manufacturers, these commercial handbooks are likely to be more up-to-date than published books. Microfiche systems are now well-established and CD-ROM and on-line systems developing fast; they are invaluable sources of both listings and actual text, comprehensive and regularly updated. Many of the documents needed in the office – regulations, standards, design guidance and product literature, even textbooks and journal articles – are now available in these media. It would theoretically be possible to reduce the paper library to a very small unit. This will of course have to be weighed against other factors – the costs, the location and portability of the information, and the need for several people to have access at the same time.

Historic information

Some familiar and very useful series – such as PSA *Advisory leaflets* and BRE *Current papers* – have been discontinued or much reduced, although often superseded by new series. They should not be ignored. They may still be found in practice libraries and institution libraries, and provide useful background and historical information. They can be helpful in giving an understanding of the background to a current situation or problem, and could be important for those researching a subject in depth. However, it would be dangerous to rely on these earlier publications as guides to current practice.

Organization of material

Four documents have been influential in improving the content and arrangement of technical and project documentation. The current versions are:

- *CIB Master list of headings for the arrangement and presentation of information in technical documents for design and construction* (CIB report 18, 1993)
- *CI/SfB construction indexing manual* (3rd edn, RIBA Publications, 1976, abridged reprint 1991
- *Common arrangement of works sections* (BPIC, 1987)
- BS 4940: *Technical information on construction products and services* (in 3 parts, BSI, 1994).

They have gradually led to the following advantages for the user of technical information:

- standardization: ease of comparison of properties, familiarity with arrangement of documents, quicker searching
- discipline: encouragement of methodical approach, aid to understanding
- checklist value: yardsticks against which to check information, reminders of matters to be considered.

Materials

Legislation, regulations and standards

These are covered elsewhere, but passing reference should be made to them here as they are vital to the subject matter of this chapter. Building Regulations and Approved Documents lay down fundamental requirements and should of course be in every library. The European context is now becoming more important through the Construction Products Regulations and the forthcoming European Technical Approvals (ETAs). Keep informed through the Agrément Board, *BSI News* and the European Construction Centre. The DoE issues *Construction monitor* (superseding *Euronews construction*, which ran from 1987 to 1993), which has been expanded to include UK construction news as well as European. This is free from the DoE (0171-276 6698), and also published in *Building*. Knight's *European construction documents* (Charles Knight Publishing) is a loose-leaf subscription service with extensive text and explanatory notes. BSI documents – standards, codes of practice, drafts for development and other publications – are essential references for specification purposes. They also form a valuable starting point for the study of materials and construction, providing a rich source of data on materials and guidance on good building practice. BS Handbook 3 *Summaries of British Standards for building* contains almost complete text of standards, in updated loose-leaf format. The *Manual of British Standards in building construction and specification* (2nd edn, Hutchinson Education, 1987) is a convenient classified compilation of key standards in book form, but is of course frozen at publication date.

Directories

The best known general directory of the industry is *Sell's building index* (annual, formerly by Sell's Publications, but now to be published by Benn Business Information Services). It includes a classified list of products and services and alphabetical lists of professional and trade organizations, trade names and companies – all very extensive. The *Barbour Index building product compendium* and the *RIBA Product selector* both contain comprehensive listings of manufacturers and trade names. *Specification* includes useful lists of organizations relevant to each chapter.

There is a wide range of specialist directories, including:

Adhesives and sealants yearbook and directory (annual, FMJ International Publications for BASA)
Adhesives directory (annual, Turret Group)
BASA Yearbook and directory (adhesives)
Buyers guide: the source of product information for the building industry (occasional, BTJ Books)
Buyers guide to the British timber industry (2nd edn, British Timber Merchants Association, 1991)
Carpet annual (Benn Business Information Services)
Concrete yearbook (annual, Thomas Telford)
Directory of precast concrete products (occasional, BPCF)
Natural stone directory (every three years, Ealing Publications)
Panel products directory (new from TRADA in 1993)
Wood equipment buyers guide (annual, formerly *Buyers guide for the woodworking industry*. Turret Group).

The professional associations issue directories of their members, both individuals and practices, and sometimes international practices. For example, the CIOB issues both the *Chartered building company directory and handbook* and the *Directory of construction consultants*. These associations may be able to identify members with special expertise. For consultants and contractors throughout Europe, arranged by country, see the *European directory of contractors and public works annual and construction industries buyers guide* (annual, Biggar and Co Publishers). For a comprehensive listing of directories, see *Current British directories* (12th edn, CBD Research, 1993).

Dictionaries

The BSI has been compiling glossaries for many years, and since the mid-1980s has been publishing them as BS 6100, in 55 Parts. They are now available as a hardback book: *Glossary of building and civil engineering terms* (1993). The long-running Penguin dictionaries have been updated: John Scott and James Maclean's *Penguin dictionary of building* (4th edn, 1993); and John Scott's *Penguin dictionary of civil engineering* (4th edn, 1991). More recent titles are: P. Marsh's *Illustrated dictionary of building* (Longman Scientific and Technical, 1982, reprinted 1989); James Stevens Curl's *Encyclopaedia of architectural terms* (Donhead, 1992); and Peter Brett's *Building terminology: an illustrated guide for students* (Oxford: Newnes, 1993). Bi-lingual and multi-lingual dictionaries, a growing necessity in Europe, include the *Dictionary of building terms in twelve languages* (published in Moscow, available London: RIBA Publications, 1986). The languages are: Russian, Bulgarian, Czech, German, Hungarian, Mongolian, Polish, Roumanian, Serbo-Croat, Spanish, French and English.

Data

Specification (EMAP Architecture, annual) must be mentioned as perhaps the most comprehensive and useful single publication, trades and materials being illustrated with numerous tables and diagrams. The *New metric handbook*, edited by Patricia Tutt and David Adler (Butterworth-Heinemann, 1979), includes chapters on materials and on structures. Henry Haverstock's *The 'Building design' easibrief* (Morgan-Grampian (Construction Press), 1993) is described as a first stop reference book for building designers: it consists of a large number of short items, originally published in *Building design* and, now updated, provides a useful introduction to various topics. In September 1992 the *Architects' journal* began a weekly series of 'Briefing guides', a number of which relate to materials and construction.

Kempe's engineers' yearbook, edited by Carill Sharpe (99th edn Benn Business Information Services, 1994) remains an extremely detailed and authoritative reference on all branches of engineering, and includes data useful to architects. Other technical reference books include: *Civil engineer's reference book* (4th edn, Butterworth-Heinemann, 1989), edited by L.S. Blake; L. Black's *Builder's reference book* (Spon, 1985); and David Doran's *Construction materials reference book* (Butterworth-Heinemann, 1992) and *Construction materials pocket book* (Butterworth-Heinemann, 1994). More specialized is Sax' *Dangerous properties of industrial materials* (Van Nostrand Reinhold), which might prove helpful on occasion. A CD-ROM format was issued in 1994, combined with Hawley's *Condensed chemical dictionary* – both very familiar to industrial health professionals.

Official publications

Building Research Establishment

The BRE publishes a range of documents in various formats making basic technical information and news of the latest developments readily available to the industry. These are all listed in the annual *BRE Bookshop catalogue*, and announced in *News of construction research* and *Publications news*. BRE *Digests* are perhaps the most important series, and design professionals ought not to be without a complete set. They cover practically every aspect of building technology, each one being a summary of the BRE's knowledge in a particular area. The slimmer (four page) Information Papers provide simple statements of the latest research results and how to apply them. *Good Building Guides*, superseding the former *Defects Action Sheets*, offer concise practical guidance on good building design and construction. The best way to ensure that you receive all of these is to subscribe to the BRE Update service.

Other publications include BRE *Reports*, giving more detailed accounts of research findings, Overseas Building Notes, video cassettes and computer software, and literature packs collating information on particular topics.

British Board of Agrément

The Agrément Board, as it was then known, was set up by the government in 1966 to provide independent and accurate assessment of materials and products for their performance in use. A complete set of Agrément Certificates now provides technical information on a formidable range of products, and there is an updating service. The BBA is the UK body that will be responsible for European Technical Approvals. As well as individual certificates, the BBA also produces a series of MOATs – Methods of Assessment and Testing – giving detailed technical requirements for the performance of various elements, e.g. MOAT No. 1: *Windows*, MOAT No. 11: *Doors*.

Product information

Product information is only mentioned briefly here. Specifiers are now well catered for with guides to available products and their types and properties. The pioneering work of the lamented *NBA Commodity file* has been developed by others, in comparative selection tables, in structured product data based on the *CIB Master list*, and in highly organized classified listings and indexes. The *Barbour Index building product compendium* (annual) and the *RIBA Product selector* (RIBA Information Services, annual) are both free to specifiers and should be in every office. The *Compendium* contains product information to a standard format, the *Selector* includes advertisements; both have comprehensive indexes. *Architects standard catalogues* (now just known as *ASC*) differs from others in containing reproductions of manufacturers' literature, not rewritten to common format; however, it includes comprehensive selection tables and an extensive section of technical information. *RIBA Product data* (RIBA Information Services) is a subscription service of loose-leaf, systematically designed product data sheets. *Specification* is a priced annual publication, now in three volumes; the Products volume is notable for its comprehensive product selection tables; a *Specification product update* is issued free to subscribers.

The text of manufacturers' catalogues has been available on microfilm for some years (through Barbour Index and Technical Indexes). The next two stages, using computers, are already well-developed: CD-ROM systems and on-line systems. Names to note are NBS *Specification manager, Construction and civil engineering index* (Technical Indexes), Prodex (Guidex Publishing), BCQ and *On Demand Information* – ODI (Building Centre). Working details and specification aids are also available on computer. RIBACAD (RIBA Information Services) is a library of manufacturers' details which can be incorporated directly into CAD drawings. Drawings and design and specification programs are also offered by individual manufacturers (see the section on Construction below for examples).

Specifying

The *National building specification* (*NBS*) is now well-established as the industry standard, with *NES* for engineering work. With comprehensive guidance notes and checklists of reference documents, *NBS* can be regarded as an important basic office reference, as well as a working document. It comes in three versions – Standard, Intermediate and Minor. The *PSA specifications* (PSA Specialist Services; from BRE Bookshop) have been written for government contracts, and care would be needed in editing for private work. There are four versions: PSA *General specification 1991*; PSA *Minor works specification 1992*; *Standard specification for estate management building works 1991* and *Standard specification for decorative works 1991*.

NBS clauses, the PSA General and Minor works clauses and the Specification clauses are also available on disk, enabling the user to edit a project specification directly on screen. In addition, NBS is linked through *Specification manager* to standards, other technical literature, trade literature and CAD details.

The *Common arrangement of work sections for building works* (BPIC, 1987) provides the classification framework for specifications (and can be used for the library arrangement of trade literature). BPIC also issued in 1987 a definitive guide to specifying – *Project specification: a code of procedure for building works*. NBS and *Specification* both include substantial introductions on the principles of specifying, as well as guidance notes related to the clauses. The long-running standard text by Arthur J. Willis, *Specification writing for architects and quantity surveyors*, first published in 1953, is now in its 10th edition (1991), revised by J. Christopher and J. Andrew Willis.

Texts

Amongst the forerunners of the modern literature on building materials was H.J. Eldridge's *Properties of building materials*. This was the first attempt to list the properties of the more important building materials according to the recommendations of the *CIB Master list*. It first appeared in the *Construction industry handbook* in 1971 and was reprinted in book form in 1974 (both by Medical and Technical Publishing – MTP). It is worth looking out for. So too is Lyall Addleson's classic *Materials for building* (Iliffe, 1972). This was in four volumes: 'Physical and chemical aspects of matter and strength of materials'; 'Water and its effects' (2 volumes); and 'Heat and fire and their effects'. Together they formed a most detailed study of materials and their properties and behaviour. Topics from this work were developed by Lyall Addleson and Colin Rice in a more recent single volume: *Performance of materials in buildings: a study of the principles and agencies of change* (Butterworth-Heinemann, 1992).

Other recent texts include: David Doran's *Construction materials reference book* (1992); Cecil Elliott's *Technics and architecture: the development of materials and systems for buildings* (MIT Press, 1992); Alan Everett's *Materials* (5th edn, in Mitchell's Building Series – see 'Construction' below, 1994); J.M. Illston's *Construction materials: their nature and behaviour* (2nd edn, Spon, 1994); and G.D. Taylor's *Materials in construction* (2nd edn, Longman Higher Education, 1994) and *Construction materials* (1991), a more advanced treatment of properties and performance. At a more specialized level, *RILEM Technical recommendations for the testing and use of construction materials* (Spon, 1994) is a compilation of 170 Technical Recommendations prepared by RILEM Technical Committees since 1975. This is intended for engineers and scientists.

Specific materials

The literature on individual materials is rather uneven in quantity. Information may have to be searched for in general books such as those already mentioned. The major source in many cases is in fact likely to be the relevant trade associations. Books on conservation and repair can also be salutary in pointing out the characteristics of a material and showing what can go wrong.

Asphalt

The Mastic Asphalt Council and Employers Federation has for many years issued popular handbooks on the use of mastic asphalt. The latest revisions are the *Roofing handbook* (1993), *Paving handbook* (1993), *Flooring handbook* (1988) and *Tanking handbook* (1994). Technical Information Sheet No. 2: *Trapped water in roofs* (1969), explaining the problems of trapped water and interstitial condensation, is also still available.

In 1989, MACEF (the contractors) joined with MAPA (the producers) to form the Mastic Asphalt Technical Advisory Centre (MATAC), which offers a comprehensive advisory service

Brick

Although brick is an apparently simple material to design for, careful selection and detailing are needed to avoid water penetration, poor weathering and other defects. It is an attractive material with a wide range of colours and textures. However, choice and availability can be badly affected by boom/recession cycles as manufacturers try to match output to demand. Selection and specification can thus raise a number of problems. Older texts to look out for are McKay's *Brickwork* (Longman, 1974) and S. Smith's *Brickwork* (2nd edn, Macmillan, 1975). Note also Gage and Kirkbride's *Design in blockwork* (3rd edn, Architectural Press, 1980). More recent is R.W. Brunskill's *Brick building in Britain* (1990). A new series, *Brickwork: history, technology and practice*, by Gerard Lynch (Donhead) offers an in-depth guide to all aspects of brickwork and bricklaying practice. Volumes I and II were published in 1994, and four more volumes are due to follow in 1995 and 1996.

The Brick Development Association (BDA) produces a wide range of publications, such as Design Guides, Engineers File Notes, Technical Information Papers (TIPs), Design Notes (DNs), Building Notes and Special Publications (SPs). Most of these deal with brick construction and structural brickwork – see below. Those that deal with bricks as a material include *Bricks: notes on their properties* (TIP7), *The use of bricks of special shape* (DN13), *A study of the dimensional deviations of clay bricks* (TIP4), *European clay brick standard takes shape* (TIP9) and *Bricks and brickwork* (SP1), a set of five wallcharts.

Concrete

Concrete is a very versatile material, but prone to defects and failure for various reasons: the individual mixing for each project, the scope for human error, the lack of understanding of mix design, dependency on quality of workmanship, and the failure to give adequate attention to finish and weathering. While the literature is extensive it is largely concerned with concrete structures rather than concrete as a material. A significant development is the revision of BS 5328: 1972 in 1991. This updated guidance on specifying concrete and introduced a new method for specifying concrete mixes. S.T. Adams' *Complete concrete, masonry and brick handbook* (Spon, 1983) is a massive guide covering all aspects of working with concrete, masonry, brick, stucco and tile. British practice is described in Orchard's *Concrete technology* (2nd edn, Applied Science, 1976), and American practice in Wadell's *Concrete construction handbook* (2nd edn, McGraw-Hill, 1974). The hazards are highlighted in P.H. Perkin's *Repair, protection and waterproofing of concrete structures* (Elsevier Applied Science, 1986).

Several publications deal with special materials or techniques. This selection illustrates the versatility mentioned above: J.D. Dewar and R. Anderson's *Manual of ready-mixed concrete* (2nd edn, Blackie Academic & Professional, 1992); *Cement admixtures* (2nd edn, Longman Higher Education, for the CCA, 1988), edited by P.C. Hewlett; *Structural lightweight aggregate concrete* (Blackie Academic & Professional, 1993), edited by J.L. Clarke; *Use of PFA in construction* (Spon, 1994), edited by R.K. Dhir and M.R. Jones – a comprehensive review of current applications; G. True's *GRC (glass fibre reinforced cement): production and uses* (Spon, 1985); John Young's *Guide to GRC for architects* (Architectural Press, 1978); and *Concrete in hot climates* (Spon, 1992), edited by M.J. Walker.

The British Cement Association (BCA) was formed in 1987, superseding the previous Cement and Concrete Association (CCA). Funded by cement companies, it produces an extensive range of publications, advice and courses useful to architects. The *BCA Catalogue* includes publications from nearly 40 concrete industry organizations – indicative of the range of interests. Again the numerous publications relate mainly to construction. Those concerned with different aspects of concrete as a material include: *Admixtures for concrete* (1984); *The properties and use of concretes made with composite cements* by T.A. Harrison and D.C. Spooner, 1987; *Impurities in concreting aggregates* by T.P. Lees, 1987; *Foamed concrete: composition and properties* (1991); and *The diagnosis of alkali-silica reaction* (report of a working party, 2nd edn, 1992).

Fixings and ironmongery

While architects have always taken an interest in architectural ironmongery – the visible parts – they have not always understood the structural and mechanical aspects of hardware and fixings. Their importance has been made apparent by a series of mishaps with wall ties, claddings and roof coverings. There are not many texts on this subject, but one recent one is Michael Wilson and Peter Harrison's *Appraisal and repair of building structures: claddings and fixings* (Thomas Telford, 1993), a practical guide to the investigation and remedy of faults in cladding, with particular emphasis on fixings.

The following is a miscellaneous selection of technical publications in this field. CIRIA Technical Note TN137 *Selection and use of fixings in concrete and masonry: interim update to CIRIA Guide G4* (1991) is a comprehensive but concise guide to current fixing techniques. Nancy R. Badoo's *Design of stainless steel fixings and ancillary components* (the Steel Construction Institute, Report SCI-P-119, 1993) gives guidance on mechanical properties, design strengths and the selection of grades. The *PSA Method of building* includes *Hardware* (the 'Blue Book', 3rd edn), now available exclusively from the Guild of Architectural Ironmongers (GAI). More advanced technical publications are issued by the Construction Fixings Association.

Two codes of practice should be mentioned: *Code of practice: architectural ironmongery suitable for use on fire-resisting, self-closing timber and emergency exit doors* (3rd edn, GAI, 1993) and *Code of practice for hardware essential to the optimum performance of fire resisting timber doorsets* (Association of Builders' Hardware Manufacturers).

Glass

The key text here is *Glass in building: a guide to modern architectural glass performance*, edited by David Button and Brian Pye (2nd edn, Butterworth-Heinemann, 1993), which explains the properties, performance and potential use of glass. See also the earlier book by G. Brand, *Principles of glazing* (Essential Structures Research Association, 1977). The Glass and Glazing Federation issues a number of datasheets on different materials and glazing techniques.

Metals

There are few general texts on the various metals – aluminium, copper, lead, steel and zinc. Most technical information comes from the respective trade associations (see below). Texts on structural steel and aluminium are dealt with below. One recent book that helps to fill the gap is John Lane's *Aluminium in building* (Gower, 1992). This describes the characteristics of the material and its many possible uses.

The various trade associations produce a number of leaflets and booklets, as well as videos. Most of these are more appropriate to construction. One to be noted here, is *The properties of aluminium and its alloys* (9th edn, 1993) by the Aluminium Federation (Alfed).

Paint

This is a highly technical subject and subject to continuous development. But here, too, there are few texts available apart from relevant chapters of *Specification* and books on finishes. However, paint manufacturers' catalogues provide excellent technical information and specification guidance.

Plastics

This is another technical subject not easy for architects to get to grips with unless they have a liking for complex chemistry. If they do, they should find books on the subject in public libraries. It is essential to understand the differences between the various plastics and their respective uses. Helpful texts are: Alec Leggatt's *GRP and buildings: a design guide for architects and engineers* (1984); *Polymeric building materials* (Spon, 1989), edited by D. Feldman; and L. Hoolaway's *Polymers and polymer composites in construction* (Thomas Telford, 1990).

Stone

This most natural of building materials is coming back into favour. Its use is encouraged by John Ashurst, F.G. Dimes and D. Honeyborne in *Stone in building: its use and potential today* (Architectural Press, 1977; reprinted by the Stone Federation). The Stone Federation publishes data and information sheets on types of stone, suitable mortars, etc., and a directory of quarry owners and stone masons. Note also *Code of practice on natural stone cladding* (*non-loadbearing*) (Stone Federation and District Surveyors Association, 1984).

Thatch

Another traditional material enjoying renewed interest is thatch, no longer a dying craft. *The thatchers' craft*, published by Cosira (the Council for Small Industries in Rural Areas – now RDC, the Rural Development Commission) is a valuable guide to methods and styles, while R.C. West's *Thatch* (David & Charles, 1987) is a detailed guide to design and maintenance.

Wood

There has been much debate recently about the use of timber. Its ecological advantages on the one hand – a renewable resource, low energy requirements for production, potential for design of energy efficient buildings – and concern at the destruction of rain forests on the other have led to conflicting advice, not helped by bogus labelling and false claims. Information is gradually becoming available to specifiers so that they can make up their own minds about the suitability and acceptability of any species. Look out for information about a new revolutionary electronic tagging system, devised by Bill Miller. A '1995 Group' of companies has been formed committed to phasing out the marketing of timber from non-sustainable sources by 1995, rejecting all existing 'green' labels but accepting Miller's. See the *Architects' journal*, 199 (15), 158 13 April 1994.

A standard work on wood, first published in 1948, is Douglas Patterson's *Commercial timbers of the world* (5th edn, Gower, 1988). This comprises a general account of the structure and properties of wood and descriptions of over 350 species. Another authoritative reference work is *Timber in construction*, edited by John Sunley and Barbara Bedding (Batsford/TRADA, 1987). Other technical guides are H.E. Desch's *Timber: its structure, properties and utilisation* (6th edn, 1991) and G.T. Tsoumis' *Science and technology of wood* (Spon, 1992), while Jack Baird adopts a more practical approach in *Timber specifiers' guide: understanding and specifying softwoods in building* (1990).

Pests and decay and the preservative treatment of timber are well-documented in technical literature. There are several recent books on the subject, such as A.F. Bravery and J.K. Carey's *Recognising wood rot and insect damage in buildings* (1992) and three published by Spon: R. Eaton and M. Hale's *Wood: decay, pests and protection* (1993); B.A. Richardson's *Wood preservation* (2nd edn, 1993) and B.V. Ridout's *Timber in buildings: decay, treatment and conservation* (an English Heritage/Historic Scotland co-publication, 1994). However, specifiers have yet more rules to learn. The British Standards Institution recommends preservatives and processes for particular components and situations. New European standards take a different approach – they are performance-based, specifying the results of treatment rather than the treatment itself. Preliminary information is given in BRE Digest 393 *Specifying preservative treatments: the new European approach* (April 1994). No doubt the trade associations and manufacturers will be providing advice and textbooks will be updated.

TRADA is a prolific source of useful and authoritative publications. For general awareness see *List of British Standards relating to timber* (1992), *TRADA Update – Standards*, a monthly updating service, and *TRADA Update – Legislation*, a monthly updating service which includes environmental issues, health and safety developments, etc. Special mention should be made of *The Building Regulations 1991: Approved Document: Timber intermediate floors for dwellings* (1992) – the first Approved Document to be prepared by an independent organization. There are numerous Wood Information Sheets. These titles indicate the range: *Structural use of hardwoods; Trussed rafters; Guide to stress graded softwood; Timber and wood-based sheet materials in fire; Introduction to timber framed housing;* and *Finishes for exterior timber*. Note also the famous Red Booklets, 'Timbers of the world' (1978 and 1979) – a series of nine pocket-sized books describing the characteristics and use of commercial timbers from different regions.

The BRE has produced *Handbook of hardwoods* (2nd edn, 1972) and *A handbook of softwoods* (1977). Forest Forever can provide current information on the availability of timber from well-managed sources.

Trade literature

Trade literature is covered in Chapter 5, but a few comments may be made here. The essentials for a working collection are that it should contain the product catalogues relevant to the work of the practice, that they can be readily identified and accessible and that they be kept up-to-date. The advantages and disadvantages of paper, microfilm, CD-ROM and on-line information – or a combination – will have to be weighed up. Electronic media have the edge on currency (including prices and company changes), as well as saving space and labour. There is a trend towards 'on-demand' information, called up as required, rather than a maintained collection.

As mentioned in the introduction, some trade catalogues make very effective textbooks. They go far beyond describing their products, giving wide and authoritative information on their subjects and extensive technical data, and are almost obligatory references. Some are in such demand that a charge is made. Well-known examples are British Gypsum's *White Book, Expandite jointing and sealing manual*, Pilkington Glass' *Specifier's guide*, Redland Roof Tiles' *Technical guides*, and the handbooks from the major paint companies such as Crown Berger and ICI Paints. Look out for Cape, Lytag, Marley, Rentokil and others. One-off books and guides are also produced, such as *Weather resistant steel: use and applications* (British Steel plc, Sections and Plates and Commercial Steels Division, revised 1994) and *Brickwork and detailing* (Ibstock, 1989).

Technical and design advisory services

Some manufacturers, such as Crown Berger and Ibstock, provide very helpful advisory services, usually free. Many now offer computer programs to develop designs and produce drawings (see below).

House journals

A useful source of information on developments and new products – and of inspiration – is the wide range of magazines produced by manufacturers and trade associations, who are normally only too happy to supply them free on request – they are often mailed to practices automatically. They are worth scanning quickly, for new products and applications, for warnings, and for examples of products in use. However, information is seldom very detailed. See under 'Periodicals' below for examples.

Samples

An in-house collection of samples, however small, is an important reference source. The minimum would be standard materials that hardly change and are constantly specified – say, timber specimens (TRADA can supply samples of various timber species, individually or as a set), textured glass samples and paint colour cards. Then add selected proprietary products, such as an ironmongery board of the most-specified range. However, the collection will need to be strictly controlled. Some products – bricks and blocks, sanitary fittings, even carpet samples – may be too bulky, and labelling and keeping up-to-date can be difficult. Temporary collections can be gathered together for individual projects at specification stage, then kept on-site and finally disposed of. Full use should be made of external sources, as it is important for designers both to see what they are specifying and to explore new products. Possible locations are national building exhibitions and specialist trade exhibitions, building centres, trade associations and manufacturers' and suppliers' showrooms, and even museums – the Geological Museum, part of the Natural History Museum in London, holds 18 000 specimens of stone in its study collections.

Structures

Roles

In a medium-sized or large building the design of the main structure will normally be carried out for the designer by a structural engineer. The designer may require a particular type of structure, or he may take the engineer's advice and agree it with him. The same will apply to building services and any other significant engineering content (see Chapter 16). Engineers and other specialists may be selected from the practice's own shortlist, from known experts or from the directories of the appropriate institutions – the ACE, ISE, ICE, RICS and CIOB (see 'Types of Materials' above). These are usually updated annually. An in-house record of specialists used and their performance will form an important part of a practice's resources.

Developments

Brick is one of the oldest structural materials, with little change for thousands of years. A variety of techniques has been developed in the last few decades, however, and the architect needs an understanding of diaphragm walls, reinforced brickwork, post-tensioned brickwork, prefabricated brick panels and brick cladding to steel frames. In the case of concrete, design procedures have been altered by new design codes, first BS 5110 in 1985, replacing CP 110 and written in limit state terms, then *Eurocode EC2* (Part 1.1 *General rules for buildings*) in 1992. Older texts on structural design may still be of value but will need to be updated. Developments in steel construction include slim floor systems, with the steel members contained within the depth of the floor, and long span steel frames. *Eurocode 3* on steel structures also appeared in 1992. The new Eurocodes, expected to be eight in number, will be the future structural design codes for the whole of the EC. See below for guides to the new codes.

Timber frame and trussed rafters continue to develop, and design tables are readily available from TRADA and from manufacturers. Other developments range from earth structures to cables and fabric. There is continuing effort to develop innovative structures and combine materials and components in new ways, whether for functional reasons, economy or elegant visual effect. Many of the references under 'Construction' will be relevant to structures as a whole. More specialized references are given here.

Reference books

Texts not already mentioned include J.A. Barker's *Dictionary of soil mechanics and foundation engineering* (Construction Press, 1981); Reynolds and Steedman's *Reinforced concrete designer's handbook* (Spon, 1988) – a specialized handbook for engineers, but useful for background understanding; the *Structural steelwork handbook* (2nd edn, BCSA, 1978); and the *Steel construction yearbook* (Thomas Telford).

CPD guides

The RIBA open-learning packages include several on structural engineering topics, intended to give architects a better understanding of structural principles and possibilities. Examples are *The corrosion and protection of structural steelwork in buildings* by Ken Johnson, and *Tension structures* by John Thornton.

Texts

Structures and structural design

A wide range of books exists. They aim at different levels of readership, and take different viewpoints, from relationship to architectural design to theoretical and technical. The *AJ handbook of building structure* (2nd edn, Architectural Press, 1980) is out of print, but provides a good introduction. Angus J. MacDonald's *Structure and architecture* (Butterworth-Heinemann, 1994), the latest addition to the subject, explains basic principles, describes structural types and links these topics to architectural design.

Several books aim to give a popular explanation, such as J.E. Gordon's *New science of strong materials: why you don't fall through the floor* (2nd edn, Penguin, 1976), *Structures: or why things don't fall down* (Penguin, 1978) and *The science of structures and materials* (New York: Scientific American Library, 1988). Similar are *Why buildings stand up: the strength of architecture* by Mario Salvadori (New York: Norton, 1980; 1990 printing with new afterword) and the more recent *Why buildings fall down: how structures fail* by Matthys Levy and Mario Salvadori (Norton, 1992). The architectural context is dealt with by several authors, including Andrew Orton in *The way we build now: form, scale and technique* (Van Nostrand Rheinhold, 1988); Mario Salvadori and Robert Heller in *Structure in architecture: the building of buildings* (3rd edn, Prentice-Hall, 1986); Bjorn Sandaker and Arne Eggen in *The structural basis of architecture* (Phaidon, 1993); and Mick Eekhout in *Architecture in space structures* (Netherlands, 1989).

This is just a selection of the many books on structural design, either fairly recent or in new editions: D. Brohn's *Understanding structural analysis* (2nd edn, BSP Professional Books, 1990); R.C. Coates and M.G. Courie's *Structural analysis* (3rd edn, Chapman Hall, 1988); N.J. Cook's *Designer's guide to wind loading of building structures* (Butterworth-Heinemann, vol I, 1986; vol II, 1990); Bryan Gauld's *Structures for architects* (2nd edn, Longman Higher Education, 1989) – a student text; Lavan and Fletcher's *Student's guide to structural design* (Butterworth-Heinemann, 1989) – a replacement for Morgan's *Student's structural handbook* of 1973; T.Y. Lin and Sydney D. Stotesbury's *Structural concepts and systems for architects and engineers* (2nd edn, Wiley, 1988); and Alec Nash's *Structural design for architects* (Gower, 1990).

Brick

Turning to more specialized texts, the BDA has issued over 20 Design Guides on retaining walls, diaphragm walls, reinforced brickwork, post-tensioned brickwork, etc.

Concrete and masonry

This vast field can be represented by C.E. Reynolds and J.C. Steedman's *Examples of the design of reinforced concrete buildings to CP110* (4th edn, Spon, 1992) and their *Reinforced concrete designer's handbook* (10th edn, Spon, 1988), available as a two volume set; P. Abeles and B.K. Bardhan-Roy's *Prestressed concrete designers' handbook* (3rd edn, Viewpoint, now Spon, 1981); and E. O'Brien's *Reinforced and prestressed concrete design: the complete process* (Longman Higher Education, 1994) – one of the first textbooks to use the new *Eurocode EC2*.

Cladding is covered in W.R. Oram's *Precast concrete cladding* (Slough:

Cement & Concrete Association, 1978) and in three books by Alan Brookes: *Concepts in cladding* (1985) – 30 case studies; *Cladding of buildings* (Construction Press, 1983); and with Chris Grech, *The building envelope: applications of new technology cladding* (Butterworth-Heinemann, 1994). An out of print title worth looking up is Michael Gage's *Guide to exposed concrete finishes* (Architectural Press/CCA, 1970). This covers more than the title suggests, giving a comprehensive description of the whole process of producing reinforced concrete.

Key texts on masonry are *Structural masonry designer's manual* (2nd edn, BSP Professional Books, 1987) by W.G. Curtin et al. and Arnold W. Hendry's *Structural masonry* (1990).

From ICE comes *Specification for piling: contract documentation and measurement* (Thomas Telford, 1988) – mainly dealing with concrete, but including steel and timber; and from ISE and ICE, *Manual for the design of reinforced concrete building structures* (ISE, 1985). More recently the BCA has issued *Precast concrete frame buildings: a design guide* by K.S. Elliott and A.K. Tovey (1992).

Foundations

Books related to foundation design include R.F. Craig's popular *Soil mechanics* (5th edn, Spon, 1992), M.J. Tomlinson's *Foundation design and construction* (5th edn, Longman, 1986, reprinted 1989) and Tomlinson's *Pile design and construction practice* (Viewpoint, 1987).

Steel and aluminium

First mention must be given to the Steel Construction Institute's *Steel designer's manual* edited by G.W. Owens, P.R. Knowles and P.J. Dowling (Blackwell Scientific Publications, 1992) – the first major revision of this manual for 20 years, based on the limit state design method and BS 5950. *Architecture and construction in steel,* edited by Alan Blanc, Michael McEvoy and Roger Plank (Spon, 1994), is a new comprehensive guide. Older familiar texts are L.V. Leech's *Structural steelwork for students* (2nd edn, Butterworths, 1988) and F. Hart et al. 's *Multi-storey buildings in steel* (2nd edn, Collins, 1985). Structural aluminium is covered by a new book by John Bull, *The practical design of structural elements in aluminium* (Gower, 1993).

The British Constructional Steelwork Association (BCSA) has published *The National structural steelwork specification for building construction*, which is increasingly the standard for specifier and fabricator. Another standard work is the *Manual for the design of steelwork structures – the Grey Book* (ISE, 1989, reprinted with corrections 1990). The Steel Construction Institute (SCI) – formerly the Constructional Steel Research and Development Organization (CONSTRADO) – promotes effective use of steel in construction and issues a number of publications. These include *Joints in simple construction, Fire protection for structural steel in buildings* and *Adaptability of steel framed buildings – design guidance for architects and clients*. The British Steel Advisory Service gives free advice to designers.

Timber

John Bull has published *The practical design of structural elements in timber* (Gower, 1989). Other texts from about the same time are J. Burchell and F.W. Sunter's *Design and build in timber frame* (Longman, 1987), C.J. Mettem's *Structural timber design and technology* (Longman, 1986); and J.A. Baird and E.C. Ozelton's *Timber designer's manual* (2nd edn, BSP Professional Books, 1989). TRADA has published several Wood Information Sheets on timber frame construction, and two books on structural aspects: *Timber frame construction* (1988) and *Timber frame housing: structural recommendations* (1989).

Special structural forms

Some out of print but seminal books are worthy of mention: *Tensile structures* (2 vols: I Pneumatic structures; II Cables, nets and membranes, London and New York: A. Tiranti, 1967; 2 vols in 1, New York: Reinhold, 1973) by Frei Otto et al.; Jurgen Joedicke's *Shell architecture* (MIT, 1963); and Rowland J. Mainstone's *Developments in structural form* (Allen Lane with RIBA Publications, 1975). More recent texts of varied interest are M.R. Terman's *Earth-sheltered housing: principles in practice* (Chapman and Hall, 1986); Chris Wilkinson's *Supersheds: the architecture of long-span large-volume buildings* (Butterworth-Heinemann, 1991); and James Harris and Kevin Li's *Masted structures in architecture* (Butterworth-Heinemann, 1994).

Technical and trade

BRE series generally include some items relevant to structures, such as Digest 315 *Choosing piles for new construction*, Digest 346 Parts 1 to 8 *The assessment of wind loads* and a whole series of reports on proprietary steel-framed houses and bungalows in the late 1980s and early 1990s. The ICE has issued *Site investigation in construction* (Site Investigation Steering Group, Thomas Telford, 1993). Between them the BCA, BDA, ICE, ISE, SCI and other bodies have published an extensive range of manuals, guides and reports, some of which are mentioned above. A number of manufacturers supply complete building structures or substantial structural components such as portal frames and precast floor units and cladding – names such as Bison, Trent, British Steel and Space Decks. Some produce very good catalogues with detailed drawings.

Construction

The basic principles of building construction are understood and good practice has been well documented. Yet buildings have been plagued with problems since the war. Recent concerns include:

- foundations: subsidence and heave, unsuitable sites
- ground gases: radon (natural) and methane (resulting from contaminated land)
- flat roofs: water penetration, condensation, thermal insulation
- pitched roofs: structural stability, secure fixing of roof covering, condensation, thermal insulation
- curtain walling and cladding: wind suction, shattering, falling, thermal movement
- sick building syndrome (SBS): complex causes, unpredictable effects
- long-term deterioration of structures and components: concrete corrosion, wall ties.

Three major causes of these problems are costs, technology and workmanship. Genuine budgetary restraints, shortage of materials and commercial cost-cutting mean that minimum standards are not achieved. New technology solves some problems but introduces new factors which were not anticipated – thinner structural materials causing thermal and sound insulation problems, for example. Workmanship is often slipshod, and may be downright fraudulent, with inferior materials being substituted or components (e.g. wall ties) being omitted altogether. There are some long-lasting standard texts which are still useful for a thorough understanding of basic principles. But new technologies and new regulations mean that literature becomes out-of-date, and updated and modern texts are vital. One new watchword is 'buildability' – closer links between design and construction, a better understanding by designers and specifiers of the building process, and a greater awareness of cost implications and of cost-effective alternative methods.

Reference books

NHBC Standards gives detailed guidance on principles for the whole design and building process, with numerous drawings, tables and references. It is published by the National House-Building Council for Registered Housebuilders and Designers, and updated frequently.

Detailing – general

There is now quite a wide range of books of drawn details. Some of these may be out of print, but they are still worth looking up as exemplars of good practice and for ideas, even though some techniques may now be out-of-date. The multi-volume *Architects' working details*, edited by Colin Boyne and Lance Wright (Architectural Press, 1977), first published in the 1960s, was the classic forerunner of other detail books. It should be readily available in libraries. More recent details from the *Architects' journal* appear in *Architects' working details* (1989) edited by David Jenkins and Louis Dezart.

The *Architects' journal* continues to include working details, often related to more extensive building studies. It is not a systematic series, but provides a variety of examples of interesting current practice. Other detail books, old and new, are: GLC's *Good practice details* (Architectural Press, 1980; Butterworth-Heinemann, 1990); GLC's *Detailing for building construction: a designer's manual of over 350 standard details* (Butterworth-Heinemann, 1980); Cecil Handisyde's *Everyday details* (Construction Press, 1976; Butterworth-Heinemann, 1979); S. Smith and P. Stronach's *Builders' detail sheets* (2nd edn, Spon, 1986) – only revised up to the 1985 Building Regulations; Wendy W. Staebler's *Architectural detailing in contract interiors* (Butterworth-Heinemann, 1988); and, most recently, Brenda and Robert Vale's *New domestic detailing* (Butterworth-Heinemann, 1994) – a guide to energy-efficient detailing.

Detailing – specific

Several detail books concentrate on particular elements: Peter Newton's *Structural detailing* (2nd edn, Basingstoke: Macmillan Educational, 1991); Roy Pepperell's *Stonemasonry detailing* (Eastbourne: Attic Books, 1991); A.K. Tovey and J.T. Roberts' *Efficient masonry housebuilding: detailing approach* (BCA, 1990), dealing with brickwork and blockwork; Duell and Lawson's *Damp-proof course detailing* (2nd edn, Architectural Press, 1983) – becoming dated, but the only one on the subject; *NBA external works detail sheets* (Architectural Press, 1977); Leslie Woolley's *Hot water details* (2nd edn, 1986) and *Drainage details* (2nd edn, 1988); and Leslie Woolley and P. Stronach's *Sanitation details* (revised edn, 1990), all from Spon; and Littlewood's *Landscape detailing* (3rd edn, Butterworth-Heinemann, 1993) – in two volumes: vol I Enclosures; vol II Surfaces.

Examples and case studies

Two new books give technical details of good modern buildings showing innovative use of materials and detailing: Alan Brookes and Chris Grech's *The building envelope: applications of new technology cladding* (new paperback edn, Butterworth-Heinemann, 1993); and their new title, *Connections: studies in building assembly* (Butterworth-Heinemann, 1993). These follow Alan Brookes's earlier book of 30 case studies, *Concepts in cladding* (1985). 'Architecture in detail' is a series of monographs, each dealing with a single building and including construction drawings. Some 20 have been issued so far; for example, David Jenkins' *Schlumberger Cambridge Research Centre: Michael Hopkins and Partners* (Phaidon, 1993).

Detail is a German bi-monthly review, each issue taking a particular structural topic and illustrating it with meticulous drawings of interesting examples (obtainable through RIBA Publications).

Texts

Buildability

For an introduction to this subject, refer to *Buildability: an assessment* (CIRIA Special Publication SP26, 1983), and Stewart Adams' *Practical buildability* (CIRIA and Butterworth-Heinemann, 1989). See *AJ*, 2 March 1994, for more on this subject.

Principles

Another classic is BRE's *Principles of modern building* (2 vols, 3rd edn, HMSO, 1959 and 1961). This authoritative and readable work is out of print, and naturally out-of-date, but still worth studying for its clear explanation of principles. A successor publication is in preparation. The *AJ Handbook of building enclosure* edited by A.J. Elder (Architectural Press, 1974), now out of print, provided a systematic presentation of all elements of building construction. The later *AJ* Element Design Guides (e.g. 'Substructure', from 26 November 1986 to 10 December 1986) formed a pioneering series which also encouraged a systematic approach and provided comprehensive checklists. Some details and references are out-of-date, but they are still useful. Another well-known text now out of print was Peter Rich's *Principles of element design* (Godwin, 1977; revised and expanded by John Streeter in 1982).

Building construction in general

'McKay', first published in 1938, is familiar to many generations of students. The current details are: W.B. McKay, revised J.K. McKay, *Building construction* (Longman), in four volumes (vol I, 5th edn, 1971; vol II, 4th edn, 1971; vol III, 5th edn, 1974; vol IV, 4th edn, 1988). Volumes are arranged to suit student course work, with information on one subject spread over more than one volume, but they still provide a useful reference on traditional construction for practising architects – particularly useful for maintenance and repair work on buildings which may well have been built in accordance with McKay. 'Mitchell' has an even longer history, going back to the beginning of the century. However, it was completely restructured and rewritten in the 1970s, and provides a very systematic presentation of modern knowledge and methods. The complete Mitchell's Building Series (Longman Higher Education) is as follows:

Introduction to building (Derek Osbourn, rev. edn, 1989)
Structure and fabric: Part 1 (Jack Foster, 5th edn, 1994)
Structure and fabric: Part 2 (Jack Foster and Raymond Harington, 5th edn, 1994)
Materials (Alan Everett, 5th edn, 1994)
Internal components (Alan Blanc, 1994)
External elements (Michael McEvoy, 1994) (the 4th edn of *Components* is now
    divided into 2 vols)
Finishes (Yvonne Dean, 3rd edn, 1989)
Environment and services (Peter Burberry, 7th edn, 1992).

Two other standard works should be mentioned: R. Barry's *Construction of buildings* (Crosby Lockwood Staples, vol I, 5th edn, 1985, rev. 1993; vol II, 4th edn, 1985; vol III, 4th edn, 1993; vol IV, 3rd edn, 1986; vol V, 2nd edn, 1988); and C.M.H. Barritt's *Advanced building construction* (2 vols, 2nd edn, Longman Higher Education, 1988).

A considerable number of other texts has been published over the years, some for TEC courses, useful at an elementary level or for ready reference. The following is just a selection. Roy Chudley has written *Construction technology* (2nd edn, Butterworth-Heinemann, 1987), a four volume textbook, and the *Building construction handbook* (Butterworth-Heinemann, 1988), a handy single volume reference. Similar in aim is Ivor Seeley's *Building technology* (4th edn, Macmillan, 1993) – an elementary introduction to basic construction techniques. Peter Roper has written or edited the following texts in Spon's 'Practical guide' series: *Builders' questions and answers* (1985); *Groundworks and foundations* (1986); *Blockwork* (1987); *Roofing* (1987); and *Windows* (1986).

The following are more general: John Eastwick-Field and John Stillman's *The design and practice of joinery* (4th edn, Architectural Press, 1973) is out of print, but should be sought out for a clear explanation of principles, albeit out-of-date in some technical details. Amongst the many books on crafts and trades are J.B. Taylor's *Plastering* (5th edn, Longman Higher Education, 1990), and William Monks' *External rendering* (8th edn, 1988). Finally, something a little different: Peter Carpenter's *Introduction to earth-sheltered development in England and Wales* (BESA, 1994).

Brickwork

BDA publications on construction include Building Notes BN1 *Brickwork: good site practice* (by Knight, 1991) and BN3 *Bricklaying in winter conditions* (by Harding and Smith, 1986) and *The BDA guide to successful brickwork* (1994), which is a substantial guide to techniques.

Concrete

Two series from the BCA are worth special mention. *Concrete on site* (originally published as *Man on the job*) is a series of 11 booklets, all dated 1993, edited by R. Tattersall; they deal with basic concreting techniques such as formwork, placing and compacting and making test cubes. *Appearance matters* is a series of nine booklets, dated 1981 to 1992, dealing with concrete finishes, weathering and defects. Examples are *Visual concrete: design and production* and *Exposed aggregate concrete finishes*, both by W. Monks, and *Efflorescence on concrete*, by D.D. Higgins.

Cladding

Two popular texts on cladding are A.J. Brookes' *Cladding of buildings* (Longman Higher Education, 1990), mentioned above, and J.M. Anderson and J.R. Gill's *Rainscreen cladding: a guide to design principles and practice* (Butterworth-Heinemann, 1988). The British Steel Strip Products publication, *Colorcoat in building: a guide to architectural practice* (1992), includes advice on the choice of cladding systems. See also under 'Windows and curtain walls' below.

Flat roofs

The well-publicized problems with flat roofs led to a number of excellent, comprehensive design manuals. The main ones are listed here.

- *Flat roofing: design and good practice* (BFRC and CIRIA, 1993), edited by Robert Cather and Steven Groak of Arup Research and Development, is the most recent and comprehensive guide, yet easy to use. It covers principles, design selection, inspection, maintenance and construction methods and details. Earlier manuals are partly superseded by this one.
- The PSA's *Flat roof technical guide* (2 vols, rev. 1987) is limited to mastic asphalt and built-up roofing, but good on analysis and defects.
- *Flat roofing: a guide to good practice* (3rd edn, Tarmac, 1995) the classic 'Blue Book' on mastic asphalt and built-up roofing, offers good coverage of site considerations.
- Bickerdike Allen Partners' *Flat roof manual: a guide to the repair and replacement of built-up felt roofs* (NHS Continuing Education Unit, IAAS, University of York, 1985) is useful in devising a general design strategy for existing roofs; goes beyond built-up roofs.
- The Foamglas *Practical guide to flat roofing* (Pittsburgh Corning Europe, 1992) is a commercial manual concerned with the use of Foamglas cellular glass insulation, but with a substantial section of useful technical information of general application.

BRE coverage includes Digest 324 *Flat-roof design: thermal insulation*, and Information Paper 2/89 *Thermal performance of lightweight inverted warm deck flat roofs.*

Floors

Specific texts on floors include Philip H. Perkins' *Concrete floors, finishes and external paving* (Butterworth-Heinemann, 1993). Another BCA publication is *Concrete ground floors* by Colin Deacon (3rd edn, 1986).

Foundations

BCA's output includes *House foundations for the builder and building designer* by G. Barnbrook (1981).

Partitions

There is more to partitions than just picking one out of a catalogue. There is a very wide range of proprietary products, as well as the possibility of traditional or specially designed construction or customized products. A thorough understanding of the performance criteria is needed (see BS 5234: Parts 1 and 2: 1992; and PSA *Method of Building* MOB P6/PS, 1993), followed by a careful assessment of available products (trade literature, showrooms).

Roofs

Roofs in general are dealt with in John Wickersham's *Manual of roofing* (David and Charles, 1987) – a comprehensive survey of roof construction and repair; and in D.T. Coates' *Roof and roofing: design and specification handbook* (Whittles Publishing, 1993) – a guide to all common roofing types.

There is plenty of guidance available on roofing materials for both flat and pitched roofs. The British Flat Roofing Council issues Technical Information Sheets and Model Specification Sheets. The Copper Development Association has issued Technical Note 32 *Copper in roofing: design and installation* (1985). Information on profiled sheets comes from the Metal Cladding and Roofing Manufacturers Association – *Profiled metal roofing design guide* (No. 6 of a series of Technical Papers, 1993); and from the National Federation of Roofing Contractors – *Profiled sheet metal roofing and cladding: a guide to good practice* (2nd edn, 1991).

Information on lead sheet in building now comes from the Lead Sheet Association (LSA), which separated from the Lead Development Association (LDA) in 1990 (the LDA deals with environmental, health and safety matters and industry representation). The LSA has produced *The lead sheet manual: a guide to good building practice* in three volumes:

I *Lead sheet flashings* (1990); II *Lead sheet roofing and cladding* (1992); III *Weathering* (1993). This is a good presentation of lead sheet merits and solutions, but does not show the full construction build-up.

Single ply roofing will still be unfamiliar to some. The Single Ply Roofing Association (SPRA) issues a number of good guides: *Guide on design criteria for single ply roofing membranes* (1990); Information Sheet No. 2: *General information* (1991) – useful information on single ply membranes and on the SPRA; and a series of Product Sheets on different materials.

Stairs

Two books deal with stairs in depth: W. Mannes' *Techniques of staircase construction* (Spon, 1986) and Alan Blanc's *Stairs, steps and ramps* (Butterworth-Heinemann, 1994).

Walls

Wall technology (CIRIA Special Publication 87, 1992) is a detailed treatment in seven volumes, including 'Performance requirements' and 'Loadbearing small units'. W.E. Anderson, J.J. Roberts and P. Watt's *Efficient masonry housebuilding: a design approach* (BCA, 1985) concentrates on design and construction rationalization – building sequence, simplification of detailing and standardization. Note also March's *Air and rain penetration of buildings* (Construction Press, 1977) and W.G. Nash's *Brickwork* (3 vols, Hutchinson, 1983).

Windows and curtain walls

Barry Josey's 'Element design guide: curtain walls' (*AJ*, **184** (30) 23 July 1986, pp. 47-65) is still largely valid. The Centre for Window and Cladding Technology (CWCT) was established in 1991 – the 'Bath Initiative' – to set standards of excellence in cladding design, manufacture and assembly in order to halt the decline in the UK cladding industry. This resulted in 1993 in the publication of *Standard and guide to good practice for curtain walling* (the Bath Standard). Other publications are planned. The older American Architectural Manufacturers Association (AAMA) issued *Aluminium curtain wall design guide manual* (1979), a collection of papers giving a historical perspective, technical information and guidance, and also *Methods of test for metal curtain walls* (1983), which deals with water penetration and includes site test procedures which were adopted in the Bath Standard.

CIBSE has produced the *Applications manual: window design* (1987), which deals with cladding as well as windows, and covers daylighting, heat gain and loss, glare, noise and other environmental matters. The Aluminium Window Association (AWA) has issued a number of low-priced booklets, including *Guide to specification of windows*. Clear advice on sealants is given in the CIRIA/BASA *Manual of good practice in sealant application* (CIRIA, 1990).

Technical and trade

BSI codes of practice provide authoritative summaries of good design and construction principles for the various elements. To conform with a European requirement they no longer have the distinctive CP reference, but the *BSI Standards catalogue* still lists all the codes of practice together and gives their new BS references.

BS 8000 *Workmanship on building sites* is very relevant to building construction. It is in 15 Parts (two of them in two sections each), issued in 1989 and 1990.

Relevant BRE documents include: *Thermal insulation: avoiding risks: a good practice guide supporting Building Regulations requirements* (2nd edn, HMSO, 1994). The Centre for Alternative Technology (CAT) can give advice and courses on self-build and on suitable materials and methods in countries overseas without an established construction industry and with limited resources.

Trade literature is relied on not only for data about products but also for guidance on construction details and specification. Many catalogues contain numerous details showing the application of products in various situations. These often extend to complete elements, such as a full height wall. They are often to scale and intended for tracing onto working drawings, or even removing and using as ready-made working drawings. These can be helpful time-savers, but should of course be used intelligently. Rather than being followed slavishly, they may need to be modified to achieve the particular design requirements. On the other hand, any departure from the published details should be checked to ensure that correct practice has not been undermined. It is also advisable to agree modifications with the manufacturers lest they disclaim responsibility for the use of their products.

Specific topics

Green issues

One of the most significant developments of the last decade is the increasing awareness of environmental issues, now almost routinely being taken into account during the design process. 'Green' issues include:

- energy conservation in production and transportation of materials and in the construction and use of buildings

- avoidance of hazardous materials
- avoidance of damage to the environment, including the atmosphere
- conservation of diminishing resources, recycling
- durability, maintenance, renewability
- full life-cycle analysis (LCA).

There is growing recognition of the need to consider the whole life of a building – initial costs vs. ongoing costs, design for low energy and minimum maintenance, ease of change of use, etc. – bringing together all the separate aspects the designer has to consider. Environmental assessment is a planning requirement for large projects, voluntary for smaller ones, but it includes technical matters as well as planning, visual and social factors. Some materials are prohibited, by government or by particular authorities and developers, and others will need careful specifying and use. A wealth of guidance is now available. It is advisable for a practice to consider its own policy and draw up its own list and guidance notes.

BRE initiatives

The BRE Environmental Assessment Method (BREEAM) sets basic voluntary standards but is widely recognized and operated. There are several versions, which are essential references:

1/93 *New offices*
2/91 *New superstores and supermarkets*
3/91 *New homes*
4/93 *Existing offices*
5/93 *New industrial units.*

A series of BRE Digests on environmental issues includes Digest 358 *CFCs in buildings* (1991; new edn, 1992). Information Papers include IP 23/89 *CFCs and the building industry* and IP 11/93 *Ecolabelling of building materials and building products*, an update on methods for assessing environmental impact and proposals for the ecolabelling of construction products.

Texts

Arup's *The green construction handbook* (J.T. Design & Build, 1993) is an A-Z summary of issues and is a good starting point (see *AJ,* 14 July 1993 for extracts). A major reference work is the Rosehaugh guide, edited by Steve Curwell, Chris March and Roger Venables, *Buildings and health: the Rosehaugh guide to the design, construction, use and management of buildings* (RIBA Publications, 1990). Other smaller works between them provide an impressive collection of data and ideas. Examples are: Steve Curwell and Chris March's *Hazardous building mate-*

rials: a guide to the selection of alternatives (Spon, 1986); Avril Fox and Robin Murrell's *Green design: a guide to the environmental impact of building materials* (Architecture Design and Technology Press, 1989); Curwell, March and R.C. Fox's *Use of CFCs in buildings* (Fernsheer, 1988); *HCFCs: hidden CFCs* (Greenpeace International, 1992); Brenda and Robert Vale's *Green architecture: design for a sustainable future* (Thames and Hudson, 1991) and *Towards green architecture* (RIBA Publications, 1991) – six case studies of green offices and housing; and David Pearson's *The natural house book* (Conran Octopus, 1989).

Organizations

The Association of Environmentally Conscious Builders (AECB) provides much useful information and a directory of contacts in Hall and Warm's *Greener building products and services directory* (1993). The Ecological Design Association is a monthly forum for the exchange of information and ideas, and issues a directory of members. Friends of the Earth has produced a number of publications on environmental issues, such as the *Good wood manual* specifying alternatives to non-renewable tropical hardwoods, while Forests Forever has produced *A real wood guide* (1990).

The Institute of Environmental Assessment (IEA) operates an environmental consultancy referral database, courses and conferences, and a quarterly magazine, *Environmental Assessment*. The UK Ecolabelling Board (UKEB) is the UK focus for the emerging European ecolabel. For other organizations consult the following directories: Michael J.C. Barker's *Directory for the environment: organisations in Britain and Ireland* (2nd edn, Routledge & Kegan Paul, 1986-87); Civic Trust's *Environmental Directory* (7th edn, 1988); *The green index: a directory of environmental organisations in Britain and Ireland* (Cassell Educational, 1990), compiled and edited by J. Edward Milner, Caril Filby and Marian Board for the Environmental Information Bureau and Acacia Productions in association with the Nature Conservancy Council; *Who's who in the environment: England* (2nd edn, the Environment Council, 1992; also Scotland, 1989; and Wales, 1991); *The LCA sourcebook* (SustainAbility, 1993); and Frances G. Gretes' *Directory of international periodicals and newsletters on the built environment* (2nd edn, USA and UK, 1986).

Defects and failures

Official

Concern at the deterioration of public-sector housing led to the establishment of a Housing Defects Prevention Unit (DPU) at the BRE. It set up a computerized Building Failures Information System (BFIS), ar-

ranged seminars and issued an occasional newsletter, *Defect news*. Its
most visible output, however, was the series of *Defect Action Sheets*
(DAS), which alerted the industry and professions to common design
faults and poor site practice. The series ran from 1982 to 1990 but was
then superseded by a new series, Good Building Guides. The DASs are
available as a book: *Housing defects reference manual* (Spon, 1991).
The Housing Association Property Mutual (HAPM), with the BRE, issued the *Defect avoidance manual: new build* (also Spon, 1991). This
was followed by the *HAPM component life manual* (Spon, 1993, with
updating service), which provides life-span assessments for a wide range
of building components. Earlier publications were the National Building Agency's *Common building defects: diagnosis and remedy* (NBA,
1983) – tabulated information on identification and remedies – and
Defects in buildings (PSA, 1989).

General

Other texts include W.H. Ransom's *Building failures: diagnosis and
avoidance* (2nd edn, Spon, 1988), Barry A. Richardson's *Defects and
deterioration in buildings* (Spon, 1991), Lyall Addleson's *Building failures* (3rd edn, Butterworth-Heinemann, 1992) and B. Harrison
McCampbell's *Problems in roofing design* (Butterworth-Heinemann,
1992) – illustrated case histories with drawings of solutions.

Specific

P. Pullar-Strecker's *Corrosion damaged concrete: assessment and repair* (Butterworth-Heinemann in conjunction with CIRIA, 1987) is one
example of the many technical articles and publications on specific problems.

Health and safety

This section overlaps with 'Green issues' above. The *Rosehaugh guide*,
for example, includes information on a number of health hazards. Under
the *Health and Safety at Work Act 1974* (and amendments) manufacturers have to produce data sheets indicating hazardous content of their
products; read them in conjunction with the Health and Safety Executive's *Occupational exposure limits* (1994) – a reference table indicating the level of risk to health. Under the *Construction (Design and
Management) Regulations 1994*, designers have a new duty to consider
the health and safety of people on-site – ensuring that the building can
be constructed safely. There has been a flood of guidance documents.
Meanwhile, a great deal of information for contractors already exists.
See *AJ*, **200** (1) & (2) 6 and 13 July 1994 pp. 23-5 and 34-6 for an
introduction to the new requirements and a summary of the existing

literature. One general study is *A guide to the control of substances hazardous to health in construction* (CIRIA in conjunction with Thomas Telford, 1993).

Guides to the new CDM regulations will be of vital importance to designer and contractor alike. HSE has published *A guide to managing health and safety in construction, Designing for health and safety in construction: a guide for designers on the Construction (Design and Management) Regulations 1994* and *Health and safety for small construction sites*. Useful guidance can be found in CIRIA's *The CDM regulations: case study guidance* and in Raymond Joyce's *The CDM explained* (Thomas Telford). Also helpful is Sylvester Bone's *Information on site safety for designers of smaller building projects* (HSE Contract Research Report 72/1995, HSE Books). All these publications came out in 1995.

Asbestos is covered by a number of publications, including: *Asbestos use in buildings: the hazards and their mitigation* (Report SHE9, Loss Prevention Council, 1993); John Delaine's *Asbestos removal, management and control* (Gower, 1988); I. Berkovitch's *Hazards of asbestos in construction practice: a review of UK sources of information and advice* (CIRIA, 1976); and *Asbestos: directory of unpublished studies* (2nd edn, Spon, 1986), edited by S. Amaducci. Advice can be obtained from the Asbestos Information Centre. Guidance on other specific hazards includes two BRE Reports, *Radon: guidance on protective measures for new dwellings* (BR 211, 1991) and *Construction on gas-contaminated land* (BR 212, 1991). SBS is treated in *Sick building syndrome: causes, effects and control* (London Hazards Centre Trust, 1990).

Fire

There are several aspects of fire – causes and prevention, fire spread, fire resistance, fire detection, means of escape, fire fighting and dealing with fire damage. Many are covered by legislation, regulations and standards. Approved Document B on *Fire safety* is by far the largest of the Building Regulations Approved Documents.

The principal Act is the *Fire precautions Act 1971*, to which has been added the *Fire safety and safety of places of sport Act 1987*. The government department responsible for fire is the Home Office, which issues a number of guides, including *Guides to the fire precautions Act 1971*: (1) *Hotels and boarding houses* (1972); (2) *Factories* (1977); and (3) *Offices, shops and railway premises* (1977). BS 5588: *Fire precautions in the design, construction and use of buildings* is a most important standard consisting of nine codes of practice, dating from 1978 to 1991. BS 4422: *Glossary of terms associated with fire* is an extensive standard also in several parts, dating from 1975 to 1990.

The Loss Prevention Council (LPC) looks at fire from an insurance point of view, while the Fire Protection Association (FPA) is recognized as the UK's national fire safety organization. The Institute of Fire Safety (IFS) was formed in 1991 from the Society of Fire Safety Engineers and the UK Chapter of the Society of Fire Protection Engineers. Relevant documents from the LPC include: *Code of procedure for the construction of buildings: insurers' rules for the fire protection of industrial and commercial buildings* (1992); *Fire protection on construction sites: a joint code of practice on the protection from fire of construction sites and buildings undergoing renovation* (with the BEC and the National Contractors Association, 1993); *Fire safety and security on construction sites* (1994), a technical handbook which complements the joint code; and a *List of approved products and services* (annual, plus updating amendments). The FPA issues a journal, *Fire Prevention*, and other publications.

Marchant's *A complete guide to fire and buildings* (Construction Press, 1972) is still worth looking up for a good introduction to fire behaviour, as is Taylor and Cooke's *Guide to the fire precautions Act in practice* (Architectural Press, 1978). Extensive treatment was also given in volume four of Lyall Addleson's *Materials for building*. However, there are several more recent works: Aqua Group's *Fire and buildings: a guide for the design team* (1984); T.J. Shields and G.W.H. Silcock's *Buildings and fire* (1987); R. Hirst's *Underdown's practical fire precautions* (3rd edn, Gower, 1990); and Paul Stollard and John Abrahams' *Fire from first principles: a design guide to building fire safety* (Chapman Hall, 1991). Trade and technical literature will normally include information relating to fire. For special products refer to the *International fire and security directory* (Blenheim Group, 1993). This has some technical text plus a directory of trade suppliers of fire and security products and what they offer.

Conservation, durability and maintenance

It is appropriate to conclude a chapter on materials and construction with a long-term view – how will the construction last? There is a wide range of aspects:

- routine cleaning and maintenance
- special cleaning
- redecoration
- alteration, modernization and conversion
- durability
- conservation
- restoration
- demolition.

These demand knowledge of current techniques, understanding of historic design and techniques, ability to identify and interpret signs of deterioration and a sensitive approach to dealing with old buildings. An understanding of the behaviour of materials and the success of building techniques as revealed in the literature on conservation and the direct study of old buildings can be very helpful to designers in detailing and specifying new work.

Conservation

Conservation is dealt with in detail elsewhere, but perhaps one series of texts could be mentioned here for their general usefulness: John and Nicola Ashurst's *Practical building conservation: traditional building materials, their repair and conservation* (English Heritage Technical Handbooks, Gower, 1988). There are five volumes: I Stone masonry; II Brick, terracotta and earth; III Mortars, plasters and renders; IV Metals; V Wood, glass and resins. Also to be noted is *Building conservation directory 1994* (Cathedral Communications), a new guide giving notes on materials and techniques, articles by experts, and listings and advertisements on suppliers to the market.

Durability

Durability is the subject of two conference proceedings: by J.M. Baker et al. (eds.), *Durability of building materials and components: proceedings of the Fifth International Conference* (Spon, 1991); and by S. Nagataki et al., *Durability of building materials and components* (Spon, 1994) – the proceedings of the 1993 conference. The *HAPM component life manual*, mentioned above, is also relevant here.

Maintenance

Building maintenance is well served by texts, ranging from Melville and Gordon's *The repair and maintenance of houses* (Estates gazette, 1973) to the more recent *Repair and refurbishment of modern buildings* by Ian Chandler (Batsford, 1992) and *Building maintenance and preservation: a guide for design and management* by Edward Mills (Butterworth-Heinemann, 1994). Particular aspects are covered by: Ashurst and F.G. Dimes' *Conservation of building and decorative stones* (Butterworth-Heinemann, 1991); *International conference on stone cleaning and the nature, soiling and decay mechanisms of stone Edinburgh, 1992* (London: Donhead, 1992) edited by Robin G.M. Webster; W.G. Nash's *Brickwork repair and restoration* (2nd edn, Eastbourne: Attic Books, 1989); Bidwell's *Conservation of old brick buildings* (Brick Development Association, 1977); and Allan Hutchinson's *Resealing of buildings* (Butterworth-Heinemann, 1994).

Facilities management

This is a growing field – largely to do with management, legal and social, but including technical maintenance. Computer-aided facilities management (CAFM) is already well-established in the United States and there is a growing number of programmes in the UK. The Centre for Facilities Management (CFM) provides support for those wishing to develop understanding and systems. The professional association is the Association of Facilities Managers (AFM), which merged with the Institute of Facilities Management in 1993. Relevant books are Reginald Lee's *Building maintenance management* (3rd edn, Collins, 1987) and Ivor H. Seeley's *Building maintenance* (2nd edn, Macmillan Educational, 1987).

Demolition

Demolition can mark both the beginning and the end of a project. The demolition of an existing building on site needs careful investigation and adequate allowance in the programme, including dealing with hazardous materials or structures, conforming with statutory requirements for notification, etc. In designing a new building, ultimate demolition must be kept in mind, considering how it will be done and preparing adequate records and instructions. BS 6187: 1982 *Code of practice for demolition* deals with procedures, methods and protective precautions. Advice can be obtained from the National Federation of Demolition Contractors (NFDC). Amongst other publications the Federation issues a useful journal, *Demolition and dismantling;* a *List of members*, which includes guidance for property/site owners; a form of contract and a demolition specification; and short bibliographies on demolition and on pre-stressed concrete demolition.

Other general sources

Periodicals

Periodicals may be used for inspiration and ideas or for hard facts. In addition, the mere scanning of headlines and advertisements can give one a feel for current issues and developments. A library should therefore acquire as many relevant titles as possible. An individual should develop a systematic approach to get the best out of them – a regular read of a few, an occasional scan of a variety of others. Relevant periodicals can come from a number of sources, such as general commercial publishers, specialist construction industry publishers, trade associations and manufacturers (see Chapter 3). *Willings's press guide* (Reed Information Services, annual) gives a comprehensive, but not complete, listing.

Most general construction industry periodicals include features or supplements on materials, construction and technology. Some specialize in product news and information. Others send packs of product cards to their subscribers from time to time. Some of the main titles are:

AJ and *AJ focus*	*Building trades journal*
Building and *Building supplements*	*RIBA journal*
Building design	*Specifier review*
Building products	*Specify*
Building specification	*What's new in building*

Periodicals on building science and science generally might be taken by a large practice, especially an interdisciplinary practice. Otherwise they may be worth an occasional browse in a public library.

Building science	*Nature*
Chemistry and industry	*New scientist*

This is just a selection of the myriad specific titles produced, from various quarters, to give an indication of the range.

Acier/stahl/steel	*Focus* (Suspended Ceilings
ARena (Adshead Ratcliffe)	Association)
	Ibstock design
Blinds and shutters	*ICE proceedings*
Brick bulletin (BDA)	*International journal of cement*
Brick matters (London Brick)	*composites*
Building research and information (CIB)	*International journal of*
	lightweight concrete
Cem-fil news	*Magazine of concrete research*
Ceramic tiles world	*Mastic asphalt today*
Concrete	*Materials and structures*
Concrete quarterly	(RILEM, France)
CoNTact (Newman Tonks)	*Precast concrete*
	Roofing, cladding and insulation
Demolition and dismantling	*Structural engineer*
	Terrapin world
FGI (Fabrication and Glazing Industries)	*World cement technology*
Flooring contractor and specifier	

Periodicals specializing in structural matters include:

Computers and structures	*Steel construction today*
International journal of solids and	*Structural engineer*
structures	
Proceedings of the Institution of Civil	
Engineers: structures and buildings	

Abstracts and indexes, databases, bibliographies

Specification includes some very extensive bibliographies at the end of each chapter, although mainly confined to official publications. Many books include bibliographies of publications on related topics. These can provide valuable guides to the literature of a particular subject. CIRIA's *Index of technical publications* (1970) has not been revised.

Most of the relevant sources have been covered in the general chapter; however, a few useful titles may be mentioned here. *Construction references*, the PSA's cumulation of the fortnightly *Current information in the construction industry*, ceased publication in June 1990 but much of its content is covered in the database ICONDA, available on Questel ORBIT and STN International, or as a CD-ROM from Silverplatter with optional Internet subscription access. *Building science abstracts* from the BRE ceased to be published in 1976 but much of the content was maintained in the Library indexes at BRE and added to ICONDA. Begun by the Institution of Civil Engineers was *ICE abstracts* which is now known as *International civil engineering abstracts* and published by CITIS (Dublin) with a CD-ROM version also available.

The general resources *Current technology index* (British) and *Applied science and technology index* (American) include many aspects of construction, as does the ISI's *Current contents in engineering technology and applied sciences*. *Engineering index* is also useful, used with *Subject headings in engineering*.

Textual databases

BCSA has produced a number of software programs for detailing all types of steel structures, with connections, and to program fabrication. The BRE Technical Consultancy has produced *Strongblow*, a program for generating design wind speed data.

Many manufacturers offer computer programs and CAD services that help put together construction drawings and specifications. A few examples are:

- Jones of Oswestry: a database of lintel profiles
- Marley Building Materials: production of a CAD drawing following discussion of the design brief; Computer-Aided Specification Scheme which checks details and produces specification clauses
- Sealmaster: Fire Legislation Expert System which checks legal requirements and building context and produces a specification
- TAC Metal Forming: Datacad, a complete suite of standard details for metal roofing and cladding applications
- The Velux Company: Velux CAD for roof window details.

Organizations and enquiries

Trade associations

These are an important source, each being regarded as the main authority for its subject. Most will assist with enquiries. Their technical literature is very extensive, and provides descriptive information, guidance on applications, drawn details and technical data. While much of this is reliable, it can be heavily biased, and should be used with care, especially when statistics are introduced. There have been famous campaigns to influence the construction industry and the house-buying public and others in favour of specific materials and techniques – timber versus masonry and concrete, gas versus electricity, different methods of thermal insulation, claims about 'green' products.

Guides to organizations

Comprehensive guides to organizations are the *CIRIA UK construction information guide* (CIRIA and Spon, 1989) and *CIRIA Guide to European Community and international sources of construction information* (CIRIA Special Publication 60, 2nd edn, 1991). They group organizations by subject as well as alphabetically, thus helping to identify organizations in unfamiliar fields, and include descriptions of each. Further detailed listings appear in several other publications, such as the Barbour Index *Building product compendium*, the RIBA *Product selector* and *Specification*. They do not have the expanded entries, but are more comprehensive. If these listings do not give you what you want then the more general directories discussed in Chapter 2 have subject indexes to the extensive A-Z listings.

Some specific organizations

A number of organizations have been mentioned above. The following checklist, by no means exhaustive, includes a number of others concerned with materials and products.

Aluminium Federation (Alfed)
Aluminium Window Association (AWA)
American Plywood Association (APA)
Asbestos Information Centre (AIC)
Brick Development Association (BDA)
British Adhesives and Sealants Association (BASA)
British Aggregate Construction Materials Industries (BACMI)
British Cement Association (BCA)
British Plastics Federation (BPF)
British Precast Concrete Federation (BPCF)
British Ready Mixed Concrete Association (BRMCA)
British Reinforcement Manufacturers' Association (BRMA)
British Woodworking Federation (BWF)

Clay Roofing Tile Council (CRTC)
Concrete Society (CS)
  with subsidiary Concrete Advisory Service (CAS)
Construction Fixings Association (CFA)
Copper Development Association (CDA)
  with Copper Roofing Advisory Service
Council of Forest Industries of British Columbia (COFI)
Glass and Glazing Federation (GGF)
Guild of Architectural Ironmongers (GAI)
Lead Sheet Association (LSA)
Mastic Asphalt Council and Employers Federation (MACEF)
Mastic Asphalt Technical Advisory Centre (MATAC)
Metal Cladding and Roofing Manufacturers Association (MCRMA)
Paintmakers Association of Great Britain (PA)
Paint Research Association (PRA)
Plastics Window Association (PWA)
Roofing Tile Association (RTA)
Single Ply Roofing Association (SPRA)
Southern Pine Marketing Council (SPMC)
Steel Window Association (SWA)
Stone Federation (SF)
Swedish-Finnish Timber Council (SFTC)
Thatching Advisory Service (TAS)
Timber Research and Development Association (TRADA)
Timber Trade Federation (TTF)
Western Wood Products Association (WWPA)
Zinc Development Association (ZDA)

CHAPTER SIXTEEN

Executing the design: energy services

STEPHEN LOYD

Introduction

Demands by occupants for a high quality environment within buildings
have increased the need for engineering services designed to maintain
comfort and health, while at the same time meeting growing environmental requirements imposed through increasingly stringent legislation.
To meet the needs of clients, building services have become a complex
and sophisticated part of the construction process, to the point where
they may be worth up to 30 per cent of a project's value.

Today, the main specialist publishers in this field – the Chartered
Institution of Building Services Engineers (CIBSE), the Building Services Research and Information Association (BSRIA) and the American
Society of Heating, Refrigerating and Air-Conditioning Engineers
(ASHRAE) – now have a wide range of guides and reference works to
help all who plan, design or equip buildings. The growth of specialist
publishing has been concurrent with a somewhat limited number of new
textbook titles from commercial publishers. However, for a relatively
small industry it still supports a surprisingly large number of periodicals, and there are plenty of standards and trade information available
covering the wide range of equipment to be found in today's buildings.
This is demonstrated by the following review of some of the most important current sources of information in the form of handbooks, trade
and technical literature, literature published by organizations and associations, abstracting and indexing publications, periodicals, databases
and standard texts.

Handbooks

The *CIBSE Guide* remains the most important design document for building services engineers. The 1986 edition came in three volumes: *Guide A: Design data*, *Guide B: Installation and equipment data*, *Guide C: Reference data*. In 1993, *Guide D: Transportation systems in buildings* extended the *CIBSE Guide* to give a useful tool for those responsible for both the design and operation of transportation systems. Further volumes of the authoritative *CIBSE Guide* are promised, each dealing with a specific subject area, such as *Energy efficiency in buildings*. The four volume *ASHRAE Handbook* has been published in a four-yearly update programme, whereby one volume is updated each year. The set consists of *Handbook: fundamentals*, *Handbook: HVAC systems and equipment*, *Handbook: HVAC applications* and *Handbook: refrigeration*.

Industrial exhaust ventilation design is presented in *Industrial ventilation: a manual of recommended practice* by the American Conference of Governmental Industrial Hygienists. This manual has found wide acceptance as a guide to the design, maintenance and evaluation of industrial ventilation.

Plumbing has changed considerably in scope and technology, with revised water bye-laws and codes of practice and this is recognized in the *Plumbing engineering services design guide* (1988) from the Institute of Plumbing.

The *IEE Wiring regulations* are recognized as the national code for the safety of electrical installations. In the 16th edition they were granted formal recognition as a British Standard (BS 7671) in 1992.

A number of dictionaries have been published in recent years. *Mechanical engineering services: a plumbing encyclopedia* (Blackwell Scientific Publications, 1989) provides definitions and explanations with many illustrations, while on a broader front David Kut's *Illustrated encyclopedia for building services* (Spon, 1993) explains over 3000 terms and presents over 200 line illustrations.

Growing internationalization of the construction industry has highlighted the need for an agreed international vocabulary and *The international dictionary of heating, ventilating and air conditioning* (Spon, 1994), now in its second edition, covers 11 languages in addition to English. Four glossaries compiled by Lee Consulting Engineers are available from CIBSE, *Glossary of terms for building services engineering* covers English/French, English/German, English/Italian and English/Spanish translations. On a more specialized topic, the International Institute of Refrigeration's *New international dictionary of refrigeration* (Paris, 1971) provides a comprehensive range of definitions and covers seven languages.

Trade and technical

Many of the manufacturers of heating, ventilation, air-conditioning and lighting equipment produce large, detailed catalogues containing a great deal of technical data and diagrams. A well-produced compilation of specifications from a range of manufacturers has made the annual *Opus* a much-used reference book. Published by Building Services Publications, it chiefly contains technical product information, a directory of suppliers and a listing of codes, standards and guides.

Trade information is often published by specialist trade organizations either as simple buyers' guides or as more detailed application documents. BSRIA's useful directory, *Information sources for building services professionals* (6th edn, 1995), will provide a starting point to approach the right organization. The annual *Specifiers guide* from EMAP is the Heating and Ventilating Contractors' Association guide to companies in heating, ventilation, air-conditioning and refrigeration.

Supplements produced by journals either within the journal itself or as stand-alone volumes such as the *Air conditioning and refrigeration news handbook* make good trade guides, particularly supplements on specific products. Trendata Publications' *H & V Index desk reference book* is an easy-to-use regularly updated guide to suppliers of industrial and commercial heating, ventilation, air-conditioning and refrigeration equipment. Its 38 main sections each cover a specific type of equipment.

The industry is well-served by more specialist trade directories and buyers' guides, many of which contain useful technical information about the industry in question. The *Insulation handbook* (Turret Group) gives the insulation properties of acoustic and thermal insulation products. The *Gas industry directory* (Morgan Grampian) is chiefly a buyer's guide to suppliers, but also includes a list of approved appliances. The *Electrical and electronics trades directory* (Peter Peregrinus) provides a guide to companies showing their main sources of manufacture and supply.

Two directories represent the fire protection and security industries: *Fire protection directory* is published by A.E. Morgan Publications and the *Security and fire protection yearbook and buyers guide* is from Paramount Publishing.

Energy-related products and services are well-covered by two comprehensive publications. The *Energy world yearbook* (H. Howland Associates) includes useful information on databases, energy management software, energy and water suppliers, a buyers' guide and technical data. The current concerns for the environment and the security of energy supplies have led to renewed interest in alternative energy, and the *European directory of renewable energy* (James & James) presents a wide range of information in the area.

Much building services design and management is now conducted on computers and finding the appropriate software may prove a difficult and time-consuming exercise. The annual selection guide *Software for building services* (BSRIA) gives descriptions of over 400 software products available in the United Kingdom. CIBSE publishes a range of 'Applications manuals', 'Commissioning codes', 'Building energy codes' and 'Technical memoranda', providing authoritative guidance on specific topics such as *Condensing boilers* (1989), *Security engineering* (1991), *Information technology and buildings* (1992), *Minimising the risk of Legionnaires' Disease* (1991) and *Maintenance management for building services* (1994).

BSRIA's publishing programme has expanded over the last decade and now a broad range of industry guides, technical information and market-related titles features in its highly indexed *Publications index*. Titles such as *The commissioning of water systems in buildings* (1992) and *Pre-commission cleaning of water systems* (1991) are examples of good industry practice, while other titles, such as *Ventilation system hygiene* (1995) and *Lightning protection of buildings and their contents* (1994), disseminate knowledge and research results.

The HVCA publishes a range of specifications for heating and ventilation ductwork, and recently issued a *Standard maintenance specification for mechanical services in buildings*. This is a five-volume guidance on the actions that need to be taken to ensure plant is adequately maintained.

Lighting design, installation, commissioning and operation are covered in *CIBSE's Code for interior lighting* (1994) and this is supported for various types of buildings and applications by CIBSE's series of Lighting Guides, such as *Lighting for offices* (1993) and *Lighting for sports* (1990). CIBSE is also supplying the lighting guides published by the Commission Internationale de L'Eclairage (CIE). The Lighting Industry Federation issues a useful *Lamp guide* (1994).

Detailed accounts of the research findings of the Building Research Establishment are presented in BRE's books and reports. *Tackling condensation* (1991) is a guide produced from monitoring results. Design advice is presented in manuals such as *Design principles for smoke ventilation in enclosed shopping centres* (1990). BRE's long running series of Digests are considered essential reference material on a wide range of topics. The concise format is a summary of BRE's knowledge in a particular area. Environmental assessment methods for buildings are defined in BRE's BREEAM publications, which cover offices, retail buildings and dwellings. (See Chapter 15.)

Good meteorological information is a fundamental pre-requisite to system design. Weather and solar data are presented in volume A of the *CIBSE Guide* and the Meteorological Office's *Tables of temperature, relative humidity, precipitation, and sunshine for the world* (HMSO, 1983) gives data for many weather stations.

British Standards contain much technical information for design, testing, installation, operation and maintenance of building services equipment, and a good annual guide to those and other standards is provided in *Opus* (Building Services Publications). ASHRAE standards describe methods of testing, specifying design requirements, and recommend standard practices.

Design and operational advice for many aspects of NHS estate is provided by a growing list of titles from NHS Estates. Health Building Notes (HBNs) are used for briefing and design for new buildings. Health Technical Memoranda (HTMs) give advice and guidance on the design, installation and operation of specialist engineering technology. A new series of Health Facilities Notes (HFNs) and specific codes for energy efficiency, ENCODE (originally published in 1986, this is being superseded by a new edition in two parts; part 1 was published in 1993, and part 2 is in preparation), and fire safety, FIRECODE, (issued in parts since 1987), complete a very comprehensive publishing programme through HMSO. Price books and services are essential tools for quoting, estimating, costing and buying. Spon's *Mechanical and electrical services price book* is an annual services engineering reference covering wage rates, materials costs and measured work prices, subdivided into mechanical and electrical installations.

Organizations and associations

There is an abundance of specialist organizations, each covering a particular technology, product or professional concern. To help identify quickly and accurately sources of information, BSRIA has compiled a directory of *Information sources for building services professionals*, which indexes over 260 organizations with addresses and telephone numbers.

Many of these bodies are active publishers of technical information and advice, such as the Heating and Ventilating Contractors Association, the HEVAC Association, the Fire Protection Association and the Lighting Industry Federation. Others develop and produce standards in their area, such as the Swimming Pool and Allied Trades Association, and the Industry Committee for Emergency Lighting.

The range and scope of government-funded organizations has been undergoing radical change in recent years with the result that growing importance is being given to industry-sponsored organizations for publishing information. The work undertaken by BSRIA has continued to expand with a growing catalogue of titles that are described and indexed in its *Publications index*. CIBSE and BRE also issue easy-to-use publications catalogues which include a selection of texts from other publishers.

Periodicals

The area of building services is served by a comparatively large number of periodicals, many of which are trade journals. Detailed, referenced technical papers are published in CIBSE's *Building services engineering research and technology*; and, from America, *ASHRAE Transactions* and *ASHRAE journal* publish many full technical papers given at its meetings. CIBSE also publishes *Building services*, which is received by all CIBSE members, while the internationally recognized quarterly, *Lighting research and technology,* and the monthly, *Electrical design,* both represent electrical and lighting interests of CIBSE. Another well-respected US periodical is *Heating, piping and air conditioning.*

BSRIA compiles an annual list of *Library periodicals,* which gives a very wide international list of periodical titles in the fields of energy use and building services. Some British titles which might be mentioned include *Building services and environmental engineer, Electrical review, Energy and buildings, Fire prevention, Heat recovery systems and CHP, Heating and ventilating engineer insulation journal, International journal of ambient energy, International journal of refrigeration, Plumbing* and *Resource. Electrical review* is the only relevant periodical to feature patent applications regularly.

Most countries have at least one periodical title on building services; some, such as Germany, Italy and France, have several long-established titles for their industries. Two useful English language titles are *Australian refrigeration, air conditioning and heating* and the *IRHACE Journal,* which are the official journals of the Australian and New Zealand institutes respectively.

Market statistics are reported in BSRIA's *Statistics bulletin,* which presents statistics from BSRIA's own database and published sources including data on production, home demand, overseas trade and company performance. Forecasts for the industry and in-depth analysis of a significant market are included each quarter.

Abstracts and indexes

Published abstracts bulletins still serve a vital current awareness role in a convenient format and present summaries of specific new articles from many sources. Although there has been a general decline in the number of such bulletins, the sector is still well served by some long-established abstracts services. BSRIA's *International building services abstracts* has been published bi-monthly since 1966 and each issue contains some 350 abstracts on all aspects of building services in the UK and overseas. Complementary to this, but focused on the requirements of building owners and occupiers is *Engineering services management* (BSRIA), which gives abstracts of English language papers on topics such as maintenance, energy management, fire protection, health and safety and security.

Energy and its applications are covered in *Fuel and energy abstracts*, published by Butterworth-Heinemann. It is an international journal published on behalf of the Institute of Energy and is based on abstracts made available from a range of other organizations on the technical, scientific, commercial and environmental aspects of fuel and energy. Reviews of selected articles, papers, patents and other material of interest to the gas and energy industries are presented in *Gas abstracts* by the US Institute of Gas Technology. Recent environmental concerns have raised the profile of refrigeration in buildings, and the *Bulletin of the International Institute of Refrigeration* gives both French and English abstracts of recent world information on this subject. The energy implications of ventilation, indoor air quality and building envelope performance are covered by the abstracts in *Recent additions to AIRBASE*, the quarterly abstracting journal of the Air Infiltration and Ventilation Centre (see below).

Electrical and electronics abstracts from the IEE brings together summarized information of recent world-wide technical developments in electrical power and installations. Useful cumulative indexes are published separately twice a year. Fire protection of buildings is included in Fire Research Station's monthly *Fire information bulletin* which contains approximately 200 references each month arranged under nine subject headings.

The *Library bulletin* issued bi-monthly by NHS Estates provides about 100 abstracts to building topics, including the internal environment, with the emphasis on healthcare buildings. Refrigeration, cooling and storage conditions for food and other commodities are the subjects covered in Cambridge Refrigeration Technology's *Library accessions list*, which also includes a list of patent applications. A safe, healthy and comfortable working environment is generally the aim of good building services design: *Safety and health at work*, the ILO-CIS bulletin from the International Labour Office in Geneva, publishes abstracts covering such topics as indoor air pollution and control of hazards from mechanical and electrical installations, lighting, industrial ventilation and control of the thermal environment.

Abstracting organizations are well placed to issue bibliographies on specific topics, and BSRIA continues to publish a range of these, from reading list style to the larger annotated texts where the abstract helps the reader make a selection from a larger number of references. The AIVC also produces reading lists on topics concerned with ventilation and the Fire Research Station publishes bibliographies on fire-related subjects.

Databases

Bibliographic databases for this diverse industry require large resources
to maintain; consequently, BSRIA's IBSEDEX database has no rivals.
Currently approaching 90 000 records and dating back to the early
1960s it offers a comprehensive international information resource. It is
available either from the host network, ESA-IRS (available in the UK
from IRS-Dialtech, The British Library Science Reference and Information Service, 25 Southampton Buildings, Chancery Lane, London
WC2A 1AW) or by direct-dial and password to BSRIA. IBSEDEX users can benefit from keyword searching using BSRIA's *Building services thesaurus* which is available either in hard copy, diskette or on-line
to direct-dial users. In recognition of specific interest areas, BSRIA make
available on diskette the *Buildings and health* database, which deals
with the health-related problems of occupying buildings; the *Database
of ASHRAE publications*, which summarizes all ASHRAE-produced material since 1980; the *CIBSE Journal electronic index*, which indexes
all the technical articles of this journal since 1978; and an electronic
index to the *Proceedings of the Institute of Refrigeration* compiled in
collaboration with Cambridge Refrigeration Technology and covering
the period 1900 to the present.

The AIVC's AIRBASE database is also distributed on diskette and
contains over 7000 abstracts of world-wide technical literature on air
infiltration and ventilation. BRE's BRIX/FLAIR on-line database includes some coverage of mechanical services as well as energy use and
fire aspects of buildings. This is hosted on ESA-IRS and searches can
also be done by BRE library staff. References to electrical installations
can be found on the IEE's INSPEC database, which is offered either in
on-line format with 4.5 million references or on CD-ROM covering 1989
onwards.

There are currently two CD-ROMs containing building services information. *ASHRAE TransText* holds the full text of *ASHRAE Transactions* for one year, together with the abstracts of the *Database of ASHRAE
publications*. The *CLIMA 2000* CD-ROM holds the complete text of all
368 technical papers presented at the 1993 CLIMA 2000 conference in
London and is available from BSRIA.

The *National engineering specification* (*NES*) is a database of specification clauses structured in accordance with the Common Arrangement of Works Sections. It is available on annual subscription and is
designed for use with either a standard word-processor package or one
of the programs written specifically for the assembly of NES project
specifications.

Texts

Long accepted as a standard reference book for both students and practitioners, Faber and Kell's *Heating and air conditioning of buildings*
(Butterworths, 1994) is now in its eighth edition and is edited by P.L.
Martin and D.R. Oughton. An up-to-date text which will appeal to students is *Introduction to building services* by C. Howard and E. Curd
(2nd edn, Macmillan, 1994). The *HVAC Engineer's handbook* by F.
Porges (Butterworths, 1991) is accepted as a concise, definitive reference for the day-to-day work of the engineer or technician employed in
designing HVAC systems, domestic hot and cold water services, gas
supply and steam services. *Mechanical services for buildings* by T.
Eastop and W. Watson (Longman, 1992) discusses heating and pressu-
rized heating systems and goes on to look at transient heat flow, moisture transfer, mass transfer and refrigeration plant. Air conditioning and
ventilation is well-served by recent texts, including *Packaged air conditioning* by Bernard Hough (Butterworths, 1993), which is an easy-to-
use guide to the design and application of these cheaper and more
flexible systems compared to the large central plant room.

Among the more recent British texts there are some titles worth noting, such as Chadderton's *Building services engineering* (Spon, 1991),
which explains the design of building services with their many calculations, and gives copious examples and student exercises. His companion volume, *Air conditioning: a practical introduction* (Spon, 1993), is
another text book aimed at students. A comprehensive introduction to
the principles and practice of refrigeration and air-conditioning is provided by Trott's *Refrigeration and air-conditioning* (Butterworths,
1989). Up-to-date information on the procedures for calculating a ventilation design can be found in Awbi's *Ventilation of buildings* (Spon,
1991), which makes a valuable contribution to the avoidance of 'sick
building syndrome. This important topic is well addressed in *Buildings
and health: the Rosehaugh guide to the design, construction, use and
management of buildings* (RIBA, 1990), a collection of 30 papers written by experts in various scientific fields associated with the quality of
the built environment.

Fan engineering, published by the Buffalo Forge Company of New
York, was first published in 1914 and is now in its eighth edition (1983)
and serves as a handbook for engineers who use fans. The fan company,
Woods of Colchester, has published *Practical guide to fan engineering*
and *Practical guide to noise control.* Although published in the 1970s
they have become standard reference books for professional engineers,
specifiers and students. Ventilation system noise can be a problem, and
Iqbal's *The control of noise in ventilation systems* (Spon, 1977) addresses
this subject.

Two books by F. Hall on plumbing, *Hot water supply and heating systems* and *Cold water supplies: drainage and sanitation* (Longman, 1994), are both now in their third edition, while his earlier work, *Design calculations for plumbing and heating engineers* (Longman, 1988), presents a number of essential calculations relating to pipe size, heat loss, boiler power and pump duty.

The selection and use of materials for heating, sanitation and fire protection of piped services is of growing importance and authoritative information is given in BSRIA's *Building services materials handbook* (Spon, 1987). Materials and fittings are of particular concern where water is flowing and a very helpful guide from the Water Research Centre entitled *Water supply byelaws guide* (Ellis Harwood, 1989) presents the text of the bye-laws with accompanying guidance. Recent legislation has increased pressure for improved maintenance and Armstrong's book, *Maintaining building services: a guide for managers* (Mitchell, 1987), deals with all aspects of maintaining and operating the plant, ranging from the responsibilities of the building owner or operator to new methods of information collection and analysis now available to help the maintenance engineer in his work. The advent of relatively inexpensive measuring instruments has made condition monitoring of engineering plant and equipment more practical, and Armstrong and Taylor's *Low-cost condition monitoring for engineering services* (Spon, 1988) provides a unique summary of techniques and instrumentation available. Benn Technical Books has a three-volume basic reference set on *Gas service technology*: volume I *Basic science and practice of gas service*; volume II *Domestic installation and servicing practice*; volume III *Commercial and industrial installation and servicing practice*.

Computerized control of building services has reached high levels of sophistication and *Building energy management systems* by G.J. Levermore (Spon, 1992) will appeal to both practising building services engineers and energy managers, while Eyke's *Building automation systems* (Blackwell Scientific Publications, 1988) aims to be a practical guide to selection and implementation.

Electrical services are a costly component in any modern building and Porges' well-established *Design of electrical services for buildings* (3rd edn, Spon, 1989) sets out a basic grounding in their design. Protection of valuable data, essential services and production process plants is necessary against power supply breaks or contamination. *Uninterruptible power supplies*, edited by J. Platts (Peter Peregrinus, 1992), is a guide to the various types of system available and how they may be specified and applied effectively. *Lighting design* by Gardner and Hannaford (Design Council, 1993) provides an international introduction to the lighting of commercial interiors and exteriors. A survey of the practical requirements of the electrical services in buildings, ranging from the preliminary negotiations with electricity supply companies through to the final inspection, testing and commissioning is provided by C. Dennis

Poole in *Electrical distribution in buildings* (2nd edn, Blackwell Scientific Publications, 1994). High technology buildings require complex cabling layouts, a subject which is covered in *Premises cabling* by Gilmore and Daly (Butterworths, 1994) and *Cable management systems* by Reeves (Blackwell Scientific Publications, 1992). Poor maintenance is often linked with outbreaks of Legionnaires' Disease, which is addressed in Brundrett's *Legionella and building services* (Butterworths, 1992).

Conclusion

In executing a design one must consider not only design guidance but maintenance and operating conditions, energy and environmental factors, capital and running costs, as well as taking due note of trends and forecasts. Consequently, a broad range of information sources must be available to practitioners. Growing complexity of engineering services is occurring alongside increasing use of passive technologies to reduce environmental damage. Together these are spawning an increasing range of guidance texts, standards and case studies, the most important sources of which this chapter has attempted to highlight.

CHAPTER SEVENTEEN

Interior design

ANTHONY J. COULSON

The completion of any major architectural project or transformation of premises normally involves an interior designer to ensure that the finished building meets the requirements and tastes of the client. The interior designer may be part of an architectural partnership or be in independent practice. In both situations the specialist's design expertise requires support from a substantial and diverse range of information sources.

Professional bodies

Interior design is a profession in its own right and forms an important part of the designers' central professional body. The Chartered Society of Designers (since its merger with the British Institute of Interior Design in 1988) has its own qualifications, publications, conferences and workshops, library and information service. The Interior Decorators and Designers Association is a professional and commercial association which maintains a directory and its own publications. Both are members of the International Federation of Interior Architects/Designers (IFI), 'the only international and non-governmental organization of the interior design profession', dedicated to raising standards, and understanding and championing the interests of the professional designer. As well as maintaining a permanent secretariat, and supporting many international meetings and committees, the IFI seeks to achieve its aims through an expanding publications programme of international significance. *International handbook* (1991) gives interior design practice and professional practice information listed by country, while *The*

Directory of Schools III (1993) gives detailed information on schools providing interior architectural and design courses. Other publications include *Model code for professional conduct for designers* (1989), *International guidelines to conditions for contracts for interior design* (1983) and *Green design checklist* (1993), as well as regular IFI Position Papers, such as *Environmental stewardship* (1993).

In a broader way, the Design Council is deeply concerned with many aspects of interior and product design through its journal, *Design* (quarterly), together with specialist services and committees. Many other Design Councils in Europe and elsewhere share this interest and so the interior designer may find it helpful to build up a collection of publications and details of services and activities offered by these bodies. Besides these central bodies there are many other national and international organizations that may need to be contacted for current information and codes of practice. There is a convenient, but now rather old, listing in the *World design sources directory (Répertoire des sources d'information en design)*, edited by the Centre de Création Industrielle, Centre Georges Pompidou, Paris, for the International Council of Graphic Design Associations (ICOGRADA) and the International Council for Societies of Industrial Design (ICSID) (Oxford: Pergamon, 1980). IFI and its affiliated societies will provide more up-to-date information.

Information sources in the practice

Most successful interior designers tend to specialize or develop particular interests. Since designers move from one practice or group to another fairly often, their knowledge and experience is frequently the main source of fresh information on problems and solutions. To support them, most practices maintain detailed and (often within very tight financial and space constraints) comprehensive libraries of samples of available materials, specialist information sources, general reference works and records of completed projects. Although few practices have a full-time librarian or information officer, most interior designers are well aware of the range of sources and materials they need.

Resources

Archives

Once a practice has been established for some time, possibly with a number of regular clients, or clients in a particular field, reference to past jobs becomes an important part of planning new work. Detailed and carefully filed records of contracts, suppliers, particular site difficulties, colour schemes/co-ordination, samples of material and special conditions demanded by the client are essential to prepare the designer adequately. As nearly all completed models and presentation plans are lodged with the client as part of the contract, the practice will need to retain details of as many of these decisions as it can within its own resources. For ease of retrieval and re-filing the archives are probably best kept according to the established system of recording a contract and samples. Detailed photographic records (prints, slides and videos) also provide essential reference materials for negotiations with current and new clients. These archive materials constitute the core of the library/information service.

Samples

Next to a firm's own records, its collection of samples is probably the most heavily used resource – both for making up sample boards for clients and for more general reference. Ideally, the designer will want to draw on as many examples of available materials available as possible to show colour, texture and other physical characteristics. This bulky and easily disorganized resource normally includes samples of carpet and other floor coverings, furnishing materials (for curtains, blinds, hangings, etc.), ceiling boards and panels, paint colour cards, plastics, tiles and ceramic finishes, light fittings, switches and handles, woods and metal, glass (for interior divisions), wallpaper and plaster, leather and textiles for furniture, lettering and graphics. It can be quite difficult ensuring that this collection only includes available material, but many practices deal with this problem by arranging with representatives and agents of contractors and suppliers to remove obsolete material when delivering fresh samples and new price information. Other samples collected on a more occasional basis need to be carefully dated and discarded or replaced regularly after a set period (rarely more than two years).

It is not normally possible to keep samples of larger items, such as furniture, readily available, and so the designer has to rely on a full range of catalogues and promotional literature. Multiple copies are useful to allow for cutting up for interior sample boards. In the case of specially imported items or pieces made to order only, it may be essential to keep details of both specification and estimated fabrication/delivery times. This information changes constantly and so a note needs to be kept of contacts (agents, shippers and manufacturers) from whom up-to-date information and news can be obtained rapidly and accurately. There are a number of product information services that, depending on the particular specialities of the practice, may help alleviate this problem to some extent: these include the Barbour Index *Building product compendium* (annual) and *Interior design product selector*, from the

Royal Institute of British Architects. Long delays or uncertainties cannot be tolerated on contracts; materials that cannot be made available relatively simply cannot be used.

Trade literature and directories

As well as the assorted collection of samples and leaflets that can be cannibalized for sample boards, the interior designer needs instant access to as full a range of manufacturers' catalogues and price lists as possible. Maintaining this collection is time-consuming, and so co-operative updating by contractors and representatives is essential. It also needs to be supported by a detailed range of current address books and directories to provide prompt access to product and supply information elsewhere. These reference books include telephone directories (alphabetical and yellow pages) and local street directories, such as *Kelly's Post Office London business directory*, as well as company and product directories, such as *Kelly's manufacturers and merchants directory*, *United Kingdom Kompass register* (Reed), *Key British enterprises* (Dun & Bradstreet), *UK trade names* (Reed).

In the case of overseas suppliers and contacts a detailed index of contacts, telephone numbers and addresses is necessary. Kompass publishes directories for many European and other countries. Many of the commercial attachés in London embassies and trade delegations can be very helpful in providing information that is more up-to-date than printed sources, particularly if this is combined with subscriptions to some of the many computer database networks providing commercial information. Dealings with a wide range of statutory and advisory bodies occur in the course of many projects. General reference works such as *Councils, committees and boards: a handbook to advisory, consultative, executive and similar bodies in British public life*, edited by I.G. Anderson (8th edn, CBD Research, 1993), provide addresses, contact names and information about the relevant bodies. These general reference works need to be supplemented by more specific directories aimed at potential clients and contractors, such as the British Carpet Manufacturers' Association's regular publication, *Index of quality names*. The problem is that there are so many associations, companies and organizations involved in the building and allied trades, but the interior design practice is always short of space. The most convenient solution is probably to invest in the general directories covering these specialist organizations, such as *Directory of British associations* (CBD Research), *Directory of European industrial and trade associations* (CBD Research) or *Trade associations and professional bodies of the United Kingdom*, rather than pile up data that may be used occasionally. Access to some of the growing number of specialist computer networks and databases may also help.

Surveys

In a more general way, it is vital to keep in touch with developments elsewhere and in other fields through some of the more general regular world-wide surveys of interior design, such as the 'International interiors' series from Thames and Hudson, e.g. *International interiors 3: Offices, studios, restaurants, bars, clubs, hotels, shops, cultural and public buildings* (1991). More general works include: Francis D.K. Ching's *Interior design illustrated* (Van Nostrand Reinhold International, 1987); and Gerd Hatje and H.Weisskamp's *Rooms by design: houses, apartments, studios, lofts* (Thames and Hudson, 1989). There are now quite a few histories of interior design – both general surveys, such as Allen Tate's *Interior design in the 20th century* (Harper and Row, 1986), Anne Massey's *Interior design of the twentieth century* (Thames and Hudson, 1990) and Mark Hampton's *Legendary decorators of the twentieth century* (Hale, 1993), and studies of particular periods, such as Patricia Bayer's *Art deco interiors: decoration and design classics of the 1920s and 1930s* (Thames and Hudson, 1990) and Jeremy Cooper's *Victorian and Edwardian furniture and interiors: from gothic revival to art nouveau* (Thames and Hudson, 1987). If particular effects or details are of interest, these could be very useful.

Journals

A much richer and more diverse source of current information and visual ideas is provided by the broad range of architectural, interior design and related journals. Advertisements can often be as valuable as features and this is why the more general architectural magazines are frequently useful.

UK

As well as the regular interior design features in such journals as the monthly *Architectural review*, there are the two monthly specialist journals, *Interior design* (Ruislip: A.G.B. Publications) and *What's new in interiors* (Morgan Grampian), as well as the more wide-ranging *The world of interiors* (11 per year, London: Pharos Publications) and various trade journals, such as *British decorator* (six per year, Harrogate: British Decorators Association). The professional will also need to draw on some of the important journals published in other countries to keep up-to-date with new developments and ideas.

USA

The relevant US journals include *Interior design* (17 per year, New York: Cahners Publishing Company), *Contract design: the business magazine of commercial and institutional interior design and architecture, planning and construction* (monthly, New York: Miller Freeman), *Inte-*

riors: for the contract design professional (monthly, New York: BP Communications), *Interior decorator's handbook* (three per year, New York: Columbia Communications), *Designers illustrated* (six per year, Los Altos: Select Communications), *Architectural digest: the international magazine of fine interior design* (monthly, Los Angeles: Knapp), *Design solutions* (four per year, Centerville, VA: Architectural Woodwork Institute), *Journal of interior design education and research* (two per year, Ithaca, NY: Interior Design Educators Council), *Today's facility manager: the magazine of facilities-interior planning teams* (10 per year, Red Bank, NJ: Group C. Communications).

Canada

In Canada the major journals are *Canadian interiors* (three per year, Toronto: Maclean-Hunter), *Contract magazine* (six per year, Downsview, Ontario: Victor Publishing) and *Designs* (four per year, Montreal: Association Communication Innovation Design).

Scandinavia

Scandinavian journals include *Bonytt/Design for living: Norsk spesialblad for arkitektur boliginnreding* (10 per year, Oslo: Forlaget Bonytt), *Design from Scandinavia: Scandinavian production in furniture, textiles, illumination, arts and crafts and industrial design* (annual, Copenhagen: World Pictures), *Avotakka* (monthly, Helsinki: A-Lehdet) and *Nordic contract: commercial furnishings and interior design* (annual, Alleroed, Denmark: NOVA Kommunikation – text in English, French and German).

Other parts of Europe

From Italy there are *Interni* (10 per year, Paderno Dugnano: Elemond) and *Home: tessile d'arredamente nell'architettura d'interni* (10 per year, Milan: Editore Galfa – text in Italian and English). From Germany come *MD* (monthly, Leinfeldin-Echteringen: Kuonradin Verlag), *DLW Nachrichte: zeitschrift für architektur und innenausbau* (annual, Bietigheim-Bissinen: DLW Aktiengesellschaft) and *Neues Wohnen* (monthly, Berlin: Verlaggesellschaft Neues Wohnen). The French journals include *Archi-Crée* (six per year, Paris: Societé d'Edition et de Presse), *Art et décoration: la revue de la maison* (eight per year, Paris: Editions Charles Massin) and *Décoration* (nine per year, Paris: Editions Rusconi).

Australia

In Australia the following journals are available on the subject: *Interiors magazine* (six per year, Balmain, NSW: Magazine Group), *The inte-*

rior (six per year, Royal Melbourne Institute of Technology Department of Interior Design) and *Australian design series* (monthly, Sydney: Australian Design Series).

Far East

The Far East has, from Japan, *Interior design* (Tokyo: Japan Interior Designers Association), and from China, *Shinei Sheji/Interior* Design (four per year, Chongqing, China: Architectural Industry Press).

Only the very largest practices will be able to afford many of these journals and so there may have to be greater reliance on mainstream architectural and design journals and on the more glossy and easily obtainable general European journals, such as *Domus: architettura, arredamento, arte* (monthly, Rozzana: Editoriale Domus) and *Casabella: rivista di urbanistica architettura e disegno industriale* (monthly, Milan: Electa); also, possibly, on some of the more popular domestic journals, such as *Homes and gardens* (monthly, London: IPC), *House and garden* (monthly, London: Conde Nast), *Ideal home* (monthly, London: IPC) and *House beautiful* (monthly, New York: Hearst Magazines). There are also many journals that concentrate on particular aspects of interior design, such as *Floors* (monthly, Purley: Maple Publications) and *Glass interiors* (four per year, London: Spotlight).

Apart from the indexes to architectural journals, such as the *Architectural periodicals index* (four per year, London: British Architectural Library), mentioned elsewhere in this book, the researcher will find that many of these journals are now indexed in detail and promptly (and in some cases retrospectively) in *Design and applied arts index* (two per year in print, four per year on CD-ROM. Mayfield: Design Documentation).

Administration and planning

Business practice and administration

Many of the considerations and problems of administering and running an architectural practice (see Chapter 20) apply to interior design practices. However, there is now a growing literature, based largely on American experience, that helps tackle particular issues confronting the interior designer. Books of advice now cover basic organization, e.g. C.M. Piotrowski's *Interior design management: a handbook for owners and management* (1992), marketing, e.g. M.V. Knackstedt's *Interior design business handbook: a complete guide to profitability* (1992), professional conduct, e.g. C.M. Piotrowski's *Professional practices for interior designers* (1989) and designer/client relations, e.g. Mary V. Knackstedt and L. Haney's *Marketing and selling design services: the designer/client relationship* (1992), all from Van Nostrand Reinhold International; and legal considerations, e.g. C.J. Berger's *Interior design law and business practices* (Wiley, 1994).

Standards

In the execution of any contract the designer needs to pay careful attention to a great range of standards, regulations and specifications that relate to products, materials, techniques and their application. Apart from local and national building and planning regulations that have been discussed in other chapters, the designer needs access to current individual standards. To help meet this requirement, the practice may need to include British Standards Institution (and possibly also European and American standards) publications in its library. The key documents here will be the *BSI Standards catalogue* (and supplements) the BSI *Annual report, BSI News* (monthly) and *Instep* (the BSI quarterly on international standards), as well as individual standards that bear directly on work in progress. One such standard might be BS 4875 *Strength and stability of furniture*. National and international standards may also be necessary but, as space is at a premium, it may be more convenient to subscribe to BSI's multilingual and multinational CD-ROM service, PERINORM (monthly, one disk: Europe, one disk: International). A more thorough knowledge of the services provided by BSI and the local libraries holding complete sets of standards will also be useful. There exists a useful summary text of relevant considerations and standards in the form of S.C. Reznikoff's *Interior graphic and design standards* (Butterworth-Heinemann, 1986). Many other organizations, such as the British Carpet Manufacturers' Association, apply their own standards and grading schemes and so information on the fundamentals of these schemes and how widely they are applied is necessary. The association concerned is the only reliable current source of this information.

Publications from consumer organizations, such as *Which?* (monthly, London: Consumers Association), and from materials testing organizations, such as the *Annual book of the ASTM standards* (Philadelphia: American Society for Testing and Materials) are also useful. The potential range of this sort of material is enormous and so only a very limited selection of material for immediate needs and special interests is likely to be possible.

Ergonomic data

To supplement the data provided by standards and regulations, some more general texts on ergonomics will help with some of the spatial and functional aspects of interior design. As well as the compact introduction provided by Stephen Pheasant's *Ergonomics: standards and guidelines for designers* (BSI, 1987), there are the established larger textbooks, such as J. Panero and M. Zelnick's *Human dimension and interior space: a sourcebook of design reference standards* (rev. edn, New York: Watson-Guptill, 1992), John A. Roebuck Jnr's *Anthropometric methods: designing to fit the human body* (Human Factors and Ergonomics Society, 1995) and Henry Dreyfuss Associates' *Measure of man and woman: human factors in design* (rev. edn, New York: Whitney Library of Design, 1993). The selection will depend on the interests of the designers. If this is a particular interest they may conveniently update their knowledge with subscriptions to *Applied ergonomics* (four per year, Butterworth-Heinemann) and *Ergonomics abstracts* (four per year, London: Taylor and Francis).

Computer-aided design

Increasingly computers are proving invaluable in planning, reviewing and presenting schemes and the practice needs to assemble advice and guides to underpin developments. As well as more theoretical works looking at potential developments, such as Robin Baker's *Designing the future: the computer transformation of reality* (Thames and Hudson, 1993), it may be sensible to keep in touch with advances in this fast-changing area through subscriptions to key journals, such as *Computer aided design* (monthly, Butterworth-Heinemann) and *Automation in construction* (quarterly, Amsterdam: Elsevier Science), or even the on-line computer database *CAD/CAM on-line* (New York: EIC/Intelligence Inc.).

The literature of general advice for the designer concerned with architectural projects is quite extensive, e.g. Dennis Neely's *User's guide to computer aided draughting and design in the design office* (Wiley, 1992), Gerhard Schmitt's *Microcomputer aided design for architectural designers* (Wiley, 1988), P.E. Perkins' *Hands on CAD: introduction to computer-aided draughting and design* (Cassell, 1989), Mark L. Crosley's *Architect's guide to computer-aided design* (Wiley, 1988) and, Antony Radford and Guy Stevens' *CADD made easy: a comprehensive guide for architects and designers* (McGraw-Hill, 1987). However, the designer will also need more detailed advice that relates directly to the minutiae of the system and software being used. As well as the many manuals directly relating to particular hardware, systems and software, there is a growing literature spelling out wider possibilities of individual systems relevant to the designer, e.g. Alastair Campbell's *The Macdesigner's handbook* (Harper-Collins, 1992) and Paul Jodard's *Paintboxed electronic graphics now* (Batsford, 1994).

Drafting

In drafting the final scheme, the designer may need to refer to basic manuals of advice, such as Donald E. Hepler's *Interior design funda-*

mentals (McGraw, 1983) and John F. Pile's *Interior design* (Abrams, 1994), but there is also a growing literature concerned with more theoretical considerations of interiors, e.g. J.M. Malnar and F. Vodvarka's *Interior dimension: a theoretical approach to enclosed space* (Van Nostrand Reinhold International, 1991). In case the designer is interested in following up these and other more theoretical design issues, it may be useful to take out subscriptions to the journals *Design studies: the international journal for design research in engineering, architecture, products and systems* (quarterly, Butterworth-Heinemann) and *Design methods, theories, research, education and practice* (quarterly, San Luis Obispo, CA: Design Methods Institute). As regards the physical drafting, such basic works as John F. Pile's *Perspective for interior designers* (Whitney Library of Design, 1989) may be useful.

Specific elements of interior design

So far the information sources discussed have a fairly general application but, within each practice, there will be a need for more specialist material on elements of design. As suggested earlier, the balance will depend on the particular needs and interests of individuals as these vary considerably from practice to practice. Information needs and sources for structural problems and services have already been discussed (see Chapter 15). In this section there will be discussion of some of the information materials to support more detailed investigation of lighting, colour, furnishing materials, furniture and fittings.

Lighting

A useful introduction to the whole subject is provided by Carl Gardner and Barry Hannaford's *Lighting design: an introductory guide for professionals* (Design Council, 1993). A number of important codes for lighting particular interiors have been developed, but these have important functional and national differences. As well as documents from general sources, such as the *Code for interior lighting* (1994) from the Chartered Institute of Building Services Engineers and their more specific lighting guides, e.g. *Office lighting* (1993) and *Lecture, teaching and conference rooms* (1991), access is needed to the more specific professional publications and information services in the field, such as those of the Lighting Industry Federation with its guides and draft standards, the Institute of Lighting Engineers with its *Lighting journal* and codes of practice and the International Association of Lighting Designers.

Fortunately, there is now a wide range of more general texts written with the designer in mind: J.L. Nuckolls' *Interior lighting for environmental designers* (3rd edn, Wiley, 1993), Lee Watson's *Lighting design handbook* (McGraw-Hill, 1990), *Calculations for interior lighting: applied method* (Paris: Commission Internationale de l'Eclairage, 1982), P.R. Boyce's *Human factors in lighting* (Applied Science, 1981), Stanley L. Lyons' *Lighting for industry and security: a handbook for providers and users of lighting* (Butterworth-Heinemann, 1992) and Prafalla C. Sorcar's *Architectural lighting for communal interiors* (Wiley, 1987); and from the Department of the Environment, *Environmental action guide, Advisory notes 6: Lighting in buildings: environmental aspects* (HMSO, 1993). There is also the journal *Architectural lighting* (four per year, New York: Miller Freeman).

Colour

As with lighting, the variety of colour systems, terminology and practices has given rise to a considerable and often confusing literature. Many standards have been published, e.g. BS 4800: 1989 *Schedule of paint colours for building purposes*, BS 5252: 1976 *Framework for colour co-ordination for building purposes*, BS 5252F: 1976 (1986) *Colour matching fans*, BS 4901: 1976 (1986) *Specification for plastics colours for building purposes*, BS 381C: 1988 *Specification for colours for identification, coding and special purposes*. Also Building Research Establishment publications have made a very important contribution, particularly H.L. Gloag and M. Gold's *Colour coordination handbook* (HMSO, 1978). As regards dyes and colouring, the publications of the Society of Dyers and Colourists provide the most useful international guide in the very large form of the *Colour index* (3rd edn, 4th revision, 9 vols with supplements and additions).

Further, there are some general guides and texts emerging, such as Susan Berry and Judith Martin's *Designing with colour* (Batsford, 1993) and B.M. Whelan's *Colour harmony 2: over 1400 new colour combinations for the designer* (Thames and Hudson, 1994), but, otherwise, the literature of colour is extremely large, complex and specialized. For more detailed technical data the designer relies on the work of the specialist bodies in the field and their publications, such as the British Colour Makers Association, the Oil and Colour Chemists Association, the Paint Research Association (publishers of the monthly *World surface coatings abstracts*) and the Paintmakers Association of Great Britain Ltd. On a more general level some texts on response to colour might be useful as a way of providing necessary context, e.g. Faber Birren's *Color and human response* (Van Nostrand, 1984), as well as works providing a historical perspective, e.g. Sarah Marberry's *Color in the office: design transformation 1950-90 and beyond* (Van Nostrand International, 1994).

Furnishing materials

Beyond the basic handbooks, such as Mortimer O'Shea's *Interior furnishings* (Manchester: Textile Institute, 1981) and William R. Hall's *Contract interior finishes: a handbook of materials, products and applications* (Whitney Library of Design, 1993), there is an extensive literature on the properties and design of individual materials. The retail/contract aspect of many materials is conveniently treated by the *Decorating contractor annual directory* (London: Kingslea Press) and the work of the British Contract Furnishing Association, which publishes *Contract furnishing* (twice yearly).

The specialist central bodies that have emerged over the last 100 years are generally the most reliable sources of current information and opinion about performance and suitability of individual types of material.

A key source of information on textiles is the Textile Institute, which publishes a very broad range of documents. As well as its more technical works, the *Journal of the Textile Institute* (quarterly), *Textile progress* (quarterly), and a variety of monographs, such as *World review of textile design 1993*, the Institute publishes the very useful guide to terminology in the form of M. Tubbs and M. and P. Daniels' *Textile terms and definitions* (9th rev. edn, Manchester: Textile Institute, 1991). Together with a few basic texts on textile design, e.g. I. Winget and J.F. Mohler's *Textile fabrics and their selection* (Prentice-Hall, 1984), W. Watson's *Textile design and colour*, seventh edition revised by E.G. Taylor and J. Buchanan (Butterworths, 1975), they provide a useful nucleus of technical information. Particular interests in the technical performance of specific fabrics will require the publications of other specialist textile associations, such as the British Textile Technology Group, Didsbury, which is associated with *World textile abstracts* (monthly, Elsevier Science), Lambeg Industrial Research Association (linen) at Lisburn, and the International Wool Secretariat.

Probably the textile form that most concerns the interior designer is the carpet. For current information and developments there are the regular journals, *Carpet and floorcoverings review* (22 per year, Tonbridge: Benn), *International carpet bulletin* (nine per year, Bradford: World Textile Publications) and the *Carpet annual* (Tonbridge: Benn). More detail will require access to the publications of the British Carpet Manufacturers' Association, particularly its monthly *Index of quality names and research* emanating from its technical centre. However, availability is often as much a problem as any technical issue.

Synthetics were touched on earlier and information on plastics will help in assessing the performance and suitability of these common but extremely diverse materials. As well as general surveys of the nature of different materials, such as Sylvia Katz' *Classic plastics: from bakelite to high-tech* (Thames and Hudson, 1985), useful journals include *Euro-*

pean plastics news (monthly, London: IPC) and *Plastics and rubber weekly* (Croydon: Maclaren). More detailed technical information will require access to the publications of RAPRA Technology (Rubber and Plastics Research Association), particularly *Progress in rubber and plastics technology* (quarterly) and *New trade names in the rubber and plastics industries* (annually), together with technical leaflets from the Plastics and Rubber Institute. If the practice can only carry a very small collection of this data there is the useful if elderly guide and directory, *Plastics and rubber: world sources of information,* edited by E.R. Yescombe (Applied Science, 1976).

Furniture and fittings

Probably even more has been published about furniture than any of the preceding topics, but fortunately there are two well-established and highly regarded journals, *Cabinet maker* (weekly, Tonbridge: Benn) and *Furniture manufacturer: the international journal for the furniture manufacturer* (monthly, Oxted: Publex International), and also the annual *Directory to the furnishing trade* (Tonbridge: Benn). For more technical issues the publications of the Furniture Industry Research Association, such as *FIRA Research journal* (quarterly), provide a valuable resource.

Some of the many historical and general surveys help to give an idea of range, shape and effects of different materials and settings, e.g. Charlotte and Peter Fiell's *Modern furniture classics since 1945* (Thames and Hudson, 1991) and John F. Pile's *Furniture: modern and postmodern: design and technology* (2nd edn, Wiley, 1990). Exhibition catalogues, such as *The modern chair: twentieth century chair design* (London: ICA, 1988), are also useful contextual materials. The selection depends a lot on the tastes and interests of the designers concerned and this is even more important in considering the information to be collected on the minor pieces of furniture (knobs, handles, switches, etc.) before going beyond the available retail and wholesale trade literature. There is a convenient general text in the form of Wendy W. Staebler's *Architectural detailing in contract interiors* (Whitney Library of Design, 1988).

If there is a clear interest, it will be worth seeking out specialist associations, such as the British Blind and Shutter Association with its quarterly *Blinds and shutters* and annual *Specifier's guide and directory.* The International Wallcovering Manufacturers Association, the Contract Flooring Association and the Wallcovering Fabric and Decor Retailers Association offer similar services. *Kompass* and the *Directory of British associations* are useful starting points for information on these and other specialist groups and companies.

Designing for particular functions and problems

Designs for specific ranges of interiors and activities, such as restaurants, shops, hotels, offices, hospitals and exhibitions, raise distinctive combinations of problems and so are served by some quite distinctive information sources. Broadly, it is possible to divide the literature serving each range into: handbooks and manuals, such as Walter Rutes and Richard Penner's *Hotel planning: a guide for architects, interior designers and hotel executives* (Butterworths, 1985), Fred Lawson's *Restaurants, clubs and bars: planning, design and investment in food service facilities* (Butterworths, 1995), James Rappoport et al.'s *Office planning and design desk reference* (Wiley, 1991) and Vilma Barr's *Timesaver details for store planning and design* (McGraw-Hill, 1994); more individual opinions and reflections, such as Rodney Fitch's *Fitch on retail design* (Phaidon, 1990) and Francis Duffy et al.'s *The responsible workplace: the redesign of work and offices* (Butterworths, 1993); and standards and bye-laws and publications of official bodies in the field concerned, e.g. the British Institute of Management 'show-case' surveys or books of examples, such as Saitoh Hideo and Joao Stroeter's *Interior design in cafés and restaurants* (Dusseldorf: Nippan, 1992) and Volker Hartkopf et al.'s *The Japanese approach to tomorrow's workplace: towards the office of the future* (Butterworths, 1992).

Journals in the field that are normally aimed at the practitioner rather than the designer include *Hospitality design* (monthly, New York: Bill Communications) and *Professional hotel and restaurant interiors* (six per year, Dorking: Scroll Communications).

There are also particular types of design problem that affect all schemes, and every designer will need to be aware of the issues. Ensuring the interior layout can meet the needs of people with physical and other problems is now more important than ever. Consequently, the designer will need to consult basic texts, such as Selwyn Goldsmith's *Designing for the disabled* (3rd edn, RIBA, 1976) and to keep in touch with more general design ideas in this area, such as those advanced in W.L. Lebovich's *Design for dignity* (Wiley, 1993), and the publications of specialist agencies such as the Disabled Living Foundation.

Conclusion

This chapter should have indicated that the interior designer may need to draw on as wide a range of information sources as the architect and contractor. The emphasis is different – the interior designer is generally an assembler and modifier rather than a constructor. The sources need to be used in a much more selective way and may vary enormously from one contract to another. In reality, the interior designer tends to specialize much more than may be supposed at first glance.

CHAPTER EIGHTEEN

Landscape

SHEILA HARVEY

All architecture is contained within some kind of landscape setting, whether urban or rural. The public concern for the environment – threats to existing landscape, effects of new developments, dereliction of land – is also the concern of the landscape architect. A welcome result of this is that it has become accepted that the landscape professional should be involved in the design process from its conception. Projects may include housing, roads, parks and urban open space, business and science parks, environmental assessment, conservation and wildlife protection, mineral workings and reclamation.

The designers, scientists and managers who make up this small but highly specialized profession together encompass a wide range of skills and knowledge, obtained over many years of academic and practical training. Inevitably, one of the problems arising from this breadth of subject matter is the sheer impossibility of containing, within any one convenient source, the range of information sources which relate to landscape architecture. The problem is compounded by the comparatively limited number of landscape architects (c.3500 in Great Britain) which makes the production of targeted reference works and databases economically unattractive.

This chapter will therefore endeavour simply to highlight the most helpful and reasonably accessible sources, but will make no attempt at comprehensive coverage of the entire range of information that could be required on landscape architecture.

Texts

There are, nowadays, many texts published throughout the world dealing with landscape subjects. The selection given here offers a basic introduction to the subject through standard works in English originating mainly in Great Britain.

Landscape design with plants edited by Brian Clouston provides comprehensive technical guidance on planting design for most conditions. Subjects covered include derelict and toxic sites, water, tropical and arid landscapes, tree planting and landscape management. Most chapters have extensive bibliographies and detailed plant lists are included. A recent paperback version will make this book more accessible to individual users.

Basic practical information, including bibliographies and lists of relevant British Standards, are to be found in the two volume *Landscape design guide* by Lisney and Fieldhouse. Volume I covers soft landscape applications, whilst volume II is on hard landscape. Also providing technical construction guidance is Littlewood's *Landscape detailing* with two volumes on enclosures and surfaces respectively, and with scale-drawn detail sheets.

Readers requiring a sound and readable introduction to land use and landscape planning should find *Landscape planning* by T. Turner invaluable. Apart from an introductory chapter on landscape theory, coverage includes the landscape of industry, reservoirs, flood control, forestry and urban landscape. Extensive references are provided for each subject described. A. Beer's *Environmental planning for site development* is a clear guide to the physical and social aspects of the site and to its planning, planting and management. *People places*, subtitled *Design guidelines for urban open spaces*, edited by Marcus and Francis is exactly that, and coverage includes urban space for neighbourhoods, housing, plazas and hospitals.

Specialist aspects

Restoration

Restoration is a constantly recurring problem and one of the standard works that summarizes most kinds of dereliction and their solutions is *The restoration of land* by Bradshaw and Chadwick. *The potential for woodland establishment on landfill sites* from the Department of the Environment is an extremely useful tool for dealing with an important aspect of this subject and contains further references.

Roads

The Department of Transport's *Design manual for roads and bridges,* volume 10, includes *The good road guide: environmental design guides for inter-urban roads.* It aims to function as a sourcebook and checklist for all aspects of road design.

In addition, McCluskey has written two books which contain clearly set out practical information augmented by technical drawings and illustrations on urban roads. They are *Parking: a guide to environmental design* and *Road form and townscape*; the latter includes comprehensive references and a list of relevant British Standards.

Play

Two useful and complementary studies are *Playgrounds: the planning, design and construction of play environments* by Heseltine and Holborn, which needs no further explanation, and R.C. Moore's *Childhood's domain: play and place in child development*, which provides valuable insights into the psychology and social aspects of play.

Forestry

The Forestry Commission's *Forest landscape design guidelines* still offers a useful basic approach, but a more comprehensive coverage of the full range of landscape work within forestry can be gained from *The design of forest landscapes* by O. Lucas. Design techniques, visual impact assessment for forestry operations and management are included.

Management

The vital importance of landscape management if a scheme is to have any chance of successful maturity and survival cannot be underestimated. The practicalities of the subject are clearly set out in Parker and Bryan's *Landscape management and maintenance.* Cobham's *Amenity landscape management: a resources handbook* explains in depth the management requirements for all kinds of sites: woodland, grassland, water. There are also bibliographies for further reading.

Habitat

With the current enthusiasm for things ecological perhaps one basic title should be included here from the range available. *A guide to habitat creation* by Baines and Smart (published in conjunction with the London Ecology Unit) also contains a guide to wildflower seed sources. *Biological habitat reconstruction* edited by G.P. Buckley provides a scientific approach to the creation, recreation and transplanting of habitats and the ecological principles involved.

History

The history of landscape and garden has generated such a vast body of literature that merely noting this fact must suffice here. However, the following books may be of particular interest in terms of landscape design. *The landscape of man: shaping the environment from prehistory to the present day* by Susan and Geoffrey Jellicoe, compiled over a period of 17 years of travel and research, provides a well-illustrated overview of the evolution of the landscape throughout the world from the ancient cultures of the East to the modern landscapes of the West. There is a select bibliography arranged by historical period. *The English garden in our time: from Gertrude Jekyll to Geoffrey Jellicoe* by Jane Brown offers a clear, well-illustrated survey of twentieth century styles and movements.

Finally, brief mention must be made of texts such as *Land and landscape: evolution, design and control* by Brenda Colvin; *The landscape of roads*, *The landscape of power* and *Garden design* all by Sylvia Crowe; and Jellicoe's wide-ranging output (a four volume edition of his collected works has recently been published). All of these have become 'classics' and continue to be reprinted and, in some cases, revised.

Periodicals

The number of specialist periodicals continues to grow but is still fairly limited in terms of landscape titles in the English language. *Landscape design* is the journal of the Landscape Institute (LI) and is published 10 times per year by the Landscape Design Trust. It contains articles on all aspects of landscape work including accounts of recent projects and in-depth technical articles. News items, reports of conferences and symposia, book reviews, LI information and an events listing are all featured. Of particular value are its special theme issues such as those on 'Environmental assessment', 'CAD', 'Urban parks' and 'Bioengineering'. As well as articles and case studies, technical and product information together with a subject bibliography are usually included. The journal is indexed annually. A monthly newspaper, *Landscape design extra*, also includes special features, such as play equipment or lighting dealt with mainly from a product viewpoint but often including relevant organizations and a bibliography. *Plant user* is published twice yearly in association with the Professional Plant Users Group as part of *Landscape design extra*. Subjects may include specification, seeding, planting techniques and management.

Landscape research is published by the Landscape Research Group three times per year and takes in academic contributions with a base that may include art, geography, literature, photography or sociology in relation to landscape subjects. It carries lengthy book reviews, and its accompanying newsletter lists the contents of related magazines, including *Landscape design*.

Landscape and urban planning (International Journal of Landscape Ecology, Landscape Planning and Landscape Design) published by Elsevier in Amsterdam has an international editorial board and covers the subjects suggested by its title throughout the world. The approach is generally academic and methodological with extensive references. Frequency varies since, though originally quarterly, whole volumes may be devoted to special conference proceedings of considerable length, e.g. wetlands, urban design, and may incorporate what would have been four separate issues.

The American Society of Landscape Architects publishes a long-established monthly journal, *Landscape architecture*, featuring lavishly illustrated articles. A 10-year database called *The Design Networ' '*as been set up covering the magazine and other ASLA publications. Another American title is *Landscape journal* published twice yearly by the University of Wisconsin. An academic journal, it fulfils a vital role by addressing the theory and philosophy of landscape and promotes discussion amongst its contributors. *Landscape Australia* published quarterly by the Australian Institute of Landscape Architects (AILA) is the most substantial of the otl English language landscape periodicals. As well as articles on (mainly) Australian landscape work and current projects, native plants and rainforest, it includes AILA policy guidance notes and practice listings.

European journals of particular interest include *Garten und Landschaft* issued monthly from Callwey in Munich and currently printed in German with English summaries. As well as articles, it carries news, reports, book reviews and competition announcements. A more recent title from the same publisher is *Topos*, subtitled 'European landscape magazine'. It appears four times per year and each issue explores a particular theme with examples from as many European countries as possible. Large format with spacious layout and colour illustrations, it is bilingual in English and German. *Anthos* is published quarterly in Zurich for the Swiss Federation of Landscape Architects with parallel texts in English, French and German and is the official organ of IFLA. The Danish landscape architects' journal, *Landskab*, is published eight times per year from Copenhagen and, whilst language is obviously a problem, English summaries are provided. It should not be confused with the similarly titled Swedish journal, *Utblick Landskap*.

There are two history journals: *Garden history* published by the Garden History Society twice yearly; and the *Journal of garden history*, an international quarterly from Taylor and Francis of London. Both have an academic approach, especially the latter, which can be extremely esoteric, with extensive references. Another title which can be of use to landscape architects is the *Arboricultural journal*, a quarterly publication from the Arboricultural Association. Subjects covered include research, tree care, urban trees, surgery and pathology.

Current awareness

Landscape periodicals are the main source here and mention has already been made of the special features in *Landscape design* and *Landscape design extra* where subjects such as CAD and Environmental Assessment (EA) are updated as necessary (e.g. EA in March 1993 was followed by EA update in June 1994). *Planning and environmental law bulletin* (Longmans) is a useful monthly source for legislation, not so much for its case studies as for its discussion and analysis of new legislation and listings of current PPGs, RPGs, and MPGs issued by the DoE (see Chapter 12).

Many government and official organizations produce catalogues of publications which are usually revised on an annual basis and provide a useful checklist of available current literature. The MAFF subjects most likely to be relevant to landscape architecture include agriculture, poisonous plants, pesticides, environmentally sensitive areas and agricultural land classification maps. As far as the Countryside Commission is concerned, there is little in its catalogue that is not of relevance, whilst the Forestry Commission also includes those items not published by HMSO. The latter's *Environmental catalogue* contains wide coverage of landscape-related subjects including legislation. *Spon's landscape and external works price book*, edited by Derek Lovejoy Partnership and Davis Langdon and Everest, is revised annually and contains sections on legislation, fees, specification, costing and British Standards relating to both hard and soft landscape.

Abstracts and indexes, databases

There are no major sources which are specifically designed for landscape architects but some coverage is given by sources originating in related subjects. The most useful of these is probably the *Architectural periodicals index* compiled by the British Architectural Library. Coverage is international and includes landscape history and design and urban design and planning. Arranged by subject headings, with an index of names and places and/or buildings, it is also available on CD-ROM and through DIALOG.

Elsevier/Geo Abstracts produce *Ecological abstracts* and *Geographical abstracts* (both human and physical volumes). These are published 12 times per year and are also available on CD-ROM from Elsevier/

Geobase. They currently comprise over 400 000 abstracts on geography, earth sciences and ecology.

The Landscape Institute Library is compiling an in-house database which currently stands at some 10 000 records drawn from journals, books and reports held. There is no plan for publication but arrangements for on-line availability are being investigated. Meanwhile, searches can be made on request for which a charge will be made. ASLA's *The Design Network* has already been cited.

Trade and technical

Within this section might usefully be included some LI publications. *The directory of registered landscape practices* is arranged by region and gives brief notes of the kind of work undertaken by each practice listed. Inclusion is restricted to firms in which one or more of the principals is a professional member of the LI. *Trees and shrubs for landscape planting,* published by the Joint Council for Landscape Industries (JCLI), aims to provide a quick and concise source of information on the culture and requirements of approximately 1200 species of cultivars and woody plants. *Herbaceous perennials for landscape planting* is intended as a companion volume giving information on non-woody plants. *A visitor's guide to 20th century British landscape design* contains brief descriptions and illustrations of over 300 schemes throughout Great Britain.

Standard information on landscape practice and contracts can be obtained from *Spon's landscape contract manual: a guide to good practice and procedures in the management of landscape contracts* and *Landscape professional practice,* both by H. Clamp. The second title is a source for codes of conduct governing landscape work, law and contract administration.

A subject of great importance is Environmental Assessment and a vast body of literature has been generated. The LI and the Institute of Environmental Assessment have jointly produced *Guidelines for landscape and visual impact assessment,* which outlines good practice, the EA process and includes a current list of environmental assessment regulations. Three basic publications – one general, the others covering specific areas – may also be of assistance: the DoE/Welsh Office's *Environmental assessment, a guide to the procedures* (this also contains the text of the EC Directive 85/337/EEC); the Forestry Commission's *Environmental assessment of afforestation projects*; and the Countryside Commission's *Environmental assessment: the treatment of landscape and countryside recreation issues.*

One compendium that has proved a valuable source of trade information in recent years is *External works* (previously known as *Landscape specification*) published by Landscape Promotions. It is a guide to products and services for the external environment for both hard and soft landscape. There is an alphabetical contents index, a register of companies and a list of useful organizations with colour illustration of many products. For soft landscape, the *Hillier manual of trees and shrubs* is a good practical guide to care and site conditions for over 9000 plants.

Organizations and associations

The Landscape Institute is the professional body for landscape architects, managers and scientists. The combined skills of these landscape professionals take in the implementation and management of landscape works, which may involve design, horticulture, ecology, nature conservation and the long-term care of the landscape including the financial and physical organization of manpower and materials. The LI aims to promote the highest standards of professional service and operates a code of professional conduct for its members. Professional membership is through recognized qualification and the LI validates landscape courses in universities to this end. It promotes and organizes an annual conference, as well as symposia, workshops and talks throughout Great Britain. Details of these and other events of interest to landscape architects are listed in each issue of *Landscape design*.

The LI secretariat will answer enquiries on professional and practice matters. There is a reference library for members and landscape students which is also available to non-students with bona-fide research enquiries by prior appointment only. Telephone enquiries will be accepted, although there may be a charge for some services.

The European Foundation for Landscape Architecture is an association of national landscape organizations within the European Community. The Landscape Design Trust publishes on its behalf an annual directory, *Landscape Europe*, which is a useful source on legislation, practice, education, organizations and international events within the member countries.

Who's who in the environment from the Environment Council is a useful guide to all organizations, whether official or unofficial, that have any connection with environmental matters.

Conclusion

It will be seen from the foregoing that the variety of information required for landscape architecture is wide, as are its possible sources. The information given here should be regarded as a starting point to set the enquirer on the right road and provide some signposts into this important subject.

Bibliography

Baines, C. and Smart, J. (1991) *A guide to habitat creation*. Chichester: Packard (for London Ecology Unit).

Beer, A. (1990) *Environmental planning for site development*. London: Spon.

Bradshaw, A.D. and Chadwick, M.J. (1980) *The restoration of land*. Oxford: Blackwell.

Brown, J. (1986) *The English garden in our time: from Gertrude Jekyll to Geoffrey Jellicoe*. Woodbridge: Antique Collectors' Club.

Buckley, G.P. (1989) (ed.) *Biological habitat reconstruction*. London: Belhaven Press.

Clamp, H. (1988) *Landscape professional practice*. Aldershot: Gower.

Clamp, H. (1986) *Spon's landscape contract manual*. London: Spon.

Clouston, B. (1990) (ed.) *Landscape design with plants*. London: Heinemann.

Cobham, R. (1990) *Amenity landscape management: a resources handbook*. London: Spon.

Colvin, B. (1970) *Land and landscape*. London: John Murray.

Countryside Commission (1991) *Environmental assessment: the treatment of landscape and countryside recreation issues*. Gloucester: Countryside Commission.

Crowe, S. (1994) *Garden design*. Chichester: Packard.

Crowe, S. (1958) *The landscape of power*. London: Architectural Press.

Crowe, S. (1960) *The landscape of roads*. London: Architectural Press.

Department of the Environment (1993) *The potential for woodland establishment on landfill sites*. HMSO.

Department of the Environment /Welsh Office (1989) *Environmental assessment: a guide to the procedures*. HMSO.

Department of Transport (1993) *Design manual for roads and bridges*. vol. 10. HMSO.

Derek Lovejoy Partnership and Davis Langdon & Everest (1994) *Spon's landscape and external works price book*. London: Spon.

Environment Council (1995) *Who's who in the environment*. London: Environment Council.

External works (1994) Stirling: Landscape Promotions.

Forestry Commission (1988) *Environmental assessment of afforestation projects*. Edinburgh: Forestry Commission.

Forestry Commission (1994) *Forest landscape design guidelines*. HMSO.

Heseltine, P. and Holborn, J. (1987) *Playgrounds: the planning: design and construction of play environments*. London: Mitchell.

The Hillier manual of trees and shrubs (1991) Newton Abbot: David & Charles.

Jellicoe, G.A. (1994-) *Collected works* 4 vols. Woodbridge: Garden Art Press.

Jellicoe, G.A. and S. (1987) *The landscape of man: shaping the environment from prehistory to the present day*. London: Thames and Hudson.

JCLI (1994) *Herbaceous perennials for landscape planting*. Reading: Horticultural Trades Association.

JCLI (1989) *Trees and shrubs for landscape planting*. London: Landscape Institute.

Landscape Institute (1994) *Directory of registered landscape practices*. London: Landscape Institute.

Landscape Institute (1994) *A visitors' guide to 20th century British landscape design*. London: Landscape Institute.

Landscape Institute and Institute of Environmental Assessment (1995) *Guidelines for landscape and visual impact assessment*. London: Spon.

Lisney, A. and Fieldhouse, K. (1990) *Landscape design guide*. 2 vols. Aldershot: Gower.

Littlewood, M. (1993) *Landscape detailing*. London: Butterworths.

Lucas, O.W.R. (1991) *The design of forest landscapes*. Oxford University Press.

McCluskey, J. (1987) *Parking, a handbook of environmental design*. London: Spon.

McCluskey, J. (1992) *Road form and townscape*. London: Butterworths.

Marcus, C. and Francis, C. (1990) (eds.) *People, places: design guide lines for urban open space*. New York: Van Nostrand Reinhold.

Moore, R.C. (1986) *Childhood's domain: play and place in child development*. London: Croom Helm.

Parker, J. and Bryan, P. (1989) *Landscape management and maintenance*. Aldershot: Gower.

Turner, T. (1987) *Landscape planning*. London: Hutchinson.

CHAPTER NINETEEN

Quality assurance in building design

LORRAINE JEFFERSON

During the 1980s, the focus on quality assurance was heightened (the concept of QA had been around for some years beforehand in diverse areas of the manufacturing industry) by the publication of the Government White Paper (1982) *Standards, quality and international competitiveness.*

As a result of the White Paper, the Government instructed the Property Services Agency (PSA) to encourage suppliers of design and construction services to adopt a BS 5750 quality system. The PSA led the way by setting an example to the industry and developing a QA system for its design arm, submitting that system to external scrutiny and by achieving certification from an external body, in line with the major recommendations of the White Paper.

The principles of QA had seemed more relevant in manufacturing industries, where the concept of quality control in relation to a product was clearly understood, but it was less clear how one could quantify 'quality' when referring to the provision of a service. BS 4778: Part 1 defines 'quality' as 'the totality of features and characteristics of a product or service that bear on its ability to satisfy stated or implied needs'. This definition requires some clarification and interpretation, particularly when it is linked to the provision of a service. There is, indeed, some disagreement as to the appropriateness of the term 'quality assurance' itself and a conviction that the word 'assurance' has misleading connotations. Some bodies, for instance the Construction Industry Research and Information Association (CIRIA) in its publication, *Quality management in construction: implementation in design services organisations*, prefer to shed the expression in favour of 'quality management', which CIRIA defines as 'the management of quality'.

Whichever controversial points have been debated during the years during which QA has been gaining acceptance in industry and commerce, the fact remains that QA is now an established procedure and the terms 'fifty-seven-fifty' and 'five-seven-five-O' are now firmly entrenched in managerial jargon.

In mid-1994, the British Standard, BS 5750, which had been adopted by the International Organisation for Standardisation (ISO 9000) and CEN, the European Standards body (EN 29000), was subjected to a process of review and renumbering. The revisions were not all completed during that year, but the most important work was concluded and five standards in the series were re-issued with their new numbering:

FORMERLY KNOWN AS	NOW KNOWN AS
BS 5750: Part 1: 1987	BS EN ISO 9001: 1994
BS 5750: Part 2: 1987	BS EN ISO 9002: 1994
BS 5750: Part 3: 1987	BS EN ISO 9003: 1994
BS 5750: Part 0: Section 0.1: 1987	BS EN ISO 9000-1: 1994
BS 5750: Part 0: Section 0.2: 1987	BS EN ISO 9004-1: 1994

The review process also introduced changes to the text to make the standards more user-friendly, to take recognisance of the needs of small businesses and to better accommodate the service sectors. BS 5750: Part 4: 1990, the standard which provided guidance to organizations seeking to comply with BS 5750: Parts 1, 2 and 3, was revised in late 1994 and came into effect in 1995, as a fully international guidance document was still some way off. BS 5750: Part 4: 1994 highlights the important aspects of BS EN ISO 9001, 9002 and 9003 to which special attention should be given in order to meet the requirements of the standards.

Why QA?

The question 'Why bother with QA?' has been, and will no doubt continue to be, debated for some time in manufacturing and commercial circles. The relevance of a 'quality system' of some kind was brought home very clearly to architects and building designers in the conclusions of a report by the Building Research Establishment, *Quality in traditional housing* (Bonshor and Harrison, 1982), in which it was revealed that at least 50 per cent of building defects were caused by errors in designs. BRE concluded that the major reasons for these errors were lack of discipline and failure to use authorized design guidance. Such salutary facts were enough to focus the minds of many designers on the need to have clear procedures for improving quality of product, by, in the words of BS 4891: 1972, 'developing their own capabilities to meet contractual requirements'.

Few practices or designers would admit to striving to achieve QA certification for purely altruistic reasons. The two most pertinent benefits of instituting a system that sets out a disciplined framework for operations are: acceptance in the commercial world – many clients, especially governmental and public bodies, now specifically cite BS EN ISO 9000 as a prerequisite when firms reply to an invitation to tender; and to safeguard against costly litigation, as far as is possible, by having improved, quantifiable working methods in place.

Auditing, accreditation, certification and registration

The quality audit

Once a quality system has been established, the Standard requires that an effective internal auditing system is put in place. This is known as the quality audit. The audit process is defined in BS 4778 *Quality vocabulary* as 'a systematic and independent examination to determine whether quality activities and related results comply with planned arrangements and whether these arrangements are implemented effectively and are suitable to achieve objectives'.

Quality audits can fall into one of three categories:

- first party audits: these are audits carried out internally by trained personnel, and are the only ones specified in order to comply with the standard. Training for the function of auditor is available from a number of commercial organizations and academic institutions.

- second party audits: these are audits which a purchaser or client may wish to carry out to satisfy themselves that the supplier does indeed perform according to the Standard.

- third party audits: These are external assessments by an independent body. It is not a requirement of the Standard that a quality system be subjected to independent audit. However, many firms or establishments, having spent a considerable amount of time and money on installing a quality system feel that exposing the system to external scrutiny gives it that extra stamp of credibility.

There are now numerous certification bodies, some with a wide sphere of operation, some of which only operate in a specialized field, from which to choose. In making that choice, guidance can in turn be obtained from various other bodies which audit the external auditors! The Institute of Quality Assurance (IQA) is the professional body which organizes and administers structured training courses and sets examination syllabuses. The IQA can give advice on the training of auditors and can supply details of opportunities for training, both on a full- or part-time basis.

Accreditation

Any certification body worth its salt will wish to be accredited. Accreditation is the process of approval of certification bodies by the Secretary of State for Trade and Industry. The organization set up to perform this function is the National Accreditation Council for Certification Bodies (NACCB), which was established in 1984 to assess the competence and impartiality of certification bodies, leading to their accreditation. The NACCB aims to ensure consistency in the performance of certification bodies so that it cannot be said that it is easier to gain certification with one body than with another. Accreditation enables certification bodies to display the National Accreditation Mark alongside their own certification marks.

The Association of British Certification Bodies (ABCB) is the national organization for independent nationally-accredited certification bodies. Its members aim to promote consistent quality by adopting a uniformly high standard of independent certification. Members represent the majority of accredited certification bodies and participate in a wide range of organizations, including the NACCB.

Certification and registration

Having begun work on the planning and implementation of the quality system, it is advisable to choose a certifying body at a reasonably early stage, if it has been decided that third-party certification is required. Although the formal contract of appointment may not be signed until some time later, informal talks and advice can take place and arrangements can be made for a mutually suitable date for the initial assessment. An internal audit programme should first be carried out and corrective action taken if necessary. If the external assessor is obliged to issue non-compliance notes, he will arrange to repeat his visit when the faults have been rectified. When all is satisfactory the assessor will recommend to his organization that certification is granted and that a Certificate of Registration is issued.

Each certification body keeps a list of firms registered with them. The *DTI Quality assurance register*, although by no means exhaustive, is a very full list of quality assured firms in the UK, and therefore also useful for checking out the registration or otherwise of quality assessed suppliers of services, competitors and potential partners in business enterprises. The *Register* is now also available on CD-ROM.

Documentation: what is needed?

BS EN ISO 9004-1 gives guidance on documentation of the quality system in clause 5.3. It states that 'all the elements, requirements and provisions adopted by an organization for its quality system should be documented in a systematic, orderly and understandable manner in the form of policies and procedures. However, care should be taken to limit documentation to the extent pertinent to the application'. It further states that the typical form of the main document used to describe a documented quality system is a 'quality manual'.

Quality system manual

This should be the strategic document which sets out the firm's approach to quality. Care should be taken to make it as succinct as possible and to avoid too much detail. It should include items such as the organization's stated commitment to QA, signed by the chief executive or similar person, organizational and management details as they relate to QA and information on how the quality system will operate in practice. Books which can advise on the writing of the quality system manual are listed in the bibliography, or it may be appropriate to employ a consultant to assist in the process.

Quality procedures

Unlike the manual, all or parts of which may be used as a marketing tool for the organization, quality procedures are internal, confidential documents which document the way in which key tasks in the design process and the associated administration procedures are to be handled. Again, care should be taken not to make these documents too unwieldy, but they should answer the question 'Who does what, when, how and why?'. RIBA *Architect's job book* is an excellent work which gives guidance on working methods for architects, although other design professions may require different procedures written on parallel lines. As working methods will evolve with time and advances in technique, the procedures system must also allow for a controlled process of change and modification of documents, or perhaps their total revision, through a regular review process. Again, guidance can be sought from published literature or from a consultant.

Where to look for help

Sources of information

It is possible to collect quite a lot of information on QA without cost, by contacting advisory agencies, particularly those that are government funded, or by using reference and lending libraries. Commercial QA organizations will also be able to supply introductory prospectuses, but these will naturally not be totally unbiased, as they are a sales vehicle for the service they offer.

Department of Trade and Industry

The DTI's *Enterprise Initiative scheme* was able to offer advice and some financial assistance to firms planning to adopt QA. This scheme is no longer available, but the DTI *Business Link network*, which is a partnership between the DTI, local Chambers of Commerce and various Enterprise Agencies, has been set up to assist businesses and give advice. The DTI's *Managing in the '90s* programme signposts the way for firms to obtain practical help and advice in essential management areas including quality. Phone the DTI Help-line on 0800 500 200 (free-phone number) for the address and telephone number of your nearest advice point. Contact the DTI, c/o Mediascene Ltd, PO Box 90, Hengoed, Mid Glamorgan CF8 9YE tel: 01443 821877, for a selection of free publications on the topic of quality and also a number of informative videos available for free loan.

The *DTI QA register (the UK register of quality assessed companies)* is available from HMSO retail outlets. It is published annually and lists those companies whose quality systems have been assessed by an accredited UK certification body. The *DTI QA register on CD ROM* is available on annual subscription from HMSO and has a quarterly updating service. Both versions of the *Register* also include the National Measurement Accreditation Service (NAMAS) *Directory of accredited laboratories*.

National Accreditation Council for Certification Bodies

The NACCB, the body which awards accredited status to certifying bodies, produces a list of these, together with the date of their accreditation. The list is available from the NACCB (Audley House, 13 Palace Street, London SW1E 5HS tel: 0171 223 7111).

Association of British Certification Bodies

The ABCB is the national organization for independent nationally-accredited certification bodies. Its membership, comprising the majority of accredited certification bodies, undertakes impartial certification of quality management systems. It plays a major role in international, European and national certification developments. The ABCB can supply a list of its members, on request, from the ABCB Secretariat (c/o Sira Ltd, South Hill, Chislehurst, Kent BR7 5EH tel: 0181 295 1128).

Institute of Quality Assurance

The IQA was established to serve the needs of all those involved in QA. The Institute organizes short courses, seminars and conferences. It offers a Diploma in Quality Assurance and can give guidance on aspects of training. It also operates the National Quality Information Centre (NQIC), which aims to help industry and commerce obtain the information they need to improve quality in their corporate activities and in the products and services they provide. Enquiries may be addressed to the IQA (PO Box 712, 61 Southwark Street, London SE1 1SB tel: (0171) 401 7227).

Association of Quality Management Consultants

The AQMC is a self-regulating body whose members, by their training, qualifications and experience, meet requirements designed to establish that they are professionally competent to act as consultants on a wide range of quality management activities. The AQMC can supply information on consultants who are in its membership and offer guidance as to which may have appropriate expertise in a particular field. Contact the AQMC Ltd. (4 Beyne Road, Olivers Battery, Winchester SO22 4JW tel: (01962) 864394).

British Standards Institution

Apart from its role in the development and publication of standards, a branch of BSI (BSI QA) is the largest accredited certification body in the UK. It also has an education and training arm, BSI International Training, which runs courses on QA, including those for internal auditors. The *BSI Quality Management Handbook* (formerly Handbook 22) is an authoritative source of quality assurance, reliability and maintainability standards in one publication. It contains executive summaries which enable a quick but thorough grasp of quality management. Contact BSI for information on the services available.

Other valuable sources of information, together with practical guides to aid the development and maintenance of a quality system, can be obtained by contacting professional institutes and technical associations in architecture and the allied disciplines.

Construction Industry Information Group

CIIG is an organization for all those interested in construction industry information. Its members come from many professions, including architects, information officers, engineers, librarians and surveyors. The *CIIG manual: a guide to good practice in construction industry information* contains a chapter on quality assurance.

CIRIA has produced a selection of books, guidance documents and a video on the subject of quality assurance, since the mid-1980s. In 1990,

CIRIA stepped in to address a situation in the construction industry which resulted in contractors having much better guidance on quality management available to them than was available to the design professionals in architecture, quantity surveying and engineering consultancies, by inviting representatives from design services organizations to participate in a project to rectify the situation. The result, *Special Publication SP88*, gives detailed guidance to quality system managers in design services organizations wishing to prepare and implement a quality system. A booklist giving information on this and other publications relating to QA is available from CIRIA.

Royal Institute of British Architects

RIBA has published various practice manuals which give clear practical instruction on running a job and has also produced a quality management manual. Occasional features in the 'Practice' section of the *RIBA Journal* deal with quality management issues.

Other professional organizations have, in the recent past, produced guidance on QA for their members, some of which is useful to any design firm preparing its own QA programme. Try the Association of Consulting Engineers, the Chartered Institute of Building and the Building Services Research and Information Association, all of which will be able to supply lists of their publications.

Monographs on QA

The development of the concept of QA and the impetus given to it in the 1980s have spawned the publication of a large number of books on the subject. A local public library or bookseller will be able to supply a list of works in print. Below are mentioned just a few items by individuals which not only document the growth of QA, but also give sound practical advice on the setting up of a system.

Sadgrove is a clear, concise guide for the layman which cuts through the jargon and takes the reader step by step through the procedures leading up to certification. Cornick's *Quality management for building design* is a stage by stage guide to quality management. Foster presents the case for QA in the industry, and Stebbing covers all QA activities including the contents of a quality programme, the quality plan, the development of a quality manual and supporting procedures. Taylor and Hosker is a valuable reference work and practical guide which demonstrates how to develop, implement and audit QA. Its authors have extensive experience as practitioners and consultants in the field.

References and bibliography

Standards, quality and international competitiveness. (Cmnd 8621) (1982) HMSO.

Bonshor, R.B. and Harrison, H.W. (1982) *Quality in traditional housing.* 3 vols. BRE.

British Standards Institution (1995) *Quality management handbook.* (3 vol. boxed set) BSI.

BS 5750: 1995: Part 4 *Guide to the use of BS EN ISO 9001 'Model for quality assurance in design, development, production, installation and servicing' (Formerly BS 5750: Part 1), BS EN ISO 9002 'Model for quality assurance in production, installation and servicing' (Formerly BS 5750: Part 2) and BS EN ISO 9003 'Model for quality assurance in final inspection and test' (Formerly BS 5750: Part 3).* BSI.

BS EN ISO 9000 1: 1994 *Quality management and quality assurance standards: Part 1: Guidelines for selection and use.* BSI.

BS EN ISO 9001: 1994 *Quality systems: model for quality assurance in design, development, production, installation and servicing.* BSI.

BS EN ISO 9002: 1994 *Quality systems: model for quality assurance in production, installation and servicing.* BSI.

BS EN ISO 9003: 1994 *Quality systems: model for quality assurance in final inspection and test.* BSI.

BS EN ISO 9004 1: 1994 *Quality management and quality system elements: Part 1: Guidelines.* BSI.

CIIG Manual: a guide to good practice in construction industry information. Construction Industry Information Group.

Cornick, T. (1991) *Quality management for building design.* Butterworths Architecture.

Cox, S. and Hamilton, A. (1988, rev. 1989) *Architect's job book.* 3 vols. RIBA.

Department for Trade and Industry *DTI Quality assurance register.* Annual. HMSO.

Department for Trade and Industry *DTI Quality assurance register on CD-ROM.* HMSO (annual subscription).

Foster, A. (1990) *Quality assurance in the construction industry.* Hutchinson.

Oliver, G.B.M. (1992) *Quality management in construction: implementation in design services organisations.* CIRIA (SP 88).

RIBA, Sound Practice Committee (1991) *Quality management: guidance for an office manual.* RIBA.

Sadgrove, K. (1994) *ISO 9000 BS 5750 made easy: a practical guide to quality.* Kogan Page.

Stebbing, L. (1986) *Quality assurance: the route to efficiency and competitiveness.* Ellis Horwood.

Taylor, M. and Hosker, H.H. (1992) *Quality assurance for building design.* Longman Scientific & Technical.

CHAPTER TWENTY

Managing the design office

SYLVESTER BONE

It is said that Japanese construction is programme led, North American construction is cost led and UK construction is design led. The success of UK construction projects is therefore particularly dependent on design management. Where designers have been successful their management of the design process must take a share of the credit. However, the higher cost and overrun contract periods that have been typical of building often arise from the failings of design management. This chapter focuses on the practical tools and the advice that have been prepared over the years to help designers manage design more effectively. It does not trace the various research projects and official reports that have highlighted the deficiencies in the management of design offices.

At each stage of a designer's work management needs to focus on specific issues. There are, however, some common themes to be kept in mind throughout. The RIBA Indemnity Research publication *Risk management for architects* lists seven such issues:

- the importance of good general management
- putting in place standard procedures
- making sure records are properly kept
- maintaining files and archives
- time-management and deciding priorities
- knowing employees' level of skill
- setting up a regular system of feedback on completed buildings.

A different (but overlapping) list of general issues is given as '10 essential steps' in *The successful management of design* published by the University of Reading:

- recognize the inherent complexity of design

- carefully manage the design-selection process
- recognize the changing design leadership role as design progresses
- integrate information supply with construction need
- obtain agreement at key decision points
- actively manage the integration of contributions
- plan, plan and plan again
- manage the interfaces
- control design development
- agreements.

Detailed information and guidance on these issues will be referred to in the paragraphs below which follow the course of a typical building project as described in the *Architect's job book: Volume 1: Job administration*. This publication on its own is a sound basis for managing the design of a building. For each stage of the work it sets out an action checklist of things that have to be done. These are followed up by 'watchpoints', drawing attention to things that can go wrong. This publication, together with the *Architect's handbook of practice management*, which covers the broader aspects of management such as selecting staff, managing office premises and partnership arrangements, form a comprehensive body of guidance for current architectural practice. Both publications give guidance on 'what has to be done' as well as specific advice on 'how to do it'. They contain some worked examples and proformas for specific records and actions.

For those who want to learn by example rather than from the theoretical approach that so often forms the basis of official guidance, the collection of papers edited by M.P. Nicholson entitled *Architectural management* shows a number of different approaches. For case studies, particularly for US practice, Ellen Shoshkes' *The design process: case studies in project development* is a useful book.

Inception

The initial appointments and agreements often take place in a tentative way before there is any certainty that the project will proceed. No-one is willing to make the necessary commitments to establish a sound basis for the project. Most publications on this subject highlight this stage as being critical to the success of the project. The CIRIA *Environmental handbook for building and civil engineering projects: Volume 1: Design and specification*, for example, puts 'gaining commitment' as the initial step. The handbook warns 'without explicit environmental commitment, any attempt to tackle environmental problems on the project are likely to be ill-considered and ultimately ineffective'. Although they are referring to the commitment to tackle environmental issues and follow with sections on environmental policy they might equally be referring to a number of other key issues such as the responsibilities of the participants in the project (appointments), health and safety standards or the investigations and studies required to establish a project's feasibility. In *Design management: a handbook of issues and methods*, edited by Mark Oakley, the commitment of the London Underground to their passengers is described:

> Traditionally the train service has been seen as the ultimate product. Now it is recognised that the product must be viewed as the entire experience that the passenger receives. Therefore product quality must be maintained not just in running the trains but in all other facets of operation that the customers see and experience.

At the inception of a project, design opportunities for a broader view occur for those commissioning designers. Mark Oakley's handbook deals with design in general terms. It focuses on the client's management of design and provides an analysis of the design process. Another book dealing with management of design in general terms, rather than exclusively for buildings, is Marcello Minale's mildly subversive *How to run a successful multi-disciplinary design company*, which gives a useful insight into the various approaches that are successful in different European countries.

The RIBA *Standard form of appointment* provides a useful checklist of design skills that can be offered, and in the *SFA Guide* there is advice on negotiating appointments.

Feasibility, outline proposals and scheme design

The development of the brief is a key activity throughout the following stages. In Frank Salisbury's book, *Architect's handbook for client briefing*, under the chapter on 'Gradually compiling the brief' he explains:

> What first looks like a final brief produced at inception stage turns out to be really an outline brief. . . As the designing begins and tentative forms or alternative arrangements of the proposed building are produced, the incentive is created which encourages both client and designer to work hard to achieve a coincidence of aims. This process is conducive to the production of a full and complete statement of requirements – a final brief.

Frank Salisbury's book provides a useful checklist on the form and composition of the brief and includes techniques for comparing the use and length of circulation routes in different design solutions.

The RIBA *Architect's handbook of practice management* describes the brief as the factual foundation of the project. It is closely linked with a programme and a budget. Where a quality management system is being operated (see Chapter 19) the brief, the budget, the programme and the interfaces with others involved in the project are all recorded in a project quality plan.

The RIBA *Handbook* deals with many of these critical design management issues, but in the short section on design management it understandably concentrates on raising awareness of potential problems rather than on specific methods of managing design. There is a risk that one style of management could be seen as leading to the creation of a particular type of building. The equivalent publication written by David Haviland for the American Institute of Architects, *The project management manual*, is much more specific about management methods and contains a set of procedures that could be transferred directly to a quality management system.

The RIBA *Handbook* also has chapters on managing people, roles and responsibilities, teamwork, pre-design and design. There are also chapters on allied subjects such as forms of practice, business management, financial management, marketing, etc. The *Handbook* is full of good practical advice on how to manage a design office, including control of design costs as the project proceeds through increasingly detailed and time-consuming design stages.

Detailed design and production information

As the design progresses and the work becomes more detailed and also more complex the need to delegate (and the difficulty of delegating) increases. Sir Richard Dowson and Richard MacCormac compare their delegation methods in 'Delegating design', an *Architect's journal* article. The same volume of *Architect's journal* describes how several other practices are run. There are also many more interfaces with other organizations to be considered. Apart from the bodies from which approvals are required and other consultants employed by the client, there are subcontractors and specialists who contribute to the design in specific areas. The co-ordination of the work requires participants in the design to accept disciplines and conventions. At a simple level the Butterworths Architecture Management Guide, *The architect's guide to running a job,* is a good explanation of what needs to be done by an architect. The University of Reading handbook on *The successful management of design* is a more objective view that pays particular attention to the things that can go wrong. Drawing conventions are spelled out in the various parts of BS 1192 *Construction drawing practice*. The co-ordination of drawings, specification and bills of quantities is dealt with in the Building Project Information Committee's publication, *Production drawings: a code of procedure for building works*. Where production drawings are being produced on computer, advice is available in S. Port's *The Management of CAD*, from BSP Professional books. The financial side of design management – described by one designer as 'when to stop' – is dealt with in Peter Barrett's book *Profitable practice management for the construction professional*, in particular the chapter on cost and time control. A useful second reference on this topic is No. 2/21 of the RIBA's open-learning packages on professional studies in British architectural practice, *Managing for profit*, available from the RIBA Education Department.

Levels of management

Construction requires different levels of design management. The client, or sometimes the client's project manager, may be managing design as a part of the overall operation of developing and managing property. They are also managing a financial investment and the progress (or programme) of development. As was said at the start of this chapter, countries differ in the importance they tend to allocate to the programme, the cost or the design. The second level is the management of the design of a specific building project which involves bringing together and coordinating the efforts of different organizations. The third level is the management of the design process within a particular organization, for example, the allocation of work and responsibilities, the keeping of records and the checking of drawings. In the BS 7000 series of guides on *Design management systems*, the different levels are recognized. The series of guides currently planned consists of:

- Part 1:1989 *Guide to managing product design* (under revision, but no fundamental changes expected)
- Part 2 *Guide to managing the design of manufactured products* (still being developed)
- Part 3:1994 *Guide to managing service design* (services include anything from a design consultancy to a bus service)
- Part 4 *Guide to managing design in construction* (publication expected in 1995)
- Part 10 *Glossary* (publication expected in 1995).

In Part 4 design management has been reduced to simple elements applying to different levels of management; it will provide a good summary of the subject and a basis for the development of quality management procedures.

Keeping up-to-date

The day-to-day management of design is affected by frequent changes in forms of contract, insurance conditions, standards, regulations and technology. Design managers need to keep up-to-date and need to see that those they employ keep up-to-date. Journals should be scanned for relevant items. The bibliographic databases which can be searched for articles are discussed in Chapters 3 and 4 . The Institute of Management at Corby can supply CD-ROMs of their database or arrange for searches on particular topics (non-members pay a fee, but the service and loan of the publications is free to members). Seminars and organized professional development courses are a source of current information and can provide clues to changes that will affect future projects. These are usually listed in *Architect's journal*, *Building* and the RIBA's *Practice information*.

Conclusion

No one book covers all aspects of design management for the full range of building projects and circumstances. Many of the publications mentioned above are strictly reference works. They are intended to be used when a problem is foreseen or when something has gone wrong. There is, however, one book of essays that is exceptionally readable. Not surprisingly many of its authors come from advertizing design, rather than from the construction industry. Edited by Liz Lydiate and published by the Design Council, its title is *Professional practice in design consultancy* and, as a taster of the down-to-earth advice provided, the chapter on 'Controlling day-to-day reality' suggests the following:

> 'there are two types of crisis; the ones which can be avoided or mitigated by contingency planning, and those which actually happen'; and 'Never answer a telephone call unless prepared to deal wholeheartedly with whatever is on the other end.'

References

Barrett, Peter (1993) *Profitable practice management for the construction professional*. London: Spon.
BS 1192 *Construction drawing practice*
BS 7000 *Design management systems*
  • Part 1: 1989 *Guide to managing product design*
  • Part 2: *Guide to managing the design of manufactured products*
  • Part 3: 1994 *Guide to managing service design*
  • Part 4: *Guide to managing design in construction*
  • Part 10: *Glossary*
The Building Project Information Committee (1987) *Production drawings: a code of procedure for building works.*
CIRIA (1994) *Environmental handbook for building and civil engineering projects: Volume 1 Design and specification*. London: CIRIA (SP 97).
(1990) Delegating design. *Architects' journal*, **192**, 25/26.

Gray, Colin, Hughes, Will and Bennett, John (1994) *The successful management of design: a handbook of building design management*. University of Reading.

Green, Ronald (1992) *The architect's guide to running a job*. 4th edn. Butterworths.

Haviland, David (1984) *Managing architectural projects: the project management manual*. New York: American Institute of Architects.

Lydiate, Liz (1992) (ed.) *Professional practice in design consultancy*. London: Design Council.

Minale, Marcello (1991) *How to run a successful multi-disciplinary design company*. Elfande Art Publishing.

Nicholson, M. P. (1992) (ed.) *Architectural management*. Spon.

Oakley, Mark (1990) (ed.) *Design management: a handbook of issues and methods*. Oxford: Blackwell.

Port, S. (1989) *The Management of CAD*. Oxford: BSP Professional Books.

RIBA (1988) *Architect's job book: Volume 1: Job administration*. London: RIBA Publications.

RIBA (1991) *Architect's handbook of practice management*. 5th edn. London: RIBA Publications.

RIBA (1990) *Managing for profit*. London: RIBA distance learning package 2/21.

RIBA (1992) *Standard form of appointment* (SFA/92). London: RIBA Publications.

RIBA (1992) *SFA guide: a guide to the standard form of agreement for the appointment of an architect* (SFA/92). London: RIBA Publications.

Risk management for architects. RIBA Indemnity Research.

Shoshkes, Ellen *The design process: case studies in project development*. Architecture and Technology Press.

Salisbury, Frank (1990) *Architect's handbook for client briefing*. Butterworths.

CHAPTER TWENTY-ONE

Contracts and liability

VINCENT POWELL-SMITH

Introduction

There are three broad divisions of information on contracts and professional liability: the general law of contract and tort, standard forms and procurement routes, and reports of cases decided in the Courts. The information sources in the specialist area of construction law are expanding constantly and there is now a wealth of specialist publications.

The architect cannot administer any building contract without an understanding of the general law of contract, and one of the standard basic texts on English contract law is *Cheshire, Fifoot and Furmston's Law of contract* (12th edn. Butterworths, 1991). Similarly, all architects should be aware of the principles governing the law of negligence, and Ray Cecil's *Professional liability* (3rd edn. Legal Studies Publishing, 1991) is a useful general guide for architects. An in-depth book on the topic is *The modern law of negligence* by R.A. Buckley (2nd cd. Butterworths, 1993). *Design liability in the construction industry* by David Cornes (4th edn. Blackwell Scientific Publications, 1994) is the leading source of reference for all architects, engineers and contractors concerned with design liability.

Other major reference texts include *Keating on building contracts*, edited by Sir Anthony May (6th edn. Sweet & Maxwell, 1995), which is the standard legal text dealing with building contracts in general. It also contains a commentary on several of the standard forms of contract. *Hudson's Building and engineering contracts* (11th edn. Sweet & Maxwell, 1995), edited by I.N.D. Wallace QC, is the classic text and is in two substantial volumes. Another major text, *Emden's Construction law* (8th edn. Butterworths, 1990), is in four loose-leaf volumes and is regularly updated. The *Building contract casebook* by Vincent Powell-Smith and Michael Furmston (3rd edn. BSP, 1996) is a compendium of the leading cases on building contracts, while a detailed explanation of all the important words and phrases used in building contracts is to be found in *Building contract dictionary* by Vincent Powell-Smith and David Chappell (3rd edn. Blackwell Scientific Publications, 1995).

For general reference – and this should be regarded as a 'must' in every architect's office library – *The Architect's legal handbook,* edited by Anthony Speight and Gregory Stone (5th edn. Butterworth-Heinemann, 1990) will be found invaluable. It contains chapters by specialist contributors on every aspect of architectural law. *Butterworths construction law manual* by Stephen Bickford-Smith and others (Butterworths, 1993) is also a useful work to have on one's shelf as a ready reference.

Building contracts are as much about procedure as about law and, while there may be minor differences in the approach of different architectural firms, there are certain standard practices which must be observed and the main elements or parts of the procedure will most probably be common to all architectural practices. The essential point is that the architect must understand and observe all the requirements of the contract and remember that in many important respects, he is expected to form an independent judgment. He must not lean in favour of his client, the employer, but must hold the scales evenly between employer and contractor. David Chappell's *Standard letters in architectural practice* (Blackwell Scientific Publications, 1994) is a useful set of some standard letters based on the RIBA *Plan of work* will be found to be a useful aid to contract administration.

Contract choice

One of the architect's functions is to advise his client on procurement methods and choice of standard form contract, and there are two useful sources of information. The first is a short book by David Chappell called *Which form of building contract?* (Longman, 1991) which is a guide with tables for choosing the right procurement system and form of contract. The second is more comprehensive. It is *Building contracts compared and tabulated* (2nd edn. Legal Studies Publishing, 1989) which contains tabular comparisons of the most common forms of contract with flow charts and a brief descriptive text. A new edition is urgently needed.

Contract procedure

Basic procedures are very well set out in two books produced by the Aqua Group: *Pre-contract practice for the building team* (8th edn. BSP, 1992) and *Contract administration for the building team* (7th edn. BSP, 1990). The former deals with the first stages of the contract, through approximate quantities and cost control, drawings, schedules, specifications, bills of quantities, sub-contractors and suppliers to obtaining tenders. The latter covers all aspects from the placing of the contract through to completion and final account. Additional chapters deal briefly with delays and disputes and with insolvency. Both are up-to-date and take account of current practice requirements.

Legal & contractual procedures for architects by R. Greenstreet and David Chappell (4th edn. Butterworths Architecture, 1994) is a very useful *vade-mecum* and contains an excellent bibliography. *The architect in practice* by David Chappell and Christopher Willis (7th edn. BSP, 1992) is a useful general reference source, and architects will find *The architect's job book* by Stanley Cox, Roderick Males, Leonard Beavan and David Dry (5th edn. RIBA Publications, 1991) very useful. The RIBA also publishes a useful *Handbook of architectural practice management* (5th edn. 1991), which offers far more than contract procedure in its pages. The section dealing with job procedures covers management of projects as well as contract procedure. It also contains the *Plan of work for design team operation* which can be obtained as a separate booklet.

The publications of the National Joint Consultative Committee for Building (NJCC) should not be overlooked. They include *Code of procedure for single stage selective tendering* and *Code of procedure for two stage selective tendering.* Revised editions of both *Codes* were issued in 1994, replacing the previous editions which were published in 1989 and 1993 respectively. The NJCC also issues *Guidance notes on joint venture tendering for contracts in the United Kingdom* and *Construction management – selection and appointment of the construction manager and trade contractors.* It also publishes two standard forms of tendering questionnaire for submission of contractors to general and select lists.

Forms of contract

Today's architect is spoiled for choice in the United Kingdom as there are many contract forms available. The standard forms can be grouped into three categories: the Joint Contracts Tribunal (JCT) standard forms; government or government-derived forms; and forms sponsored by other bodies. The pre-eminence of the JCT – which is a committee and not a tribunal in the legal sense – has been challenged in recent years because the working of its standard forms is complex and unclear and has resulted in endless and costly litigation. However, the JCT forms are widely used and are amended from time to time.

JCT forms of building contract

The JCT – which consists of representatives from the RIBA, BEC, RICS and certain local authority and other organizations – licenses the RIBA to publish its growing family of standard forms of contract which are designed for the most commonly used methods of procurement.

The basic form – designed for use where the works are architect designed – is *The JCT standard form of building contract,* 1980 edn. (revised 1995), which is commonly called 'JCT 80'. It is regularly amended when decisions of the courts reveal defects. It consists of the following variants:

- Private version with Quantities
- Private version with Approximate Quantities
- Private version without Quantities
- Local authority versions as above.

It is essential to obtain the latest edition, including all relevant amendments. A major problem is that the contract as revised is very seldom reprinted in its amended form and copies of the unamended form have to be read in light of a bulky series of numbered amendments, although copies of these are supplied free of charge.

Additional documents to be used in conjunction with JCT 80 are:

- Sectional completion supplement
- Contractor's designed portion supplement
- Scottish supplement – This adapts JCT 80 for use under Scots law.
- Fluctuations supplement
- Formula rules for fluctuations.

Very importantly, the RIBA publishes NSC/4: *Nominated sub-contract* designed for use where sub-contractors are nominated under JCT 80, together with an essential series of supporting documents to give effect to the nomination procedure, a revised version of which was introduced in 1991. The revised procedure is explained in *Revised procedure for nomination of a sub-contractor* (May 1991) which also contains sample copies of the various forms and the Guidance Notes. There is also a series of forms for nomination of suppliers.

In addition, there are various standard certificates and forms which are intended to be used in conjunction with JCT 80 and which can be obtained from the RIBA. A related sub-contract form, *The sub-contract conditions for use with domestic sub-contract DOM/1,* (1980, revised 1992) is published by the BEC.

The RIBA also publishes, for the Joint Contracts Tribunal, a great many other forms. These include:

- IFC 84: Intermediate form and supporting documentation
- CD 81: Standard form of building contract with contractor's design and supporting documents.
- MC 87: JCT Management contract and supporting works contractors
- MW 80: Agreement for minor works 1980
- Standard form of prime cost contract 1992 and relevant documents
- MTC 89: Measured term contract.

(The latest amendments to forms and notes can usually be traced in the *Architect's reference annual* from RIBA Publications or by contacting RIBA Publications – Editor's note)

There are various guides to the standard forms of contract and sub-contract, not all of which are particularly helpful. *The JCT 80 standard form of building contract* by Vincent Powell-Smith (3rd edn. 1995) is a straightforward guide to JCT 80 and contains a clause-by-clause commentary. There are three major books on IFC 84: *The architect's guide to the JCT intermediate form of contract* by Stanley Cox (2nd edn. RIBA Publications, 1989), which is a straightforward guide to the provisions at its date; *A commentary on the JCT intermediate form of building contract* by Neil Jones and David Bergman (2nd edn. Blackwell Scientific Publications, 1990); and *The JCT intermediate form of contract – a practical guide* by David Chappell and Vincent Powell-Smith (2nd edn. Legal Studies Publishing, 1991).

The best guide to the JCT management contract, *The JCT management contract* by Vincent Powell-Smith and John Sims (Kluwer Publications, 1988) is unfortunately out of print. However, there is a comprehensive guide to the JCT 'design and build' form – *The JCT design and building contract* by David Chappell and Vincent Powell-Smith (Blackwell Scientific Publications, 1993). *The shorter forms of building contract,* by Hugh Clamp (3rd edn. Blackwell Scientific Publications, 1993), is a good treatment of MW 80.

Government sponsored forms

In 1989 the PSA published the long-awaited revision of the Government Standard Form of Contract – *The General conditions of contract of building and civil engineering – GC/Works/1* – in a lump sum, with quantities version. The current revised edition is dated 1990, and also available is a variant for 'design and build'. Unfortunately, there is no related sub-contract. The government conditions differ in many important respects from the JCT conditions and are generally regarded as being better-drafted, possibly because they are in plain English.

A variant intended for use in the private sector is called *PSA/1* and was published in 1994. These forms are available from HMSO. Vincent Powell-Smith has written a straightforward guide to GC/Works/1 called *GC/Works 1/Edition* 3 (BSP, 1990).

Other forms of contract

In 1984 the Association of Consultant Architects (ACA), whose members were dissatisfied with JCT 80, published *The ACA form of building agreement,* which contains many novel features and is written in simple English. It exists in two variants:

- ACA 2 (2nd edn, 1984, revised 1990)
- ACA/BPF (1984)

The ACA form is not widely used and is said to be unpopular with contractors.

Civil engineering contracts present special problems and most architects will not get involved in civil engineering projects. The principal form of contract in civil engineering projects is issued by the Institution of Civil Engineers (ICE), the Federation of Civil Engineering Contractors and the Association of Consulting Engineers: *Conditions of contract and forms of tender, agreement and bond for use in connection with works of civil engineering construction* (6th edn. revised ICE, 1991). There is also a variant for use with 'design and construct', as well as a shorter form called *The ICE conditions of contract for minor works 1988* intended for use where the contract value does not exceed £100 000 (at 1988 values). There is also a non-traditional form of contract known as *The new engineering contract,* the use of which was endorsed enthusiastically by Sir Michael Latham in his July 1994 report on the ills of the construction industry.

For use on civil engineering work outside the United Kingdom, there is the FIDIC *International civil engineering conditions,* 4th edition, 1987 and 1992, which is based on the English form.

Various books on civil engineering contracts are available. They include Brian Eggleston's *The ICE conditions of contract sixth edition: a user's guide* by Brian Eggleston (Blackwell Scientific Publications, 1994). The international conditions are dealt with by E.C. Corbett in *FIDIC 4th: a practical legal guide* (Sweet & Maxwell, 1990), which is also available in disk form as part of the 'FIDIC's Red Book' package available from Powerdoc Systems (37 Broomleaf Road, Farnham, Surrey GU9 8DG).

Claims and disputes settlement

Claims by contractors for extra payment and/or extensions of time are inevitable on almost any project, and much of the architect's time can be taken up dealing with these matters. The standard forms of contract in current use all contain provisions for dealing with these issues and, unfortunately, disputes often end in arbitration.

Useful sources of reference are *Building contract claims* by Vincent Powell-Smith and John Sims (3rd edn. BSP, 1995), *Construction arbitrations: a practical guide* by the same authors (Legal Studies Publishing, 1989) and Brian Eggleston's *Liquidated damages and extensions of time in construction contract* (Blackwell Scientific Publications, 1992).

Law reports

Law reports are a most important source of information, but they require specialist knowledge to interpret, and most architects and other construction professionals will not need a full set in their office library. There are two main series of 'specialist' law reports: *Building law reports,* a quarterly publication by Longman; and *Construction law reports,* published by Butterworths almost bi-monthly. Both contain complete judgements of recent cases relevant to building contracts which are not generally available elsewhere. Another useful series for comparative purposes is *Asia-Pacific construction law reports* (Butterworths Asia, Singapore), which covers cases from Australia, Brunei, Hong Kong, New Zealand, Malaysia and Singapore. *Construction law journal,* a quarterly publication (Sweet & Maxwell), publishes edited reports of cases, as well as articles of general legal interest.

The Times and *The Independent* newspapers publish daily reports of a wide variety of cases.

Most construction professionals will be well informed by two quick references: *Construction law digest,* issued 10 times a year by Blackwell Scientific Publications and very topical, also available on CD-ROM and in PC compatible disk format; and *Construction industry law letter* (Legal Studies Publishing), which is published at similar intervals. The former contains useful and sometimes provocative comment, as well as details of contract amendments, book reviews and so on, while the latter gives abbreviated reports of recent decisions, most of which will be later published in full in either *Building law reports* or *Construction law reports.*

Current information

Professionals must keep abreast of changes in both the law and the practice and the best and quickest way to keep up-to-date is by reading the half page 'Contract' section in *Building* or by scanning the 'Construction Notes' issued to RIBA *Product data* subscribers. *Architects' journal, Building* and *Contract journal* all contain regular articles and news about contract, liability and case law development and one or other of these must be regarded as essential reading as the law changes almost daily. The *Architects' journal* 'Practice' pages are particularly useful.

A more comprehensive source of current information is available by subscribing to *Building: law information subscriber service* (Wardour House, King Street, Knutsford, Cheshire WA16 6PD), a weekly publication which abstracts information from various publications and which can provide case details on request.

From 1994 onwards, Lloyds of London Press has issued a *Construction law yearbook,* edited by John Uff QC, which amongst other things contains a good digest of construction law cases supported by an excellent index. It includes reports of otherwise unreported decisions as well as articles and some construction industry arbitration awards.

The indexing and abstracting services cover construction contracts — in particular, the *Architectural periodicals index* has a sub-heading 'Contract' that brings together useful articles in the architectural press. The CIOB's *Building management abstracts* cites references from a wide range of other journals, including *Contract journal* and *Quantity surveyor.* For information published recently *Current information in the construction industry* is useful, and contract in its broader sense and the general law is well covered in the *Index to legal periodicals.*

Other information

CIOB publishes several series of occasional papers which will be found useful, while there are various RIBA publications, including various 'open-learning' packages. They include:

- *Group practice and consortia, 1987*
- *Starting up in practice, 1992*
- *Guide to employment practice, 1987*
- *The architect as arbitrator, 1987*
- *Code of professional conduct, 1991*
- *Responsibilities for insurance under the JCT standard forms of building contract* by Peter Madge (1989)
- *Principles and procedures associated with sub-contractors and suppliers* (1989).

The *RIBA publications catalogue,* which is published annually, includes all the items published by RIBA or for which they are the distributors. This includes material published by the JCT, BEC, RICS, Landscape Institute, NJCC, Ecclesiastical Architects and Surveyors Association and the Chartered Society of Designers.

There is a useful bibliography and list of addresses to contact for further information in *Legal and contractual procedures for architects* by Bob Greenstreet and David Chappell (4th edn. Butterworths Architecture, 1994), which is also useful in its own right. No bibliography can be fully up-to-date as new information and guides issue constantly from the press. Construction professionals must be fully up-to-date with changes as actions for professional negligence are on the increase. Advice and assistance is always obtainable from the appropriate professional institute. But construction professionals must remember that this is an area where, if there is any shade of doubt, legal advice should be sought from a lawyer specializing in construction law. There are a growing number in this category.

CHAPTER TWENTY-TWO

Practice information provision

ANNETTE O'BRIEN

Introduction

Why have a practice library?

Whether specializing in the planning, funding, design, construction or
operation of a building or structure, each professional and technician
involved relies on information in the broadest sense. Many individuals
hold this information on a personal basis; it is a cumulation of initial
education/training, experience and continuing information-gathering
in a variety of ways. For the individual who works alone, this can be a
satisfactory approach, provided that the information-gathering process
is maintained on a regular basis.

To replicate such individual collections even in a modestly sized practice is not cost-effective either in terms of space or of time. This approach has the additional hazard that it is possible (all too likely) for
some individuals to be working from out-of-date or from conflicting
information. This can cause confusion and wasted time in the office,
problems and abortive work on site, and is often the base cause of disputes that lead to arbitration or litigation.

Insurance against these problems comes from having a properly established and managed library/information source within the office. It
must be established to reflect the interests and activities of the host practice; it must acknowledge the scale and variety of work undertaken; it
must be managed to reflect changes in the industry and in the context of
the practice in which the work is done; it must be funded (including the
funding of staff) to an appropriate level.

Context

Such a library must always be an integral part of the design office – it is no more an optional extra than is an office manager or an accountant. Its aims and objectives must be synonymous with those of the practice. Its scope and operation should be as familiar to all members of staff as, say, the procedures for claiming expenses or the office conventions for labelling drawings.

Role

In considering the possible role and function of a practice library, as well as its content and coverage, information can be gathered from a variety of sources – some of which will be more pertinent than others. An awareness of what other practices do is helpful, and this can be gathered from articles in periodicals such as the *Architects' journal* (1) and *RIBA journal* (2). But the needs of the specific practice are paramount, and thorough consultation and consideration are essential in determining what these are. There then arises the more difficult question of which can be met, given other constraints.

In determining the role of a practice library, several questions must be considered, but often the most basic ones are forgotten. The fundamental questions are:

- What can we not afford to have by way of information?
- What can a library/information service do for this practice?
- What can realistically be budgeted for this activity?

Personnel

Many practices assume that it is too expensive or difficult to have a professional/experienced librarian dealing with their information, and so allocate the task to an existing member of staff. This can work well, largely because of the involvement of the individual in the day-to-day work of the practice and their enthusiasm for the task, based on a recognition of its purpose and importance.

There are, however, several potential drawbacks. Without awareness of available information and knowledge of current practice, time can be wasted in re-inventing systems for many routine tasks such as organizing/classifying publications. More importantly, a non-librarian has a different set of priorities within the practice: someone trained as an architect will always concentrate on fee-earning design work rather than on weeding out old product information, and rightly so. For information professionals, there is no such conflict as their priority is to have up-to-date information available and accessible.

Increasingly in the UK, practices are using part-time librarians where they cannot currently justify the employment of a full-time one. This can be on the basis of the librarian being employed by a single practice on a part-time basis or being contracted as a consultant to do specific tasks. Such consultants are usually working for a variety of clients, not all in construction, and usually offer a variety of types and levels of services. Using such consultants can allow a greater degree of flexibility in the time (and therefore cost) of library staff; the occasional concern for confidentiality and possible conflict of interests has to be resolved on an individual basis. Directories of professionals who work in each of these ways are available from Information Market-makers (3) and the Construction Industry Information Group (4). Agencies such as Aslib and TFPL also offer a recruitment service, as does the Library Association (LA).

Policy

While there should be no question about the provision of information within the practice, there is a need to formulate a policy as to how this is to be done and at what level. Input from an experienced librarian is invaluable at this point, to ensure that all relevant aspects have been considered, that the practice is aware of all the options as to how to achieve the desired objective. Such consultants (who can be located through the directories mentioned above) can also be a source of leads to personnel. A regular review of the library policy and the manner in which it is being implemented is also essential. This would, in part, be an aspect of the review of staff involved, but a review of the policy itself is also important, to determine whether or not it is still relevant and effective. Such reviews should be undertaken on a two to three year cycle.

Budget

The budget for information must be in line with the overall budget and business plan of the practice, and so will reflect changing circumstances. Given proper recognition of the basic need for information, the budget for its provision should never be cut to the point where a reliable service is no longer possible. Cutting information services totally is neither realistic nor cost-effective. Frequently, a practice which is short of work will cut back on information provision, and concentrate on looking for work. Even in times of recession, the balance between public relations expenditure (the means of getting new work) and information provision (the means of dealing effectively with work in hand) is a delicate one — but balance there must be.

Sources and guidebooks

General texts

Because of the specialized nature of information provision for the construction industry as a whole, sources of information relating to general librarianship and information provision are relevant only in the broadest sense. Two of the more useful are *Practical information policies on managing information flow* by E. Orna (5) and *Management skills for the information manager* edited by A. Lawes (6). The *Aslib Handbook of special librarianship and information work*, edited by P. Dossett (7), is a useful, broad-based guide to all aspects of special library operations.

Construction-specific texts

Advice on very practical aspects of establishing a construction information library, down to the various methods of storing material, are covered in *Office library systems: a guide for the construction industry* by R. Hargrave (8). Though a few years old now, it is a valuable source of ideas as well as a checklist of aspects which should be considered in setting up a library.

The recently published *Construction Industry Information Group manual*, edited by P. Adderley and A. O'Brien (9), with contributions from a range of experienced construction information specialists, is probably the most relevant source available. It covers traditional library topics such as cataloguing and classification in a manner which makes them accessible to the non-specialist. A suggested basic collection offers a useful guide, and the section on IT is a good starting point for establishing an approach to using IT in information provision. This manual also deals with information topics which are often considered more in a management context: project filing, archiving and QA, for example.

The choice of technical publications to hold in the library is partly dictated by the nature of the practice and the type of work undertaken. Documents relating to the regulation of design and construction are essential. Building regulations, standards and codes of practice, and regulations concerning health and safety must be available, as well as guides to their application. In contrast, information on products and materials and the way they function could be acquired or borrowed at the point at which they are needed. Publications illustrating the built environment are always popular, and can provide useful stimulation – but they are expensive, and their real contribution to the functioning of the office must be assessed carefully.

A variety of basic or suggested book lists appear from time to time – there is one in the *CIIG manual* mentioned above – and they can be a useful starting point. But they are usually based on a specific practice, which will rarely be a mirror image of your own. Only one thing is sure – the cost of the appropriate basic book list for any practice will be more than anyone expects.

Identifying possible texts

Printed publications, such as *British national bibliography* (10), which has entries arranged by subject, provide access to relevant texts covering all aspects of information provision. The CD-ROM *BookFind-CD* (11) covers the output of nearly 300 publishers world-wide. It has useful additional information including an indication of the likely level of readership, and includes forthcoming publications.

The *Architect's reference annual* compiled by P. Adderley (12), published as a supplement to the RIBA's *Handbook of practice management*, includes a basic book list (the RIBA's list of recommended books) and a list of the most relevant EC Directives, with source information. Publications lists from specialist publishers such as Thomas Telford, RIBA Publications, British Cement Association and others, as well as subject lists from other publishers, are useful. The actual stock of specialist bookshops such as RIBA, Building Centre, Triangle can provide useful ideas; for those who cannot get there in person, the list of titles held can be a useful alternative. Also helpful are the contents lists of collections available on microfiche or CD-ROM. Again, it is essential to remember that these are aimed at a wide target audience, and will hold much more than many practices need.

General journals

Information on general (but applicable) aspects of handling information can be found in a variety of library and information journals, particularly those from the professional associations and their constituent groups. Also valuable are journals such as *Managing information* (13) and *Library management* (14), which have informative articles on topics such as the potential for IT applications which can be relevant to practice libraries. None that I am aware of will assist with identifying useful subject-specific publications. These journals are indexed in *Library and information science abstracts* (LISA – 15) and *Information management and technology abstracts* (16).

Construction-specific journals

Mainstream construction journals regularly have reviews of new publications as well as relevant technical series from time to time. Over the last few years, the *Architects' journal* has regularly included single page 'Briefings' covering a wide range of topics, but always giving a list of references and/or sources of further information. These can be useful indicators of possible stock for a practice library. Henry Haverstock's 'Easibrief' series in *Building design* (17) gave a mix of practical guidance and possible further sources of information and the *RIBA Journal* also touches on such matters occasionally.

Each professional will have access to the main relevant journals, usually as part of membership of an appropriate institution. Covering the wider areas is more problematic – both in time and in cost. Using other libraries to browse through current journals is important, as is awareness of the indexing and abstracting services which cover the topics of interest.

Identifying possible journals

The mainstream journals can be identified quite easily by visiting a specialist library or bookshop. To search for more specialist journals or foreign titles, there are directories such as *Willing's press guide* (18), *Ulrich's international periodicals directory* (19), and *Pims UK media directory* (20). Another approach is to search the UnCover database, made available by Blackwells, which records information from the contents pages of thousands of journals. From this it is possible to identify journals which regularly cover the relevant topics; it is also possible to place an on-line order for a copy of articles to be delivered by fax (see Chapter 4).

All of these journals, and many more, are indexed in the *Architectural periodicals index* (21) and *Avery index to architectural periodicals* (22). These can be not only a means of identifying specific articles, but also of determining those journals that should be held in the practice. It is important to remember that these are bibliographies, not full text; you only identify relevant information, getting hold of it involves another step. Although the RIBA's British Architectural Library does provide a photocopy order service for articles indexed in the *API*.

Internal information

Staff within the practice can be a useful guide to what could or should be in the collection. It is important that suggestions from such sources be taken seriously, in the context of the predetermined library policy and budget. However, it should never be the case that the interests of any individual (and that must include partners and directors, not to mention the librarian) be allowed to subvert library policy and budget by forcing the purchase of publications that are peripheral or irrelevant in the context of the practice library.

Other subject coverage

Often, specialized information is required which relates more closely to the project or client than to the construction industry. Good leads to possible sources of information can be found in the *Directory of British associations* (23) and the *Yearbook of international organisations* (24). Where listed organizations offer information services or a range of publications, this is identified along with an indication of access and charging policy.

Increasingly, information is required on companies – potential clients, possible tenderers or suppliers. Basic information on companies can be found in directories such as *The Times 1000* (25), *Kompass* (26), and *Who owns whom* (27), the last two of which have various national and regional issues. More detailed information is available from specialist services such as those offered by Dun and Bradstreet. While institutions such as London's City Business Library are invaluable to those who have access to it, it is increasingly possible to find similar services offered by local public libraries.

Guides to other libraries

Though these give an indication of subject coverage and services offered, perhaps the most important use of these guides is to indicate what is available in professional institutions, research organizations, etc., and which therefore can perhaps be omitted from the practice collection. It is important to ensure both that the practice has access through membership or subscription, and that this degree of rather remote access is sufficient. Increasingly, such libraries are having to restrict the level of service available to members (let alone non-members) and are charging for access and services. The *CIIG manual* lists many such organizations, and gives an indication of their charges for services. The days of 'free' information are largely a thing of the past, and this can require careful calculation to indicate not only a pragmatic but also a cost-effective way forward.

Arranging the collection

Why classify?

While there is no doubt that the usefulness of retained information is absolutely related to the ease of retrieval, there is much discussion and contention as to how this is best achieved. The long-standing joke about users most frequently remembering (and identifying) a book by size and colour is not apocryphal. Unfortunately, no sufficiently clear classification scheme for so arranging publications has yet been published – though the practice is not unknown in domestic situations.

Classification schemes: general

Guidance on application and procedures is available within the most commonly used classification schemes in varying degrees, as well as in a plethora of guides. Two of the general schemes, *Dewey decimal classi-fication* and the *Library of Congress classification*, are rarely used in practice information provision in the UK.

The *Universal decimal classification scheme* (28) is more often found in large practice libraries and those in research and professional institu-tions, where it is more usual to find staff with training and experience in its use. It is, as its name implies, designed for wide-ranging application, so every area of information can be accommodated; it can be used sim-ply or in a complex manner, depending on the size of the collection and the need for precise recall and retrieval. Despite the new edition, there are still areas of interest to the construction industry which are not dealt with as clearly and precisely as might be hoped. The continual emer-gence of new topics (business parks, for example) and conjunctions of topics (environmental aspects of refurbishment of buildings and rein-statement of adjacent water in an integrated way) probably mean that either independent decisions as to feasible location must be made or cumbersome conflations of class marks will always be required.

Classification schemes: construction

On the other hand, the *CI/SfB construction indexing manual* (29), de-signed specifically for the construction industry, has no pretension to generality but aims to relate use of the scheme to office practice. While its schedules have not kept up-to-date with new concepts or technology, it is still widely considered the best option. Sadly, the recent reprint has ap-peared without any updating of the schedules or expansion of the index.

For some librarians (though not for its originators), the *Common ar-rangement of work sections for building works* (CAWS – 30) offered an alternative method of arranging technical and product information which is related closely to providing information for specifications. Some work has been done on developing CAWS for library applications, and a detailed index has been prepared to support such applications: *Index to common arrangement of work sections* by J. Hargrave and A. O'Brien (31).

New developments

Largely as a result of the attempts to use CAWS in this way, the Building Project Information Committee (BPIC) has sponsored investigations into a possible new approach to classification for construction, to be called Universal Classification for the Construction Industry (UCCI). Three factors in particular influenced this decision: awareness of work being undertaken in other centres; the need for greater coherence and consist-ency within Europe; and the ever increasing use of computers in apply-ing and using such systems.

Recently, what is planned as part of the first section of UCCI has been published; this is European Product Information Co-operation (EPIC).

This provides *Construction product grouping* (32), a system of grouping products and identifying specific products by a unique number – which, it is expected, will lead to greater consistency in product identification. The first edition is in English, with editions in other languages to follow. In its present form, the EPIC system is intended for computer use, and its terminology needs to be refined; a print version for UK use will be prepared in late 1994. Its intended use is for organizing product information in collections and libraries. When the EPIC scheme is available in all the major European languages, it will also become an invaluable multilingual thesaurus, which is much needed.

Other schemes

One other specialist scheme is the *Landscape filing index* (33), which is available in its full version and also as a subset relating to photographic and product information.

In a modest practice collection, use of a formal classification scheme is not always necessary; it can be sufficient to group material by source (particularly useful for publications from organizations such as Building Research Establishment (BRE), British Standards Institution (BSI) and similar) with monographs and other documents arranged by author. However, it is always advisable to have a catalogue which identifies what is held and where it is located. This avoids wasting time searching for a document which is not held or purchasing duplicate copies.

Current awareness

Getting information on current news and events of relevance, including possible projects, is potentially a very time-consuming practice. News cuttings agencies can give broad or specific coverage, as required, but only as indicated in advance. One of the real skills of information practitioners working in the context of a specific practice is to be able to identify potentially relevant information, and to send it to the most appropriate individual(s) or have it available as and when required.

The more up-to-date method of providing this service is to search one of the on-line databases of newspaper contents, such as TEXTLINE. This is a full text service, so it is possible to print the text of any article. Similarly, the on-line version of the *Official journal* (34) is often preferred to the hard copy, though searches do not always produce clean and clear information.

Abstracts & indexes/databases

Databases of the holdings of universities, professional institutions and research organizations are increasingly available via national and international networks such as JANET and the Internet. While these are used for locating specific publications, they can also be used to produce a bibliography relating to a particular topic.

It is very difficult to keep up with the currently available databases, as more and more information is re-packaged and made accessible in this way. A listing such as the *Gale directory of databases* (35) is useful.

The increased availability of IT has resulted in an understandable move from the use of printed indexes to their electronic version – though many are available in both forms. A useful alternative is the growing availability of a CD-ROM version of these databases. This allows initial searching and refining of the search strategy without the time/cost constraints of being on-line – which can then be used to update the search results. Not every practice will feel the need to have access to on-line databases – though the advent of the 'information superhighway' may change that in the near future. It is always possible to have searches of these databases carried out by another library on your behalf. Most of the professional institutions and research bodies will do this, as will the Science Reference and Information Service (SRIS) and most public libraries.

The table below includes the databases mentioned in this chapter, plus a few others. It gives the producer and host, where relevant.

Database	Producer	Host
ACCOMPLINE	London Research Centre	ESA-IRS
Architecture Database	BAL (CRIBA)	DIALOG
BCIS	BCIS	
BRIX	BRE	ESA-IRS
CACTI	BCA	
COMPENDEX	Ei	DIALOG
CRIB	Longmans	(CD-ROM)
FLAIR	FRS	ESA-IRS
IBSEDEX	BSRIA	ESA-IRS
ICC		DIALOG
ICONDA	Silver Platter	(CD-ROM)
INFOCHECK		ESA-IRS
Information Science Abstracts		DIALOG
INSPEC	IEE	DIALOG
INSTRUCT	ISE	ISE only
KOMPASS		DIALOG
LISA	LA	DIALOG
NTIS		DIALOG
PERINORM	BSI	(CD-ROM)
STANDARDLINE	BSI	ESA-IRS
TEXTLINE		DIALOG
TRIS	TRL (in part)	DIALOG
UNCOVER	Blackwells + CARL Systems	
URBALINE	London Research Centre	ESA-IRS

WELDASEARCH   TWI   ORBIT

Trade and technical information

Sources

Trade or product information forms a larger proportion of the collection in small practices. It is important, but produces problems. Identifying manufacturers of product types requires directories of one sort or another. Most practices are familiar with the *RIBA Product selector* (36) and the *Barbour compendium* (37). Engineers, both civil and structural, and contractors have found the slightly different coverage of *Specification* (38) suits their needs, while *Opus: building services design file* (39) is aimed at mechanical engineers. In addition, *Kompass* and *Kelly's* (40) provide wider coverage, and *Europages* (41) provides some European coverage.

Collection coverage

Holding a collection of product information can be time- and space-consuming – even without storing samples. A decision must be made as to the method of organizing the material. Classified arrangement, whether to an established system or an in-house system, makes retrieval easier, but can cause problems, especially when a single publication covers products separated in the classification scheme. A good catalogue is necessary to help locate information from manufacturers within the scheme. Especially in the case of an in-house system, clear and up-to-date documentation on the structure and implementation of the system is required.

Alphabetical arrangement by manufacturer is generally considered the simplest and least error prone method of filing product information. Again, it requires detailed indexing to enable easy retrieval. Increasingly, practices are looking to IT to help with this problem, and services do exist which supply product information on microfiche (Barbour), on CD-ROM (BCQ) or printed from a central database as required (On Demand Information – ODI). The microfiche system has a long track record and exercises editorial control over inclusion; the choice consists of information of high technical content and that of the market leaders in relevant fields. CD-ROM and ODI services, where inclusion is on the basis of payment per page, still have a long way to go to provide the range and quality of information required at a price which is affordable by the majority of practices.

Research and conferences

Libraries/information in general

A full programme of conferences and training courses is available – though much of it at a level of charging which construction information professionals find difficult to meet. The professional institutions, the Library Association and the Institute of Information Scientists, along with commercial organizations such as TFPL, are among the leading providers. Library Association groups such as the Library Association Industrial Group (LAIG) also arrange conferences and informative visits. Aslib is one of the few organizations, along with the LA, which undertake substantial research in information fields; the other main players are university departments.

Construction information

The various professional institutions organize conferences aimed at highlighting topics of interest and supporting their requirement for continuing professional development of their members. Few of them undertake research, but many have an involvement in research undertaken by bodies such as CIRIA and BRE. The British Standards Society, through its four subgroups, arranges a series of forums on matters related to the content and use of standards and codes of practice.

Construction-specific conferences are organized by CIIG. For some of these, papers are published. Because CIIG is a non-commercial organization, and has no secretariat, its programme is modest. Two other specialist groups, the Fire Information Group (FIG) and Property Information Group (PIG), operate in the same way and at the same level. It has long been recognized that technical research in the construction industry is not undertaken at the necessary level. Increasingly, research projects are managed by the research organizations (CIRIA, BRE, BSRIA, SCI, etc.) but carried out by practices or individuals under contract.

Publications such as *Research focus* (42) offer useful summaries of current and recent research, with names and telephone numbers of contacts for further information. A broader view can be obtained from the CRIB database either on-line or on CD-ROM.

Conclusion

The planning, implementation and management of a well focused information centre provide a practice with a wide range of opportunities, not only to consider its information needs, but to examine, and chart if possible, the way information flows within the practice. This can identify gaps in the system and service, areas of interaction and duplication of provision. Sorting out these discrepancies, as part of establishing the system, can only be beneficial.

Increasingly, the integration of all information within a practice has led to a beneficial broadening of the areas of responsibility of librarians. The disciplines of organizing, recording and retrieving information, which are the home ground of the librarian, can be applied to a wider range of information than just printed material. This presents an opportunity not to be missed.

References

1. *Architects' journal*. Weekly. London: Emap Business Communications.
2. *RIBA Journal*. Monthly. London: RIBA Journals.
3. Information Marketmakers (1994) *Directory of information brokers and consultants*. London: Effective Technology Marketing & Information Marketmakers.
4. Construction Industry Information Group (1994). *Directory of members*. London: CIIG.
5. Orna, E. (1990) *Practical information policies on managing information flow*. London: Gower.
6. Lawes, A. (1993) (ed.) *Management skills for the information manager*. London: Ashgate Publishing.
7. Dossett, P. (1992) (ed.) *Aslib handbook of special librarianship and information work*. London: Aslib.
8. Hargrave, R. (1987) *Office library systems: a guide for the construction industry*. London: Architectural Press.
9. Adderley, P. and O'Brien, A. (1994) (eds.) *Construction Industry Information Group manual*. London: CIIG.
10. *British national bibliography*. Weekly, with monthly and annual cumulations. British Library Bibliographic Services Department.
11. *BOOKFIND-CD* (CD-ROM). London: Book Data (Producer).
12. Adderley, P. (ed.) *Handbook reference manual: supplement to the RIBA handbook of practice management*. Annual. London: RIBA Publications.
13. *Managing information*. Bi-monthly. London: Aslib.
14. *Library management*. Seven issues per year. Bradford: MCB University Press.
15. *Library and information science abstracts*. Monthly. London: Bowker-Saur.
16. *Information management and technology abstracts*. Monthly. Bradford: MCB University Press.
17. *Building design*. Weekly. London: Morgan-Grampian, (Construction Press).
18. *Willings press guide*. Annual. East Grinstead: Reed Information Services.
19. *Ulrich's international periodicals directory*. Annual. New York: Bowker.
20. *Pims UK media directory*. Annual, monthly or quarterly updates. London: PIMS.
21. British Architectural Library. *Architectural publications index*. Quarterly, with annual cumulations. London: RIBA Publications.
22. Avery Architectural Library. *Avery index to architectural periodicals*. Boston: G.K. Hall.

23. *Directory of British associations*. Annual. Beckenham: CBD Research.
24. Union of International Associations (ed.) *Yearbook of international organizations*. 2 vols. Annual. Munich, NY, London, Paris: Saur.
25. *The Times 1000*. Annual. London: Times Books.
26. *Kompass*. 2 vols. Annual. East Grinstead: Reed Information Services.
27. *Who owns whom Volume 3 United Kingdom, Volume 4 Ireland*. Annual. High Wycombe: Dun & Bradstreet.
28. British Standards Institution (1993) BS 1000 M *Universal decimal classification. International medium edition. English text.* 2nd edn. 2 parts. BSI.
29. Ray-Jones, A. and Clegg, D. (1976, repr. 1982) *CI/SfB construction indexing manual*. London: RIBA Publications.
30. Co-ordinating Committee for Project Information (1987) *Common arrangement of works sections for building works*. London: Building Project Information Committee.
31. Hargrave, J. and O'Brien, A. (1988) *Index to Common arrangement of work sections*. Unpublished.
32. European Product Information Co-operation (1994) *Construction product grouping. Version 1.0*. London: RIBA Information Services.
33. Landscape Institute (1988) *Landscape filing index*. 3rd edn. London: Landscape Institute.
34. *Official journal of the European Communities, C series, Information and notices*. Daily. Luxembourg: Commission of the European Communities.
35. Marcaccio, K.Y. (1994) (ed.) *Gale directory of databases*. Detroit: Gale Research.
36. RIBA Services. *RIBA Product selector*. Annual. London: RIBA Information Services.
37. Barbour Index. *Barbour compendium*. Annual. Windsor: Barbour Index.
38. *Specification*. 3 vols. Annual. London: Emap Architecture.
39. Chartered Institution of Building Services Engineers. *Opus: building services design file*. Annual. London: Builder Group.
40. *Kelly's*. Annual. East Grinstead: Reed Information Services.
41. *Europages*. Biennial. Paris: Euredit.
42. *Research focus: building and civil engineering*. Monthly. London: Institution of Civil Engineers.

CHAPTER TWENTY-THREE

Conservation

KEITH PARKER

Conservation is a wide-ranging subject, drawing information from a variety of disciplines, from art history to engineering. As with other practical disciplines, however, there are two basic sources of information: either experts, or specialist bodies, can provide it, or the literature of the subject can be examined. During recent years, interest in conservation has grown considerably; concerned bodies have grown in number and in publishing activity, and this in turn has brought some specialists into greater prominence.

We consider first the traditional, printed sources, however. In the absence of a nearby specialist library, bibliographies will probably form the easiest entry to the subject. Major texts in the field, which are considered next, can usually offer another approach. Unfortunately, such publications are obsolescent as soon as they are published, so the following section looks at methods of updating or supplementing the information they contain, whether through periodicals, current awareness and indexing services, or databases and other IT resources. Finally we shall consider the kinds of specialist organizations and libraries which may be consulted.

Bibliographies

Generally, bibliographies are much-neglected tools and are grossly under-used by all except librarians. This is a pity, as they can be extremely valuable in giving direction to the search for information. Conservation bibliographies come in different types: some have attempted to cover the whole field of architectural conservation, some touch on it while dealing with a related subject area, and others are specialist dealing with one small facet of the subject. It is well to be aware of this when using them.

While specialist bibliographies continue to appear, there are few which attempt to cover the whole field of architectural conservation (especially if we extend that term to include both town planning and landscape garden aspects, as we do in this chapter). Of those which have attempted to look comprehensively at the subject, the major survey is still John Smith's *Critical bibliography of building conservation* (1). That it has not been revised since appearing in 1978 is perhaps at once a tribute to the huge effort involved in such a milestone publication, and a comment on the growth of writing on the subject since. An additional factor is no doubt the growth of IT: first, on-line databases, and now CD-ROMs have become available to offer the searcher a rapid and wide-ranging (though not critical) overview of the literature. Inevitably, then, we must seek to add other information sources to this historic work. *British and Irish architectural history: a bibliography and guide to sources of information* by Ruth Kamen offered the next step in 1981. In addition to the bibliography, it contains sections on how to find out about architects and buildings from published and unpublished sources, from indexes and catalogues. Other sections list organizations, including sources of architectural photographs. While some of this material, too, is inevitably out of date, it remains of great value as a guide to possible paths to follow.

General bibliographies in English, but published abroad, can also be useful, but naturally their emphasis will lie more in the country of origin. While this may be seen as a drawback for the British conservation scene, it is also a virtue in that publications overlooked in British records will be listed there. Thus Mary Vance's *The conservation and restoration of buildings: monographs in the English language, 1978-88* (2) is an excellent source, especially for North American publications of that decade.

Aspects of conservation can be found scattered throughout the literature of planning, so any guides to information sources in this field can be called into service. Bodies with a special interest in conservation may also be responsible for issuing what amount almost to specialized guides to available publications. Thus *The Conservation Areas of England* (3) by the Historic Buildings and Monuments Commission for England, more commonly known as English Heritage, is a five volume set which can also act as a directory to local authority records on the topic.

Bibliographies dealing with one specialist aspect of conservation, often the most useful for either the practitioner or the student, can be found in many places. Smith in his *Critical bibliography* records more than 50 on subjects ranging from brick to damage by tree roots. While these are inevitably outdated, they may still offer a useful starting point, or at least suggest paths of enquiry, as may directories of groups active in the field. Ministries and official research bodies may produce such specialist bibliographies, although they may be neither well-publicized nor widely distributed, as they are often intended mainly for internal use, or produced only on an ad hoc basis. It would nevertheless be worthwhile to approach their libraries (in Britain, for example, those of the Department of the Environment and Building Research Establishment). The United States National Park Service has produced and distributed widely a five part *Historic building materials bibliography* (4) covering wood, masonry, painting, concrete and 20th century building materials; this has uses far beyond the borders of the USA.

Non-government organizations also produce specialist bibliographies reflecting their particular concern. These can deal specifically with conservation or be relevant to some branch of it. A very useful series on the scientific and technical aspects of conservation appeared between 1955 and 1985 in issues of *Art and archaeology technical abstracts*. Each volume contained a supplement devoted to a particular topic, and while many are of a more museological interest, others examined subjects such as stone conservation or stained glass. Similarly, *APT Bulletin* includes bibliographies and book reviews.

Reference has already been made to one of Mary Vance's bibliographies. From 1978 to 1990 over 2000 bibliographies were produced in both the Architecture Series and the Public Administration Series, many of them relevant to conservation interests. They may be found, or at least a selection of them, in some of the architectural libraries in the UK.

Frequently the architect, conservator or student may be faced with a building type the literature of which, if it exists, would best be sought in a more general bibliography. For example, aspects of the conservation of vernacular buildings might best be sought in something like the Vernacular Architecture Group's *Bibliography on vernacular architecture* (5) and its supplements. The *Encyclopedia of vernacular architecture of the world* (6) announced for autumn 1995 promises an entire volume devoted to the subject. Information on early industrial buildings might also be sought in such publications, as well as in the pages of journals such as *Industrial archaeology* (7) or in histories or encyclopaedias of the subject or, above all, in the extensive bibliography published in *The Blackwell encyclopedia of industrial archaeology* (8). For buildings of archaeological importance, or for those where conservation has archaeological implications, *British archaeological abstracts* (9) is probably of greatest help.

Unfortunately, many classes of buildings, including that large and very important class, churches, do not have specific bibliographies or lists devoted to them, and advice on them will have to be sought from journals or from a specialist institution. Alternatively, help may be found in bibliographies included in such specialized works as – for churches – *Treasures on earth*, edited, by Peter Burman (10), which has an outstanding bibliography on conserving churches and their contents.

The conservation of historic gardens and landscapes has not been a subject of wide concern for as long as that of buildings and monuments, though the major study of *The historical literature of the garden in Britain* by Blanche Henrey (11) pre-dates the comparable studies of British architectural literature.

The *Conservation reading list* by J. Gallagher and P.H. Goodchild (12) and R. Desmond's *Bibliography of British gardens* (13), both from 1984, mark the beginnings, in print, of the contemporary movement in the conservation of historic gardens and landscapes. Others soon followed: the National Trust's *Policy and practice in National Trust gardens: a reading list* (14); the US National Park Service's *Preserving historic landscapes* (15) in the following year; and Parks Canada's *Selected bibliography for garden history in Canada* (16). In view of the French contribution to landscaping, and as just one example of how our subject crosses national and linguistic frontiers with great ease, special mention should be made of *Bibliographie de l'art des jardins* by de Ganay and Mosser (17) which examines five and a half centuries of French garden literature.

This is not the place to consider the history of architecture, building, or landscape and garden (see the relevant chapters) but mention has to be made of the value of historical publications as discussed and listed by Archer, or Harris and Savage in their works on British architectural publications from the mid-16th to the mid-19th centuries. Similarly, the appearance of the British Architectural Library's catalogue, *Early printed books 1478-1840*, is of inestimable value to specialists seeking writings of the period. For those seeking landscaping sources, Blanche Henrey's work serves the same purpose, and like Archer, and Harris and Savage, helps even more by providing a variety of locations for the works listed. In this respect they all act as union catalogues for their subjects too. It may sometimes be necessary to consult the original book (which itself requires conservation and protection) but there is also the possibility that reprints have been made which, for most purposes, are perfectly adequate. Facsimiles have been available for some time, in paperbacks such as those of Dover Press, or in hardback like the Gregg Press architectural facsimiles of the 1960s-1970s or the Garland series, *The English landscape garden,* of recent years. Such ventures have given libraries the opportunity to furnish their public shelves with works that otherwise would be firmly shut into rare book collections.

Microforms have also allowed such wider access to rare collections, ranging from the *Fowler collection of early architectural books* (18) in the Johns Hopkins University, microfilmed by Research Publications

International, to the photographic collection of the Archaeological survey of India (19), on microfiche from Emmett Publications. These, however, may prove rather more difficult to find.

A recent publishing venture of some interest is the *Literary sources and documents* series from Helm Information (20). Each title comprises an extensive introduction to its subject, with bibliography and other editorial apparatus, followed by selective reprints from a large number of primary works. All of these can guide the architect and conservator to early pattern books, craftsmen's handbooks, or to the literary and theoretical works of the period, which can be of great value. Accurate descriptions, early photographs or other illustrations can equally be of great help during conservation work.

Although works such as Pevsner's *Buildings of England* series may be useful for providing an outline history of a building, conservation work requires more detail than this excellent series can offer. More valuable, where they exist, are the architectural descriptions and scale plans appearing in the *Victoria county histories* (VCH – 21) and the *Inventories* of the Royal Commissions on the Historical Monuments (RCHM) of England, Scotland and Wales (22). There used to be considerable overlap between these bodies, but in the more recent volumes the VCH has tended to leave detailed architectural coverage to the RCHM. In surveying an area the RCHM takes large numbers of high quality photographs, which can be up to 90 years old in the earliest volumes. These are then deposited with the National Monuments Record (NMR), which also holds large collections of other photographs and measured drawings. It may be worth supplementing the information provided in the RCHM inventories by an inspection of the original survey cards which are often in more detail. Regional offices of the RCHME in Cambridge, Salisbury and York retain the survey records of any current work; files for work which has been published are sent to the Headquarters at Swindon. Inspection of these records may be made by prior arrangement. The Commission is also actively developing computer applications to improve access to its records. The National Register of Archives has surveyed many regional and private archives, and between 1969 and 1974 published five lists of additions with entries by architect, place and subject (23). There are other institutions which hold drawings, plans, photographs or descriptions of individual buildings. The Council for the Care of Churches has a file on every Anglican church in the country and the contents of these may range from a few odd photographs to complete surveys and detailed records of previous conservation work. Similarly, the Society for the Protection of Ancient Buildings (SPAB) holds over 10 000 files on individual buildings; it may be possible to arrange permission to consult these. The RIBA British Architectural Library Drawings Collection holds many thousands of architectural drawings recorded in its

20 volume *Catalogue* (24).

The 19th century architectural and building periodicals are also a good source for measured drawings of historic buildings, and are often valuable in that they can show them in a pre-restoration state. Foremost among these was *The Builder* – now *Building* – and the eagerly awaited index to the drawings which it published between 1843 and 1883 has now appeared (25). For illustrations in other journals of the period the index produced early in this century by the Victoria and Albert Museum, *The topographical index to measured drawings of architecture which have appeared in the principal architectural publications* (26), is still of great value.

Very useful also is the modern general guide by Maurice W. Barley, *A guide to British topographical collections* (27). This is a county-by-county index of collections, many of which include illustrations of buildings, in public repositories and some private collections in England, Scotland and Wales. It is by no means exhaustive, but it is still very useful. For early illustration of country houses, there is also John Harris' *A country house index* (28) which indexes 'over 2000 country houses illustrated in 107 books of country views published between 1715 and 1872'. Although superseded to a large extent by Michael Holmes' *The country house described* (29), Harris' work still has references which do not appear in the later book, as his pamphlet is not restricted to works in the Victoria and Albert Museum, as is the other.

At the local level it is well worth enquiring at the area record or archive office to see if any relevant plans or illustrations exist, and for churches, at the local diocesan record office, which in many cases is the same place. It is fortunate that for churches, plans and drawings deposited with earlier faculty applications often survive, as do many hanging on the walls of church vestries. Sometimes useful background material may be located through enquiries via the local historical, archaeological or amenity society.

The garden conservator must make similar searches, and some of the publications mentioned above can be called upon for help. A valuable guide to the wide range of documents, published and unpublished, and of repositories, is provided by David Lambert's *Researching a garden's history from documentary and published sources* (30). The same author has reported on a pilot study to build up a *Record of documentary sources for British gardens, gardening and landscape design* (31), a project which is being carried further at the Centre for the Conservation of Historic Parks and Gardens at York, where a large amount of data has already been collected. This Centre also played a large part in developing English Heritage's *Register of parks and gardens of special historic interest in England* (32), one of a series of inventories which cover the UK. The Welsh Register is still in progress. The National Trust has a Garden Survey Team which produces valuable reports on its properties, as do private consultants contracted to or supported by English Heritage to survey estates private or public.

Texts

Principles

Access to such information is, however, only one part of the problem for conservators. How should they act when such preparations must turn to practice? Generally accepted guiding principles can be found in a series of agreements and declarations, from the *Venice charter* of 1964 (for monuments and sites) and the *Florence charter* of 1982 (for historic gardens) to the *Burra charter of* 1988 (33). All such declarations up to 1984 are recorded in *ICOMOS 1964-84* (34) and the International Council on Monuments and Sites (ICOMOS) headquarters in Paris, or the national committees, can be approached for copies of them all. A recent study of policies and practices since the 18th century in four different countries can be found in W.F. Denslagen's book, *Architectural restoration in Western Europe: controversy and continuity,* together with a lengthy and polyglot bibliography (35).

General practice

The standard work for architectural conservators, *Conservation of historic buildings* by Sir Bernard Feilden, was first published in 1982, and the second edition has recently appeared in an abbreviated form (36). While retaining the chapters on general practice, and also a bibliography of considerable importance, certain sections on repair have been deleted because of the publication of what has become another standard work: *Practical building conservation,* by John and Nicola Ashurst for English Heritage (37). The five volumes consider Stone masonry; Brick, terra-cotta and earth; Plasters, mortars and renders; Metals; Wood, glass and resins; and once again there is a 40 page technical bibliography and directory of organizations. Publications such as these provide for all of us some of the expertise at the disposal of English Heritage. Works of similar authority may be found among the publications of the International Centre for the Study of the Preservation and Restoration of Historic and Cultural Property (ICCROM).

Alongside such monographs, the increased publishing activity of many bodies involved in conservation has produced a steady flow of shorter papers which extend and update them. Besides English Heritage's *Listed buildings guidance leaflets* (38), the Georgian Group, SPAB, the Victorian Society and others are now all issuing advisory notes (variously titled) on such things as Georgian mouldings or Victorian and Edwardian fireplaces. In the United States, the National Park Service provides a similar stream of *Preservation briefs* (39) and other technical notes. The same office's *National Register bulletins* offer a regular flow of guidance on researching, evaluating and documenting historic sites, from houses to battlefields to navigation aids – e.g. *Guidelines for evaluating and registering historic archaeological sites and districts* (40). Although aimed at researchers on sites intended for the US National Register of Historic Places, the clear listing of suggested research methods, evaluation criteria, recommended bibliographical and other sources make this series a model for such activities elsewhere.

Gardens and landscapes

The case of historic gardens and landscapes has not yet produced such a wealth of guidance, but help is available, whether in Tom Wright's *Large gardens and parks* (41) or *Heritage gardens: care, conservation and management* by S.M. Goulty (42). For those with access to the *National Register bulletins* just discussed, there are also bulletins dealing with historic landscapes, designed or rural, as well as cemeteries and burial places.

Law

Guidance on principles and practice is often transferable from country to country even though it may need adapting to different circumstances. One type of information, however, is quite specific and non-transferable: the law of the land must be observed, whatever the practice in other countries. In addition to the texts of the laws themselves, governments may produce other guidance. Thus in England the Department of the Environment has issued Planning Policy Guidance notes 15: *Planning and the historic environment* (43) and 16: *Archaeology and planning* (44), while in the United States, the National Park Service publishes a guide, *Federal historic preservation laws* (45), revised as occasion demands.

Basic guides are not restricted to government publications of course. They may come from other official bodies, like Cambridgeshire County Council's guide to historic building law (46), or individuals such as Charles Mynors (47) or Roger Suddards (48). In 1982 the US National Committee of ICOMOS began an ambitious series, *Historic preservation in foreign countries* (49), surveying the situation in (to date) 10 European countries, including a historical overview of legislation.

Periodicals

The knowledge contained in books can be extended either in terms of case studies, or in terms of updating information, by articles in periodicals, the next information source to be considered. For general architectural, or planning, or landscape and garden journals, as for most practices, conservation is only one of many interests. They cannot therefore be expected to supply a large proportion of writings in this field, although they are the ones to which most libraries tend to subscribe. We shall therefore refer readers to other chapters for a consideration of general periodicals (*Architectural review, Town planning review,* etc.) and restrict ourselves, with one exception, to more specialist titles. The exception is *Country life* (50), since it frequently carries articles on conservation issues, with regular features on historic houses and gardens (a cumulative index appears regularly).

The Association for Studies in the Conservation of Historic Buildings (ASCHB), a body composed largely of conservation architects, issues regular newsletters outlining the work of the association and providing good conservation book reviews. Its annual *Transactions* (51) is a more formal publication containing longer articles with a high proportion of conservation case studies. Containing much that is of practical value to a conservation architect, they deserve to be more widely known.

Churches are dealt with in the annual publication *Churchscape* (52), issued from 1981 onwards by the Council for the Care of Churches. This contains articles on all aspects of the care of churches and is issued mainly for the guidance of diocesan advisory committees. Up to half of each issue can consist of book reviews and so acts as an extension to the bibliography in P. Burman's work mentioned earlier. *Churchscape* and its predecessors from 1964-1980 can be found in some architectural libraries, along with other publications by the Council. The *Annual reports* of SPAB (53) go back to 1878, with thousands of reports on individual buildings. In 1980 their cumulative indexes were supplemented by Phillipa Bassett's listing of all case records up to that time (54). The society also issues *SPAB News* (55), a quarterly which is an essential item for any library with building conservation interests. The same can be said for the *Transactions* (56) of the Ancient Monuments Society, and their *Newsletter* (57), while the Civic Trust's *Urban focus* (58), like its variously-named predecessors, deals more with general urban and village conservation themes.

Journals of such voluntary bodies, like those of the architectural and planning professions, can be expected to contain relevant articles. Enquirers do not always think of another possible source: the literature of engineering. Such journals as the *Proceedings* of the Institution of Civil Engineers (59) or the *Structural engineer* (60) do not contain a large number of articles in this area, but those which appear are usually clearly and methodically set out, the structure, defects and conservation programme being analyzed in turn. The *Transactions* of the Newcomen Society (61) often provides valuable articles on the history of structural engineering practices and processes, while the more recent *Construction history* (62) does the same for the building industry.

At the moment, those seeking information on the conservation of historic gardens must still rely mainly on more general journals, such as *Landscape design* or *Garden history*. Since 1991, short articles on conservation have also been available in the *AA garden conservation newsletter* (63); although addressed primarily to the students and alumni of the course at the Architectural Association, it may also be found at some libraries.

Articles on the law of conservation can be found scattered throughout the range of journals, usually just before or after the enactment of legislation, or during some particular controversy; the indexes referred to later in this chapter will help locate them. There is one periodical specializing in the field, the *Journal of planning and environment law* (64). If this cannot be found nearby for regular consultation, using a basic guide, such as those by Cambridgeshire County Council or others mentioned earlier, and then scanning the general weekly journals can help you keep up-to-date. Again, if it is possible to find it, the monthly *List of publications* of the Department of the Environment (see below) announces publications such as the summaries of official policy which began in Departmental circulars and are now continuing in *Planning policy guidance* notes (65). A number of journals deal with the fittings and furnishings of historic buildings, often those that concern themselves with the science and technology of conservation. This is very much the area of concern of *Studies in conservation* (66), the quarterly published by the International Institute for the Conservation of Historic and Artistic Works (IIC). It contains many very technical articles, including such subjects as the conservation of wall paintings and the treatment of polychromed sculpture. Many of its contributors work in conservation laboratories, often attached to major museums, so the conservation of artifacts in controlled or museum environments tends to predominate. A similar publication, but maybe more directly useful to architectural conservators, is the *Conservator* (67) from the United Kingdom Institute for Conservation (UKIC). This too contains much on museum conservation, but also articles on structural conservation in situ, for example, of church monuments.

Many specialist societies devote themselves and their journals to the history and conservation of particular artifacts or materials. There are too many to list but as one example we may cite *Stained glass: the journal of the British Society of Master Glass Painters* (68). Possibly the most recent group of this kind to appear in conservation is the Building Limes Forum, with its journal, *Lime news* (69). British societies of this kind may be traced through the *Conservation sourcebook* mentioned below. Specialist publications from such societies outside the country may be sought (as indeed may all kinds of periodicals) in guides such as

Ulrich's international periodicals directory (see Chapter 3). If no recent mention can be found, records of older publications or societies might be found either in Smith's *Critical bibliography* or Kamen's *British and Irish architectural history,* mentioned above.

In the UK such voluntary or private bodies have long been associated with the conservation movement, and their counterparts can be found in many countries. Another perspective on the state of conservation in a country is afforded by the publications of government or official bodies. These may appear in news-sheet form, like the RCHME *Newsletter* (70) or *Preservation in action* (71); they may carry more detail, like English Heritage's *Conservation bulletin* (72) with its occasional supplement, *Scientific and technical review* (73). The annual reports of such bodies are also well worth looking out. For those concerned with the practicalities of managing the heritage, the US National Park Service's *CRM* (74) offers both general and specific studies, from considerations of principles to dealing with lead-based paints (**17** (4), 1994).

In the international field three bodies in particular stand out: the International Council on Monuments and Sites, the Getty Conservation Institute (GCI), and the Association for Preservation Technology International (APT). From 1967 to 1984 ICOMOS produced *Monumentum* (75) succeeded until 1990 by *ICOMOS Information* (76); both contained authoritative articles on conservation world-wide, but *ICOMOS news* (77) which followed them is primarily a members' newsletter announcing and reporting on activities. It does, however, record new ICOMOS publications, as well as additions to the World Heritage List, whose records ICOMOS keeps. There are hopes a new *Scientific journal* may yet continue what *Monumentum* began, and a first issue has already appeared (78). The Getty Conservation Institute's activities are primarily practical and educational, but we should mention *Conservation: the GCI newsletter* (79). Recording the Institute's activities, it also notes its publications, whether proceedings of conferences or reports of conservation projects.

APT, based in North America but world-wide in scope, produces *APT Bulletin* (80) and *Communique* (81). The latter is mainly the Association's newsletter, but carries useful notes of recent publications; the former consists of detailed studies, very practical and wide-ranging, from locks or heating systems to special issues such as 'Conserving historic landscapes' (**24** (3-4), 1992). Other journals have appeared or been announced recently which, if they are successful, should extend international coverage still further. Among these are the *International journal of heritage studies* (82) and *Journal of architectural conservation* (83).

Current awareness

It would be possible to keep abreast of much current book production in conservation by consulting national bibliographies or book trade listings. They are usually to be found in public as well as academic libraries, but extracting specialist information from such general lists can be extremely tedious. Many libraries will also collect the catalogues of publishers active in this area. Official bodies like HMSO, English Heritage and the Building Research Establishment issue annual lists of publications for sale while the Department of the Environment has a monthly *List of publications* (84). Many societies have also become active in publishing, and their lists can also be consulted (e.g. SPAB in the UK or Preservation Press, the publishing arm of the National Trust for Historic Preservation, in the USA). Catalogues can also be obtained from commercial publishers which specialize in architecture, such as Butterworths Architecture, or Donhead, a recent arrival which has already built up an impressive list specifically on conservation.

The book reviews to be found in the relevant journals (see above) are of course a valuable supplement to such lists, adding an informed and independent opinion on the value of the works reviewed. Better still, if possible, is to visit a good architectural library. Naturally, the value of this will depend on the quality of the library, its staff and stock, but the recent increase of interest in conservation, and courses on it, has improved the prospects of success. The principal architectural library in the UK is of course the British Architectural Library (BAL) at the Royal Institute of British Architects. Its accessions list was separately published from 1979 to 1982, and since then has appeared as an appendix to *Architectural periodicals index (API)*, so it is not even necessary to visit the Library to keep up with additions to its stock.

Finding recent periodical articles might seem a more difficult problem, given the bulk of the literature and the way writings are scattered through a large number of publications. There are, however, several aids to success which make it easier than might be thought. Most large public and academic libraries will hold some of the general indexes to periodicals in the arts, humanities or technology, even if specialist indexes are not to hand (or, if they are, the general ones can help widen the search). Specialist abstracting and indexing publications do exist, though, and some at least should be available in architecture libraries. In the UK, the first place to look is the *API* (85), which indexes, with one line annotations, articles in the journals received by the BAL. The *API* has been published since 1972, but searches can be taken back to 1946 through its more selective predecessors. It is arranged by subject keyword, and users need to remember to check more than the simple heading, such as 'Preservation, restoration' ('conservation' is not used). The term can also be used as a subheading for another keyword – that of a building type, for example. A general warning might be given, indeed, for searches in any kind of literature, that other headings which might relate to the problem in hand should be checked as a matter of course: building type, area, material, technique, etc.

The alternative to *API*, its American counterpart, is the *Avery index to architectural periodicals* (86) from the Avery Library of Columbia University, like BAL one of the world's great architectural libraries. Begun in 1934 (but going back, selectively, into the 19th century) the printed index is a multi-volume work, with supplements. Retrospective indexing has continued, so even supplements may contain entries for earlier years. These two are of course indexes to architectural periodicals in general ('architecture' being defined broadly, and including, for example, town planning and landscape gardening). More specialized than these is *Art and archaeology technical abstracts (AATA)* (87), the special supplements of which are mentioned above. Published by the GCI and IIC, this six-monthly journal provides much more of architectural interest than its title might suggest. Sections on architectural conservation and building materials are part of the classified arrangement, alongside others on the conservation of artifacts, museum storage and recording techniques, which might be expected. *AATA* provides abstracts not only for periodical articles but also for conference papers, books, and even chapters of some multi-authored works. Until recently there was no direct equivalent of these for people interested in gardens and their conservation (other than sections in *API* or *Avery*). An index to articles and book reviews in over 200 journals since 1992 is now available in *Garden literature* (88). Strongest on North American publications, it has good international coverage, and may be found in some UK libraries.

Databases

Printed indexes of the sort discussed above now have electronic counterparts. As books and journals from a variety of disciplines can be helpful to conservators, so many databases can supply valuable information. This section looks at a few which are more directly relevant. Just as *API* is probably the first print index consulted in UK architectural circles, so BAL's *Architecture database* (89), its electronic counterpart, is likely to be the most familiar at present. It holds references to articles since 1978 and to books since 1984, updated monthly, and is available on-line through DIALOG. A CD-ROM version, *APId*, is now available too. The *Avery index on disc* (90) provides a cumulated list of articles since 1977, with annual update. The third list discussed above, *AATA*, is available on-line like *API*, but in this case from the Canadian Heritage Information Network (CHIN) under the title *Conservation information network (CIN)* (91). Originally developed at the GCI in collaboration with

ICCROM, ICOMOS, the International Council of Museums (ICOM), the Smithsonian Institution's Conservation Analysis Laboratory, and the Canadian Conservation Institute (CCI) as well as CHIN, *CIN* is a network of four databases, of which the most immediately relevant is *BCIN*, the bibliographic database. This is not just an electronic version of *AATA* from volume one onwards, as it also contains extra data from the ICCROM database and from the libraries of the other partners. At CHIN a separate bibliographic database on heritage law is also being compiled, updated twice-yearly, as well as one on museology. Plans are under way to make *CIN* and CHIN databases available to each other's subscribers.

One database, available from UNESCO on CD-ROM, does not correspond to a print version: *ICOMMOS* (92) is made up of about ten years' input from ICOM and ICOMOS. It is, however, markedly smaller than *BCIN,* with about 26 000 references compared with about 120 000, and the museological content is high (about 50%).

Conferences and research

The literature of conference and research activities, like much else in conservation, must often be sought through more general reference works or databases which list conference proceedings, reports or theses. Alternatively, access may come via the bodies which organize the events, such as the Council of Europe, whose series *Architectural heritage reports and studies* (93) publishes the proceedings of a succession of seminars and colloquia. From the European Community comes *European cultural heritage newsletter on research* (94), which reports on very technical aspects of conservation science. A calendar of forthcoming events can be found in the newsletter from ICOMOS, while those of GCI and ICCROM report on meetings in which they have been involved or whose proceedings they have published. UNESCO's *List of documents and publications* (95) includes both conference proceedings and reports of expert missions (though well-nigh submerged in the flood of the other publications of this many-sided world body).

Research by individuals pursuing private interests is inevitably more difficult to track down, but two works show what can be offered by specialist groups. Both the Garden History Society and the Society of Architectural Historians of Great Britain compile a register (96/97) of work by members, and include also some work in academic institutions. They appear only at intervals, but are a helpful guide to research in progress. The growth of interest in conservation in university departments of architecture, landscape and planning has led also to an increasing number of theses. It is sometimes possible to acquire lists of such work (from the Architectural Association, for example, or the Institute of Advanced Architectural Studies at York): it is always worth enquiring.

Organizations and associations

The most likely organization to approach either for information or for directions as to where to send enquiries, is the library. In the UK, the best existing library for architecture and conservation is the BAL. It is, however, the RIBA's private library, though non-members may use its reference collection on payment of a fee. Reference has already been made to its collection of early architectural works. This, together with its current collection and large stock of periodicals, makes it one of the world's major architectural libraries. The libraries of the other related professions may likewise offer help, but to most people, especially those not in the capital, the most readily available collections will be in the nearest university to have a relevant department or school. These will probably be freely available at least for reference. Other specialist libraries, such as those of the Civic Trust, Council for the Care of Churches, or SPAB, are usually, like the BAL, private collections. The serious searcher should try approaching them, however; with prior notice it is often possible to arrange access if other sources have failed.

Specialist bodies such as these may of course need to be traced first, before enquiries can be addressed to them. In the field of conservation the UK is fortunate in having several guides which can confidently be offered to enquirers. The *Conservation sourcebook* (98), issued by the Conservation Unit of the Museums and Galleries Commission, lists several hundred bodies, indexed in 44 subject categories ranging from gardens to wall paintings, and also includes a list of full-time courses in aspects of conservation from buildings to paper. Other directories, for subjects such as planning and environment list groups ranging from government departments and agencies to voluntary, professional and trade associations. One example is Frisch's *Directory for the environment* (99).

One specific and very important aspect of conservation is the financial one. Information on this can be sought in English Heritage's *Directory of public sources of grants for the repair and conservation of historic buildings* (100), which is issued in loose-leaf form to accommodate occasional updates; or in general guides to charities and grant-making bodies.

Any directory of libraries and information bureaux may help searchers, but a particularly valuable list of European contacts has been prepared by the Council of Europe: *Architectural heritage documentation centres in Europe* (101). Nearly 200 centres in 26 countries are listed, with details of their collections, size, coverage, accessibility, etc., in loose-leaf form for updating. In each country the situation will vary, of course, but even if such specific guides may be lacking, government, professional or voluntary bodies may be approached, either for details of their own collections, publications or activities, or for suggestions of other possible contacts.

Conclusion

The main sources of information in conservation are the literature, specialist bodies and individual experts. Bibliographies will help provide the literature, and their inevitable obsolescence can be overcome by using the means of updating mentioned above. Advisory bodies may be located through the *Conservation sourcebook* and similar directories, while the indexes to the literature and the specialist bodies can combine to help trace the experts.

References

1. Smith, J. F. (1978) *Critical bibliography of building conservation.* London: Mansell.
2. Vance, M. (1988) *The conservation and restoration of buildings: monographs in the English language, 1978-88.* Monticello, IL: Vance Bibliographies.
3. English Heritage (1988) *The Conservation Areas of England.* 5 vols. London: English Heritage.
4. United States National Park Service (1993) *Historic building materials bibliographies.* 5 vols. Washington, DC: National Park Service.
5. Vernacular Architecture Group (1972-92) *Bibliography on vernacular architecture.* Newton Abbot: David & Charles, with supplements: *A current bibliography of vernacular architecture.* York: VAG; and A *bibliography of vernacular architecture,* Vol. III. Aberystwyth: VAG.
6. Oliver, P. (1995) (ed.) *Encyclopedia of vernacular architecture of the world.* 4 vols. Oxford: Blackwell.
7. *Industrial archaeology* (1964-) Tavistock: Graphmitre.
8. Trinder, B. (1993) (ed.) *The Blackwell encyclopedia of industrial archaeology.* Oxford: Blackwell.
9. *British archaeological abstracts* (1968-) London: Council for British Archaeology.
10. Burman, P. (1994) (ed.) *Treasures on earth: Good Housekeeping guide to churches and their contents.* London: Donhead.
11. Henrey, B. (1975) British botanical and horticultural literature before 1800. . . a history and bibliography. 3 vols. London: OUP.
12. Gallagher, J. and Goodchild, P. H. (1984) *Conservation reading list: the conservation of historic parks and gardens with special reference to Great Britain.* York: Institute of Advanced Architectural Studies.
13. Desmond, R. (1984) *Bibliography of British gardens.* Winchester: St. Paul's Bibliographies.
14. National Trust (1989) Polica and practice in National Trust gardens: reading list. London: National Trust.
15. United States National Park Service (1990) *Preserving historic landscapes: a bibliography.* Washington, DC: National Park Service.
16. Parks Canada (1994) *Selected bibliography for garden history in Canada.* Rev. edn. Ottawa: Parks Canada.
17. Ganay, E. de and Mosser, M. (1989) *Bibliographie de l'art des jardins.* Paris: Bibliotheque des Arts Decoratifs.
18. Johns Hopkins University (1982) *Fowler collection of early architectural books, 1485 through the early 1800s.* 86 reels of microfilm. Reading Research Publications International.

19. Archaeological Survey of India (1993) *Archaeological survey of India photographs in the India office collections in the British Library.* 230 microfiches. Haslemere: Emmett Publishing.
20. Charlesworth, M. (1993) (ed.) *The English garden: literary sources and documents.* 3 vols. Mountfield, East Sussex: Helm Information.
21. *Victoria History of the counties of England* (1901-) London: Institute of Historical Research.
22. Royal Commission on the Historical Monuments of England (1910-) *Inventories, etc.* London: HMSO. (Two other Royal Commissions cover Scotland and Wales.)
23. National Register of Archives (1969-74) *Architectural history and the fine and applied arts: sources in the National Register of Archives.* London: National Register of Archives.
24. Royal Institute of British Architects (1969-89) *Catalogue of the drawings collection.* 20 vols. Farnborough: Gregg International.
25. Richardson, R. and Thorne, R. (1994) (eds.) *The Builder illustration index.* London: Hutton and Rostron.
26. Victoria and Albert Museum (1908) *The topographical index to measured drawings of architecture which have appeared in the principal architectural publications.* HMSO.
27. Barley, Maurice W. (1974) *A guide to British topographical collections.* London: Council for British Archaeology.
28. Harris, J. (1971) *A country house index.* Shalfleet: Pinhorns.
29. Holmes, M. (1986) *The country house described.* Winchester: St. Paul's Bibliographies.
30. Lambert, D. (1991) *Researching a garden's history from documentary and published sources.* Reigate: Landscape Design Trust.
31. Lambert, D. (1991) *Record of documentary sources for British gardens, gardening and landscape design: report on a pilot study. 1989-90.* York: Institute of Advanced Architectural Studies.
32. English Heritage (1984-92) *Register of parks and gardens of special historic interest in England.* 49 vols. London: HBMCE.
33a. International Council on Monuments and Sites (1964) *International charter for the conservation and restoration of monuments and sites (Venice charter).* Venice: ICOMOS.
33b. International Council on Monuments and Sites (1982) *Charter on historic gardens (Florence charter).* Paris: ICOMOS.
33c. International Council on Monuments and Sites, Australian National Committee (1988) *The Australia ICOMOS charter for the conservation of places of cultural significance (Burra charter).* 3rd edn. Sydney: ICOMOS Australia.
34. International Council on Monuments and Sites (1984) *ICOMOS 1964-84.* Paris: ICOMOS.
35. Denslagen, W.F. (1994) *Architectural restoration in Western Europe: controversy and continuity.* Amsterdam: Architectura and Natura.
36. Feilden, B.M. (1994) *Conservation of historic buildings.* 2nd edn. Oxford: Butterworths Architecture.
37. Ashurst, J. and Ashurst, N. (1988) *Practical building conservation.* 5 vols. Aldershot: Gower.
38. English Heritage (undated) *Listed buildings guidance leaflets.* London: English Heritage.
39. United States National Park Service (1975-) *Preservation briefs.* Washington, DC: USGPO.
40. United States National Park Service (1993) *Guidelines for evaluating and registering historic archaeological sites and districts.* Washington, DC: National Park Service.

41. Wright, T.W.J. (1982) *Large gardens and parks: maintenance, management and design.* St. Albans: Granada.
42. Goulty, S.M. (1993) *Heritage gardens: care, conservation and management.* London: Routledge.
43. Department of the Environment and Department of National Heritage (1994) *Planning, and the historic environment.* (Planning Policy Guidance 15). HMSO.
44. Department of the Environment (1990) *Archaeology and planning* (Planning Policy Guidance 16). HMSO.
45. United States National Park Service (1993) *Federal historic preservation laws.* Rev. edn. Washington, DC: USGPO.
46. Cambridgeshire County Council (1995) *The Cambridgeshire guide to historic buildings law.* 8th edn. Cambridge: County Council.
47. Mynors, C. (1994) *Listed buildings and conservation areas.* 2nd edn.
48. Suddards, R. (1995) *Listed buildings: the law and practice of historic buildings, ancient monuments and Conservation Areas.* 3rd edn. London: Sweet & Maxwell.
49. International Council on Monument and Sites, US National Committee (1982-) *Historic preservation in foreign countries.* Washington, DC: US/ICOMOS.
50. *Country life.* (1897-) London: Country Life.
51. Association for Studies in the Conservation of Historic Buildings (1973-) *Transactions.* London: ASCHB.
52. *Churchscape: annual review of the Council for the Care of Churches* (1981-) London: CCC.
53. Society for the Protection of Ancient Buildings (1878-) *Annual reports.* London: SPAB.
54. Basset, P. (1980) *List of the historical records of the Society for the Protection of Ancient Buildings.* Birmingham: Centre for Urban and Regional Studies.
55. *SPAB News* (1980-) London: SPAB.
56. Ancient Monuments Society (1953-) *Transactions.* New series. London: AMS.
57. Ancient Monuments Society (1973-) *Newsletter.* London: AMS.
58. *Urban focus* (1992-) London: Civic Trust.
59. Institution of Civil Engineers (1920-) *Proceedings.* London: ICE.
60. *Structural engineer* (1922-) London: Institution of Structural Engineers.
61. Newcomen Society for the Study of the History of Engineering and Technology (1922-) *Transactions.* London: Newcomen Society.
62. *Construction history:* journal of the Construction History Society (1985-) Ascot: Chartered Institute of Building.
63. *AA garden conservation newsletter.* (1991-) London: Architectural Association.
64. *Journal of planning and environment law.* (1948-) London: Sweet & Maxwell.
65. *Planning policy guidance.* (1988-) HMSO.
66. *Studies in conservation.* (1952-) London, etc.: IIC.
67. *Conservator.* (1977-) London: UKIC.
68. *Stained glass: the journal of the British Society of Master Glass Painters.* (1924-) London: BSMGP.
69. *Lime news: the journal of the Building Limes Forum.* (1992-) York: IOAAS.
70. Royal Commission on the Historical Monuments of England (1989-) *Newsletter.* London: RCHME.
71. *Preservation in action.* (1984-) London: Architectural Heritage Fund.
72. *Conservation bulletin* (1987-) London: English Heritage.
73. *Scientific and technical review.* (1992-) London: English Heritage.
74. *CRM: cultural resources management.* (1976-) Washington, DC: National Park Service.
75. *Monumentum.* (1967-84) Leuven, etc.: ICOMOS.
76. *ICOMOS Information.* (1985-90) Paris: ICOMOS.
77. *ICOMOS News.* (1991-) Paris: ICOMOS.

78. *Scientific journal.* (1993-) Leuven: ICOMOS. (pilot issue produced in Madrid by Ediciones Doce Calles)
79. *Conservation: the GCI newsletter.* (1986-) Marina del Rey, CA: GCI.
80. *APT Bulletin.* (1969-) Ottawa: APT.
81. *Communique.* (1972-) Ottawa: APT.
82. *International journal of heritage studies.* (1994-) University of Plymouth Press.
83. *Journal of architectural conservation.* (1995-) London: Donhead. To these new titles might also be added the following, the list is increasing annually:
83a. *Conservation and management of archeological sites.* London: James & James.
83b. *European heritage.* Strasbourg: Council of Europe.
84. Department of the Environment. *List of publications* (1970-) London: DoE.
85. *Architectural publications index.* (1972-) London: RIBA.
86. *Avery index to architectural periodicals.* (1975-) 2nd edn. and supplements. Boston: G.K. Hall.
87. *Art and archaeology technical abstracts.* (1955-) Marina del Rey, CA: Getty Conservation Institute and International Institute of Historic and Artistic Works.
88. *Garden literature: an index to periodical articles and book reviews.* (1992-) Boston: Garden Literature Press.
89. *Architecture database.* London: RIBA. Available on DIALOG. *APId.* London: RIBA.
90. *The Avery index on disc.* New York: G.K. Hall.
91. *Conservation information network.* Ottawa: Canadian Heritage Information Network.
92. *UNESCO databases on CD-ROM.* (1994) 2nd edn. Paris: UNESCO.
93. *Architectural heritage reports and studies.* (1984-) Strasbourg: Council of Europe, Division for Cultural Heritage.
94. *European cultural heritage newsletter on research.* (1986-) Brussels: Commission of the European communities, DG XII.
95. UNESCO (1972-) *List of documents and publications.* Paris: UNESCO.
96. Garden History Society (1992) *Registers of research.* 5th edn. Cheltenham: GHS.
97. Society of Architectural Historians of Great Britain (1994) *Research register no. 6.* Leeds: W.S. Money (for SAHGB).
98. Museum and Galleries Commission, Conservation Unit (1991) *Conservation sourcebook.* 2nd edn. HMSO.
99. Frisch, M. (1994) *Directory for the environment.* London: Green Print.
100. English Heritage (1988-) *Directory of public sources of grants for the repair and conservation of historic buildings.* London: English Heritage.
101. Council of Europe (1993) *Architectural heritage documentation centres in Europe.* Strasbourg: Council of Europe.

CHAPTER TWENTY-FOUR

Buildings, people, places: architectural history

MARGARET CULBERTSON AND MARY NIXON

Fascinating background information on buildings, people and places can be found in a wide variety of sources. This chapter will present the major sources and tools for research on historical and contemporary architects and architecture, as well as examples of some of the specialized sources that may help when the information needed is more elusive. It also suggests how to translate your information need into search terms and strategies that will facilitate a successful search.

The ease with which you can find information, as well as the quality and quantity of material that exists, will vary with your enquiry. Many architects and some key buildings have entire books devoted to them that can easily be identified through library catalogues. Even when information is located in periodical articles or within books on broader subjects, many architectural history enquiries can be answered with relative ease by searching standard indexes and bibliographies. However, it is important to remember that creativity, flexibility and the instincts of a detective are invaluable assets in research.

Planning your search

The more you know about a subject, the easier it becomes to find even more information about it. If you know that your architect is an obscure 16th century practitioner from Suffolk, you can skip several steps of the basic search strategy, such as looking for books or checking reference books that do not cover the appropriate period, such as *Contemporary architects*. As you learn more about your subject during the search process, it is important to take particular note of information that might prove helpful in identifying additional sources or different search terms. Aspects of each subject that may facilitate a search are given under the headings below.

Buildings

Who was the architect or designer?
Information about buildings is most often retrievable through the architect's name.
When was it built?
Since many information sources concentrate on specific periods, and others are organized by period, knowing the date or general period of your building's construction may be useful.
What is its use or function? (Is it an office building, church, school?)
You can frequently search catalogues and indexes by building type.
Does it have a distinctive name? Has the name changed?
Some information sources provide access by building name, but be aware that the format, order, and language used may vary. For example, the following headings have all been used in different sources for the museum building in Paris designed by Piano and Rogers: Centre Beaubourg, Centre National d'Art et de Culture Georges Pompidou, Centre Georges Pompidou, Pompidou Centre.
Has the address of the building changed?
For many buildings the only definite way to identify them is by address or legal description. Check to see if the street name or numbers of your building have been changed if you are having difficulty finding information.
If you cannot find anything specifically on your building, you may have to widen the search to any or all of the following:

- buildings by the same architect
- buildings of the same period and type
- buildings of the same construction method
- buildings in the same area.

People

Are there possible variations in the form of the name?
Some people's names are not listed in the same form in all reference works and indexes. Michelangelo is listed in the 'M's' under 'Michelangelo' in some sources and in the 'B's' under 'Buonarotti' in others. Le Corbusier can be found in the 'L's' and also in the 'J's' under his given name 'Jeanneret-Gris, Charles-Edouard.' The editors of reference sources and library cataloguers have serious theoretical reasons for choosing the name forms that they use but, unfortunately, the inconsistencies between sources require flexibility on the part of the researcher. Try alternative name forms before moving to another source. People are

not always consistent about the way they spell their names, and printed sources, particularly newspapers, may make mistakes. Remember to check possible variants, e.g. Pearce, Pierce, Piers. When doing a computer search, even common variants, such as Brown/Browne may be missed. In Victorian Britain, in particular, it was not uncommon for men to change their surnames, usually in order to benefit from an inheritance. This change might take the form of inserting another surname before their existing one, so what looks like a second forename may be the first element of the surname. For example, M.H. Baillie Scott may appear under Baillie or Scott. Herbert Duncan Appleton changed his name to Searles-Wood, and he might be listed under any of these three surnames in reference sources.

Does the person practise in a firm or in partnership with another architect?

Flexibility is needed when looking for information on contemporary architects practising in firms. Articles on Gordon Bunshaft can be found under his own name, as well as under the name of the firm Skidmore, Owings and Merrill. Some sources list Jean Nouvel in the 'N's' under his last name, while others list him in the 'J's' under the firm name, 'Jean Nouvel, Emanuel Cattani et Associés.'

Another complication derives from the frequent changes in the names of architectural practices and in their personnel. William Alsop's practice was Alsop & Lyall, then Alsop Lyall & Stormer, and then Alsop & Stormer within a couple of years. Foster Associates became Sir Norman Foster & Partners when the senior partner received his knighthood. Some firms prefer to be known by their initials, but this may not be their legal title. For example, the same firm could be listed as CZWG or as Campbell Zogolovitch Wilkinson & Gough or as Piers Gough. Whether you are using an index, a library catalogue, or an encyclopaedia, try searching under alternative name forms if you are not finding anything.

When did the person live?

Since many biographical sources cover specific time periods, you can save time by avoiding sources that do not cover the relevant period.

When did the person die?

Obituaries in professional publications, as well as in newspapers, often prove to be rich sources of information about a person's accomplishments. Local newspapers can be a good source of obituaries of people not famous enough to have obituaries in the national press.

Where was the person born, and where did the person work?

In addition to the geographic focus found in many books and reference sources, several major indexes, particularly the *Architectural periodicals index*, subdivide architects by country before they list them by name. (Bear in mind that architects do, and did, move about frequently.)

Was the person a member of a professional organization?

Directories published by professional organizations may include biographical information or lists of works. Clients, as well as architects, may be members of professional associations, with their own directories, such as the *Law list* or *Crockford's clerical directory*, and specialist periodicals. If the client has any letters after his name, it is worth checking what they mean and whether he was a member of a society that may keep records of its members' activities.

Places

Could there be alternative spellings or ways of listing the place name?

There are many possible variations in the way place names may be listed in reference sources. If you are looking for information on a city, it may be listed directly under the city name, or it may be listed after the name of a larger geographic division within which it lies, such as 'France, Paris' or 'Illinois, Chicago'. A foreign place name may be listed under the native language form (e.g. Venezia) or under the anglicized form (e.g. Venice).

Local government boundary changes in the UK mean that some towns are no longer in the same county. Bournemouth, for instance, should be searched for under Hampshire as well as Dorset, while Bath will be under Somerset in books dating from before the creation of Avon. This mutability extends to other boundaries. Many new Church of England dioceses were founded in the 19th and early 20th centuries, and some church records may be located with the records for the previous diocese or jurisdiction.

Is there a local library or a research library in the place?

Many libraries have local history departments or specialized indexes or collections of materials relating to their city, county, state or province. In Britain, each public library service has one or more designated local history libraries, while each county (England and Wales) or region (Scotland) has a record office that houses both public records and private archives of local significance.

Basic sources

The following basic sources are excellent starting points, whether you are looking for information about an architect, a building or a place.

Encyclopaedias

Check appropriate encyclopaedias for articles on your architect or building. Encyclopaedia entries can provide useful background information and bibliographic listings of additional sources to check. One of the most important encyclopaedias for architectural history is the *Macmillan encyclopedia of architects*, which provides 2450 substantial biographies of architects, past and present. The entries usually include lists of built works as well as bibliographies of additional sources. There is also an index by building name. *Contemporary architects* is not limited to living architects but includes major architects of the 20th century. The bibliographies and lists of works are quite extensive. The *International dictionary of architects and architecture* is primarily historic in its focus, although significant 20th century architects are included. Major buildings are featured in one volume and architects in the other, but unfortunately there are no indications in the architects' entries if any of their buildings are featured in the other volume. The biographical section of the *Illustrated dictionary of architects and architecture* is followed by general articles on periods and styles of construction, illustrated with relevant examples. The *Encyclopedia of architecture* contains some biographical articles but is more useful for its information on the history of aspects of architectural technology and building types.

Library catalogues

Check library catalogues to find books on your architect, building or place. With the advent of computerized library catalogues and their widespread availability through networks and electronic communications, searching your own library's catalogue is only the beginning of a search for books. The ability to search the computerized catalogues of libraries, such as the Avery Architectural and Fine Arts Library at Columbia University and the British Architectural Library, significantly expands a researcher's capabilities to determine what has been published on a subject. It is also possible to search databases of shared catalogue information from multiple libraries. The *WorldCat* database, available from OCLC, contains over 30 million records from 18 000 libraries, and the RLIN database (Research Libraries Information Network) contains citations to over 22 million titles from more than 200 institutions. Both of these databases are based in the United States, but they have international membership and users. With a citation from a library catalogue or database in hand, the staff of your local Inter-library Loans Office may then be able to identify more conveniently located libraries that may lend the material.

If a subject search is unsuccessful in a library's catalogue, be sure to investigate the free text search capabilities if it is a computerized catalogue. Free text searching can be invaluable when the official subject headings prove elusive, as when books on Roman baths are listed under the term 'Public Baths' or books on town squares are listed under 'Plazas'. If free text searching is not available, find out if there is a list of official subject terms that might provide helpful references from your subject to the term used in the catalogue. The *Library of Congress subject headings* and the *Art and architecture thesaurus* are examples of such lists that may prove useful in determining search terms.

Most computerized library catalogues still do not provide subject access to book chapters or the full variety of subjects that may be included within the pages of a book. A welcome exception is the British Architectural Library catalogue of books (1984 to the present), which is available through DIALOG File 179 along with the *Architectural periodicals index*. The analytical cataloguing provides access to chapters of books and to specific buildings featured within books. The CD-ROM version, APId appeared in 1995 and is updated quarterly. If you do not have access to the British Architectural Library's catalogue, you may still find relevant information within books on broader subjects by checking bibliographic citations from encyclopaedias, periodical articles and other books, as well as by searching for books on related or inclusive subjects that might logically contain relevant information.

Periodicals

Two major indexes provide subject access to articles in most of the important periodicals in architectural history: the *Architectural periodicals index (API)*, produced by the British Architectural Library, and the *Avery index to architectural periodicals*, produced by the Avery Architectural and Fine Arts Library. Both are available in print, on-line and CD-ROM versions. Even though there is some duplication in their indexing, if you are doing a comprehensive search, you will want to look for your subject in both in order to determine the full range of articles published in architecture journals. When searching the on-line versions through DIALOG, it is even possible to do a joint search of the *Avery index* and the *Architecture database*, which includes the *API* and the British Architectural Library's catalogue of books. If you need to look for articles that may have been indexed before 1979 in the *Avery index*, you will need to consult the printed volumes of the index. Articles indexed by the British Architectural Library before 1973 were published in the *RIBA Library bulletin*. A list of *Current periodicals indexed in API* is available from the British Architectural Library, as is the library's complete *List of periodical holdings*.

The *Architectural index* covers only 8–10 periodicals, but these are among the major US periodicals, and the index is priced within the budget of even very small firms and libraries. The *Design and applied arts index*, published twice yearly, includes quite a lot of information on architecture as well as on allied decorative arts. It combines subject headings (such as building types) and designers' names in one alphabetical sequence. The *Burnham index to architectural literature*, compiled from 1919 to the mid-1960s in the Ryerson and Burnham Libraries of the Art Institute of Chicago, is particularly useful for its coverage of architectural periodicals during the period before the introduction of the *Avery index* in 1934, but it continued to index materials not covered by *Avery* until it was discontinued.

Art history periodicals also publish important articles on architectural history. The *Art index* (available in print and CD-ROM versions) and *Bibliography of the history of art* (BHA) (and its predecessors, *RILA* and the *Repertoire d'art et d'archeologie*) are the major indexes to art history periodicals. For ancient architecture the *Archaologische bibliographie* is useful. General periodicals and history periodicals also include articles on buildings, people and places. A few of the major indexes to these include *Readers' guide to periodical literature, Periodical abstracts, Historical abstracts, America: history and life* and *British humanities index*. (Many of these indexes are available for computerized searching, either on-line or on CD-ROM.)

Nineteenth-century periodicals

A few architectural periodicals of the 19th century are indexed in the printed 15 volume set of the *Avery index*, and others are included in the *Burnham index*, but many nineteenth-century architecture periodicals are not fully indexed. *Poole's index to periodical literature 1802-81* and *19th century readers' guide to periodical literature 1890–1899, with supplementary indexing, 1900-1922* do index 19th century general periodicals, but their coverage of architectural articles is uneven. A few specialized indexes provide detailed access to architectural material published in 19th century periodicals. A useful example is *The Builder illustrations index 1843-1883*, compiled by Richardson and Thorne, which gives unprecedented access to the 12 000 illustrations that appeared in *The Builder* over its first 40 years. It is possible to search by designer, building name, place and type of construction. *American house designs, an index to popular and trade periodicals 1850-1915* provides access by architect's name and geographic location to over 6000 illustrations of house designs that were published in ladies' magazines, house and garden magazines and periodicals of the building trade. Unpublished indexes can also be found in some libraries, including an index to the 19th century periodical on church architecture, the *Ecclesiologist*, which is kept in the British Architectural Library.

Newspapers

Newspapers may contain notices of building construction, reviews of completed buildings, obituaries and articles on architects. Many indexes to newspapers exist in print or computerized form, including *The Times* and the *New York Times*. A separate index to the obituaries in *The Times* contains the obituaries from 1951 to 1975 in three volumes. The *New York Times obituaries index* covers the years 1858-1978. Many regional and local newspapers do not have published or computer-searchable indexes but may contain useful information. To find out where British newspapers are accessible, check P.E. Allen's *Catalogue of the news-*

paper collection in the British Library and *Local newspapers and periodicals of the nineteenth century: a checklist of holdings in provincial libraries.* For holdings in the United States and Canada, check *Newspapers in microform: United States 1948-1983.* Remember that there may be locally-produced, unpublished indexes to a town's newspapers in the local public library or newspaper office.

Specialized sources

When the aforementioned sources prove insufficient, there is an abundant array of more specialized sources and search strategies. The sections below provide descriptions of some of those that are most frequently consulted.

Bibliographic guides

Several bibliographic guides list useful sources for research on architects and buildings. Guides to a wide variety of architectural sources include Ehresman's *Architecture*, the *RIBA list of recommended books*, and the bibliographies published in the Architecture series of Vance Bibliographies. The major guide to British sources is Ruth H. Kamen's extensive *British and Irish architectural history: a bibliography and guide to sources of information.* American architecture is included in Karpel's *Arts in America* and Sokol's *American architecture and art.* As the American examples indicate, guides to the literature of architectural history are often included within guides to the literature of art history for specific periods or countries.

People

Architects as well as clients, developers and historical figures associated with a building may be found in general biographical encyclopaedias, such as the *Dictionary of national biography*, for British biographies, and the *Dictionary of American biography* for those of the United States. The *Biography and genealogy master index* (available on CD-ROM as well as in print and on-line) indexes both of these sources as well as over 670 other biographical dictionaries of historical and contemporary figures, including *Who's who* and *Who was who.* Library catalogues should be used to identify other, more specialized biographical sources, and the indexes discussed in Chapter 3 can be used to identify articles about people in periodicals and newspapers.

Architects

Architects and designers form the major category in architectural research on people, and there are many specialized sources devoted to them. If you have tried the *Macmillan encyclopedia of architects, Contemporary architects,* library catalogues and the indexes described in Chapters 2 and 3 without finding what you need, the dictionaries listed below may help. In addition to these, catalogues of architectural drawings and archives described in the next section often contain basic biographical information about architects.

The *Avery obituary index of architects* is international in its coverage and contains over 17 000 entries for obituaries in 19th and 20th century architectural periodicals and selected newspapers. If your German is up to it, consult the very thorough dictionary of artists, *Allgemeines Lexikon der bildenden Kunstler,* edited by Thieme and Becker, which covers architects and those who contributed to buildings in other ways, such as sculptors and mural painters. (This dictionary is in the process of being updated and expanded.) Most other biographical dictionaries are devoted to architects of specific countries or periods and vary in the amount of detail they give.

British architects

Harvey's *English mediaeval architects: a biographical dictionary down to 1550* includes everyone involved in the building process, from patrons to masons. Colvin's *Biographical dictionary of British architects 1600-1840* gives full lists of works with bibliographic references, location of extant drawings and even details of portraits of the architects. Ware's *A short dictionary of British architects* and Gray's *Edwardian architecture* are less detailed but give at least summary lists of works. The British Architectural Library's *Directory of British architects 1834-1900* and Wodehouse's *British architects, 1840-1976* do not give lists of works but do give references to literature. If you know that an architect was connected with a particular area, you can search local directories and sources such as Pike's *Contemporary biographies* published in county volumes at the turn of the century. For some areas, there are extremely good local dictionaries of architects, such as Brown's *Dictionary of architects of Suffolk buildings 1800-1970* and Linstrum's *West Yorkshire architects and architecture,* but these are unfortunately the exception rather than the rule.

American architects

Krantz's *American architects* provides brief information on 400 contemporary American architects who have received awards for their work, while *Master builders* profiles 39 famous historic American architects. Withey's *Biographical dictionary of American architects (deceased)* gives brief biographical information on 2000 American architects living between 1740 and 1952, many of whom are not included in any other published sources. Wodehouse's two bibliographies on American architects give annotated bibliographical references to literature on the architects and sometimes report locations of archival material. Unfortunately, there are only a few regional dictionaries of architects, such as the excellent *Biographical dictionary of Philadelphia architects, 1700-1930* by Sandra Tatman. Histories of the architecture of specific states, regions or cities also may include information on local architects.

Architects' drawings and archives

For a very few major architects there are complete editions of all of their extant drawings, pulled together from separate collections, such as the Wren Society's 20 volume catalogue of Sir Christopher Wren's drawings. For other major architects, the complete contents of specific collections of their drawings have been published. Garland Publishing has produced several of these, including 32 volumes of Le Corbusier drawings from the collection of the Fondation Le Corbusier, and 20 volumes of Mies van der Rohe drawings in the Museum of Modern Art. These catalogues can be easily identified when you search library catalogues for books by, and about, your architect.

It is more of a challenge to find drawings by less well-known architects. If the books or other sources on your architect do not guide you to a drawings collection, you should search the published catalogues of likely collections, such as the *Catalogue of the Drawings Collection of the Royal Institute of British Architects*. Additional volumes of this catalogue are in preparation, but until they are completed, the card catalogue in the Drawings Collection is the only complete index to the drawings. Microfilm of the drawings contained in the published catalogue are available from World Microfilms. For the United States, the *National Union index to architectural records*, a computerized index to collections throughout the country, is maintained by the Prints and Photographs Division of the Library of Congress. Enquiries for information from the *Index* may be made to the Prints and Photographs Division by mail or telephone. Some of the information from the *Index* has also been published in several guides to architectural research in specific cities, including New York City, Philadelphia, Boston, Chicago and San Francisco. John Harris' *Catalogue of British drawings for architecture, decoration, sculpture and landscape gardening 1550-1900 in American collections* is also a useful source of information. Catalogue records for architectural drawings held in many research libraries, including the Avery Architecture and Fine Arts Library, can be searched on-line within the visual materials (VIM) file of the RLIN database.

Access to architectural drawings will undoubtedly improve in the future as the catalogues of more collections become available for computer searching and as the efficiency of storing images in computerized form increases. A pioneer effort in this direction is the Avery Architectural and Fine Arts Library's creation of AVIADOR, an interactive system that links videodisk images of 41 000 architectural drawings from the Avery collection to their on-line catalogue descriptions on RLIN.

Archival collections of architects' manuscripts and firm records are included in many of the guides and directories described above, but specialized guides to archives also exist. In Britain, the National Register of Archives holds information on the whereabouts of some architects' drawings and office papers. Most record offices and other archival collections produce handlists or more detailed catalogues and indexes of some of their material. Angela Mace's *Royal Institute of British Architects: a guide to its archives and history* is an example of such a source, but it is important to remember that it is a guide to the archive of the organization, not to RIBA's collection of architects' manuscripts. A guide to the letter was in preparation in 1995. *Record repositories in Great Britain*, published by the Royal Commission on Historical Manuscripts, lists county and other record offices with brief details of their holdings. The AMC (Archival and Manuscripts Control) file of RLIN may be searched by subject or personal name to identify archival holdings in hundreds of member libraries in the United States and internationally.

Buildings

Extensive resources on individual buildings may be found within books or articles about the architect or within the catalogues of collections of drawings described above. Books about the architecture of a period or a country or about particular building types also frequently discuss individual buildings at length. Even though books devoted to individual buildings are relatively rare, it is worth checking for your building in library catalogues. In addition to books and pamphlets on specific buildings published by many different publishers over the years, a few publishers have published series of books of consistently high quality on individual buildings. *Global architecture* is a series of well-illustrated monographs on significant examples of modern architecture, including James Stirling's Leicester Engineering Building and Louis Kahn's Yale University Art Gallery. The text in many of the volumes is fairly limited, but the photographs are large format and high quality, and plans and sections are routinely included. The periodical *Blueprint* has produced some *Blueprint extra* volumes on buildings, including Nicholas Grimshaw's British Pavilion for Expo 92. In 1992 Phaidon Press began publishing an excellent series of monographs on individual buildings entitled *Architecture in detail*. The series has featured primarily 20th century buildings, but a few 19th century examples include the Crystal Palace and Gaudi's Sagrada Familia. Photographs, plans, sections and details for each building are included as well as a substantial text.

Architectural surveys of particular areas and catalogues of historic buildings may contain very detailed information on individual buildings. For buildings in Great Britain, three major series provide considerable information about historic buildings. The 43 volumes of the *Survey of London* include the history of areas and individual buildings, maps, plans and photographs for such historically important areas as the Strand and Piccadilly and, rather surprisingly, the Isle of Dogs. Whole volumes are devoted to individual buildings such as the Queen's House at Greenwich, but less than half of central London has been covered by the published volumes of the *Survey*. The *Victoria county histories* are produced on a county-by-county basis, some being almost complete, while others have barely been started. These volumes contain general historical information as well as descriptions of notable buildings. The *Inventories of historical monuments* of the Royal Commissions on the Historical Monuments of England, Scotland and Wales are also published by counties, but whole volumes (sometimes several of them) are devoted to the buildings of historic towns such as Cambridge, York and Stamford. The *Inventories* were published on microfilm under the title *Historic buildings in Britain*.

More geographically comprehensive, although less exhaustive, is the *Buildings of England (Scotland, Ulster and Wales)* published by Penguin and frequently referred to by the name of its originator as 'Pevsner'. A CD-ROM has been produced by Oxford University Press that supplies a general index to the volumes for England (excluding London), thus opening up numerous possibilities for cross-referencing information. Less thorough, but still very useful, are the *Shell guides*, which like Pevsner are arranged by county. For country houses, Holmes' *The country house described* lists both articles in *Country life* and illustrations of country houses in topographical works of the 19th century and earlier, which can be useful for finding out what a house looked like before alterations were made. Another source for early illustrations of buildings is William Upcott's *A bibliographical account of the principal works relating to English topography*, which lists the contents of topographical books with both national and local coverage. This includes country houses and also other notable buildings, such as churches, up to the end of the 18th century.

For buildings in the United States, the Historic American Buildings Survey contains measured drawings, photographs and research notes on thousands of historic structures. The collection is kept on file in the Prints and Photographs Division of the Library of Congress. The photographs and research notes have been published on microfiche by Chadwyck-Healey. The measured drawings for California, New York and Texas were published by Garland Publishing, and may be available in your local library or through Inter-library Loan. If you are interested in a building located in another state or do not have access to the Garland volumes, copies of any of the measured drawings are available from the Library of Congress. The National Register of Historic Places contains information about thousands of buildings that have been recognized by the US Government as significant historically, architecturally or culturally. Brief summary information on these buildings is published in the *National register of historic places, 1966-1994* or in the *Federal register* for properties added later. The full textual information and photographs are on file in the Washington office of the National Register of Historic Places, and copies of the information on the properties in each state are also on file with the State Historic Preservation Officer for that state. The full set of information has also been published on microfiche by Chadwyck-Healey.

The *Buildings of the United States* series was modelled after Pevsner's *Buildings of England*, but only four volumes had been published as of 1994. A multitude of architectural guidebooks have been published on specific cities, counties and states, and they include many buildings that are not documented in other sources. The information may be brief, but it can provide some basic facts and clues for further research. Local historical societies or libraries may also have special files on local buildings or local architectural surveys. Since many historic buildings are under government protection or ownership, checking indexes to government publications may also yield results.

Information about a building may also be held by another relevant body; for example, the archives of the Incorporated Church Building Society, held at the Lambeth Palace Library, include thousands of plans of churches. Educational institutions, learned societies and commercial firms may maintain their own archives, which contain details of buildings, even those which they have ceased to occupy. Ruth H. Kamen's *British and Irish architectural history* gives details of over 200 organizations, from government departments to local museums, which hold relevant material, and lists a further 70 or so sources for architectural photographs and slides.

If you need to find illustrations of a building or its plan, Teague's *World architecture index* and *Index to Italian architecture* guide you to illustrations of buildings within standard books on architecture. For more elusive buildings, photographic archives, several of which have been published on microfiche, may help. Plans and photographs of many historic buildings can be found in the *Alinari photo archive*, which illustrates works of architecture and art in Italy, the *Marburger index*, which does the same for Germany, *L'Index photographique de l'art en France*, and the Conway Library's photographic research library for art history, which includes British and European architecture. A few microfiche collections concentrate exclusively on architecture, including *Ancient Roman architecture* and *Armenian architecture*.

When one is trying to date a building that has not been researched before, government records are important but time-consuming resources. The chapter on 'The paper trail' in Howard's *How old is this house?* provides a very helpful guide to using public records to date buildings in the United States.

For technical information about a building, *Construction references* (ceased 1990), published by the now defunct Property Services Agency, contains references to buildings arranged by UDC classification. It is principally concerned with more technical aspects of construction, and references may be found under a particular aspect of a building's construction, rather than under building type.

Places

To find historical information about a place and the development of its built environment, many of the basic sources already discussed, such as library catalogues and indexes to periodicals and newspapers, are essential. Many of the specialized sources discussed in the section on 'Buildings' are also useful, particularly the *Victoria county history* (VCH) for England. Specialized guides include W.B. Stephens' *Sources for English local history* and P.W. Filby's *Bibliography of American county histories*. Anthony Sutcliffe's *History of urban and regional planning* lists publications on the planning history of 104 individual cities throughout the world.

For information about English towns, a noteworthy source is the series of three books that were derived from Alec Clifton-Taylor's series of television programmes for the BBC. This series, consisting of *Six English towns, Six more English towns*, and *Another six English towns*, gives a chapter each to smaller historic towns, including Warwick and Chichester.

Maps and historic views of cities provide invaluable information but are often easy to miss since many are either not included in library catalogues or are only included under a series title or publisher's name. Small, but useful maps were also often included in historic travel guidebooks, such as Karl Baedeker's guides to cities, regions and countries that were published in the 19th and early 20th centuries. David A. Cobb's *Guide to US map resources* lists libraries with significant map collections and provides a subject index by collection strengths.

For US cities, thousands of extremely detailed maps were created for the insurance industry and were updated frequently over the years, thereby providing an impressive record of the physical growth of cities, as well as enabling researchers to determine when individual buildings were constructed. The Sanborn Map Company was the primary producer of these maps, and 11 000 volumes of its maps are owned by the Library of Congress (LC). The checklist of the LC collection is entitled *Fire insurance maps in the Library of Congress*. Many of the maps have also been published on microfilm by Chadwyck-Healey and University Publications of America.

Historic views of towns and cities recorded an amazing amount of detail, often showing every building, street and open space within a community. John W. Reps' *Views and viewmakers of urban America* contains a catalogue of over 4000 separately published lithographic city views of the United States and Canada. Collections that own the views are indicated in each entry.

Contemporary urban mapping has been revolutionized by the use of computer technology with aerial photography to create amazingly detailed and accurate maps. Marsilio Editore has published atlases utilizing this technology to document Rome, Venice and Florence. The volumes for Rome and Venice contain aerial photographs and corresponding line maps at a scale of 1:500. The volume for Florence contains photographs and line maps at a scale of 1:1000.

Historical publications

Historical architectural literature is essential to the researcher who is interested in the professional and intellectual world in which an architect developed and practised. It can also provide an insight into the design sources and the technology that were available to the architect. Major bibliographies that list historic architectural publications include Eileen Harris's *British architectural books and writers 1556-1785*, John Archer's *Literature of British domestic architecture, 1715-1842* and Henry Russell Hitchcock's *American architectural books; a list of books, portfolios, and pamphlets on architecture and related subjects published in America before 1895*.

Historical trade catalogues, the actual sales catalogues of firms selling building materials or services, may also prove useful. Bibliographies of trade catalogues include Romaine's *Guide to American trade catalogs: 1744 through 1900, Trade catalogues at Winterthur* and Ross's *Guide to architectural trade catalogues from Avery Library, Columbia University on microfiche*.

Associations

Specialist organizations and associations dealing with the history of architecture include the following:

- Society of Architectural Historians, whose major publications are the *Journal of the Society of Architectural Historians* and *Newsletter of the Society of Architectural Historians*
- Vernacular Architecture Forum, which publishes *Vernacular architecture newsletter*
- National Trust for Historic Preservation, which publishes *Historic*

> *preservation, Preservation forum* and *Preservation news*
> • Society of Architectural Historians of Great Britain, publishing *Architectural history* and its *Newsletter*.

Conclusion

The strategies and sources for architectural history research are as varied as the possible enquiries. This chapter presents some of the important reference sources and provides examples of points to consider when planning your strategy. However, it is important to remain alert and flexible in your research, since new sources continue to be created and since new technologies are transforming existing sources as well as the research process.

References and bibliography

Alinari photo archive. (1983) Zug, Switzerland: Inter Documentation microfiche.

Allen, P.E. (1975) *Catalogue of the newspaper collection in the British Library.* London: British Museum Publications.

Allgemeines Kunstlerlexikon. (1983-) Leipzig: Seemann; Munich: Saur.

America: history and life. (1964-) Santa Barbara, CA: ABC-CLIO. Also available online through the DIALOG Service and on CD-ROM from ABC-CLIO.

Ancient Roman architecture: photographic index on microfiche. (1979) Munich & New York: Saur.

Archaologische bibliographie. (1914-) Berlin: De Gruyter.

Archer, John (1985) *Literature of British domestic architecture, 1715-1842.* Cambridge, MA: MIT Press.

Architectural index. (1950-) Boulder, CO: Architectural Index.

Architectural publications index. (1973-) London: RIBA Publications for the British Architectural Library. Also available through the DIALOG Service as part of File 179, the *Architecture database.* It is published on CD-ROM as part of *Architectural publications index on disc (APId)* by RIBA Publications.

Architectural records in Boston. (1983) New York: Garland.

Architectural records in the San Francisco Bay area: a guide to research. (1988) New York: Garland.

Architectural research materials in New York City: a guide to resources in all five boroughs. (1977) New York: Committee for the Preservation of Architectural Records.

Architectural research materials in Philadelphia: a guide to resources. (1980) New York: Committee for the Preservation of Architectural Records.

Architecture series. (1978-) Monticello, IL: Vance Bibliographies.

Armenian architecture: a documented photo-archival collection on microfiche. (1980) Zug, Switzerland: Inter Documentation.

Art and architecture thesaurus. (1994) New York: Oxford University Press. Also available in an electronic edition from Oxford University Press.

Art index. (1930-) New York: H.W. Wilson. Also available on-line and on CD-ROM from H.W. Wilson.

Atlante di Venezia. An atlas of Venice: the form of the city on a 1:1000 scale photomap and line map. (1990) 3rd edn. Venice: Comune di Venezia; London: Architecture Design and Technology.

Avery index to architectural periodicals. (1973-) Boston: G.K. Hall. Also available on-line through RLIN, Research Libraries Group and through the DIALOG Service and on CD-ROM from G.K. Hall.
Avery Library (1980) *Avery obituary index of architects.* 2nd edn. Boston: G.K. Hall.
AVIADOR: Avery videodisc index of architectural drawings on RLIN. (Mountain View, California: Research Libraries Group).
Bibliography of the history of art (BHA)/Bibliographie de l'histoire d'art. (1991-) Santa Monica, CA: J. Paul Getty Trust, Getty Art History Information Program.
Biography and genealogy master index. (1980-) Detroit: Gale Research. Also available on-line through the DIALOG Service and on CD-ROM from Gale Research.
British Architectural Library (1993) *Directory of British architects 1834-1900.* London: Mansell.
British Architectural Library catalogue of books. Available through the DIALOG Service as part of File 179, the *Architecture database.* It is published on CD-ROM as part of *Architectural publications index on disc (APID)* by RIBA Publications.
British humanities index. (1963-) London: The Library Association.
Brown, Cynthia et al. (1991) *Dictionary of architects of Suffolk buildings 1800-1970.* Ipswich: Brown, Haward & Kindred.
Buildings of the United States. (1993-) New York & Oxford: Oxford University Press.
Burnham index to architectural literature. (1989) New York: Garland.
Catalogue of the drawings collection of the Royal Institute of British Architects. (1968-1989) London: Gregg.
Clifton-Taylor, Alec (1984) *Another six English towns.* London: British Broadcasting Corporation.
Clifton-Taylor, Alec (1978) *Six English towns.* London: British Broadcasting Corporation.
Clifton-Taylor, Alec (1981) *Six more English towns.* London: British Broadcasting Corporation.
Cobb, David A. (ed.) (1990) *Guide to US map resources.* Chicago: American Library Association.
Colvin, Howard Montagu (1978) *A biographical dictionary of English architects, 1660-1840.* London: Murray; New York: Facts on File.
Construction references. (1970-1990) London: Property Services Agency.
Contemporary architects. (1994) 3rd edn. Chicago & London: St. James Press.
Conway Library, the Courtauld Institute of Art, the University of London: Photographic research library for art history. (1987) Haslemere, Surrey: Emmett Publishing.
Culbertson, Margaret, (1994) (ed.) *American house designs: an index to popular and trade periodicals, 1850-1915.* Westport, CT: Greenwood.
Cummings, Kathleen Roy (1981) *Architectural records in Chicago.* Art Institute of Chicago.
Current periodicals indexed in API. (1994) London: British Architectural Library.
Design and applied arts index (1987-) Gurnleys, East Sussex: Design Documentation. Also available on CD-ROM from Design Documentation.
Dictionary of American biography. (1928-1958) New York: C. Scribner's Sons.
Dictionary of national biography. (1908-1909) London: Smith, Elder.
Ehresmann, Donald L. (1983) *Architecture: a bibliographic guide to basic reference works, histories, and handbooks.* Littleton, CO: Libraries Unlimited.
Encyclopedia of architecture: design, engineering, and construction. (1988-1990) New York: John Wiley & Sons.
Filby, P. William (1985) *A bibliography of American county histories.* Baltimore: Genealogical Pub. Co.
Fire insurance maps from the Sanborn Map Company archives, 1900s-1990. (1992-1993) Bethesda, Maryland: University Publications of America.
Gray, Alexander Stuart (1985) *Edwardian architecture: a biographical dictionary.* London: Duckworth.
Hanford, Sally (1983) *Architectural research materials in the District of Columbia.*

Washington, DC: American Institute of Architects Foundation.

Harris, Eileen (1990) *British architectural books and writers, 1556-1785.* Cambridge & New York: Cambridge University Press.

Harris, John (1971) *A catalogue of British drawings for architecture, decoration, sculpture and landscape gardening 1550-1900, in American collections.* Upper Saddle River, NJ: Gregg Press.

Harvey, John (1984) *English mediaeval architects: a biographical dictionary down to 1550: including master masons, carpenters, carvers, building contractors, and others responsible for design.* 2nd rev. edn. Gloucester: A. Sutton.

Henry Francis du Pont Winterthur Museum (1984) *Trade catalogues at Winterthur: a guide to the literature of merchandising, 1750 to 1980.* New York: Garland.

Historical abstracts. (1955-) Santa Barbara, California: ABC Clio. Also available on-line through the DIALOG service and on CD-ROM from ABC-CLIO.

Historic American buildings survey. (1980) Microfiche. New York: Chadwyck-Healey.

Historic buildings in Britain. (1977) New York: Chadwyck-Healey, microfiche.

Hitchcock, Henry Russell (1962) *American architectural books; a list of books, portfolios, and pamphlets on architecture and related subjects published in America before 1895.* Minneapolis: University of Minnesota Press.

Holmes, Michael (1986) *The country house described: an index to the country houses of Great Britain and Ireland.* Winchester: St Paul's Bibliographies in association with the Victoria & Albert Museum.

Howard, Hugh (1989) *How old is this house?* New York: Farrar, Straus and Giroux.

Illustrated dictionary of architects and architecture (1991) London: Headline.

Index photographique de l'art en France. (1981) Munich: K.G. Saur.

International dictionary of architects and architecture. (1993) Detroit & London: St. James Press.

Kamen, Ruth H. (1981) *British and Irish architectural history: a bibliography and guide to sources of information.* London: Architectural Press.

Karpel, Bernard (1979) *Arts in America: a bibliography.* 4 vols. Washington, DC: Archives of American Art, Smithsonian Institution.

Krantz, Les (1989) *American architects: a survey of award-winning contemporaries and their notable works.* New York: Facts on File.

Le Corbusier (1982) *Le Corbusier archive.* New York: Garland Pub.; Paris: Fondation Le Corbusier.

Library of Congress, Geography and Map Division, Reference and Bibliography Section (1981) *Fire insurance maps in the Library of Congress: plans of North American cities and towns produced by the Sanborn Map Company: a checklist.* Library of Congress.

Library of Congress subject headings. (1995) Library of Congress, Cataloging Distribution Service.

Linstrum, Derek (1978) *West Yorkshire architects and architecture.* London: Lund Humphries.

Local newspapers and periodicals of the nineteenth century: a checklist of holdings in provincial libraries. (1973) Leicester University, Department of Victorian Studies.

Mace, Angela (1986) *The Royal Institute of British Architects: a guide to its archive and history.* London & New York: Mansell.

Macmillan encyclopedia of architects. (1982) New York: Macmillan.

Marburger index: photographic documentation of art in Germany. (1976-) Munich: K.G. Saur.

Master builders: a guide to famous American architects. (1985) Washington, DC: Preservation Press.

Mies van der Rohe, Ludwig (1986) *The Mies van der Rohe archives.* New York: Garland.

National register of historic places. (1976) Washington, DC: US Department of the Interior, National Park Service.

National register of historic places, 1966-1994. (1994) Washington, DC: Preservation Press.

National register of historic places, parts I & II. (1984, 1992) Alexandria, VA: Chadwyck-Healey, microfiche.

New York Times CD-ROM. Ann Arbor, MI: University Microfilms.

New York Times obituaries index 1858-1968. (1970) New York Times.

Newspapers in microform: United States 1948-1983. (1984) Library of Congress.

Nineteenth century readers' guide to periodical literature, 1890-1899, with supplementary indexing, 1900-1922. (1944) New York: H.W. Wilson.

Obituaries from The Times: 1951-1975. (1975-1979) Reading: Newspaper Archive Developments; Westport, CT: Meckler Books.

Periodical abstracts. CD-ROM. Ann Arbor, MI: University Microfilms.

Pevsner, Nikolaus, (1951-) (ed.) *Buildings of England.* London: Penguin.

Poole's index to periodical literature 1802-81. (1891) Boston: Houghton. (Reprinted 1963. Gloucester, Massachusetts: P. Smith).

Pike, W.T. (1898-1911) *Contemporary biographies.* Brighton: Pike. (Reprinted as *Dictionary of Edwardian biography.* Edinburgh: Bell, 1983-87; Interfiche, 1987).

Reader's guide to periodical literature. (1905-) New York: H.W. Wilson. Also available on-line and on CD-ROM from H.W. Wilson.

Répertoire d'art et d'archeologie. (1910-1989) Paris: Centre de Documentation Sciences Humaines.

Reps, John William (1984) *Views and viewmakers of urban America: lithographs of towns and cities in the Unites States and Canada, notes on the artist and publishers, and a union catalog of their work, 1825-1925.* University of Missouri Press.

RIBA list of recommended books, now included in the *Architect's reference annual.* London: RIBA Publications.

Richardson, Ruth and Thorne, Robert (1994) *The Builder illustrations index 1843-1883.* Guildford: Hutton & Rostron.

RILA: International repertory of the literature of art. (1975-1989) Williamstown, MA: Sterling and Francine Clark Art Institute.

Romaine, Lawrence B. (1960) *A guide to American trade catalogs, 1744-1900.* New York: R.R. Bowker.

Ross, Norman A. (1989) *Guide to architectural trade catalogues from Avery Library, Columbia University on microfiche.* Frederick, Maryland: UPA Academic Editions.

Royal Commission on Historical Manuscripts, (1994) *Record repositories in Great Britain.* HMSO.

Royal Institute of British Architects: the drawings collection. (1969-) London: World Microfilms.

Sanborn fire insurance maps. (1983) Alexandria, VA: Chadwyck-Healey, microfiche.

Sokol, David M. (1976) *American architecture and art: a guide to information sources.* Detroit: Gale Research.

Stephens, W.B. (1981) *Sources for English local history.* rev. and expanded edn. Cambridge & New York: Cambridge University Press.

Survey of London. (1900-) London: Athlone Press, University of London, etc.

Sutcliffe, Anthony (1981) *The history of urban and regional planning: an annotated bibliography.* New York: Facts on File.

Tatman, Sandra L. (1985) *Biographical dictionary of Philadelphia architects, 1700-1930.* Boston: G.K. Hall.

Teague, Edward H. (1992) *Index to Italian architecture: a guide to key monuments and reproduction sources.* New York: Greenwood Press.

Teague, Edward H. (1991) *World architecture index: a guide to illustrations.* Westport, CT: Greenwood Press.

Thieme, Ulrich and Becker, Felix (1907-1950) *Allgemeines Lexikon der bildenden Kunstler von der Antike bis zur Gegenwart.* Leipzig: E.A. Seemann.

Upcott, William (1978) *A bibliographical account of the principal works relating to English topography.* Wakefield, England: EP Publishing.

Victoria history of the counties of England. (1900-) London: Constable, later volumes published by Oxford University Press.

Ware, Dora (1967) *A short dictionary of British architects*. London: Allen & Unwin.

Withey, Henry F. (1970) *Biographical dictionary of American architects (deceased)*. Facsimile edn. Los Angeles: Hennessey & Ingalls.

Wodehouse, Lawrence (1976) *American architects from the Civil War to the First World War: a guide to information sources*. Detroit: Gale Research.

Wodehouse, Lawrence (1977) *American architects from the First World War to the present*. Detroit: Gale Research.

Wodehouse, Lawrence (1978) *British architects, 1840-1976: a guide to information sources*. Detroit: Gale Research.

WorldCat. Dublin, Ohio: OCLC Online Computer Library.

Wren Society (1924-1943) *Catalogue of Sir Christopher Wren's drawings*. 20 vols. Oxford University.

Appendix A

Organizations and associations

This list contains details of all organizations and information providers to which reference is made in the text. It is by no means exhaustive. Not all organizations have fax, e-mail or internet addresses given, either because they do not possess them or such information has not been given to the editor. Although some of the details here have been checked by the editor, most have been entered as received from the contributors and the information is quoted in good faith. The directories discussed in earlier chapters will give current information on most of those listed below. Format is standardized as far as possible. Countries are named only where they are not necessarily well known, thus DC and NY in the USA and better known parts of Great Britain have no country name, but other states and a few lesser known locations in the UK do state the country. US and Canadian telephone numbers start with a three-digit number in brackets, for example, (123) and all others begin with the recognized country code for international dialling, for example, +44.

A Positive Approach Inc.
366 UN, New Bedford, MA 02740-
3667, USA
Tel: (508) 994 5866

AIA/ACSA Council on Architectural
Research
1735 New York Ave. NW
Washington, DC 20006
Tel: (202) 626 7300
Fax: (202) 626 7420
Air Infiltration and Ventilation Centre,
University of Warwick Science Park

Barclays Venture Centre
Sir William Lyons Road
Coventry CV4 7EZ
Tel: +44 1203 692050
Fax: +44 1203 416306

Aluminium Federation
Broadway House, Calthorpe Road
Five Ways, Birmingham B15 1TN
Tel: +44 121 456 1103
Fax: +44 121 456 2274/1897

Aluminium Window Association
Suites 323/324 Golden House
28–31 Great Poulteney Street,
London W1R 3DD
Tel: +44 171 494 4650
Fax: +44 171 287 9010
Fax: technical enquiries:
+44 121 4429 8460

American Architectural Manufacturers
Association
1540 E. Dundee Road, Suite 310
Palatine, IL 60067-8321, USA
Tel: (708) 202 1350
Fax: (708) 202 1480

American Automobile Association
811 Gatehouse Road, Rm 335
Falls Church, VA 22047 USA
Tel: (703) 222 6000

American Concrete Institute
PO Box 19150
22400 West Seven Mile Road
Detroit, MI 48219, USA
Tel: (313) 532 2600
Fax: (313) 538 0655

American Institute of Architects
1735 New York Ave. NW
Washington, DC 20006
Tel: (202) 626 7300
Fax: (202) 626 7420

American Institute of Certified Planners
1776 Massachusetts Ave. NW
Washington, DC 20036-1997
Tel: (202) 872 0611
Fax: (202) 872 0643

American Library Association
50 East Huron Street
Chicago IL 60611-2795, USA
Tel: (312) 944 6780
Fax: (312) 440 9374

American National Standards Institute
11 West 42nd St., 13th floor
New York, NY 10036
Tel: (212) 642 4900
Fax: (212) 398 0023

American Planning Association
1776 Massachusetts Ave. NW
Washington, DC 20036-1997
Tel: (202) 872 0611
Fax: (202) 872 0643

American Plywood Association
now APA Engineered Wood Products
Association

American Society for Photo- grammetry
& Remote Sensing
5410 Grosvenor Lane, Ste 210,
Bethesda, MD 20814-2160, USA
Tel: (301) 493 0290
Fax: (301) 493 0208

American Society of Heating,
Refrigerating and Air-Conditioning
Engineers
1791 Tullie Circle NE
Atlanta, Georgia 30329 – 2305
Tel: (404) 636 8400
Fax: (404) 321 5478

American Society of Interior Designers
608 Massachusetts Ave. NE
Washington, DC 20002
Tel: (202) 546 3480
Fax: (202) 546 3240
American Society of Landscape
Architects
4401 Connecticut Ave. NW,
5th floor,
Washington, DC 20008-2302
Tel: (202) 686 2752
Fax: (202) 686 1001

American Society of Mechanical
Engineers
345 E 47th St.
New York, NY 10017
Tel: (212) 705 7722
Fax: (212) 705 7674

American Society for Testing &
Materials
1916 Race St., Philadelphia, PA 19103-
1187, USA
Tel: (215) 299 5400
Fax: (215) 977 9679

Ancient Monuments Society
St. Ann's Vestry Hall, 2 Church Entry,
London EC4V 5HB
Tel: +44 171 236 3934

APA Engineered Wood Products
Association
65 London Wall,
London EC2M 5TU
Tel: +44 171 638 1414
Fax: +44 171 638 4545

Arboricultural Association
Ampfield House
Romsey, Hampshire SO51 9PA
Tel: +44 1794 368717
Fax: +44 1794 368978

Architectural Association
36 Bedford Square
London WC1B 3ES
Tel: +44 171 636 0974
Fax +44 171 414 0782
Architectural Cladding Association
60 Charles Street
Leicester LE1 1FB
Tel: +44 1162 536161
Fax: +44 1162 514568

ARLIS/NA Art Libraries Society of
North America
4101 Lake Boone Trail, Suite 201,
Raleigh, NC 27607 USA
Tel: (919) 787 5181,
(800) 89-ARLIS
Fax: (919) 787 4916
e-mail: pdepas@mercury.interpath.net

ARLIS/UK Art Libraries Society (United
Kingdom & Ireland)
c/o 18 College Rd., Bromsgrove, Worcs.
B60 2NE
Tel: +44 1527 579 298
Fax: +44 1527 579 298

Arup Geotechnic
Bede House, All Saints
Newcastle-upon-Tyne NEI 2EB
Tel: +44 191 261 6080

Asbestos Information Centre Ltd
St Andrews House, 22–28 High Street,
Epsom, Surrey KT19 8AH
Tel: +44 1372 742055

Aslib: The Association for Information
Management
20–24 Old Street, London
EC1V 9AP
Tel: +44 171 253 4488
Fax: +44 171 430 0514

Association of Builders' Hardware
Manufacturers
Heath Street, Tamworth
Staffordshire B79 7GH
Tel: 01827 52337
Fax: +44 1827 310827
Association for Computer Aided Design
Ltd
Suite 1002, 10th floor,
91 York Street,
Sydney, NSW, Australia

Association for Computing Machinery
(SIGGRAPH)
1515 Broadway, New York
NY 10036-5701
Tel: (212) 869 7440
Fax: (212) 944 13188

Association of Environmentally
Conscious Building
Windlake House, The Pump Field
Cooley, Gloucester
Tel: +44 1453 890757

Association of Facilities Managers
Now British Institute of Facilities
Management

Association Française de Normalisation
Tour Europe
92049 Paris La Defense Cedex
Tel: +33 1 42 91 55 55
Fax: +33 1 42 91 55 56

Association for Geographic Information
12 Great George Street
London SWIP 3AD
Tel: +44 171 222 7000 x 226
Fax: +44 171 334 3791

Association of Independent Information
Professionals
245 5th Ave., Suite 2103
New York, NY 10016
Tel: (212) 779 1855
Fax: (212) 481 3071

Association for Preservation Technology
International
904 Princess Anne Street,
PO Box 8178, Fredericksburg, Virginia
22404 USA
Tel: (703) 373 1621
Fax: (703) 373 6050

Association of Progressive
Communications
c/o greenNet
23, Bevenden Street,
London N1 6BH
Tel: +44 171 608 3040
Fax: +44 171 253 0801
e-mail: support@gn.apc.org

Association for Studies in the
Conservation of Historic Buildings
Institute of Archaeology
2 Morwell Street
London WC1B 3AR (no Tel:)

Automobile Association
Fanum House, Basingstoke
RG21 2EA
Tel: +44 1256 21023
Fax: +44 1256 493389

Avery Architectural and Fine Arts
Library
Columbia University
New York, New York 10027
Tel: (212) 854 3501
Fax: (212) 854 8904
email: giral@columbia.edu

Barbour Index Ltd
New Lodge
Drift Road
Windsor Sl4 4RQ
Tel: +44 1344 884121
Fax: +44 1344 884845

Bartholomew Times
now Harper Collins Cartographic

B H Blackwell Ltd.
Hythe Bridge Street,
Oxford OX1 2ET
Tel: +44 1865 261362
Fax: +44 865 791438

Brick Development Association
Woodside House,
Winkfield, Windsor,
Berkshire SL4 2DX
Tel: +44 1344 885651
Fax: +44 1344 890129

British Adhesives and Sealants
Association
33 Fellowes Way, Stevenage
Hertfordshire SG2 8BW
Tel: +44 1438 358514

British Aggregate Construction
Materials Industries
156 Buckingham Palace Road
London SW1W 9TR
Tel: +44 171 730 8194
Fax: +44 171 730 4355

British Architectural Library
Royal Institute of British Architects
66 Portland Place
London W1N 4AD
Tel: +44 171 580 5533
Fax: +44 171 631 1802

British Board of Agrément
PO Box 195,
Bucknalls Lane,
Garston, Watford,
Hertfordshire WD2 7NG
Tel: +44 1923 670844
Fax: +44 1923 662133

British Cartographical Society
13 Sheldrake Gardens, Hordle
Lymington, Hampshire SO41 0FJ
Tel: +44 1425 618679

British Cement Association
Telford Avenue
Crowthorne
Berkshire RG11 6YS
Tel: +44 1344 762676

British Coal, Property Division
Bretby Business Park,
Ashby Road
Burton-on-Trent, Staffordshire DE15
0YZ
Tel: +44 1283 554400

British Computer Society
PO Box 1454,
Station Road, Swindon,
Wiltshire SN1 1TG
Tel: +44 1793 480269
Fax: +44 1793 480270

British Constructional Steelwork
Association
4, Whitehall Court
London SW1A 2ES
Tel: +44 171 839 8566
Fax: +44 171 976 1634

British Earth Sheltering Association
Caer Llan Bern House,
Lydart, Monmouth,
Gwent NP5 4JJ
Tel: & Fax: +44 1600 850359

British Flat Roofing Council
38 Bridlesmith Gate
Nottingham NG1 2GQ
Tel: +44 1159 507733
Fax: +44 1159 504122

British Geological Survey
Information Systems Group
Keyworth,
Nottingham NG12 5GG
Tel: +44 115 936 3100
Fax: +44 115 936 3200

British Institute of Facilities
Management
67 High Street,
Saffron Walden,
Essex CB10 1AA
Tel: +44 1799 513371
Fax: +44 1799 51237

British Library, Document Supply Centre
Boston Spa,
Wetherby,
West Yorkshire LS23 7BQ
Tel: +44 1937 546060
Fax: +44 1937 546333

British Library Science Reference &
Information Service
25 Southampton Buildings
Chancery Lane
London WC2A 1AW
Tel: +44 171 323 7494/6
Fax: +44 171 323 7495

British Plastics Federation
6 Bath Place,
Rivington Street
London SW1X 8PD
Tel: +44 171 457 5000
Fax: +44 171 457 5038

British Precast Concrete Federation
60 Charles Street
Leicester LE1 1FB
Tel: +44 116 253 6161
Fax: +44 116 251 4568

British Reinforcement Manufacturers'
Association
Now: The Reinforcement Group of the
British Independent Steel Producers
Association which is now known as the
British Iron and Steel Producers
Association
5 Cromwell Road,
London SW7 2HX
Tel: +44 171 581 0281
Fax: +44 171 589 4009

British Ready Mixed Concrete
Association
The Bury, Church Street,
Chesham, Bucks. HP5 1JE
Tel: +44 1494 791050
Fax: +44 1494 791140

British Society of Master Glass Painters
6 Queen Square
London WC1N 2AR
Tel: +44 1322 67000 (evenings)

British Standards Institution
Linford Wood
Milton Keynes MK14 6LE
as of October 1994
BSI will be at
389 Chiswick High Road
London W4 4AJ
Tel: +44 181 996 7111
Fax: +44 181 996 7048

British Standards Institution
Technical Help for Exporters
See above

British Standards Society
39 Raglan Gardens, Oxhey
Watford, Hertfordshire WD1 4LJ
Tel: +44 1923 252361

British Steel Advisory Service
Sections (+44 1642 474111)
Plates (+44 1698 266233)
Tubes (+44 1536 404120)
Stainless steel (+44 1742 440060)

British Woodworking Federation
82 New Cavendish Street
London W1M 8AD
Tel: +44 171 580 5588
Fax: +44 171 436 5398

The Building Centre
26 Store Street
London WC1E 7BT
Tel: +44 171 637 1022
Fax: +44 171 580 9641

Building Cost Information Service
85–87 Clarence Street
Kingston-on-Thames, Surrey KT1 1RB
Tel: +44 181 546 7554
Fax: +44 181 547 1238

Building Law Information Subscriber
Service
James R Knowles Construction
Contracts Consultants
Wardour House, King Street
Knutsford, Cheshire WA16 6PD
Tel: +44 1565 654666
Fax: +44 1565 654990

Building Limes Forum
c/o Institute of Advanced Architectural
Studies

Building Materials Market Research
Baden House, 7 St Peter's Place
Brighton BN1 6TB
Tel: +44 273 680041/2
Fax: +44 273 606588
Building Project Information Committee
The Building Centre
26 Store Street,
London WC1E 7BT

Building Research Establishment
Garston, Watford
Hertfordshire WD2 7JR
Tel: +44 1923 894040
Fax: +44 1923 664010

The Building Services Research and
Information Association
Old Bracknell Lane West, Bracknell,
Berkshire RG12 7AH
Tel: +44 1344 426511
Fax: +44 1344 487575

Business Link network
c/o Regional Government office
or, Department of Trade and Industry
2, Marsham Street, London SW1
Tel: +44 171 276 3000

CADDETC (CAD/CAM Data Exchange
Technical Centre)
Arndale House, Headingley, Leeds LS6
2UU
Tel: +44 1132 305 005
Fax: +44 1132 304 488

Cambridgeshire County Council
Shire Hall, Castle Hill
Cambridge CB3 0AP
Tel: +44 1223 317111
Fax: +44 1223 317201

Cambridge Refrigeration Technology
140 Newmarket Road
Cambridge CB5 8HE
Tel: +44 1223 461352
Fax: +44 1223 461522
Canadian Conservation Institute
1030 Innes Road, Ottawa
Ontario K1A 0C8 Canada
Tel: (613) 998 3721
Fax: (613) 998 4721

Canadian Heritage Information Network
365 Laurier Avenue West,
12th Floor, Ottawa,
Ontario K1A 0C8 Canada
Tel: (613) 992 3333
Fax: (613) 952 2318

CARL Systems Inc.
Ste 200, 3801 E Florida Avenue
Denver CO 80210 USA
Tel: (303) 758 3030
Fax: (303) 758 5946

CCTA (Government Centre for
Information Systems)
156–161 Millbank, London SW1P 4RT
Tel: +44 171 217 3338
Fax: +44 171 217 3449

Cement and Concrete Association
now the BCA

Centre for Accessible Environments
60 Gainsford Street
London SE1P 3NY
Tel: +44 171 357 8182
Fax: +44 171 357 8183
Formerly Centre on the Environ-ment for
the Handicapped

Centre for Alternative Technology
Llangwern Quarry
Machynlleth, Powys SY20 9AZ
Tel: +44 1654 702400
Fax: +44 1654 702782

Centre for the Conservation of Historic
Parks and Gardens
see Institute of Advanced Architectural
Studies

Centre for Facilities Management
Strathclyde Graduate Business School,
University of Strathclyde
199 Cathedral Street,
Glasgow G4 0QU
Tel: +44 141 553 4165
Fax: +44 141 552 7299

Centre for Window and Cladding
Technology
University of Bath,
Claverton Down, Bath BA2 7AY
Tel: +44 1225 826541
Fax: +44 1225 826556

Chartered Institute of Building
Englemere, Kings Ride
Ascot, Berkshire SL5 8BJ
Tel: +44 1344 23355
Fax: +44 1344 23467

Chartered Institution of Building
Services Engineers
Delta House,
222 Balham High Road
London SW12 9BS
Tel: +44 181 675 5211
Fax: +44 181 675 5449

Chartered Institute of Public Finance and
Accountancy
3 Robert Street,
London WC2N 6BH
Tel: +44 171 895 8823
Fax: +44 171 895 8825

Chas E. Goad
Salisbury Square, Old Hatfield
Hertfordshire AL9 5BJ
Tel: +44 1707 271171
CIM Institute (Computer Integrated
Manufacturing Institute)
Cranfield Institute of Technology,
Cranfield, Bedfordshire
MK43 0AL
Tel: +44 1234 754073
Fax: +44 1234 750852

City Business Library
1 Brewers Hall Gardens
London EC2V 5BX
Tel: +44 171 638 8215
Fax: +44 171 260 1847

Civic Trust
17 Carlton House Terrace
London SW1Y 5AW
Tel: +44 171 930 0914
Fax: +44 171 321 0180

Clay Roofing Tile Council
Federation House,
Station Road,
Stoke on Trent,
Staffordshire ST4 2SA
Tel: +44 1782 744631
Fax: +44 1782 744102

Colleges of Further and Higher
Education group of the UK Library
Association
c/o Library Association
7, Ridgmount Street
London WC1E 7AE
Tel: +44 171 636 7543
Fax: +44 171 436 7218

Comité Européen de Normalisation
Secrétariat Central,
rue de Stassart 36
B-1050 Bruxelles
Tel: +32 2 519 68 11
Fax: +32 2 519 68 19
Commission of the European
Communities
200 rue de la Loi
1049 Brussels, Belgium
Tel: +32 2 235 11 11
Fax: +32 2 235 01 22/23/24
Telex 21877

Commission for Local Democracy
200–208 Tottenham Court Road
London W1P 9LA
Tel: +44 171 323 4770
Fax: +44 171 637 3530

Computer Graphics Suppliers
Association
8 Canalside, Lowesmoor Wharf
Worcester WR1 2RR
Tel: +44 1905 613 236
Fax: +44 1905 291 38

Concrete Society
Framewood Road,
Wexham Springs, Slough, Berkshire SL3
6PJ
Tel: +44 1753 662226
Fax: +44 1753 662126
Concrete Advisory Service
(subsidiary of Concrete Society)
Tel: +44 1443 23721

Conseil International du Batiment pour
la Recherche, l'Etude, et la
Documentation (CIB)
Kruisplein 25, Postbus 1837
NL – 3014 DB Rotterdam, Netherlands
Tel: +31 10 411 0240
Fax: +31 10 433 4372

Construction Industry Computing
Association
Guildhall Place,
Cambridge CB2 3QQ
Tel: +44 1223 311246
Fax: +44 1223 62865

Construction Fixings Association
a group of the Federation of British
Hand Tool Manufacturers
Light Trades House, 3 Melbourne
Avenue, Sheffield S10 2QJ
Tel: +44 114 266 3084
Fax: +44 114 267 0910

Construction Industry Information
Group
26 Store Street,
London WC1E 7BT
Postal enquiries only

Construction Industry Research and
Information Association
6 Storey's Gate, Westminster
London SW1P 3AU
Tel: +44 171 222 8891
Fax: +44 171 222 1708

Construction Specifications Institute
601 Madison St.
Alexandria,
VA 22314-1791
Tel: (703) 684 0300
Fax: (703) 684 0465

Cooperative Network for Building
Researchers
c/o Peter Edwards
Department of Building & Construction
Economics
Royal Melbourne Institute of
Technology
GPO Box 2476V,
Melbourne 3001, Victoria, Australia
Tel: +61 3 660 3478
Fax: +61 3 663 2891
email: edwards@rmit.edu.au
email address for list:
cnbr-l@kanga.edc.rmit.edu.au

Copper Development Association
Orchard House, Mutton Lane
Potters Bar,
Hertfordshire EN6 3AP
Tel: +44 1707 650711
Fax: +44 1707 642769

Copper Roofing Advisory Service see
CDA

Council of Forest Industries of British
Columbia
131–3 Upper Richmond Road
Putney, London SW15 2TR
Tel: +44 181 788 4446

Council for British Archaeology
Bowes Morrell House
11 Walmgate, York YO1 2UA
Tel: +44 1904 671417
Fax: +44 1904 671384

Council for the Care of Churches
83 London Wall
London EC2M 5NA
Tel: +44 171 638 0971/2
Fax: +44 171 638 0164

Council of Europe, Division for Cultural
Heritage
BP 431 R6, 67006 Strasbourg Cedex,
France
Tel: +43 88 41 20 00
Fax: +43 88 41 27 88
Telex 870943 F

Council on Tall Buildings and Urban
Habitat
Lehigh University, Fritz Engineering
Laboratory,
13 Packer Avenue, Bethlehem, PA 18015
Tel: (215) 758 3515
Fax: (215) 758 4522

Countryside Commission
John Dower House,
Crescent Place, Cheltenham,
Gloucestershire GL50 3RA.
Tel: +44 1242 521381
Fax: +44 1242 584270.

The Data Consultancy
7 Southern Court South Street
Reading RG1 4QS
Tel: +44 1734 588181

Data-star DIALOG Europe
Haymarket House, 1 Oxendon Street,
London SW1Y 4EE
Tel: +44 171 930 7646
Fax: +44 171 930 2581

Defense Mapping Agency
Office of Distribution Services, Attn.
DOA.
Washington, DC 20315-0010

Department of Energy (DOE)
1000 Independence Ave. SW
Washington, DC 20585
Tel: (202) 586 5000

Department of the
Environment (DoE)
2 Marsham St.
London SW1P 3EB
Tel: +44 171 276 3000
Fax: +44 171 276 0818
Telex: 22221

Department of the
Environment (DoE)
Map and Air Photograph Library (as
above)

Department of National Heritage
2–4 Cockspur Street
London SW1Y 5DH
Tel: +44 171 211 6043

Design Access
National Building Museum
401 F St. NW, Suite 322
Washington, DC 20001
Tel: (202) 272 5427
Fax: (202) 272 5432

Design Council
The Design Centre,
28 Haymarket
London SW1Y 4SU
Tel: +44 171 839 8000
Fax: +44 171 925 2130

Direccion General de Geografia del
Territorio Nacional
San Antonio Abad No. 124, Mexico 8,
DF

Dun and Bradstreet International
Holmers Farm Way,
High Wycombe
Buckinghamshire HP12 4UL
Tel: +44 1494 422000
Fax: +44 1494 422260

Earth Resources Observation Systems,
Data Center
EROS Building, Sioux Falls,
SD 57198 USA
Tel: (605) 594 6123,
(800) USA-MAPS
Fax: (605) 594 6589

ECHO
PO Box 2373, L-1023 Luxembourg
Tel: +352 34 98 1200
Fax: +352 34 98 1234

EDICON
PO Box 111, Aldershot
Hampshire GU11 1YW
Tel: +44 1252 336318
Fax: +44 1252 333901

Ecclesiastical Architects and Surveyors
Association
(Group of RIBA)
Scan House, 29 Radnor Cliff
Folkestone,
Kent CT20 2JJ
No Tel:

Ecological Design Association
Stroud, Gloucestershire
Tel: +44 1453 765575
Fax: +44 1453 752987

Energy Efficiency Office
Dept of the Environment
2 Marsham Street,
London SW1B 3EB
Tel: +44 171 276 3000
Fax: +44 171 276 3746

Energy Technology Support Unit
Harwell Laboratory
Didcot, Oxon OX11 ORA
Tel: +44 1235 821000
Fax: +44 1235 432923
Helpdesk on renewable energy, Tel: +44
1235 433601
on energy efficiency, Tel: +44 1235
436747

English Heritage
Historic Buildings and Monuments
Commission
for England
Fortress House
Saville Row, London W1X 2HE
Tel: +44 171 973 3000
Fax +44 171 973 3001
Telex 892091 HBMCFHG

English Nature
Northminster House
Peterborough PE1 1UA
Tel: +44 1733 340345
Fax: +44 1733 68834

The Environment Council
80 York Way, London N1 9AG
Tel: +44 171 278 4736.

Environmental Design Research
Association
PO Box 24083, Oklahoma City, OK
73124
Tel: (405) 843 4863

Environmental Protection Agency
401 M St. SW
Washington, DC 20460
Tel: (202) 260 2090
Internet address: URL: gopher://
gopher.epa.gov:70/11

Ergonomics Information Analysis Centre
University of Birmingham
School of Manufacturing and
Mechanical Engineering
Edgbaston,
Birmingham B15 2TT
Tel: +44 121 414 4239
Fax: +44 121 414 3476

Ergonomics Society
Devonshire House,
Devonshire Square
Loughborough,
Leics LE11 3DN
Tel: +44 1509 234904
Fax: +44 1509 234904

ESA/IRS c/o IRS-Dialtech
The British Library,
Science Reference and Information
Service
25 Southampton Buildings, Chancery
Lane
London WC2A 1AW
Tel: +44 171 323 7951/7946
Fax: +44 171 323 7954

ESRC Data Archive
University of Essex,
Wivenhoe Park
Colchester, Essex CO4 3SQ
Tel: +44 1206 872001
Fax: +44 1206 872003

European Computer Manufacturers
Association
Rue de Rhone 114
Geneva,
Switzerland CH-1024
Tel: +41 22 35 3 634
Fax: +41 22 86 5 231

European Environment Agency
Rue de la Loi 200
1049 Brussels, Belgium
Tel: +32 2 236 8815

European Foundation for the
Improvement of Living and Working
Conditions
Loughlinstown House
Shankill, Co. Dublin, Ireland
Tel: +353 1 826888

Founded by EC regulation in 1975
European Foundation for Landscape
Architecture
Avenue Brugmann 52
060 Brussels, Belgium

Eurostat
Batiment Jean Monnet B3/105
LUXEMBOURG L -2920
Tel: +352 4301 33088

European Organisation for Technical
Approvals
rue du Trone 12,
Troonstraat, B-1050 Brussels
Tel: +32 2 502.69.00
Fax: +32 2 502.38.14
European Union of Agrément
Centre Scientifique et Technique du
Bâtiment
4 avenue du Recteur-Poincaré, 75782
Paris,
Cedex 16
Tel: +33 (1) 40 50 28 28
Fax: +33 (1) 45 25 61 51

Federation of Environmental Trade
Associations
Sterling House,
6 Furlong Road,
Bourne End,
Buckinghamshire SL8 5DG
Tel: +44 1628 531186/7
Fax: +44 1628 810423

Fire Information Group
c/o London Fire and Civil Defence
Authority
Albert Embankment,
London SE1 7SD
Tel: +44 171 587 6340

Fire Protection Association
140 Aldersgate Street
London EC1A 4HX
Tel: +44 171 606 3757
Fax: +44 171 600 1487

Fire Research Station
Garston,
Watford
Hertfordshire WD2 7JR
Tel: +44 1923 894040
Fax: +44 1923 664050

Forestry Commission
231 Corstorphine Road, Edinburgh
EH12 7AT
Tel: +44 131 334 0303.

Forest Forever
c/o TTF (qv)
Friends of the Earth
26–28 Underwood Street
London N1 7JQ
Tel: +44 171 490 1555
Fax: +44 171 490 0881

General Register Office for Scotland
Ladywell House,
Ladywell Rd
Edinburgh EH12 7TF
Tel: +44 131 334 0380

Geological Survey of Canada
Energy, Mines and Resources, 601 Booth
St.
Ottawa,
Ontario K1A 0H3,
Canada

Georgian Group
37 Spital Square
London E1 6DY
Tel: +44 171 377 1722
Fax: +44 171 247 3441

Getty Art History Information Program
401 Wilshire Boulevard,
Suite 1100, Santa Monica, California
90401-1455 USA
Tel: (310) 395 1025
Fax: (310) 451 5570

GisDATA
262, Regents Park Rd
London N3 3HN
Tel: +44 181 343 2573

Glass and Glazing Federation
44–48 Borough High Street
London SE1 1XB
Tel: +44 171 403 7177
Fax: +44 171 357 7458

Garden History Society
5 The Knoll
Hereford HR1 1RU
Tel: +44 1432 354479
No fax

Getty Conservation Institute
4503 Glencoe Avenue
Marina del Rey,
California 90292-6357
Tel: (310) 822 2299
Fax (310) 821 9409

Government Printing Office
North Capitol and H Streets, NW
Washington, DC 20401 USA
Tel: (202) 512 0000
or
Superintendent of Documents,
Government Printing Office
Washington, DC 20402 USA
Tel: (202) 783 3238

GreenNet
See Association for Progressive
Communications

Guild of Architectural Ironmongery
8 Stepney Green, London E1 3JU
Tel: +44 171 790 3431
Fax: +44 171 790 8517

Harper Collins Cartographic
PO Box Glasgow G4 0NB
Tel: +44 141 772 3200
Fax: +44 141 762 0451

Health and Safety Executive
Baynards House Chepstow Place
London W2 4TF
Tel: +44 171 7176090
Also, at six other major UK cities.

Heating and Ventilating Contractors
Association
ESCA House, 34 Palace Court
London W2 4JG
Tel: +44 171 229 2488
Fax: +44 171 727 9268

HEVAC Association
Sterling House
6 Furlong Road
Bourne End
Buckinghamshire SL8 5DG
Tel: +44 16285 31186/7
Fax: +44 1628 810423

Highways Agency
Jefferson House
27 Park Place,
Leeds LS1 2SZ
Tel: +44 1132 541141
Fax: +44 1132 541005

HM Land Registry
Lincoln's Inn Fields
London WC pH
Tel: +44 171 917 8888
Fax: +44 171955 0110

Industrial Society
Quadrant Court,
49 Calthorpe Road
Edgbaston,
Birmingham B15 1TH
Tel: +44 121 454 6769
Fax: +44 121 456 2715
London office
Tel: +44 171 262 2401

Industry Committee for Emergency
Lighting Ltd
Swan House,
207 Balham High Road,
London SW17 7BQ
Tel: +44 181 675 5432
Fax: +44 181 673 5880

Infonorme London Information
Index House, Ascot,
Berkshire SL5 7EU
Tel: + 44 1344 874343
Fax: + 44 1344 291194

Information Handling Service Inc.
15 Inverness Way East,
PO Box 1154,
Englewood, CO 80150-1154, USA
Tel: (800) 241 7824
Fax: (303) 397 2599

Institute for Research in Construction of
the National
Research Council of Canada
Montreal Road, Ottawa,
Ontario K1A OR6
Tel: (613) 991 5917
Fax: (613) 952 7671

Institute of Advanced Architectural
Studies
University of York
King's Manor,
York YO1 2EP
Tel: +44 1904 433966
Fax +44 1904 433949

Institute of Civil Engineering Surveyors
26 Market Street,
Altrincham
Cheshire WA14 1PF
Tel: +44 161 928 8074
Fax: +44 161 841 6134

Institute of Consumer Ergonomics
75, Swingbridge Road
Loughborough,
Leics LE11 OJB
Tel: +44 1509 236161
Fax: +44 1509 610725

Institute of Energy
18 Devonshire Street
London W1N 2AU
Tel: +44 171 580 7124
Fax: +44 171 580 4420

Institute of Environmental Assessment
Fen Road, East Kirkby
Lincolnshire PE23 4DB
Tel: +44 1790 763613
Fax: +44 1790 763630

Institute of Gas Technology
3424 S State, Chicago, Illinois
Tel: (312) 949 3810
Fax: (312) 949 3776

Institute of Geological Sciences
renamed British Geological Survey,
London Information Office
Natural History Museum Earth Galleries
Exhibition Road,
South Kensington,
London SW7 2DE
Tel: +44 171 589 4090
Fax: +44 171 584 8270

Institute of Grocery Distribution
Letchmore Heath
Watford WD2 8DQ
Tel: +44 1923 857141
Fax: +44 1923 852531

Institute of Hydrology (a unit of
Natural Environment Research Council)
Maclean Building,
Crowmarsh Gifford
Wallingford,
Oxfordshire OX10 8BB
Tel: +44 1491 838800
No fax

Institute of Information Scientists
44 Museum Street
London WC1A 1LY
Tel: +44 171 831 8003
Fax: +44 171 430 1270

Institute of Management
Management House,
Cottingham Road
Corby, Northants NN17 1TT
Tel: +44 1536 204222
Fax: +44 1536 201651

Institute of Plumbing
64 Station Lane, Hornchurch
Essex RM12 6NB
Tel: +44 1708 472791
Fax: +44 1708 448987

Institute for Scientific Information,
European Branch
Brunel University,
Uxbridge UB8 3PQ
Tel: +44 895 270016
Fax: +44 895 256710

Institute of Sport and Recreation
Planning and Management
University of Technology,
Ashby Road, Loughborough,
Leics LE11 3TU
Tel: +44 1509 263171 or 223289
Fax: +44 1509 231776

Institute of Terrestrial Ecology
Environmental Information Centre
Monks Wood, Abbots Ripton
Huntingdon,
Cambridgeshire PE17 2LS
Tel: +44 1487 773 381
and
Merlewood Research Station
Grange-over-Sands
Cumbria LA11 6JU
Tel: +44 15395 32264

Institution of Civil Engineers
1 Great George Street
London SW1P 3AA
Tel: +44 171 222 7722
Fax: +44 171 222 7500

Institution of Electrical
Engineers
Savoy Place,
London WC2R 0BL
Tel: +44 171 240 1871
Fax: +44 171 240 7735

Institution of Electrical & Electronics
Engineers
345 East 47th Street
New York 10017
Tel: (212) 705 7900

IEEE Computer Society
1730 Massachusetts Avenue NW
Washington DC 20036
Tel: (202) 371 0101
or
10662 Los Vaqueros Circle,
PO Box 3014,
Los Alamitos,
CA 90720-1264 USA

Institution of Fire Safety (membership
body of
Federation of British Fire Organisations)
12 Ranmore Avenue
Croydon CR0 5QA
Tel: +44 181 654 2582
Fax: +44 181 654 2583

Institution of Structural Engineers
11 Upper Belgrave Street
London SW1X 8BH
Tel: +44 171 235 4535
Fax: +44 171 235 4294

International Centre for the Study of the
Preservation and Restoration of Cultural
Property
13 via di San Micheli
00153 Rome, Italy
Tel: +39 6 587265
Fax +39 6 5884265
Telex: 613.114

International Conference of Building
Officials
5360 S. Workman Mill Road
Whittier,
CA 90601 USA
Tel: (213) 699 0541
Fax: (213) 692 3853

International Council of Museums
UNESCO House,
1 rue Miollis
75732 Paris
Cedex 15, France
Tel: +33 1 47 34 05 00
Fax +33 1 43 06 78 62
Telex: UNESCO 270 602 /
204 461

International Council on Monuments and
Sites
75 rue du Temple
75003 Paris, France
Tel: +33 42 77 35 76
Fax +33 42 77 57 42
Telex: 249018 Trace F ref.617

IFLA International Federation of
Landscape Architects
4 rue Hardy,
78009 Versailles-Cedex,
France
Tel: +33 30 21 13 15
Fax: +33 39 53 53 16

International Federation of Library
Associations
c/o British Library Document Supply
Centre
Boston Spa, Wetherby
West Yorkshire LS23 7BQ
Tel: +44 1937 546123 / 843434
Fax: +44 1937 546236
&
c/o Postbus 95312, NL 2509 CH The
Hague
The Netherlands
Tel: +31 70 314 0884
Fax: +31 70 383 4827

International Institute for the
Conservation of Historic and Artistic
Works
6 Buckingham Street
London WC2N 6BA
Tel: +44 171 839 5975
Fax +44 171 976 1564

International Institute of Refrigeration
177, Boulevard Malesherbes
75017 Paris, France
Tel: +33 (1) 42 27 32 35
Fax: +33 (1) 47 63 17 98

International Society of Interior
Designers
433 S. Spring St., 10th floor
Los Angeles, CA 90013
Tel: (213) 680 4240
Fax: (213) 680 7704

International Standards Organisation
Central Secretariat, 1 rue de Varembé,
Case postale 56
CH-1211 Genève 20, Switzerland
Tel: +41 22 749 01 11
Fax: +41 22 733 34 30

International Union of Architects
51, rue Raynouard
F-75016 Paris, France
Tel: +33 (1) 45 24 36 88
Fax: +33 (1) 45 24 02 78
UK Section c/o RIBA

Kingswood
449 Chiswick High Road
London W4 4AU
Tel: +44 181 994 5404

Landscape Design Trust
13a West Street, Reigate
Surrey RH2 9BL
Tel: +44 1737 221162
Fax: +44 1737 224206.

Landscape Institute
6/7 Barnards Mews
London SW11 1QV
Tel: +44 171 738 9166
Library +44 171 978 5037.
no fax

Lawrence Berkeley Laboratory
US Department of Energy
University of California
Berkeley, CA 94720 USA
Tel: (510) 486 5771
Internet address: URL: http://
www.lbl.gov

Lead Development Association
42–46 Weymouth Street
London W1N 3LQ
Tel: +44 171 499 8422
Fax: +44 171 493 1555

Lead Sheet Association
St John's Road, Tunbridge Wells
Kent TN4 9XA
Tel: +44 1892 513351
Fax: +44 1892 535028

Library Association
7 Ridgmount Street
London WC1E 7AE
Tel: +44 171 636 7543

Library Association Industrial &
Commercial Information Group
c/o Chair: Jackie Berry
Bacon & Woodrow
Parkside House,
Ashley Road, Epsom,
Surrey KT18 5BS
Tel: +44 1372 733897
Fax: +44 1372 733991

Library Information Technology Centre
South Bank Tecnopark
90 London Road,
London SE1 6LN
Tel: +44 171 815 7872
Fax: +44 171 815 6699

Lighting Industry Federation
Swan House,
207 Balham High Road,
London SW17 7BQ
Tel: +44 181 675 5432
Fax: +44 181 673 5880

Liverpool University,
Department of Civic Design
PO Box 147
Liverpool L69 3BX
Tel: +44 151 794 3128/3112
Fax +44 151 708 6502
Telex: 627095 UNILPL G

London Research Centre, Research
Library
81 Black Prince Road,
London SE1 7SZ
Tel: +44 171 627 9661
Fax: +44 171 627 9674

Longman GeoInformation
now GeoInformation International
307 Cambridge Science Park
Milton Road, Cambridge CB4 4ZD
Tel: +44 223 423020
Fax: +44 223425787

Loss Prevention Council
140 Aldersgate Street
London EC1A 4HY
Tel: +44 171 606 1050
Fax: +44 171 600 1487

Macaulay Land Use Research Institute
Resource Consultancy Unit
Craigiebuckler,
Aberdeen AB9 2QJ
Tel: +44 224 318611
Fax: +44 224 311556

Martin Centre for Architectural and
Urban Studies
University of Cambridge
School of Architecture Cambridge CB2
1TN
Tel: +44 223 337733
Fax: +44 223 332983

Mastic Asphalt Council and Employers
Federation and
Mastic Asphalt Technical Advisory
Service
Lesley House, 6–8 Broadway
Bexleyheath, Kent DA6 7LE
Tel: +44 181 298 0411
MATAC: +44 181 298 0414
Fax: +44 181 298 0381

Metal Cladding and Roofing
Manufacturers Association
18 Mere Farm Road, Noctorum
Birkenhead, Merseyside L43 9TT
Tel: +44 151 652 3846
Fax: +44 151 653 4080
Meteorological Office
London Road, Bracknell
Berkshire RG12 2SZ
Tel: +44 1344 420242
Fax: +44 1344 854412

Ministry of Agriculture,
Fisheries and Food
Whitehall Place,
London SW1A 2HH
Tel: +44 171 270 8080.
Fax: +44 171 270 8125

MR Data Graphics
Dukes Way,
Teeside Industrial Estate
Thornaby, Cleveland TS17 9LT
Tel: +44 1483 575312
Multimedia Special Interest Group
c/o N. Sandford, MM-SIG
Co-ordinator,
The Old Office Block,
Elmtree Road
Middlesex TW11 8ST

Museums and Galleries Commission.
Conservation Unit
16 Queen Anne's Gate
London SW1H 9AA
Tel: +44 171 233 3683
Fax +44 171 233 3686

National Association for Aerial
Photographic Libraries
Information House,
20–24 Old Street
London EC1V 9AP
Tel: +44 171 253 4488
Fax: +44 171 430 0514

National Building Specification
NBS Services
Mansion House Chambers
The Close,
Newcastle upon Tyne NE1 3RE
Tel: +44 191 232 9594
Fax: +44 191 232 5714

National Cartographic Information
Center
US Geological Survey, 507 National
Center
Reston, VA 22092
Tel: (703) 860 6045

National Computing Centre
Oxford House, Oxford Road
Manchester M1 7ED
Tel: +44 161 228 6333
Fax: +44 161 236 8049

National Contractors Group
82 New Cavendish Street
London W1M 8AD
Tel: +44 171 580 5588
Fax: +44 171 631 3872

National Engineering Specification Ltd
Southgate Chambers
37/39 Southgate Street
Winchester SO23 9EH
Tel: +44 1962 842058
Fax: +44 1962 868982

National Environmental Technology
Centre
Air Quality Section,
Culham Laboratory, Abingdon,
Oxfordshire OX14 3DB
Tel: +44 235 463040
Fax: +44 235 463005

National Federation of Demolition
Contractors
1a New Road, The Causeway
Staines, Middlesex TW18 3DH
Tel: +44 1784 456799
Fax: +44 1784 461118

National Federation of Roofing
Contractors
24 Weymouth Street
London W1N 3FA
Tel: +44 171 436 0387
Fax: +44 171 637 5215

National Geographic Society
17th & M Streets NW, Washington DC
20036
Tel: (202) 857 7000
Fax: (202) 775 6141

National House Building Council
Chiltern Avenue,
Amersham
Buckinghamshire HP6 5AP
Tel: +44 1494 434477
Fax: +44 1494 728521

National Institute of Standards and
Technology
Department of Commerce
Route I-270 & Quince Orchard R
Gaithersburg,
MD 20899 USA
Tel: (301) 975 3058
Fax: (301) 869 6787
Internet address: URL: gopher://
zserve.nist.gov

National League of the
Blind and Disabled
2 Tenterden Road,
London N17 8BE
Tel: +44 181 808 6030
Fax: +44 885 3235

National Oceanic and Atmospheric
Administration
US Dept. of Commerce, Washington, DC
20230 USA
Tel: (202) 482 2985
Fax: (202) 482 6203

National Park Service, Office of Public
Affairs
Department of the Interior,
PO Box 37127
Washington, DC 20013-7127
Tel: (202) 208 6843
Fax: (202) 219 0916

National Playing Fields Association
25 Ovington Square
London SW3 1LQ
Tel: +44 171 584 6445
Fax: +44 171 581 2402

National Remote Sensing Centre now
NRSC Ltd
Delta House,
Southwood Crescent
Southwood, Farnborough
Hampshire GU14 0NL
Tel: +44 1252 541464
Fax: +44 1252 375016

National Rivers Authority
Kingfisher House, Goldhay Way
Autumn Gold Hay
Peterborough PE2 52P
Tel: +44 1733 371811
Fax: +44 1733 231840

Natural Slate Quarries Association
26 Store Street,
London WC1E 7BT
Tel: +44 171 323 3770
Fax: +44 171 323 0307

National Society of Professional
Engineers
1420 King Street
Alexandria, VA 22314-2715
Tel: (703) 684 2800
Fax: (703) 836 4875

National Technical Information Service
5285 Port Royal Road
Springfield,
VA 22161 USA
Tel: (703) 487 4604
Fax: (703) 321 8547

National Trust
36 Queen Anne's Gate
London SW1H 9AS
Tel: +44 171 222 9251
Fax +44 171 222 5097

National Trust for Historic Preservation
1785 Massachusetts Avenue, NW.
Washington, DC 20036
Tel: (202) 673 4000
Fax: (202) 673 4058

Natural Environment Research Council
Polaris House,
North Star Avenue
Swindon SN2 IEU
Tel: +44 1793 411500
Fax: +44 1793 411501

Newcomen Society for the Study of the
History of Engineering
and Technology
c/o The Science Museum
London SW7 2DD
Tel: +44 171 589 1793
Fax: +44 171 589 1793

NHS Estates
Department of Health
1 Trevelyan Square
Boar Lane,
Leeds LS1 6AE
Tel: +44 1532 547000
Fax: +44 1532 547299

Nordic Timber Council
17 Exchange Street, Retford
Nottinghamshire DN22 6BL
Tel: +44 1777 716616
no fax

OCLC Europe
7th Floor, Tricorn House
51–53 Hagley Road
Birmingham B16 8TP
Tel: +44 121 456 4656
Fax: +44 121 456 4680

OCLC Online Computer
Library Inc.
6565 Frantz Road, Dublin
Ohio 43017-3395, USA
Tel: (614) 764 6000

Office of Population Censuses &
Surveys
10 Kingsway, London WC2B 6JP
Tel: +44 171 242 0262
Fax: +44 171 242 2167

On Demand Information
8 Gemini Park,
Sheepscar Way,
Leeds LS7 3JB
Tel: +44 1132 469611
Fax: +44 1132 448796

Ordnance Survey (GB)
Romsey Road, Maybush
Southampton SO9 4DH
Tel: +44 1703 792773
Fax: +44 1703 792452

Ordnance Survey (Northern Ireland)
Colby House,
Stanmillis House
Belfast BT9 5BJ
Tel: +44 1232 661244

Paintmakers Association of Great Britain
Ltd
now part of British Coatings Federation
Alembic House,
93 Albert Embankment
London SE1 7TY
Tel: +44 171 582 1185
Fax: +44 171 735 0616

Paint Research Association
8 Waldegrave Road, Teddington
Middlesex TW11 8LD
Tel: +44 181 977 4427
Fax: +44 181 943 4705

Parks Canada
Jules Leger Building – TLC
25 Eddy Street, Hull
Quebec K1A 0H3, Canada
Tel: (819).994.2231
Fax (819) 953 4909

Plastics Window Association Ltd
2 Everglade Road, Priorslee Park
Telford, Shropshire TF2 9QS
Tel: +44 1952 613965

Powerdoc Systems Ltd (FIDIC)
37 Broomleaf Road
Farnham, Hampshire GU9 8DG

Property Information Group
c/o Secretary, David Robbins
Gerald Eve, 7 Vere Street
London W1M 0JB
Tel: +44 171 333 6359
Fax: +44 171 491 1825

Property Intelligence
Ingram House
13–15 John Adam Street
London WC2N 6LD
Tel: +44 171 839 7684
Fax: +44 171 839 1060
Property Services Agency (PSA)
PSA Projects now TBV Consult

Questel-Orbit
18 Parkshot,
Richmond on Thames TW9 2RG
Tel: +44 181 332 7888
Fax: +44 181 332 7449

Rendel Geotechnics
58–72 John Bright Street
Birmingham B1 1BN
Tel: +44 121 627 1777
Fax: +44 121 627 1778

Research Libraries Group, Inc.
1200 Villa St., Mountain View
California 94041-1100 USA
Tel: (800) 537 7546
Fax: (415) 964 0943

Roofing Tile Association
60 Charles Street
Leicester LE1 1FB
Tel: +44 1162 536161
Fax: +44 1162 514568

Royal Architectural Institute of Canada
55 Murray St., Suite 330
Ottawa, Ontario, K1N 5M3
Tel: (613) 241 3600
Fax: (613) 241 5750

Royal Commission on the His-torical
Monuments of England and National
Monuments Record
National Monuments
Record Centre,
Kemble Drive,
Swindon SN2 2GZ
Tel: +44 1793 414700 (RCHME)
Fax: +44 1793 414707 (RCHME)
Tel: +44 1793 414600 (NMR)
Fax: +44 1793 414606 (NMR)
Royal Institute of British Architects
(RIBA)
66 Portland Place
London W1N 4AD
Tel: +44 171 580 5533
Fax: +44 171 255 1541

RIBA Publications Ltd
39 Moreland Street
London EC1V 8BB

Royal Institution of Chartered Surveyors
12 Great George St
London SW1P 3AD
Tel: +44 171 222 7000
Fax: +44 171 222 9430

Royal Town Planning Institute
26 Portland Place
London W1N 4BE
Tel: +44 171 636 9107
Fax: +44 171 323 1582

Rubber & Plastics Research Association
now RAPRA Technology
Shawbury, Shrewsbury Shropshire SY4
4NR
Tel: +44 01939 250383
Fax: +44 01939 251118

Rural Development Commission
141 Castle Street, Salisbury
Wiltshire SP1 3TP
Tel: +44 1722 336255
Fax: +44 1722 332769

School of Leisure and Food Management
Sheffield Hallam University
Pond Street,
Sheffield
Tel: +44 742 720 911
Fax: +44 742 533343

Secretaria de Programacion y
Presupuesto
Direccion General de Geografia del
Territorio Nacional
San Antonio Abad No. 124, Mexico 8,
D.F.

Single-Ply Roofing Association
36 Bridlesmith Gate
Nottingham NG1 2GQ
Tel: +44 115 924 0499
Fax: +44 115 950 4122

Smithsonian Institution Conservation
Analysis Laboratory
4210 Silverhill
Suitland, MD 20746 USA
Tel: (301) 238 3712
Fax: (301) 238 3709

Society of Architectural Historians
1232 Pine Street
Philadelphia, PA 19107 USA
Tel: 215 735 0224
Fax: 215 735 2590

Society of Architectural Historians of
Great Britain
23b Home Park Road,
London SW19 7HP
Tel: +44 181 946 4445

Society for the Protection of Ancient
Buildings
37 Spital Square, London E1 6DY
Tel: +44 171 377 1644
Fax: +44 171 247 5296

Society of Motor Manufacturers and
Traders
Forbes House, Halkin Street
London SW1X 7DS
Tel: +44 171 235 7000
Fax: +44 171 235 7112
Soil Survey and Land
Research Centre
Cranfield University,
Silsoe Campus
Silsoe, Bedford MK45 4DT
Tel: +44 1525 860428
Fax: +44 1525 8611147

Southern Pine Council & Western Wood
Products Association
Regent Arcade House,
19–25 Argyll Street
65 London Wall,
London EC2M 5TU
Tel: +44 171 638 1234
Fax: +44 171 588 8855

Sports Council
16, Upper Woburn Place
London WC1H
Tel: +44 171 388 1277
Fax: +44 171 383 5740

Steel Construction Institute
Silwood Park, Ascot
Berkshire SL5 7QN
Tel: +44 1344 23345
Fax: +44 1344 22944 or 872775

Steel Window Association
c/o Building Centre
26 Store Street,
London WC1E 7BT
Tel: +44 171 637 3571
Fax: +44 171 637 3572

STN International
(The Scientific and Technical
Information Network)
Postfach 2465.
76012 Karlsruhe,
Germany
Tel: +49 7247 808 513
Fax: +49 7247 808 131

Stone Federation Great Britain
82 New Cavendish Street
London W1M 4AD
Tel: +44 171 580 5588
Fax: +44 171 631 3872

Swimming Pool and Allied Trades
Association
SPATA House,
1a Junction Road
Andover,
Hampshire SP10 3QT
Tel: +44 1264 356210
Fax: +44 1264 332628

Technical Help for Exporters
SEE British Standards Institute

Technical Indexes Ltd
Willoughby Road,
Bracknell,
Berkshire RG12 8DW
Tel: +44 1344 426311
Fax: +44 1344 424971

Thomas Telford Ltd
1 Heron Quay,
London E14 9XF
Tel: +44 171 987 6999
Fax: +44 171 538 5746

TFPL Ltd
17 Britton Street,
London EC1M 5NQ
Tel: +44 171 251 5522
Fax: +44 171 251 8318

Thatching Advisory Service
29 Nine Mile Ride, Finchampstead
Wokingham,
Berkshire RG11 4QD
Tel: +44 1734 734203
Fax: +44 1734 328054

Tiles & Architectural
Ceramics Society
c/o Centre for the Arts & Contemporary
Studies
H Block Room H317,
Leeds Metropolitan University
City Campus,
Leeds LS1 3HE
Tel: +44 1532 832600
Fax: +44 1532 425733

Timber Research and Development
Association
Chiltern House, Stocking Lane
Hughenden Valley
High Wycombe,
Bucks. HP14 4ND
Tel: +44 1494 563091
Fax: +44 1494 565487

Timber Trade Federation
Clareville House,
20–27 Oxendon Street
London SW1Y 4EL
Tel: +44 171 839 1891)
Fax: +44 171 930 0094

TNO Building and
Construction Research
PO Box 49, 2600 AA Delft,
The Netherlands

UK Ecolabelling Board
Eastbury House,
30–34 Albert Embankment
London SE1 7TL
Tel: +44 171 820 1199
Fax: +44 171 820 1104

The UK Land and Hydrographic Survey
Association Limited
33 Catherine Place
London SWIE 6DY
Tel: +44 171 828 0933
Fax: +44 171 834 5747
UNIDO – United Nations Indus- trial
Development Organisation
Vienna International Centre,
PO Box 300,
A-1400 Wien, Austria
Tel: +43 1 211 310
Fax: +43 1 23 21 56

Underwriters Laboratories
333 Pfingsten Road
Northbrook, IL 60062
(708) 272 8800

United Kingdom Institute for
Conservation
6 Whitehorse Mews,
Westminster Bridge Road
London SE1 7QD
Tel: +44 171 620 3371
Fax +44 171 620 3371

United Nations Educational, Scientific
and Cultural Organisation (UNESCO)
7 place de Fontenoy
75700 Paris 07 SP, France
Tel: +33 45 68 10 00
Fax: + 33 43 06 16 40
Telex: 204461 PARIS

United States Coast and
Geodetic Survey
National Oceanic and Atmospheric
Administration
Washington Science Center, Building 5,
6010 Executive Blvd.,
Rockville, MD 20852 USA
Tel: (301) 713 3163

United States Geological Survey, Public
Affairs Offices
119 National Center, Reston,
VA 22092 USA
Tel: (703) 648 4000
Fax: (703) 648 5427
United States National Park Service
Preservation
Assistance Division
PO Box 37127
Washington, DC 20013-7127
Tel: (202) 343 9561

Urban Land Institute
625 Indiana Ave. NW, #400
Washington, DC 20004-2930
Tel: (202) 624 7000
Fax: (202) 624 7140

Valtio Teknillinen Tutkimuskeskus
Statens Tekniska Forskningscentral
(Technical Research Centre
of Finland)
Vuorimiehentie 5, SF-02150 Espoo,
Finland

Vernacular Architecture Forum
109 Brandon Road
Baltimore, MD 21212 USA
Tel: (410) 296 7538

Victorian Society
1 Priory Gardens
Bedford Park,
London W4 1TT
Tel: +44 181 994 1019
Fax: +44 181 995 4895

Visual Resources Association
Tappan Hall, Rm. 20,
Ann Arbor, MI 48109 USA
Tel: (313) 763 6114
Fax: (313) 747 4121

Western Wood Products Association
See also Southern Pine Council
Yeon Building, 522 Fifth Avenue
Portland,
Oregon 97204-2122 USA
Tel: (503) 224 3930
Fax: (503) 224 3934

Wimpey Environmental
Hargreaves Road, Swindon
Wiltshire SN2 5AZ
Tel: +44 1793 725766
Fax: +44 1793 706604

Zinc Development Association
42–46 Weymouth Street
London W1N 3LQ
Tel: +44 171 499 6636
Fax: +44 171 493 1555

Appendix B

Acronyms and abbreviations

Most of the acronyms and abbreviations which appear in the text should appear here: not all relate to organizations but most do. In some contexts there are several interpretations for the same abbreviation: e.g. IFLA relates to the International Federation either of Library Associations or of Landscape Architects according to the context – this will always be clear. Generally only those acronyms which authors have flagged for inclusion are included here.

AA	Arboricultural Association
AA	Architectural Association
AA	Automobile Association
AAA	American Automobile Association
AAMA	American Architectural Manufacturers' Association
AATA	Art and Archaeology Technical Abstracts
AAT	Art and Architecture Thesaurus
ABHM	Association of Builders' Hardware Manufacturers
ACA	Architectural Cladding Association
ACADS	Association for Computer Aided Design
ACI	American Concrete Institute
ACM	Association for Computing Machinery
AEC	architecture, engineering and construction
AECB	Association of Environmentally Conscious Builders
AFM	Association of Facilities Managers
AFNOR	Association Française de Normalisation
AGI	Association for Geographic Information
AIA	American Institute of Architects
AIA/ACSA	Council on Architectural Research
AIC	Asbestos Information Centre
AICP	American Institute of Certified Planners

AIIP	Association of Independent Information Professionals
AIVC	The Air Infiltration and Ventilation Centre
AJ	*Architects' Journal*
ALA	American Library Association
Alfed	Aluminium Federation
ANSI	American National Standards Institute
APA	American Planning Association
APA	American Plywood Association
APC	Association of Progressive Communications
API	*Architectural Publications Index*
APT	Association for Preservation Technology International
ARLIS/UK	Art Libraries Society (United Kingdom & Ireland)
ARLIS/NA	Art Libraries Society of North America
ASC	Architects Standard Catalogue
ASCHB	Association for Studies in the Conservation of Historic Buildings
ASID	American Society of Interior Designers
ASLA	American Society of Landscape Architects
ASLIB	Aslib: The Association for Information Management
ASHRAE	The American Society of Heating, Refrigerating and Air-Conditioning Engineers
ASME	American Society of Mechanical Engineers
ASTM	American Society for Testing & Materials
AWA	Aluminium Window Association
BACMI	British Aggregate Construction Materials Industries
BAL	British Architectural Library
BASA	British Adhesives and Sealants Association
BBA	British Board of Agrément
BC	Building Centre
BCA	British Cement Association (previously the Cement Association – CCA)
BCartS	British Cartographical Society
BCompS	British Computer Society
BCQ	BCQ Poulter Communications
BCSA	British Constructional Steelwork Association
BDA	Brick Development Association
BEAB	British Electrotechnical Approvals Board
BESA	British Earth Sheltering Association
BFRC	British Flat Roofing Council
BI	Barbour Index
BGS	British Geological Survey (previously the Institute of Geological Sciences – IGS)
BLDSC	British Library, Document Supply Centre
BLSRIS	British Library, Science Reference Information Service
BPCF	British Precast Concrete Federation
BPF	British Plastics Federation
BPIC	Building Project Information Committee
BQ	bill of quantities
BRE	Building Research Establishment
BRMA	British Reinforcement Manufacturers' Association
BRMCA	British Ready Mixed Concrete Association
BSI	British Standards Institution
BSRIA	Building Services Research and Information Association
BSS	British Standards Society

BSAS	British Steel Advisory Service
BWF	British Woodworking Federation
CAD	computer-aided design
CADD	Computer-aided design and drafting
CADDETC	CAAD/CAM Data Exchange Technical Centre
CADCAM	computer-aided design and manufacturing
CAE	computer-aided engineering
CAE	Centre for Accessible Environments
CAFM	computer-aided facilities management
CAS	Concrete Advisory Service (subsidiary of Concrete Society)
CAT	Centre for Alternative Technology
CBA	Council for British Archaeology
CBL	City Business Library
CC	Countryside Commission
CCA	see BCA
CCI	Canadian Conservation Institute
CCPI	see BPIC
CDA	Copper Development Association (and Copper Roofing Advisory Service)
CDM	Construction Design and Management Regulations
CECC	Electronic Components Committee
CEN	European Committee for Standardization
CENELEC	European Committee for Electro-technical Standardization
CERCO	Comité Européen de Responsable Cartographie Officielle
CFA	Construction Fixings Association
CFC	chlorofluorocarbon
CFM	Centre for Facilities Management
CGSA	Computer Graphics Suppliers Association
CHIN	Canadian Heritage Information Network
CIB	Conseil International du Batiment pour la Recherche, l'Etude et la Documentation (International Council for Building Research, Studies and Documentation)
CIBSE	Chartered Institution of Building Services Engineers
CICA	Construction Industry Computing Association
CIIG	Construction Industry Information Group
CIM	computer integrated manufacturing
CIMI	Computer Integrated Manufacture Institute
CIN	Conservation Information Network
CIOB	Chartered Institute of Building
CIPFA	Chartered Institute of Public Finance and Accountancy
CIRIA	Construction Industry Research and Information Association
CI/SfB	Construction Indexing/Samarbetskommitten for Byggnadsfragor
CLD	Commission for Local Democracy
CNBR	Cooperative Network for Building Researchers
CNS	Chinese National Standards
CoBoP	Catalogue of British Official Publications not published by HMSO
CoFHE	Colleges of Further & Higher Education Group of the Library Association

COFI	Council of Forest Industries of British Columbia
CP	code of practice (BSI)
CPI	coordinated project information
CRAS	Copper Roofing Advisory Service – see CDA
CRT	Cambridge Refrigeration Technology
CRTC	Clay Roofing Tile Council
CS	Concrete Society
CSA	Canadian Standards Association
CSI	Construction Specifications Institute
CSO	Central Statistical Office (UK)
CTBUH	Council on Tall Buildings and Urban Habitat
CWCT	Centre for Window and Cladding Technology
DA	Design Access
D&B	Dun & Bradstreet
D B Z	Deutsche Bauzeitschrift
DC	Design Council
DC	Drafts for Comment (BSI)
DGGTN	Direccion General de Geografia del Territorio Nacional
DIN	Deutsches Institut für Normung
DMA	Defense Mapping Agency
DOE	Department of Energy (USA)
DoE	Department of the Environment (UK)
DoT	Department of Transport
EA	Environmental Assessment
EASA	Ecclesiastical Architects and Surveyors Association
EC	European Community/European Commission
ECMA	European Computer Manufacturers Association
EDA	Ecological Design Association
EDM	engineering data management
EDRA	Environmental Design Research Association
EEO	Energy Efficient Office
EFILWC	European Foundation for the Improvement of Living and Working conditions
EFLA	European Association for Landscape Architects
EIA	Environmental Impact Assessment
EIAC	Ergonomics Information Analysis Centre
EN	Euronorm (European standard)
EPA	Environmental Protection Agency
EROS	Earth Resources Observation Systems
ES	Environmental statement
ES	Ergonomics Society
ESA-IRS	European Space Agency – Information Retrieval Service
ETA	European Technical Approval
ETSU	Energy Technology Support Unit
EU	European Union
FC	Forestry Commission
FETA	Federation of Environmental Trade Associations
FF	Forest Forever
FIDIC	Powerdoc Systems Ltd
FIG	Fire Information Group
FoE	Friends of the Earth
FPA	Fire Protection Association

FPRL	Forest Products Research Laboratory
FRS	Fire Research Station
GAI	Guild of Architectural Ironmongery
GCI	Getty Conservation Institute
GGF	Glass and Glazing Federation
GPO	Government Printing Office
GPS	Global Positioning Systems (satellites)
GRC	glass reinforced cement
GS	Georgian Group
GSC	Geological Survey of Canada
GSS	Government Statistical Service
HMSO	Her Majesty's Stationery Office
HSE	Health & Safety Executive
HVCA	Heating and Ventilating Contractors Association
ICBO	International Conference of Building Officials
ICCROM	International Centre for the Study of the Preservation and Restoration of Cultural Property
ICE	Institution of Civil Engineers
ICE	Institute of Consumer Ergonomics
ICEL	Industry Society for Emergency Lighting
ICES	Institute of Civil Engineering Surveyors
ICOM	International Council of Museums
ICOMOS	International Council for the Conservation of Monuments and Sites
IE	Institute of Energy
IEA	Institute of Environmental Assessment
IEE	Institution of Electrical Engineers
IEEE	Institution of Electrical & Electronic Engineers
IFLA	International Federation of Library Associations
IFLA	International Federation of Landscape Architects
IFS	Institute of Fire Safety
IGD	Institute of Grocery Distribution
IGS	see BGS
IGT	Institute of Gas Technology
IHS	Information Handling Service
IIC	International Institute for the Conservation of Historic and Artistic Works
IIR	International Institute of Refrigeration
IIS	Institute of Information Scientists
ILI	Infonorme London Information
ILL	Inter-library Loans
IM	Institute of Management
IP	Institute of Plumbing
IRC,NRC	Institute for Research in Construction (National Research Council, Canada)
IS	Industrial Society
ISE	Institution of Structural Engineers
ISI	Institute for Scientific Information
ISID	International Society of Interior Designers
ISO	International Standards Organization
ISRPM	Institute of Sport and Recreation Planning & Management

JAPA	Journal of the American Planning Association
JISC	Japanese Industrial Standards Committee
LA	Library Association
LAIG	Library Association Industrial Group
LBL	Lawrence Berkeley Laboratory
LCA	life-cycle analysis (or assessment)
LDA	Lead Development Association
LDT	Landscape Design Trust
LI	Landscape Institute
LIF	Lighting Industry Federation
LITC	Library Information Technology Centre
LPC	Loss Prevention Council
LR	Land Registry (UK)
LSA	Lead Sheet Association
MACEF	Mastic Asphalt Council and Employers Federation
MAFF	Ministry of Agriculture, Fisheries & Food
MATAC	Mastic Asphalt Technical Advisory Centre
MCAUS	Martin Centre for Architectural and Urban Studies
MCRMA	Metal Cladding and Roofing Manufacturers Association
MO	Meteorological Office
MOATS	Methods of Assessment & Technical Specifications (BBA)
MoHLG	Ministry of Housing & Local Government
MoPBW	Ministry of Public Building & Works
NAPP	National Aerial Photography Program
NBS	National Building Specification
NBS	National Bureau of Standards (USA)
NCC	National Computing Centre
NCG	National Contractors Group
NCIC	National Cartographic Information Center
NES	National Engineering Specification
NF	French standards from AFNOR
NFDC	National Federation of Demolition Contractors
NFPA	National Fire Prevention Association (USA)
NFRC	National Federation of Roofing Contractors
NRSC	National Remote Sensing Centre
NHBC	National House-Building Council
NHS	National Health Service
NIST	National Institute of Standards and Technology
NLBD	National League of Blind & Disabled
NMR	National Monuments Record
NOAA	National Oceanic and Atmospheric Administration
NPFA	National Playing Fields Association
NPS	National Park Service
NRC	National Research Council of Canada
NRSC	National Remote Sensing Centre
NSQA	National Slate Quarries Association
NTIS	National Technical Information Service
ODI	on demand information
OPCS	Office of Population Censuses and Surveys
OS	Ordnance Survey

PA	Paintmakers Association of Great Britain
PIG	Property Information Group
PLUS	Private List Update Service (BSI)
PRA	Paint Research Association
PSA	Property Services Agency
PWA	Plastics Window Association
RAIC	Royal Architectural Institute of Canada
RAPRA	Rubber & Plastics Research Association
RCHM	Royal Commissions on Historical Monuments (of England, Scotland and Wales)
RDC	Rural Development Commission
RIBA	Royal Institute of British Architects
RILEM	Reunion Internationale des Laboratoires d'Essais et de Recherches sur les Materiaux et les Constructions (International Union of Testing and Research Laboratories for Materials and Structures)
RLG	Research Libraries Group
RLIN	Research Libraries Network
RTA	Roofing Tile Association
RTPI	Royal Town Planning Institute
SAA	Standards Association of Australia
SASO	Saudi Arabia
SBS	sick building syndrome
SC	Sports Council
SCI	Steel Construction Institute
SCOOP	Standing Committee on Official Publications (UK)
SEA	strategic environmental assessment
SF	Stone Federation
SFTC	Swedish-Finnish Timber Council
SIGGRAPH	A division of ACM
SLFM	School of Leisure & Food Management
SMM	standard method of measurement
SMMT	Society of Motor Manufacturers and Traders
SPAB	Society for the Protection of Ancient Buildings
SPATA	Swimming Pool & Allied Trades Association
SPMC	Southern Pine Marketing Council
SPRA	Single Ply Roofing Association
SRIS	British Library Science Reference & Information Service
SSP	Secretaria de Programacion y Presupuesto
STEP	Standard for the Exchange of Product Model Data
SWA	Steel Window Association
TACS	Tiles and Ceramics Society
TAS	Thatching Advisory Service
Ti	Technical Indexes
TT	Thomas Telford Ltd
TNO	TNO Building and Construction Research
TRADA	Timber Research and Development Association
TTF	Timber Trade Federation
UEAtc	European Union of Agrément
UDC	Universal Decimal Classification

UIA	International Union of Architects
UKEB	UK Ecolabelling Board
UKOP	UK Official Publications (CD-ROM from HMSO)
UL	Underwriters Laboratories
ULI	Urban Land Institute
UNESCO	United Nations Educational, Scientific and Technical Organisation
UNIDO	United Nations Industrial Development Organisation
USC&GS	United States Coast and Geodetic Survey
USGS	United States Geological Survey
VDE	Verband Deutscher Elektrotechniker
VRA	Visual Resources Association
VS	Victorian Society
VTT	Valtio Teknillinen Tutkimuskeskus
WWPA	Western Wood Products Association
ZDA	Zinc Development Association

Index

Biography master index, 71
Biological abstracts, 62
BIOSIS, 73
Birmingham Public Libraries, 143, 153
Blackwells, 75
BLAISE, 63, 113
Blinds, 341
BLISS, 92, 378
Blockwork, 301
BMCIS, 252
Book review digest online, 68
Book reviews, 406
Bookbank, 9
Bookdata, 68
Bookfind, 9
Bookfind CD, 68, 385
Books in print, 14, 67
Books on screen, 72
Bouw-CD, 65
BQs SEE Bills of quantities
Brad, 87
BRE digests, 89, 118, 284
BREEAM, 306, 320
Brick, 287, 293, 295
Brick Development Association, 90,
    287, 295, 297, 301
Brickwork, 293, 301, 396
British archaeological abstracts, 397
British Architectural Library SEE
    Royal Institute of British Architects
British Blind & Shutter Association,
    341
British Board of Agrément, 90, 100–1,
    117, 281, 284
British books in print, 14, 67
British Carpet Manufacturer's
    Association, 332, 336, 340
British Cartographic Society, 185
British Cement Association, 121, 288,
    296, 297, 302, 385
British Coal, 191
British Colour Makers Association,
    339
British Computer Society, 184, 185,
    214
British Constructional Steelwork
    Association, 248, 270, 296, 314
British Contract Furnishing
    Association, 340
British education index, 268
British Electrotechnical Approvals
    Board, 100
British Flat Roofing Council, 302, 303
British Geological Survey, 131, 132,
    171, 191

British Gypsum, 292
British humanities index, 268, 269,
    421
British Institute of Interior Design,
    329
British Library, 14, 75, 121, 141, 220,
    422
British library directory, 42
British Library, Document Supply
    Centre, 10, 40, 59, 114
British Library, Science Reference &
    Information Service, 63, 84, 324,
    390
British Museum, 141, 143
British national bibliography, 14, 385
British Standard Codes of practice
    SEE Codes of practice
British Standards Institution, 31, 73,
    90, 94 et seq, 106–7, 216, 270,
    336, 359, 389
British Standards Society, 392
British Steel, 297, 302
British technology index, 66
British Textile Technology Group, 340
BRIX / FLAIR, 64, 324
Brochures, 80
Brown University, 155
BS 5750 SEE Standards, quality
BSI Catalogue, 98, 101, 104, 305,
    336
BSI news, 94, 98–101, 106, 281, 336
Budget, information, 383
Buildability, 298, 300
Building, 48, 87, 93, 99, 101, 209,
    253, 255, 269, 281, 368, 377, 400,
    421
*Building and construction resource
    directory*, 35
Building bulletins, 113
Building Centre, 5, 90, 94, 279, 385
Building Centre Trust, 213
Building contracts SEE Contracts
Building Cost Information Service
    SEE BCIS
Building design, 87, 283, 386
Building design and construction, 48
Building economist, 253
Building Education Council, 374, 378
Building Employer's Federation, 249
Building Environmental Performance
    Analysis Club, 214
Building law information service, 378
Building Limes Forum, 404
Building Maintenance Cost
    Information Service SEE BMCIS

Staff SEE Personnel
Stairs, 304
Standard Method of Measurement,
    248, 249
Standard periodicals directory, 70
Standard phraseology, 247
Standardline, 67, 97
Standards, 90, 92, 95 passim, 117,
    221, 367, 384
Standards and specifications (US), 67
Standards Association of Australia,
    107
Standards Infodisk, 107, 269
Standards, Australia, 107
Standards, bibliographical references,
    19
Standards, CAD, 216
Standards, Canada, 106, 107
Standards, colour, 339
Standards, construction drawing, 216,
    249, 366
Standards, databases, 67, 269
Standards, ergonomic, 265, 267
Standards, Europe, 101–104
Standards, French, 106
Standards, German, 106
Standards, GIS, 185
Standards, interior design, 336
Standards, international, 104–106
Standards, Japanese, 106, 107
Standards, landscape, 344, 345, 348
Standards, manufacturing design, 367
Standards, materials, 281, 336
Standards, NATO, 106
Standards, NHBC, 298
Standards, office equipment, 266
Standards, partitions, 303
Standards, quality, 354, 359
Standards, reports, 21–22
Standards, Saudi Arabia, 107
Standards, section numbering, 23
Standards, structures, 281, 293, 305
Standards, theses, 21–22
Standards, timber, 291
Standards, trade literature, 80–81, 92,
    281
Standards, types of buildings, 258
Standards, wiring, 318, 321
Standards, workmanship, 305
Stanford Center for Design Research,
    212
State Historic Preservation, 427
Statistical Information Service (USA),
    69
Statistics, 69, 119–122, 253, 322

Statute law database, 116, 122
Statutes, 114–118, 229, 309
Statutes, UK, indexes, 116
Steel, 270, 289, 294, 296, 297
Steel Construction Institute, 262, 289,
    296, 297, 392
Steel designer's manual, 296
STEP, 215, 216
STN, 63, 64, 76, 314
Stone, 290, 401
Stone Federation, 290
Storage, maps, 144
Storage, slides, 156–157, 170
Strategic Mapping, 195
Streetscape slides, 156
Strongblow, 314
Structural design, 294–312
Structures, 221, 293 et seq
Subcontractors, 366
Subject collections, 41
Subsidence, 298
SuDOCs, 123
Supplier's information SEE Trade
    literature
Survey of London, 426
Survey, databases, 66
Survey, texts, 246, 333
Surveyors, 245–247
Surveys, as built, 180
Sustainable development, 239 See also
    Green issues
Sweet directories, 56, 65, 86
Swimming Pool and Allied Trades
    Association, 321
Swiss Federation of Landscape
    Architects, 347
Symbols, in drawing, 150
Synthetic materials, 340
System George, 65
Systems Development Corporation, 62

Tactician, 195
Tactics International, 195
Tall buildings, 267
Tarmac Ltd, 302
Technical advice, 31
Technical data, 88, 283, 297–298,
    305–306, 391
Technical Help to exporters, 107, 270
Technical Indexes Ltd, 84, 92, 105,
    106, 107, 285
Technical information microfile, 92
    See also RIBA/Ti
Techniques, drawing, 147, 149–150
Technophobia, 218